MW00965475

School Psychology
A Social Psychological Perspective

SCHOOL PSYCHOLOGY

A series of volumes edited by
Thomas R. Kratochwill and James E. Ysseldyke

Lawrence Erlbaum Associates, Inc., Publishers
365 Broadway
Hillsdale, New Jersey 07642

Library of Congress Cataloging-in-Publication Data

Medway, Frederic J.
   School psychology : a social psychological perspective / Frederic
J. Medway, Thomas P. Cafferty.
      p.   cm.
   Includes bibliographical references and index.
   ISBN 0-8058-0536-2
   1. School psychology – United States. 2. Social psychology – United
States. I. Cafferty, Thomas P. II. Title.
LB1027.55.M43 1992
370.15 – dc20   91-14483
                                           CIP

Printed in the United States of America
10 9 8 7 6 5 4 3 2

School Psychology
A Social Psychological Perspective

Edited by

Frederic J. Medway
Thomas P. Cafferty
University of South Carolina

LEA   **LAWRENCE ERLBAUM ASSOCIATES, PUBLISHERS**
1992   **Hillsdale, New Jersey**   **Hove and London**

This book is dedicated with love to our wives, Marcia and Loretta, and our children, Scott, Lauren, Carolyn, and Brendan, whose enduring support, encouragement, and interest in our careers has sustained and nourished our personal and professional lives.

CONTENTS

LIST OF CONTRIBUTORS

Oscar A. Barbarin, III
Associate Professor
School of Social Work and Department
of Psychology
University of Michigan
Ann Arbor, Michigan 48104

Jack I. Bardon
Excellence Foundation Professor of
Education
School of Education
University of North Carolina
Greensboro, North Carolina 27412

Thomas P. Cafferty
Associate Professor
Department of Psychology
University of South Carolina
Columbia, South Carolina 29208

Laurie Chassin
Professor
Department of Psychology
Arizona State University
Tempe, Arizona 85287

Jane Close Conoley
Professor and Chairperson
Department of Educational Psychology
University of Nebraska—Lincoln
Lincoln, Nebraska 68588

Patrick J. Curran
Department of Psychology
Arizona State University
Tempe, Arizona 85257

John M. Davis
School of Education
University of California—Davis
Davis, California 95616

William P. Erchul
Associate Professor
Department of Psychology
North Carolina State University
Raleigh, North Carolina 27695

Maribeth Gettinger
Associate Professor
Department of Educational Psychology
University of Wisconsin
Madison, Wisconsin 53706

David S. Goh
Professor
Graduate Program in School Psychology
Queens College, City University of
    New York
Flushing, New York 11367

Mary Henning-Stout
Assistant Professor
Counseling Psychology
Lewis and Clark College
Portland, Oregon 97219

Jan N. Hughes
Professor
Department of Educational Psychology
Texas A & M University
College Station, Texas 77843

Robert J. Illback
REACH Inc. and Associate Professor
Spalding University
Louisville, Kentucky 40272

Ruth Ann Johnson
Assistant Professor
Psychology Department
Augustana College
Rock Hill, Illinois 61201

Judith LeCount
Department of Educational Psychology
University of Minnesota
Minneapolis, Minnesota 55455

Maurice J. Levesque
Department of Psychology
University of Connecticut, U-20
Storrs, Connecticut 06268

Charles A. Lowe
Professor
Department of Psychology
University of Connecticut, U-20
Storrs, Connecticut 06268

Geoffrey Maruyama
Professor
Department of Educational Psychology
University of Minnesota
Minneapolis, Minnesota 55455

Frederic J. Medway
Professor
Department of Psychology
University of South Carolina
Columbia, South Carolina 29208

Christopher Peterson
Department of Psychology
University of Michigan
Ann Arbor, Michigan 48109

Clark C. Presson
Assistant Professor
Department of Psychology
Arizona State University
Tempe, Arizona 85287

Jayne Ross
Department of Psychology
Augustana College
Rock Hill, Illinois 61201

Daniel W. Russell
Associate Professor
Center for Health Services Research
College of Medicine and Graduate College
University of Iowa
Iowa City, Iowa 52242

Jonathan Sandoval
Professor
School of Education
University of California—Davis
Davis, California 95616

Steven J. Sherman
Professor
Indiana University
Bloomington, Indiana 47405

Paula Skedsvold
Department of Psychology
University of South Carolina
Columbia, South Carolina 29208

James M. Weyant
Professor
Department of Psychology
University of San Diego
San Diego, California 92110

Gwen M. Williams
School Psychologist
Fonda–Fultonville Central Schools
Fonda, New York 12068

Kevin J. Williams
Assistant Professor
Psychology Department
State University of New York at Albany
Albany, New York, 12222

Roland K. Yoshida
Professor of Special Education
Queens College, City University of
   New York
Flushing, New York 11367

FOREWORD

School psychology has a long and consistent history of self-discovery after the fact. Due to its extremely applied nature, its practitioners tend to act first, responding to the needs of others, and then to reflect upon what it is they have done and the foundational bases for their actions. Strongly influenced by clinical psychology, school psychology most often has adopted the view that it is a specialty concerned mainly with individual differences; with persons in need of direct or indirect assistance for a wide variety of problems of the human condition as they occur in a place called school. The field's training programs have accepted as basic to the education of their students the substantive content areas expected in any professional psychology training program, including demonstration of competency in the social bases of behavior. But specialization has tended to emphasize those aspects of psychology dealing primarily with personality, abnormality, and individual behavior, in keeping with the emphasis on the troubled-person-as-client.

Yet, if you think about it, it seems obvious that the one area of psychology that may be most pervasive in school psychology, broadly speaking, is the field of social psychology. Can you think of any aspect of the work of the school psychologist that is not influenced in important ways by the presence of others, whether actual, imagined, or implied? What is there that school psychologists do that is apart from how they are perceived; how those with whom they work think and feel about them? What are the elements of the phenomenon we call *rapport*, an essential factor influencing whether or not our assessment results tell us something valid about the persons we are trying to understand? What are the contexts in which teachers, administrators, and parents use our findings, advice, and interventions? How do we get others to hear what we have to say and to use the information we provide? Involved in all these questions are problems to be solved relating intrapersonal concerns to interpersonal, intragroup, and intergroup factors.

Of all practitioner psychologies, with the possible exception of industrial/organizational psychology, school psychology practice is most intimately tied to a particular kind of complex social setting that serves to define the specialty. We are not "school" psychologists for nothing. We are set apart from other psychologists by the social organization with which we are identified, and the problems posed by those who administer, teach, and learn in educational environments. The success of whatever it is we do is dependent on what others think about and do with our findings, suggestions, and ideas. We are primarily an indirect service delivery specialty, and that means we are helpful to the extent that others hear, respect, and work with us. These "others" we try to assist work in educational organizations or are concerned with teaching and learning, which is always an interactive process.

What is the nature of the problems others bring to us? Mostly they are problems about failure in interaction or failure in learning or behaving in a group, whether it be the classroom, home, or community. What are the impediments to being heard and used well by teachers, parents, and administrators? Do they not include attitudes toward children, misunderstandings, attributions of motives and perceptions? What factors affect how well we perform? Given that we have basic competencies in assessment, intervention methods, and evaluation, is it not our ability to get people to trust us, to understand us, and to use the good things we have to offer them because we have been able to overcome the differences between or among us?

In our psychological language, these questions relate back to a knowledge base that includes knowing about attitude formation and attitude change, interpersonal attraction and social acceptance, gender and race issues, organizational behavior, attributions, group dynamics, and interpersonal relations. In other words, if you think about it, social psychology may be the key foundational base in psychology that undergirds our ability to offer assistance to others. Whatever else we may know, whatever skills we may have, we cannot accomplish much without directly or implicitly understanding that we function in a social psychological world.

Throughout my career, I have recognized the importance of a social psychological perspective, mostly due to the good fortune of having an applied social psychologist as my mentor and teacher in graduate school. But, as a trainer of school psychologists, it did not occur to me to include social psychology as a requirement for my students, much less consider it as a major aspect of their formal education and training, although some of my students wisely chose to include course work in social psychology as electives in their graduate programs. Perhaps there is something about the field of social psychology itself that contributed to this gap between my implicit understanding of its importance to me as a school psychologist and my failure to view it as an important foundation area for my students. The field of social psychology has struggled for decades with issues of scientific purity versus social action. Much of its literature has been specialized, dominated by laboratory research whose relevance has not been made clear to those of us who think of ourselves as human service providers. The literature in applied social psychology concerned with the social psychology of schooling is limited, and much of it has not had direct appeal to psychology practitioners.

Frederic J. Medway, a school psychologist with a social psychological background, and Thomas P. Cafferty, a social psychologist who teaches school psychologists in training, have undertaken to correct this imbalance. The book you are about to read, to my knowledge, is the first serious attempt in school psychology literature to provide a social psychological perspective to the clinical and social problems with which we work every day. It is a monumental undertaking that is long overdue.

Most books we read do not break new ground, but this book offers school psychologists an opportunity to shift perspectives from seeing clients as isolated entities who need to be treated to seeing them as social beings who virtually are never away in fact or in thought from others who populate their lives. As I understand the authors' intent, their book is a way for those in training or in the field to consider how they can better use this important body of knowledge—social psychology—to increase sensitivity to others and effectiveness as professional psychologists. It may also serve to encourage students to take additional course work in social psychology.

We all know we are living in a rapidly changing world, and we have chosen to be part of a rapidly changing profession. One of the critical changes taking place throughout the world involves greater recognition of the interrelatedness of people. More and more we realize how dependent we are on each other. Global education is no longer something others should be concerned about. Environmental issues involve interactions among societies and persons. We have witnessed only recently how shifts in attitudes and attributions influence world events and world order. In our small part of this world—school psychology—we too gradually have come to recognize the importance of interpersonal, interorganizational, and contextual factors in our work. We never function in isolation from those components that form the subject matter of social psychology, as professionals and as citizens.

Understanding and using the knowledge base and skills related to social psychological phenomena in our work may well make the difference between helping or not helping our clients, consultees, and our educational systems to make best use of our services. This is a book to read carefully; to think about as we go about our daily professional assignments as educator, student, or practitioner. If enough school psychologists read this book and take its content seriously as a way of shaping a more socially perceptive perspective, it could positively influence our ability to continue to be part of a rapidly changing profession in a rapidly changing educational system in a rapidly changing world in which social psychological factors are always in operation.

Jack I. Bardon

PREFACE

*Although clinical psychology is clearly related to medicine, it is quite as closely
related to sociology and pedagogy*

—Lightner Witmer

In 1907 Lightner Witmer conceived of a new profession using clinical methods
in the examination and treatment of individuals with psychological disorders.
Witmer termed the new profession *clinical psychology* because the word "clinical" best described his view of employing systematic observation and experimentation to effect change in individuals. Witmer saw mostly children
drawn from schools in Pennsylvania and is credited with founding school psychology as well as clinical psychology.

Lightner Witmer, like many of his contemporaries, viewed the study of
sociology and social psychology as critical to the diagnostic and treatment
process. However, during the last century, and especially within the last 30
years, school psychology has moved away from its early sociological roots
so that today few school psychologists have taken more than one survey
course in social psychology. And, it is our belief that even fewer recognize
the importance of social psychology for school psychologists.

It is with a great sense of pride and excitement that we have attempted
to reintroduce the contributions of social psychology to school psychology
in *School Psychology: A Social Psychological Perspective*. The book itself
represents a merging and cross-fertilization of our own professional identities, the first author being primarily identified with school psychology and
the second author with social psychology.

The origins of this book go back many years and reflect our own career development. For nearly 20 years, Frederic Medway has been interested in the application of social psychology in school settings. Dr. Medway was studying for his PhD in social psychology at the University of Connecticut when, in 1972, he was offered an NIMH-sponsored internship in Long Beach, New York, under the supervision of Dr. Victor B. Elkin. Dr. Elkin's support and encouragement allowed him to spend a year functioning as a social psychologist in several school districts doing organizational consultation, modifying learning environments, and providing in-service training in group process skills to school staff. Returning to Connecticut to complete his dissertation, he was encouraged by several faculty members to try and integrate social psychology with educational practice. The most influential members of this faculty were Charles A. Lowe and Reuben M. Baron, to whom special thanks are due. Since 1975 Dr. Medway has been affiliated with the school psychology program of the University of South Carolina, where he has continued to train students in social psychological processes.

Dr. Thomas Cafferty was trained as an experimental social psychologist at a time when many in the field were becoming concerned about the loss of relevance for applied areas. He benefitted from the resurgence of interest represented by the program at Purdue, particularly in the work of Sigfried Streufert and his associates. Coming to the University of South Carolina in 1972, he was assigned to teach a graduate seminar in social psychology to graduate students, the majority of whom were in school and clinical psychology programs, and has continued to do so every year since. He brings a unique perspective of having discussed many social psychological principles with school psychologists in training and a sensitivity to the needs of applied psychologists.

The idea for this volume did not come until 1987 when we received an invitation by Drs. Terry B. Gutkin of the University of Nebraska at Lincoln and Cecil R. Reynolds of Texas A & M University to contribute a chapter on the contributions of social psychology to school psychology for the second edition of the *Handbook of School Psychology* (Gutkin & Reynolds, 1990). In working on that chapter we realized that the interface between the two disciplines was broad and far reaching, and that one chapter could not capture all the many ways that social psychology impacts on school psychology practice. We realized that a need for a more detailed treatment existed and felt that both the theories and methods of social psychology were very important for effective functioning in school psychology. Thus, we owe a special debt to Drs. Gutkin and Reynolds, for recognizing the importance of social psychology for school psychologists and starting us on our initial collaborative writing, an effort that set the stage for this volume. Once a general idea for the book was developed, Drs. Thomas R. Kratochwill and James Ysseldyke were most supportive in encouraging us to pursue the project in conjunction with the ongoing school psychology series of Lawrence Erlbaum and Associates.

We made a decision early in the development of this book to focus it on school psychology and have contributors write for this audience. This is reflected in the title we chose. Our contributors were specifically asked to cover the classical, contemporary, and cutting-edge research and theory in their respective areas and to address, where applicable, the applications for school psychology. The volume is not as broad or basic in presentation as most existing introductions to school psychology; on the other hand, it is not as narrow as books that deal with one specific skill or technique, be that assessment, consultation, therapy, or other area. Thus, we see the book as most appropriate as a text in an advanced seminar course, as a supplemental book in an introductory course, and certainly, as an essential reference tool for all school psychologists.

There are three major sections in *School Psychology: A Social Psychological Perspective*. The first section is entitled "Theoretical Perspectives on Applying Social Psychology to Educational Practices." This section contains eight chapters that cover basic areas of social psychology (e.g., history, attitudes, attribution, attraction, research methods). These chapters review the basic research on which subsequent chapters build and contain many illustrations from educational practice.

The second section is entitled "Applying Social Psychology to Clinical Interventions in the Schools." It contains chapters covering many of the traditional areas of school psychology role and function including assessment, therapy, and consultation. Each of these areas are considered from a uniquely social psychological view.

The final section is called "Applications to Clinical and Social Problems." It covers specific educational and social problems, many of which only receive scant coverage in basic school psychology texts. Here important topics such as substance abuse, loneliness, and integration are reviewed with reference to the latest social psychological models.

We have put a great deal of effort into selecting contributors for this volume. The contributors include a combination of applied social psychologists knowledgeable about school psychology, and school psychologists who have made extensive use of social psychology in their research and practice. We feel that we have a nice mix of social and school psychologists, both university and school affiliated. In fact, this book is the first of which we are aware to include both school and social psychologists in relatively equal numbers.

Many individuals assisted in putting this volume together. We wish to thank Dr. Lester Lefton, our department chair, for his encouragement of our scholarship. Camilla Tezza and Dan McNiff aided us in many aspects of editorial work and index development, and Taffy Lemox who provided invaluable help in typing parts of the manuscript. We also wish to express our appreciation to staff members at Lawrence Erlbaum Associates, particularly Christopher Pecci and Hollis Heimbouch for their tireless efforts in the editorial and production work.

Finally, we wish to offer our appreciation and love to the most important people in our lives, our wives, Marcia Medway and Loretta Cafferty, and our children, Scott and Lauren Medway and Carolyn and Brendan Cafferty. To you, this book is dedicated.

Frederic J. Medway
Thomas P. Cafferty

PART

I

THEORETICAL PERSPECTIVES ON APPLYING SOCIAL PSYCHOLOGY TO EDUCATIONAL PRACTICES

The purpose of this volume is to demonstrate the many contributions of social psychology to the profession of school psychology. Part I consists of eight chapters providing overviews of important developments, theories, and methods of social psychology and their extension to the practice of psychology in schools. These chapters deal with important applications of social psychology in working and conducting research with individual children, their parents and families, teachers, and the school as a social system.

Chapter 1 by Medway reviews the history and growth of social psychology and school psychology. Medway describes how social and school psychology developed from common origins in philosophy and psychophysics research, and how the first social psychologists were interested in the application of their work to educational issues. This chapter describes the cross-fertilization of the two fields and how each has been shaped by similar social and political occurrences, including the migration of large numbers of immigrants to the United States at the turn of the 20th century, prevailing philosophies of education, two World Wars and their aftermath, and the social movements of the last three decades.

Chapter 2 by Cafferty deals with the nature of attitudes and attitude change. The study of attitudes has been a major social psychological topic, and, at one time virtually defined the field. For school psychologists, understanding the nature of attitudes is important in numerous contexts. These include understanding educators' and the public's attitudes toward school psychology, attitudes of school staff toward particular practices such as intelligence testing, behavior modification, and consultation, and the attitudes of schoolchildren toward school policies, academic work, teachers, their families, and their own abilities. Cafferty reviews issues in measuring such attitudes and some of the theoretical models underlying effective attitude change programs.

In chapter 3 Levesque and Lowe focus on two particular types of beliefs and inference processes: causal attributions and expectations. Since the 1970s attribution research has been a major topic in social psychology. Attributional propositions have been widely employed in school psychology; for example, in consultation, in studies of diagnostic labels and their effects, in research on teachers' attributions and behaviors, and in investigations of children's school achievements and learning difficulties. Levesque and Lowe offer a model for understanding a variety of theories and findings in attribution and expectation research. They emphasize the antecedents, consequences, and cyclical nature of social perception. They differentiate between category and target-based expectancies, and mastery versus learned helplessness attributions. Throughout the chapter they highlight the educational applications.

Chapter 4, coauthored by Maruyama and LeCount, reviews the nature of interpersonal attraction in educational settings. Interpersonal attraction is discussed in regard to both cognitive and reinforcement models. Several of the theories covered in this chapter (e.g., dissonance, social influence) also are cited in chapters in Part II on clinical interventions. Maruyama and LeCount also cover the sources of initial impressions, and the maintenance and development of long-term relationships, including friendship formation and its measurement.

In chapter 5, Henning-Stout and Conoley show the importance of gender in school psychology. These authors point out that training and practice in school psychology has virtually ignored gender considerations even though gender expectations can and do influence the delivery of psychological services. This chapter covers theories of gender-linked behavior, and how schools, communities, peers, and the media often socialize students into rigid sex-typed roles. Henning-Stout and Conoley raise a provocative question, namely, to what extent does school psychology, by its practices, serve to perpetuate gender stereotyping?

Chapter 6, by Barbarin, and chapter 7, by Illback, examine the nature of families and schools, respectively, both from the point of view of systems theories. Barbarin introduces how family roles are interdependent, and how this affects the process of change in the family system. He provides some specific ways to measure family functioning and discusses the role of school professionals in effecting family change. Illback reviews the history of industrial-organizational psychology and its application to schools. Illback discusses the work of Daniel Katz, a social psychologist with a psychoanalytic orientation, who, after devoting many years to research on attitudes, addressed problems of organizations. Illback provides an integrative model from which to view schools as social organizations, focusing on both structures and processes. He concludes his chapter with a review of organizational development.

The last in this section, chapter 8, by Medway and Skedsvold, describes the use of social psychological research methods in school psychology. The authors examine the prevailing research problems in the fields, existing research paradigms, and the "social psychology" of school experimentation including experimental biases, deception, and data evaluation. In addition, Medway and Skedsvold present a selective review of social psychological research methods useful for school psychologists such as observational techniques, survey procedures, archival methods, and naturalistic inquiry. The authors conclude that many social psychological research methods that traditionally have been underutilized in school psychology hold great promise for advancing future school-based research and evaluation.

1

THE RAPPROCHEMENT OF SOCIAL PSYCHOLOGY AND SCHOOL PSYCHOLOGY: A HISTORICAL ANALYSIS

Frederic J. Medway
University of South Carolina

Imagine that you have just walked into an elementary school, turned and entered the first classroom on the left, and sat down. In front of you are children taking turns winding fishing reels as fast as they can. Some children wind alone, others in small groups, alternating these situations. An adult watches them and patiently records the winding time. The purpose is to determine if there is a change in individual, solitary performance when others are present.

Now suppose you are told that a psychologist set up this situation, and you are asked to guess his or her expertise. What criteria would you use to make your determination? Would you choose a school psychologist because the event takes place in a school or exclude school psychologist because of your beliefs that school psychologists do not work with classroom groups and are usually engaged in individual testing. Would you choose a developmental or educational psychologist because the subjects are children and the topic is educationally relevant or dismiss these groups because developmental levels are not studied and many variables are uncontrolled? Furthermore, would you choose a social psychologist because the event deals with the effects of social influence or exclude a social psychologist because of beliefs that they typically study college students on campus rather than school-children.

In actuality, the study described is considered the first social psychology experiment and was conducted by Triplett (1897–1898) at schools in Indiana. The study is one of many illustrating that there are few distinct boundaries between many psychological subspecialties. Nor are there many distinct boundaries between psychology and other social sciences, including sociology, management science, political science, and cultural anthropology. However, in the last decade, and especially since World War II, social psychology and school psychology have developed their own unique interests, foci, viewpoint, and scholarship. Each discipline now has its own textbooks, journals, research topics, perspectives, and political influences with which it has to deal. However, in this chapter, I consider the common ground of social and school psychology, their mutual contributions, and how the identities of both fields have been shaped by similar political and social ideologies of the last century. My intent is to show that a full appreciation of contemporary school psychology is impossible without reference to the history of studies of society generally and without knowledge of social psychological propositions, propositions described in detail in following chapters of this text.

Table 1.1 presents an outline of the landmark events that have shaped the development of social psychology and school psychology. As is described, both fields are rooted in the writings of ancient Greek philosophers who initially applied rudimentary scientific methods, rather than religious or supernatural concepts, to the study of man in society. The lineage of social psychology springs from social philosophy, and the lineage of school psychology springs from clinical psychology, which in turn is rooted in studies of individual differences and ancient writings in philosophy and medicine.

The 1990s mark the 100th anniversary of both social psychology and psychology applied to education. At the turn of the last century, the professions of social and school psychology did not exist. Armchair theorizing about the individual and society had been recorded for approximately 2,000 years, and important work was underway in psychophysics and evolution. However, psychological experimentation was just beginning in the laboratories of Wilhelm Wundt (1832–1920) in Liepzig, Germany in 1879; Sir Francis Galton (1822–1911) in Britain in 1884; and William James (1842–1910) in the late 1870s at Harvard. With the exception of Galton's work, there was essentially no applied psychology. As we enter the 1990s there are approximately 5,000 social psychologists (American Psychological Association Directory, 1986) and approximately 16,000 school psychologists (National Association of School Psychologists Directory, 1989). Both fields have developed a distinct body of literature (Allport, 1985; Fagan, 1986) and standards for training. There are accreditation, certification, and licensure regulations in school psychology. The number of training programs for school psychologists increased from 45 in 1962 to 211 in 1984 (Brown & Minke, 1986).

TABLE 1.1
Landmarks in Social and School Psychology

Social Psychology		School Psychology	
		2200 BC	Chinese initiate testing programs for public officials
400 BC	Plato and Aristotle discuss the origins of social behavior	400 BC	Plato discusses the relationship between ability and employment
1870s	Tarde discusses imitative learning	1869	Galton studies individual differences and heredity
		1888	Cattell, student of Galton, describes mental test
		1891	Hall commences studies of children and adolescents
		1894	Binet develops modern intelligence test
1895	LeBon discusses crowd behavior		
1897	Triplett conducts first social psychology experiment	1896	Lightner Witmer calls for psychologists to work in schools
		1899	Centers for testing and counseling school children developed in Chicago
1900	Wundt and Durkheim describe social organization and group mind, respectively		
		1902	Dewey initiates progressive education movement
1908	McDougall and Ross publish first social psychology texts	1909	Mental health reforms initiated by Beers
1910-1920	Nietzsche, Adler, Freud discuss the role of "ego" in psychology	1915	Gesell appointed first school psychologist
		1917	World War I: Development of Army intelligence tests
1928	Thurstone introduces study of attitude measurement	1930	New York University offers first graduate program in school psychology
1934	Moreno develops sociometry	1935	State departments of education begin certifying school psychologists
1936	Sherif studies group influence		
1937	Whyte studies street corner gangs in Boston using "participant observation"		
1939	Lewin studies leadership atmosphere in schools; initiates program of action research		
1942-1945	World War II: Social psychology applied to war issues such as attitude change, propaganda, etc.	1942-1945	World War II: Clinical psychologists recruited for diagnosis and treatment

(Continued)

TABLE 1.1
(Continued)

	Social Psychology		School Psychology
		1940s	Emergence of humanism and behaviorism
1947	Clark and Clark publish studies of racial preference in children	1947	Division of School Psychology started in APA
1949	Hovland studies mass communication and attitude change	1949	Wechsler Intelligence Scale for Children published
1949-1954	Sherif studies intergroup relations	1954	Standards for psychological tests developed by APA
1951	Asch publishes studies on group pressure		
1954	Festinger develops social comparison theory	1954	Thayer conference on education and training of school psychologists
1954	*Handbook of Social Psychology* published		
1957	Festinger develops "cognitive dissonance" theory	1957	Russians launch Sputnik; Cowen introduces primary mental health project in Rochester, New York schools
1958	French and Raven describe types of social power		
1963	Milgrim publishes studies on conformity	1963	First issue of *Journal of School Psychology*; Caplan publishes work on consultation
1965-1970	Development of "attribution theory"	1965	Elementary and Secondary Education Act provides increased school funding and demand for school psychologists
		1969	National Association of School Psychologists formed
1970s	Calls for more relevance and applied research in light of Vietnam conflict, race relations, women's movement, ecological concerns	1970s	Rapid growth in states certifying school psychologists and university training programs; increasing interest in cognitive behaviorism
		1975	Passage of PL 94-142
		1975-1980	Professional "guild issues" dominate school psychology; Calls for social activism, child advocacy, and ethics in school psychology
1980s	Social psychologists study behavioral aspects of health and medicine	1980s	Emergence of accountability in education; minimum competency testing; preschool evaluation; family involvement
		1982	*Handbook of School Psychology* published
		1986	Passage of PL 99-457

DEFINING THE FIELDS

What is Social Psychology?

Nearly all introductory textbooks in social psychology attempt to define the field. G. Allport (1985) offered the most popular definition. Allport defined social psychology as "an attempt to understand and explain how the thought, feeling, and behavior of individuals are influenced by the actual, imagined, or implied presence of others" (p. 3). Allport focused on the actions of individuals within a social context. This definition embraces the following major research topics in social psychology over the last 40 years: (a) attitudes; (b) cognitive processes including social perception; (c) interpersonal relations, including attraction, aggression, and altruism; (d) social and sexual roles; (e) small group behavior; (f) the relationship between environment and behavior; and (g) social variables in health, law, and education.

However, Allport's definition is embedded in the psychological perspective that takes the individual as the primary unit of analysis. Another definition was provided by Elwood (1925) utilizing a sociological perspective. Elwood defined social psychology as "the study of social interaction . . . based upon the psychology of group life" (p. 16). The emphasis here is not on how individuals are affected by social phenomenon but rather how societies and institutions are organized and develop. A "sociological" social psychology attempts to study roles, culture, complex social structures, and deviance.

What is School Psychology?

Unlike social psychology, no one has proposed a widely accepted definition of school psychology (cf. Reynolds, Gutkin, Elliott, & Witt, 1984). This is due in part to changes and fluctuations in the field that have occurred in the last 25 years. School psychology is no longer just the practice of clinical psychology in child guidance clinics and schools. It has been expanded to include services to individuals below and above school age, has concerned itself with social, emotional, and vocational services as well as educational ones, and has broadened to include indirect services to caregivers and social systems besides diagnosis and treatment of individual clients. Borrowing heavily from Reynolds et al. (1984), we can define school psychology as an applied psychological discipline designed to enhance the educational and psychological welfare of learners (child and adult) through prevention, diagnosis, intervention, research, and training.

By definition and tradition, school psychology is firmly embedded in psychology and its scientific method. School psychologists look to the science of psychology to provide answers to practical, educational problems, and problems that commonly are intertwined with certain social contexts. Thus, social psychology's concern with how individuals perceive, feel about, and respond to events must be shared by anyone in school psychology.

HISTORICAL DEVELOPMENT OF SOCIAL AND SCHOOL PSYCHOLOGY: THE SEARCH FOR COMMONALTIES

Ancient Philosophical Roots

Common to both social and school psychology is the reliance on scientific method to address human behavior. Initial thinking about the origins and nature of social behavior can be traced back to the ancient Greeks, particularly the philosophers Plato (427–347 B.C.) and Aristotle (384–322 B.C.). Plato was concerned with how individuals and societies functioned in harmony. Plato proposed that social behavior is a function of man's biological nature and the predominance of head (intellect), heart (volition), and stomach (appetite). Particularly relevant to school psychology was Plato's claim that societies functioned best when individuals occupied places and held positions for which they were most aptly suited. Testing programs to identify individual abilities of prospective public officials had in fact been initiated in China some 1,500 years earlier, and Plato's equating of ability levels and employment status was quite consistent with the purposes to which assessment would be put for the next 1,800 years (French & Hale, 1990). Further, both Plato and Aristotle were nativists who claimed that intelligence and other capacities were inborn. Both lived in a society with distinct social classes and barriers to advancement. Aristotle, however, did place some emphasis on the role of environment in determining social behavior. Thus, Plato and Aristotle were the first to begin to articulate the so-called "nature–nurture" controversy that, in the last half century, has been debated in the intelligence test arena.

Sahakian (1974) noted that Aristotle was the first to begin to study the social psychology of attitudes and persuasion. Aristotle considered persuasion to be a function of the speaker's personal characteristics, the type of audience, and the nature of the message. Many of Aristotle's propositions were incorporated in the groundbreaking work of Theodore M. Newcomb (1943) and Carl Hovland and associates (Hovland, Janis, & Kelley, 1953). Set in motion by events following World War II, the study of attitude change and persuasion would dominate the field of social psychology from the mid-1950s to the mid-1970s (McGuire, 1969).

Simple and Sovereign Theories

For a period of about a century, commencing in the mid-1700s, social philosophy was dominated by what has been called "simple and sovereign theories," overarching and all-sufficient explanations of social behavior. Three leading theories dominated the latter half of the nineteenth century, theories that continue, in modern form, to be central to both social and school psychology. These are hedonism, egoism, and imitation.

Hedonism. Jeremy Bentham (1748–1832) borrowing from the earlier writings of Epicurus, Aristippus, Hobbes, and Adam Smith, offered the idea of hedonism, which stated simply that individuals act to maximize pleasure or happiness and avoid pain. Further, Bentham noted that such pleasure could be measured by examining the hedonistic consequences of an act. The reader will no doubt recognize Bentham's influence on Sigmund Freud's (1856–1939) discussion of the pleasure principle and tension reduction. Freud's contributions to the clinical enterprise were monumental; however, he also made important contributions to social psychology in works such as *Totem and Taboo* (1913) and *Civilization and Its Discontents* (1930), in which he described the cultural basis of conscience development via imitation, the basis of religion, and the relation of man and society.

Of particular interest to school psychologists was Herbert Spencer's (1820–1903) adoption of hedonism in relation to Charles Darwin's (1809–1882) theory of evolution and natural selection. Spencer, arguing for individualism and natural selection processes, was firmly opposed to social legislation in England. He opposed the establishment of free public education in Britain, and his protests delayed this important social welfare program until 1873.

Hedonism also finds expression in the "law of effect," the foundation of instrumental conditioning. Edward L. Thorndike (1874–1949) in the late 1800s, like Spencer before him, employed hedonism and Darwinian theory to provide one of the first "scientific" treatises on the heritability of intelligence. As Thorndike (1899) put it, "He who learns and runs away, will live to learn another day" (p. 91). Hedonism underlies all the modern-day motivational theories of social psychology such as balance theory (Heider, 1959), dissonance theory (Festinger, 1957), and French and Raven's (1959) field theory of social power, although none of these theories were proposed as all encompassing as was hedonism.

Egoism. Egoism, espoused by Thomas Hobbes (1588–1679) and others, was a theory of social behavior that viewed egoistic drives for power over others as even more basic than pleasure seeking. Hobbes, writing during the Renaissance period, offered a pessimistic view of man that, like the earlier views of Plato and Aristotle, was essentially rooted in constitutional and biological factors. Hobbes (1651) offered some insightful observations regarding ego drives that foreshadowed modern writings on self-concept and self-defensive motives: "For such is the nature of men, that howsoever they may acknowledge many others to be more witty, or more eloquent, or more learned; Yet they will hardly believe that there be many so wise as themselves" (p. 82).

The importance of ego strivings and self-image would be resurrected in the writings of many future writers, most notably those of the cultural psychoanalytic school who would merge cultural anthropology and sociology with psychiatry (e.g., Karen Horney, Alfred Adler, and Harry Stack Sullivan; see Sahakian, 1974). However, a point not to be missed is that Hobbes' formulations dealt with collective behavior whereas the psychiatric concern was with individual variation and abnormal behavior, which reflects the influence of Hippocrates (460–377 B.C.).

Imitation. Since the beginnings of the individual disciplines, both social and school psychologists have been concerned with accounting for the conformity of one person's behavior to another, be it child for parent, peers for one another, followers to leaders, or observers to actors on film or video. The French writer, Gabriel Tarde (1843–1904), was a noted philosopher, criminologist, and statistician, who offered the first insights into collective behavior, generally and criminal behavior specifically. Tarde (1903) viewed criminals as persons reared by criminals, and he boldly asserted, "Society is imitation and imitation is a kind of somnambulism" (p. 87). Tarde equated the power of imitation with the power of hypnosis being studied by fellow Frenchman Charcot. Tarde, in his influential book *The Laws of Imitation*, described several important elements of the imitation process, including the observations that inferiors imitate superiors and that imitation occurs within cultures that are similar rather than different.

Although Tarde's writings set the stage for much of the modern-day writings on social learning theory advanced by Miller and Dollard, Bandura, and others, the link between imitation theory as social philosophy and the emerging discipline of school psychology is seen most clearly in the writings of James Mark Baldwin (1861–1934). Baldwin can be credited as the first to apply social psychology to the study of the child in his three-volume series, *Dictionary of Philosophy and Psychology* (1901–1906). It was Baldwin rather than G. Stanley Hall, noted for his contributions to the study of adolescence, who was the first psychologist to argue that individual genetic development recapitulated the history of mankind, although the idea itself must be credited to Darwin.

Studying Individual Variation: The French Connection

Sahakian (1974) noted that it was the French social theorists who were the most influential investigators of collective behavior, in particular Auguste Comte (1790–1857), considered the founder of sociology, Tarde; Gustave Le

Bon (1841–1931), who wrote of the irresistible urges and suggestibility seen in mass collectives in his book *The Crowd* (1896), and Emil Durkheim (1858–1917), who offered important views on collective behavior in general and social causes of suicide in particular. Both Tarde and LeBon were heavily influenced by Charcot's work using hypnosis to cure neuroses as was Freud. In the late 1800s, there was little demarcation between those interested in abnormal psychology and those interested in social psychology.

It is no coincidence that the same intellectual climate that nurtured French social psychology also provided the impetus to advance understanding retardation and emerging statistical techniques. Jean Marc Gaspard Itard's (1774–1838) work with Victor, the so-called "Wild Boy of Aveyron," who had lived in the woods of France for about 8 years and was considered an "idiot," set the stage for French interest in intelligence and retardation (MacMillan, 1982). British social scientists Sir Frances Galton (1822–1911) and Karl Pearson (1857–1936) are credited with developing the statistical techniques that would spur America's mental testing movement and thereby school psychology; however, several years earlier Lambert A. J. Quetelet sought to measure intelligence using crude statistical methods. Quetelet's work predated Galton's publication in 1890 of "Mental tests and measurements" by nearly half a century. Quetelet proposed measurements focusing on physical and sensory reactivity, methods that would dominate intelligence testing until Alfred Binet added tests of acquired knowledge in the last decade of the nineteenth century.

Wundt and Witmer

Perhaps one of the most interesting and best kept secrets in the history of school psychology involves Wilhelm Wundt (1832–1921), the acknowledged founder of experimental psychology, and Lightner Witmer (1867–1956), the acknowledged founder of clinical and school psychology. Wundt is credited with establishing the first laboratory of psychology in Leipzig in 1879, and James McKeen Cattell was his first assistant. What is less often recognized is that Wundt made a decision early in his career to devote the first part to the study of physiological differences in sensation and perception, and the second half to the investigation of what he called *folk psychology* (the study of language, myth, and custom). Wundt was strongly influenced by the earlier writings of Darwin and Spencer, and published his writings on social psychology in the last decade of his life when he already was a dominant figure in psychology. However, his work had little impact on mainstream social psychology, partly because he placed social psychology in an ancillary role relative to individual psychology, partly because his orientation was historical rather than analytical, and partly because it was never translated into English.

In 1892 Lightner Witmer was awarded his PhD in psychology under the direction of Wilhelm Wundt (see McReynolds, 1987, for an excellent account of Witmer's career). Witmer had been one of Cattell's students at the University of Pennsylvania studying individual differences in reaction time, and Cattell's taking a job at Columbia University led Witmer to complete his doctorate under Wundt, Cattell's and G. Stanley Hall's former mentor. Although Witmer returned to America as an experimental psychologist, within 5 years he would inaugurate course work in clinical psychology, mental retardation, and criminology at the University of Pennsylvania, establish the first psychological clinic dealing with children's school problems, coin the name *clinical psychology* (which at the time was synonymous with school psychology), and develop the first private practice. One can only speculate about the influence of Wundt on Cattell's and ultimately Witmer's thinking. Wundt was a hereditarian in his ideology, and Witmer only gradually shifted to an environmental position late in his career. Wundt had interests in applied psychology, especially criminology and social organization; Witmer devoted much of his career to emotionally troubled youth and was very concerned with family and living environments in his prescribed treatments. In addition, both men basically were antagonistic to the growing impetus of the mental testing movement. Thus, Witmer shared many of Wundt's interests in applied psychology and its social nature.

The Early Years: 1900–1935

During the period from 1880 to 1920 the United States was faced with problems caused by massive immigration from Central and Southern European countries and the migration of the populace from rural, agrarian centers to urban, industrial ones (Fagan, 1985). The school population doubled and the schools themselves were far different than they had been a generation earlier. Graded classes replaced the traditional "one-room schoolhouse" in the middle of the nineteenth century, and progression from grade to grade was based on lesson mastery. However, because schools were not prepared to deal with the large numbers of culturally diverse children, many of whom had language barriers, many students were retained in grade (Larson, 1955). The conditions of urban life were poor and many communities set up settlement houses staffed with social workers.

The early 1900s ushered in a number of important social reforms affecting women and children (especially child labor legislation and the passage of compulsory school attendance laws). There was an increasing reliance on science as a partner in the move toward industrialization and national efficiency.

By 1908 the seeds had been planted that would serve to separate clinical/school psychology from social psychology. In 1905 Binet and Simon produced the first intelligence test, and this was translated into English by Henry Goddard in 1911. Goddard, director of research at the New Jersey

Training School for Feeble-Minded Boys and Girls at Vineland, was a strong advocate of mental testing and, after Witmer, a prominent figure in the development of school psychology. Within a few years, several major metropolitan areas would develop child guidance clinics to deal with the growing numbers of children considered retarded, maladjusted, or delinquent (many of whom did not fit the conventional mold of the schools of the day, see Fagan, 1985).

On July 28, 1914, Austria–Hungary declared war on Serbia and World War I began. That same year, a number of research studies appeared examining groups of children (e.g., Black–White) with Goddard's version of the Binet test. On April 6, 1917, the United States entered the war on the side of the Allies. In that year Goddard, Thorndike, Lewis Terman, and others developed the Army Alpha and Beta intelligence tests used to screen nearly 1.7 million recruits in World War I (French & Hale, 1990). When the war ended a year and a half later, these tests were widely used in schools and industry, and school psychology was heavily invested in individual diagnosis and treatment.

The war also greatly changed the nature of psychological thought. Psychoanalysis became the dominant perspective, and out of this orientation grew an interest in measuring unconscious material. In 1921 Rorschach published his inkblot test, and in 1935 Morgan and Murray published the Thematic Apperception Test. In the intervening years, John Watson and Mary Cover Jones reported early experiments with behavior therapy with children suffering from phobias (the famous cases of Little Albert and Peter). Floyd Allport's (1924) text *Social Psychology* had a behavioristic stance; however, behaviorism would not catch on in mainstream psychology until the 1960s.

From Witmer and Goddard's work prior to and after the war, for the next quarter of a century clinical/school psychology was concerned almost exclusively with assessment, and most work was done with retarded, maladjusted, and delinquent children. Psychologists in adult-oriented clinics often were relegated to positions of testers for psychiatrists.

By the late 1920s the city of Chicago had developed a number of clinics for testing and counseling schoolchildren. In the same city John Dewey (1859–1953) and Margaret Mead (1901–1978) were teaching social psychology at the University of Chicago. Dewey's thinking was influenced by Tarde and Baldwin (Sahakian, 1974). Dewey was the consummate pragmatist, deeply concerned with the application of social philosophy. His progressive education movement's emphasis on "whole-person learning" forced the public schools to take a broader role in education. This, along with advances made in intelligence testing of recruits during World War I, set school psychology on its present applied course.

During this same time period, social psychology was separating from its philosophical and sociological roots. In 1908 the first two textbooks on social psychology were published by McDougall and Ross. Following Triplett's lead, within the next 5 years there would be calls for a more scientific and less "armchair" social psychology (Sahakian, 1974). In 1918 the University of South Carolina only offered two psychology courses, and one was in social psychology (Furchtgott, 1984). The professor, Josiah Morse, was a student of Hall, another example of the early convergence of developmental, clinical, and social thinking. However, compared to the clinical enterprise, social psychology as a discipline would witness little growth and development over the next 20 years.

The influence of psychoanalysis was felt in social psychology as the 1920s saw further cross-fertilization between clinical and social psychology. In 1921 the *Journal of Abnormal Psychology* was renamed as the *Journal of Abnormal and Social Psychology*. The 1920s began with economic prosperity and ended in economic collapse. There would be a rise in anti-Jewish, -Catholic, and -Negro sentiment as the decade marked the rise of the Ku Klux Klan in the South. There was fear that liberalism and economic prosperity would undermine the country's traditional beliefs and values. John Scopes was indicted for teaching evolution in high school. Such events led social psychologists to ask questions about social influence, attitudes toward racial and religious groups, and social class differences.

Starting in the late 1920s and continuing right up through World War II, advances were being made in attitude measurement by L. L. Thurstone, Emory S. Borgadus, and Rensis Likert. The primary focus of these men was on racial and cultural attitudes. Further, the nature of the questions tells much about the tenor of the times. For example, in one survey Likert (1932) inquired, "In a community where the negroes outnumber the whites, a negro who is insolent to a white man should be: (a) excused or ignored, (b) reprimanded, (c) fined and jailed, (d) fined, jailed, and given corporal punishment (e.g., whipping), and (e) lynched."

Social psychology in the 1920s and 1930s, following Tripplet's lead, also was very concerned with schooling issues. Jacob Moreno (1889–1974), rejecting the antireligious stances of Marxism and Freudianism, developed sociometry, psychodrama, and group psychotherapy in nine books published between 1919 and 1925. Sociometry, an important measurement tool widely used in school psychology (see Medway & Skedsvold in this volume), was advanced by the early work of Quetelet and directly originated in the work of James Mark Baldwin and particularly John Dewey (Moreno, 1953). Moreno and Helen Hall Jennings' early studies of sociometry were done in schools. Moreno himself tested sociometric methods in schools in 11 states in the Northeastern, Midwestern, and Western United States. Moreno (1953), in discussing the first sociometric test, recalled: "In the sociometric test given at PS 181, Brooklyn, N. Y., in the winter of 1931 the seating order in the classroom imposed upon the children by extraneous authority was confronted with the seating order which the children expressly preferred. Every sociometric test brought out the contrast between an authoritarian and a democratic pattern of grouping"(p. xxi). Dewey's influence in this work is unmistakable.

Gardner Murphy (1895–1979), one of Moreno's proteges and a founder of the Society for the Psychological Study of Social Issues, provided important insights on the use of discipline in education (Murphy, 1958). In fact, Moreno credited Murphy with the acceptance of sociometry in the United States. Rensis Likert was one of Murphy's students.

Both Kurt Lewin (1890–1947), considered the founder of experimental social psychology, and Fritz Heider (1896–1987), the originator of attribution theory, were trained in the Gestalt tradition, and both would migrate to the United States in the early 1930s. Lewin worked with Wertheimer (Lauretta Bender took designs that Wertheimer originally used for research purposes in developing the Bender Visual-Motor Gestalt Test, a widely used instrument in clinical and school psychology) and Kohler. Both Lewin and Heider worked with William Stern in Berlin. Stern was preoccupied with the study of individual differences and, in 1912, introduced the idea of the mental quotient. Stern no doubt influenced Lewin's consideration of person as well as environmental variables in social behavior.

Lewin's impact on social psychology was broad and far-reaching both in terms of his direct contributions and the influence he exerted through his students, including Leon Festinger, Ronald Lippitt, Harold Kelley, and John Thibaut. He introduced field theory, concepts of life space, the interrelationships between person and environment, the study of group processes, level of aspiration, and social influence. Lewin was much in the pragmatic mold of Dewey. In the years when most of the allied nations were involved in World War II, Lewin, Lippitt, and White (1939) conducted a series of classic studies on social climate in which they demonstrated how leadership styles (autocratic, laissez faire, and autocratic) influence group behavior.

The 1940s

In the late 1940s psychology had begun to lose much of its earlier apolitical nature as both school and social psychology were beginning to be wedded to vested interest groups through school psychology's alignment with the educational establishment and social psychology's growing need for research funding. A $500 gift from an unknown donor interested in the causes of antisemitism led Nevitt Sanford, a psychoanalyst with interests in social psychology, to study the Authoritarian Personality in 1943 at the University of California at Berkeley. This research program subsequently was accused of making unwarranted generalizations about the nature of prejudice in the United States (Sahakian, 1974), and the controversy engendered the interest of Donald T. Campbell to study for his doctorate at Berkeley (Evans, 1980).

Social psychology maintained a very applied focus in the years just prior to the war and typically dealt with issues with direct political overtones. In the days just prior to America's entrance into World War II, the Associated Press asked Moreno to predict Hitler's future. Psychologists like Lewin believed that social psychology could solve social problems. Lewin's emigration to the United States from Germany was accompanied by shifts in his research, from early work in topological psychology, field theory, and level of aspiration in Berlin to social climates and group dynamics in Iowa. With the outbreak of war, his work would be directly tied to the war effort, most notably in a series of studies examining the effectiveness of group techniques in convincing consumers to buy less desirable cuts of meat and provide better nutritional care for their children (Lewin, 1947).

World War II transformed the face of clinical/school and social psychology. Applied psychologists now found themselves involved in military hospitals working with adults rather than children and doing therapy as well as assessment, whereas social psychologists were enlisted to change attitudes and counter Nazi propaganda. A separation of clinical from school psychology that Witmer never envisioned occurred in the years from 1944 to 1947 as separate divisions of the American Psychological Association were established. During these years clinical psychology underwent massive growth and development, establishing new patterns of training (the so-called Boulder model) some 10 years before school psychologists would convene at the Thayer Hotel in West Point, New York to chart their field's course.

The Postwar Years

Cartwright (1979) offered a telling observation about social psychology after World War II: "It is difficult for anyone who did not experience it to appreciate the magnitude of the impact of the war upon American social psychology. . . . When the war was over, the field was incomparably different from what it had been just three or four years before" (p. 84).

Cina (1981) argued that the military reorganized social psychology through a series of contractual arrangements, establishments of research institutes, and support of professional organizations. She claimed that social psychology was used to serve the purposes of psychological warfare. This is not unlike the flourishing of the mental testing industry following World War I (Kamin, 1974).

The years immediately following World War II brought a concern for the problems of adults returning home from overseas and less emphasis on children's needs. Social psychologists during the war had invested heavily in studying attitudes and communications research employing soldiers in the Army as subjects. As they returned home and took university positions, they continued to study attitudes and social influence but instead used laboratory settings and turned to the readily available supply of college students, many of whom were funded by the G. I. Bill. After the war, social psychology took root in traditional research universities in metropolitan areas (Jones, 1968) such as Columbia, Yale, Harvard, and Michigan. Steiner (1974) observed: "By the late 1950s, social psychology had turned inward. It had largely renounced its concern for larger states and processes; . . . what happened to the group, and why" (p. 94)? One answer to Steiner's question is that group-oriented psychologists socialized by Lewin had left the field to study planned organizational change. Ronald Lippitt, Kenneth Benne, and Leland Bradford developed laboratory or T-group training in 1947, which became one of the main instruments for organizational change and development (see chapter 7 in this volume).

Pennsylvania, New York, and Ohio developed certification programs for school psychologists before the war, but after many school psychologists had difficulty finding employment in schools, partly because demand for testing children had waned. This demand would not return to prewar levels until school psychology was wedded with special education in the 1970s. School psychology programs also were located in metropolitan areas but in education colleges rather than psychology departments. Both school and social psychology had trouble penetrating the conservative South until the mid-1960s. As of 1963 there were only two universities awarding the PhD in school psychology in the South (Furchtgott, 1984).

Although social and school psychology were as far apart after the war as they would be, one event occurred in 1954 that brought the disciplines together. Lawyers from the NAACP were about to introduce legislation to challenge the constitutionality of the "separate but equal" doctrine in schools established by Plessy versus Ferguson in 1896. In order to prove psychological damage of segregation, they turned to a group of social psychologists, initially contacting Otto Klineberg of Columbia University. Klineberg put the attorneys in touch with Kenneth F. Clark, who completed his PhD in social psychology at Columbia in 1940. Clark summarized the literature on the effects of prejudice on children for the NAACP and included the results of his wife Mamie's master's thesis showing an aversion of black children for black dolls (Clark & Clark, 1947). The monograph was appended to the brief for the Brown versus Board of Education case heard by the U.S. Supreme Court in 1954. Based partly on social science data, the notion of separate but equal was overturned and racially discriminating schools were ruled illegal. Of interest is the fact that within 3 years of the decision Festinger (1957) postulated the theory of cognitive dissonance. Dissonance predicts attitude change in conformity with behavior. By the Supreme Court's decision, a wave of legislation started where social behavior was legislated and where it was anticipated that social attitudes would follow. The Brown decision paved the way for other laws, such as Public Law 94–142, allowing public school access to handicapped children, and with this legislation too it was hoped that attitudes toward the handicapped would change. Thus, the work of Clark and other social psychologists would set in motion forces that would ultimately impact on all of school psychology.

Developments in the 1960s and 1970s

By the late 1950s school psychology's identity as an applied area of psychology would be firmly established. In the period from 1956 to 1964, the number of school psychology training programs increased 900% (Brown & Minke, 1986), and the field produced its first journal, the *Journal of School Psychology*, and early textbooks. The orientation of course work was focused heavily on clinical courses and practica, much of which reflected the dominance of behaviorism beginning in the 1950s. Whereas the child guidance clinics established in the 1920s and 1930s focused psychologists toward community work integrating agencies involved with education, health, and family matters, school and clinical psychology from 1940 until today has been oriented toward treating mental illness.

Within social psychology behaviorism would not play a key role, another phenomenon that had its roots in World War II. Before the war, Carl Hovland researched Hullian's behavioral theory and helped develop the frustration–aggression hypothesis. However, during and after the war, his research interests shifted to the persuasion process (Jones, 1985). Hovland was a significant figure in the history of social psychology, and collaborated with a number of prominent researchers including Harold Kelley, Jack Brehm, and William McGuire. By the end of the 1960s, the study of social psychology would be synonymous with the study of attitude change.

Behaviorism also had a difficult time taking hold in social psychology because of its disregard of internal, inferential processes. Even prior to the war the Gestalt tradition, with its emphasis on phenomenology, dominated social psychology in the work of Lewin, Heider, Muzafer Sherif (1936), and Soloman Asch (1956). Social psychology developed outside the mainstream of American psychology that was dominated by the S–R behavioral tradition of Watson, Hull, and Skinner. From the 1930s to present day, social psychology has been heavily influenced by a cognitive orientation, seen most readily in the interest in attribution theory (see chapter 3, this volume). By comparison, clinical and school psychology embraced, although not uncritically, the dominant theories of the time, especially client-centered therapy and social learning theory. It was not until the 1970s that cognitive theories of psychology would be given much attention in school psychology (Craighead, 1982), an outgrowth of the cognitive revolution in experimental psychology.

As the Vietnam War, the sexual revolution, crime, inadequate health care, environmental neglect, and drug abuse dominated the attention of the American people, so did it occupy the attention of both the social and school psychologists. The same factors that caused social psychologists to broaden their research interests away from the dominancy of attitude paradigms in the 1950s and early 1960s caused school psychologists to be trained in consultation, organization development, crisis intervention, group and family counseling, vocational methods, and legal and ethical concerns. However, despite the contributions of social psychology to school consultation (e.g., Sarason, Levine, Goldenberg, Cherlin, & Bennett, 1966) and isolated calls for social psychologists to be hired by schools (Lighthall, 1969; Medway, 1975), the two fields have stayed on relatively parallel courses and have not witnessed the rapprochement evident at the turn of the century.

EPILOGUE

The purpose of this chapter was to provide some insight into the development of social and school psychology over the last century. As seen, each field has been molded by the winds of social, political, and economic change, and each bears the particular imprint of dynamic personalities like Hobbes, Freud, Wundt, Witmer, Binet, Dewey, and Lewin, to name a few. Each field has been shaped by global unrest and attempted to raise public awareness and concern for children, to encourage environmental preservation, to recognize unrepresented groups (such as minorities and the handicapped), and to promote an end to violence and aggression.

Whereas social and school psychology have been products of their past, they also are likely to be products of their future. Although the social class barriers and obstacles to vocational advancement taken for granted during the days of Plato and Aristotle have long been dismantled, the tearing down of ideological and geographical barriers that have prevented the free exchange of ideas on a worldwide basis is just beginning. Social psychology and school psychology have both grown apart during periods of conflict including two World Wars, the Vietnam War, and the wars for human equality irrespective of race, sex, color, age, and physical endowment. The next decade appears to be the only one in modern history where leaders of nations are talking peace and not preparing for war. The prevailing winds of peace offer a new promise and challenge to once again integrate social and school psychology so that each can bring unique strengths to addressing societal and educational problems over the next century.

REFERENCES

Allport, F. H. (1924). *Social psychology*. Boston: Houghton Mifflin.
Allport, G. W. (1985). The historical background of social psychology. In G. Lindzey & E. Aronson (Eds.), *Handbook of social psychology* (Vol. 1, 3rd ed., pp. 1–46). New York: Random House.

American Psychological Association. (1986). *Biographical directory of the American Psychological Association*. Arlington, VA: Author.

Asch, S. E. (1956). Studies of independence and conformity. *Psychological Monographs, 70,* 1–70 (whole).

Baldwin, J. M. (Ed.), *Dictionary of philosophy and psychology* (3 vols.). New York: MacMillan, 1901–1906.

Brown, D. T., & Minke, K. M. (1986). School psychology graduate training: A comprehensive analysis. *American Psychologist, 41,* 1328–1338.

Cartwright, D. (1979). Contemporary social psychology in historical perspective. *Social Psychology Quarterly, 42,* 82–93.

Cina, C. (1981). *Social science for whom?: A structural history of social psychology.* Doctoral Dissertation, State University of New York at Stony Brook.

Clark, K. B., & Clark, M. P. (1947). Racial identification and preference in Negro children. In T. M. Newcomb & E. L. Hartley (Eds.), *Readings in social psychology* (pp. 169–178). New York: Holt, Rinehart, & Winston.

Craighead, W. E. (1982). A brief clinical history of cognitive-behavior therapy with children. *School Psychology Review, 11,* 5–13.

Elwood, C. A. (1925). *The psychology of human society.* New York: Appleton.

Evans, R. I. (1980). *The making of social psychology.* New York: Gardner Press.

Fagan, T. K. (1985). Sources for the delivery of school psychological services during 1890–1930. *School Psychology Review, 14,* 378–382.

Fagan, T. K. (1986). The evolving literature of school psychology. *School Psychology Review, 15,* 430–440.

Festinger, L. (1957). *A theory of cognitive dissonance.* Stanford, CA: Stanford University Press.

French, J. L., & Hale, R. L. (1990). A history of the development of psychological and educational testing. In C. R. Reynolds & R. W. Kamphaus (Eds.), *Handbook of psychological and educational assessment of children: Intelligence and achievement* (pp. 3–28). New York: Guilford Press.

French, J. R. P., & Raven, B. (1959). The bases of social power. In D. Cartwright (Ed.), *Studies in social power* (pp. 15–167). Ann Arbor, MI: Institute for Social Research.

Freud, S. (1913). *Totem and taboo.* New York: W. W. Norton.

Freud, S. (1930). *Civilization and its discontents.* Garden City, New York: Doubleday.

Furchtgott, E. (1984). *History of Psychology at the University of South Carolina.* Paper presented at the meeting of the Southern Society for Philosophy and Psychology, Columbia, SC.

Gottlieb, J., & Leyser, Y. (1981). Friendship between mentally retarded and nonretarded children. In S. Asher & J. Gottman (Eds.), *The development of children's friendships* (pp. 150–181). Cambridge, MA: Cambridge University Press.

Heider, F. (1946). Attitudes and cognitive organization. *Journal of Psychology, 21,* 107–112.

Hennigan, K. M., Flay, B. R., & Cook, T. D. (1980). "Give me the facts": Some suggestions for using social science knowledge in national policy-making. In R. F. Kidd & M. J. Saks (Eds.), *Advances in applied social psychology* (Vol. 1, pp. 113–147). Hillsdale, NJ: Lawrence Erlbaum Associates.

Hobbes, T. (1651). *Leviathan.* (Reprint of 1st ed. Cambridge: Cambridge University Press, 1904).

Hovland, C. I., Janis, I. L., & Kelley, H. H. (1953). *Communication and persuasion: Psychological studies of opinion change.* New Haven: Yale University Press.

Jones, E. E. (1985). Major developments in social psychology during the past five decades. In G. Lindzey & E. Aronson (Eds.), *Handbook of social psychology* (Vol. 1, 3rd ed., pp. 47–108). New York: Random House.

Kamin, L. J. (1974). *The science and politics of I.Q.* New York: Halstead Press.

Larson, R. E. (1955). *Age-grade status of Iowa elementary school pupils.* Unpublished doctoral dissertations, State University of Iowa.

Le Bon, G. (1896). *The crowd.* London: T. Fisher Unwin.

Lewin, K. (1947). Group decision and social change. In T. M. Newcomb & E. L. Hartley (Eds.), *Readings in social psychology* (pp. 330–344). New York: Henry Holt.

Lewin, K., Lippitt, R., & White, R. K. (1939). Patterns of aggressive behavior in experimentally created "social climates." *Journal of Social Psychology, 10*, 271–299.

Lighthall, F. F. (1969). A social psychologist for school systems. *Psychology in the Schools, 6*, 3–12.

Likert, R. (1932). A technique for the measurement of attitudes. *Archives of Psychology, 140*, 1–55.

MacMillan, D. L. (1982). *Mental retardation in school and society*. Boston: Little, Brown.

McDougall, W. (1908). *Introduction to social psychology*. London: Methuen.

McGuire, W. J. (1969). The nature of attitudes and attitude change. In G. Lindzey & E. Aronson (Eds.), *Handbook of social psychology* (Vol. 3, 2nd ed., pp. 136–314). Reading, MA.: Addison-Wesley.

McReynolds, P. (1987). Lightner Witmer: Little known founder of clinical psychology. *American Psychologist, 42*, 849–858.

Medway, F. J. (1975). A social psychological approach to internally based change in the schools. *Journal of School Psychology, 13*, 19–27.

Moreno, J. L. (1953). *Who shall survive?: Foundations of sociometry, group psychotherapy, and sociodrama*. Beacon, New York: Beacon House.

Murphy, G. (1958) *Human potentialities*. New York: Basic Books.

National Association of School Psychologists (1989). *Membership directory*. Washington, DC: Author.

Newcomb, T. M. (1943). *Personality and social change*. New York: Dryden.

Reynolds, C. R., Gutkin, T. B., Elliott, S. N., & Witt, J. C. (1984). *School psychology: Essentials of theory and practice*. New York: Wiley.

Ross, E. A. (1908). *Social psychology*. New York: MacMillan.

Sahakian, W. S. (1974). *Systematic social psychology*. New York: Chandler Publishing.

Sarason, S. B., Levine, M., Goldenberg, I. I., Cherlin, D. L., & Bennett, E. M. (1966). *Psychology in community settings: Clinical, educational, vocational, social aspects*. New York: Wiley.

Sherif, M. (1936). *The psychology of social norms*. New York: Harper & Row.

Steiner, I. D. (1974). Whatever happened to the group in social psychology? *Journal of Experimental Social Psychology, 10*, 94–108.

Tarde, G. (1903). *The laws of imitation*. New York: Henry Holt.

Thorndike, E. L. (1899). *The associative processes in animals*. Biological lectures from the Marine Biological Laboratory at Woods Hole. Boston: Atheneum.

Triplett, N. (1897–1898). The dynamogenic factors in pacemaking and competition. *American Journal of Psychology, 9*, 507–533.

2

MEASURING AND CHANGING ATTITUDES IN EDUCATIONAL CONTEXTS

Thomas P. Cafferty
University of South Carolina

Schools, like all complex organizations, are attitude arenas. Members of several diverse groups—public, parents, teachers, students, administration, and staff—develop and maintain attitudes toward each other and toward policies and practices relevant to school functioning. Such attitudes may include racial and ethnic attitudes; attitudes toward those with physical, mental, and emotional handicaps; toward school in general; toward particular aspects of school such as the disciplinary policy, extracurricular activities or homework; toward subject material, such as reading or mathematics; toward curriculum design; and even toward school psychology. These attitudes in turn are thought to play a directive role in the production of behavior, thus affecting the implementation of policy and the outcome of practice. In many instances, such attitudes are of direct or indirect concern to the school psychologist.

This chapter is designed to provide an overview of some important attitude issues as they may be related to the work of the school psychologist. These issues include a definition of terms in the field, generally accepted methods of measuring attitudes, some models that suggest strategies for developing attitude change campaigns, and some thoughts about the outcome of such campaigns, including the relationship between attitudes and behavior.

DEFINITIONAL ISSUES

There are numerous definitions of attitude in the social psychological literature. Some differ in only minor points, whereas others are widely divergent.

They often seem to reflect major emphases in the general field of social psychology at the time of their formulation (e.g., behavioral vs. cognitive orientation) or the primary interest of their formulator (e.g., measurement vs. change). Thus what in one publication is termed *attitude* may well be viewed as something quite different in another. The choice of one over another is probably less important for the practitioner than a recognition that such differences exist.

Although definitions differ, there is general agreement that the literature can be organized around three interrelated aspects of the concept of an attitude. One aspect (the cognitive aspect) concerns the thoughts one may have about the attitude object. A second (the affective aspect) concerns the emotional response one may have regarding the attitude object. For many attitude researchers (e.g., Fishbein & Ajzen, 1975), this affective response to the attitude object is the single identifying characteristic of the attitude. Moreover, the major attitude measurement techniques, such as those of Thurstone (1931), were developed to measure the level of affect experienced in response to an attitude object. The third aspect (the behavioral aspect) concerns the behavioral tendencies one may possess toward the attitude object. The term attitude object may refer to virtually any concept, and as Fishbein and Ajzen (1975) pointed out, ambiguity in the specification of the object has been the source of considerable misunderstanding in the field, especially with respect to the prediction of behavior from assessed attitudes.

We can illustrate these aspects of attitude with reference to a topic of potential interest for a school psychologist such as "student attitudes toward mathematics." A student's definition of mathematics (i.e., what subject material is involved) would be a part of the cognitive aspect of the attitude. Perhaps of greater interest would be other cognitions, such as the student's belief about how difficult the subject is for them, how useful it might be, how much homework is involved, and how important it is to do well. Whatever these cognitions, the student's level of liking or disliking mathematics as they understand it would reflect the affective aspect of the attitude. Finally the student's tendencies or intentions to engage in behavior that is either positive or negative with respect to mathematics would comprise the behavioral aspect of the attitude. Such behavioral intentions might involve positive behaviors such as working diligently in mathematics classes, devoting time to math homework, or assisting others with math problems. Alternatively they might involve negative behaviors such as skipping or disrupting math class, failing to complete math homework, or rejecting efforts of assistance with math problems.

These distinctions between the cognitive, affective, and behavioral aspects of attitude form the basis for a number of issues to follow. In discussing the measurement of attitudes, it is important to specify which aspect of attitude is assessed by which measurement technique. Effective planning and evaluation of attitude change efforts often rest on assumptions about the ways in which the three aspects are interrelated. At least one major approach to improving the prediction of behavior from an assessment of attitude relies on a scheme for conceptual coordination between aspects.

MEASUREMENT

General Issues

This section is a summary of the major methods for the measurement of attitudes with reference to their use in educational contexts. It contains general descriptions of the techniques and an indication of their applicability to school psychology issues. Discussion of psychometric properties such as reliability and validity is not included, nor are specific procedures for instrument development that can be found in more extended treatments (cf. Dawes & Smith, 1985; Edwards, 1957; Mueller, 1986).

In view of the preceding discussion, it should be noted that the measures to be discussed can be seen as assessing one or another of the aspects of attitude. This is an important consideration for the school psychologist confronted with the need to "assess attitudes" toward some object or issue. If interest is confined to determining whether respondents like or dislike the issue under investigation, then a relatively simple measure of affect may be all that is needed.

Frequently, however, we are not only interested in whether respondents like or dislike an attitude object, we are also interested in what they think about the object. In fact, in many cases we have a good idea of the affect. Our primary interest is in the cognitions, on the assumption that knowing the cognitions will help us understand the basis for the affect. In these cases we may turn to other instruments described next that fully explore the respondent's cognitions about the attitude object. Realize, however, that some measures of cognition such as statements of belief do not directly yield affective information and, therefore, do not give an indication of whether the respondent likes or dislikes the attitude object. For instance, a respondent's endorsement of the statement "Knowledge of mathematics is important for job success today" does not render evidence regarding their degree of liking for the subject.

Finally there may be some cases where we are only interested in behavioral tendencies or intentions as they may relate to the accurate prediction of behavior. The issue of attitudes and behavior is discussed in a later section. For the present, simply note that, although measures of behavioral intention are the best predictors of actual behavior (cf. Fishbein & Ajzen, 1975), they may yield little direct information about either affect or cognition with respect to the attitude object. Thus, for the school psychologist faced with the task of assessing attitudes toward some issue, an important initial step involves determining which aspects of the attitude are of primary interest. Depending on this determination, he or she can choose or develop an appropriate instrument.

Self-Report Measures

Self-report measures are by far the most common means for assessing attitudes as well as characteristics related to attitudes. Administration of the measures commonly involves a paper-and-pencil questionnaire format. Less common are face-to-face or telephone surveys. As the name implies, self-report measures rely on the respondent's (a) ability and (b) willingness to report his or her reactions to attitude-relevant stimuli.

In the case of paper-and-pencil self-report measures, "ability" is usually thought of in terms of how well the respondent comprehends the items. Intelligence and reading level are the two factors most commonly considered and are particularly salient in work with children or those with intellectual deficits. When the items are read to the respondent, as in telephone surveys, reading level is obviously not of concern, although comprehension of the items is still dependent on level of intellectual functioning. In addition to reading level and intellectual functioning, ability to respond may also refer to the familiarity of the respondent with the response format. When simple agreement with a statement or choice from among alternative statements is required, this is generally not an issue. However, when the response format requires percentage allocation, ranking among alternatives, graphic representation of position on a line between alternatives, or use of machine-scored forms, there may be a considerable loss of information. Relevant to the educational setting, children present a variety of problems related to ability. Simplified wording or pictorial presentation of the item stem may be necessary as well as modification of the response format. For some measures, response alternatives are presented as schematic faces ranging from happy to sad. For others, counting techniques such as pennies deposited in a jar have been used. Literature on the effectiveness of such techniques is sparse. The problem is particularly serious when the researcher is interested in administering age-appropriate forms of the same scale across a range of grade levels.

More recently social psychologists have become concerned with the respondent's ability from a more fundamental perspective. Based on theory and research in the area of social cognition, Nisbett and Wilson (1977) suggested that in many instances the respondent may not have access to the information needed to answer questions about mental processes. Instead, they create plausible answers based either on what they think must have occurred or on conventional wisdom. In giving responses, they are often "telling more than they can know." Although there has been considerable debate about these propositions as originally stated (Smith & Miller, 1978; White, 1980), the position of Nisbett and Wilson suggests caution when developing and interpreting self-report measures.

Willingness of the respondent can become an issue when the information requested could potentially have negative consequences for them or for others with whom they are associated. Areas of interest to the school psychologist, where such a problem could arise, include student attitudes toward drug abuse, teacher attitudes toward the school administration, and administration attitudes toward legislatively mandated programs. In some cases, willingness may be affected by the perceived social desirability of the true response. Responses indicating racial prejudice or aversion to the physically handicapped may be avoided because the respondent recognizes that such responses are socially disapproved. Often, willingness can be enhanced by assurances of confidentiality. Where practical, guarantees of anonymity may be even more effective in securing respondent cooperation.

If only group level data is needed, a set of techniques called *randomized response techniques* may be adapted for use with traditional attitude measures (Dawes & Smith, 1985). Based on techniques originally developed to gather sensitive economic information (e.g., cheating on income tax returns), randomized response guarantees not anonymity but the impossibility of ascertaining any respondent's answers as true of them. With a predetermined level of probability, the respondent is instructed to respond to an item either truthfully or with a specified answer. The researcher is blind with respect to what the respondent has been told. Any given respondent's pattern of answers is therefore some unknown combination of true responses and artificially generated responses. Whereas the pattern for an individual is meaningless, the distribution of responses for the group can be determined by taking into account the distribution expected on the basis of the predetermined probabilities.

One other technique developed to overcome the unwillingness of the respondent to give true answers is called "the bogus pipeline" (Jones & Sigall, 1971). This technique involves the use of a pretest to obtain a respondent's attitude ratings on a few topics. Later, and in an unrelated context, the respondent is led to believe by an elaborate deception using their pretest ratings that some device can detect their true response even when they give a false one. This is followed by a presentation of the questions of primary interest on which the subject is challenged to estimate his or her true response. Although the technique has proven successful in some contexts (e.g., Sigall & Page, 1971), the use of deception, the need for a plausible apparatus, and the requirement that the respondent be pretested for the sample questions all make this a problematic technique for educational settings. However, its development and use underscore the considerable problems posed by situations in which the respondent may be unwilling to give true responses.

Traditional Scales

Four types of scales—Thurstone, Likert, Guttman, and semantic differential— are considered the traditional means of assessing attitudes. All are basically designed to measure affect for or against the attitude object. The first three more properly refer to specific techniques for the construction of scales that meet certain psychometric requirements. Requirements and techniques differ, resulting in scales that appear different and require different types of response to their items. Specific items will differ depending on the attitude object under investigation. The semantic differential simply consists of a basic set of bipolar adjectives that can be applied to any given attitude object. Thus a different scale does not have to be constructed for each attitude object.

In the following sections, each scale is briefly described in terms of its form and administration. Techniques for construction are too lengthy to be included in this chapter. An excellent treatment of these techniques can be found in several sources (e.g., Edwards, 1957; Mueller, 1986).

Thurstone Scales

Although earlier measures of attitudes (or concepts similar to attitudes, such as social distance) were proposed by others (e.g., Allport & Hartman, 1925; Bogardus, 1925), L. L. Thurstone is usually credited with developing the first generally accepted set of techniques for the construction of attitude scales (Thurstone, 1927, 1928, 1931; Thurstone & Chave, 1929). Based on traditional psychophysical scaling techniques, the scales were designed to measure affect for or against some object. Construction involved the use of several judges and time-consuming calculations on their judgments to select the final set of items that constituted a scale pertaining to a specific attitude object. Each item was assigned an empirically determined value on an equal interval scale, with the value being an indicator of how much relative positive or negative affect toward an attitude object was conveyed by that item. Thurstone and his associates offered scales for a number of attitude objects.

Administration of a Thurstone scale is quite simple. The respondent is presented with a set of items (usually 10 to 20) in the form of opinion statements. He or she is then asked to read over the statements and endorse the one that best reflects their own position. If they cannot decide on one, they are asked to select the two or three that best reflect their position, and the researcher calculates the median or mean value of the chosen statements.

The statements are usually arranged in a random order, and the respondent is not aware of their scale values. In any case, the respondent's attitude is assigned the value of the chosen statement or statements. Thus, the respondent's task is to read over a limited set of statements and choose one or more as best reflecting his or her own opinion.

A major advantage of a Thurstone scale is the simplicity of administration and scoring. As a measure of the affective aspect of attitude, it rests on some carefully articulated psychometric theory. A major disadvantage is the labor involved in the construction of the scale. Although computer technology makes the extended calculations relatively easy, gathering data from the judges is still quite time consuming and labor intensive. Perhaps of greater concern to the practitioner, responses on the scale do not yield information about anything other than the intensity and direction of affect toward the attitude object. Information about cognition or behavioral intention would have to be gathered from other instruments.

Likert Scales

Whereas Thurstone techniques were widely recognized as measures of attitude, the effort required to construct acceptable Thurstone scales precluded their extensive use. In 1932, Likert introduced a technique for attitude scale construction that greatly reduced the effort involved, and at the same time produced scales that correlate highly with Thurstone scales dealing with the same topics. On Likert's scales, each item offered a set of alternative responses. The items comprising each scale were selected and modified using item analysis to assess whether any given item discriminated among respondents in a manner consistent with the scale as a whole. The respondent was required to respond to each item by selecting the alternative that best represented their position on the item. The alternatives were assigned values based on pretesting and intuition. A respondent's attitude was indicated by the sum or average of the alternatives selected. Thus, if the scale consisted of 20 items, each with 5 alternatives with values from 1 to 5, the highest (summated) score would be 100, and the lowest score would be 20.

Scales constructed using Likert's methods continue in widespread use today. They are easy to administer and score, and their format is familiar to most respondents (especially in school settings), resembling in many cases a multiple-choice test. Although not an essential feature of a Likert scale, most items contain alternatives worded on a continuum of approval ("strongly approve" to "strongly disapprove") or agreement ("strongly agree" to "strongly disagree"). The actual number of alternatives is arbitrary and depends on various considerations of the researcher. A major problem in the proper construction of a Likert scale is that it requires pretesting and an item analysis, which today involves item intercorrelations. Use of optical scan answer sheets and mainframe computers makes the item analysis quite simple, but without them the task can be difficult.

Like Thurstone scales, Likert scales are designed to measure affect for or against an attitude object as a whole. The attitude object, however, may be a multidimensional concept, eliciting different levels of affect on different dimensions. The item analyses involved in the construction of a Likert scale permit comparisons among responses to different dimensions of the attitude object. Thus, some information about cognitive structure may be obtained. To the extent that an item included on a scale involves a behavioral intention or preference, information may also be derived about behavior. It is important to note, however, that information about cognitive or behavioral aspects of the attitude object are incidental to the primary task of ascertaining affective responses.

Guttman Scales

Thurstone and Likert scales yield a score that reflects overall affect toward or against the attitude object. Any given score, however, cannot be identified with any specific pattern of item responses (unless only a single item is endorsed on the Thurstone scale). In 1944, Louis Guttman proposed a technique for attitude scale construction that under appropriate conditions could scale both items and respondents simultaneously. The practical implication was that it would be possible to associate (with a given level of accuracy) a respondent's score on the scale with a particular pattern of responses. This property of Guttman scales was called *reproducibility*. Furthermore, the level of reproducibility achieved was considered an indicator of whether attitude toward the object could be measured along a single dimension.

Administration and scoring of a Guttman scale is similar to that of a Likert scale. The respondent simply reads each item and responds with the choice of an alternative. As previously indicated, a respondent's score reflects both the level of affect for or against the attitude object and the approximate pattern of responses chosen.

Although Guttman's techniques were not necessarily more difficult or complex than those for Thurstone and Likert scales, and although they possess some advantages, they have not been widely adopted by psychologists interested in measuring attitudes. Concerns about reproducibility may have simply not outweighed the intuitive appeal or utility of the Likert scales. Furthermore, Guttman scales are found more frequently in the sociological literature on attitudes and may, therefore, be less accessible than the others. Finally, the uncertainty about whether one might obtain a unidimensional scale after following the scale construction techniques perhaps discourages potential users.

Semantic Differential

Whereas the Thurstone, Likert, and Guttman techniques were developed for the measurement of attitudes, the semantic differential technique was a by-product of an extensive investigation into the measurement of meaning by Osgood and his associates (Osgood, Suci, & Tannenbaum, 1957). In an effort to discover the dimensions of connotative meaning, these investigators had respondents rate various concepts (e.g., mother, house, religion) on a number of bipolar adjectives (e.g., good–bad, weak–strong, heavy–light). When they factor analyzed the adjective pairs, they found three primary dimensions: evaluation (with high loadings on pairs such as good–bad), potency (with high loadings on pairs such as weak–strong), and activity (with high loadings on pairs such as active–passive). Osgood et al. noted that the evaluative dimension, which accounted for the highest percentage of the variance in meaning, was conceptually similar to the notion of affect in attitudes. Subsequent research strengthened their belief that the adjective pairs on the evaluative dimension measured attitude affect and led to widespread adoption of the technique as a means to measure attitudes.

Administration of a semantic differential measure of attitude simply involves presenting a respondent with the attitude object to be rated at the top of a sheet of paper, followed by a series of bipolar adjectives. The adjective pairs are chosen from those that load most highly on the evaluative dimension of Osgood et al.'s original measure (e.g., good–bad, kind–cruel, awful–nice). Additional pairs are sometimes included depending on the special interests of the researcher or to simply provide fillers to disguise the real intent of the scale. Each pair is separated by seven blanks. The respondent's task is to give a spontaneous response to the attitude object by placing a check on one of the blanks between the adjectives, indicating whether the object rates closer to one of the adjectives or the other. Depending on the location of the check, the respondent is assigned a score from 1 to 7 on each adjective pair. A total score is calculated as the sum of the scores on all the relevant adjective pairs.

Construction of a semantic differential measure of attitude simply involves specifying the attitude object and selecting the appropriate pairs of bipolar adjectives. Such scales can be made up very quickly and with little effort or material requirements. Administration is relatively easy, making minimal demands on the respondent's reading ability. There are, however, two major drawbacks. First, many respondents find the task difficult to understand. For instance, they might not be sure how an adjective pair such as kind–cruel would apply to a concept like mainstreaming. Careful instruction and examples on completing the items can usually overcome this problem. Second, the technique generally reveals very little about the cognitive or behavioral aspects of the attitude object. Other measures would be required to obtain that information.

Extensions of Traditional Scales

The traditional attitude scales described previously are used to assess affect toward or against an attitude object considered along a single dimension. However, as Guttman scaling techniques imply, an attitude object may have many facets, and one may be interested in attitudes toward these facets considered separately. The problem here is that one must first determine what these facets are. In some cases, practical interest or theoretical considerations dictate the facets of interest. For instance, a school subject like English might be broken into constituent activities as defined by the curriculum, with interest in attitudes toward each of the constituent activities, such as reading or composition. In other cases, the facets may have to be uncovered by multidimensional scaling techniques performed on the respondent population prior to constructing the attitude scales. This might be the case for attitudes toward handicapped students, where perceptions of handicaps may differ on a number of dimensions. However the facets are determined, the point is that full exploration of an attitude issue may involve several scales embedded in a single instrument.

General Rating Scales

As previously mentioned, the traditional scales are more appropriately viewed as procedures for the construction of attitude scales that assess the degree of affect toward or against some object of concern. Very often, however, a researcher is not so interested in measuring affect as in gathering information on a respondent's perception of the attitude object (e.g., what teachers view as the most important function of the school psychologist) and/or his or her preferences from among several alternative courses of action (e.g., what type of disciplinary action is appropriate to a given infraction). In these circumstances, the researcher may construct or adopt a self-report measure of this information that looks formally like an attitude scale (usually a Likert scale, with multiple alternatives for each of several items). In fact, many of the recommendations for the construction of sound attitude items, which can be found in several sources dating back to Likert (e.g., Likert, 1932; Mueller, 1986; Selltiz, Wrightsman & Cook, 1976), apply equally to items on these more general measures.

Depending on the aims of the researcher, such measures may be entirely appropriate, but they may not be measuring what is generally considered attitude. Confusion arises when a measure of a respondent's perception of an object is interpreted by the researcher as an indicator of attitude toward the object. Chapter 16 by Chassin, Presson, Sherman, and Curran in this volume illustrates the danger of this problem with respect to substance abuse. Two students may both endorse an item such as "Students who use crack are social outcasts." One, however, may view this situation negatively and the other positively, depending on the value system of their group.

Keeping the preceding considerations in mind, there are numerous attitude scales and measures of attitude related concepts for use in educational settings. Unfortunately, locating these scales can be difficult, because many are found only in original publications, or worse, in unpublished files of the researchers who used them. Nevertheless, there are some sources for such instruments, with the best general source contained in an annotated bibliography in Mueller's (1986) volume.

Other Self-Report Techniques

Although paper-and-pencil scales and rating forms as described previously are the most popular self-report methods for measuring aspects of attitudes, there have been alternative techniques suggested from time to time as partial solutions to some of the problems mentioned before. One technique involves the analysis of projective answers to unstructured stimuli, patterned methods used for the measurement of personality characteristics using the Thematic Apperception Test (cf. Kidder, 1981; Mueller, 1986). Such a projective technique might prove useful when dealing with material on which the respondent is unwilling or unable to give overt unpopular or socially disapproved responses. One form of projective technique that has been developed for use with children has involved doll play (Walker, 1973). The lack of evidence for reliability or validity of the measures, however, makes the technique a little used one.

This and other alternatives to the traditional format are often classified as *indirect measures* of attitude. Most lack reliability and validity information, and could occasionally create ethical concerns over deception used in presenting these techniques as something other than attitude measures. Good general reviews of these techniques are found in Kidder (1981) and Kidder and Campbell (1970).

Objective Measures

In addition to the self-report techniques, there are several other techniques for the measurement of attitudes that are not dependent on respondent self-report. None are nearly as popular as the traditional scales or rating forms, but they have some advantages that might make them a preferred mode of measurement in certain situations.

Physiological Indices. Because affect is a central aspect of attitude, and because there are a number of somatic manifestations of affect, it appears reasonable to assume that one might be able to develop a measure of attitude that would be based on a somatic manifestation. The best known of these measures uses dilation and constriction of the pupil of the eye as an index of liking or disliking for a visual stimulus. Developed by Hess (1965), this measure has conceptual appeal in that it bypasses the need for verbal self-report from the respondent. It does, however, require special equipment and a carefully controlled environment for appropriate measurement of pupil size, making it generally impractical for use in an educational setting. In addition, reviews of the literature on studies using the technique raise concerns for the impact of nonattitudinal factors on pupil response (Petty & Cacioppo, 1983; Woodmansee, 1970).

Other physiological indicators of arousal or interest such as galvanic skin response, heart rate, or respiration, either individually or in combination, have been suggested as possible indicators of attitude. The classic objection to such physiological techniques is that, although they may be valid indicators of intensity of affect, they do not adequately distinguish direction of affect. This may not be as critical a problem as it first appears, because in context the direction of affect can easily be otherwise assessed or assumed. Furthermore, it is important to note that recent advances in physiological measurement techniques and their analysis have addressed a number of previous objections to their use (Petty & Cacioppo, 1983; Tursky & Jamner, 1983; Wegener, 1982). Nevertheless, practical considerations such as the availability or portability of equipment and the need for testing personnel are likely to limit the use of such techniques on a widespread basis in educational context, at least for the foreseeable future.

Behaviors. The fact that for many attitude researchers the concept of attitude has a behavioral component leads to the suggestion that some measurable aspect of behavior might be used as an index of a corresponding attitude. Indeed, the responses to the items on a scale or rating form can be considered behavioral indicators of an attitude. Of more substantive interest are characteristics of behavior that can be used as indicators of attitude in place of scale responses. These might include a number of traditional behavioral measures such as: response choice (e.g., fruit versus candy for a school lunch), time on task, number of responses, rate of responding, and strength of response. Such behaviors can be measured as they occur, they can be videotaped for later examination, or they can be recorded by trained observers via behavior checklists (Henerson, Morris, & Fitz-Gibbon, 1978). The use of such measures may be particularly appealing when, for reasons of age or disability, the subjects of the research are unable to respond on a standard scale or rating form.

The problem with such measures is that conceptually *behavior is not attitude.* In any given situation, behavior has multiple determinants, only one of which may be the attitude in question. As discussed next, behavior may constitute the bottom line in many educational contexts. The school psychologist may simply be interested in changing a pattern of behavior. Such an aim certainly justifies identifying and using a suitable behavioral measure. It is important, however, not to confuse the outcome obtained on the behavioral measure with the outcome that might exist for the corresponding attitude.

Behavioroid Measures. As an alternative to unwieldy and often expensive behavioral measures of dependent variables in social psychology, Aronson, Brewer, and Carlsmith (1985) advocated the use of what they called *behavioroid* measures. Behavioroid measures involve measures of the subject's willingness or intention to perform some behavior without the necessity of actually doing so. The use of such measures in attitude research is illustrated in a classic study of prejudice conducted by DeFleur and Westie (1958), in which White subjects were first given a paper-and-pencil measure of their attitudes toward Blacks. In a subsequent session, subjects were asked to sign as many of a graded series of release agreements as they preferred, indicating their willingness to have their picture taken in an interracial situation as part of a campaign to promote racial harmony. The number of releases signed was the primary dependent variable. No further behavior was required and the study concluded. Similar measures have included willingness to volunteer time to solicit for some cause, to help another in need, and to donate varying amounts of money to a cause. In no case were subjects actually required to make good on these agreements.

Although it might be argued that behavioroid measures are in fact behaviors, there is an important difference in that they are not the behaviors of primary interest. As behaviors, they are subject to most of the same concerns raised in the previous section. Because they are usually measures of behavioral intention, they are subject to some reservations raised in the following section concerning the attitude–behavior relationship. On the other hand, they have an advantage in that they can be collected more efficiently and effectively than other behavioral measures. In most cases, they are paper-and-pencil measures themselves and may be particularly attractive if trying to obtain behavioral information from a large number of respondents without the need to observe each individually.

Unobtrusive Measures. All attitude measures reviewed in the preceding sections intrude to some extent into the respondent's awareness, thus possibly changing the pattern of responses from what it would otherwise be. The final set of measurement techniques are designed to be unobtrusive and have been proposed as such by Webb, Campbell, Schwartz, Sechrest, & Grove (1981). Most involve the creative use of traces of the behaviors of interest to infer the attitudes involved. These traces are often left on physical material that has been the object of the behavior in question. In educational settings, these could include the presence and content of graffiti left on school property, other property damage to school facilities, and normal but selective wear and tear on books and equipment. School records of rates of repair, of library withdrawals, of cafeteria expenditures, and of levels of attendance are also among sources of unobtrusive measures. Webb et al. (1981) offered an array of such measures, many of which could be readily adapted to educational settings. Usually such measures are readily available, particularly for those already in a school system. They circumvent the problem of respondent awareness, because they are usually collected well after the behavior in question has occurred, and they generally (but not always) preserve anonymity because they are measures of aggregate behaviors.

Problems with unobtrusive measures are similar to those with other behavioral measures reviewed previously. In fact, unobtrusive measures are often more remote from the cognitive and affective aspects of attitudes than other behavioral measures, thus making inferences about the attitudes that produced the traces quite tentative. Nevertheless, they are an underutilized means of obtaining often informative data about aggregate attitudes toward various school issues.

MODELS FOR ATTITUDE CHANGE

General Considerations

There are many circumstances in which the school psychologist is not merely interested in measuring attitudes toward some issue but also in developing strategies for changing those attitudes. To some extent, the choice of a strategy is dependent on the purpose for attempting the attitude change. In many instances, the attitude change is related to some specific behavior change (e.g., increasing cooperative and decreasing competitive behaviors). In other cases, the interest may be more in the strength of the behavior (e.g., the enthusiasm with which a new teaching technique is adopted). In still other cases, the interest may be in promoting a general positive climate that is assumed to affect a wide and nonspecific range of behaviors (e.g., public opinion of the school system). A single approach to changing attitudes may not be equally applicable to all these situations. In practice, many attitude change campaigns are quite eclectic in their use of strategies derived from the available social psychological literature.

The study of attitude change has long been a topic of interest in the field of social psychology (McGuire, 1985), and social psychologists have established a number of approaches to the problem. These approaches can be categorized in many ways, but for the purpose of this chapter they will be distinguished in terms of the method of change. First, some attitude change takes place as a result of direct experience with the attitude object. This experience can be haphazard or it can be planned. For instance, students might find themselves paired by chance with others of different race, sex, or ethnicity on some class project. On the other hand, they may be deliberately assigned to groups that are sexually, racially, or ethnically diverse. In either event, attitude change may take place as a result of experiences brought about by such contact. In other instances, students may change their attitudes toward subject areas as a result of good or bad experiences with teachers, texts, or class activities. Dissonance, self-perception, and reinforcement theories all address ways that attitude change might occur in these situations, and all suggest strategies that might be useful for arranging situations that promote change. Weyant (chapter 18, in this volume) reviews the literature on some of these strategies as they apply to reducing negative attitudes toward culturally different and handicapped students in school integration efforts. Therefore, this chapter does not further elaborate on these change techniques.

The second way that attitudes can be changed is through the development of communications designed to persuade the recipients to accept a given position or follow a recommended course of action. Such communications are widely found in school settings and are integral components in campaigns such as those designed to combat drug abuse, promote patriotism, encourage civic participation, and enhance school morale. They may also be used to rally public support for school policy and program funding. As with other aspects of attitude change, there are several approaches to the design and analysis of such persuasive communications. In the sections that follow, three models, one traditional and two somewhat more recent, are briefly reviewed, with an emphasis on their practical implications for the school psychologist interested in promoting attitude change.

The Yale Communications-Persuasion Paradigm

The classic approach to the analysis of attitude change communications was one Hovland developed and used as the basis for an extensive program of research at Yale University in the decade following World War II (Hovland, Janis, & Kelley, 1953). Hovland's original relatively simple paradigm was elaborated through the research, and a more comprehensive version is thoroughly reviewed by McGuire (1985). The basic idea is that in a persuasive communication, a communicator delivers a message over some medium to an audience with the intent of producing some desired effect. These components (communicator, message, medium, audience, and destination) may be thought of as antecedent or independent variables that can be manipulated singly or in combination along a number of dimensions. The communication may result in various outcomes including attention to the message, comprehension, retention, and acceptance, all of which may be thought of as dependent variables that can be measured in a number of ways.

The literature derived from and pertinent to the model contains several findings with major implications for the development of attitude change campaigns in educational settings, many of which are discussed at length in McGuire's (1985) review of the literature. More important than the specific findings, however, is the fact that the model provides a clear conceptual framework for the design of persuasive communications, allowing the change agent to simultaneously consider several aspects of a potential campaign. For instance, choice of an effective communicator may rely not only on characteristics of the communicator themselves (e.g., factors that enhance credibility) but also on the message to be conveyed, the medium over which it is to be conveyed, the intended audience, and the desired outcome. Furthermore, "effectiveness" may be assessed in terms of any of several effects, such as attention to the message, comprehension of its content, retention of the desired content, acceptance of the message, and perhaps action consistent with the intent of the message.

Theory of Reasoned Action

A more recent model that more explicitly links attitudes to behavior is derived from their theory of reasoned action (Ajzen & Fishbein, 1980; Fishbein & Ajzen, 1975). According to this model, beliefs constitute the bases for attitudes that in turn are a major determinant of behavioral intentions, and behavioral intentions are a major determinant of behavior. Thus, to change attitudes, behavioral intentions, or behaviors, it is necessary to change beliefs.

According to Fishbein and Ajzen, there are several types of beliefs that play a role in producing change. First, there are *primary* beliefs that directly support the attitudes, intentions, or behaviors of interest. Primary beliefs are those that must be changed in order to achieve desired change in the other components. For instance, high school students may have a primary belief that drinking alcoholic beverages promotes social acceptance, and this belief might be a major determinant of a positive attitude toward alcohol usage. Second, there are *target* beliefs that are identified by the source of a communication which must be changed to change the other components. Note that the target beliefs should be, but may not turn out to be, the primary beliefs. If they are not, then any effort to change the target beliefs is unlikely to have the desired effect on the attitudes, intentions, or behavior of interest. Thus, changing a target belief that drinking is harmless would be ineffective if that belief is not also a primary one. Furthermore, in many situations target beliefs and primary beliefs may be impossible to change directly. Instead, other beliefs that are more easily addressed in attitude communications are changed first, with the assumption that changes in these beliefs will result in an inference process that results in the change of related primary beliefs. The more easily accessible beliefs are called *proximal* beliefs and are assumed to be most closely associated with the information content of the message. Thus, rather than try to directly change the primary belief that drinking promotes social acceptance, a persuasive communication may show some socially undesirable character drinking, with the aim of establishing a proximal belief that social outcasts are alcohol users, and assuming that such a belief will lead to a change in the belief that drinking promotes social acceptance. However, in addition to the intended proximal and target beliefs, a persuasive communication may unintentionally change other beliefs not related to the content of the communication. These beliefs are called *external* beliefs. Changes in external beliefs can have either positive or negative impact on the receipt of the communication. In the example used, a communication designed to depict a social outcast as one who uses alcohol may unintentionally lead students to infer that only the alcohol identified (e.g., beer) will lead to social rejection, or the outcast may be presented in such a way as to make the whole communication humorous or insincere, thus producing a negative impact on attitudes.

The implication of this analysis of beliefs is that attitude change may fail to occur, because the target beliefs were not the primary belief, because the communication did not produce the effect on the proximal beliefs that would affect the target beliefs or because the communication affected external beliefs that had a negative impact on the desired change. In any event, the analysis represents an important contribution to the design of persuasive communications.

Elaboration-Likelihood Model

One of the most recent additions to attitude theory and research, the Elaboration-Likelihood model (Petty & Cacioppo, 1981), is based on evidence indicating that attitudes may change according to two different sets of mental processes. First, attitudes may change via a central route that involves cognitive effort to process the communication and/or the issue to which the communication is addressed. The cognitive effort or elaboration may or may not result in attitude change or may even result in a boomerang effect, depending on a number of factors such as strength of the arguments. If attitude change is achieved, however, it is likely to be long lasting.

Second, attitudes may be changed via a peripheral route that involves primarily an immediate response to cues in the situation promoting the desired change. There is little cognitive effort involved, so the change tends to be superficial and relatively short-lived. Such change via the peripheral route, however, can lead to further interest in the issue, which might lead to processing additional information via the central route.

The model has interesting implications for changing attitudes in an educational context. Very often persuasive communications must be delivered in a context of competing attractions for students or teachers. The use of techniques often used in the mass media to grasp attention can be very effective, but lasting change is unlikely unless initial peripheral change is followed by measures to elicit elaboration of message content or of the issue in question. Furthermore, care needs to be exercised so that elaboration does not in fact lead to strengthening of original positions, thus creating even more difficult attitude change problems for the future.

Outcomes: The Bottom Line

The three approaches to persuasive communications discussed previously, as well as others in the literature, are not only useful in the design of attitude change campaigns. They also raise questions about the purpose of the campaigns, that is, what the change agent is trying to achieve. Some campaigns may be addressed to specific behavior changes, such as food choice in a school cafeteria or choice of a handicapped or minority student as a co-worker on a cooperative classroom task. Others may be addressed toward more general classes of behaviors, such as teacher implementation of a recommended instructional program or increased student involvement in extracurricular activities. Still others may be directed at building a positive or negative climate within which participants operate, such as campaigns for citizen support for public education or programs to promote student antagonism to substance abuse behaviors. The nature of these aims and the difficulty of achieving them must be taken into consideration when evaluating the success of the campaign.

Using an analysis taken from Fishbein and Ajzen (1975) as described previously, attitude change campaigns may be evaluated as failures because (a) they failed to change the attitudes they were designed to change; (b) they changed the attitudes, but the attitudes did not produce the desired behavior change; or (c) the changed attitudes produced the desired behavior change, but the behavior change failed to produce the desired result. An example can be drawn from efforts to promote racial harmony in an integrated school. An attitude change campaign might be directed toward the reduction of prejudiced attitudes between groups of White and Black students with the aim of increasing cross-race choices on cooperative classroom projects, which is thought to reduce racial hostilities. The campaign may be unsuccessful because it is ineffective in reducing prejudice. This could be due to problems with the communicator or the message. It could be due to misidentification of the target beliefs. It could be due to the fact that any change obtained was too fleeting to have a real impact. But the campaign may also be unsuccessful even if it does reduce prejudice because this reduction does not lead to increased cross-race choices in the classroom. As Fishbein and Ajzen (1975) pointed out, behavior is affected by more than just attitudes toward the behavior. Social norms and motivations to comply with them also have powerful effects on behavior. Finally, even if cross-race choices occur in the classroom, there may be no general reduction in racial hostility unless conditions such as equal status contact (chapter 18, in this volume) are met.

ATTITUDE–BEHAVIOR LINK

In educational settings, the primary outcome of interest is most often the production of a desired change in behavior as a function of a change in corresponding attitudes. It is therefore critical to establish that attitudes determine behavior. A commonsense notion of attitude would suggest a link with consequent behavior; yet there has been a long history of controversy in sociology and social psychology over whether such a link exists. Rather than review this history, it seems more instructive to point out that the question in social psychology is no longer whether there is a link between attitudes and behavior, but under what conditions the link is strong or weak.

One condition that appears to affect the link is the specificity of the measurement of attitude and behavior. Fishbein and Ajzen (1974) argued that behavior occurs in context that can be specified with respect to action, location, time, and object. For instance, a student may choose a specific handicapped classmate as a partner for an activity in a science class on a specific day. Such behavior can then be generalized over any and all of these factors. Thus, choice as a partner can be generalized by considering all positive interpersonal behaviors a student could perform toward his or her handicapped peer. Similarly, the specific handicapped peer could be generalized by considering all handicapped peers, the science class by considering all classes, and the specific day by considering all days.

Just as the behavior has specific referents that can be generalized, the attitude measure can also have specific or general referents. One can ask the student about his or her attitude toward choosing a specific handicapped peer as a partner in a science class on a specified day. Of course, attitude measures are usually taken for more general referents. Fishbein and Ajzen (1974) argued that attitudes predict behavior best when the level of specificity of the attitude measure matches the level of specificity of the behavior to be predicted. One of the most common problems in many attitude studies occurs when a general measure of attitude is used to predict behavior at a more specific level, as when a general measure of attitude toward the handicapped is used to measure students' selections of handicapped peers as partners on a science project. Fishbein and Ajzen (1974) recommended either a more specific attitude measure or a more general indicator of positive interpersonal behavior toward the handicapped in this instance.

A second condition that affects the degree to which appropriately measured attitudes affect behavior is the degree of direct involvement of the respondents in the attitude issue. Fazio (1986; Fazio & Zanna, 1981) argued that behavior is best predicted from measured attitudes for those who have had direct involvement. So students who have had prior experience with handicapped peers, either through family, friends, or other school activities, should show higher correlations between attitudes toward the handicapped and subsequent behavior.

A third condition concerns the degree to which the attitudes are salient at the time the behavior is performed. For those who have thought about their attitudes immediately prior to engaging in related behavior, the correlation between measured attitude and behavior is higher than for those who have not thought about their attitudes.

Much of the research in this area is relatively recent, and new conditions may be found to facilitate the attitude–behavior link. At this point, it seems fair to say that the old issue of whether attitudes predict behavior can no longer be framed in such simple terms. The individual interested in achieving attitude change with an eye to changing behavior must consider a number of factors that can promote or obscure the link.

CONCLUSION

There are three major conclusions that can be drawn from this treatment of attitude measurement and change in educational settings. First, a lack of conceptual clarity about what constitutes an attitude continues to present problems in interpretation of findings in the field. A clear differentiation of terms would greatly facilitate communication in this area. Second, the techniques of measurement largely remain the traditional techniques, with little change or improvement over the past 30 years. This may be a testimony to their utility in meeting the needs of attitude researchers in the schools. However, it should be noted that there have been dramatic advances in scaling and measurement that have not generally been incorporated into practical programs involving attitudes of relevance to the school psychologist. Third, theoretical advances in the analysis of persuasive communications and in delineating the attitude–behavior link offer promising leads for the design and evaluation of attitude change campaigns in school settings.

REFERENCES

Ajzen, I., & Fishbein, M. (1980). *Understanding attitudes and predicting social behavior.* Englewood Cliffs, NJ: Prentice-Hall.

Allport, F., & Hartman, D. A. (1925). Measurement and motivation of a typical opinion in a certain group. *American Political Science Review, 19,* 735–760.

Aronson, E., Brewer, M., & Carlsmith, J. M. (1985). Experimentation in social psychology. In G. Lindzey & E. Aronson (Eds.), *Handbook of social psychology* (3rd ed., Vol. 1, pp. 441–486). New York: Random House.

Bogardus, E. S. (1925). Measuring social distance. *Journal of Applied Sociology, 9,* 299–308.

Dawes, R. M., & Smith, T. L. (1985). Attitude and opinion measurement. In G. Lindzey & E. Aronson (Eds.), *Handbook of social psychology* (3rd ed., Vol. 1, pp. 509–566). New York: Random House.

DeFleur, M. L., & Westie, F. R. (1958). Verbal attitudes and overt acts: An experiment on the salience of attitudes. *American Sociological Review, 23,* 667–673.

Edwards, A. L. (1957). *Techniques of attitude scale construction.* New York: Appleton-Century-Crofts.

Fazio, R. H. (1986). How do attitudes guide behavior? In R. M. Sorrentino & E. T. Higgins (Eds.), *The handbook of motivation and cognition: Foundations of social behavior* (pp. 204–243). New York: Guilford.

Fazio, R. H., & Zanna, M. P. (1981). Direct experience and attitude–behavior consistency. In L. Berkowitz (Ed.), *Advances in experimental social psychology* (Vol. 14, pp. 161–202). New York: Academic Press.

Fishbein, M., & Ajzen, I. (1974). Attitudes toward objects as predictors of single and multiple behavioral criteria. *Psychological Review, 81,* 59–74.

Fishbein, M., & Ajzen, I. (1975). *Belief, attitude, intention, and behavior: An introduction to theory and research.* Reading, MA: Addison-Wesley.

Guttman, L. (1944). A basis for scaling qualitative data. *American Sociological Review, 9,* 139–150.

Henerson, M. E., Morris, L. L., & Fitz-Gibbon, C. T. (1978). *How to measure attitudes.* Beverly Hills, CA: Sage.

Hess, E. H. (1965). Attitude and pupil size. *Scientific American, 212,* 46–54.

Hovland, C. I., Janis, I. L., & Kelley, H. H. (1953). *Communication and persuasion.* New Haven: Yale University Press.

Jones, E. E., & Sigall, H. (1971). The bogus pipeline: A new paradigm for measuring affect and attitude. *Psychological Bulletin, 76,* 349–364.

Kidder, L. H. (1981). *Selltiz, Wrightsman and Cook's research methods in social relations* (4th ed.). New York: Holt, Rinehart, & Winston.

Kidder, L. H., & Campbell, D. T. (1970). The indirect testing of social attitude. In G. F. Summers (Ed.), *Attitude measurement* (pp. 333–385). Chicago: Rand McNally.

Likert, R. (1932). A technique for the measurement of attitudes. *Archives of Psychology, 140,* 44–53.

McGuire, W. J. (1985). Attitudes and attitude change. In G. Lindzey & E. Aronson (Eds.), *Handbook of social psychology* (3rd ed., Vol. 2, pp. 233–346). New York: Random House.

Mueller, D. J. (1986). *Measuring social attitudes: A handbook for researchers and practitioners.* New York: Teachers College Press.

Nisbett, R. E., & Wilson T. D. (1977). Telling more than we can know: Verbal reports on mental process. *Psychological Review, 84,* 231–259.

Osgood, C. E., Suci, G. J., & Tannenbaum, P. H. (1957). *The measurement of meaning.* Urbana: University of Illinois Press.

Petty, R. E., & Cacioppo, J. T. (1981). *Attitudes and persuasion: Classic and contemporary approaches.* Dubuque, IA: Brown.

Petty, R. E., & Cacioppo, J. T. (1983). The role of bodily responses in attitude measurement and change. In J. T. Cacioppo & R. E. Petty (Eds.), *Social psychophysiology: A sourcebook* (pp. 51–101). New York: Guilford.

Selltiz, C., Wrightsman, L. S., & Cook, S. W. (1976). *Research methods in social relations* (3rd ed.). New York: Holt, Rinehart, & Winston.

Sigall, H., & Page, R. (1971). Current stereotypes: A little fading, a little faking. *Journal of Personality and Social Psychology, 18,* 247–255.

Smith, E. R., & Miller, F. D. (1978). Limits on perception of cognitive processes: A reply to Nisbett and Wilson. *Psychological Review, 85,* 355–361.

Thurstone, L. L. (1927). Psychophysical analysis. *American Journal of Psychology, 38,* 268–389.

Thurstone, L. L. (1928). Attitudes can be measured. *American Journal of Sociology, 33,* 529–554.

Thurstone, L. L. (1931). The measurement of attitudes. *Journal of Abnormal and Social Psychology, 26,* 249–269.

Thurstone, L. L., & Chave, E. J. (1929). *The measurement of attitude.* Chicago: University of Chicago Press.

Tursky, B., & Jamner, L. D. (1983). Evaluation of social and political beliefs: A psychophysiological approach. In J. T. Cacioppo & R. E. Petty (Eds.), *Social psychophysiology: A sourcebook* (pp. 102–121). New York: Guilford.

Walker, D. K. (1973). *Socioemotional measures for preschool and kindergarten children.* San Francisco: Jossey-Bass.

Webb, E. J., Campbell, D. T., Schwartz, R. D., Sechrest, L., & Grove, J. B. (1981). *Nonreactive measures in the social sciences* (2d ed.). Boston: Houghton–Mifflin.

Wegener, B. (1982). *Social attitudes and psychophysical measurement.* Hillsdale, NJ: Lawrence Erlbaum Associates.

White, P. (1980). Limitations of verbal reports on internal events: A refutation of Nisbett and Wilson and of Bem. *Psychological Review, 87,* 105–112.

Woodmansee, J. J. (1970). The pupil response as a measure of social attitudes. In G. F. Summers (Ed.), *Attitude measurement* (pp. 514–533). Chicago: Rand McNally.

3

THE IMPORTANCE OF ATTRIBUTIONS AND EXPECTANCIES IN UNDERSTANDING ACADEMIC BEHAVIOR

Maurice J. Levesque
Charles A. Lowe
University of Connecticut

INTRODUCTION

Although both attributions and expectancies can serve as *determinants* of academic behaviors, the central concern of this chapter is the role that attributions and expectancies play in the *understanding* of academic behaviors. When a student receives an A (or an F) for the marking period, passes (or fails) an exam or responds correctly (or incorrectly) to a teacher's query, what do these behaviors mean to the student or to his/her teacher?

In summarizing the theory and research pertaining to this question, this chapter is both integrative and selective. Borrowing liberally from several attribution theories, a general model depicting the cognitive processes involved in understanding academic behavior and explicating the relationships between attributions and expectancies is presented. In the literature reviews that follow, this general model is employed as an organizational guide to select representative studies whose results elucidate the theoretical principles relevant to students' and teachers' understanding of academic behavior.

AN ATTRIBUTION MODEL FOR UNDERSTANDING ACADEMIC BEHAVIOR

Fritz Heider is widely recognized as the father of attribution theory. In his book, *The Psychology of Interpersonal Relations*, Heider (1958) laid the foundations of what has become one of the more influential and widely used theories in the area of social psychology by describing a set of concepts (e.g., can, try, ability, effort, etc.) and the relationships among these concepts that laypersons use to interpret behavior. The premise of Heider's "naive psychology" is that we come to understand another's behavior by referring that behavior to "relatively unchanging underlying conditions, the so-called dispositional properties of (our) world" (p. 79). According to Heider, behavior per se remains meaningless until we attribute a cause for that behavior; for example, Heider (1958) explained: "John's good grades make sense when we refer his achievement, a relatively momentary event, to his high intelligence, a more or less permanent property, and we then believe we are safe in predicting a successful college career." (p. 80) Conversely, if John's good grades are referred (i.e., attributed) to an "easy teacher" or to the fact that the material on which his grades are based is "easy," then we would be much less confident in predicting his success in college. Heider's contention was that the way in which John's teachers or parents "understand" his "good grades" will affect their behaviors toward John, which in turn could influence John's future academic performance. Indeed, the way John himself understands his good grades could influence his future academic behavior.

The richness of Heider's naive psychology is evidenced by the large number of attribution theories that have emerged over the past several years (see reviews by Harvey & Weary, 1981; Ross & Fletcher, 1985). Several of these theories are relevant to understanding academic behavior. The attribution theories of Edward Jones and his colleagues are especially important, because these theories focus on the determinants of personal attributions (Jones & Davis, 1965), the differences between attributions made for our own behavior compared to the behavior of others (Jones & Nisbett, 1972), and the important role that expectancies play in determining the extent to which we hold others responsible for their behaviors (Jones & McGillis, 1976). As will be demonstrated, we rely heavily on Jones's work in our discussion of the "antecedents of causal attributions."

Jones' focus on personal attributions has been nicely augmented by the work of Harold Kelley, who has been concerned primarily with environmental attributions. In his anova cube model, as will be demonstrated, Kelley (1967) identified the observational criteria that we use to determine whether a behavior is environmentally caused or, by inference, personally caused. In his later work, Kelley (1972a, 1972b) identified several cognitive "principles" or "schemata" that observers employ when they attempt to understand behavior, principles involving covariation, augmentation, and discounting. Kelley's work is especially relevant in our discussions of the "observation of academic behavior" and the "inferences regarding covariation." Finally, the work of Bernard Weiner and his colleagues (Weiner, 1974, 1979; Weiner, Frieze, Kukla, Reed, Rest, & Rosenbaum, 1972) attempted to apply attribution theory to the area of academic achievement. Weiner was concerned with the differences between high and low achievers in the attributions they employ to explain their achievements and with the role that these attributions play in subsequent achievement behaviors. As will be demonstrated, Weiner's work has been extremely useful in our discussion of the various perceived causes and consequences of academic behavior.

The model presented in Fig. 3.1 integrates a number of attribution principles drawn from the attribution theories cited previously. The model identifies three component processes—observation, inference, and attribution—as well as the general determinants and consequences of these processes. In the context of this discussion, *academic behavior* refers to any behavior that can be presumed to reflect a student's academic ability or motivation. Obvious examples are performances on exams, homework assignments, special projects, and the like. Less obvious examples are spontaneous answers to questions in class, the amount of time spent on homework assignments, or the intrinsic interest exhibited for particular academic subjects.

Antecedents of Causal Attributions

Most of the time, neither students nor teachers observe an academic behavior without some prior knowledge. Whether this knowledge involves information about the situation (e.g., the relative difficulty of an exam or the relative performance of other students) or information about a particular student (e.g., the student's past performance or his/her academic strengths and weaknesses), it clearly influences both the type and extent of attribution processes that are necessary to explain an observed behavior. For most perceivers, this prior knowledge is summarized in the form of an expectancy that a particular student will (or will not) do well on a particular academic task; in short, *expectancies are the antecedents of attributions.*

In their integrative reappraisal of Jones and Davis's (1965) correspondent inference theory and Kelley's (1967) attribution cube model, Jones and McGillis (1976) proposed two general types of expectancies. First, *category-based expectancies* derive from the perceiver's knowledge that the target person is a member of a particular class, category, or reference group. Like Kelley's (1967) *consensus criterion* discussed later, category-based expectancies compare a particular student with other students by his/her group membership. For example, simply because a particular student is categorized as slow or bright, male or female, black or white, disadvantaged or advantaged, teachers and eventually the student him/herself may develop expectancies regarding the student's academic behaviors.

Teachers have access to and are encouraged to use category information in grouping students (e.g., slow vs. fast readers); thus, certain category-based expectancies may play a relatively major role in teachers' understanding of students' academic behaviors. By contrast, because students do not have ac-

ANTECEDENTS	OBSERVATION OF BEHAVIOR	INFERENCES about CONVARIATION	ATTRIBUTION of CAUSE(S)	CONSEQUENCES
Type of Expectancy	Behavioral Criteria	Type of Information	Locus of Cause	Type of Consequence
Category-Based *IQ *Gender *Race	Success vs. Failure	Consensus Distinctiveness Consistency	Personal Forces *ability *effort	Affective (feelings)
		Covariation Principles Discounting Augmentation		Cognitive (expectancies)
Target-Based *Past performance *Peak performance *Pattern of performance	Expected vs. Unexpected	Causal Schemata Multiple Necessary Multiple Sufficient	Environmental Forces *task *teacher	Behavioral (actions)

FIG. 3.1. An attribution model for understanding academic behavior.

cess to this comparative information, at least early in their education, category-based expectancies may play a relatively minor role in students' understanding of their own academic behaviors.

Second, Jones and McGillis (1976) described *target-based expectancies* as deriving from prior information about a specific individual student. Like Kelley's (1967) *distinctiveness criterion* discussed later, target-based expectancies compare a particular academic behavior with other academic behaviors of the same student. For example, a student who does well in the first grade may be expected to do well in the second grade; a student who does well on a reading comprehension test may be expected to do well on a vocabulary test; or a student who usually has answered questions correctly may be expected to continue to do so.

Target-based expectancies, which summarize a student's past academic performance, undoubtedly play an important role in both teachers' and students' understanding of academic behavior. Both students and teachers expect that past academic performance will predict future performance; therefore, both may develop and employ attributional patterns that insure the perception of consistency over time. For example, students have been shown to employ "learned helplessness" and "mastery" attributional patterns—the former leads students to internalize failure, whereas the latter allows students to take credit for success. Similarly, teachers have been shown to exhibit a "teacher expectation" attribution pattern, where teachers give the benefit of the doubt in interpreting the academic performances of high-expectancy students compared to low-expectancy students (Rejeski & McCook, 1980).

Observation of Academic Behavior

Regardless of its particular form, any academic behavior is typically categorized by the observer on a *success/failure* continuum and an *expected/unexpected* continuum. These categorizations immediately define the observed behavior as relatively positive (or negative) and as relatively surprising (or unsurprising) and may influence both the extent and type of attribution processing that will be used to understand the observed behavior. For example, behaviors that are extreme on the success/failure continuum (as compared to neutral behaviors) and behaviors that are unexpected (as compared to expected) are more likely to instigate attribution processing (see Ross & Fletcher, 1985). In short, we notice and seek to explain the exceptional and the unusual, whereas the mediocre and commonplace are often ignored.

Inferences Regarding Covariation

Once a behavior has been performed and observed, the next step in understanding that behavior is to determine which of several causes may have been present or absent when that behavior occurred. According to the attribution *principle of covariation* (Kelley, 1972a), perceivers will attribute a behavior to the one cause of its possible causes with which over time it covaries.

When the observed behavior is expected, the covariation principle essentially describes a *confirmation* of causal covariation. For example, when a student who is expected to do well because she is known to be gifted does succeed, her success will be attributed to her giftedness, a cause that is both salient and sufficient to explain her behavior, even when other causes (e.g., her considerable effort) may have contributed to her success. When the observed behavior is unexpected, the covariation principle describes a *search* for causal covariation, a search where two additional attribution principles may be employed. Kelley's (1972a) *discounting principle* states that the role of any one cause in producing a behavior is discounted if other plausible causes are also present. For example, when an intelligent student studies hard and passes an easy exam, the observer will be less confident that any one of these three plausible causes (ability, effort, easy exam) produced the success than when only one of these causes is present. Conversely Kelley's (1972a) *augmentation principle* suggests that, when a student succeeds, the role of a facilitatory cause (e.g., ability) is judged to be greater when a plausible inhibitory cause (e.g., a difficult exam) is also present than when the facilitatory cause alone is present. For example, a student will be judged to have more ability when he or she passes a difficult exam than when he or she passes an easy exam.

To determine the presence or absence of one or more plausible causes, observers may employ three covariation criteria: *consensus, distinctiveness,* and *consistency* (Kelley, 1967). Each of these criteria may be used to obtain information about the situation (i.e., the exam) and, by extension, about the student. The general types of attributions that result from the several combinations of consensus, distinctiveness, and consistency are shown in Table 3.1.

Given that a student has failed a spelling test, for example, employing the *consensus criterion,* the observer (either the student or the teacher) determines whether many students or few students have failed the same test. If most students have failed (i.e., *high consensus*), an *environmental attribution* is implied—the observer may conclude that the spelling test is hard and, further, could infer that the student in question is not necessarily lacking in the ability to spell correctly. By contrast, if only a few students fail (i.e., *low consensus*), a *personal attribution* is implied—the observer concludes that the test could not be that difficult and, therefore, that the student in question does not have much spelling ability relative to his or her peers. Compared to students and their parents, consensus information is more readily available to teachers, an availability that often leads teachers to evaluate the academic performance of a particular student in relation to the academic performances of other students.

Employing the *distinctiveness criterion,* an observer determines whether

TABLE 3.1
ANOVA Cube Analysis (Kelley, 1967) of Student Failure

Behavioral Criteria			Type of Attribution	
Consistency	Distinctiveness	Consensus	Stability	Locus
	HIGH	HIGH	stable	environmental
		LOW	stable	personal or environmental
HIGH	LOW	HIGH	stable	personal or environmental
		LOW	stable	personal
	HIGH	HIGH	unstable	environmental
		LOW	unstable	personal or environmental
LOW	LOW	HIGH	unstable	personal or environmental
		LOW	unstable	personal

Note: As an example, suppose that the observed behavior is a student's failure on one spelling test; then . . .

HIGH Consistency = fails most other spelling tests.
LOW Consistency = passes some spelling tests and fails other spelling tests.
HIGH Distinctiveness = passes most tests in other academic areas.
LOW Distinctiveness = fails most tests in other academic areas.
HIGH Consensus = most other students fail the same spelling test.
LOW Consensus = most other students pass the same spelling test.

this particular student fails only in spelling or fails in other academic areas as well. If a student does well in most areas but fails only in spelling (i.e., *high distinctiveness*), an *environmental attribution* is indicated. Rather than see the student as lacking in general academic ability, the observer could conclude that the level of spelling required is too difficult. By contrast, if a student fails not only in spelling but also in other academic areas as well (i.e., *low distinctiveness*), a *personal attribution* is implied. The observer concludes that the difficulty level of the spelling test is not sufficient to account for the student's failure and may infer that the student in question does not have much academic ability. Compared to teachers, students (and their parents) probably have more complete distinctiveness information, which would lead students and their parents to judge current academic performance in relation to past academic performances.

Finally, employing the *consistency criterion*, an observer determines whether the performance of a particular student in spelling is consistent or inconsistent over time or over different types of spelling tests (e.g., written vs. oral). Consistent performance (i.e., *high consistency*) enables the observer to make an attribution to *stable causes*, either personal or environmental, depending on consensus and distinctiveness information. For example, when a student fails every type of spelling test (i.e., high consistency) *and* is the only student to do so (i.e., low consensus) *and* fails tests in other academic areas (i.e., low distinctiveness), the observer could confidently attribute the student's poor performance to his lack of ability—a personal attribution. Conversely, when a student fails all spelling tests (i.e., high consistency) *and* other students also fail all spelling tests (i.e., high consensus) *and* the student passes tests in other academic areas (i.e., high distinctiveness), the observer could confidently attribute the student's poor performance to the difficulty level of the spelling tests—an environmental attribution. By contrast, inconsistent performance (i.e., *low consistency*) precludes attributions to stable causes. In these instances, the observer begins to search for the exception to the rule. For example, a student's inconsistent failure in spelling, regardless of that student's performance on tests in other academic areas and regardless of other students' performances on these spelling tests, should be attributed to variable causes such as the student's mood, the noise level in the classroom, particular items on particular tests, the pressure of an oral spelling bee, or even the teacher's ambiguous instructions.

Environmental attributions result from high consistency, high consensus, and high distinctiveness information; personal attributions result from high consistency, low consensus, and low distinctiveness information. However, because different types of information may be relatively more available to teachers or to students (and their parents), conflicting evaluations of the same academic behavior may occur (Jones & Nisbett, 1972). For example, consensus information often informs teachers that a particular student is not performing as well as other students, and because teachers know that the student is below par, they logically assign a low(er) grade. Further, teachers may begin to categorize such a student as "slower" or "below grade level," categorizations that define category-based expectancies for future academic behavior. By contrast, distinctiveness information may inform students and their parents that they are performing better than they have in the past. Employing this information, students (and their parents) may develop target-based expectancies for success—because they know that they are doing better than they have done in the past, they logically expect to receive high(er) grades.

In addition to employing the behavioral criteria of consensus, distinctiveness, and consistency, Kelley (1972b) suggested that observers may employ different rules or schemata in their attempts to understand different types of academic behaviors (e.g., successful versus unsuccessful behaviors and/or expected versus unexpected behaviors). Kelley (1972b) defined *causal sche-mata* as relatively permanent conceptions held by perceivers of the manner in which two or more causes interact to produce behavior. When a *multiple necessary* causal schema is employed, the presence of two or more causes are felt to be necessary to produce the outcome (e.g., both ability and effort are felt to be necessary to produce an unusually high grade on an exam). When a *multiple sufficient* causal schema is employed, the presence of any one of several causes is felt to be sufficient to produce the outcome (e.g., either inability or lack of effort is felt to be sufficient to produce failure on an exam). Over an extended range of task difficulty levels, Kun and Weiner (1973) found that multiple necessary causal schema are elicited by successful outcomes or by unexpected outcomes (e.g., success at a difficult task or failure at an easy task), and that multiple sufficient causal schema are elicited by unsuccessful outcomes or by expected outcomes (e.g., failure at a hard task or success at an easy task).

Attribution of Causes for Academic Behavior

Heider (1958) initially distinguished between personal causes (e.g., ability, effort) and environmental causes (e.g., task difficulty, luck). Following Heider, Weiner, Frieze, Kukla, Reed, Rest, and Rosenbaum (1972) proposed that the causes of academic behavior could be categorized along two dimensions[1]—a *locus of control* dimension (i.e., internal vs. external) and a *stability* dimension (i.e., stable vs. unstable) (see Table 3.2).

Based on Heider's (1958) assumptions that perceivers prefer stability and that environmental causes are relatively more permanent than personal causes, the theoretical predictions for attributional preferences are clear: *Stable causes and environmental causes should be preferred over unstable causes and personal causes.* In theory therefore, perceivers' preferences for stability should lead them to make ability (rather than effort) attributions and task difficulty (rather than luck) attributions. Similarly, perceivers' preferences for environmental causes should lead them to make task difficulty (rather than ability) attributions and luck (rather than effort) attributions.

Empirically, however, these predictions have not been confirmed. One reason is that some specific causes cannot be categorized unambiguously. For example, although effort is theoretically an unstable factor, effort may be seen as a stable quality of a person; similarly, whereas luck is theoretically an environmental factor, lucky may be seen as a personal quality. A second reason is that perceivers can be biased (Jones & Nisbett, 1972). For example, as self-perceivers students tend to attribute success to personal causes

---

[1]A third dimension called "intentionality" (Rosenbaum, 1972) or "controllability" (McClelland, 1987) has been suggested but has received little empirical attention and is not discussed.

TABLE 3.2
Perceived Causes of Academic Behavior

		Stability of Cause	
		Stable	Unstable
	Internal	ability	effort (unstable)
	or	effort (stable)	mood
	Personal	personality traits	fatigue
SOURCE			illness
OF			
CAUSE			
	External	task	luck
	or	teacher	weather
	Environmental	parents	
		peers	

and failure to environmental causes (Frieze & Weiner, 1971). Similarly, as other perceivers who have a stake in their students' successes, teachers tend to take at least partial credit for their students' successes and to avoid blame for their students' failures (Beckman, 1970; Johnson, Feigenbaum, & Weiby, 1964).

Consequences of Causal Attribution

The central focus of attribution theories has been on the perception or understanding of behavior rather than on discovering the determinants of behaviors (cf. Kelley, 1973). According to McClelland (1987), attribution theory cannot be an adequate theory of behavior because it starts with behavior that is already ongoing and asks for explanations of this behavior after it has occurred: "A student receives a D on an examination. . . . How the person interprets such events has consequences for what the person chooses to do next, but it does *not* explain why the behavior occurred in the first place" (p. 498, emphasis added). Yet as McClelland stated, it is not unreasonable to assume that one's understanding of the past might influence what one feels, thinks, and does in the future.

Research by Weiner and his colleagues shows that students' attributions for past academic behaviors mediate a wide range of *affective reactions* (Weiner, Russell, & Lerman, 1978), establish or modify *expectancies* for future academic behaviors (Weiner, Heckhausen, Meyer, & Cook, 1972), and influence future *behaviors* like students' choices of academic tasks and their levels of persistence at those tasks (Weiner, 1974). Similarly, teachers' attributions for students' academic behaviors have been shown to influence teachers' *feelings* toward their students, teachers' *expectations* for their students' future academic behaviors, and teachers' *behaviors* toward students for whom they hold different expectancies (Cooper, 1979; Jussim, 1989).

Expectancies and Attributions

Expectancies and attributions are closely related. On the one hand, *expectancies are the antecedents of the attribution process*. At the level of observation, expectancies may influence the aspects of a particular academic behavior or the situation that are noticed or remembered. At the level of inference, because expectancies imply a presumed cause(s) for a behavior, they may preclude attributional processing when an observed academic behavior is expected and may mandate attributional processing when an observed academic behavior is unexpected.

On the other hand, *expectancies are one consequence of the attribution process*. As such, both self-expectancies and other-expectancies can become mediating links between one's understanding of past academic performance and one's potential influence on future academic performance. According to Heider (1958), what we expect of ourselves and what others expect of us can have a substantial impact on our behavior: "What we can do is influenced by what we think we can do, and what we think we can do is influenced by what other people think we can do. Therefore, what we can do is influenced by what other people think we can do" (p. 97). Thus, students who themselves expect to do well or who believe that their teachers expect them to do well may behave differently (try harder, persist longer, etc.) than students who expect to do poorly or who believe that their teachers expect them to do poorly. Also teachers may behave differently toward a student whom they expect to do well (e.g., listen more closely, favorably interpret an answer, forgive careless mistakes) than toward a student whom they expect to do poorly, and these differences in teachers' behaviors may affect students' future academic performances.

STUDENTS' UNDERSTANDING OF ACADEMIC BEHAVIOR

Developmental Aspects of Causal Attributions

The attribution model presented previously is based largely on data obtained from "adult-like" college students. A fundamental question is whether or not younger children have the cognitive abilities necessary to process information relevant to understanding their academic behaviors.

Generally, the answer seems to be that children's cognitive abilities are somewhat limited (see Ruble & Rholes, 1981, for a review). Although Shultz and Mendelson (1975) found that young children can infer covariation between cause and effect, other research suggests that this ability may be limited to those situations where cause and effect are *not* separated temporally (Siegler, 1975) or where there is some visible rationale for the time lapse (Mendelson & Shultz, 1976). For this reason, younger students may require immediate verbal feedback on their performance from the teacher. At higher grade levels, when students can infer covariation over time, effective feedback on student performance may be and often is delayed for substantial periods of time.

Similarly, although younger children are able to use consensus, distinctiveness, and consistency information appropriately, this ability is limited by the manner in which this information is presented. In research where written scenarios have been employed as stimuli, young children (e.g., first graders) made limited use of consistency and distinctiveness information (DiVitto & McArthur, 1978) and could not use consensus information appropriately (Boggiano & Ruble, 1979; Nicholls, 1978). However, in research where videotaped scenarios have been employed as stimuli, young children could infer that an actor who made a nonconsensual choice was driven by personal causes (Ruble, Feldman, Higgins, & Karlovac, 1979). Further, when behavioral stimuli have been presented perceptually using animated cartoons, children as young as kindergarteners can make attributions predicted by the augmentation principle (Kassin & Lowe, 1979) and by the discounting principle (Kassin, Lowe, & Gibbons, 1980). Thus, it appears that young children do understand many behaviors that they can observe but do not understand these same behaviors when they are presented to them in a verbal or written description. Indeed, it may also be the case that young children do not have the verbal skills to adequately communicate their understanding.

However, even when visual stimuli are used, children younger than 6 rely almost exclusively on multiple necessary schemata to explain achievement and are unable to use multiple sufficient schematas that require an inverse compensation pattern; that is, an attribution pattern where more ability is taken to mean less effort and more effort is taken to mean less ability. Until about 12 years of age, children tend to see effort and ability as covarying— they employ both effort and ability to explain success (Kun, 1977; Nicholls, 1978). At about 12 years of age, children are able to perceive ability and effort as compensatory (Nicholls, 1978), especially with regard to inferring more effort when less ability is present (Kun, 1977).

Finally, although Shaklee (1976) showed that children can use past performance information accurately when judging the behavior of others, there is considerable evidence that young children cannot use past performance information to make self-attributions (Nicholls, 1979; Rholes, Blackwell, Jordan, & Walters, 1980; Ruble, Parsons, & Ross, 1976). This evidence may reflect young children's positive attitudes and/or high expectations with regard to their own academic abilities, which leads them to be reluctant to decrease ratings of their own academic ability following academic failure. As children develop they become more realistic (often more pessimistic) about their abilities. Thus, whereas younger children give a uniformly positive interpretation to their academic behavior, older children react differently to success and failure and begin to rely on consistency and distinctiveness information to explain their academic performance.

To summarize, it appears that relatively young children are somewhat limited in the extent to which they are able to use information relevant to understanding their own academic behavior. These limitations appear to involve children's inability to process consensus information, to employ multiple sufficient schemata, and to adjust self-ratings of ability following failure. Although these limitations may be partly a function of the particular methods that are typically employed to assess children's understanding of behavior (i.e., methods that rely on cognitive/verbal abilities rather than perceptual/visual abilities), by the age of 12, children appear to be fully capable of making adult-like attributions for academic behaviors.

Children's Attributional Patterns

Empirical evidence suggests that there are two general patterns that characterize students' attributions for their academic behaviors: a *mastery pattern*[2] and a *learned helplessness* pattern (Diener & Dweck, 1978). With a mastery attributional pattern, students attribute success internally, especially to ability, and attribute failure to external factors or to lack of effort (see Miller & Ross, 1975, for a review). Thus, the mastery attributional pattern enables students to take credit for their successes thereby protecting themselves from the potentially damaging effects of (internalized) failure. By contrast, with a learned helplessness attributional pattern, students make stable attributions, especially to lack of ability, to explain their failures and tend to externalize success. These types of attributions presume that attempts to alter future outcomes will be unsuccessful; therefore, the student remains helpless to effect a change in his/her performance outcomes (see chapter 14, this volume, for an extended discussion of learned helplessness).

Whether a student employs a mastery pattern or a learned helplessness pattern depends on the student's expectancy for success or failure at a particular academic task. For example, Feather (1969) tested whether college students' initial confidence that they could pass an anagram test would bias their subsequent attributions. Feather (1969) found that students who initially were confident internalized their success and externalized their failure

---

[2]Our use of mastery is quite similar to Diener and Dweck (1978), who used "mastery" to describe those students who, following failure, focus on strategies to succeed. Our use of mastery refers to students who, following failure, implicitly assume that they have the ability to succeed and that their failures were caused by low effort or the use of inappropriate strategies. In both definitions, mastery students retain the belief that they are capable of succeeding in the future.

(i.e., a mastery attributional pattern) and that students who initially were not confident externalized their success and internalized their failure (i.e., a learned helplessness attributional pattern). In a similar study, Gilmor and Minton (1974) replicated these results. Thus it would appear that students' initial expectations interact with variations in outcome to produce an expectancy confirmation or disconfirmation that lead to attributions that are quite similar to the two general attributional patterns (i.e., mastery and learned helpless) discussed previously. In the sections that follow, the bases for expectancies of academic success and failure and their relation to these attributional patterns are examined.

Antecedents of Causal Attributions

Although researchers have examined a variety of antecedent factors that influence attributions for academic behavior, past performance information is undoubtedly the most salient and influential factor affecting children's attributions for their current academic behaviors. We propose, however, that this influence is not direct; rather we believe that the past performance–attribution link is mediated by expectancies. In short, a student's past performance outcomes and the perceived causes of those outcomes are summarized in the student's expectations concerning future performance and its likely causes.

Further, compared to the expectancies held by older adult-like students, younger students' expectancies may rely exclusively on past performance information, in part because younger children may not be able to process consensus information necessary to form category-based expectancies and in part because younger children may not have developed an accurate awareness that they are members of a particular group (e.g., the slow reading group or the accelerated reading group) and that all members of this group can be expected to perform less well or better than members of other groups. In short, younger students probably neither understand nor explain their academic behaviors as a function of their belonging to a particular group. Thus, among younger students, category-based expectancies should play a relatively minor role in their attributions for academic behavior than would target-based expectancies that rely on past performance information.

Category-Based Expectancies

Category-based expectancies rely on the perceiver's knowledge that he or she is a member of a particular social class, category, or reference group. Although expectancies based on race, socioeconomic status, and gender have been shown to influence teachers' attributions, there has been relatively little research on category-based expectancies and their effects on students' attributions for their own academic behaviors.

Gender Differences. In the area of academic achievement, few findings have raised as much concern as the discovery that males and females differ in their relative achievement in math and reading. Perhaps as a result, attribution researchers have focused on the differences between males and females in their attributions for these academic outcomes.

One of the more controversial hypotheses is that males tend to use a mastery attributional pattern whereas females tend to use a learned helplessness attributional pattern. For example, Nicholls (1975) found that, on an angle matching task, female students attributed failure to lack of ability more than did male students and that male students attributed failure to bad luck more than did female students. Moreover, whereas male students responded to their success by raising their expectations (female students did not do so), female students responded to their failure by lowering their expectations (male students did not do so). This latter finding is especially problematic, because lowered expectations following failure may further reinforce the use of a learned helplessness attributional pattern for future failures.

These findings have not gone unchallenged. For example, a meta-analytic study examining gender differences in attributions found no evidence for cross-study sex differences in attributions for academic behaviors (Sohn, 1982). Moreover, Sweeney, Moreland, and Gruber (1982) found that, although both male and female students internalized success, female students externalized failure more than did male students. Thus, the question of whether or not there are systematic gender differences in attributional patterns (i.e., mastery vs. learned helplessness) is still open.

A second focus of attribution researchers has been on those situational factors that may elicit gender differences in attributions. One such factor is the "maleness"/"femaleness" or the sex-role appropriateness of the task for which attributions are to be made. Stein, Pohly, and Mueller (1971) argued that the attainment value of a task and expectancy for success are influenced by sex-role standards. Thus, compared to females, males could be expected to perform better and have more ability in culturally determined male domains, whereas the reverse pattern could be expected in culturally determined female domains.

Etaugh and Ropp (1976) had third- and fifth-grade male students and female students play with a game labeled appropriate for either males or females. The authors found no support for the influence of the sex appropriateness of the task on subsequent attributions but did obtain a learned helplessness attributional pattern among females; specifically females, as compared to males, attributed failure more to ability regardless of the sex appropriateness of the game. However, because the "female" game was similar to basketball and could have been viewed as a "male" game, the results could be interpreted as supporting the sex-appropriateness hypothesis.

Other research speaks more directly to the issue of whether males and females make different attributions for academic sex-linked tasks. For example, Gitelson, Petersen, and Tobin-Richards (1982) used spatial and verbal tasks that they assumed were appropriate for males and females, respectively. Their results indicated that male students had higher expectations for success than female students on both tasks and that female students evaluated their performance less highly and attributed less ability on the spatial task than did males. A second study by Parsons, Meece, Adler, and Kaczala (1982) found that female students were not more likely than were male students to attribute according to the learned helplessness pattern for mathematical tasks, although females did have slightly lower expectations for math performance than did males.

Although the link between sex appropriateness and attribution remains tenuous, research has shown that task sex-role appropriateness does influence task performance (Mazurkiewicz, 1960; Dwyer, 1974). The sex appropriateness of an academic task does have some effect on academic performance; thus, the mediating role of attributions should be especially important. Yet the attribution research just reviewed leaves many questions unanswered as to the role of attributions in explaining math and reading performance. We do not know if sex-linked achievement differences are the result of different attributions, nor do we know if male and female students do in fact use different attributional patterns (i.e., mastery vs. learned helplessness) to explain their academic behaviors.

Target-Based Expectancies

Past Performance. Target-based expectancies derive from students' information about their prior academic performances. At the very least, students who have done well (or poorly) in the past might expect to do well (or poorly) in the future. Theoretically, these target-based expectancies could influence attributions for current academic behavior; specifically, current academic performance that is consistent with past performance should lead to attributions to stable factors like ability or task difficulty/ease, whereas current academic performance that is inconsistent with past performance should lead to attributions to unstable factors like luck or effort. For example, Ames, Ames, and Felker (1976) examined attributions for performance outcome among sixth-grade male students performing a task at two different sessions. The results showed that consistent success increased attributions to ability and task ease (i.e., stable causes), whereas inconsistent performance increased attributions to effort and luck (i.e., unstable factors).

The sequence of success and failure has also been studied as a determinant of attributions. Results tend to show a strong primacy effect such that early rather than later successes lead to attributions of ability (Jones, Rock, Shaver,

Goethals, & Ward, 1968). For example, Feldman and Bernstein (1977) examined the effects of performance outcome and sequence on fourth graders' attributions by manipulating performance outcomes on two series of shape location puzzles. The results supported the hypothesized primacy effect for ability ratings—success on the initial series resulted in increased ability inferences.

However, it should be noted that the results of studies where past performance is manipulated experimentally should be interpreted with caution. Such manipulations usually involve limited trials, identical tasks, and very short periods of time; thus, these manipulations may not represent the kinds of experiences that are available to students in real-life classroom settings. In the classroom, some students may experience rather consistent outcomes across several different types of academic behaviors and over considerable periods of time. Theoretically, this real-life consistency should lead to the development and use of attributional patterns to explain current academic performance; specifically, students who experience consistent failure should develop a learned helplessness attributional pattern, whereas students who experience consistent success should develop a mastery attributional pattern.

In fact, attribution research has focused on three naturally occurring groups of students who do seem to experience relatively consistent academic outcomes—high (vs. low) need achievers, learning disabled (vs. normal) students, and students with high (vs. low) self-concepts. We suggest that students in each of these groups, based primarily on their records of consistent past successes (or failures), develop expectancies regarding their future academic behaviors. One could argue, because these groups are naturally occurring, that expectancies for a student's performance as a member of one of these groups are category based. Indeed, for teachers who evaluate a student's performance based on the fact that the student *is* a "high achiever" or *is* "learning disabled," these expectancies are category based. However, for students themselves who evaluate their own performance based on their consistent past performance, these expectancies are more target based than category based. Of course, over a period of years, students' target-based expectancies may become category-based expectancies if and when they begin to view their own behaviors as the result of their membership in a learning disabled or high achievement group.

Need Achievement. Need achievement is a relatively stable internal trait disposing a person to strive for success in achievement situations (Atkinson, 1964). One distinction between high and low achievers is that the former are more likely to have a history of success. Thus, over time, high achievement should increase the expectancy for success whereas low achievement should increase the expectancy for failure, and these differences in expectancies should affect attributions. A number of studies have shown that need achievement and attribution are related. For example, Weiner and Kukla (1970) found that high achievers (especially males) tended to make internal attributions for success. Further, research by Weiner and Potepan (1970) showed that the internal ascription for success most strongly associated with high need for achievement was ability and that children who were high need achievers were less likely to attribute failure internally, especially to inability, than were children who were low need achievers. Again, these relationships were most striking for male subjects. In another study, Stipek and Hoffman (1980) sought to determine if attributions varied by achievement level rather than level of need achievement motivation. Third-grade teachers were asked to divide their students into high, average, and low achievers. These students then performed an anagram task that was impossible to solve, thus assuring failure, a situation where high and average achievers who are expected to show mastery patterns should have been less likely to attribute failure to lack of ability than low achievers. Some support for this mastery attributional pattern was found, but only for male students. Low-achieving male students used lack of ability more than high achievers and had lower initial expectancies.

Learning Disabled.   It is assumed that learning disabled students have past performance histories that contain relatively more failure experiences than do non-learning disabled students. According to Licht (1983), this history of failure leads learning disabled students to believe that they lack ability and that continued effort is fruitless because little perceived covariation exists between effort and outcome. In short, learning disabled students could be expected to use a learned helplessness attributional pattern. For example, Jacobsen, Lowery, and DuCette (1986) had seventh- and eighth-grade LD (learning disabled) and NLD (non-learning disabled) students attribute causes for hypothetical academic and social outcomes. LD students used task ease and luck to account for success more than did NLDs. Also LD students used ability attributions more for failure than for success, whereas NLD students used ability attributions more for success than failure. In a second study, LD students were observed to use a multiple necessary schema to explain success so that, although ability and effort ratings increased with success, so did external attributions. This use of a multiple necessary schema to explain success dilutes the positive effects of taking relatively more credit for success than failure. Taken together with the results of other similar studies, there seems to be considerable evidence that LD students do not take credit for success, and that they take relatively more blame for failure compared to NLD students (e.g., Licht, Kistner, Ozkaragoz, Shapiro, & Clausen, 1985; Palmer, Drummond, Tollison, & Zinkgraff, 1982).

Self-Concept.   Self-concept may also predispose students to infer the causes of success and failure in different ways. Self-concept is defined as a set of beliefs concerning one's self-efficacy (i.e., one's ability to attain desired goals or outcomes) and competence (Epstein, 1973). Weiner (1974) argued that a high self-concept includes information concerning a past history of success, perceived high ability, and better outcomes compared to others. Thus, based on their past performance, we could expect that high self-concept students would attribute success internally, whereas low self-concept students would internalize failure.

A number of studies have supported this contention (e.g., Ames, 1978; Fitch, 1970; Nicholls, 1976). Most recently Marsh, Cairns, Relich, Barnes, and Debus (1984) found that high self-concept children internalize success but not failure and prefer ability attributions to explain success. Further, the relationship between failure attributions and self-concept was partially clarified by Ickes and Layden (1978), who found that high self-concept subjects attributed failure either externally or ambiguously—by rating all causes as unlikely—whereas low self-concept subjects attributed failure internally.

Evidence from experimental studies tends to confirm the preceding correlational findings. Ames and Felker (1979) found that high self-concept sixth graders rated skill as more important in success than did low self-concept students. Both groups attributed failure to lack of skill; however, low self-concept children endorsed more self-punitive statements following failure than did high self-concept children. Although both groups internalized failure, this result may be an artifact of the attribution measure that allowed only skill or luck attributions. For example, Wong and Weiner (1981) found that luck was the least used among ability, effort, task difficulty, and luck attributions, suggesting that the skill–luck scale used by Ames and Felker (1979) may have been inappropriate.

Summary. The evidence pertaining to target-based expectancies demonstrates that children who have been relatively successful in their academic undertakings tend to exhibit a mastery attributional pattern. Specifically, high achievers, non-learning disabled students, and students with positive self-concepts tend to take credit for their successes by attributing these successes to their ability, thus reinforcing their expectancies for continued success. Failure is relatively unexpected for these students; therefore, they tend to attribute failure either to external causes or to a lack of effort, and the latter attribution implies that, with increased effort, future outcomes could be successful. By contrast, students who have experienced relatively more failure (i.e., low achievers, learning disabled students, students with low self-concepts) tend to show a learned helplessness attributional pattern. Instead of bolstering their self-concepts, these students give themselves less credit for success and take more blame for their failure. Their attributions for failure to lack of ability reinforce their expectations for failure in the future and, because ability is relatively stable, imply that future outcomes could not be changed.

Consequences of Causal Attributions

In explaining their academic performance, some children tend to use one or the other of two general attributional patterns: either a learned helplessness or a mastery attributional pattern. These patterns are invoked by students who have relatively consistent histories of either failure or success, respectively. There is suggestive evidence that these two attributional patterns that involve rather different attributions also have an effect on students' affective reactions regarding their past academic performances, on students' expectancies regarding their future academic performances, and on students' academic behaviors that could affect their future academic performances.

Affective Reactions

Weiner (1974) argued that affective reactions to success or failure are intensified when the behavior is attributed to personal rather than to environmental causes. More recently, Weiner et al. (1978) showed that some affective reactions following success and/or failure were outcome dependent; specifically, success led to feelings of happiness, satisfaction, and contentedness, whereas failure resulted in uncheerfulness, displeasure, and upset.

According to Weiner et al. (1978), other affective reactions are attribution dependent. For example, effort attributions for success elicit feelings of pride, delirium, or activation, whereas attributions to (lack of) effort for failure result in shame. Ability (or inability) attributions to account for success (or failure) are related to feelings of competence or incompetence, respectively. Attributions to task ease to account for success lead to feelings of hopefulness and safety, but attributions to task difficulty to account for failure did not produce a unique affective reaction. Finally, surprise is the predominant response when either success or failure is attributed to luck, a finding that should not be very surprising.

These results Weiner et al. (1978) reported suggest that attributions to internal causes—specifically to effort or to ability—are most crucial for academic outcomes, because these attributions produce affective reactions that bear directly on children's self-concepts. For example, Covington, Spratt, and Omelich (1980) found that college students who role played being a student who failed because of stable low effort rated themselves as being less motivated and as being less persistent than did high-effort students. The implication of these results is that attributions to either effort or ability to account for success or failure produce affective reactions that over time may become an important part of a student's more stable view of his or her academic prowess. Thus, students who employ a learned helplessness attributional pattern would feel incompetent as a result of their failures because they are attributed to inability, and would not feel competence as a result of their successes because they are attributed to external causes. By contrast, students who employ a mastery attributional pattern would feel competent as a result of their successes because they are attributed to both ability and effort, and would not feel incompetent as a result of their failures because they are attributed to lack of effort or to external causes. Over the course of formal schooling, we could expect that these immediate reactions to academic outcomes would be incorporated into students' academic self-concepts.

Expectancies

In addition to being an antecedent to attributions for academic behavior, there is considerable evidence that expectancies are also one result of academic performance outcomes and the specific attributions that are made to account for these outcomes. Weiner (1974, 1979) proposed that expectancies are based primarily on stable attributions, specifically task difficulty or ability. If success is attributed to either task difficulty or ability, then expectancies for success in the future increase (Rosenbaum, 1972; Weiner, Nierenberg, & Goldstein, 1976). If failure is attributed to either task difficulty or lack of ability, then expectations for success in the future decline (Fontaine, 1974). By contrast, attributions to unstable factors to account for success produce a decrease in expectations for future success (McMahan, 1973), whereas attributions to unstable factors to account for failure may actually produce an increase in expectations for success in the future (Nicholls, 1975).

These results suggest that students who employ a learned helplessness attributional pattern (i.e., attribute their failures to lack of ability) may develop persistent expectancies that they cannot succeed in the future, expectancies that may obviate any motivation to exert effort to succeed. By contrast, students who employ a mastery attributional pattern (i.e., attribute their failures to a lack of effort rather than to their inability) actually raise their expectations for success in the future, developing expectations that would lead them to exert considerable effort to succeed.

It should be noted that for both affect and expectancies, younger children seem to be relatively immune to the effects described previously. With regard to affective reactions, Ruble, Parsons, and Ross (1976) found that, whereas negative affect following failure increased with age, 6-year-olds did not feel bad following failure. With regard to expectancies, Nicholls (1979) found that young children tend to overestimate their achievement and thereby maintain high expectations for success in the future.

Behaviors: Task Persistence and Task Choice

The direct effects of attributions on academic behavior has been demonstrated on task persistence and task choice. Dweck and Repucci (1973) found that continual failure lowered persistence on subsequent tasks. Moreover, the specific attributions exhibited by students who employ a learned helplessness attributional pattern also have lowered task persistence. For example, attributions to lack of ability to account for failure were shown to severely reduce task persistence (Diener & Dweck, 1978; Weiner, 1979). In fact, Licht et al. (1985) found a negative correlation between attributions to inability to account for failure and persistence on a reading task among learning disabled students. Moreover, attributions for previous academic behavior have been shown to influence task choice. For example, Riemer (1975) found that students who attributed success to ability chose to try a more difficult task than did students who attributed success to factors other than ability.

TEACHERS' UNDERSTANDING OF STUDENTS' ACADEMIC BEHAVIOR

Teachers' Self-Ascribed Role in Students' Performance

Teachers obviously play an important role in a student's academic performance. Objectively, good teaching is one important factor that contributes to a student's success whereas poor teaching could be a sufficient cause for a student's failure. However, because teachers want their students to do well and direct considerable effort toward this end, teachers' perceptions may be biased. For example, elementary education majors estimate higher grades for students and view the quality of instruction as a more important factor in academic performance than do psychology majors (Cooper, Baron, & Lowe, 1975).

Much of the research in this area was focused on whether or not teachers are objective in evaluating their causal role in a student's academic performance. The self-protective hypothesis assumes that teachers take personal credit for their student's success and avoid personal blame for their failure. For example, Beckman (1970) found that prospective teachers (i.e., undergraduate education majors) mentioned themselves as a cause for their students' success and cited situational factors to explain their students' failure more than did observers. By contrast, the counterdefensive hypothesis proposes that teachers should take some blame for student failure and give students some credit for their success. When real teachers (Ross, Bierbrauer, & Polly, 1974) or cross-age tutors (Medway & Lowe, 1980) were the instructors, teacher factors were rated as more important following student failure and student factors were rated as more important following student success.

However, Tetlock (1980) suggested that this counterdefensive attributional pattern may be explained in part by teachers' self-presentation concerns rooted in cultural norms that require teachers to take responsibility for student failures and to encourage and credit students for their successes. For example, Tetlock (1980) found that college students rated teachers who gave counterdefensive attributions for students' performances as more competent and more likable than teachers who gave defensive attributions for students' performances. This issue is far from settled, however. It remains for future research to determine whether teachers are in fact self-protective or counterdefensive in their attributions and to identify the positive or negative consequences of teachers' attributions for particular groups of students.

Antecedents of Teachers' Attributions

Category-Based Expectancies. Generally, teachers' attributions for students' academic behavior parallel those of students. Yet despite the fact that both student and teacher attributions are influenced by expectancies based on students' past academic performances (i.e., on target-based expectancies), teachers are often compelled to rely more heavily on category-based expectancies. On the one hand, teachers are concerned with many students and at times may be unable to process all of the available target-based information relevant to each individual student. On the other hand, the consensus information on which category-based expectancies are based is readily available to teachers, and categorization of students is encouraged by educational practices such as "tracking." The net result is that teachers' attributions for their students' academic behaviors are heavily influenced by category-based expectancies, expectancies that depend on task difficulty information and consensus (i.e., race, socioeconomic status, and gender) information.

Task Difficulty Information. Cooper and Lowe (1977) investigated the effects of having task difficulty information available. Undergraduates who role played as teachers were required to evaluate the academic performance (i.e., success or failure) of a hypothetical smart, average, or dull student with task difficulty information (i.e., that students succeeded 50% of the time) either present or absent. The results of this study suggest that task difficulty information may have different effects on teachers' attributions for different students. For average students, teachers attribute less ability to successful performances when task difficulty information is available compared to when such information is unavailable; for smart students, task difficulty information appears to have little effect on teachers' attributions.

Race and Socioeconomic Status (SES). Although the effects of race and SES on teachers' attributions has received little attention, there is some suggestion that teachers generally hold White, middle-class children more responsible for their academic outcomes than minority students. For example, Cooper, Baron, and Lowe (1975) found that preservice teachers and college students expected lower class students to receive poorer grades than middle-class students and held Black students less personally responsible for their failures than White, middle-class students. These results together with those of other studies (Baron, Tom, & Cooper, 1985; Wiley & Eskilson, 1978) suggest that teachers expect Black students and lower class White students to fail more than White, middle-class students.

One minority group that may benefit from stereotyped beliefs held by teachers is Asian–Americans. For example, elementary school teachers attribute the academic success of both White, middle-class, and Asian students to internal factors and academic failure to external factors, a pattern that is not found for lower class White students (Tom & Cooper, 1986). Moreover, compared to White students, Asian–American students are rated as more academically competent (Wong, 1980), and their academic performance is evaluated more favorably (Tom, Cooper, & McGraw, 1984).

Student Gender.   Surprisingly little research has been conducted to determine if teachers use gender as a basis for attributions. A study by Bernard (1979) found that teachers rated successful academic performance in a sex-inappropriate domain more positively than the same behavior in a sex-appropriate domain. Specifically, male students were evaluated more highly in English than were female students, a pattern that suggests that the importance of personal causes is augmented when a student performs well in a sex-inappropriate domain. At present, there is virtually no empirical evidence to suggest that teachers differentiate systematically between the causes of male and female students' academic behaviors (Heller & Parsons, 1981; Wiley & Eskilson, 1978).

Target-Based Expectancies: Past Performance

Much of the research that investigates teachers' attributions seeks to determine the effects of information regarding students' past academic behavior on teachers' attributions for students' current academic behaviors. Generally the results of this research show that past-performance information creates target-based expectancies that lead teachers to make attributions that are nearly identical to the mastery and learned helplessness attributional patterns observed among students' attributions for their own academic behaviors.

One consistent finding is that teachers' attributions are strongly influenced by whether or not teachers "expect" success or failure. For example, Cooper and Lowe (1977) compared teachers' attributions for the successes and failures of students whom teachers nominated as being either below or above average with the successes and failures of students nominated as being average. Teachers attributed both the successes and the failures of above-average students to personal factors. However, compared to their attributions for the successes and failures of average students, teachers were less likely to attribute the successes of below-average students to personal factors and were more likely to attribute the failures of below-average students to personal factors.

Although the previous results relied on general personal and environmental attributions, subsequent research has clarified the more specific attributions used by teachers to account for the expected and unexpected successes and failures of students. For example, Rejeski and McCook (1980) found that teachers attributed the successes of "high reading group" students to ability and the failures of "low reading group" students to inability. By contrast, teachers attributed the failures of high reading group students to task difficulty (i.e., an environmental cause for this unexpected behavior) and the successes of low reading group students to effort (i.e., an unstable cause for this unexpected behavior). In another study, Cooper and Burger (1980) compared teachers' attributions for students who were expected to succeed or fail. For students expected to succeed, teachers used ability and acquired characteristics to explain their successes but used teacher factors and immediate effort to explain their (unexpected) failures. For students expected to fail, teachers used lack of ability and low stable effort to explain their failures and used teacher effort, student interest, and task ease to explain their successes.

Similar to the mastery attributional pattern found for some students (e.g., high achievers), teachers ascribe continued student success to internal factors and unexpected student failure to external factors. In short, students who teachers expect to do well are credited with success and excused from failure. Similar to the learned helplessness attributional pattern found for other students (e.g., LD students), teachers ascribe continued failure to inability and do not use ability to explain unexpected success. In short, students who teachers expect to do poorly are blamed for their failures and not given lasting credit for their successes. These similarities suggest that teachers and students base their attributions on much the same information, that teachers and students process this information in much the same way, and perhaps that teachers may exert some influence on students' self-attributions for academic behaviors.

Consequences of Causal Attributions

Because teachers are personally involved in the education process, they have a personal stake in their students' successes or failures. Although there is relatively little empirical work on how teachers in vivo come to understand students' academic behaviors, there has been considerable research on how teachers react to students' academic behaviors. This research has focused on the effects of students' academic performances, on teachers' affective and behavioral reactions, and on teachers' expectancies.

Affective and Behavioral Reactions

Much like students themselves, teachers have a number of different affective reactions to their students' performances. These affective reactions have been linked to particular attributions. For example, Covington, Spratt, and Omelich (1980) found that teachers felt happy following student success and disappointed following student failure, although these feelings were less strong for low-ability and/or low-effort students who were expected to fail. More specifically, teachers felt angry when bright students and/or students who tried hard failed and were surprised when low-ability students and/or students who did not try hard succeeded. Finally, teachers experienced gratitude when students showed an increase in effort, pride when a low-ability student put forth effort, and guilt when a high-ability student failed or when effort expenditure declined.

The pattern that emerges from the preceding results suggests that teachers' affective responses are linked to effort. In fact, Covington argued (Covington et al., 1980; Covington & Omelich, 1979) that, although students prefer ability inferences in their self-perceptions, teachers use effort more than ability to evaluate students. Paradoxically, whereas students prefer ability over effort to account for their academic successes, teachers use effort as a basis for their reactions to students' academic behaviors.

Teachers' reliance on effort information is apparent in their behavioral reactions to students' academic behaviors; that is, teachers seem to use the amount of effort a student expends together with performance outcome as the major criteria for distributing rewards and punishments. For example, Weiner and Kukla (1970) found that the tendency of college students role playing as teachers to reward success and punish failure was mediated by the effort expended; specifically, students who tried were rewarded more and punished less than those who did not try, especially when the outcome was success. Understandably, in allocating rewards and punishments, teachers may rely on students' effort expenditure, because effort, as opposed to ability, is more visible and is more easily influenced by the teacher.

Teacher Expectancies for Students' Academic Behavior

The theoretical relationship between attributions and teachers' expectancies for student performance is clear. Weiner (1974) theorized that attributions to stable factors (ability and task difficulty) increase expectations after success and decrease expectations after failure, whereas attributions to unstable factors (effort or luck) decrease expectations after success and increase expectations after failure. However, there is little empirical evidence to support these theoretical predictions other than a study by Rolison and Medway (1985), who found that less than 14% of the variance in teachers' expectations could be accounted for by teachers' attributions. This lack of empirical evidence is particularly surprising given the attention that teacher expectancies have received in the literature. Since Rosenthal and Jacobsen's (1968) work on Pygmalion in the classroom, which showed that teachers' expectancies could function to raise students' scores on a standardized IQ test, researchers have sought to document the mediating role of teachers' behaviors in this teacher expectancy–student performance relationship.

Several studies have found that teachers do behave differently towards students for whom they hold different expectancies. With regard to high versus low achievers, teachers create a warmer socioemotional climate (Babad, Inbar, & Rosenthal, 1982; Chaikin, Sigler, & Derlega, 1974), respond more favorably to questions (Cooper, 1979; Good, Sikes, & Brophy, 1973), and give more useful feedback (Good et al., 1973) to high than to low achievers. With regard to racial groups, Yee (1968) found that teachers' behaviors toward Black students are similar to their behaviors toward low achievers, whereas teachers' behaviors toward White students are similar to teachers' behaviors toward high achievers. However, other research suggests that the differences in teachers' behaviors due to race may be minimal (Taylor, 1979). With regard to gender groups, teachers' behaviors are influenced more by the sex stereotype of the subject matter (i.e., math versus reading) than by the gender of the student. Specifically, female students receive high achievement-like feedback from their teachers in reading, whereas male students receive more positive treatment in math (Good & Findley, 1985). Although these differences parallel the attributional patterns used by teachers to explain the successes and failures of these various groups of students, the apparent link between attributions and teachers' behaviors has not been established.

There is considerable evidence that these differences in teachers' behaviors toward different students are noticed by other students (Weinstein, 1985; Weinstein & Middlestadt, 1979). That students can discern these differences further strengthens the assumption that teachers' behaviors can influence student achievement—an influence that has been labeled a self-fulfilling prophecy in the literature. Given that teachers do hold different expectancies and that these expectancies do influence teachers' behaviors, the question still remains whether or not teachers' expectancies affect student achievement. Although the results have not been consistent across studies, there does appear to be sufficient evidence supporting a teacher behavior–student achievement link to warrant concern (Crano & Mellon, 1978; Brophy & Good, 1974). This link, however, is at least partly dependent on teacher characteristics. Whereas Babad and others (Babad et al., 1982; Brattesani, Weinstein, & Marshall, 1984) found that certain teachers were more likely to behave differentially toward students, it is also important to note that certain differences in teachers' behaviors may be necessary. For example, low achievers may be "taught less" simply because they require more structure and more time to achieve the same outcome as high achievers.

It seems clear that attributions should play an important role in the teacher expectancies–student performance relationship, specifically, that teachers' behaviors should influence students' attributions and thus affect academic performances. Cooper (1979, 1985) proposed that teacher expectancy effects may influence students' beliefs about the covariation between effort and outcome. He argued that teachers use criticism, especially with low achievers, to maintain control over student–teacher interactions and student performance. This repeated use of criticism that is not contingent on performance leads students to believe that they will be criticized regardless of their behavior, that any amount of trying will lead to the same outcome—criticism from the teacher. Although Cooper provided some evidence for the link between teacher expectancies and student attributions, the more general links between the teacher expectancy literature and the attribution literature has not been established. This failure should not be taken as evidence that such links do not exist but rather as an indication that these two literatures have not been aggressively integrated.

Summary

Theoretically, determining the cause of an academic outcome is a complex process involving the search for and integration of information related to cause–effect covariation and resulting in an inference about the most likely cause(s). However, the research on this process indicates that much of the knowledge necessary to make an inference is summarized and available to teachers and students in the form of outcome expectancies. Generally, students utilize target- or self-based expectancies derived from the relative consistency of past outcomes, whereas teachers use both target-based and category-based expectancies, integrating information about students' past performances with information about the performances of other students in various social and educational groups. Based on these expectations, teachers and students interpret present outcomes as successful or unsuccessful and as expected or unexpected. Mastery attributions are derived from expectancies for success and consist of stable, internal attributions for success and unstable or external attributions for failure. Learned helplessness attributions derive from expectancies for failure and consist of stable, internal attributions for failure and unstable or external attributions for success.

Teachers and students appear to employ these attributional patterns fairly consistently according to their performance-based expectancies, and their use results in different affective and behavioral reactions to performance. Mastery students feel competent and happy, and they show task persistence and a desire to seek out new challenges. Learned helplessness students feel relatively incompetent, guilty, and unhappy, and they tend to persist less and to avoid new challenges. These attribution patterns are also self-perpetuating in that, regardless of present outcome, mastery students consistently expect successes, whereas learned helplessness students consistently expect failures, expectations that are mirrored by teachers. Further, these attributions for academic behavior are cyclical in nature, such that each new performance is understood in terms of past performances in a manner that maintains current attributional patterns. This cycle is perpetuated by the reciprocal influence between teachers and students and perhaps also by the influence of parents and peer groups, although the impact of these latter sources has received little empirical attention.

Throughout the chapter, particular inconsistencies or gaps in current knowledge have been noted. One shortcoming is the lack of evidence that bears on the relationship between teachers' attributions and expectancies and students' performances, attributions, and expectancies. A second important issue is the different methodological practices that have contributed to many of the inconsistencies in this literature. The use of children as subjects requires increased sensitivity to issues related to whether subjects can adequately understand the information given as well as the questions asked of them. Rather than written scenarios, for example, videotapes and/or naturalistic observations seem to be a more appropriate way to present causally relevant information. Perhaps more importantly, measurement techniques that force subjects to choose between causes or attribute causality among a predetermined and limited set of causes impose an artificial phenomenology that could lead to misleading results and false conclusions. Rather than follow these trends established by previous research, future research should attempt to identify the categories of causes, the meanings of causes, and the relationships among causes that are used by students and teachers to explain academic behavior.

Perhaps the most basic and important application of the attribution model and literature reviewed in this chapter is that students' and teachers' understanding of academic behaviors is much more important than students' performances per se. Whether or not a student succeeds or fails is not as important as how either of these academic behaviors is understood. Success per se does not guarantee continued success unless the student is able to attribute that success to internal causes like effort and ability. Similarly, the additional help and increased attention from the teacher following student failure may not improve performance if the student continues to attribute in a learned helplessness manner. Of course, simply altering students' attributions may have little benefit unless a relationship between effort and outcome can be established, and this relationship depends on whether or not the student is taught the skills and is given a task where the difficulty level matches the student's competencies. Related to this issue, chapter 14 in this volume details attributional retraining procedures and how these techniques may enhance performance.

Beyond their importance in improving academic behavior, attributions may also help to explain and perhaps rectify potential conflicts between teachers and parents. Although parents rely on target-based information and consequently see their child as steadily improving, teachers måy have access to consensus information that consistently places the child in the low-achievement group relative to his/her peers. Educational programs that de-emphasize category-based information (e.g., individualized computer learning programs) may eliminate many parent–teacher misunderstandings and focus more attention on the student's progress relative to his or her own past performance.

Attributional differences between teachers and students may also result in difficulties. Teachers typically rely on student effort to administer rewards and punishments, but students prefer to explain their academic success with reference to ability, a preference that leads them to expend only minimal effort in an attempt to avoid inferences of low ability when they fail. In this respect, emphasis by teachers on effort and acquired skills as covarying rather than as inversely related phenomena could be beneficial. This emphasis would enable students to attribute their success to both ability and effort, attributions that would result in a feeling of pride in personally caused success. Further, this emphasis would enable students to attribute their failure either to a lack of effort or to a lack of acquired ability, attributions that should lead them to believe that their failures can be rectified with increased effort and/or assistance from others in acquiring the appropriate skills.

Finally, more research should be conducted to establish what role parents and peers play in determining students' attributions. Combined with additional data on the interplay between teachers' and students' explanations of achievement, interventions based on attribution retraining may be more successful and useful on a larger scale that would involve teachers, parents, and peers. If children come to understand their performance in ways that are both realistic and adaptive relatively early in the schooling process, it is likely that self-esteem would be enhanced and future performance would improve.

REFERENCES

Ames, C. (1978). Children's achievement attributions and self-reinforcement: Effects of self-concept and competitive reward structure. *Journal of Educational Psychology, 70,* 345–355.

Ames, C., Ames, R., & Felker, D. (1976). Informational and dispositional determinants of children's achievement attributions. *Journal of Educational Psychology, 68,* 63–69.

Ames, C., & Felker, D. (1979). Effects of self-concept on children's causal attributions and self-reinforcement. *Journal of Educational Psychology, 71,* 613–619.

Atkinson, J. W. (1964). *An introduction to motivation.* Princeton, NJ: Van Nostrand.

Babad, E. Y., Inbar, J., & Rosenthal, R. (1982). Pygmalion, galatea, and the golem: Investigations of biased and unbiased teachers. *Journal of Educational Psychology, 74,* 459–474.

Baron, R. M., Tom, D., & Cooper, H. (1985). Social class, race and teacher expectations. In J. Dusek, V. Hall, & W. Meyer (Eds.), *Teacher expectancies* (pp. 251–269). Hillsdale, NJ: Lawrence Erlbaum Associates.

Beckman, L. (1970). Effects of students' performance on teachers' and observers' attributions of causality. *Journal of Educational Psychology, 61,* 76–82.

Bernard, M. E. (1979). Does sex role behavior influence the way teachers evaluate students? *Journal of Educational Psychology, 71,* 553–562.

Boggiano, A. K., & Ruble, D. N. (1979). Perceptions of competence and the overjustification effect: A developmental study. *Journal of Personality and Social Psychology, 37,* 1462–1468.

Brattesani, K. A., Weinstein, R. S., & Marshall, H. H. (1984). Student perceptions of differential teacher treatment as moderators of teacher expectation effects. *Journal of Educational Psychology, 76,* 236–247.

Brophy, J., & Good, T. (1974). *Teacher–student relationships: Causes and consequences.* New York: Holt, Rinehart, & Winston.

Chaikin, A., Sigler, E., & Derlega, V. (1974). Nonverbal mediators of teacher expectancy effects. *Journal of Personality and Social Psychology, 30,* 144–149.

Cooper, H. (1979). Pygmalion grows up: A model for teacher expectation communication and performance influence. *Review of Educational Research, 49,* 389–410.

Cooper, H. (1985). Models of teacher expectation communication. In J. Dusek, V. Hall, & W. Meyer (Eds.), *Teacher expectancies* (pp. 135–158). Hillsdale, NJ: Lawrence Erlbaum Associates.

Cooper, H., Baron, R., & Lowe, C. (1975). The importance of race and social class in the formation of expectancies about academic performance. *Journal of Educational Psychology, 67,* 312–319.

Cooper, H., & Burger, J. (1980). How teachers explain students' academic performances: A categorization of free response academic attributions. *American Educational Research Journal, 17,* 95–109.

Cooper, H., & Lowe, C. A. (1977). Task information and attributions for academic performance by professional teachers and roleplayers. *Journal of Personality, 45,* 469–483.

Covington, M. V., & Omelich, C. (1979). Effort: The double-edged sword in school achievement. *Journal of Educational Psychology, 71,* 169–182.

Covington, M. V., Spratt, M. F., & Omelich, C. L. (1980). Is effort enough, or does diligence count too? Student and teacher reactions to effort stability in failure. *Journal of Educational Psychology, 72,* 717–729.

Crano, W., & Mellon, P. (1978). Causal influences of teacher's expectations on children's academic performance: A cross-lagged panel analysis. *Journal of Educational Psychology, 70,* 39–49.

Diener, C. I., & Dweck, C. S. (1978). An analysis of learned helplessness: Continuous changes in performance, strategy, and achievement cognitions following failure. *Journal of Personality and Social Psychology, 36,* 451–462.

DiVitto, B., & McArthur, L. Z. (1978). Developmental differences in the use of distinctiveness, consensus, and consistency information for making causal attributions. *Developmental Psychology, 14,* 474–482.

Dweck, C., & Repucci, D. (1973). Learned helplessness and reinforcement responsibility in children. *Journal of Personality and Social Psychology, 25,* 109–116.

Dwyer, C. A. (1974). Influence of children's sex role standards on reading and arithmetic achievement. *Journal of Educational Psychology, 66,* 811–816.

Epstein, S. (1973). The self-concept revisited: On a theory of a theory. *American Psychologist, 28,* 404–416.

Etaugh, C., & Ropp, J. (1976). Children's self-evaluation of performance as a function of sex, age, feedback, and sex typed task label. *Journal of Psychology, 94*, 115–122.

Feather, N. T. (1969). Attribution of responsibility and valence of success and failure in relation to initial confidence and perceived locus of control. *Journal of Personality and Social Psychology, 13*, 129–144.

Feldman, R. S., & Bernstein, A. G. (1977). Degree and sequence of success as determinants of self-attribution of ability. *Journal of Social Psychology, 102*, 223–231.

Fitch, G. (1970). Effects of self-esteem, perceived performance, and choice on causal attributions. *Journal of Personality and Social Psychology, 16*, 311–315.

Fontaine, G. (1974). Social comparison and some determinants of expected personal control and expected performance in a novel task situation. *Journal of Personality and Social Psychology, 29*, 487–496.

Frieze, I., & Weiner, B. (1971). Cue utilization and attributional judgments for success and failure. *Journal of Personality, 39*, 591–606.

Gilmor, T. M., & Minton, H. L. (1974). Internal versus external attribution of task performance as a function of locus of control, initial confidence and success–failure outcome. *Journal of Personality, 42*, 159–174.

Gitelson, I. B., Petersen, A. C., & Tobin-Richards, M. H. (1982). Adolescents' expectancies of success, self-evaluations, and attributions about performance on spatial and verbal tasks. *Sex Roles, 8*, 411–419.

Good, T., & Findley, M. (1985). Sex-role expectations and achievement. In J. Dusek, V. Hall, & W. Meyer (Eds.), *Teacher expectancies* (pp. 271–300). Hillsdale, NJ: Lawrence Erlbaum Associates.

Good, T., Sikes, J., & Brophy, J. (1973). Effects of teacher sex and student sex on classroom interaction. *Journal of Educational Psychology, 65*, 74–87.

Harvey, J. H., & Weary, G. (1981). *Perspectives on attributional processes.* Dubuque, IA: Brown.

Heider, F. (1958). *The psychology of interpersonal relations.* New York: Wiley.

Heller, K. A., & Parsons, J. E. (1981). Sex differences in teachers' evaluative feedback and students' expectancies for success in mathematics. *Child Development, 52*, 1015–1019.

Ickes, W., & Layden, M. A. (1978). Attributional styles. In J. Harvey, W. Ickes, & R. Kidd (Eds.), *New directions in attributional research* (Vol. 2, pp. 119–152). Hillsdale, NJ: Lawrence Erlbaum Associates.

Jacobsen, B., Lowery, B., & DuCette, J. (1986). Attributions of learning disabled children. *Journal of Educational Psychology, 78*, 59–64.

Johnson, T. J., Feigenbaum, R., & Weiby, M. (1964). Some determinants and consequences of the teacher's perception of causation. *Journal of Educational Psychology, 55*, 237–246.

Jones, E. E., & Davis, K. E. (1965). From acts to dispositions: The attribution process in person perception. In L. Berkowitz (Ed.), *Advances in experimental social psychology* (Vol. 2, pp. 219–266). New York: Academic Press.

Jones, E. E., & McGillis, D. (1976). Correspondent inferences and the attribution cube: A comparative reappraisal. In J. Harvey, W. Ickes, & R. Kidd (Eds.), *New directions in attribution research* (Vol. 1, pp. 389–420). Hillsdale, NJ: Lawrence Erlbaum Associates.

Jones, E. E., & Nisbett, R. E. (1972). The actor and the observer: Divergent perceptions of the causes of behavior. In E. Jones, D. Kanouse, H. Kelley, R. Nisbett, S. Valins, & B. Weiner (Eds.), *Attribution: Perceiving the causes of behavior* (pp. 79–94). Morristown, NJ: General Learning Press.

Jones, E. E., Rock, L., Shaver, K. G., Goethals, G. R., & Ward, L. M. (1968). Pattern of performance and ability attribution: An unexpected primacy effect. *Journal of Personality and Social Psychology, 10*, 317–340.

Jussim, L. (1989). Teacher expectations: Self-fulfilling prophecies, perceptual biases, and accuracy. *Journal of Personality and Social Psychology, 57*, 469–480.

Kassin, S. M., & Lowe, C. A. (1979). On the visual perception of the augmentation principle: A developmental study. *Child Development, 50,* 728–734.

Kassin, S. M., Lowe, C. A., & Gibbons, F. X. (1980). Children's use of the discounting principle: A perceptual approach. *Journal of Personality and Social Psychology, 39,* 719–728.

Kelley, H. H. (1967). Attribution theory in social psychology. In D. Levine (Ed.), *Nebraska Symposium on Motivation* (Vol. 15, pp. 192–238). Lincoln: University of Nebraska Press.

Kelley, H. H. (1972a). Attribution in social interaction. In E. Jones, D. Kanouse, H. Kelley, R. Nisbett, S. Valins, & B. Weiner (Eds.), *Attribution: Perceiving the causes of behavior* (pp. 1–26). Morristown, NJ: General Learning Press.

Kelley, H. H. (1972b). Causal schemata and the attribution process. In E. Jones, D. Kanouse, H. Kelley, R. Nisbett, S. Valins, & B. Weiner (Eds.), *Attribution: Perceiving the causes of behavior* (pp. 151–174). Morristown, NJ: General Learning Press.

Kelley, H. H. (1973). The processes of causal attribution. *American Psychologist, 28,* 107–128.

Kun, A. (1977). Development of the magnitude-covariation and compensation schemata in ability and effort attributions of performance. *Child Development, 48,* 862–873.

Kun, A., & Weiner, B. (1973). Necessary versus sufficient causal schemata for success and failure. *Journal of Research in Personality, 7,* 197–207.

Licht, B. G. (1983). Cognitive-motivational factors that contribute to the achievements of learning disabled children. *Journal of Learning Disabilities, 8,* 483–490.

Licht, B. G., Kistner, J. A., Ozkaragoz, T., Shapiro, S., & Clausen, L. (1985). Causal attributions of learning disabled children: Individual differences and their implications for persistence. *Journal of Educational Psychology, 77,* 208–216.

Marsh, H. W., Cairns, L., Relich, J., Barnes, J., & Debus, R. (1984). The relationship between dimensions of self-attribution and dimensions of self-concept. *Journal of Educational Psychology, 76,* 3–32.

Mazurkiewicz, A. (1960). Social-cultural influences and reading. *Journal of Developmental Reading, 3,* 254–263.

McClelland, D. C. (1987). *Human motivation.* Cambridge: Cambridge University Press.

McMahan, I. D. (1973). Relationships between causal attributions and expectancies of success. *Journal of Personality and Social Psychology, 28,* 108–114.

Medway, F. J., & Lowe, C. A. (1980). Causal attribution for performance by cross-age tutors and tutees. *American Educational Research Journal, 17,* 377–387.

Mendelson, R., & Shultz, T. (1976). Covariation and temporal contiguity as principles of causal inference in young children. *Journal of Experimental Child Psychology, 22,* 408–412.

Miller, D. T., & Ross, M. (1975). Self-serving biases in the attribution of causality. Fact or fiction? *Psychological Bulletin, 82,* 213–225.

Nicholls, J. G. (1975). Causal attributions and other achievement-related cognitions: Effects of task outcome, attainment value and sex. *Journal of Personality and Social Psychology, 31,* 379–389.

Nicholls, J. G. (1976). Effort is virtuous, but it's better to have ability: Evaluative responses to perceptions of effort and ability. *Journal of Research in Personality, 10,* 306–315.

Nicholls, J. G. (1978). The development of the concepts of effort and ability, perception of academic attainment, and the understanding that difficult tasks require more ability. *Child Development, 49,* 800–814.

Nicholls, J. G. (1979). The development of perception of own attainment and causal attribution for success and failure in reading. *Journal of Educational Psychology, 71,* 94–99.

Palmer, D. J., Drummond, F., Tollison, P., & Zinkgraff, S. (1982). An attributional investigation of performance outcomes for learning-disabled and normal-achieving pupils. *Journal of Special Education, 16,* 207–219.

Parsons, J. E., Meece, J. L., Adler, T. F., & Kaczala, C. M. (1982). Sex differences in attributions and learned helplessness. *Sex Roles, 8,* 421–432.

Rejeski, W. J., & McCook, W. (1980). Individual differences in professional teachers' attributions for children's performance outcomes. *Psychological Reports, 46*, 1159–1163.

Rholes, W. S., Blackwell, J., Jordan, C., & Walters, C. (1980). A developmental study of learned helplessness. *Developmental Psychology, 16*, 616–624.

Riemer, B. (1975). Influence of causal beliefs on affect and expectancy. *Journal of Personality and Social Psychology, 31*, 1163–1167.

Rolison, M., & Medway, F. (1985). Teachers' expectations and attributions for student achievement: Effects of label, performance pattern, and special education intervention. *American Educational Research Journal, 22*, 561–573.

Rosenbaum, R. M. (1972). *A dimensional analysis of the perceived causes of success and failure.* Unpublished doctoral dissertation, University of California.

Rosenthal, R., & Jacobson, L. (1968). *Pygmalion in the classroom: Teacher expectation and pupils' intellectual development.* New York: Holt, Rinehart, & Winston.

Ross, L., Bierbrauer, G., & Polly, S. (1974). Attribution of educational outcomes by professional and nonprofessional instructors. *Journal of Personality and Social Psychology, 29*, 609–618.

Ross, M., & Fletcher, G. J. (1985). Attribution and social perception. In G. Lindzey & E. Aronson (Eds.), *The handbook of social psychology* (Vol. 2, pp. 73–122). New York: Random House.

Ruble, D. N., Feldman, N. S., Higgins, E. T., & Karlovac, M. (1979). Locus of causality and use of information in the development of causal attributions. *Journal of Personality, 47*, 595–614.

Ruble, D. N., Parsons, J. E., & Ross, J. (1976). Self-evaluative responses of children in an achievement setting. *Child Development, 47*, 990–997.

Ruble, D. N., & Rholes, W. S. (1981). The development of children's perceptions and attributions about their world. In J. H. Harvey, W. Ickes, & R. F. Kidd (Eds.), *New directions in attribution research* (Vol. 3, pp. 3–36). Hillsdale, NJ: Lawrence Erlbaum Associates.

Shaklee, H. (1976). Development in inferences of ability and task difficulty. *Child Development, 47*, 1051–1057.

Shultz, T. R., & Mendelson, R. (1975). The use of covariation as a principle of causal analysis. *Child Development, 46*, 394–399.

Siegler, R. S. (1975). Defining the locus of developmental differences in children's causal reasoning. *Journal of Experimental Child Psychology, 20*, 512–525.

Sohn, D. (1982). Sex differences in achievement self-attributions: An effect-size analysis. *Sex Roles, 8*, 345–357.

Stein, A., Pohly, S., & Mueller, E. (1971). The influence of masculine, feminine and neutral tasks on children's achievement behavior, expectancies of success, and attainment values. *Child Development, 42*, 195–207.

Stipek, D. J., & Hoffman, J. M. (1980). Children's achievement-related expectancies as a function of academic performance histories and sex. *Journal of Educational Psychology, 72*, 861–865.

Sweeney, P. D., Moreland, R. L., & Gruber, K. L. (1982). Gender differences in performance attributions: Students' explanations for personal success or failure. *Sex Roles, 8*, 359–373.

Taylor, M. (1979). Race, sex, and the expression of self-fulfilling prophecies in a laboratory teaching situation. *Journal of Personality and Social Psychology, 37*, 897–912.

Tetlock, P. E. (1980). Explaining teacher explanations of pupil performance: A self-presentational interpretation. *Social Psychology Quarterly, 43*, 283–290.

Tom, D., & Cooper, H. (1986). The effect of student background on teacher performance attributions: Evidence for counterdefensive patterns and low expectancy cycles. *Basic and Applied Social Psychology, 7*, 53–62.

Tom, D., Cooper, H., & McGraw, M. (1984). The influences of student background and teacher authoritarianism on teacher expectations. *Journal of Educational Psychology, 76*, 259–265.

Weiner, B. (1974). Achievement motivation as conceptualized by an attribution theorist. In B. Weiner (Ed.), *Achievement motivation and attribution theory* (pp. 3–48). Morristown, NJ: General Learning Press.

Weiner, B. (1979). A theory of motivation for some classroom experiences. *Journal of Educational Psychology, 71*, 3–25.

Weiner, B., Frieze, I., Kukla, A., Reed, L., Rest, S., & Rosenbaum, R. (1972). Perceiving the causes of success and failure. In E. Jones, D. Kanouse, H. Kelley, R. Nisbett, S. Valins, & B. Weiner (Eds.), *Attributions: Perceiving the causes of behavior* (pp. 95–120). Morristown, NJ: General Learning Press.

Weiner, B., Heckhausen, H., Meyer, W., & Cook, R. E. (1972). Causal ascriptions and achievement behavior: A conceptual analysis of effort and reanalysis of locus of control. *Journal of Personality and Social Psychology, 21*, 239–248.

Weiner, B., & Kukla, A. (1970). An attributional analysis of achievement motivation. *Journal of Personality and Social Psychology, 15*, 1–20.

Weiner, B., Nierenberg, R., & Goldstein, M. (1976). Social learning (locus of control) versus attribution (causal stability) interpretations of expectancy of success. *Journal of Personality, 44*, 52–68.

Weiner, B., & Potepan, P. A. (1970). Personality characteristics and affective reactions toward exams of superior and failing college students. *Journal of Educational Psychology, 61*, 144–151.

Weiner, B., Russell, D., & Lerman, D. (1978). Affective consequences of causal ascriptions. In J. Harvey, W. Ickes, & R. Kidd (Eds.), *New directions in attribution research* (Vol. 2, pp. 59–90). Hillsdale, NJ: Lawrence Erlbaum Associates.

Weinstein, R. S. (1985). Student mediation of classroom expectancy effects. In J. Dusek, V. Hall, & W. Meyer (Eds.), *Teacher expectancies* (pp. 329–350). Hillsdale, NJ: Lawrence Erlbaum Associates.

Weinstein, R. S., & Middlestadt, S. E. (1979). Student perceptions of teacher interactions with male high and low achievers. *Journal of Educational Psychology, 71*, 421–431.

Wiley, M. G., & Eskilson, A. (1978). Why did you learn in school today? Teachers' perceptions of causality. *Sociology of Education, 51*, 261–269.

Wong, M. C. (1980). Model students? Teachers' perceptions and expectations of their Asian and white students. *Sociology of Education, 53*, 226–246.

Wong, P. T., & Weiner, B. (1981). When people ask questions and the heuristics of the attributional search. *Journal of Personality and Social Psychology, 40*, 650–663.

Yee, A. (1968). Interpersonal attitudes of teachers and advantaged and disadvantaged pupils. *Journal of Human Resources, 3*, 327–345.

4

THE ROLE AND IMPORTANCE OF INTERPERSONAL ATTRACTION AND SOCIAL ACCEPTANCE IN EDUCATIONAL SETTINGS

Geoffrey Maruyama
Judith LeCount
University of Minnesota

Establishing relationships and interacting within social groups are prominent and common parts of everyday life. Whether the interactions are at work, home, or elsewhere, they can be characterized by the interplay of common social forces and individual responses to those forces. In interactions with family, friends, and co-workers, individuals deal with an array of social influences. Various individuals respond differently to those forces, and their responses affect their friendships, their successes, and their power and influence.

A school classroom provides a good setting for illustrating the responses of different individuals to a group. Within virtually any classroom, individual students differ widely in the number of classmates they consider friends, the number of classmates who consider them to be a friend, and the extent to which they view the class as socially important. Consequences of these different orientations to the class are easily visible. An observer of school classrooms in an unstructured situation is likely to find most students situated in a number of social clusters, some large, others relatively small, with certain clusters viewing others as rivals, competitors, or even enemies. Still other students will not belong to any one cluster, some because they are widely accepted and can move between clusters, others because they are rejected or ignored. In effect, the social clusters reflect friendships, peer groups, and involvement in the group culture that the class provides.

Insofar as groups tend to display characteristic patterns of behavior, observers of groups are likely to notice particular types of behavior. In a school classroom, for example, whether observers are parents, school personnel, or social science researchers, many of their curiosities about friendship patterns in school classrooms are likely to center around the same specific issues. Common questions include: (a) How did the groups within the class get to be the way they are?; (b) what drew different individuals to different groups?; and (c) what are the consequences of being a member of different groups? Parents may be interested because they want their children to belong to the "right" groups, school personnel because they want to identify highly talented children or children who misbehave or who are likely to be depressed or use drugs, or because they want to exert more control over particular students. Despite asking the same questions, researchers typically are much less driven by concerns about facilitating performance or controlling negative behaviors of individuals. Their primary issues more likely relate to explaining overall patterns of group members' behavior and to obtaining findings that generalize to other groups. Thus, researchers would address the preceding questions as ways to examine processes of friendship selection and group formation as well as the consequences of friendships and groups.[1]

Because attraction and friendship formation among group members is an everyday social occurrence, it should not be surprising to find that social psychologists have a history of studying interpersonal attraction, friendship and group formation, and the socialization processes that occur in groups. This chapter reviews and overviews much of that research as we discuss how social psychologists have studied interpersonal attraction as well as the implications of social psychological research for education professionals.

Social psychologists have brought several orientations to the study of attraction. First, they have tried to look at processes occurring within individuals (i.e., at the intraindividual level), particularly at how individuals react to cues from others such as dress, attractiveness, body posture, attentiveness, and so on (e.g., Berscheid & Walster, 1978; Maruyama & Miller, 1981). This literature has been called research on impression formation. Second, they have looked at interpersonal or interindividual behaviors, namely, how an individual's reactions to another person affect the latter person's reactions to the first person (e.g., Snyder, Tanke, & Berscheid, 1977), as well as how long-term interactions among individuals affect earlier impressions (e.g. Snyder &

---

[1]Whether researchers are studying groups or other phenomena, a central issue for them is determining if they are studying phenomena that involve cause–effect relationships. In the context of school classes and children's interactions with one another, the consequences and causes of friendships are of interest. Said differently, understanding how friendships form may be interesting in its own right, but it would be even more important if friendship formation is related to school academic and social outcomes, and much more important if research could establish that friendship formation *causes* changes in school academic and social outcomes. In effect, understanding and explaining social phenomena are important, but they become more important if the specific phenomenon of interest is interrelated to and impacts other phenomena.

Swann, 1978). Third, they have looked beyond individuals to groups, studying, for example, the pressure that groups put on individuals as well as the ways that groups exert pressure (Asch, 1952; French & Raven, 1959). This work in particular has been tied to schools, for it provided one model to guide school desegregation (e.g., Maruyama, Miller, & Holtz, 1986). Fourth, they have looked in detail at the development and consequences of peer relationships (e.g., Hartup, 1983). In effect, a number of complementary approaches have combined to provide a broad perspective for viewing interpersonal attraction and interpersonal relationships in group settings. This chapter tries to summarize those approaches, beginning with a discussion of the importance of interpersonal attraction.

IMPORTANCE OF INTERPERSONAL ATTRACTION

First, interpersonal attraction can aid in processes of socialization. Socialization occurs in families, in church and community groups, in neighborhoods, and in schools; because the present volume is oriented to issues of school psychology, we focus on socialization in schools. Educators have described a number of important functions that schools serve beyond teaching academic skills. Socialization, acculturation, and value transmission are prominent examples. These functions often have been addressed implicitly and given labels like *the hidden curriculum*; they also have been explicit parts of broad curriculum orientations (e.g., the common school movement). Most commonly, socializing school children in ways of the United States has been both explicit and implicit; classes in civics and social studies have helped pass on our culture and values, but many aspects of schools that are just assumed to be "right" also transmit values and culture. Furthermore, friendships and role models also have important roles in socialization.

Important to the study of interpersonal relations is the ways in which values are passed as well as effectiveness in passing them. For example, children need to be socialized to behave appropriately both inside and outside of school. Although behavior can be controlled by means of rewards or punishment, such means of control are external to the individuals being socialized, and, therefore, once these means are removed, behavior reverts back to old patterns. Alternatively, behavior that emerges when children voluntarily model their teachers or peers is behavior that becomes internal to the children,[2] especially if the behavior is affirmed through acceptance by the individual whose behavior is modeled. Thus, one important facet of interpersonal attraction is that it is a very effective way of passing values. Anecdotes

---

[2]Later conceptual discussion of this point covers bases of power and transmission of values/social influence processes.

of peer groups dictating hairstyle, clothing types, mannerisms, or even drug use and other misbehavior are easy to find; they attest to the power of attractive individuals or groups in shaping the beliefs and behaviors of others who want to be accepted by them.

In sum, interpersonal attraction provides one means of controlling behavior; people model the behaviors of attractive individuals and groups in order to be accepted by them. Clearly, such influence can work well for professionals working in schools, for it allows them to change the behavior of others without using material rewards or forms of punishment. In addition, attractive groups and individuals shape the attitudes and values of others; attitudes and values change with or following from the behavioral changes described previously.

Second, interpersonal attraction can help shape and build social skills necessary for experiencing successful interpersonal relationships. Although the nature and meaning of interpersonal attraction change somewhat across the school years (e.g., Hartup, 1983), learning adaptive social behavior provides a strong base for building successful relationships. Given the sometimes inaccurate messages about competence and cultural desirability that influence even initial interactions with any other, it seems clear that an important part of successful socialization involves attending to available cues and using them to behave in acceptable if not desirable ways.

The "flip side" of successful interpersonal relationships, namely, unsuccessful interpersonal relationships, provides a third aspect of interpersonal attraction. Individuals who fail to "fit," regardless of the reason, experience greater stress and less life satisfaction. Unfortunately, individuals are too often ostracized or ignored for reasons other than their unwillingness to abide by group norms and values. Individuals who are physically disfigured, lower class, or ethnic racial minority, as examples, hold lower social status and are less frequently looked to as friends (see, e.g., Johnson & Johnson, 1989).

In summary, we have attempted to provide a rationale for studying interpersonal attraction. Next, we discuss *why* attraction operates the way it does, presenting conceptual models that help explain interpersonal attraction. First we tie back to earlier discussions of power and social influence and then cover theories directly addressing interpersonal attraction.

POWER AND SOCIAL INFLUENCE

Bases of Power

French and Raven (1959) provide a widely cited model of different types or bases of power that individuals have available. In terms of the present discussion, it makes sense to think of their bases of power as clustering into three types. The first is related to norms and expectations for societal roles. Teachers, for example, have power to give grades or to enforce discipline and have power stemming from knowledge they acquired to prepare themselves for their job. Second, there is power that comes from shaping and controlling outcomes (reward and punishment). Third, there is power in possessing attributes that make one socially attractive. Importantly, French and Raven note that this last type of power, which they call referent power, is most desirable, for it not only produces compliance but also changes the targets' beliefs and liking for the person with power. Referent power is the power held by people and groups whom we want to accept us; we modify our behavior (often by modeling theirs) in order to be accepted by them. Note, for example, the influence exerted by social groups (e.g., fraternities) or by professional groups (e.g., corporations with "dress for success" norms).

Social Influence Processes

Referent power provides the basis for a second conceptual model discussed later, namely, one Deutsch and Gerard (1955) called normative and informational social influence processes. Deutsch and Gerard (1955) suggested that socially attractive individuals shape others' behaviors and attitudes in two ways. The first, called *informational social influence*, occurs as attractive individuals provide others with enough information to compare their behaviors and beliefs to the attractive individuals. (Note that competent or expert individuals who are unattractive also have this type of social influence.) Individuals can model the successful behaviors of others as they attempt to modify their own behavior. For example, an individual wanting to learn how to play golf can learn some aspects of how to play just by watching good golfers play and trying to model their behavior. In school settings, adaptive and successful behaviors of teachers and high-achieving students can show other students ways of behaving that increase their successes. To the extent that those other children try to behave in the ways they have seen, informational social influence is exerted. The second, called *normative social influence*, requires that the persons displaying adaptive behavior be seen as attractive by the others, so that the modeling is done not only to perform more effectively but also to be accepted by the attractive others. In the language of French and Raven, the attractive individuals are granted referent power that helps to shape the behaviors of others. Importantly, then, normative social influence is powerful because the persons influenced not only see behavior modeled but also are motivated to change their beliefs and behaviors in order to be accepted.

Social Comparison Theory

The model of Deutsch and Gerard (1955) seems implicitly to be built on or at least complements yet another social psychological theory, namely Festinger's (1954) theory of social comparison processes. Festinger's (1954) model described how in interpersonal situations individuals cope with the uncer-

tainty produced when individuals are not sure about the validity of their beliefs or the quality of their behaviors. In such situations, individuals use the
reactions and behaviors of others to judge the adequacy of their own performance or their own beliefs. For the discussion of interpersonal attraction and
social influence processes, social comparison theory provides a mechanism
that drives individuals to attempt to perform better (Festinger argues that
for abilities individuals compare most often with others of higher but still similar skill levels) and adopt more normative beliefs (when belief discrepancies
occur, there is a strong tendency for individuals with non-normative beliefs
to conform to the views of others). Further, it is through processes of social
comparison that individuals and groups come to be seen as competent and/or
attractive. Individuals viewed as competent gain informational social influence; those viewed as attractive gain normative social influences.

ATTRACTION THEORIES

Theories of interpersonal attraction are considered to be of two major types:
cognitive theories, primarily cognitive consistency theories, and reinforcement theories (Berscheid, 1985). Reinforcement theories, which have played
the dominant role in interpersonal attraction research, are examined first.
They maintain that our attraction behavior results from the effects of rewards
and punishments dispensed to us directly from others or from our environment or from the expectation that we will receive rewards for our behavior.
These theories also have been termed social exchange theories because of
their premise that social interaction is based on the principles of an exchange
of rewards and punishments. Although some reinforcement theories are true
to a behaviorist/operant tradition (e.g., Homans, 1961; Lott & Lott, 1974),
for many the focus on reinforcements is blended somewhat with perception
and expectations. In effect, the distinction between reinforcement and cognitive theories is somewhat blurred. We have chosen to split theories at equity theory, which we discuss with the cognitive consistency theories (cf.,
Berscheid, 1985).

Consistency theories, in contrast to the reinforcement theories, view interpersonal attraction as resulting from the need to realize consistency between our experiences and our thoughts and beliefs about people and objects.
From a consistency theory perspective, cognitions of attraction or repulsion
may predispose individuals to interpret behaviors in certain ways and therefore are often instrumental in shaping the social interaction. Both consistency theory and reinforcement theory orientations have made important contributions to the study of interpersonal attraction, and recent approaches to
attraction tend to be an amalgamation of reinforcement and cognitive consistency theories (e.g., Kelley, 1979).

Reinforcement Theories

Homans' Social Exchange Theory. The principles of Homans' (1961) social exchange theory are modeled after economic transactions that utilize rewards, costs, and alternatives. When one individual gives, the recipient is supposed to provide something in return. An imbalance between what is given and what is received places one or the other in debt and thus promotes continuity of a reciprocal exchange. Even children at a preschool level have been found to engage in reciprocal exchange of positive reinforcers. Nursery school-children who gave the most positive social reinforcers to peers were the ones who received the most in return (Charlesworth & Hartup, 1967).

Although exchange theory assumes that the goods exchanged are comparable in value, fair exchanges do not necessarily engender liking. Rather, liking may be seen as resulting from the exchange of positive reinforcers. Attractive exchanges are those that are most rewarding, least costly, and the best bargains. Furthermore, attractiveness of the exchange can generalize beyond the actual goods exchanged to the exchange situation and participants.

A second aspect of exchanges relates to costs incurred in producing goods. Thus, part of establishing the value of a good is the effort and cost expended in producing it. Costs involve both the negative behaviors that we receive and the positive behaviors that we think we deserve but don't receive (Williams, 1979). Likewise, rewards usually involve positive behaviors but may also consist of expected negative events that are avoided. Interestingly, incurring even major costs is not necessarily bad because of the potential rewards we may obtain from "investing" in the costs.

One difficulty in establishing equitable exchanges comes from our "egocentric bias" (Ross & Sicoly, 1979), a tendency to take more credit for investments and costs than is warranted; that is, we tend to overestimate the personal contributions and costs resulting from our share of a given activity.

Finally, there are two other points worth noting. First, Homans assumes that, even though in social transactions we want to maximize our gains and minimize our losses, not all gains are valued equivalently. For example, the more something costs us to obtain, the higher the value we may place on it. The scarcer a valued reward, the higher the price a person can exact for giving it. Thus, a reward that is easily obtained may be less valuable than one that is difficult to secure (Homans, 1961). Second, Homans resurrected the Aristotelian principle of distributive justice to suggest that, the more heavily invested we are, the more angry we would become if the reciprocal exchange were not realized.

Byrne's Similarity Attraction Model. Byrne (1971) argued we would find others with attitudes similar to our own to be generally attractive. The attraction results because similar people socially validate our attitudes. His similarity attraction paradigm generated a tremendous amount of research about the effects of attitude similarity on attraction to strangers (e.g., Byrne, 1973).

Clore and Byrne (1974) proposed a model of attraction and reinforcement in which liking is based on association of rewards. The rewards need only be associated with another person, not necessarily received directly from that person. A rewarding experience that generates a positive affective response can produce an evaluative response, such as liking, for the person responsible for the initial favorable stimulus. In the language of Byrne, London, and Reeves (1968), "Attraction toward X is a positive linear function of the proportion of positive reinforcements received from X or expected from X" (p. 261).

Lott and Lott's Reward-Attraction Model.   Lott and Lott (1974) developed the model of reward-attraction most directly tied to behavioral principles of learning. They viewed attractive others functioning as secondary reinforcers and documented generalizability of reinforcers. They demonstrated "liking by association" in classroom situations with small groups of young children playing an imaginary war game. Children rewarded by reaching the goal showed greater liking for their teammates regardless of whether or not the others were instrumental in reaching the goal or even intended to help them achieve the goal. Thus, not only does reward increase the attractiveness and liking of others, but liking can occur when an individual experiences reward merely in the presence of a person, even if that person is not responsible for the reward.[3] When teachers systematically reward their students, the classmates' liking for each other increases significantly more than children who are ignored or treated unfavorably by their teachers (Lott & Lott, 1968). Lott and Lott (1974) also were interested in clarifying the different types of reward that could be used. They maintain that there are basic categories of rewards that increase our interpersonal attraction for others. These categories include the intrinsic characteristics the other persons possess that are rewarding to us (e.g., their beauty, sense of humor, intelligence), rewarding behaviors coming directly from others (e.g., sex, attention, consolation in times of distress), and the types of concrete resources potentially available to us through others (e.g., prestige, money, other people).

Thibaut and Kelley's Social Interdependence.   Thibaut and Kelley (1959) interpreted attraction behavior in dyadic interactions as involving principles of reinforcement and social exchange; in the interactions each individual depends on the other's behavior to attain desired outcomes. The value of the outcome of any behavior is affected by the other's response to that behavior.

---

[3]This argument fits the Deutsch (1950) theory of cooperation, competition, and individualization. Deutsch argued that experiencing success with others produces positive cathexis, which in turn produces positive affect and liking for others.

Based on the average of outcomes experienced in the past, one estimates what outcomes can be expected in the future. This comparison level (or CL) for expected outcomes becomes the individuals' standard from which they evaluate the rewards and costs of future social exchanges. Satisfaction and attraction are dependent on both the actual outcome and the individuals' CL and are hypothesized to be favorable when outcomes are above the CL; outcomes and relationships below the CL will be considered relatively unattractive.

According to Thibaut and Kelley, individuals evaluate their outcomes against a "comparison level for alternatives" (CLalt) that defines the lowest level of outcomes acceptable to them as compared with the outcomes elsewhere. Whether these alternatives are actually available or not does not matter. It is the belief about the alternative that is important. For example, high school students considering dropping out of school may remain in circumstances regarded as unsatisfactory (school) and continue to interact with others whom they regard as unattractive (peers), provided they perceive no better alternative. If they believe, however, that outcomes associated with dropping out are more attractive than outcomes tied to staying in school, they are likely to drop out.

To summarize, we have briefly overviewed four reinforcement theories that affirm the importance of reinforcers in determining attractiveness. Viewed from the framework of French and Raven, these theories provide guidance in judging what is rewarding and how rewards are viewed in the context of costs. Importantly, they point to nontangible, nonmaterial reinforcers that affect impressions and liking, to reasons why common backgrounds and orientations are rewarding and produce attraction, and to the ways reinforcement histories set baselines (comparison levels) for judging present rewards.

Cognitive Theories

Equity Theory. Equity theory uses a social exchange perspective to explain behavior but defines equity/inequity at the individual perception level. In dyads, an individual compares his or her ratio of outcomes to inputs in a relationship to the ratio of the other's outcomes to inputs. If inequity is perceived by either individual, some attempt (possibly cognitive as well as behavioral) is made to restore equity (see Adams, 1965; Walster, Walster, & Berscheid, 1978). The under-rewarded person obviously will want to reestablish equity; in addition, however, the over-rewarded person should feel uncomfortable because cultural norms of fairness have been violated. To relieve this distress, the reestablishment of equity can be accomplished in several ways (Adams, 1965; Walster et al., 1978): by altering the inputs through reducing or increasing one's contributions; by withdrawing from the relationship (i.e., "leaving the field"; Hatfield, Ute, & Traupmann, 1979); or by developing psychological equity. Attaining psychological equity involves changing one's perception of the circumstances by convincing oneself that equity does exist even though inputs and outcomes remain unchanged, through belief that the partner deserves the better deal (McDonald, 1981), or by diminishing the importance of the relationship.

Equity theory has been applied to long-term and intimate as well as casual interpersonal relationships (e.g., Walster et al., 1978). Not surprisingly, equity and reciprocity seem most important in the beginning stages of and in casual relationships; over time and in more intimate relationships individuals are less likely to demand or expect immediate return, recognizing that they can be rewarded at a later time. Nonetheless (e.g., Lloyd, Cate, & Henton, 1984), equity plays an important role even in enduring relationships.

Equity theory can easily be applied to personal relationships in educational settings. For example, interactions among regular classroom teachers, school psychologists, and special education teachers can be stressful if some individuals feel that their input/output ratio is much different than the ratios of others. At the same time, such relationships can be improved when clear school norms define expected (and, implicitly, equitable) roles and behaviors for all individuals.

A liability of equity theory is that it defines equity in terms of the individuals' perceptions. Thus, its ability to predict outcomes is limited because psychological equity can be attained despite seemingly inequitable circumstances (and vice versa). To the extent changes may be internal to individuals, shifts in equity/inequity can occur with no observable change in manifested behaviors. Further, equitable norms do not guarantee that individuals will perceive their situation as equitable.

Heider's Balance Theory. Heider's (1958) theory of cognitive balance assumes that people desire consistency or balance and are motivated to maintain balance in their beliefs, cognitions, and feelings. Inconsistency disrupts balance, produces a feeling of discomfort, and results in a tendency to shift toward balance. Heider suggests that social perception and interpersonal behaviors can be explained through simple cognitive configurations (viz. a P–O–X triad) describing by attitude the positive or negative relationship of a person P to another person O, or to an impersonal entity X that may be any situation, event, idea, or thing. Thus, there are three relations, P–O, the person's liking for or evaluation of the other; P–X, the person's evaluation of the object, and O–X, the person's perception of the other's evaluation of the object. A P–O–X triad is balanced when all relations are positive or when two of the three relations are negative. In other situations, with one or three negative relations, a change is necessary to restore consistency within the P–O–X triad.

Importantly, Heider's model takes the orientation of the person and judges consistency only in terms of the person's perception of the other and attitude object. Thus, if we were trying to assess consistency of a P–O–X triad, we would assume that the person's perception of the other is reciprocated. As an example, consider how a school psychologist might view a teacher–student situation. If the school psychologist ("person") likes the teacher ("other"), balance would occur if they agree about how to most effectively deal with the situation (the "attitude object" would be their beliefs about some disposition of the situation). Note that balance occurs regardless of whether or not the psychologist and teacher both like or dislike the disposition as long as they both agree. If imbalance occurs, the person should be motivated to restore balance to the P–O–X triad.

Heider's balance theory has received support when individuals feel positively toward each other, but limitations to the theory's predictive value occur when people do not like each other. First, under conditions of dislike, balancing forces are relatively weak, resulting in "nonbalanced" situations (Newcomb, 1968) such that subjects generally become less involved (Crano & Cooper, 1973) and prefer imbalance (Crockett, 1974). Second, people seem to show more preference for agreeing rather than disagreeing on an attitude issue whether they like each other or not; this predilection toward a positivity bias (the tendency to express positive evaluations more often than negative evaluations; see Sears & Whitney, 1973) also limits the balancing forces of Heider's theory.

Heider's (1958) model operates at a very specific level and does not explicitly provide guidance for aggregating across the array of attitude objects. Nonetheless, the notion of consistency restoration or maintenance is an appealing one, and it seems reasonable to assume that inconsistency evokes motivation to resolve that inconsistency, that unresolved inconsistency is unpleasant and should produce negative affect that reduces liking, and that individuals whose views about attitude objects are consistent with one another should experience balance and like each other.

Newcomb's A–B–X (Strain-Toward-Symmetry Theory) Model. Newcomb's (1953, 1961) cognitive consistency theory is a modification of Heider's balance theory to incorporate the simultaneous orientation of two individuals toward each other (A < – > B). This modification assumes that personal relations with objects of communication (A– > X) are influenced by others' orientations to the object (B– > X). In a manner similar to Heider's forces pushing toward a balanced state, Newcomb expects that there are persistent and strong forces, resulting from imbalance, impinging upon the A–B–X system that "strain" the system toward preferred states of equilibrium. The more similar A's and B's orientations toward X, the more symmetrical the A–B–X configuration. Symmetrical systems should be rewarding insofar as they provide information validating the individuals' orientations. In effect, individuals gain more confidence in their own cognitive and evaluative orientations via reinforcement from similar others; thus, symmetry is likely to acquire secondary reward value.

The major implication of this approach for interpersonal attraction (and of course, an implication of Byrne's similarity–attraction paradigm as well) is that people are likely to be attracted to and seek out the company of others who are similar to them (e.g., Newcomb, 1961). Research in desegregated schools has certainly provided support for such a view; in the absence of interventions that force intergroup contact, students associate with similar others and stratification of groups can occur (e.g., Maruyama, Petersen, & Knechel, in press).

Cognitive Dissonance. Festinger's (1957) cognitive dissonance theory has strongly shaped social psychologists' ways of thinking about the outcomes of interpersonal attraction in relationships. The basic assumption is that individuals' behavior will be consistent with the cognitions they hold (and also that groups seek to optimize consistency of their interpersonal relations). When cognitions are dissonant, the individual is psychologically uncomfortable and is motivated to reduce the dissonance to attain consonance.

Dissonance theory predicts that a person who voluntarily has made a significant contribution to a relationship, and yet who is dissatisfied with that relationship, would experience dissonance. One way to reduce this dissonance would be to positively evaluate the relationship, as when an individual who knows of the negative aspects of a relationship voluntarily decides to invest in it even further. As an example, school professionals may continue to work on tasks they should drop because they need to justify efforts they have already expended.

Also, individuals who perceive themselves as kind and yet harm others unjustly will experience dissonance. Commonly, they will come to dislike the others or believe that the persons deserved to suffer (Davis & Jones, 1960). In effect, punishment can be accompanied by a negative label that may justify future punishments. The belief that people get what they deserve ("just world") stimulated research that suggests that attraction is decreased for others who have been treated unjustly by fate or other people (Lerner & Miller, 1978).

To summarize, the three consistency theories argue: (1) that we evaluate our relationships in terms of consistency between our attitudes/feelings and our past and present behaviors; (2) that similarity in beliefs can produce consistency that engenders positive feelings and liking; (3) that inconsistency can be resolved by changing attitudes and perceptions as well as behaviors. The implications of consistency theories can be extended to broad patterns of behavior as individuals face the need to attain consistency across issues and behaviors as well as within them.[4]

---

[4]This is not intended to imply that individuals are driven to integrate all aspects of their lives. There is much inconsistency that is unresolved simply because individuals are not attentive to it and therefore have no awareness of it.

A SEQUENTIAL PROCESS
OF INTERPERSONAL ATTRACTION

Attraction to others can be viewed as changing as contact with them increases. This section looks at factors shaping both first impressions and longer term interactions.

DETERMINANTS OF FIRST IMPRESSIONS

Initial impressions of others are strongly influenced by potent observable variables such as physical attractiveness, appearance, body type, and kinesic, paralinguistic, or facial cues. These immediately evident bases for evaluation exert bias independently of explicit attempts to exchange information and can be instrumental in determining a person's social standing in many kinds of groups.

Physical Attractiveness

One of the first dimensions on which evaluations are made is physical attractiveness, for it is immediately apparent. Effects of attractiveness on individuals' behavior and on the behavior of others toward them begins early in socialization and continues into adulthood (Berscheid & Walster, 1974). For example, physically unattractive preschool children are considered by their peers to be "meaner" (Dion, 1972). Similarly, adult judgments of children's misbehavior seem also to be strongly influenced by the children's attractiveness. Unattractive children who committed a serious transgression were judged as being antisocial in character, whereas attractive children behaving the same way were excused as having temporary mood changes (Dion, 1972).[5]

Elementary schoolchildren's evaluations of prospective teachers are also highly influenced by the teachers' attractiveness. Children judged photographs of attractive female teachers as being nicest, happiest, prettiest, and teachers from whom they would learn the most; they judged the unattractive photographs as teachers who would punish their students more when they misbehaved (Hunsberger & Cavanagh, 1988).

Previous research provides a great deal of evidence for a general "what is beautiful is good" attractiveness stereotype (Dion, Berscheid, & Walster, 1972). For example, physically attractive individuals exhibit desirable behaviors, such as being more socially skilled (Goldman & Lewis, 1977; Lerner & Lerner, 1977), having more social mobility (Elder, 1969; Taylor & Glenn,

---

[5]In contrast, when misbehaviors were mild, attractiveness did not influence evaluations.

1976), having more positive self-concepts (Adams, 1977; Agnew, 1984; Chaiken, 1979; Kaats & Davis, 1970; Lerner & Karabenick, 1974; Lerner & Stuart, 1973), and being less delinquent (Agnew, 1984). Attractive persons affect the behavior of others on a number of dimensions: Others have been more reinforcing toward them (Barocus & Karoly, 1972), have helped more frequently (Athanasiou & Greene, 1972; Mims, Hartnett, & Nay, 1973), have approached them for help less frequently (Stokes & Bickman, 1974), have rated them as more popular (Dion & Berscheid, 1974), and have provided them with greater amounts of personal space (Dabbs & Stokes, 1975). These studies provide additional evidence that attractiveness affects behaviors as well as attitudes in the early stages of interactions.[6]

Physical attractiveness affects the favorability of outcomes in a wide variety of educational settings. Clifford and Walster (1973), for example, found that fifth-grade teachers had higher expectations for attractive children than for less attractive ones (see also Ross & Salvia, 1977). Because teachers judged potential of unknown students from file information only, the results are attributable to attractiveness and not to other attributes of the children. This attractiveness bias in teachers may also heighten report card grades of attractive children (Agnew, 1984; Salvia, Algozzine, & Sheare, 1977) and lead to greater numbers of referrals of attractive children for psychological assessment (Barocas & Black, 1974). Even though attractive children are referred for psychological assessment more often than unattractive children, Elovitz and Salvia (1982) found that school psychologists have an attractiveness bias and recommend attractive children to less stigmatizing programs and for more integration into regular classes. Also, attractive children were considered inappropriate for classes for mild mental retardation; conversely, unattractive pupils were judged to be more appropriate for mildly retarded classes and were expected to have more difficulties in future peer relationships and poorer functioning upon further evaluation.

Body Type

Body type is another potent and immediately observable variable that affects not only individuals' first impressions but also their self-concept and peer acceptance. Fat and skinny individuals tend to be viewed less favorably. For example, when elementary schoolchildren are shown pictures of thin (ectomorphic), chubby (endomorphic), and muscular (mesomorphic) physiques, they ascribed positive attributes (brave, neat, helpful) to their preferred body type, the mesomorph, and negative attributes (sloppy, lazy, stupid) to the endomorphic body type (Staffieri, 1967). Correspondingly, mesomorphic chil-

---

[6]No sex differences have been found with respect to the use of the attractiveness stereotype (Chaikin, Gillen, Derlega, & Wilson, 1978; Dion, 1973; Hunsberger & Cavanagh, 1988; Lerner & Lerner, 1977).

dren tend to be more popular in the classroom than ectomorphs and particularly endomorphs (Lerner, 1969). The most stressful time for peer rejection based on having an endomorphic body type may be first grade, when weight percentile significantly predicts low sociometric ratings (Summerville, Cohen, & Klesges, 1987).

The timing of puberty has important and differing social consequences for boys and girls. Early-maturing girls are temporarily less popular (Clausen, 1975; Faust, 1960) and end up with body types less similar to current norms for attractiveness. In contrast, early-maturing boys are perceived to be more attractive, masculine, sociable, and enjoy continuing popularity and respect into adulthood (Jones & Bayley, 1950). Late-maturing males tend to feel socially inadequate, inferior, and uncertain (Livson & Peskin, 1980). It appears that particularly for males early maturation is associated with differential treatment and long-lasting social consequences.

Names

Differential attraction to persons with unconventional names has found cautious support through correlational studies in the late 1960s and early 1970s. McDavid and Harari (1966) found that 10- and 12-year-old children with names determined to be attractive (e.g., Steven, John, Susan, Kim) were rated as more popular by their peers than children with unusual and less attractive names (e.g., Herman, Chastity). Consonant with these findings, teachers' expectations for higher achievement were found to be higher for children with attractive names (Harari & McDavid, 1973). These findings of Harari and McDavid (1973) are of course subject to alternative interpretations. Perhaps a child with an unattractive and unusual name may be ostracized by his or her peers not because of the name per se, but because of a lack of social skills or because of peculiar behaviors encouraged by the caregiver who selected the unusual name. At the same time, however, the well-documented effects of appearance suggest that other superficial cues like names could have a marked impact on evaluation received from others.

DETERMINANT OF LONGER TERM IMPRESSIONS

As relationships move beyond first impressions, obviously there is substantially more information available than for first impressions. Notably, information about values, attitudes, beliefs, interests, personality, occupation, and so forth become available. First, then, we should ask how this later information affects first impressions. Perhaps surprisingly, there are strong tendencies to maintain first impressions; persons distort later information to make it remain consistent with their initial views (e.g., Aronson, 1969; Asch, 1946; Dion, 1972; Miller & Campbell, 1959).

Over and above the tendency to maintain one's initial views, there are factors that impact impressions and move acquaintanceships forward to more interdependent and committed relationships. Prominent among those factors are mechanisms we described earlier regarding social influence and social comparison processes, availability of varying types of rewards, the role of reward in attraction, plus cognitive processes involved in integrating disparate positions.

First, it is no surprise to note that we are attracted to others who reward us. Importantly, attraction seems driven by two types of rewarding information, one, possession of culturally desirable attributes, and, two, high similarity. The reward value of culturally desirable attributes is fairly obvious, for those connote power and influence. In addition, as argued earlier, the affirmation and validation of one's views produced by similarity of others is also rewarding. Thus, we are likely to build relationships with others who are like us and who have relatively high status.

Second, in situations in which we are uncertain about our views and abilities, we need others for comparison. In the process of comparing opinions and abilities, we tend to seek out others similar to us for opinions and somewhat superior to us for abilities. In addition to strengthening our understanding of our attitudes and abilities, however, social comparison processes also build bonds as we are attracted differentially to others who we believe share common beliefs with us and who perform the way we want to perform. The differential attraction allows those others to have extra opportunities to give us rewards and therefore increases the likelihood that friendships will form around opinion and ability similarity or co-orientation.

Once we decide that certain individuals or groups are attractive and that we want to be accepted by them, we grant them referent power as well as reward power, and, by their use of that power, our beliefs and values could easily change to conform with theirs. Importantly, groups with referent power shape individuals who want to be accepted and, even after individuals are accepted by them, those groups continue to dictate appearance, values, etc. Furthermore, if individuals' acceptance by the group remains tentative, they are at the mercy of high-status others who shape their behavior.

To summarize, this section reaffirms why reward–attraction models have been so appealing to relationship researchers; much of attraction can easily be reduced to the rewards given by or anticipated from others with whom we choose to associate. We choose the people we associate with based on their similarity and valued attributes they possess. Further, once we associate with them, we provide them with increased opportunities to reward us, and, therefore, our attraction can increase further. As a consequence, friendships of all ages are characterized by reciprocal liking and behavioral involvement (McGuire & Weisz, 1982) that reward participants with a sense of security (Schwartz, 1972) and with affection, trust, and pleasure.

RELATIONSHIP DEVELOPMENT

At this point, we briefly touch on the relationship of age to friendship development. Not surprisingly, as children get older the principles of exchange and reward that shape friendships become more complex as their general cognitive and language skills develop (Hartup, 1983).

Even though young preschool children have limited verbal ability to describe friendships, their friendship preferences are readily demonstrated by more responsive behaviors extended to preferred playmates or "strong associates" than to acquaintances (Hinde, Titmus, Easton, & Tamplin, 1985). Preferred playmates exhibit more positive reinforcers (Masters & Furman, 1981) and have proportionally fewer negative exchanges (see Guralnick & Groom, 1988; Hinde et al., 1985). The importance of these reciprocal exchanges is indicated in Guralnick and Groom's (1988) observation that mildly developmentally delayed preschool children who rarely exhibit reciprocal friendships tend to remain isolated in mainstreamed playgroups. Unfortunately, peer rejection is relatively stable (Coie & Dodge, 1983), and children who are not accepted by peers may be at risk for later difficulties in social and emotional development (Hartup, 1983).

Thus far, we have argued that the processes of attraction and reciprocity are necessary for establishing children's friendships. Connected with these processes, children's expectations for their friendships may vary according to a developmental (or stage) approach (Bigelow, 1977): (a) *Reward–cost stage* occurs about second or third grade when friends have similar expectations about play; (b) *Normative stage* emerges about fourth or fifth grade when friends are expected to cooperate and share possessions, are loyal and helpful, and avoid fighting (Berndt, 1981); (c) *Empathic stage* develops about fifth to seventh grade when friends share similar interests and attempt to understand each other; by sixth grade attraction to peers is affected by reciprocity of self-disclosures (Rotenberg & Mann, 1986). Adolescents extend the equity norms to include a sense of "shared identities" of "we" (Hartup, 1983) and choose friends whom they can count on for understanding and for intimate emotional support (Smollar & Youniss, 1982). In sum, the quality of early peer relations may predict later social adjustment (Parker & Asher, 1987) necessary for friendships and supportive intimate relationships in life (e.g., Kelley et al., 1983).

MEASUREMENT OF FRIENDSHIP PATTERNS

Given all the work building theoretical models of attraction, it is safe to assume that comparable energy has been expended in developing ways of effectively measuring interpersonal attraction and friendships. First and most prominent among such techniques are what have been called sociometric methods. Sociometric methods were developed by Moreno (1953) for assessing along a single dimension, such as liking, the positive, negative, and neutral patterns of interpersonal relations existing within a group.

In effect, sociometric techniques assess patterns of friendships as well as status of individuals within peer groups. They yield information about the overall popularity of individuals and have the potential for defining subgroups (called cliques), high-status groups, social stars, social isolates, and rejected group members. Because popularity is highly dependent on the specific domain assessed, the subjects being tested need to know the limits of the group being assessed and the specific criteria for which they are choosing and rejecting. Said differently, sociometric assessment needs to carefully define the area being measured because choices for teammates on sports teams differ markedly from choices for work or schoolwork colleagues or from choices for friends.

Ideally, subjects should be allowed an unlimited number of choices of picks and rejects in order for the researcher to distinguish between an unchosen person and the social isolate who neither chooses nor is chosen (Lindzey & Byrne, 1968), but typically researchers limit their data to most and/or least preferred group members. For example, students in a preschool group might each be asked privately to point to photographs of three classmates with whom they most liked to play and three classmates with whom they did not like to play (Hayvren & Hymel, 1984). A major strength of limited choice approaches is that they force subjects to be selective, thus distinguishing close friends from other friends. At the same time, however, that strength can be a liability because it doesn't measure friendships other than close. Consider, for example, a child with three close friends. Ideally, sociometric assessment would not only show the existence of those strong friendships but also would show which of the other children are friendly with that child and which other children that child likes. Such other friendships, which could be labeled *casual* or *peripheral*, seem particularly important in heterogeneous classrooms, for they provide substantial information about class stratification. Further, such casual friendships are more transient and thus more sensitive to changes in class climate. In effect, an intervention designed to improve intergroup relations may not penetrate close friendships yet markedly reshape casual relationships.

An alternative sociometric technique, often called a *roster rating* approach, requires individual subjects to rank each member of the group with respect to one or more dimensions, such as aggressiveness or friendliness. As suggested previously, this approach assures assessment of group peer acceptance by allowing the researchers to see how each group member is perceived by all individual group members and by the group as a whole, yet it avoids some of the problems of peer nomination. The beauty of this technique is that the subjects are not explicitly asked to state whom they dislike (Asher & Dodge, 1986), yet it permits the researcher to identify children who are actively rejected by their peers because rejectees acquire low ratings.

Sociometric data are often used to categorize subjects into particular classes (e.g., Bukowski & Newcomb, 1985; Coie & Krehbiel, 1984; Venable, 1954). Principal sociometric categories into which a child might fall are:

1. *Sociometric stars*, children who receive the most positive nominations and are rejected by few. These are children who are well liked by their peer group.

2. *Amiable, accepted*, or *popular*, children who receive fewer nominations than sociometric stars, but for whom most of the nominations are positive.

3. *Isolates* or *neglectees*, who receive few nominations of any kind. They are neither actively liked nor disliked but are ignored by their peers. Eventually they may be "accepted" or even achieve the status of sociometric star should they enter a new class or a new play group (Coie & Dodge, 1983; Coie & Kupersmidt, 1983). These are children who probably have the basic social skills necessary to become accepted by their peers.

4. *Rejectees*, who receive many negative nominations and who are actively disliked and receive very low ratings on measures of likability and friendliness. It is the rejected child rather than the isolate who faces the greater risk of suffering serious adjustment problems later in life (Cowen, Pederson, Babigan, Izzo, & Trost, 1973; Roff, 1974). Rejectees feel more lonely than isolated children (Asher, Hymel, & Renshaw, 1984; Asher & Wheeler, 1985) and are most likely to remain rejected (Coie & Dodge, 1983).

5. *Controversials*, who are clearly accepted by a sizeable number of peers but actively disliked by many others (Bukowski & Newcomb, 1985; Coie & Dodge, 1983). These children have notably inconsistent social behaviors and may be prosocially inclined but high in aggression and antisocial activities, such as selective exclusion of peers from play activities. Newcomb and Bukowski (1984) found that nearly 60% of children initially classified as controversial had achieved another status in the peer group over an interval of one month. The particular brevity of this sociometric status illustrates the mercurial nature of peer group acceptance, variability in sociometric categories, and dynamics of interpersonal attraction processes associated with the controversials, as they either befriend those who initially disliked them and become "acceptees" or alienate those who liked them and become "rejectees."

In sociometric assessment of interpersonal attraction between individuals, the focus of the questions should be on A's liking for B (i.e., as a companion, friend, guest, etc.), not on A's evaluation of B's leadership potential or physical strength (Lindzey & Byrne, 1968). The consistency with which sociometric testing actually measures the variable in question may increase as the age of the subjects increases, decrease with longer time spans between testing and retesting (Horowitz, 1962), or vary when assessing perceived attraction of children with variable social profiles (Bukowski & Newcomb, 1985). Also, assessment of same-sex ratings are more valid in young elementary schoolchildren than cross-sex ratings (Bukowski & Newcomb, 1985; Coie, Dodge, & Coppotelli, 1982).

School administrators seem to have developed a reluctance about allowing researchers to use sociometric techniques, especially techniques identifying individual students as liked or disliked. In particular, there has been concern about children making choices about children they dislike because the request to identify such children contradicts the authority figure's usual tendency of rejecting disparaging remarks from children about their peers (Moore, 1967) and may legitimize not accepting peers. Further, children may perceive encouragement to state negative opinions as license to behave more negatively toward their unliked peers. To this point, however, there is no evidence that sociometric assessments produce negative effects. Hayvren and Hymel (1984) reported that preschool children who made negative sociometric peer nominations did not exhibit more negative verbal interaction toward their less preferred peers, nor did they change their behavior toward preferred and nonpreferred peers in the 10 minutes immediately following testing. Bell-Dolan, Foster, and Sikora (1989) obtained similar results with fifth-grade subjects and suggested that the risk of negative peer nomination sociometric measures to elementary school-aged children may be minimal. Clearly, because there are only two studies to date, additional information is necessary before suggesting indiscriminate application of sociometric peer nomination in the classroom in place of other methods of social preference data.

There are a number of other methods similar to sociometric measures that provide information about interpersonal attraction in groups including (see Lindzey & Byrne, 1968): self-rating analyses ("Who do you think will choose you?"), scaling methods (forced-choice comparisons), the "guess who" technique (naming who "fits" particular behavioral descriptions), and ratings of interpersonal attractiveness (open-ended questions, adjective checklists, ordinal rating scales, social distance measures, etc.). Although these methods do not follow exactly Moreno's (1953) criteria for the sociometric measure, they are similar social-choice measures that involve simple rating scales or direct questions about attraction.

GENERAL EDUCATIONAL IMPLICATIONS OF
RESEARCH ON INTERPERSONAL ATTRACTION

Although readers already may have thought about links to education of the research we have described, at this point we focus explicitly on what we think are some prominent implications of the research. We begin with first impressions, then discuss how perceived similarity in conjunction with social comparison processes drives attraction, and then look at how social power within peer groups operates. Finally, we suggest a class of interventions that holds promise for reshaping peer friendship structures.

Perhaps the initial dilemma for education professionals like school psychologists is recognizing how visible cues like attractiveness affect both the students' perceptions of each other and also educators' perceptions of students and other educators. Physically attractive children are treated better, rewarded more for their performances, and more highly accepted (e.g., Maruyama & Miller, 1981). As a consequence, they build up expectations of being rewarded, and in many circumstances do receive better outcomes. To the extent that one's self-concept reflects past outcomes, attractive children should have positive self-concepts, whereas unattractive children may have lower self-concepts (e.g., Adams, 1977; Chaiken 1979; Kaats & Davis, 1970). Our recommendation for educators with respect to attractiveness is beguilingly simple: Recognize how much attractiveness shapes our perceptions as well as the perceptions of our students. With respect to colleagues, it is important to acknowledge that attractiveness affects adult interactions too, and that collegial relations may be better understood by looking at attractiveness and its potential impacts. With respect to students, try to treat all children as if they are attractive. Notably, Cavior and Dokecki (1973) found that one's self-concept is strongly related to how attractive *one believes oneself to be*. As students get to know one another, a major determinant of attraction is similarity of attitudes and values. Said simply, we tend to seek out people we think are going to be like us. As argued by social comparison theory, we are drawn to similar others for purposes of social comparison; they reduce our uncertainty about our opinions and abilities by providing us with normative information. In addition, similar others are likely to agree with us, and the affirming information from them has reward value. Finally, similar others are attractive because their higher level of agreement reduces conflict that results from disagreements and lessens the need for conflict resolution.

Although attraction to similar others is common within our society, its implications for heterogeneous groups are not uniformly positive. For example, if students in a heterogeneous classroom are all attracted to similar others, the classroom would likely be highly stratified and students would experience conflict. There are available, however, strategies for reducing intergroup conflict and building relationships with dissimilar others. Most widely documented are strategies involving cooperative learning techniques (e.g., Johnson & Johnson, 1989), particularly those that provide a structure for disagreement. Before discussing them further, however, we tie in issues of power.

At several points in this chapter, we have attended to the value of referent power, namely, that it not only changes behaviors but also shapes attitudes so the behavioral changes endure. Perhaps ironically, of French and Raven's (1959) power bases, it is the only one not generally available to teachers and school psychologists. Imagine, for example, being able to change students' misbehaviors without having to continually monitor them to be sure the misbehaviors are not reemerging. Given its potential value, referent power should seemingly be the "power of choice." Unfortunately, however, it must be granted by the individuals influenced as they aspire to be like or to be accepted by attractive others. Thus, school professionals have referent power only insofar as they are viewed as attractive and their group is viewed as attractive and aspired to. Further, if individuals changing their attitudes and behavior in attempts to conform to a group or school professional feel rejected or ignored by that group or school professional, their behaviors and attitudes are likely to change again and become less similar to that group or school professional.

In sum, issues of referent power are quite complex. In order for school professionals to use referent power, children have to want to be like the professionals. Thus, children who view authority figures negatively will not give them much referent power; some researchers have argued that such patterns of behavior are common even for high-status children (e.g., Bronfenbrenner, 1979). Similarly, peer referent power is fragile because acceptance by the desired group is ultimately necessary. Given the hierarchical status patterns of most classes plus the minimal intergroup interactions as children cluster with similar others, student referent power may do little to shape attitudes and behaviors except within small and independent friendship clusters.

What can school professionals do to counter fragmented and encapsulated peer groups, most of which are homogeneous and many of which view authority figures neutrally or negatively? Without suggesting that there is a panacea for these problems, we believe that reorienting children's ways of interacting and thinking about conflict are highly promising. First, use cooperative learning groups *that are heterogeneous* (e.g., Gettinger, this volume; Johnson & Johnson, 1989). Successes of these groups lead children to view the others who share in and contribute to their successes in positive ways (Deutsch & Collins, 1951; Lott & Lott, 1974). The positive associations with dissimilar others should help to lessen intergroup conflicts. Second, structure controversy as part of the cooperative groupings (e.g., Johnson & Johnson, 1987). Structured controversy not only teaches students how to disagree; it teaches them that dissimilar others can provide important information that helps them improve the accuracy and validity of their views (e.g., Maruyama et al., in press). In the context of social comparison theory, one might argue that Festinger (1954) described general tendencies to seek out similar others without being prescriptive or restrictive. Individuals are not good at seeking out dissimilar others and using information that would force them to change their beliefs (e.g., Einhorn & Hogarth, 1978), even though they would be better decision makers if they could. Thus, teaching students about the value of alternative views and the need to seek out dissimilar others is important. Furthermore, with respect to interpersonal attraction, being rewarded by and interacting more with dissimilar others should help increase the likelihood of friendships that cross group lines.

To summarize, we have argued first that school professionals need to attend to effects of variables like attractiveness and, second, that schools, like other social structures, frequently encourage friendship patterns marked by homogeneity/similarity and in which intergroup contact is minimal. For this latter issue, use of cooperative learning techniques with structured controversy offers promise for reshaping patterns of peer friendships.

The preceding discussion has additional direct implications for practicing school psychologists. Most importantly, it is clear that all individuals, through their reinforcement histories, their social comparison processes, and their striving for cognitive consistency, end up with idiosyncratic and egocentric perspectives. Those perspectives predispose them to view others in biased ways. The biases are further augmented by the effects of superficial cues like appearance on first impressions. Unless divergent perspectives and visible differences are recognized as cues that affect perceptions, attaining a good understanding of interpersonal relations would be impossible. For example, a very attractive staff person may have difficulty interacting with others because the attractiveness affects others' perceptions of similarity, competence, and power. At the same time, extended direct contact has the potential of lessening the effects both of visible cues and of predisposing stereotypes.

CONCLUDING DISCUSSION

In beginning this chapter, we focused on everyday interactions with family, friends, and colleagues. Then, throughout the chapter, we have tried to explain how and why social psychologists have looked at interpersonal attraction within these interactions in the ways they have. First, given the array of transient interactions in our society, analyzing the determinants of first impressions is both reasonable and important. Second, our focus on social influence processes and social comparison processes should have helped explain (a) why we are attracted to similar others and (b) why similarity is so rewarding. Further, it hopefully illustrated how intuitively appealing a reward attraction approach is as well as how rewards coupled with referent power potentially produce marked attitudinal as well as behavioral changes. Finally, the cognitive consistency approaches have helped to explain why first impressions endure and why relationships tend to endure across time.

Understanding processes underlying friendship selection also helps to focus attention on limitations of friendship patterns. Most notably, intergroup friendships (i.e., friendships with others perceived as dissimilar) are not fostered by the processes described. Thus, one challenge for educational professionals including school psychologists is to provide a school climate that fosters positive intergroup relations. In this regard, our focus was on cooperative learning techniques and structured controversy.

In closing, we look to the future and issues related to interpersonal attraction in schools of the future. First, it seems that schools would have a difficult time fostering intergroup friendships unless the staff is heterogeneous and models such patterns. Second, heterogeneity of schools seems likely to increase: Lower class and non-White birth rates are relatively high; immigrant populations are becoming more diverse; more children with gay and lesbian parents and from single-parent families are increasing diversity; and "crack" children present potential concerns. In sum, these two points bring us back to a major challenge for schools, namely, maintaining a positive interpersonal climate where children interact effectively with one another and build friendships rather than rivalries or hatreds. Hopefully, work of social psychologists and other social scientists has helped in understanding processes of interpersonal attraction well enough that we can structure classroom environments in ways that effectively shape positive peer relationships. Although the work to date is most promising, only with time and further research will we know for sure.

ACKNOWLEDGMENTS

The authors would like to acknowledge support provided to the first author by US Department of Education Grant G008730255. Thanks also are due to Laureen O'Brien, Laura Tiede, and Diane Koski for their assistance in manuscript preparation.

REFERENCES

Adams, G. R. (1977). Physical attractiveness, personality, and social reactions to peer pressure. *Journal of Psychology, 96*, 287–296.

Adams, J. S. (1965). Inequity in social exchange. In L. Berkowitz (Ed.), *Advances in experimental social psychology* (Vol. 2, pp. 266–300). New York: Academic Press.

Agnew, R. (1984). The effect of appearance on personality and behavior: Are the beautiful really good? *Youth and Society, 15* (3), 285–303.

Aronson, E. (1969). Some antecedents of interpersonal attraction. In W. J. Arnold & D. Levine (Eds.), *Nebraska Symposium on Motivation, 17* (pp. 143–173). Lincoln: University of Nebraska Press.

Asch, S. E. (1946). Forming impressions of personality. *Journal of Abnormal Social Psychology, 41*, 258–290.

Asch, S. E. (1952). *Social psychology*. Englewood Cliffs, NJ: Prentice-Hall.

Asher, S. R., & Dodge, K. A. (1986). Identifying children who are rejected by their peers. *Developmental Psychology, 22*, 444–449.

Asher, S. R., Hymel, S., & Renshaw, P. D. (1984). Loneliness in children. *Child Development, 55*, 1456–1464.

Asher, S. R., & Wheeler, V. A. (1985). Children's loneliness: A comparison of rejected and neglected peer status. *Journal of Consulting and Clinical Psychology, 53*, 500–505.

Athanasiou, R., & Greene, P. (1972). Physical attractiveness and helping behavior. *Proceedings of the 81st Annual Convention of the American Psychological Association, 8*, 289–290.

Barocas, R., & Black, H. K. (1974). Referral rate and physical attractiveness in third grade children. *Perceptual and Motor Skills, 39*, 731–734.

Barocas, R., & Karoly, P. (1972). Effects of physical appearance on social responsiveness. *Psychological Reports, 31*, 495–500.

Bell-Dolan, D. J., Foster, S. L., & Sikora, D. M. (1989). Effects of sociometric testing on children's behavior and loneliness in school. *Developmental Psychology, 25*, 306–311.

Berndt, T. J. (1981). Age changes and changes over time in prosocial intentions and behavior between friends. *Developmental Psychology, 17*, 408–416.

Berscheid, E. (1985). Interpersonal attraction. In G. Lindzey & E. Aronson (Eds.), *Handbook of social psychology* (Vol. 2, 3d ed., pp. 413–484). New York: Random House.

Berscheid, E., & Walster, E. (1974). Physical attractiveness. In L. Berkowitz (Ed.), *Advances in experimental social psychology* (Vol. 7, pp. 158–215). New York: Academic Press.

Berscheid, E., & Walster, E. (1978). *Interpersonal attraction* (2d ed.). Reading, MA: Addison-Wesley.

Bigelow, B. J. (1977). Children's friendship expectations: A cognitive developmental study. *Child Development, 48*, 246–253.

Bronfenbrenner, U. (1979). Contexts of child rearing: Problems and prospects. *American Psychologist, 34*, 844–850.

Bukowski, W. M., & Newcomb, A. F. (1985). Variability in peer group perceptions: Support for the "controversial" sociometric classification group. *Developmental Psychology, 21*, 1032–1038.

Byrne, D. (1971). *The attraction paradigm*. New York: Academic Press.

Byrne, D. (1973) Interpersonal attraction. *Annual Review of Psychology, 24*, 317–336.

Byrne, D., London, O., & Reeves, K. (1968). The effects of physical attractiveness, sex and attitude similarity on interpersonal attraction. *Journal of Personality, 36*, 259–271.

Cavior, N., & Dokecki, P. (1973). Physical attractiveness, perceived attitude similarity, and academic achievement as contributors to interpersonal attraction among adolescents. *Developmental Psychology, 9*, 44–54.

Chaiken, S. (1979). Communicator physical attractiveness and persuasion. *Journal of Personality and Social Psychology, 37*, 1387–1397.

Charlesworth, R., & Hartup, W. W. (1967). Positive social reinforcement in the nursery school peer group. *Child Development, 38*, 993–1002.

Clausen, J. A. (1975). The social meaning of differential physical maturation. In D. Drugastin & G. H. Elder (Eds.), *Adolescence in the life cycle* (pp. 25–47). New York: Halsted Press.

Clifford, M. M., & Walster, E. (1973). The effects of physical attractiveness on teachers' expectations. *Sociology of Education, 46*, 248–258.

Clore, G. L., & Byrne, D. A. (1974). A reinforcement-affect model of attraction. In T. L. Huston (Ed.), *Foundations of interpersonal attraction* (pp. 143–170). New York: Academic Press.

Coie, J. D., & Dodge, K. A. (1983). Continuities and changes in children's social status: A five-year longitudinal study. *Merrill-Palmer Quarterly, 19,* 261–282.

Coie, J. D., Dodge, K. A., & Coppotelli, H. (1982). Dimensions and types of social status: A cross-age perspective. *Developmental Psychology, 18,* 557–570.

Coie, J. D., & Krehbiel, G. (1984). Effects of academic tutoring on the social status of low-achieving, socially rejected children. *Child Development, 55,* 1465–1478.

Coie, J. D., & Kupersmidt, J. B. (1983). A behavioral analysis of emerging social status in boys' groups. *Child Development, 54,* 1400–1416.

Cowen, E. L., Pederson, A., Babigan, H., Izzo, L. E., & Trost, M. A. (1973). Long-term follow-up of early detected vulnerable children. *Journal of Consulting and Clinical Psychology, 41,* 438–446.

Crano, W. D., & Cooper, R. E. (1973). Examination of Newcomb's extension of structural balance theory. *Journal of Personality and Social Psychology, 27,* 344–353.

Crockett, W. H. (1974). Balance, agreement, and subjective evaluations of the P–O–X triads. *Journal of Personality and Social Psychology, 29,* 102–110.

Dabbs, J. M., Jr., & Stokes, N. A., III. (1975). Beauty is power: The use of space on the sidewalk. *Sociometry, 38,* 551–557.

Davis, K. E., & Jones, E. E. (1960). Changes in interpersonal perception as a means of reducing cognitive dissonance. *Journal of Abnormal Social Psychology, 61,* 402–410.

Deutsch, M. (1950). A theory of cooperation and competition. *Human Relations, 2,* 129–152.

Deutsch, M., & Collins, M. E. (1951). *Interracial housing: A psychological evaluation of a social experiment.* Minneapolis: University of Minnesota Press.

Deutsch, M., & Gerard, H. B. (1955). A study of normative and informational social influences on individual judgments. *Journal of Abnormal and Social Psychology, 51,* 629–636.

Dion, K. K. (1972). Physical attractiveness and evaluations of children's transgressions. *Journal of Personality and Social Psychology, 24,* 207–213.

Dion, K. K. (1973). Young children's stereotyping of facial attractiveness. *Developmental Psychology, 9,* 183–188.

Dion, K. K., & Berscheid, E. (1974). Physical attractiveness and peer perception among children. *Sociometry, 37,* 1–12.

Dion, K. K., Berscheid, E., & Walster, E. (1972). What is beautiful is good. *Journal of Personality and Social Psychology, 24,* 285–290.

Einhorn, H. J., & Hogarth, R. M. (1978). Confidence in judgment. Persistence of the illusion of validity. *Psychological Review, 85,* 395–416.

Elder, G. H., Jr. (1969). Appearance and education in marriage mobility. *American Sociological Review, 34,* 519–533.

Elovitz, G. P., & Salvia, J. (1982). Attractiveness as a biasing factor in the judgments of school psychologists. *Journal of School Psychology, 20,* 339–345.

Faust, M. S. (1960). Developmental maturity as a determination of prestige in adolescent girls. *Child Development, 31,* 173–184.

Festinger, L. (1954). A theory of social comparison processes. *Human Relations, 7,* 117–140.

Festinger, L. (1957). *A theory of cognitive dissonance* (pp. 260–266). Stanford, CA: Stanford University Press.

French, J. R. P., Jr., & Raven, B. (1959). The bases of social power. In D. Cartwright (Ed.), *Studies in social power* (pp. 150–167). Ann Arbor, MI: Institute for Social Research.

Goldman, W., & Lewis, P. (1977). Beautiful is good: Evidence that the physically attractive are more socially skillful. *Journal of Experimental Social Psychology, 13,* 125–130.

Guralnick, M. J., & Groom, J. M. (1988). Friendships of preschool children in mainstreamed playgroups. *Developmental Psychology, 24,* 595–604.

Harari, H., & McDavid, J. W. (1973). Teachers' expectations and name stereotypes. *Journal of Educational Psychology, 65,* 222–225.

Hartup, W. W. (1983). Peer relations. In P. H. Mussen (Series Ed.) & E. M. Hetherington (Vol. Ed.), *Handbook of child psychology: Vol. 4. Socialization, personality, and social development* (pp. 103–196). New York: Wiley.

Hatfield, E., Ute, M. K., & Traupmann, J. (1979). Equity theory and intimate relationships. In R. L. Burgess & T. L. Huston (Eds.), *Social exchange in developing relationships* (pp. 99–133). New York: Academic Press.

Hayvren, M., & Hymel, S. (1984). Ethical issues in sociometric testing: Impact of sociometric measures on interaction behavior. *Developmental Psychology, 20,* 844–849.

Heider, F. (1958). *The psychology of interpersonal relations.* New York: Wiley.

Hinde, R. A., Titmus, G., Easton, D., & Tamplin, A. (1985). Incidence of "friendship" and behavior toward strong associates versus nonassociates in preschoolers. *Child Development, 54,* 234–245.

Homans, G. C. (1961). *Social behavior: Its elementary forms.* New York: Harcourt, Brace, & World.

Horowitz, F. D. (1962). The relationship of anxiety, self-concept, and sociometric status among fourth-, fifth-, and sixth-grade children. *Journal of Abnormal Social Psychology, 65,* 212–214.

Hunsberger, B., & Cavanagh, B. (1988). Physical attractiveness and children's expectations of potential teachers. *Psychology in the Schools, 25,* 70–74.

Johnson, D. W., & Johnson, R. T. (1987). *Creative conflict.* Edina, MN: Interaction Book.

Johnson, D. W., & Johnson, R. T. (1989). *Cooperation and competition: Theory and research.* Edina, MN: Interaction Book.

Jones, M. C., & Bayley, N. (1950). Physical maturing among boys as related to behavior. *Journal of Educational Psychology, 41,* 129–148.

Kaats, G. R., & Davis, K. E. (1970). The dynamics of sexual behavior among college students. *Journal of Marriage and the Family, 32,* 390–399.

Kelley, H. H. (1979). *Personal relationships: Their structures and processes.* Hillsdale, NJ: Lawrence Erlbaum Associates.

Kelley, H. H., Berscheid, E., Christensen, A., Harvey, J. H., Huston, T. L., Levinger, G., McClintock, E., Peplau, L. A., & Peterson, D. R. (1983). *Close relationships.* New York: W. H. Freeman.

Lerner, M. J., & Miller, D. T. (1978). Just world research and the attribution process: Looking back and ahead. *Psychological Bulletin, 85,* 1030–1051.

Lerner, R. M. (1969). The development of stereotyped expectancies of body build relations. *Child Development, 40,* 137–141.

Lerner, R. M., & Karabenick, S. A. (1974). Physical attractiveness, body attitudes, and self-concept in late adolescence. *Journal of Youth and Adolescence, 3,* 307–316.

Lerner, R. M., & Lerner, J. V. (1977). Effects of age, sex, and physical attractiveness on child–peer relations, academic performance, and elementary school adjustment. *Developmental Psychology, 13,* 585–590.

Lerner, R. M., Karabenick, S. A., & Stuart, J. (1973). Relations among physical attractiveness, body attitudes, and self-concept in males and female college students. *Journal of Psychology, 85,* 119–129.

Lindzey, G., & Byrne, D. (1968). Measurement of social choice and interpersonal attractiveness. In *The handbook of social psychology* (2nd ed., pp. 452–510). Reading, MA: Addison-Wesley.

Livson, N., & Peskin, H. (1980). Perspectives on adolescence from longitudinal research. In J. Adelson (Ed.), *Handbook of adolescent psychology* (pp. 47–98). New York: Wiley.

Lloyd, S. A., Cate, R. M., & Henton, J. M. (1984). Predicting premarital relationship stability: A methodological refinement. *Journal of Marriage and the Family, 46,* 71–76.

Lott, A. J., & Lott, B. E. (1968). A learning theory approach to interpersonal attitudes. In A. G. Greenwald, T. C. Brock, & T. M. Ostrom (Eds.), *Psychological foundations of attitudes* (pp. 67–88). New York: Academic Press.

Lott, A. J., & Lott, B. E. (1974). The role of reward in the formation of positive interpersonal attitudes. In T. Huston (Ed.), *Foundations of interpersonal attraction* (pp. 171–192). New York: Academic Press.

Maruyama, G., & Miller, N. (1981). Physical attractiveness and personality. *Progress in Experimental Personality and Research, 10*, 203–280.

Maruyama, G., Miller, N., & Holtz, R. (1986). The relation between popularity and achievement: A longitudinal test of the lateral transmission of value hypothesis. *Journal of Personality and Social Psychology, 51*, 730–741.

Maruyama, G., Petersen, R., & Knechel, S. (in press). The impact of role reversal and minority empowerment strategies in decision-making in numerically unbalanced cooperative groups. In N. Miller & R. Hertz-Lazarowitz (Eds.), *Interaction in cooperative groups: The theoretical anatomy of group learning.*

Masters, J. C., & Furman, W. (1981). Popularity, individual friendship selection, and specific peer interaction among children. *Developmental Psychology, 17*, 344–350.

McDavid, J. W., & Harari, H. (1966). Stereotyping of names and popularity in grade school children. *Child Development, 37*, 453–459.

McDonald, G. W. (1981). Structural exchange and marital interaction. *Journal of Marriage and the Family, 43*, 825–839.

McGuire, K. D., & Weisz, J. R. (1982). Social cognition and behavioral correlates of preadolescent chumship. *Child Development, 53*, 1478–1484.

Miller, N., & Campbell, D. T. (1959). Recency and primacy in persuasion as a function of the timing of speeches and measurements. *Journal of Abnormal and Social Psychology, 59*, 1–10.

Mims, P. R., Hartnett, J. J., & Nay, W. R. (1973). Interpersonal attraction and help volunteering as a function of physical attractiveness. *Journal of Psychology, 89*, 125–131.

Moore, G. S. (1967). Correlates of peer acceptance in nursery school children. In W. W. Hartup & N. L. Smothergill (Eds.), *The young child: Reviews of research* (pp. 229–247). Washington, DC: National Association for the Education of Young Children.

Moreno, J. L. (1953). *Who shall survive? Foundations of sociometry, group psychotherapy and sociodrama* (2d ed., pp. 48–57). Beacon, NY: Beacon House. (1st ed. published 1934.)

Newcomb, A. F., & Bukowski, W. M. (1984). A longitudinal study of the utility of social preference and social impact sociometric classification schemes. *Child Development, 55*, 1434–1447.

Newcomb, T. M. (1953). Communicative acts: The A–B–X system (the acquaintance process). *Psychological Review, 60*, 393–404.

Newcomb, T. M. (1961). *The acquaintance process.* New York: Holt, Rinehart, & Winston.

Newcomb, T. M. (1968). Interpersonal balance. In R. P. Abelson et al. (Eds.), *Theories of cognitive consistency: A sourcebook* (pp. 25–51). Chicago: Rand, McNally.

Parker, J. G., & Asher, S. R. (1987). Peer relations and later personal adjustment: Are low-accepted children at risk? *Psychological Bulletin, 102*, 357–389.

Roff, M. F. (1974). Childhood antecedents of adult neurosis, severe bad conduct, and psychological health. In D. F. Ricks, A. Thomas, & M. Roff (Eds.), *Life history research in psychopathology* (Vol. 3, pp. 131–162). Minneapolis: University of Minnesota Press.

Ross, M., & Salvia, J. (1977). Attractiveness as a biasing factor in teacher judgments. *American Journal of Mental Deficiency, 80*, 96–98.

Ross, M., & Sicoly, F. (1979). Egocentric biases in availability and attribution. *Journal of Personality and Social Psychology, 37*, 322–336.

Rotenberg, K. J., & Mann, L. (1986). The development of the norm of the reciprocity of self-disclosure and its function in children's attraction to peers. *Child Development, 57*, 1349–1357.

Salvia, J., Algozzine, B., & Sheare, J. (1977). Attractiveness and school achievement. *Journal of School Psychology, 15*, 60–67.

Schwartz, J. C. (1972). Effects of peer familiarity on the behavior of preschoolers in a novel situation. *Journal of Personality and Social Psychology, 24*, 276–284.

Sears, D. O., & Whitney, R. E. (1973). Political persuasion. In I. deS. Pool, F. W. Frey, W. Schramn, N. Maccoby, & E. B. Parker (Eds.), *Handbook of communication.* Chicago: Rand McNally.

Smollar, H., & Youniss, J. (1982). Social development through friendships. In K. H. Rubin & H. S. Ross (Eds.), *Peer relations and social skills in childhood* (pp. 279–298). New York: Springer–Verlag.

Snyder, M., & Swann, W. B. (1978). Behavioral confirmation in social interaction: From social perception to social reality. *Journal of Experimental Social Psychology, 14,* 148–162.

Snyder, M., Tanke, E., & Berscheid, E. (1977). Social perception and interpersonal behavior: On the self-fulfilling nature of stereotypes. *Journal of Personality and Social Psychology, 35,* 656–666.

Staffieri, J. R. (1967). A study of social stereotype of body image in children. *Journal of Personality and Social Psychology, 7,* 101–104.

Stokes, S. J., & Bickman, L. (1974). The effect of the physical attractiveness and role of the helper on help-seeking. *Journal of Applied Social Psychology, 4,* 286–294.

Summerville, M. B., Cohen, R., & Klesges, R. (1987, March). The relationship of body type, sociometric ratings, and self-perceptions in children. Paper presented at the *Annual Meeting of the Southeastern Psychological Association,* Atlanta, GA.

Taylor, P., & Glenn, N. (1976). The utility of education and attractiveness for females' status attainment through marriage. *American Sociological Review, 41,* 484–498.

Thibaut, J. W., & Kelley, H. H. (1959). *The social psychology of groups.* New York: Wiley.

Venable, T. C. (1954). The relationship of selected factors to the social structure of a stable group. *Sociometry, 17,* 355–357.

Walster, E., Walster, G. W., & Berscheid, E. (1978). *Equity: Theory and research.* Rockleigh, NJ: Allyn & Bacon.

Williams, A. M. (1979). The quantity and quality of marital interaction related to marital satisfaction: A behavioral analysis. *Journal of Applied Behavior Analysis, 12,* 665–678.

5

GENDER: A SUBTLE INFLUENCE IN THE CULTURE OF THE SCHOOL

Mary Henning-Stout
Lewis and Clark College

Jane Close Conoley
University of Nebraska

Suppose you were asked to describe your next-door neighbor.

> "Well, he's a furniture salesman for Smith's downtown. I guess some people would say he's attractive. He seems nice enough—a little boring. He lives with a woman who's a hairdresser. They've started paying a little more attention to the yard lately. That's nice."

or,

> "She's a ceramics engineer. I'm not sure where she's working now—somewhere across the river. Her husband's an engineer too—optics I think. They have a little girl who's three or four."

From such descriptions, we get just enough information to begin construct-ing pictures of the people described. Each additional bit of information modi-fies our impression somewhat. With each description, the initial and central concept onto which the additional information is hooked is the person's bio-logical gender. By the end of the two descriptions, we've imagined two wom-en, two men, and a preschool girl.

Why is it that, whenever we encounter another person, gender is the first bit of information we record? Sandra Bem (1974, 1981) described gender as the primary cognitive category activated in person perception. In her gender schema theory, she suggests that social emphasis on gender combines with cognitive developmental processes to firmly establish gender as a powerful schema early in children's experience. What is known as "gender constancy" occurs at a time when children are making sense of their worlds by applying simple categories (Kohlberg, 1966). The cognitive activity of which these children are now capable is influenced significantly by the culture's emphasis on some categories (e.g., sex) over others. According to this theory, the children develop the process and the culture determines the most salient content. The research and theory development of Sandra Bem and other notable scholars (e.g., Belenky, Clinchy, Goldberger, & Tarule, 1986; Chordorow, 1978; Gilligan, 1982; Jacklin, 1989; Katz, 1985, 1987; Maccoby & Jacklin, 1974) has led to better understanding of the role that gender plays in the broad array of human behaviors.

An academic area of psychology that allows for specific consideration of the socialization and enculturation of sex-typed behavior is social psychology. In contrast to sociological studies that focus on the behaviors of groups (e.g., "women supported one cause while men supported another one"), social psychology involves the study of how group membership influences individual behavior. To what extent are our behaviors influenced by being female or male—by being members of one of those two socially recognized, culturally central groups? Equally important: To what extent is our behavior toward other people influenced by our perceptions of their gender category?

The purpose of this chapter is to explore the role that gender plays in the cognitions and behaviors of adults and children in schools. Why is this of interest to school psychologists? As earlier chapters have indicated, we cannot divorce ourselves from the social situations in which we provide our services. As we work with students, teachers, and parents, we often consider the social groups with which they identify. Like any of the people we serve, we too are influenced by our membership in a variety of groups, both actively organized and socially defined.

Until recently, little has appeared in the school psychology literature addressing issues of gender (Alpert & Conoley, 1988; Conoley & Henning-Stout, 1990). In contrast to other areas of psychology where gender issues have become a primary focus of research and theory, school psychology has seemed essentially unresponsive to gender as an academic area or matter of concern. Attention to gender questions will allow school psychology to join the other areas of psychology that have been enriched already by adding to their knowledge base scholarship specific to women. Alpert and Conoley (1988) stated: "As a result of [the] interest in women, previously unexplored topics are subjects of attention, mainstream concepts have been redefined, and traditional theory has been reformulated" (p. 1).

In school psychology, we have gathered an impressive store of empirical knowledge relevant to our practice. There has been, however, little theoretical or research consideration of the way in which gender influences that practice. As Rhoda Unger (1988) observed, "One cannot simply 'add women and stir' " (p. 29). Fortunately, such a facile response has not been opted for by our profession. Instead, we are beginning to take a careful, self-critical look at our training and practice through the lens of gender concerns.

The importance of such a perspective is further illustrated by this quote from a practitioner (Ali, 1988) writing in a recent edition of the *Communique*, the official newsletter of the National Association of School Psychologists (NASP):

> During my training as a school psychologist, the issue of sexism was never ad-
> dressed. I was taught developmental issues regarding sex differences and I
> learned that the sex of the examiner could potentially have an impact on the
> students being evaluated. I did not learn that the sex of the student could have
> an impact on the examiner although there are many [other] fundamental is-
> sues regarding the biases and prejudices that school psychologists must con-
> sider in evaluating children from different cultural, racial, and ethnic groups.
> (p. 2)

The author went on to describe instances in which her own gender-based biases influenced assessment decisions. This retrospective is important as an illustration of how expanding our understanding of the cultural constructions attached to sex can lead to better (more responsive and fair) training and practice in school psychology.

In the following pages, we attempt to articulate the gender issues that have bearing on the practice of school psychology. We briefly review the prevailing theoretical explanations of gender-linked behavior. The influences of the media and family values as reflections of some of these theories follow. We consider the influence of school culture on the development of sex-typed behavior, and, throughout, we make reference to the ways gender-linked expectations and social conventions affect the delivery of psychological services in the schools.

THEORIES OF GENDER-LINKED BEHAVIOR

What we are calling "gender-linked" behavior includes the behaviors and affectations attributed variously to one sex or the other. Myriad studies have reflected the sex-linked expression of attributes such as aggressiveness, nurturance, verbal ability, and spatial reasoning (e.g., Benbow & Stanley, 1980; Eccles & Jacobs, 1986; Gilligan, 1982; Maccoby & Jacklin, 1974). To facilitate our exploration of social stereotypes, Bem (1974) developed a list of attributes culturally associated with one sex or the other (e.g., sensitivity as feminine; authority as masculine). This instrument has become a mainstay of research into the way gender influences person perception and expectation. In spite of the fact that greater variation has been found within each sex than between sexes (Fausto-Sterling, 1985; Hyde, 1981; Jacklin, 1989) and that the differences between sexes has been quite small (in terms of statistical effect size, Hyde, 1981; Hyde & Linn, 1988), theoretical musings on gender difference have continued. Four approaches to explaining gender-linked behaviors are reviewed briefly in the following sections.

Physiological Theory

Of the four main schools of psychological thought applied to explaining gender-linked behaviors, studies exploring the biological basis for gender differences have probably received the most attention. The two primary foci of these studies are genetic and hormonal comparisons. Genetic studies have established the physical vulnerability of the male fetus (e.g., Gualtieri & Hicks, 1985; Jacklin & Maccoby, 1982; Kraemer, Korner, Anders, Jacklin, & Dimicelli, 1985). More males are conceived and more spontaneously abort due to genetic abnormalities that preclude viability. Males experience more difficulty during the birth process and are more likely to be born with birth defects. The vulnerability of males in these areas has been given clear empirical demonstration; however, the impact of this vulnerability on later behavioral patterns has received little research attention (Jacklin, 1989).

The second focus of biologically based research is hormonal variation. Differences in hormonal makeup are the most frequently cited causes for gender differences in behavior (Jacklin, 1989). In her recent review of the status of research on gender differences in children, Jacklin acknowledges the relationship between hormonal levels and emotional behavior. She describes the most recent findings in this area indicating that anger is more clearly associated with variations in the circulating levels of testosterone (a sex-steroid hormone found in both sexes, more so in males) than with mean levels of that hormone. The findings relating hormonal activity to behavior continue to disallow a clear understanding of which is the cause and which the effect. To emphasize this point, Jacklin (1989) stated:

> A word of warning: Correlations between hormones and behavior are typically interpreted as cases in which the biological causes the psychological. It fits our predispositions to assume that hormones cause behavioral outcomes. The hormone system is an open system. Much more empirical work is needed before the direction of the causal arrows are (sic) understood. (p. 130)

An illustration of such faulty reasoning is the historical tendency for researchers to attribute to biology the observed differences in performance on tasks designed to reflect cognitive ability and achievement (e.g., Benbow & Stanley, 1980; Lehrke, 1972; Seller, 1981). Maccoby and Jacklin's (1974) landmark review of literature revealed four areas in which gender differences were statistically verified. Their review indicated that males did better in mathematics, had better spatial skills, were more physically aggressive, and had lower verbal skills than females. Fausto-Sterling (1985) has made an important observation relative to the first two of these findings. When the statistics as presented by Maccoby and Jacklin are extrapolated to vocational representation, we might expect that males would outnumber females by 10 to 7 (10:7) in fields such as engineering. The ratio in such careers is far greater than this with very few women employed in those areas. It is difficult to deny a social/cultural component to the sex-segregation in the professional world.

What Fausto-Sterling described as the confounding of culture and biology is evident for each of the differences observed by Maccoby and Jacklin. Although aggression may be linked with testosterone, there is convincing evidence that, from birth, girls and boys are responded to differently, that is, reinforced for different behaviors (Fagot, 1985). Ember (1973) observed that when boys in a Kenyan village were expected to do more "feminine" tasks of child care and housework, the frequency of their aggressive behaviors decreased by 60%. Fausto-Sterling (1985) summarized this point when she wrote:

> For each individual born into this world a set of action–reaction–interactions becomes established. Many factors other than sex play a role including, no doubt, biological differences in reactivity, social circumstances of the family and the society, birth order within the family, and so on ad infinitum. For some forms of behavior, small average differences resulting from sex-related systems may become measurable. Whether this is the case for aggression is still far from clear. (p. 153)

For aggression as for observed differences in cognitive achievement the extent to which biological predispositions influence these behaviors remains, at best, unclear. Recent meta-analytic consideration of the gender-difference literature has revealed no significant differences in the cognitive areas identified by Maccoby and Jacklin (Hyde, 1981; Hyde & Linn, 1986, 1988). With so little information on the extent and nature of interaction between biological state and social environment, the findings in support of a physiological explanation for gender differences remains weak in practical utility.

Psychoanalytic Theory

Psychoanalytic theory has gained in popularity among theoreticians as it has lost popularity among research psychologists (Jacklin, 1989). Object relations theory, a psychological theory that focuses on the role of interpersonal relationships in the development of personality, has been viewed by many theorists as central to clear understanding of gender-linked behaviors (e.g., Alpert, 1986; Chordorow, 1978; Gilligan, 1982; Miller, 1976). However, the empirical (i.e., traditional scientific) basis for this theory is missing and some conflicting evidence has been found. For example, Maccoby and Jacklin (1974) found that identification with the same-sex parent was not significantly related to the child's sex-typed behavior, and Adams and Sarason (1963) found both boys and girls to behave more like their mothers than their fathers.

Jean Baker Miller (1976) suggested that psychoanalysis emerged to bring attention to "the basic emotional connections between an individual and other people" (p. 22). Miller suggested that these emotional aspects of relationship have been culturally associated with females. She also maintained that this area of the total human experience had, prior to Freud's work at the turn of the last century, been largely ignored. She suggested that it is precisely the feminine focus of psychoanalytic theory that has made it uncomfortable for most modern scholars in psychology. Miller (1976) asserted that: "Psychoanalysis has been doing 'women's work,' but it has not recognized it for what it was. It had to undertake 'women's work' in the first place because the dominant culture did not do this work or take it into consideration. Therein lie its problems" (p. 26).

Cognitive-Developmental Theory

Kohlberg's (1966) cognitive developmental theory attributed sex-typed behavior to the natural emergence of children's cognitive capacity for categorization and conservation. Stangor and Rubel (1987) suggested that, as children gain gender constancy (generally between the ages of 3 and 7), "they develop an increased interest in and responsiveness to gender-related information and become actively interested in learning about their own gender roles" (p. 18). Bem (1983) agreed that this exaggerated assimilation of sex-typed behavior occurs but questions the potence of gender *qua* gender over any other categories into which people can be divided. Children at the age of gender constancy are cognitively ready to understand the world in terms of categories. The culture, however, determines which categories are emphasized. This suggests that the emphasis on gender has social utility and tradition strong enough to remain a central influence in the epistemology of the culture and its participants.

Social Learning Theory

Bem's theory is a mixture of the Kohlbergian cognitive developmental perspective and social learning theory (Bandura, 1977). Social learning theory maintains that our behaviors are formed through social reinforcement. From this perspective, sex-typed behavior is no different from any other behavior.

The behavioral differences we observe across the genders are learned with girls learning to behave in a "feminine" manner and boys learning to behave in a "masculine" manner. The decision about which behaviors constitute each manner is arbitrary and enculturated. It stands to reason that the forces of cultural tradition would influence our choice of the specific behaviors we reinforce in children and other adults.

The focus of this text and of this chapter is social psychology in the schools—the influence of group membership on individual behavior. The remainder of this chapter considers whether membership in the female or male "group" influences either individual behavior or behavior of others toward the individual. As evident in the summaries presented earlier, the tradition of gender-linked expectations for behavior is well established. Our, likely unwitting, participation in perpetuating these expectations as we carry out our professional duties is a matter worthy of careful scrutiny.

SOCIAL MEDIATORS OF DEVELOPMENT

Anthropologists have long emphasized the importance of considering social and environmental factors when consistent differences in behavior or cognition are noted across groups (Goetz & Grant, 1988; Mead, 1964). How do social contexts vary from person to person as a function of gender membership? How are these differences reflected in behavior and cognition? This perspective on gender invites us to sidestep the reflexive attribution of behavior to an individual's traits (e.g., gender), considering instead the more complex system of the person and personality in a social context.

Two influences external but related to the school culture are family and the media. Phyllis Katz (1987) has considered the influence of family on the development of gender schemata in children. She discusses this influence in terms of distal and proximal variables.

> Distal variables are demographic and structural characteristics of families such as socioeconomic level, ethnicity, marital status, employment status of mothers, and family size. . . . In contrast, proximal variables concern familial socialization processes that can be measured directly, such as parental attitudes, personality patterns, and specific child-rearing techniques. (pp. 40–41)

Some of the distal and proximal influences of family described by Katz are presented in Table 5.1. We gain insight into the cultural sources of sex-typed behaviors through this information. The propositions of biological predisposition for such behavior begin to pale when we have evidence that children from families in which the mother works, children with less access to money and power, and children of divorce are less stereotyped in their

TABLE 5.1
Family Variables Associated with Children's Gender Stereotyping

Distal Variables	Proximal Variables
Socioeconomic Level (SES) Lower SES preschool children (Walker, 1982) middle class elementary and adolescent children (Emmerich & Shepard, 1983) less stereotyped.	Paternal Attitude Predicts young children's cognitions but not their behavior (Barry, 1980; Weinraub et al., 1984)
Ethnicity Extensive theory (Scott-Jones & Nelson-LeGall, 1986), no conclusive evidence.	Parental Personality Patterns Evidence too sparse to allow meaningful conclusion.
Family Constellation Boys of single parents (Heatherington, 1979) and preschoolers in mothers' custody (Brenes, Eisenberg, & Helmstadter, 1985) less stereotyped.	Parental Socialization Patterns The more traditional the other sex parent's practices, the more stereotyped the child's behavioral choices (Katz & Boswell, 1986).
Maternal Employment Children of working mothers less stereotyped (Huston, 1983; Katz & Boswell, 1986).	
Sibling Status Only girls and children with other-sex siblings less stereotyped (Katz & Boswell, 1986).	

Note: Information in this table summarized from Katz (1987).

gender-linked expectations than their peers. It is also instructive that parents with more democratic parenting styles tend to have children who are less likely to be limited to traditional gender-linked behaviors (Katz & Boswell, 1986).

Other powerful vehicles for socialization are the media. With children spending an average of 2 to 4 hours every day in the presence of an operating television set (Wright & Huston, 1983), the influence of this medium is perhaps most illustrative of the power all media have as transmitters (and, therefore, perpetuators) of both the enriching and limiting features of our culture.

The statistics on the relative frequency of appearance and the comparative roles of females and males on television (as summarized in Table 5.2) mirror the inequities of the society. It is disconcerting to note that, even on Sesame Street and among the Muppets, casts of visually generic characters include few females. Those characters that are female are known by their stereotyped behaviors (e.g., Miss Piggy and Betty Lou). The decision to make a Cookie Monster, a Big Bird, or a Kermit male seems entirely arbitrary until considered within the context of cultural tradition and power distribution.

TABLE 5.2
Comparative Roles of Females and Males on Television

Males	Females
85% of adult roles.	15% of adult roles.
67% of characters in children's programs.	33% of characters in children's programs.
powerful	subservient
dominant	deferent
active	passive
task oriented	socioemotional
In Occupations:	(frequently hold no identifiable job)
police officers	secretaries
doctors	nurses
musicians	entertainers
diplomats	maids
	When employed, usually not portrayed in family role.
	Single women more often victims of male aggression than are married women.
	Working women more often portrayed as villains than housewives.
As Sex Objects:	
9% of commercial programs.	35% of commercial programs.

Note: Summarized from Calvert & Huston, 1987.

Calvert and Huston (1987) interpreted the data on relative frequency of appearance of female and male characters with the nature of their roles as supporting their contention that, "television conveys the message that men are more powerful, authoritative, and important than women" (p. 76). The content of television programs is based largely on traditional gender stereotypes, thereby exaggerating and amplifying socially constructed gender differences.

Repeated exposure to these messages can have significant impact on a child's developing understanding of the world. Children collect regularities from experience to form abstract general representations or schemata (Fiske & Taylor, 1984). When children repeatedly see exaggerated portrayals of traditional gender stereotypes, the salience and accessibility of these concepts is increased (List, Collins, & Westby, 1983). Calvert and Huston (1987) reported extensive research in this area demonstrating that children who are heavy television viewers are more likely to make traditional gender-linked attributions than are light and nonviewers.

But, the reader may ask, why does this matter? This information on family and media influence is intriguing, but what does this mean for psychologists in the schools? The best response at this point in our narrative seems to be a question. What can we learn from considering patterns in the relationships between sex-typed behavior and social structures and practices (e.g., family and the media) that will shed light on the ways in which we perpetuate exaggerated gender-linked expectations in the schools?

SOCIALIZATION IN SCHOOLS

Children come to elementary school from the culture of the family. Increasingly, their entry into this setting does not represent their first educational experience outside the home (Clarke-Stewart, 1989). With 50% of the infants in the United States today having employed mothers (Clarke-Stewart, 1989), many children experience the influence of the culture outside the family for most of their lives. These demographic facts illustrate the significant role educational settings play in the socialization of children. Research focused on the socialization of gender-linked behaviors and expectations in schools indicates that messages perpetuating traditional gender roles pervade almost every aspect of children's school experiences (Meece, 1987).

Title IX

When Title IX of Educational Amendments of 1972 was enacted, the most apparent of these messages came under fire. The purpose of this law was to encourage sex-equitable educational experiences by making federal funding dependent on compliance with the provisions of the act. "No person . . . shall, on the basis of sex, be excluded from participation in, be denied the benefits of, or be subjected to discrimination under any education program or activity receiving federal financial assistance. . . ." (Title IX, 1972)

Perhaps the most obvious influence of Title IX has been in athletic programs. The law prohibits segregation of participants by sex in physical education classes. However, as Geadelmann (1985) pointed out, this restriction can be sidestepped by claiming segregation based on ability, a practice allowed in Title IX and reflected in the composition of most high-profile athletic teams.

Academic and career counseling also have been influenced by the passage of Title IX. Prior to its enactment in 1972, such practices as counseling girls away from more advanced courses in math and science were common (Meece, 1987). Thomas and Stewart (1971) reported evidence that, at the time of their research, it also was common for females with career goals at odds with prevailing social expectations to be referred for additional counseling. Although such overt differences in the treatment of students according to their sex are less common since the enactment of Title IX, more subtle transmission of gender stereotyped expectations continues. Recent observations by Goetz and Grant (1988) reflect this state of affairs:

> Gender expectations permeate educational organizations, just as they do all social organizations. Structures in schools mirror structures in society. Even when school staff attempt to intervene [as with the enactment of Title IX], traditional gender patterns persist. Persistence is explained by residual structural barriers [such as norms, roles, and values] in educational settings and by the uneven pace of change between men and women. Women may change attitudes toward their places in society, but it is men who control the resources to achieve those places. (p. 186)

The danger with Title IX is that of creating the impression that the problem has been solved when in fact practices of gender inequality continue to abound. The pervasiveness of traditional gender messages in the school culture is undeniable. The enforcement of Title IX deserves challenge. At this point, Title IX has served only as a weak support for sex equitable education and may have had the additional effect of inviting complacency on the part of policy makers who erroneously believe this legal policy is sufficient to rectify inequitable practices rooted deeply in our cultural history.

School Culture

In today's schools, children are asked to line up by sex, are assigned to tasks according to gender, are asked questions with content that varies based on the child's sex. What seem to be harmless routines of school life serve as components of a larger, more systematic socialization process. Understanding the role that enculturated gender bias plays in the development and perpetuation of practices like these is central to our understanding of ways schools maintain and can modify the sex-typed behavior and beliefs of children. As we have argued, the schools are primary arenas of socialization. Consideration of school culture from the perspective of gender-stereotyped messages is instructive.

Curriculum. Students spend the largest portion of their instructional time with curricular materials that convey specific information via some form of text (books, auditory cassettes, video tapes, films, etc.). The cultural themes repeated in these texts tend to portray males and females in sex-stereotypic ways. Meece (1987) summarizes a U.S. Commission on Civil Rights report reflecting these concerns:

> The focus of this criticism has been the greater representation of males in a broader range of family and work roles. Roles represented for women were

primarily traditional female pursuits such as nurse, teacher, telephone opera-
tor, and secretary. In addition, males were more often featured in stories with
"active mastery themes," whereas girls were central characters in stories with
"passivity" and "dependence" themes. (p. 62)

Informal review of children's books reveals the adventurers are male and
the nurturers are female. Neither of these is an inherently "bad" role, but
the message is clear because of the consistency of the casting that boys behave in one way and girls behave in another. The force of the tradition that
supports this stereotyped characterization is illustrated in the outcome of a
trial in Tennessee in which the judge ruled in favor of a group of fundamen-
talist parents who protested the content of a second-grade basal that failed
"to portray women in traditional roles" (Holden, 1987).

Teacher Practices.   In addition to the themes in the curricula, there continue to be instances of assignment of chores and instructional or group activities according to gender stereotypes (Grant, 1983; Hallinan & Sorensen,
1987; Meece, 1987). In these assignments, boys tend to be encouraged to rely
on their own resources, whereas girls are encouraged to check in with regular-
ity to make certain their behaviors conform with expectation (Lee & Gropper, 1974). Stipek and Sanborn (1985) presented evidence that preschool
teachers interact with girls and handicapped children in ways that encourage
passive learning, docile conduct, and attendant lack of initiative and
perseverance.

In science classrooms, boys tend to be asked questions requiring more abstract reasoning, whereas girls are more likely to be asked factual questions
requiring less sophisticated and independent thought (Morse & Handley, 1985).
In a study of ability grouping in math classes, Hallinan and Sorensen (1987)
found systematic differences in the assignment of boys and girls to groups.
Girls with high aptitude were less likely to be assigned to high-ability groups
than were similarly capable boys. Oakland and Stern (1989) recently reported that measurements of children's aptitude and achievement levels revealed
no gender effect predicting over or underachievement. The authors note this
lack of distinction between the sexes conflicts with the prevailing practice;
that is, boys are significantly more likely than girls to be identified as over
or underachievers.

Consistent with the findings of Brophy and Good (1974), Sadker and Sadker (1984) have found that boys receive more acknowledgment, approval,
criticism, corrective comments, encouragement, and praise than do girls.
Meece (1987) suggested these responses to boys have the effect of prolong-
ing intellectual exchanges with teachers and encouraging subsequent
interaction.

Substantive exchanges between students and their teachers are precisely
what we want to have happening in education. However, the problem is that

females are restricted in their access to equal opportunities for intellectual development. As teachers carry forth educational traditions, they also perpetuate subtle but profoundly discrepant academic treatment of females and males. The educational system has been sluggish, at best, in responding to these demonstrated inequities. Meece (1987) has observed: "If the schools are to be faulted, it is because they do very little to actively reduce and eliminate unnecessary gender distinctions" (p. 67).

Special Education. The evidence seems to indicate that boys in "regular" classrooms receive greater access to opportunities for intellectual growth; but, what occurs with boys who are referred for special education? Why do boys outnumber girls by over 2:1 in learning-disabilities classifications and by nearly 4:1 in classifications as emotionally disturbed (Office of Civil Rights, 1987)? In a study by Schlosser and Algozzine (1979), teachers rated boys' disturbing behaviors as more troubling than girls' disturbing behaviors. They interpreted this evidence as indicating an interpersonal ecology in the classroom that has as its by-product a higher rate of referring boys for special education.

Silvern and Katz (1986) reported findings supporting the notion that behaviors typical of boys are more likely to be incongruous with the "feminine" atmosphere of elementary school that rewards compliance and docility (Silvern, 1978). Gold and Reis (1982) have explored the variation in learning atmospheres across elementary classrooms instructed by males or by females. They found no difference in boys' behaviors based on the gender of the teacher and conclude the predominance of female teachers in elementary schools is not a significant contributor to the "feminine" atmosphere. Rather, the value for compliance and docility is deeply ingrained in the culture of these schools.

Just as this atmosphere may be "hostile" toward boys, girls who have difficulty succeeding in school may not be as obvious because of their behavioral match with environmental expectations. Silvern and Katz (1986) suggested that, whereas boys may be identified as troubled more frequently than girls due to their externalized, disturbing behavior, girls may also suffer from their gender roles by withdrawing and developing passive learning styles. The girls' behavioral tendencies are less likely to result in their being labeled as *troubled*, because they are less offensive to the established school culture.

Thus it appears that boys who behave in acceptable ways have the greatest access to educational opportunity, whereas boys who behave in disturbing ways are removed from the regular classroom and receive special services. In general, girls are given less encouragement and support academically and may also be less likely to qualify for special services because of their passive behaviors.

There is a growing literature documenting the relative absence of gender difference in intellectual ability (e.g., Fausto-Sterling, 1985; Feingold, 1988; Hyde, 1981; Hyde & Linn, 1988). This evidence supports the likelihood that the distribution of learning problems should be comparable across genders. So, why are there more boys than girls placed in special education? The sociocultural forces evident in such imbalances can no longer be ignored.

Staffing Patterns in Schools. A clear illustration of socialized gender differentiation is apparent in the staffing patterns in elementary and secondary schools. Patricia Schmuck (1987) provided a useful summary of recent statistics on staffing patterns in schools. Her data showed that, in 1983, over 68% of the teachers in public and private schools were women. At the elementary level women made up over 83% of the teachers. The numbers of women and men teaching at the secondary level were more equal but varied significantly across disciplines. Over two-thirds of the math, science, and vocational education teachers were men, whereas almost two-thirds of the English, foreign language, and business education teachers were women. Schmuck also noted that math and science classes in secondary schools are composed primarily of male students.

Although women generally outnumber men in the teaching profession, they are significantly outnumbered among administrators (Schmuck, 1987). Based on figures from 1982, 96% of all superintendents and assistant superintendents and 84% of all principals were men. Women administrators were concentrated primarily in the elementary schools. Women principals were found in 18% of the nation's elementary schools, 3% of the junior high schools, and 2% of the high schools (Metha, 1983).

These patterns provide striking evidence of institutionalized sex segregation among professional educators. They replicate the stereotypes that women are nurturers and have good verbal skills, and that men are the best models of reasoning and have aptitude for the logic underlying math and science. Men are leaders, women are helpmates. The suggestion made earlier about repeated exposure to gender stereotypes on television programs (List et al., 1983) applies equally well here. As children continue to see adults structuring the world according to gender, the stereotypic material in their gender schemata grows increasingly salient and is applied as a way of making meaning of the world; that is, schools and television shows are "run" by men, making power distributions between men and women quite apparent to children.

Issues of the representation of women and minorities in school organizations were addressed in recent interviews conducted by Patricia and Richard Schmuck (personal communication, June 5, 1989) with over 250 teachers, administrators, and school board members in small school districts across the country. Of those interviewed, only two respondents seemed to have given the matter any thought. If the issue is not even within the professional consciousness of people running the schools, the likelihood that children will have opportunities within those systems for breaking from traditional molds is obviously limited.

Peer Influences. Evidence that socialization of sex stereotypes continues is provided in the research on peer influence among grade school children. Both sociometric and observational studies indicate that elementary and middle-school children consistently segregate themselves into gender groups for friendship and for school work (Meece, 1987). When asked to describe the appropriate behavior for their friends, girls tended to indicate value for obeying classroom rules and complying with teacher requests, whereas boys tended to endorse noncompliance and resistance to authority (Grant, 1983).

Intriguing related findings indicate that contriving or requiring cross-gender grouping in classroom situations does not reduce sex-typed behavior for children at these ages (Lockheed, 1985). When mixed-sex groups are formed, the girls tend to choose supportive, "helpmate" roles and the boys tend to assume leadership, especially among high-ability children (Meece, 1987).

As just mentioned, children's sex-typed behaviors become more pronounced as they enter grade school and achieve what cognitive developmentalists refer to as "gender constancy" (see Katz, 1985, for a detailed model of the development of gender identity). At this point, children are developmentally predisposed to categorize the world, and the pervasive social category of gender takes swift hold of children's attention to become firmly established among their most potent and well-defined cognitive categories. This might explain the tenacity of adherence to gender-linked expectations among children of elementary and middle school age (Katz, 1985).

Paradoxically, this preference for affiliation with same-sex peers could provide opportunity for expanding the behaviors of children beyond sex-stereotyped boundaries. As they assume a variety of roles in their same-sex groups, they come to acquire more flexible behavioral expectations for themselves and members of their group (e.g., girls experiencing leadership and boys practicing providing support). These outcomes mirror goals articulated by proponents of single-sex education (e.g., Howe, 1984).

Katz (1987) suggested the flexibility or rigidity of stereotyping to which children are exposed prior to acquiring gender constancy is seen again as they move into adolescence. Once gender identity is clearly established, less stereotyped attitudes tend to develop. Children become more likely to say that both men and women can do a wide variety of behaviors traditionally assigned to one sex or the other (Signorella & Liben, 1985). These findings suggest that complete attainment of gender constancy leads to more rather than less flexibility in gender-linked expectations. Perhaps having identity well in hand reduces the threat of entertaining notions of gender-role flexibility (Urberg, 1982).

Given the press of social tradition described in this chapter, evidence that cognitive development might allow students within the school culture to develop gender-related cognitions beyond those modeled in that setting gives reason for optimism. At the same time, the fact of such limiting environments should be of concern to school psychologists who are well aware of the many children who do not develop cognitive capacity (or accrue reinforcement history, or gain ego strength) sufficient to override these forces. The role of education in providing opportunities for such development must be of great interest in our profession.

PSYCHOLOGY IN THE SCHOOLS

In the midst of all these blatant and subtle sociocultural influences, we offer our services as school psychologists. To what extent do we perpetuate oppressive stereotypes? How do we respond differently to the girls and boys, the women and men with whom we work? These are questions for personal introspection as well as professional concern. Recent research in the area of women's psychology has given us insight into the psychological experiences of women and girls.

Among the child-focused work that has application to our work as school psychologists is the research of Carol Gilligan and her colleagues (Gilligan, 1982; Gilligan, Ward, Taylor, & Bardige, 1989). Gilligan's work provides an amplification of Kohlberg's theory of moral development. After working extensively with Kohlberg, Gilligan began to wonder why girls consistently scored lower than their male age-mates on measures of moral development (e.g., Kohlberg & Kramer, 1969).

Kohlberg's model can be described as depicting an ethic of justice that informs moral decision making and develops toward a point of "blind justice" that is completely fair and objective. Gilligan's research suggested a second path of moral growth, one based more on relationship. This model has been described as an ethic of care. Moral decisions emerging from this ethic are oriented toward the well-being of the relationship. Gilligan maintains this type of moral development, which she has found more frequently in women than in men, has been neglected.

Research findings from the studies subsequent to Gilligan's have been mixed. Many have found no gender differences in achieved morality as measured by Kohlberg's model (e.g., Kohlberg, 1984; Snarey, 1985; Walker, 1984). Perhaps the gender differences reflected in Kohlberg's early work were due to his coding system (now substantially revised), or perhaps they have dissipated. The fact remains that certain legitimate ways of developing moral sensibility were overlooked prior to the research of Gilligan and others (e.g., Belenky et al., 1986) who have studied female development. Just as Kohlberg's theory elucidates aspects of male and female experience, theories coming from studies of female development have similar generalizability. As with all explanations of sex-typed social behavior, there are more similarities than differences. Development of an ethic of justice (Kohlberg, 1966) *and* an ethic of care (Gilligan, 1982) are possibilities for any person.

A significant implication of this work (and much work in the psychology of women and minorities) is that psychological practice based on research with White boys and men (e.g., Kohlberg & Kramer, 1969) does not provide sufficiently generalizable information for "best" practice (Miller, 1976). What haven't we learned from girls and women by excluding them from research consideration? Much of the research and practice in school psychology is based on classic studies in learning and development that had unrepresentative samples. This should be of concern.

A perusal of research reports in recent volumes of professional journals in school psychology indicates that efforts seem to have been made to include girls and women among the subjects of these studies. The most significant exceptions are found in studies involving children classified for special education. Often, only males are used in these studies (e.g., Kehle, Clark, Jenson, & Wampold, 1986). More frequently, males greatly outnumber females (e.g., Hall, Reeve, & Zakreski, 1984; McConaghy, 1985; Shinn, 1986). Justification for this discrepancy would likely refer to the fact of higher representation of boys in special education classrooms. However, this justification does not take into account the possibility that the selection process is inaccurate; that is, the process may overlook girls and overqualify boys. Research into special educational programming is best when it considers the experiences of all children. It makes little sense to practice male-centered psychology in an environment where most of the adults and half the children are female.

At the same time, it makes little sense to act as if there are differences based on arbitrary and unsubstantiated categorical differences like gender. This issue is illustrated in the differential expectations and encouragement of girls and boys in academic areas such as math, science, and home economics. There is no convincing evidence to support any but social explanations for any aptitude differences that emerge in those areas (Eccles & Jacobs, 1986; Fausto-Sterling, 1985; Hyde & Linn, 1986, 1988).

Writing in the area of philosophy of science, Evelyn Fox Keller (1985) suggested that to reduce the issue of gender to a question of uniformity versus difference is to miss the question:

> It is only in a world perceived as ordered by a common (and commonly available) source of power, and in which separation of spheres is a strategy of exclusion, that difference becomes a matter to contest; it is claimed by the haves and denied by the have-nots. An important question for us to ask, then, is how the categories . . . are constructed. . . . Perhaps an even more important question to ask is whether . . . there really are two sides or two camps. (pp. 17–18)

What we need is a psychology that is responsive to the variety of children and adults we serve in schools. In our practice, we must be able to "count past two" (Keller, 1985). The force of gender as a subtle and deeply engrained cognitive filter on our perceptions represents a threat to our being able to respond to children's individual needs. Bem's (1974, 1981) suggestion that the potency of gender categories is a social construction is useful for raising our consciousness. The question remains how to function outside of that construction.

OPTIONS FOR GENDER-FAIR PRACTICE

The preceding discussion has demonstrated that gender bias in the schools is much more than an abstract political issue. The perpetuation of this or any other inequitable educational practice should be of great concern to school psychologists. Both girls and boys—women and men—are adversely affected by cultural practices that restrict their options for learning. The following suggestions are offered as ways to take initial steps toward the elimination of sex stereotyping from education.

1. As we participate in school culture, we can take opportunities to recognize where, due to gender, children are discouraged from expressing/developing potential skills. As patterns are identified, we can apply our skills in consultation and program development to counter those restrictive and biased practices.

2. In order to have an impact in the consultation and program development activity suggested previously, we must monitor our own patterns of sex stereotyping. We must take critical perspective of our work by asking ourselves if we are systematically varying our service delivery based on a child's gender. Given the subtlety of the cultural press of these stereotypes and the fact that each of us is a product of that culture, such vigilance over our own work is extremely challenging. Peer supervision may be necessary.

3. In our interaction with children, teachers, and administrators, we can help to decrease the emphasis on gender by consistently emphasizing children's skills, talents, strengths, etc. instead of gender-stereotypical qualities.

4. When we are called on to complete formal testing, we must use only those formal assessment tools with representative standardization samples. This is, of course, an ethical obligation on our part. We must ensure the generalizability of any instrument we use to all the children to whom we administer it.

5. With service delivery at all levels (counseling with children, consultation with teachers, program development), we can help to develop interven-

tions encouraging the establishment and expression of positive behaviors characteristic of both sexes (e.g., sensitivity and assertiveness; nurturance and leadership).

6. As a part of our regular functioning, we can take every opportunity to change the expectations of the system. By making the implicit themes of gender expectation explicit and illustrating the adverse and inequitable effects of these expectations, we can begin to influence the behavior if not the beliefs of educators. Teacher inservice and parent programs provide two outlets for this type of information.

In individual and group interactions on the subject of gender inequities in the schools, techniques as varied as Caplan's (1970) theme interference reduction and the behavioral approach of differential reinforcement of incompatible responses might be employed to interrupt the traditional gender-linked expectations. In addition, as mentioned before, specific program development of programs aimed at countering these practices and evaluation of current programs for their implicit gender biases can contribute to the enhancement of gender equity.

7. Finally, we must always be asking questions in the face of continued evidence of sex-stereotyped expectations and gender-biased practices inside and outside the schools. The institutionalized practices themselves and the complacency surrounding official responses to correct them are both barriers to the educational and vocational opportunities that should be accessible to all people.

Having made these suggestions, we recognize that such a small and generally stated list is entirely too simplistic in the face of such deeply enculturated expectations. We would be naive to think that adherence to these suggestions alone will change the culture. But we do believe in the change agency of school psychologists and the integrity of our professional commitment to working toward providing each child with the best possible educational opportunity. Given this principled foundation, the preceding suggestions may provide important options for beginning to interrupt and reduce gender inequity in the schools.

CONCLUSION

We write this chapter with the assumption that to arbitrarily limit any individual's intellectual, emotional, or career options is unfair. In school psychology, we attempt to provide children who have less success in school with opportunities to develop skills for gaining access to that array of options. The information we have summarized indicates that there seem to be deeply enculturated and separate scripts for females and males. We have some evidence that this socialization occurs, in large measure, in schools (Meece, 1987). To practice our profession well, we must be interested in ways to make educational opportunity equally available to all children. Knowing what happens in families, understanding the influences of media, and continually confronting school practices that maintain oppressive gender-linked expectations and behaviors are all quite consistent with the mandate of our profession. In the final analysis, our own behaviors and attitudes will "speak" most cogently to our clients.

As psychologists confront issues of gender in schools, it is important to exhibit conviction tempered with tolerance. Educators, children, and families need us for the understanding we can construct with them. Their different starting points for addressing gender inequities are best taken not as evidence of socialized pathology, but as challenges to our expertise. In meeting these challenges, school psychologists can influence the reduction and elimination of gender bias in schools.

REFERENCES

Adams, E. B., & Sarason, I. G. (1963). Relation between anxiety in children and their parents. *Child Development, 34,* 237–267.

Ali, S. L. (1988). Sexism. *Communique, 17,* (4) 2.

Alpert, J. L. (Ed.). (1986). *Psychoanalysis and women: Contemporary reappraisals.* New York: Analytic Press.

Alpert, J. L., & Conoley, J. (Eds.). (1988). Miniseries: Women and school psychology: Issues in the professional life cycle. *Professional School Psychology, 3,* (1).

Bandura, A. (1977). *Social learning theory.* Englewood Cliffs, NJ: Prentice-Hall.

Barry, R. J. (1980). Stereotyping of sex role in preschoolers in relation to age, family structure, and parental sexism. *Sex Roles, 6,* 795–806.

Belenky, M. F., Clinchy, B. M., Goldberger, N. R., & Tarule, J. M. (1986). *Women's ways of knowing: The development of self, voice, and mind.* New York: Basic Books.

Bem, S. L. (1974). The measurement of psychological androgyny. *Journal of Consulting and Clinical Psychology, 42,* 155–162.

Bem, S. L. (1981). Gender schema theory: A cognitive account of sex typing. *Psychological Review, 88,* 354–364.

Bem, S. L. (1983). Gender schema theory and its implications for child development: Raising gender-aschematic children in a gender schematic society. *Signs, 8,* 598–616.

Bem, S. L. (1985). Androgyny and gender schema theory: A conceptual and empirical integration. In T. B. Sonderegger (Ed.), *Nebraska symposium on motivation: Vol. 32. Psychology and gender.* Lincoln: University of Nebraska Press.

Benbow, C. P., & Stanley, J. C. (1980). Sex differences in mathematical ability: Fact or artifact? *Science, 210,* 1262–1264.

Brenes, M. E., Eisenberg, N., & Helmstadter, G. C. (1985). Sex role development of preschoolers from two-parent and one-parent families. *Merrill-Palmer Quarterly, 31* (1), 33–46.

Brophy, J., & Good, T. (1974). *Teacher–student relationships: Cause and consequences.* New York: Holt, Reinhart, & Winston.

Calvert, S. L., & Huston, A. C. (1987). Television and children's gender schemata. In L. S. Liben & M. L. Signorella (Eds.), *Children's gender schemata* (pp. 75–88). San Francisco: Jossey-Bass.

Caplan, G. (1970). *The theory and practice of mental health consultation.* New York: Basic Books.

Chordorow, N. (1978). *The reproduction of mothering: Psychoanalysis and the sociology of gender.* Berkeley: University of California Press.

Clarke-Stewart, K. A. (1989). Infant day care: Maligned or malignant? *American Psychologist, 44,* 266–273.

Conoley, J. C., & Henning-Stout, M. (1990). Gender issues in school psychology. In T. R. Kratochwill (Ed.), *Advances in school psychology* (Vol. 7). Hillsdale, NJ: Lawrence Erlbaum Associates.

Eccles, J. S., & Jacobs, J. E. (1986). Social forces shape math attitudes and performance. *Signs, 11,* 367–389.

Ember, C. (1973). Feminine task assignment and the social behavior of boys. *Ethos, 1,* 424–439.

Emmerich, W., & Shepard, K. (1982). Development of sex-differentiated preferences during late childhood and adolescence. *Developmental Psychology, 18,* 406–417.

Fagot, B. I. (1985). Beyond the reinforcement principle: Another step toward understanding sex role development. *Developmental Psychology, 21,* 1097–1104.

Fausto-Sterling, A. (1985). *Myths of gender: Biological theories about women and men.* New York: Basic Books.

Feingold, A. (1988). Cognitive gender differences are disappearing. *American Psychologist, 43,* 95–103.

Fiske, S. T., & Taylor, S. E. (1984). *Social cognition.* Reading, MA: Addison-Wesley.

Geadelmann, P. (1985). Sex equity in physical education and athletics. In S. Klein (Ed.), *Handbook for achieving sex equity through education* (pp. 319–337). Baltimore: Johns Hopkins University Press.

Gilligan, C. (1982). *In a different voice: Psychological theory and women's development.* Cambridge, MA: Harvard University Press.

Gilligan, C., Ward, J. V., Taylor, J. M., & Bardige, B. (Eds.). (1989). *A contribution of women's thinking to psychological theory and education.* Cambridge, MA: Harvard University Press.

Goetz, L. P., & Grant, L. (1988). Conceptual approaches to studying gender in education. *Anthropology and Education Quarterly, 19,* 182–196.

Gold, D., & Reis, M. (1982). Male teacher effects on young children: A theoretical and empirical consideration. *Sex Roles, 8,* 493–514.

Grant, L. (1983). Gender roles and statuses in school children's peer interactions. *Western Sociological Review, 14,* 58–76.

Gualtieri, T., & Hicks, R. E. (1985). An immunoreactive theory of selective male affliction. *The Behavioral and Brain Sciences, 8,* 427–441.

Hall, R. J., Reeve, R. E., & Zakreski, J. R. (1984). Validity of the Woodcock–Johnson Tests of Achievement for learning-disabled students. *Journal of School Psychology, 22,* 193–200.

Hallinan, M. T., & Sorensen, A. B. (1987). Ability grouping and sex differences in mathematics achievement. *Sociology and Education, 60,* 63–72.

Heatherington, E. M. (1979). Divorce: A child's perspective. *American Psychologist, 34,* 851–858.

Holden, C. (1987). Textbook controversy intensified nationwide. *Science, 235,* 19–21.

Howe, F. (1984). *Myths of coeducation.* Bloomington: Indiana University Press.

Huston, A. C. (1983). Sex typing. In D. H. Mussen (Ed.), *Handbook of child psychology: Vol. 4. Socialization personality, and social behavior* (4th ed., pp. 387–467). New York: Wiley.

Hyde, J. S. (1981). How large are cognitive gender differences? A meta-analysis using ω^2 and d. *American Psychologist, 36,* 892–901.

Hyde, J. S., & Linn, M. C. (1986). *The psychology of gender: Advances through meta-analysis.* Baltimore: Johns Hopkins University Press.

Hyde, J. S., & Linn, M. C. (1988). Are there sex differences in verbal abilities?: A meta-analysis. *Psychological Bulletin, 104,* 53–69.

Jacklin, C. N. (1989). Female and male: Issues of gender. *American Psychologist, 44,* 127–133.

Jacklin, C. N., & Maccoby, E. E. (1982). Length of labor and sex of offspring. *Journal of Pediatric Psychology, 7,* 355–360.

Katz, P. A. (1985). Gender-identity: Development and consequence. In R. D. Ashmore & F. K. Del Boca (Eds.), *The social psychology of female–male relations* (pp. 21–67). New York: Academic Press.

Katz, P. A. (1987). Variations in family constellation: Effects on gender schemata. In L. S. Liben & M. L. Signorella (Eds.), *Children's gender schemata* (pp. 39–56). San Francisco: Jossey-Bass.

Katz, P. A., & Boswell, S. L. (1986). Flexibility and traditionality in children's gender roles. *Genetic, social, and general psychology monographs, 112*, 105–147.

Kehle, T. J., Clark, E., Jenson, W. R., & Wampold, B. E. (1986). Effectiveness of self-observation with behavior disordered elementary school children. *School Psychology Review, 15*, 289–295.

Keller, E. F. (1985). Gender and science: Why is it so hard for us to count past two? *Berkshire Review*, 7–21.

Kohlberg, L. (1966). A cognitive developmental analysis of children's sex role concepts and attitudes. In E. E. Maccoby (Ed.), *The development of sex differences* (pp. 82–173). Stanford, CA: Stanford University Press.

Kohlberg, L. (1984). *Essays on moral development: Vol. II. Education and moral development.* New York: Harper & Row.

Kohlberg, L., & Kramer, R. (1969). Continuities and discontinuities in childhood and adult moral development. *Human Development, 12*, 93–120.

Kraemer, H. C., Korner, A. F., Anders, T., Jacklin, C. N., & Dimicelli, S. (1985). Obstetric drugs and infant behavior: A reevaluation. *Journal of Pediatric Psychology, 10*, 345–353.

Lee, P., & Gropper, N. (1974). Sex role, culture, and educational practice. *Harvard Educational Review, 44*, 369–410.

Lehrke, R. G. (1972). *Sex linkage: A biological basis for greater male variability in intelligence.* In R. T. Osborne, C. E. Nobel, & N. Weyle (Eds.), *Human variation: The biopsychology of age, race, and sex* (pp. 171–198). New York: Academic Press.

List, J. A., Collins, W. A., & Westby, S. (1983). Comprehension and inferences from traditional and nontraditional sex-role portrayals on television. *Child Development, 54*, 1579–1587.

Lockheed, M. (1985). Some determinants and consequences of sex segregation in the classroom. In L. C. Wilkinson & C. B. Marrett (Eds.), *Gender influences in classroom interactions* (pp. 167–184). New York: Academic Press.

Maccoby, E. E., & Jacklin, C. N. (1974). *The psychology of sex differences.* Stanford, CA: Stanford University Press.

McConaghy, S. H. (1985). Using the child behavior checklist and related instruments in school-based assessment of children. *School Psychology Review, 14*, 479–494.

Mead, M. (1964). *Continuities in cultural evolution.* New Haven, CT: Yale University Press.

Meece, J. L. (1987). The influence of school experiences on the development of gender schemata. In L. S. Liben & M. L. Signorella (Eds.), *Children's gender schemata* (pp. 57–73). San Francisco: Jossey-Bass.

Metha, A. A. (1983). Decade since Title IX: Some implications for teacher education. *Action in Teacher Education, 5*, 21–27.

Miller, J. B. (1976). *Towards a new psychology of women.* Boston: Beacon Press.

Mischel, W. (1970). Sex typing and socialization. In D. H. Mussen (Ed.), *Charmichael's manual of child psychology* (Vol. 2, 3d. ed.). New York: Wiley.

Morse, L. W., & Handley, H. M. (1985). Listening to adolescents: Gender differences in science classroom interactions. In L. C. Wilkinson & C. B. Marrett (Eds.), *Gender influences in classroom interaction* (pp. 37–56). New York: Academic Press.

Oakland, T., & Stern, W. (1989). Variables associated with reading and math achievement among a heterogeneous group of students. *Journal of School Psychology, 27*, (2), 127–140.

Office of Civil Rights. (1987). *1986 elementary and secondary school civil rights survey.* (Contract No. 300-86-0062). Washington, DC: Department of Education.

Sadker, M., & Sadker, D. (1984). *Promoting effectiveness in classroom instruction.* Final report to National Institute of Education, Department of Education, Washington, DC (ERIC Document Reproduction Service No. ED 257 819).

Schlosser, L., & Algozzine, B. (1979). The disturbing child: He or she? *Alberta Journal of Educational Research, 25,* 30–36.

Schmuck, P. A. (Ed.). (1987). *Women educators: Employees of schools in western countries.* Albany, NY: State University of New York Press.

Scott-Jones, D., & Nelson-LeGall, S. (1986). Defining black families: Past and present. In E. Seidman & J. Rappaport (Eds.), *Redefining social problems* (pp. 83–98). New York: Plenum Press.

Seller, M. (1981). G. Stanley Hall and Edward Thorndike on the education of women: Theory and policy in the progressive era. *Educational Studies, 11,* 365–374.

Shinn, M. R. (1986). Does anyone care what happens after the refer–test–place sequence: The systematic evaluation of special education program effectiveness. *School Psychology Review, 15,* 49–58.

Signorella, M. L., & Liben, L. S. (1985). Assessing children's gender-stereotyped attitudes. *Psychological Documents, 15,* 7.

Silvern, L. E. (1978). Masculinity–femininity in children's self-concepts: The relationship to teachers' judgments of social adjustment and academic ability, classroom behaviors, and popularity. *Sex Roles, 4,* 929–949.

Silvern, L. E., & Katz, P. A. (1986). Gender roles and adjustment in elementary school children: A multidimensional approach. *Sex Roles, 14,* 181–202.

Snarey, J. R. (1985). Cross-cultural universality of social-moral development: A critical review of Kohlbergian research. *Psychological Bulletin, 97,* 202–232.

Stangor, C., & Rubel, D. N. (1987). Development of gender role knowledge and gender constancy. In L. S. Liben & M. L. Signorella (Eds.), *Children's gender schemata* (pp. 5–22). San Francisco: Jossey-Bass.

Stipek, D. J., & Sanborn, M. E. (1985). Teachers' task-related interactions with handicapped and nonhandicapped preschool children. *Merrill–Palmer Quarterly, 31,* 285–300.

Thomas, A. H., & Stewart, N. R. (1971). Counselor response to female clients with disparate and conforming career goals. *Journal of Counseling Psychology, 18,* 352–357.

Title IX of the Education Amendments of 1972, 34 CFR ss 100.6–100.11 (1975).

Unger, R. K. (1988). Integrating sex and gender into school psychology. *Professional School Psychology, 3,* 29–31.

Urberg, K. A. (1982). The development of the concepts of masculinity and femininity in young children. *Sex Roles, 6,* 659–668.

Walker, L. J. (1984). Sex differences in the development of moral reasoning: A critical review. *Child Development, 53,* 1330–1336.

Walker, S. J. H. (1982). *The relationship of parental educational levels, race, and sex to sex role stereotyping in young children.* Unpublished doctoral dissertation, East Texas State University.

Weinraub, M., Clemens, L. P., Sockloff, A., Ethridge, T., Gracely, E., & Myers, B. (1984). The development of sex role stereotypes in the third year: Relationships to gender labeling, gender identity, sex-typed toy preference, and family characteristics. *Child Development, 55,* 1493–1503.

Wright, J. C., & Huston, A. C. (1983). A matter of form: Potentials of television for young viewers. *American Psychologist, 38,* 835–843.

6

FAMILY FUNCTIONING AND SCHOOL ADJUSTMENT: FAMILY SYSTEMS PERSPECTIVES

Oscar A. Barbarin
University of Michigan

FAMILY IMPACT ON SCHOOL ADJUSTMENT

Discussing conceptions of family functioning may at first glance appear tangential and unrelated to the day-to-day concerns of school personnel. However, the relevance of family systems theory, which owes much to social psychology, becomes more apparent when we consider how much family life influences the psychological adjustment and academic functioning of the child (e.g., see Amerikaner & Omizo, 1984; Freidman, 1973; Gurman, 1970). The quality of family life is widely regarded as causally related to psychological adjustment in general and school adjustment in particular (Campos et al., 1985; Cramer, 1987; Sameroff & Chandler, 1975). Problems of school adjustment such as academic failure, underachievement, and disciplinary problems often arise from a combination of information-processing difficulties, attention deficit disorders, school or performance anxiety, and low motivation (Green, 1989). These problems in turn have been linked to specific domains of family life (e.g., family conflict, communication and organization). What relationships are asserted between family functioning and academic performance? In a review of educational and social psychological literature, the following relationships between family and school adjustment have been examined although the evidence supporting them is mixed:

1. Learning disabilities, poor task orientation, attention deficits, and low academic achievement are related to underorganized and unstable family

life (Green, 1989). Underorganized families are characterized by global, erratic or aversive control styles, in which conflicts are handled through threats and counterthreats. In addition, these families tend to rely on hierarchical control, communicate poorly, and apply contingencies to the child's behavior inconsistently (Green, 1989). Parents of children with learning disabilities are more authoritarian and controlling in their child-rearing attitudes than parents of normal children (Humphries & Bauman, 1980). Also, parents of children in learning-disabled and emotionally impaired classes rated their families as less adaptable and cohesive than parents of children in normal classrooms (Amerikaner & Omizo, 1984).

2. Problems of underachievement are associated with parent–child conflicts, low levels of parental availability and guidance, and a lack of openness in parent–child relations (Gurman, 1970).

3. Underachievement, obsessional worry, performance anxiety, procrastination, and passive–aggressive behavior in school are related to overorganized family styles in which parents are overprotective, restrictive, intrusive, controlling, and dominating (Green, 1989).

4. As a consequence of their disappointments and lost dreams about a child, parents may develop and promote family paradigms about the child that are negative and expressed in terms of labels such as *defective* and *incompetent* (Margalit, 1982). These paradigms denigrate the ability or effort of the child and become a demoralizing self-fulfilling prophesy.

5. Some parents develop a posture of over or underresponsibility for their child's education, maintain an adversarial relationship, or promulgate attitudes of dissatisfaction with the educational system. The net effect is that the child becomes alienated from and adjusts poorly to school (Klein, Altman, Dreizen, Friedman, & Powers, 1981).

This chapter describes theoretical conceptions of families as systems, particularly those concepts that provide a framework for understanding and intervening in the nexus between family life and adjustment of children in school. The discussion is expanded beyond family systems theory to include emerging theories of family stress and coping that provide additional insights about how families operate under duress. Finally, the chapter briefly describes the dilemmas faced by school staff in adopting a family systems approach to deal with problems arising in schools.

DEFINING FAMILY

A starting point for our discussion of family systems is a consideration of current trends in family structure and functions. Historically, the family has been the principal social organization responsible for procreation, child rearing and preparing children for adult life, transmitting religious and cultural values, teaching problem-solving and coping skills, providing for affiliation and intimacy needs, and promoting psychological growth and bolstering self-esteem. In addition, the family serves important economic, recreational, emotional, social, and educational functions for its members. As a consequence of complex economic and social forces, American families are increasingly diverse in form. High rates of divorce and remarriage have made extended- and blended-family structures commonplace. At the same time the increased proportion of births to adolescents has combined to raise the percentage of American families with young children headed by young single mothers. In a related development, decreases in the American standard of living and structural barriers to earning an income sufficient to support three people above the poverty level has decreased the likelihood that many of these young mothers will every marry (Commission on Work, Family, and Citizenship, 1988; Wilson, 1987). Multigenerational households have become more commonplace. For increasing numbers of children a series of foster home placements sadly constitutes the only experience of family life they will ever know. The resulting diversity of family forms significantly reduces the relevance of definitions of family that are structural in focus and that treat the two-parent nuclear family structure as normative. Systems theory provides an alternative approach to conceptualizing family that transcends the limits of definitions based on the nuclear family and accommodates differences in family structure by emphasizing processes and functions.

Accordingly, family is conceived as a living system that over time evolves a set of rules, rituals, roles, hierarchy, coalitions, and ways of communicating and supporting one another. Thus, families can be thought of as rule-governed organizations with patterned coordinated activity that spawns loyalty and a sense of connection whereas at the same time permitting members to function autonomously. Within the context of the family, sexually expressive and parent–child relationships develop and promote a bond or attachment unlike that common in other social relations.

Although families have much in common with respect to functions and expectations, each family evolves its own unique emotional climate, processes, and relationships. The emphasis on process and relationships emanating from family systems theory does not require that a blood relationship or even a legal bond exist among the people constituting a family. People may come together as a family through in-law relationships and through a long-term commitment to one another. These process-based definitions of family are slowly gaining legal recognition. In two separate cases heard in 1989, the New York State Supreme Court upheld the claims by persons unrelated by blood or marriage for rights and safeguards afforded to family members primarily because they lived together like a family.

Understanding Family as a System

If a theory of family functioning is to be useful, it must help us identify, characterize, and evaluate how families perform even the mundane aspects of family life. Family theory then should discern and clarify patterns in how family members play, work, love, endure life's hardships, and embrace life and its satisfactions within a set of the relationships that give meaning to their experiences together. It should contribute to our understanding of whether and how families use self-regulatory mechanisms to handle stress with equanimity and respond to threats with a sense of balance and perspective.

Theories and conceptual approaches to characterizing the psychological properties and functioning of individuals are readily available and familiar to many. For example, we draw on concepts depicting psychological defenses, coping strategies, attributional styles, self-concepts, communication skills, and personality traits. Making the transition from an analysis of individual traits to a family or systemic analysis is difficult. It is far easier to characterize family process in terms of the individual behavior of its members than it is to view family in its relational context. Extrapolations of individual constructs to depict family functioning are ipso facto, imprecise, and violate the most fundamental tenet of family systems theory, namely, that family functioning is something more than the combination of the styles, traits, and behaviors of its individual members. Simple extensions of individual theory fail to capture the interdependence, the reciprocal causality of individual feelings, motivations, and behaviors of members. In other words, the family as a collective entity has a set of processes, a life, and a character all its own. Accordingly, it is more than an accumulation of the features of its members.

Integral to a systemic approach is an emphasis on reciprocal over linear causality. Linear models of causality account for less of family interactional patterns than reciprocal models of causality. Reciprocal causality means that observed effects in families are mutually determined rather than flowing from a single causal factor. Each event or response to some prior event itself precipitates or elicits subsequent events or responses. The responses of one family member thus becomes a cause initiating still another sequence of responses. Family members develop interdependent responses that over time contribute to discernible family patterns. Interlocking, multiperson motivational systems, whereby one person carries part of the motivations and psychology of another, are only vaguely understood but clearly a part of family dynamics. When two or more persons are in close relationship, they often form a compact in which they implicitly agree to carry psychic functions for one other. These implicit compacts often make for a stable complementary relationship that may take the form of "You be scared, I, brave"; you be overresponsible, so that I am free to be under-responsible"; "you be careful, I, carefree"; "you be penurious; I spendthrift"; "you forgetful, I, mindful" (Ackerman, 1958). These interactional sequences cannot arise from, be maintained by, or be predicted from the behavior of one person alone. Consequently, if the interactional pattern is judged to be problematic, no single member of a family alone is the cause of the problem. In problematic family interactions it is rare to find a single victim, a single perpetrator. Patterson (1982), in his study of aggressive children, demonstrates how parents are both victims and unwitting architects of mutually coercive cycles of noncompliance with their children. Each family member suffers from and has the capacity to help solve family problems and conflicts.

A myriad of family systems constructs have been proposed to characterize the diverse aspects of family functioning. Though varied they can be construed as belonging to one of three broad dimensions: (a) interdependence (i.e., structuring relationships, to balance between closeness and independence in relations); (b) homeostasis (i.e., maintaining stability and enacting controls over the behavior of family members); and (c) adaptability (i.e., responding to forces of change). Most are derived from observations of distressed families in therapy and to a lesser extent on studies of nonclinical families (e.g., see Walsh, 1982). These dimensions are best conceived not as fixed properties or traits but as functional demands or tasks that challenge families as they devise idiosyncratic responses to the universal socioemotional tasks of structuring relationships among family members and family environments, providing continuity for its members, and managing change. Performance of these tasks constitutes the most basic elements of family functioning. Examination of the basic patterns, processes, or methods by which families carry out these socioemotional tasks accomplishes two goals: to describe family functioning and evaluate family effectiveness and its relation to outcomes such as child adjustment. Our discourse on systems concepts of family functioning is organized around the issues related to three family tasks (see Table 6.1).

Structuring Family Relations

When families are highly cohesive, interactions often involve a common dance, a reciprocally determined pattern of behavior and concomitant emotions that follows implicit laws and dominates family interactions over time (Minuchin, 1974; Minuchin & Fishman, 1982). These unspoken but highly influential family laws or rules capture the organized patterns, establish expectations, define roles, and prescribe what constitutes acceptable family behavior. The degree of interdependence among family members may be so encompassing that any change reverberates throughout the unit. Accordingly, family members are so intimately connected to one another that change in one part of the system or in one member will inevitably influence how the family as a whole functions. Thus, what affects one member affects all. Inter-

TABLE 6.1
Assessment Questions Related to Basic Family Tasks

Structuring Relationships:

How are relationships among family members structured?
How does the family balance between connecting and separating, between closeness and distance, between involvement and disengagement, between unity and autonomy?
How does the family pattern relationships to regulate emotional distance?
How intimate and emotionally close is the family?

Maintaining Stability:

What practices, rituals, expectations does the family employ to maintain continuity and provide a stable environment for its members?
How does the family control or curb deviant behavior and keep the behavior of family members within acceptable limits?

Managing Change:

How does the family adapt to altered circumstances, changes in its members or its environment?
How does the family copy with the demands of normative transitions, catastrophic upheavals, or atypical crises?
What are the methods by which the family adapts to internal and external changes over time?
How well does the family confront and solve difficult problems?

---

dependence is often evident in the strength of attachment and identification with and loyalty to family. At the same time there exists an ineluctable tension between dependence as expressed in cohesion or emotional closeness and independence as expressed in autonomy, individuation, and distance. Striking a balance between closeness and distance, between well-placed concern and anxious involvement and between cohesion and individuation is essential for family well-being.

Support and differentiation depict specific aspects of family interdependence. These dimensions of family life also figure prominently in characterizations of families as functional or dysfunctional. For example, support as an expression of interdependence is synonymous with kindness, understanding, and acceptance in relations among family members. It includes family sharing, expression of affection and encouragement, and concern about the physical well-being of family members. It is evidenced in the degree of attachment, regard, and interpersonal cohesion that characterizes family life. Families high in support express unconditional affection for and actively nurture members. On the other hand, unsupportive families do not effectively demonstrate its valuing of its members or sensitivity to their distress. Relations among family members is also evidenced in the way a family organizes itself to conduct its business and perform its routine work. Complementarity of instrumental tasks and socioemotional functions is a very useful way to describe this aspect of family relatedness. For example, a family might adopt

socially prescribed assignments for functions related to household management, income earnings, bill paying, car repair, child care, communication
with extended family, and so forth. This division of labor within a family may
increase efficiency and result in the most optimal use of individual competencies. However, rigid adherence to such a specialized role may contribute to
family conflict and tension, particularly if it results in perceptions of unequal
burden sharing by family members. Such tensions are rather commonplace in
periods of role shifting as mothers increase their participation in the work force.

To be healthy, the family must manage these tensions, maintain emotional closeness with one another, but not be so undifferentiated that family members blur the distinctions among themselves in role and functions inhibiting
their capacity for autonomous functions. Subgroups within the family such
as the marital dyad, the parental figures, the executive decision-making group,
and the siblings require a degree of autonomy in order to function. In other
words, family members need enough freedom from interference to carry out
their unique family roles effectively (Minuchin, 1974). Thus, in order to function well families must counteract excessive dependence that violates individual autonomy. This autonomy is dependent on development and observance
of boundaries that separate a functional subgroup from the rest of the family
and protect it from those who might constrain its functioning. *Differentiation*
is a term used to depict the diffusion or rigidity of functional and role boundaries among family members and the degree of emotional individuation within the family (Bowen, 1978).

Emotional differentiation involves the closeness and intensity of emotional exchanges in the family. It includes the extent to which family members
are fused emotionally with one another and assesses the similarity of their
psychological experiences of the world. It is a gauge of how tightly connected family members are emotionally and cognitively with one another and
of the similarity of family members' attitudes, feelings, and reactions to their
world. It refers to the extent to which family members experience the emotions of other family members as their own, interrupt or speak for one another,
and observe rules that establish family hierarchy and preserve family role
distinctions.

Highly differentiated families respect the functional autonomy of family
members, accept or even encourage differences, and tolerate disagreement.
Relationships are characterized by a close emotional bond, genuine intimacy, autonomy, and freedom from being constricted by the emotional system
of the family. Conversely, undifferentiated families are characterized by
permeable boundaries, emotional contagion, and suppression of individual
identity. They evidence an absence or diffusion of functional or emotional
boundaries within the family. These families suppress conflict, demand compliance, cover over the inevitable differences in family life, and have such
emotionally intense relations that the capacity for individualized responding

is extinguished. Undifferentiated families are characterized by an extreme, symbiotic attachment resulting in low emotional autonomy and individuation. In these families tension is always lurking beneath the surface, never to be addressed or resolved. They are caught in a web of emotional entanglement that leads the family to eschew differences or suffer the consequence of rejection. Family members intuit what the others feel, have common fantasies, and react in emotionally identical ways to the external world. Families low in differentiation are so closely connected with one another that they have the same wishes, dreams, and fantasies and react to the experience of other family members as if those experiences were their own (Bowen, 1978). Differentiation of family members is also reflected in a host of observable processes that occur in both functional and dysfunctional families such as overinvolvement in one another's lives, sibling or spousal competition, jockeying for status, position, or attention in the family, currying favor by giving in to the pressure to please, regression to infantile or dependent behavior, and being bound or getting caught up emotionally over an admittedly trivial issue. These behavior patterns are not necessarily evident when family members are outside the field of action or influence of the family system.

Stability

Optimal functioning of a system is facilitated by stability of its internal and external environment. Instability and chaos make extraordinary demands on the system to adjust, are inherently distressing, deplete system resources and thus impair the system's ability to function well. However, systems by their nature resist most pressures to change them. In fact, systems theory posits the principle of homeostasis to account for the processes by which living organisms maintain a steady state, a sense of constancy and equilibrium at the biological, behavioral, and psychological levels (Bertalannfy, 1968).

How is the stabilizing homeostatic process theorized to work its influence on family functioning? Families are governed by the explicit injunctions, admonitions, dictates, and proscriptions established by the leadership or authority structure of the family. In addition, families, like other social systems, are guided by rules derived from the implicit understanding they have about the ways they should behave toward one another. These family rules emerge from and are expressed in the regularities characterizing a wide range of mundane family activity, such as when and how to get up, retire, eat, express affection, play, work, worship, and achieve. Rules are the redundancies of family life that become evident in and take the form of family routines, role expectations, myths, rituals, and customs. Moreover, they reveal what is important to a family, what events or times are to be celebrated, and how they are to be memorialized. Family members influence each other's behavior and keep it within an acceptable range by the enforcement and support of family expectations, rules, norms, and rituals. The enforcement of family rules does not have to be coercive. Adherence to family expectations is voluntary and given willingly as the price for cohesion, order and predictability in family life.

Explicit control by the family authority structure, or as Minuchin (1974) called it, the executive subsystem, represents an additional but conceptually narrower strategy for promoting stability of family life. In this light control refers to the processes by which some family members actually direct and sanction the behavior of other family members. Control by the executive unit of the family can be aversive or positive, coercive or inductive, authoritarian or lax, and overt or psychological. Baumrind (1971) has provided a useful conceptualization of patterns of parental control that are empirically related to differential child developmental outcomes. Her patterns include rigid or authoritarian control, authoritative control, and laissez-faire or lax control. Authoritarian control occurs when influence is based on coercion and power to the exclusion of reasoning. A developmentally optimum pattern of control is described as authoritative. Although far from democratic, this approach is participatory and is characterized by inductive reasoning, persuasion, and reciprocity of influence. Lax control refers in the most extreme case to the complete lack of influence, rules, direction, or guidance in itself or the absolute failure to enforce rules if they exist. Families low in control are clearly lax in the imposition and enforcement of rules. In these families, behavioral injunctions may be issued but no meaningful consequence is associated with compliance or non-compliance. Baumrind (1966) suggests that authoritative styles in which parental figures relate to children with a combination of emotional support, reasoning, and control are very effective developing children's social competence.

In addition, physical illness or psychological problems have sometimes served to maintain stability in families. For example, Miller and Westman (1964) argue that psychogenic learning difficulties distract the family from other more disturbing sources of conflict and thus contribute to equilibrium or stability in the family. As noted earlier in the research of Patterson on aggressive children, the ability to influence the behavior of family members does not reside exclusively in the hands of a parent. Children through their ability to induce positive and negative mood states in adults possess a powerful mechanism of control. Thus, they too can influence parental behavior to maintain some steady state in the family. In essence, control provides an avenue for keeping the behavior of family members within a certain acceptable range. It is an ostensibly corrective force that protects the family from widespread and potentially deleterious deviations.

The family may have unstated norms or rules, for example about independence, achievement, separation, expressing feelings, religious expression, dealing with conflict, sexuality, use of leisure, family cohesion, etc. When forces of change within or outside the family elicit behavior from family members that transgress family norms or that lie outside the accepted range of behavior, a reaction is set into motion to negate the change. In other words, violations by a family member of these expectations are met with a controlling response by the family to restore the errant behavior back to the accepted norm. This controlling reaction is sometimes referred to by systems theorists as negative or deviation-minimizing-feedback. This negative feedback loop is a reactive balancing of forces to maintain the status quo. In this way, change is countered by an effort to co-opt, resist, or otherwise neutralize the precipitant of change. Efforts to change the family triggers responses to counter the change and to maintain the status quo. Control processes within the family are the primary means of attaining this end.

Managing Change

If the resistance to change is so great, how do families reconcile the inescapable transformations of family life? Clearly, circumstances arise that require accommodations in the family's typical ways of operating. For example, change occurs naturally as part of major life transitions in the life of family members (viz., birth, adolescence, marriage, entry to school or work, retirement). Each of these transitions potentially affects the family's rules and patterned interactions. In addition, this natural evolution of family life requires that the family adjust and situate itself somewhere along the continuum of simplicity–complexity in structure. Some families handle this adaptational task through a process of differentiation. For example, as the family increases in size it may develop a more complex organization with highly specialized role assignments to carry out the many functions involved in keeping a large family going. Similarly, as the family contracts in size, as children grow and leave, the family returns to a more simple structure with less differentiated roles. Ways in which the family uses information from its environment, solves problems, manages resources, establishes family roles, and negotiates the boundary between itself and the external world are indices of adaptability in family life.

Variations in family life also occur in response to problems such as episodes of chronic illness, substance abuse, and mental disorders. As a consequence, the value of order and stability for competent family functioning does not negate the necessity of adaptability in responding to change. Just as homeostasis and resistance to change are seen as the cornerstone of family survival, adapting just enough to accommodate the forces of change serves this same purpose. In other words, situations arise in which the very survival and well-being of family members hinge on the ability of the family to adopt a flexible stance toward crisis situations, to changes in family membership (e.g., kids getting older, illness, income loss by parent), or to changes in the environment (e.g., economic downturns, increasing community violence). Each new situation or transition presents the family with a set of problems it must solve. It can respond by ignoring the need for change and persist in its old ways of doing things or it can respond by changing. Flexibility is therefore an important characteristic of family life. It refers to the degree of a family's resistance to change, its willingness to try out new things, and its adaptability to new situations. Families high in flexibility are likely to report accommodating effectively to change and using feedback to alter its rules or ways of behaving. Flexibility permits the family to generate multiple solutions to problems encountered in family life. Low flexibility or rigidity suggests that families have difficulty integrating environmental feedback, resist change, and feel uncomfortable in novel situations.

Family Functioning Under Stress

Up to this point we have discussed ways system theory conceptualizes aspects of normal or typical family functioning. Understanding how families structure relations, closeness, and distance, and how families maintain stability and adapt to change reveals much of what is important in describing family functioning under normal conditions. These issues are captured primarily in the patterns or processes by which families deal with the tension between family cohesion and individual autonomy and the flexibility the family displays in adapting to ineluctable forces of change while providing a stable and consistent environment. To extend our understanding of normal family functioning to functioning of families under stress requires knowledge of several additional family processes. For example, it is important to know how families respond as a unit to a common stress, how they construe a stressor (e.g., as a loss, a threat of loss, or as a challenge to be overcome), how they mobilize the resources available to them, and how they manage the emotional and instrumental demands of stressful situations.

Stress is an event, situation, or stimulus that places excessive demands on an individual or group, disrupts ongoing functioning, and leads to a state of heightened emotional arousal and the subjective experience of strain. Stress is of concern because of its link to enduring negative psychosocial outcomes. The likelihood that stress will be associated with negative outcomes in the long run hinges largely on how the individual and the family cope with the situation.

In contrast to models of individual stress and coping, models of family stress and coping emphasize the shared nature of the stressor and the role-determined experience of and response to the stress. Family stress takes such varied forms as parental joblessness, chronic illness, marital dissolution, substance abuse, natural and manmade disasters, changes in family composition, and crime victimization. In keeping with the assertions about interdependence and reciprocal determinism so central to family systems theory, the behavior of one family member provides the context for the responses of other family members. Even though family members have individualized responses to a stressor, they do not implement coping strategies in isolation. Their coping is linked to and, to an extent, shaped by the family context. A somewhat different set of notions and constructs are needed to depict and understand how families function under stress.

Barbarin (1983) described family coping as the coordinated and adaptive response of a family to a shared stress. This suggests that the family evolves a group-level adaptation to stress that might involve the alteration of family expectations, rules, structure, role assignment, etc. The result may be a delineation of specific duties, equitable redistribution of responsibilities, and sometimes a division of labor. Family coping is dependent on teamwork, interdependent roles, and an implicit agreement about goals and strategies. When families cope well, members pursue a common goal and coordinate their responses in order to use shared resources (e.g., time, money, and emotional energies) in an efficient manner. Coordination of family coping responses occurs in the form of behavioral turntaking, joint problem solving, and task redistribution. It involves the demonstration of emotional empathy and understanding of the feelings and needs of other family members. Moreover, it implies the ability to anticipate and respond to the needs of family members before assistance is requested.

Coping is also expressed in efforts to promote family cohesion and to preserve a semblance of stability and continuity in family life. In addition to behavioral coordination and collaborative problem solving, families may also adopt joint socioemotional and cognitive strategies by which they interpret or give meaning to the stress. David Reiss and his colleagues have demonstrated that families can and often do develop a shared paradigm. Moreover, they have empirically linked these paradigms to families' problem-solving styles (Reiss, 1981; Reiss & Oliveri, 1980). These paradigms provide a common way of viewing reality for the family. Conceivably, paradigms influence such dimensions as family optimism, fatalism, and humor. For example, family paradigms reflect a family's disposition to focus exclusively on the hopeful side of an issue and selectively screen out distressing information. Moreover, a feeling of well-being under stress may be maintained by downward comparisons in which the family compares its situation to the problems of families who are ostensibly worse off. Families may also lower their expectations about what is possible or desirable and become willing to settle for less. Other aspects of family paradigms include the amount of hope with which the family approaches or construes the stressor, the extent to which the family expects to have control over the stressful situation, and the source to which the responsibility for the problem and solution is attributed. In turn, these beliefs may eventually influence the degree to which the family blames itself for problems and how actively they involve themselves in working toward a solution. Finally, coping is often enhanced cognitively by resorting to transcendental or religious paradigms that permit the family to give meaning to their current circumstances and thereby experience amelioration of distress.

To be acceptable, formulations of family coping must include several *sine qua non* features: (a) focus on a shared stressor, (b) emphasis on the mutual influence of family members on each others' coping behavior, and (c) reliance on family or group level to describe adaptation (Barbarin, 1983). Hill (1949) proposed that the relationship between the stressful situation and the psychological dysfunction experienced by a family is mediated by the family's appraisal of the stressor and the availability of social resources such as economic and social supports. McCubbin (1979) went farther and argued the importance of including a temporal dimension in coping with chronic stress. He distinguished between the family's initial response to a stressor and the family's pattern of long-term adaptation. The disruption and strain in families arising from stressors such as a family member sickness, job loss, divorce, remarriage, and shared custody arrangements present a challenge whose duration may not be appreciated at first. Take as an example the situation of a family with school-age children in which a family member is diagnosed with a serious life-threatening illness such as cancer or sickle cell disease. In the period immediately following the diagnosis of a life-threatening chronic illness, families view and treat the situation as a time-limited crisis. Accordingly, they mobilize themselves and redirect much of their resources away from routine life demands to deal with the crisis. If the ill family member is an adult, the nonill adult may be so concerned about the survival of the partner and may be so burdened by having to balance household responsibility and caring for the ill family member that any semblance of order and family routines falls by the wayside. The children may be too distraught to concentrate on and be motivated to perform school work. In some cases the children may return from school to be alone without anyone to carefully check school performance and provide the needed assistance. They may be shuttled from relative to relative or friend to friend while parents spend time with the ill family member in the hospital. In these and other similarly distressing situations, the family may be so emotionally preoccupied that they are unable to monitor adequately and play their accustomed role in facilitating the child's adjustment. Once it becomes apparent that the condition will not resolve quickly, the family may respond adaptively by shifting to a long-term strategy that permits them to turn to other pressing family obligations and tasks. If the family is adaptive, they assimilate the stressor into existing routines or develop new routines to accommodate its demands.

Family Stress and Personal Adjustment

Because the family is a primary arena in which the child acquires a capacity to cope with life demands, it figures prominently in whether the child acquires adaptive or maladaptive approaches to life in general. The effectiveness with which families deal with stress is often reflected in development by the child of social competence and is associated with positive school adaptation (Clark, 1983). If the family responds adaptively to stressful situations, it provides a foundation for secure attachments, reinforces a sense of mastery and personal importance, models reciprocity in social relations, and teaches the child to forego immediate gratification for some greater long-term goal and at times to forego personal needs in the interest of some common good. Children growing up in distressed families in which interactions are impaired by conflict, excessive criticism, frequent expression of negative emotions, substance abuse, and affective disorders are at higher risk of developing a variety of problems related to psychological adjustment (Leff & Vaughn, 1985). In this case, family dysfunction impedes the acquisition by the child of a range of important psychosocial competencies. When family life is disrupted by stress, school adjustment may suffer. Thus, distress emanating from family life may be etiological in the development of serious adjustment problems in the school (Miller & Westman, 1964). Consider the case of Tony Zimmer that illustrates how family stress negatively impacts school adjustment.

The Case of Tony Zimmer

Tony has stopped caring about school. Hardly a day passes without his being sent down to the principal's office for misconduct. As a 13 year-old in the fifth grade, he does not stand out because of his diminutive stature. He talks out of turn, refuses to do homework, fails to complete tests and assignments, disturbs other students by tossing paper airplanes at their desks or tripping students walking by his desk. His reading skills are on a first grade level.

As early as the second grade, teachers were cognizant of deficient math and reading achievement, but they thought things would eventually work themselves out. He was not a behavioral problem then and did not create a nuisance in the class. Tony appeared a little shy but otherwise unremarkable. Until the fifth grade the school thought it best to promote him with his peers to avoid the stigma of retention.

The behavior problems the school is just recognizing are the consequences of personal difficulties and dysfunctional family processes dating back to his entry to school. Tony was the victim of several accidents at home and school that kept him out of school for crucial periods in the beginning of the first and second grade. He never did really get started or truly invested in school. Because of a series of problems and limited social resources, the family was not functioning well enough to meet the challenges of helping Tony overcome the unavoidable events contributing to his poor start and subsequently to make a healthy adjustment to school.

Family dysfunction was also an outcome of a set of unfortunate circumstances. The year before Tony entered school, his father, an employee of an asbestos manufacturer, died of lung cancer at age 33, leaving behind four children ages 11 to 4. At that time, Tony's mother, age 31, was pregnant with their fifth child. Unable to make ends meet, she found employment as a cashier in a book store soon after the birth of Tony's younger brother. She had almost no friends and social outlets with the exception of occasional visits to church. Over the years her routine was to retreat to her bedroom when she returned home from work. Anxious and depressed, she felt overwhelmed by the burden of caring for a large family alone. It took a great deal of energy to gain compliance from her children at home, energy she often lacked. The attachment and emotional bond among family members was unmistakable. Nevertheless, family interactions were often characterized by fights, bickering, and yelling, with relatively little open expression of positive emotion. Moreover, few family rituals existed to bring them together, and for the most part family members tended to go their own ways. In her depression, Mrs. Zimmer had little energy to supervise Tony carefully and ultimately felt helpless about Tony's early school failures. Instead of helping, Tony's older brothers often made fun of him by pointing out that the baby could read better than Tony could. The school in turn, by focusing only on Tony, was unable to connect enough to mediate the problem. Had the school adopted a family systems perspective, it might have understood the difficulties occurring in the family.

Tony is by no means an exceptional case. Many children like Tony come from families that are struggling with problems related to employment, marital discord, drug abuse/dependence, neighborhood violence, poverty, and chronic illness. Like ominous clouds, they hang over the child, diffusing intellectual effort and creating a self-perpetuating cycle of school failure.

Expanded Role of School in Promoting Adjustment.

Adjustment is a multidimensional construct referring to functional status as evidenced in the presence or absence of: (a) anxiety, psychophysiological complaints, or depressive symptoms; (b) behavioral disorders that make a child disturbing to others; or (c) health in the form of self-esteem, social competence, maturation, hardiness, coping, and resilience (see Table 6.2). Academic maladjustment represents a complex of multidetermined problems. Consequently, effective solutions for these problems require collaboration among family, school, and community. Unfortunately, agencies mandated to serve these problem groups often are set up to deal with singular aspects of what are clearly multifaceted problems. For example, schools focus primarily on academic adjustment, child guidance clinics focus on psychological adjustment, family service agencies focus on housing or financial needs, and substance abuse agencies on the addictions of individual family members. These

TABLE 6.2
Domains of Adjustment at School

Psychopathology:

Affective or thought disorders including symptoms such as anxiety or depression, phobias, loss of emotional control.

Conduct Disorder:

High rates of socially inappropriate or disruptive behavior, inattention, hyperactivity, impulsivity, chronic non-compliance and aggression.

Positive Mental Health:

Favorable and realistic self evaluation, self esteem, self-efficacy, zest for life, enthusiasm, optimistic view of the world.

Psychosocial Maturation:

Attainment of developmental milestones in cognitive, motor and affective domains. It includes development of personal autonomy, a sense of responsibility and a firm identity. Ability to delay gratification, tolerate frustration, work planfully to overcome obstacles, regulate emotional arousal, planning and problem solving.

Social Competence:

Ability to maintain positive social ties, to engage in co-operative behaviors with peers and adults. This relates to the degree of participation in social activities, the development of friendship and ability to engage in reciprocal co-operative relationships. Its counterpart includes social isolation, shyness, loneliness, social withdrawal.

are treated as independent issues instead of as related components of a single phenomenon. Recognition of the interdependent relationship among components of adjustment, adolescent pregnancy, school dropout, and poverty has resulted in a push to expand the role of the school in addressing these problems. Accordingly, schools can become the locus of programs for prevention of problems such as chemical dependency, teenage pregnancy, suicide, sexual abuse, and delinquency. Wittingly or unwittingly, the school is part of a larger network of services addressing the physical and psychosocial needs of children and adolescents. Still another hurdle remains in the delivery of services to school-aged children. In the past mental health professionals concerned with problems of children made a fundamental error in serving the child but excluding the family. As long as the family was ignored, not much headway could be made in dealing with children's problems. The family systems view has gradually been adopted as a guide to serving children. If school personnel are to avoid the same pitfall of focusing too narrowly on the individual child, they too must recognize that child adjustment is fundamentally connected to the functioning of the family. This expansion of roles requires a close working relationship with families and the use of a family-oriented approach in its work. This means looking not only at the child but the family and the other social institutions involved with the family. Given the pervasiveness of these social problems and the obstacles that they present, the role of the school has been expanded to help society respond to these problems more effectively. As a society we have come to recognize the contributions that schools can make as promoters of personal adjustment and guardians of the physical health of children. Consequently, the role of the school has expanded beyond a limited focus on basic academic skills to encompass concern about a range of social problems that threaten the psychological adjustment and physical well-being of children.

In addition to understanding and addressing the problems of distressed families that may interfere with school functioning, school psychologists can also look to families as an important resource in carrying out the educational mission of the school. Efforts to identify and build upon family strengths to improve the functioning of children at school require ways to assess and remediate interactional processes with family. By joining forces with and involving families, school psychologists increase the likelihood of understanding and having some influence on the factors that may mediate related adjustment difficulties. In addition, by involving the family as partners the schools have available the opportunity to reinforce their efforts in the home. For example, early childhood education programs such as Head Start have long recognized and capitalized on the important role the family can play in promoting children's cognitive and motor development. For similar reasons, federal and state laws (e.g., PL 94–172 and PL 99–457) mandate parental involvement in planning educational programs for their children, particularly those with special needs. Even distressed families are not *ipso facto* incapable of effectively nurturing their children. Many families that are impaired by multiple problems continue to promote an orientation toward high achievement, a favorable self-evaluation, social competence, prosocial behavior, self-control, and effective strategies for solving problems and moderating emotional distress. Even families in which the quality of functioning may be less than optimal can be invaluable resources to school psychologists.

Although dysfunctional families can develop a mutually beneficial collaboration with school staff around problems of school adjustment, differences among families in domains and levels of competence must be understood and calculated as part of the collaborative equation. It is important to assess accurately their strengths and weaknesses in order to develop a contract around collaboration that will work. Initial efforts to assess domains of family competence took the form of seeking patterns that distinguish clinical from nonlabeled families in the quality of relationships and the processes through which they operated (Riskind, 1982; Walsh, 1982). Riskind (1982) found that no single pattern of relationship or operational processes significantly differentiated normal from dysfunctional families. Moreover, functional families do not all look alike. Researchers have observed much diversity among families labeled competent and normal (Lewis, Beavers, Gossett, & Phillips, 1976). Competent family functioning and its sequelae, healthy development of children and marital satisfaction, can be achieved through different processes. Many different patterns, arrangements, structures, and processes can lead to high levels of functioning and good outcomes for family members.

Evaluating Family Functioning

Effective family functioning can be described in terms of coordinated adaptive responses fashioned to deal with a significant stressor that impacts on the entire family. Ability to utilize community resources and to collaborate with community institutions are also marks of family competence. Such competence is a derivative of skills and patterns families develop in dealing with the tasks of family life enumerated before: management of internal family relationships and balancing between adaptation to change and maintenance of continuity and managing personal relationships with nuclear and extended family and friends. Effectiveness in functioning requires team work, the fashioning of interdependent roles, and the formation and execution of an implicit agreement about goals and strategies. Under the rubic of effective family functioning is included such dimensions as emotional support, open communication, loyalty, cohesion, flexible problem solving, conflict resolution, existence of family hierarchy, strong parental coalition, parental involvement in monitoring and socializing children, and efficient decision making within the family. When families function effectively, they are able to set aside conflicts and diversions of their own interest for the sake of family unity. Competence in families with school-aged children may be especially evident in the approach the family takes to its socialization and child-rearing functions. Competent families modify expectations so that they are congruent with and appropriate to abilities and resources of family members. Several dimensions stand out as especially important indices of effective family functioning:

1. *Support.* Family members behave toward one another in a way that reflects support, intimacy, and caring.

2. *Cohesion.* Family members collaborate and work jointly in handling normative demands of daily living and in responding to crisis.

3. *Differentiation.* Family respects each member's personal need for autonomy and privacy but at the same time reaches out to communicate with empathy and candor.

4. *Flexibility.* The family adapts over time, flexibly realigns roles, and redistributes tasks as the demands on the family members change and as children mature and develop.

5. *Order and use of rituals.* The family creates a semblance of normality in situations that are sometimes abnormal such as divorce or serious chronic illness. In these cases the family maintains its routines, customs, and celebrations that involve children along with adults as fully as possible and when necessary develops new routines or rituals to provide a foundation for family togetherness and to create a sense of order in family life.

This list of domains is not exhaustive nor are the items mutually exclusive. They do, however, represent key indices of family competence, and together they constitute a sensitive barometer of the resources and intervention targets in working with families around problems of school adjustment. Although the constructs presented previously concerning interdependence, stability, and change introduce ways of thinking about family functioning, questions may remain about how to apply these ideas to generate a picture of family life. Given this theoretical prescription, it is important then to figure out how we can assess the extent to which families excel in any of these domains or the extent to which they may exhibit deficits amenable to training, education, consultation, or other forms of intervention. Professionals experienced in working with families often rely on dimensions of family functioning derived from family systems theory to construct an implicit framework for evaluating families. Such a framework may not be as evident to those less experienced in thinking from a systems perspective. For that reason, a sample framework used to train psychology and social work interns for family-focused work with families of children with cancer or sickle cell disease is included in Insert A. These provide an explicit approach to operationalizing general systems concepts for the purpose of assessing families. In other words, they illustrate how systems concepts can be used to summarize features of family functioning deemed important by family systems theory. The family rating scales can be used by school psychologists and social workers as a tool for recording impressions of a family and to document the family's strengths and limitations. Documenting the family's areas of competence via these rating scales is a good starting point in the planning of family interventions. The domains captured in the rating scale have implications for how the family might be approached by outsiders, how they might respond, and the coping styles they are most likely to employ in confronting difficult situations.

Family-Focused Approaches to School-Related Problems. Learning problems and the discrepancy between a child's potential to achieve and actual achievement are among the most thorny problems facing educators (Green, 1989). Typically, when a child experiences learning difficulty in school, the initial response is to consider what resource within the school can be brought to bear in remediating the difficulty. Less frequently is the initial response

Family Interview Rating Form
University of Michigan
Family Development Project

Family Name

Date

Part A
FAMILY ATMOSPHERE DURING THE INTERVIEW

Please rate the psychological climate experienced with family during the interview. To what extent did you experience the family in the following ways:

Friendly	9 8 7 6 5 4 3 2 1	Hostile
Relaxed	9 8 7 6 5 4 3 2 1	Tense
Emotional	9 8 7 6 5 4 3 2 1	Unemotional
Disclosing Personally	9 8 7 6 5 4 3 2 1	Guarded Secretive
Invested in interview	9 8 7 6 5 4 3 2 1	Uninvested
Humorous	9 8 7 6 5 4 3 2 1	Serious, Sober
Orderly	9 8 7 6 5 4 3 2 1	Chaotic

Part B
FAMILY INTERACTION STYLES

Please rate the following qualities of the family based on observations of their interactions and comments made during the interview.

Supportive	9 8 7 6 5 4 3 2 1	Hostile
Differentiated	9 8 7 6 5 4 3 2 1	Undifferentiated
Cohesive	9 8 7 6 5 4 3 2 1	Distant
High Control	9 8 7 6 5 4 3 2 1	Low Control
High Parental Involvement	9 8 7 6 5 4 3 2 1	Low Parental Involvement
Strong Parental Coalition	9 8 7 6 5 4 3 2 1	Weak Parental Coalition
Flexible, Adaptive	9 8 7 6 5 4 3 2 1	Rigid, Unchanging
Open To Help	9 8 7 6 5 4 3 2 1	Closed/Help

centered on how to utilize the family as a resource in dealing with the problem. Awareness of the crucial role played by families in the well-being of children has stimulated a variety of methods for working with families. These include systemic therapy with individual families, multifamily groups, family network meetings, home visits, multiagency consultations around a specific family, parent education, and preventive programs of support for families in distress (Speck & Attneave, 1973). To what extent can these models be adopted by schools to address issues of school adjustment? Clearly, family-focused services are attractive to school staff because of growing evidence demonstrating their beneficial effects on the child's development. Education-based programs that target intervention on the family as well as the child are more effective in achieving their goals than programs that focus on the child alone (Shonkoff & Hauser-Cram, 1987). A notable example is the Parent Advisor program that offers ongoing family support and counseling for families of developmentally delayed and physically impaired children. The program achieved remarkable improvement in the children's language development and general school adjustment by providing assistance to the family in coping with problems that created significant strain in family life (Buchan, Clemerson, & Davis, 1988).

Because of the complexity of the issues, embarking on a family-oriented approach is not to be undertaken lightly. It involves dealing with and resolving several dilemmas regarding the nature of the relationship between the family and the school. Sometimes adoption of a family-oriented stance is made difficult because of the incompatible roles school staffs are required to play. For example, out of desire to protect children from dysfunctional and abusive parents, schools are legally required to monitor and report suspected child abuse and neglect. Similarly, schools may be required to act as an enforcement agency with respect to child immunization, truancy, or drug abuse. These incompatible functions sometimes place the school in an adversarial relation with the family who may come to view school staff with suspicion. The absence of trust makes family-focused intervention difficult at best. Families also may have grave concerns that intimate and sometimes embarrassing details of their lives will become known by persons in their social worlds with whom they interact regularly. For these reasons, the use of family-focused intervention can be risky for both the family and the school. The schools must develop practices and guidelines regarding confidentiality that adequately safeguard the family's privacy and specify ahead of time the limits of confidentiality. No matter how effective the protection of privacy, the trust and confidence on the part of the family may be not great enough to make family-focused work possible. In these cases referral to collaborating family therapists outside the school may be a preferred strategy. Clearly the effort expended to resolve these dilemmas is well worth the potential benefit. In the long run schools that help the family provide an adequate environment for the child contribute to the success of their educational mission.

Whereas the use of interventions modeled strictly after family therapy may not be appropriate for school psychologists, there are approaches already within their repertoire that can be transformed or altered somewhat to incorporate a family systems perspective. The effectiveness of teacher conferences and consultation might be increased if the school adopted a family approach (Fish & Jain, 1985). In addition, the increased use of home visits can be a valuable extension of existing services.

CONCLUSION

In adopting a family systems perspective in dealing with school-age children, we must caution against the tendency to take a hostile attitude toward and attribute blame to the family when a child experiences adjustment problems in school (Kaslow & Cooper, 1978; Lusterman, 1985). Given the available evidence, it would be simplistic and premature to assert that associations between family dysfunction and problems of school adjustment mean that family functioning is the major etiological or causal factor. In addition, a truly systemic formulation emphasizes the role of individual, familial, and institutional factors in accounting for problems of school adjustment. This is a social psychological perspective. For example, the discrepancies and conflicts between the needs of the individual and the needs of the educational systems, the conflict of school and family culture, may be at the core of adjustment problems (Pharr & Barbarin, 1981). The likelihood of reciprocal determinism in this case must also be considered. For example, the occurrence of problems such as dyslexia, learning disabilities, underachievement, or conduct problems may reverberate throughout the family and itself precipitate parent–child conflict, excessive control, hostility or withdrawal, and poor family communication (Ditton, Green, & Singer, 1987; Humphries & Bauman, 1980). Accordingly, problems of school adjustment may precede and contribute to negative family relations and to problems within the family. For this reason the family itself may be in need of support. The school must resist the inevitable temptation to absolve itself of any role in a child's difficulty and impute responsibility of the difficulty totally to the family. Such a posture is not only incorrect; it also opens the possibility the school may consider its hands tied. If the school is unable to accept its contribution to the problem, as part of the system interacting with the child and family, it is less likely to visualize its proper role in working toward a solution.

ACKNOWLEDGMENTS

Preparation of this Chapter was made possible by a Faculty Scholar Award from the WT Grant Foundation and Grant #1R01 HD23968 from the National Institute of Child Health and Human Development.

REFERENCES

Ackerman, N. W. (1958). *Psychodynamics of family life.* New York: Basic Books.

Amerikaner, M. H., & Omizo, M. M. (1984). Family interaction and learning disabilities. *Journal of Learning Disabilities, 17,* 540–543.

Barbarin, O. (1983). Coping with ecological transitions by Black families: A psychosocial model. *Journal of Community Psychology, 11,* 308–322.

Baumrind, D. (1966). Effects of authoritative control on child behavior. *Child Development, 37,* 887–907.

Baumrind, D. (1971). Current patterns of parental authority. *Developmental Psychology Monographs, 4,* 1–102.

Bertalannfy, L. von (1968). *General systems theory.* New York: Braziller.

Bowen, M. (1978). *Family therapy in clinical practice.* New York: Jason Aronson.

Buchan, L., Clemerson, J., & Davis, H. (1988). Working with families of children with special needs: The parent adviser scheme. *Child Care, Health and Development, 14,* 81–91.

Campos, J. J., Barrett, K. C., Lame, M. E., Goldsmith, H. H., & Stenberg, C. (1985). Socioemotional development. In M. M. Haith & J. J. Campos (Eds.), *Handbook of child psychology: Infancy and developmental psychology* (pp. 783–916). New York: Wiley.

Clark, R. (1983). *Family life and school achievement: Why poor Black children succeed or fail.* Chicago: University of Chicago Press.

Commission on Work, Family, and Citizenship, William T. Grant Foundation. (1988). *The forgotten half: Pathways to success for America's youth and young families.* Washington, DC: WT Grant Commission.

Cramer, B. B. (1987). Objective and subjective aspects of parent–infant relations: An attempt at correlation between infant studies and clinical work. In J. D. Osofosky, (Ed.), *Handbook of infant development* (2d ed., pp. 1037–1058). New York: Wiley.

Ditton, P., Green, R. J., & Singer, M. T. (1987). Communication deviances: A comparison between parents of learning-disabled and normally achieving students. *Family Process, 26,* 75–87.

Fish, M. C., & Jain, S. (1985). A systems approach in working with learning disabled children: Implications for the school. *Journal of Learning Disabilities, 18,* 592–595.

Freidman, R. (1973). *Family roots of school learning and behavior disorders.* Springfield, IL: Charles C. Thomas.

Green, R. J. (1989). "Learning to learn" and the family system: New perspectives on underachievement and learning disorders. *Journal of Marital and Family Therapy, 15* (2), 187–203.

Gurman, A. S. (1970). The role of the family in underachievement. *Journal of School Psychology, 8* (1) 48–53.

Hill, R. (1949). *Families under stress.* New York: Harper & Row.

Humphries, T. W., & Bauman, W. (1980). Maternal child rearing attitudes associated with learning disabilities. *Journal of Learning Disabilities, 13,* 54–57.

Kaslow, F. W., & Cooper, B. (1978). Family therapy with the learning disabled child and his/her family. *Journal of Marriage and Family Counseling, 3,* 41–49.

Klein, R. S., Altman, M. A., Dreizen, K., Friedman, R., & Powers, L. (1981). Restructuring dysfunctional parental attitudes toward children's learning and behavior in school: Family-oriented psychoeducational therapy: Part I. *Journal of Learning Disabilities, 14,* 15–19.

Leff, J. P., & Vaughn, C. F. (1985). *Expressed emotion families: Its significance for mental illness.* New York: Guilford Press.

Lewis, J. M., Beavers, W. R., Gossett, J. T., & Phillips, V. A. (1976) *No single thread: Psychological health in family systems.* New York: Brunner-Mazel.

Lusterman, D. D. (1985). An ecosystemic approach to family–school problems. *The American Journal of Family Therapy, 13,* 22–30.

Margalit, M. (1982). Learning disabled children and their families: Strategies of extension and adaptation of family therapy. *Journal of Learning Disabilities, 15,* 594–595.

160

BARBARIN

McCubbin, H. (1979). Integrading coping behavior in a family stress theory. *Journal of Marriage and the Family, 41,* 237–244.
Miller, D. R., & Westman, J. C. (1964). Reading disability as a condition of family stability. *Family Process, 1* (1), 66–76.
Minuchin, S., (1974). *Families and family therapy.* Cambridge, MA: Harvard University Press.
Minuchin, S., & Fishman, C. (1982). *Family therapy techniques.* Cambridge, MA: Harvard University Press.
Patterson, G. W. (1982). *Coercive family processes.* Eugene, OR: Castalia.
Pharr, O. M., & Barbarin, O. A. (1981). School suspensions: A problem of personal environment fit. In O. Barbarin, P. Good, O. Pharr, & J. Siskind (Eds.), *Institutional racism and community competence* (pp. 76–90). Rockville, MD: U.S. Department of Health and Human Services.
Reiss, D. (1981). *Family's construction of reality.* Cambridge, MA: Harvard University Press.
Reiss, D., & Oliveri, M. E. (1980). Family paradigm and family coping: A proposal for linking the family's intrinsic adaptive capacities to its responses to stress. *Family Relations, 29,* 431–444.
Riskind, J. (1982) Research on nonlabeled families: A longitudinal study. In F. Walsh (Ed.), *Normal family process* (pp. 67–93). New York: Guilford Press.
Sameroff, A. J., & Chandler, M. J. (1975). Perinatal risk and the continuum of caretaking casualty. In F. Horowitz, M. Hetherington, S. Scarr-Salapatek, & G. Siegel (Eds.), *Review of child development research* (Vol. 4, pp. 187–244). Chicago: University of Chicago Press.
Shonkoff, J. P., & Hauser-Cram, P. (1987). Early intervention for disabled infants and their families—A quantitative analysis. *Pediatrics, 80,* 650–658.
Speck, R., & Attneave, C. (1973). *Family networks.* New York: Vintage Books.
Walsh, F. (1982). Conceptualizations of normal family functioning. In F. Walsh (Ed.), *Normal family processes* (pp. 3–42). New York: Guilford Press.
Wilson, W. J. (1987). *The truly disadvantaged: The inner city, the underclass, and public policy.* Chicago: University of Chicago Press.

Glossary for Constructs:
FAMILY INTERVIEW RATING FORM
University of Michigan
Family Development Project

Part A:

FRIENDLY/HOSTILE: Friendliness refers to the degree of warmth emanating from the family. Did they make you feel at home, did they treat you as a guest, were they solicitous and did they look out for your comfort (9,8,7) or did they let you fend for yourself (3,4,5)? Were they happy and pleased (1), accepting (7,6), indifferent (4,5), or resentful, angry, sultry (1,2)? Did they show irritation or impatience about your being there (3,4)?

RELAXED/TENSE: How anxious or at ease did the family seem to feel about the situation? Did the parents continuously show discernible signs of tension, nervousness, or anxiety (9,8,7), occasional or moderate anxiety (6,5,4), or were they completely at east except for a brief period of discomfort (3,2,1)?

EMOTIONAL/UNEMOTIONAL: Did family members show or openly express emotions of sadness or joy, outbursts of crying, laughing throughout the interview even when questions or topics were not particularly evocative (9,8,7)? Were they even tempered and somewhat emotionally expressive, particularly during emotionally evocative topics (6,5,4), or were they very rational and highly controlled throughout the interview (3,2,1)?

DISCLOSING PERSONALLY/GUARDED: Did the family openly reveal private and sometimes not very positive information about self (9,8,7), or did the family respond to question fully for the most part but did not volunteer information (i.e., answer only what was asked) (6,5,4), or did they seem suspicious, secretive, unusually guarded, and did not respond fully to questions, giving the impression that they were withholding information or that there were secrets they did not want to disclose (3,2,1)?

INVESTED/UNINVESTED: Did some family members, particularly parents, seem eager and motivated to respond to question, putting forth a lot of energy to recall information responsive to questions (9,8,7), or did they seem somewhat motivated and willing (6,5,4), or did they seem disinterested, preoccupied, somewhere else mentally, and unwilling to put much energy into responding to question (3,2,1)?

HUMOROUS/SERIOUS, SOBER: Did the family or significant family members overuse humor to avoid dealing with problem, make light of everything, not take anything seriously (9,8), or did the family seem to have a good sense of humor, make light of themselves and their foibles, appreciate the light side of life and not take themselves or their circumstances too seriously and use humor to keep things in perspective rather than to avoid problems (7,6,5), or did they seem bereft of a sense of humor, evidence little or no smiling or lightheartedness, and approach the world with a serious demeanor (4,3), or was the family completely humorless, pessimistic, and sad (2,1)?

ORDERLY/CHAOTIC: To what extent was the interview able to be carried out in an orderly fashion, with the family tracking and responding to questions posed (9,8,7) with few significant interruptions from the outside (telephones, visitors); or within (television blaring, noisy environment, family unprepared to begin interview) that the family resolves quickly (6,5,4), or with multiple preventable interruptions or jumping all over the place in content because of failure to track and respond to the interviewers' questions) (3,2,1)?

Part B

SUPPORTIVE/HOSTILE is based on the extent to which family interactions are characterized by overt caring, praise, reassurance, and verbal or nonverbal expressions of love, affirmation, or valuing (9,8), a generally caring attitude or nonovert but implied acceptance (7,6), neutral regard that is neither positive nor negative (5,4), affective flatness or indifference (3), or criticism, faultfinding, putdowns, disqualifying statements, bitter recriminations, direct or veiled hostility (2,1).

DIFFERENTIATED/UNDIFFERENTIATED DIMENSIONS is evidenced in tolerance of differences among family members, comfort with disagreement or lack of unity, respect for individual autonomy; members speaking their own minds; emotional closeness and mutual concern combined with respect for individual autonomy; (9,8,7); slight tendency to minimize family differences balanced by modest tolerance of differences among family members in attitudes or behavior, the existence of different expectation depending on age and capacities of members, occurrence but resistance to cognitive binding of family members by the family unit (i.e., coercion to act or speak in lockstep with family), and interruptions, willingness to talk openly about problems rather than being secretive and lack of conflict resolution (6,5); emotional stuck-togetherness, speaking for each other, continuing each other's ideas, interruptions, emotional overinvolvement and excessive identification with one another, family members' reports of being preoccupied with family when separated from them, loss of individual identity, expectations of each member are the same (3,4); triangulation, scapegoating, and alternate between being overly close and distant from one another; similarity of family reactions, contagion or sharing of emotional responses, high level of cognitive binding, coercive control through guilt and blaming and pseudomutuality, a pretense of being close or alienated (1,2).

COHESIVE/DISTANT is the extent to which the family describes itself as having frequent joint activities and enjoying being with one another (9,8,7); or do little to create or avoid time together and seem satisfied when together; do many ordinary things together (e.g., meals, vacations, church service) (6,5,4); operate completely independently, each member in his/her own separate world, have few common activities, spend little time together, and even avoid contact (3,2,1).

HIGH/LOW CONTROL refers to authoritarian, despotic control, discernible leadership by which any deviations from the party line are brought back to position through coercion, or persuasion (9,8,7); lack of leadership and direction, family is without rules, parents adopt a laissez-faire attitude, the situation is chaotic with no one responsibly taking charge (3,2,1).

HIGH/LOW PARENTAL INVOLVEMENT is evidenced by parents knowing a great deal about what is happening in their children's lives, attending school activities, taking an active role in imparting values and guiding, becoming familiar with friends and other people in their world (9,8,7); or being completely shut out of the child's life and experiences outside of the home (3,2,1).

STRONG/WEAK PARENTAL COALITION is the degree parents work together or align with children versus other parent, parental agreement, cooperation (cohesion in the dyad; could be with one parent and another adult in the executive system of the family. If no other adult in the family, respond with NA) open to help/difficulty in accepting help: impression by what is said, use of resources.

FLEXIBLE/RIGID rating assesses the family's ability to tolerate ambiguity, accept and deal with the unexpected by generating and testing alternative solutions for new or unanticipated problems, to seek out and consider new resources when available ones are inadequate, to roll with the punches (9,8,7) or be unable to respond to change, to try new ways, stuck with old unworkable solutions (3,2,1).

OPEN/CLOSED TO HELP FROM OUTSIDE assesses the extent to which the family is able to acknowledge that it may face demands that exceed its capacity to respond and accepts help (9,8,7); is unable to admit need and ask for help but is willing to accept it, to let others enter its life space if an outsider defines a problem and offers aid (6,5,4); is so private, guarded, unable to admit need, fixated on the belief that it should be self-sufficient, unable to ask for or accept help (3,2,1).

Note: If evidence for a domain is insufficient, respond with NA.

7

ORGANIZATIONAL INFLUENCES ON THE PRACTICE OF PSYCHOLOGY IN SCHOOLS

Robert J. Illback
Spalding University

Increasingly, school psychologists recognize that the process of schooling involves complex interactions between a range of personal, social, and ecological variables, occurring in an organizational context (Maher, Illback, & Zins, 1984). This recognition has led to concern that school psychologists be able to conceptualize problems and psychological interventions from an organizational perspective (Illback & Maher, 1984) and become more active participants in planned organizational change in schools and community settings (Maher & Illback, 1983). Seen as complementary to individual- and group-level approaches, the practice of organizational-level school psychology can assist in the development and improvement of the school organization as a service delivery system.

Following a brief description of the principles and history of industrial/organizational psychology, this chapter delineates characteristics of schools as human service organizations, within which the practice of school psychology occurs. An integrative perspective that specifies organizational domains, functions, and elements is provided to facilitate discussion about organizational assessment and intervention strategies. Through a case illustration (preschool handicapped services), the perspective is applied to problems faced by school psychologists at individual (e.g., child, teacher), small group, (e.g., classroom, family), and organizational (e.g., department, building, district) levels.

FOUNDATIONS IN INDUSTRIAL/
ORGANIZATIONAL PSYCHOLOGY

Industrial and organizational (I/O) psychology has evolved from various sub-disciplines within psychology, including applied, personnel, psychometrics, organizational, vocational, engineering, management science, human factors, and systems psychology, to name but a few. From this diverse background, I/O psychology has become a highly developed area with strong theoretical and conceptual foundations, based in systematic psychology. Concommitantly, there is an extensive and growing literature on the practice of I/O psychology. Testimony to the breadth of the field as a distinct specialty area is found in the content coverage of the *Handbook of Industrial and Organizational Psychology* (Dunnette, 1976), as seen in Table 7.1.

Industrial/organizational psychology is one of four applied professional specialty areas recognized by the American Psychological Association, with clinical, counseling, and school psychology. I/O psychologists are trained in schools of psychology, business, management, or administrative science within a scientist-professional model, with emphasis on general psychological science, research design and methodology, quantitative and qualitative methodology, and psychological measurement.

According to the Specialty Guidelines for the Delivery of Services by Industrial/Organizational Psychologists, I/O psychologists also receive training in applications of their discipline to "problems of organizations and problems of individuals and groups in organizational settings. The purpose of such applications to the assessment, development, or evaluation of individuals, groups, or organizations is to enhance the effectiveness of these individuals, groups, or organizations." (American Psychological Association, 1981). Examples of problem areas in which I/O psychologists practice include selection and placement of employees, organization development, training and development, personnel research, motivation, and work environment design.

In general, the methods and strategies of I/O psychology parallel school psychological applications. I/O psychologists observe and describe problems of individuals, groups, and organizations; measure, analyze, and hypothesize about these problems; and develop intervention programs to bring about change. Although the unit of analysis and setting for these problems may be different, given that I/O psychologists typically work in business and industrial settings, I/O work is comparable to school psychological services in its diversity and broad-based applicability.

Most central to this chapter is the knowledge base within I/O psychology regarding organizations, including characteristics, design, and methods for promoting change and development. Based within general systems theory (Bertalanffy, 1950; Miller, 1965), organizations are described by I/O psychologists as systems of interdependent components that work in harmony. Var-

TABLE 7.1
Content of Handbook of Industrial and Organizational Psychology (1976)

A. Theory development and theory application
B. Research strategies and research methodology
C. Theories of individual and organizational behavior
D. Job and task analysis
E. Attributes of persons
F. Taxonomies
G. Engineering psychology
H. Occupational and career choice and persistence
I. Individual and group performance measurement
J. Validity and validation strategies
K. Attributes of organizations
L. Communication in organizations
M. Organizational socialization processes
N. Behavioral responses by individuals
O. Job attitudes and satisfaction
P. Problem solving and decision making
Q. Assessment of persons
R. Selection and selection research
S. Strategies of training and development
T. Strategies of organization change
U. Consumer psychology
V. Cross-cultural issues

ious levels of systems, from the suprasystem (molar) level of large societal institutions to the subsystems (molecular) level of individuals and small groups, are seen as integrally related to one another. As open systems, organizations engage in a continuous process of change in response to surroundings (adaptation), and therefore changes in one system lead to changes in related systems. Organizational systems engage in self-regulation and maintenance activities, seek homeostasis, and grow and develop over time (Berrien, 1976).

Organizations may vary in dimensions such as size, complexity, formality, and purpose. However, all organizations share common features by exhibiting identifiable boundaries, patterned behavioral regularities, systems of authority and decision making, communications systems, and mission (Hall, 1977). Any organization can be described in relation to these dimensions.

For example, a business organization such as a manufacturing firm has boundaries delineated through: (a) its mission statement, expressed in documents such as articles of incorporation and annual reports to shareholders; (b) the physical environment in which it is housed (e.g., factory production area, administrative offices); (c) its relationship to other organizations and individuals in its environment (e.g., suppliers, consumers, regulators); and (d) the resources (human, financial, informational, technological) that make up the organization and their relationship to one another (e.g., subunits within the organization defined by function, such as production, research and development, sales, and management).

Also, people in the organization engage in behavioral routines established by their roles and functions and interact with one another in predictable ways as they carry out responsibilities. The organization has an organizational chart that specifies lines of authority for decisions the organization must make on a regular basis. The careful observer will note that there are informal human influence processes at work in the organization that affect decision making, as well. Information is regularly transmitted across the boundaries of subunits of the organization (e.g., departments), both in a formal hierarchical manner and in less formal (and sometimes unpredictable) ways. Actual communication and decision making in an organization may or may not reflect the formal authority structure.

Organizational mission refers to a shared set of beliefs and attitudes regarding the overall task that the organization has been established to accomplish (Katz & Kahn, 1966). Most organizations promulgate mission and goal statements. To the extent these are explicit, operational policies and procedures can be derived to enhance goal attainment by focusing organizational effort.

In business organizations, profit and economic viability are central to organizational goal statements, from which flow more explicit actions, such as specifying the markets that will be targeted, the kinds of products or services that will be provided, and the overall vision of the organization in relation to related businesses and the business environment as a whole. Human service (typically nonprofit) organizations, such as schools, are more difficult to describe in terms of mission, as intended outcomes focus on ambiguous concepts such as adjustment, adaptation, thinking processes, and values; at best, these are difficult to specify, measure, and link together.

SCHOOL ORGANIZATIONS: INFLUENCES ON PRACTICE

This section discusses the special features of schools as human service organizations and their influence on the practice of school psychology.

Human Service Organizations

Katz and Kahn (1966) described four broad, overlapping classes of organizations in society. *Productive or economic organizations* are those that create wealth, manufacture goods, and provide services to the public such as food, clothing, and shelter. These can be further subdivided into farming and mining, manufacture and processing, and service and communication. *Adaptive organizations* create knowledge, develop and test theories, and apply information to problems, such as research and development programs in universities. Organizations concerned with the control and coordination of resources, such as regulatory agencies, political parties, labor unions and other special interest/function groups, are labeled *managerial/political organizations.*

The fourth type, *maintenance (human service) organizations,* are those that involve: (a) socialization of people into various roles and functions in society, such as educational, religious, and other training institutions; and (b) restoration functions, as in health, welfare, reform, and rehabilitation. These activities are aimed at preventing society from disintegrating and can therefore be seen as extensions of the family system. Schools serve both socialization and rehabilitative functions in society. Within the education community, of course, elements of governmental, production, and knowledge generation are also evident.

In their social, educative, and rehabilitative roles, *human service organizations* (e.g., schools) all assume that: (a) clients have needs that emanate from developmental, familial, and societal tasks and demands; (b) meaningful helping activities (e.g., teaching) can be delineated and targeted to facilitate growth and development; (c) services can be comprehensive and accessible to all who are eligible (e.g., school-age children); (d) services can be integrated in a systemic fashion (e.g., K–12 curriculum scope and sequence); and (e) service providers can be accountable to consumers and society (Baker, 1974).

Unique Features of School Organizations

Fullan, Miles, and Taylor (1980) described features of school organizations that distinguish them from other human service organizations. This uniqueness can often lead to organizational complexity, uncertainty, unresponsiveness, and occasionally immobilization in accomplishing the mission of educating children.

Social, Political, Cultural Factors. As open social systems, schools organize themselves to respond to inputs from a range of external sources. The regulatory/bureaucratic environment is one such source and consists of a broad array of federal and state legislative mandates (e.g., education for handicapped and disadvantaged students, school reform), judicial mandates (e.g., desegregation, equal access, equalization of effort), department of education implementing regulations (e.g., accreditation standards, program guidelines), and less formal directives and interactions with members of the bureaucracy. At the local school district level, little is undertaken without considering the parameters established by the regulatory environment, because program funding is often at stake. In fact, many school programs are explicitly designed to conform to the standards and guidelines established by the bureaucracy, resulting in a "patchwork quilt" of programs and practices at the local level.

Another external source of influence for schools is the education community as a whole, consisting of professional and paraprofessional groups, organizations, and individuals that affect the manner in which school personnel go about their task. For example, regional-, state-, and national-level organizations representing teacher, administrator, and school board groups are active in promoting standards and guidelines for practice. Such groups have been instrumental in the school reform movement by publishing high-profile reports detailing various problems faced by public schools, such as low achievement scores, high dropout rates, functional illiteracy, and the like. Similarly, school organizations tend to be inextricably linked to training institutions (e.g., colleges of education), where many staff members pursue advanced study while they work. More formalized influences exist when groups of school employees form unions that bargain collectively with management on issues of compensation and working conditions.

The cultural, political, and social context of the local community is a further source of powerful influence on the school system, despite widely varying circumstances. Schools in rural, agrarian settings differ from those in urban areas with respect to subcultural values, tax base and per pupil expenditure, availability of goods and services, and prospective employment opportunities. In many rural communities, the school system is heavily politicized because it is the primary employer and one of the central institutions that define the community (along with local government and churches). In contrast, schools in urban and suburban areas may play a different role in their communities, expressing the subcultural norms and beliefs attendant to these settings. In both rural and urban settings, the influence of the community as a whole permeates the school operation.

The impact of local events can be most readily seen through the local Board of Education, which governs the operation of the school and is the formal mechanism that the community expresses its wishes regarding the education of its children, given the parameters imposed by other institutions (e.g., federal and state regulations). Local Boards of Education set policy, hire superintendents and staff, and are involved in every phase of program operation. In addition to curricular issues, Boards of Education and school management must concern themselves with transportation, cafeteria programs, personnel matters, revenue generation and expenditure (fiscal responsibility), athletics, buildings and grounds, and a host of seemingly noneducational matters. Because all these decisions affect members of the public (e.g., setting of tax rates), the local community seeks to exert influence over these decision processes, often leading to competition, conflict, and tension. It is not unusual, in fact, to find that community issues not technically related to schooling have impact on the dynamics of the school–community interface.

Social and political influence processes operate also at the individual, classroom group, school building, departmental, and school system levels through all the interactions between community members and school staff. External change facilitators, such as school psychologists, may be insensitive to these subtle processes unless they immerse themselves in the system.

Overpermeable Boundaries. Given these external influences, school organizations are highly susceptible to high-rate inputs that may be conflicting, inconsistent, or otherwise troublesome. School personnel, especially teachers, are continually asked to accommodate to new regulations or procedures, revised methods and materials, the latest trend in instruction, dissatisfied parents, scheduling and logistical problems, increasingly specialized duties and responsibilities, special requests, and various other interruptions and discontinuities. These greatly affect the educational process because schools are prone to have overpermeable boundaries, a characteristic associated with high job stress, overload, and dysfunctional organizations (Forman, 1981).

On the one hand, overpermeable boundaries can cause immobilization within the school organization by making personnel fearful of taking actions that may alienate one or another constituency in the natural environment. On the other hand, overpermeable boundaries make school personnel vulnerable to the latest political or educational fads, that may not be grounded in sound instructional design and/or may be inconsistent with current successful practice within the organization.

Goal Diffuseness, Low Accountability, High Autonomy. Goal diffuseness refers to poorly specified input (e.g., teaching strategies), throughput (e.g., learning processes), and output (e.g., achievement, adjustment) variables. School organizations often rely on mission and goal statements that are global in their orientation and that serve political but not necessarily accountability functions. For example, a sentiment often stated is that the purpose of schooling is to enable "each child to attain his or her fullest potential." Although admirable, this is hardly evaluable because it is impossible to determine what an individual's full potential may be. From the perspective of the school, however, this built-in ambiguity may serve to quell criticism of the organization itself for the perceived underachievement of students and reduce scrutiny and control by external sources (a goal of all organizations).

Loose Means–Ends Relationship. A related problem is that it is not always possible to link school programs and services to goal attainment with any degree of certainty, a necessary prerequisite if school organizations are to be held accountable for educational outcomes. As in any natural environment, there are so many variables operating in schools that can account for changes (multiple treatment interference), the design problems inherent in attributing change to specific teaching and learning practices are daunting (Brophy & Good, 1986). Nonetheless, there are available methods for this task within the emergent field of school program evaluation (Illback, Zins, Maher, & Greenberg, 1989). School program evaluation approaches seek to improve organizational functioning through activities such as evaluability assessment, program (treatment) specification, needs assessment, implementation evaluation, and outcome determination. However, school organizations have resisted program planning and evaluation efforts, and departments of research, planning, and evaluation are generally found only in large school systems where their efforts focus on high-profile projects and programs (often federally funded).

Minimum Interdependence of Employees and Lack of Competition. A characteristic of school organizations that can lead to fragmented, disjointed programming, misunderstanding, and conflict is low degree of interdependence between employees. This is especially notable at the level of the classroom, the most fundamental unit of analysis for actual teaching and learning. Teachers are among the most isolated of all professionals in that they spend almost their entire day with students, with minimal time for planning and virtually no time for systematic interaction with other professionals. They are assigned a group of students for a period of time, given some general guidelines and materials, visited rarely, and receive little performance feedback about their activities from supervisors (Forman & Cecil, 1986). Because there is no direct means for measuring teacher performance in regard to pupil achievement, nor is there universal agreement as to what practices constitute "good teaching" (although a database for this is now beginning to emerge), teachers largely depend on their own judgment as to the appropriateness and success of their teaching. Efforts to address this problem have focused on team teaching to increase collegial interaction and planning, the development of "quality circles" to promote standards and innovation at the classroom level (Maher & Illback, 1984), and the use of master teachers and "clinical supervision" to improve performance feedback. Nevertheless, isolation and low interdependence remain pervasive problems.

A final characteristic of public schools is that, in general, they hold the franchise for public education, with the exception of parochial, private, and home schooling options, which are unavailable to many citizens. As such, there are no natural competitors in the environment to serve as motivation for improving organizational performance. This may lead to complacency and resistance to innovation. Recognizing this, some have suggested alternatives such as tuition tax credits, voucher systems, and special incentive plans to increase the competitive atmosphere within school organizations and thereby improve performance (National Commission on Excellence in Education, 1983).

APPLICATIONS OF ORGANIZATIONAL SCHOOL PSYCHOLOGY

In this section, a perspective from which to view school organizations is presented, followed by a discussion of organizational assessment and intervention strategies in relation to educational services and programs. A case illustration demonstrates how these strategies can be applied at individual, small group, classroom, building, and school system levels.

School Organizations: An Integrative Perspective

A model for viewing schools as organizations that can lead to more effective intervention strategies is provided by Maher, Illback, and Zins (1984) and shown in Fig. 7.1. The model posits three interactive domains of organization functions and their related elements: structure, process, and behavior. The constitutent elements and the variables that comprise these, shown within each organizational domain, often are the targets for organizational change programs.

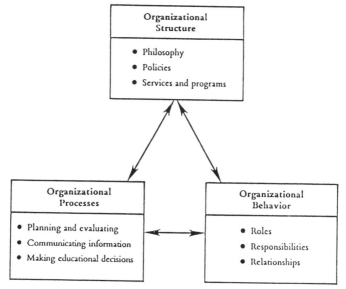

FIG. 7.1. Framework for viewing schools as organizations. From *Organizational psychology in the schools: A handbook for professionals* (p. 10) by C. A. Maher, R. J. Illback, & J. E. Zins, (1984), Springfield, IL: Charles C. Thomas. Copyright 1984 by Charles C. Thomas. Reprinted by permission.

Organizational Structure. Organizational structure refers to enduring and basic elements of the school organization, the foundation on which other functions rest. Schools provide structure in order to focus organizational processes and behavior. Structure is provided through philosophy, policy and procedures, and services and programs.

Organizational Philosophy emanates from mission and goal statements of the organization, as described earlier. For example, the mission statement of a Department of Student Services in a school system may state that the overall purposes of the department include: nondiscriminatory assessment of children with special needs; placement of identified children in the least restrictive educational environments; maximum integration of general, remedial, and special education instructional and related service programs; and recruitment, selection, and development of program professionals and paraprofessionals with broad-based instructional skills and the ability to interact effectively with one another.

Given the focus provided by the preceding mission statement, more specific *policies and procedures* are formulated to operationalize the overall perspective. Thus, in the area of student evaluation and classification, elaborate guidelines to ensure a broad database for decision making, the use of team approaches, and a process for conflict resolution are specified. Similarly, to ensure that sound and integrated instructional interventions are developed for each identified client, policies and procedures that describe the planned and ongoing collaboration between general and special educators, features of acceptable instructional approaches, and methods for regular review are stated.

Policies and procedures also articulate formal authority (power) relationships within the organization. A policy handbook in a school system, for example, states the authority (and limitations) of the Board of Education and its role in regard to the administration and operation of the school. The duties of the Superintendent, who serves at the pleasure of the Board, are also described. Documents are available that delineate lines of authority throughout the organization, including the "chain of command" (subordinate–superordinate relationships), possibly in the form of an organizational chart.

The specific *services and programs* provided by the organization, and their relationship to one another, comprise the third element of organizational structure. Table 7.2 provides a sample description of common educational services and programs organized into five subdomains: assessment, instruction, related, personnel development, and administrative services. These subdomains represent a generic means of categorizing seemingly disparate programs and practices, demonstrating how they are interrelated.

Specification of educational services and programs makes them more manageable, evaluable, and comprehensible to staff and others. Targeted structural interventions, as is described later, seek to improve organizational performance by enhancing these underlying elements of the school organization.

TABLE 7.2
Educational Services and Programs

Assessment services
- Psychoeducational assessment of children with learning and behavior problems
- Speech and language assessment
- District-wide assessment of pupil progress (standardized testing)
- Classroom-based informal assessment by teachers
- Annual review of an individual's IEP

Instructional services
- Classroom-based services delivered by a teacher
- Remedial reading and mathematics
- Career awareness and development
- Vocational education
- Special education
- Gifted and talented education
- Substance abuse education
- Computer education
- Social skills training
- Extracurricular activities

Related services
- Maintenance and custodial
- Secretarial and office support
- Community involvement
- Athletics
- Media
- School psychology
- Guidance and counseling
- Physical therapy
- Speech therapy
- Occupational therapy
- Health

Personnel development services
- Parent education and training
- In-service education for staff members
- Clinical supervision
- Peer review and peer consultation
- Self-supervision
- Employee individual action (goal) plans

Administrative services
- Program planning and evaluation
- Curriculum development and management
- Mediation and negotiation (conflict management)
- Management information system
- Records management
- Property management (buildings and grounds)
- Personnel management

Organizational Process. Organizational processes are ongoing actions (patterned behavioral regularities) that occur within the context of organizational structure. These processes allow for the enactment of policies, procedures and programs, in addition to providing stability (homeostasis) for the organization. As shown in Fig. 7.1, organizational processes include planning and evaluating, communicating information, and making decisions.

Actions involving *planning and evaluating* are central to effective and efficient delivery of educational services and programs. These processes refer to the ongoing management of resources within the school setting, including monitoring and revising existent programs and developing new ones. Teachers, for example, deliver services in classrooms and are therefore responsible for the self-management of the program they deliver (e.g., ninth-grade biology program). Based on the overall intent as understood from available curriculum documents, the teacher routinely plans and implements a sequence of lessons, assesses their impact on student learning, revises content and presentation accordingly, and then develops new materials and approaches to enhance the course. Similarly, the manager of the school psychological service program, the school psychologist, implements a building-based consultation program, reviews the effectiveness of the interventions developed as a consequence, and assesses the impact on related processes such as teacher and parent satisfaction and referral rate.

Actions involving *communication of information* are also highly salient in school organizations. Schools, which by their nature are in the business of information utilization, transmit a vast amount of both verbal and written information in a patterned manner on a regular basis. Information transmitted about students may include daily work, progress reports, attendance, participation in extracurricular activities, grade reports, and correspondence with parents. Teachers process information such as cafeteria menus, daily bulletins, curricular updates, attendance rosters, grade books, media forms, and instructional planning materials regularly. At the district level, central office personnel process fiscal reports, attendance and achievement data, policy revisions, employment-related documents (e.g., benefits), and curriculum material. School psychologists process referrals, test data, evaluation reports, intervention plans, and program documents. All these formal information processes yield extensive student, employee, and program records, which also need to be managed and accessed.

In addition to formal information transmission, there is an informal information process at work in school organizations that does not usually correspond directly to the established authority structure. People in schools are microcosms of the communities in which the school is embedded, and there are untold information connections between persons who would appear to be structurally unrelated. Sometimes these connections are obvious, such as the supervisor who is the spouse of one of the principals, or the teacher who is related to the superintendent. Oftentimes, however, the interpersonal connections are subtle and related to proximity (e.g., neighbors), history (e.g., growing up together), or circumstance (e.g., working on an extra-school project). An understanding of informal information networks within a particular school organization is essential to the change process.

Decision Making. The process of making decisions is the third element of organizational process. People in organizations make decisions daily. Teachers decide how to teach a particular lesson based on the information they have available to them. Administrators decide how to deal with problems of discipline and behavior. School psychologists decide which referrals to consider as priorities. Other types of decisions are more long term, such as deciding which curricular materials to adopt, which programs to fund or cut back, and how services can be most effectively organized.

There are certain regularities to decision processes, including clarifying the decision problem; specifying decision rules, procedures, and criteria; selecting a decision alternative; and assessing the decision outcome. Effective school organizations tend to be more systematic in this regard.

Organizational Behavior. This element relates to the activities, duties, and interactions people in schools exhibit as they provide services, communicate information, and make decisions. Organizations have been shown to have structure and process; it should not be forgotten that, most fundamentally, schools organizations are aggregations of people interacting in certain ways. The element of organizational behavior, then, seeks to portray individual actions as they occur in the context of structure and process.

In well-functioning organizations, each individual perceives clear guidance about the *role(s)* he or she is to perform (e.g., teacher, psychologist, principal). Some roles may be highly circumscribed, such as the business office worker who processes benefits data. However, many education roles are complex, involving responsibility for assorted program tasks and frequent crossing of boundaries between subunits of the organization. Organizational roles are prescribed by history and tradition (e.g., "we always did it this way"), needs and circumstances (e.g., new regulatory requirements), and personal preferences (e.g., particular employee strengths).

Responsibilities are more specific than roles, although they can be expected to derive from the overall role category that the person fulfills in the organization. Responsibilities are usually established through an explicit job description, but at the very least are communicated through systematic interaction with a superordinate, such as a direct supervisor (McInerney, 1985). For example, the key responsibilities of a school psychologist may include establishing and managing a referral system, evaluating students with special needs, planning and facilitating psychoeducational interventions, and consulting with administrators and parents. Ancillary responsibilities may include program planning and evaluation, training and supervision of paraprofessionals, and grant writing.

The final, and perhaps most essential, element of organizational behavior is *relationships*. Organizational health and survival is highly dependent on effective interactive between people in accomplishing the mission. This is overlooked by those who focus reform efforts exclusively on the technology or content of the educational process. Harmonious group interaction involves the ability to identify problems, share responsibilities, collaborate, and manage conflict situations.

Organizational Assessment and Intervention

Organizational change efforts are challenging to conceptualize and difficult to organize and implement. Often, these efforts meet with resistance as the school organization struggles to maintain homeostasis, leading to failure and frustration (Derr, 1976). Organizational change fails because of: (a) insufficient information about the problem areas and inadequate diagnosis (poor problem clarification); (b) inattention to organizational readiness for change; (c) simplistic intervention strategies and procedures; and (d) lack of follow up (Fullan, Miles, & Taylor, 1980). This section therefore provides a conceptual analysis of planned organizational change efforts in school settings that seeks to address the problems inherent in such endeavors.

Some assumptions that underlie this discussion include that: (a) School organizations are continually changing and evolving in response to both internal and external factors, implying the need to accurately perceive and utilize this ongoing process in the change effort; (b) change efforts that apply multiple methods and strategies are more likely to reflect organizational complexity than are approaches that rely on narrow methods and strategies targeted toward specific aspects of the organization, resulting in more meaningful and durable change; (c) successful change efforts involve balancing and controlling a large number of mediating variables involving people, procedures, and processes; (d) successful change efforts in schools are heavily dependent on timely, accurate, and continuous assessment information about organizational functioning; (e) some school organizations are more ready for change than others, and it may be appropriate to defer the change initiative until the organization can be made more hospitable to the intervention; (f) organizational change efforts may lead to unintended effects due to the interdependency of the organization's elements; (g) meaningful change is most likely to occur when people within the school organization achieve a sense of "ownership" of the organizational change effort; and (h) an overriding goal of planned organizational change in school organizations is the facilitation of self-evaluation and self-renewal processes, which become a part of the routine of a more functional organization. (For a more thorough discussion of these principles, see Illback & Zins, 1984). Reflection on these principles reveals that they bear a striking similarity to the active elements of psychotherapeutic change initiatives with individuals.

Case Illustration: Preschool Handicapped Services. For the purposes of describing the application of organizational change principles and procedures, the case of Public Law 99–457 (Education of the Handicapped Act Amendments of 1986) is used to illustrate an organizational problem presently confronting school organizations. Briefly stated, this legislation mandates a significant departure for schools from past practices by requiring that they identify and provide assessment and intervention services to children ages 3 to 5 with handicapping conditions. The organizational obstacles associated with this change are enormous, including problems of program structure (e.g., policies and procedures), integration with pre-existing programs (e.g., responsibilities and relationships), selection and support of staff members with proper expertise, determination of assessment technologies, and relevant educational programming that can be effective at this stage of development.

Organizational Diagnosis. As with individuals, effective organizational intervention is more likely to occur when reliable and valid information is available about the identified organizational problems (needs) and the context in which they are embedded. Organizational assessment may be the most important stage of the intervention process in that assessment culminates in selection of the variables that will be targeted for intervention and thereby focuses the change effort (Hersey & Blanchard, 1982).

Most of the writing in the area of organizational diagnosis of schools is found within the organizational development literature, beginning with the Project on Organization Development in Schools at Columbia University (Schmuck & Miles, 1971). There have been a number of other organization development initiatives with elements of diagnosis, most prominent of which is the ongoing work of Schmuck and associates at the University of Oregon (Schmuck, Runkel, Arends, & Arends, 1977). Organizational diagnosis is typically conceived as the first stage of a larger intervention process, as for example when applied to the development of organizational problem-solving skills in a school faculty (Schmuck, Runkel, & Langmeyer, 1969) and used in conjunction with the Proactive/Interactive Change Model (Zaltman, Florio, & Sikorski, 1977) and Collective Decision Intervention (Cooke & Coughlan, 1979). (Fullan, Miles, & Taylor, 1980, provided an excellent overview of organizational diagnosis in the context of organization development interventions.)

The initial diagnostic process is difficult to separate from intervention processes because it is continuous, leads to problem reframing and goal setting, and promotes a sense of collaboration and problem ownership on the part of those involved with the assessment. This argues for the inclusion of key organizational members in the process of change from the earliest stage (Beer, 1980).

In conducting diagnostic assessments of school organizations, change facilitators have available a range of methods. They can review *documents and permanent products* available in the organization, such as policy and procedure manuals, descriptive literature about programs and practices (e.g., curricula, mission statements), and routinely collected data such as attendance and achievement information. *Interviews and direct observation* methods can provide important qualitative information about process variables within the organization, such as interaction patterns and decision making. Many change facilitators also rely on more formal diagnostic instrumentation, including *questionnaires, surveys, and ratings*. These are often standardized and well-researched procedures that assess global variables (see Table 7.3) such as organizational climate (e.g., Organizational Climate Description Questionnaire; Organizational Climate Index), communication (e.g., Survey of Effective School Processes; Effective School Battery), stress (e.g., Teacher Stress Inventory), leadership (e.g., Leadership Effectiveness and Adaptability Description), and general health (e.g., Quality of School Life; Profile of a School). Alternatively, change facilitators may choose to develop measurement instruments that focus on the particular variables under investigation, but which are unvalidated. For a thorough discussion of practical issues in the development of such instrumentation, the reader is referred to the Program Evaluation Kit (Herman, 1988). Moos (1979) provided an excellent overview of conceptual, technical, and practical issues in assessing educational environments.

Critical to the process of organizational assessment is the formulation of assessment questions. When presented with a presumed problem of organizational functioning, such as the need to respond to a new federal preschool handicapped services mandate, the change facilitator must first conceptualize the questions that will focus the assessment. Examples of some evaluation questions might include:

1. How large a preschool handicapped population is to be served? With what needs? How are these to be identified?

2. Which service delivery systems will the preschool needs assessment focus on? Families? Classrooms? Department of special education? School system? With what staff? Disciplinary bases? Organizational features?

3. What special services staff are available to deal with preschool handicapped services?

4. Do available staff possess the skills to deal effectively with the needs of this population? If not, can they be provided with adequate training? How will this be accomplished? Are additional staff needed? In what areas?

TABLE 7.3
Examples of Organizational Diagnosis Instrumentation

Organizational climate assessment
- *Organizational Climate Description Questionnaire,* Halpin & Croft, 1962
  64-item scale of teacher ratings regarding their teaching colleagues and the principal. Teacher factors measured include intimacy, disengagement, esprit, and hindrance. Principal ratings focus on thrust (dynamic characteristics), consideration, aloofness, and production emphasis.
- *Organizational Climate Index,* Stern, 1970
  Questionnaire that yields data on six organizational climate factors from teacher judgments (true/false) about their school setting. Factors include intellectual climate, achievement standards, personal dignity (supportiveness), organizational effectiveness, orderliness, and impulse control. Provides contrast between *development press* (support for intellectual and interpersonal activity) and *control press* (orderliness and structure).

School effectiveness
- *Survey of Effective School Processes,* Institute for Development of Educational Activities (/I/D/E/A/)
  Extensive school effectiveness assessment procedure involving structured interviews, direct observation, and questionnaires. Assesses numerous variables and provides a mechanism to provide systematic feedback to school personnel.
- *Effective School Battery,* Gottfredson, 1984
  Student and teacher survey that measures 34 indicators of school performance, focusing on secondary schools. Provides four profiles of the school in relation to a normative sample, describing both perceptions and descriptions of students and teachers.

Stress
- *Teacher Stress Inventory,* Fimian, 1985
  Composed of 49 stress-related and 9 optional demographic items, with norms for various teacher groups. Measures five stress factors (time management, work-related stress, professional distress, discipline and motivation, and professional investment) and five stress manifestation factors (emotional, fatigue, cardiovascular, gastronomic, and behavioral).

Leadership
- *Leadership Effectiveness and Adaptability Description* (LEAD), Hersey & Blanchard, 1982
  Based on the authors' theory of situational leadership, provides a paper and pencil measure of leadership skills, focusing on balance between task behavior and relationship behavior of the leader in relation to maturity of organizational participants.

General organizational health
- *Quality of School Life,* Epstein & McPartland, 1976
  27-item scale for use with students K–12 to assess: (1) general satisfaction with school, commitment to school work, and (3) attitudes toward teachers.
- *Profile of a School* (POS), Likert & Likert, 1978
  Yields information relevant to six organizational characteristics, including: (1) leadership processes, (2) motivational forces, (3) communication processes, (4) decision-making processes, (5) goal-setting processes, and (6) control processes. Relates these data to management styles in the organization, such as exploitive–authoritative, benevolent–authoritative, consultative, and participative.

5. Do any programs presently exist that address the needs of the preschool handicapped population, either within or outside the organization? How are these organized?

6. What human, financial, informational, and technological resources will be required to develop and implement a program? Is there adequate funding? What additional funding will be required? What evidence is there to support various types of educational programming for this population?

7. What organizational routines will be affected by program development and implementation?

- How ready is this particular school organization for the changes required by this legislation?
- Which staff have expertise that can be used to develop and implement the program?

In planning for organizational change in special services, a multidimensional needs assessment framework that examines the recipients of services (and their psychoeducational needs) in relation to available resources within various organizational units of the school organization is recommended (see Maher & Illback, 1982, for a more thorough description of the needs assessment framework). In utilizing this approach, the process of organizational needs assessment includes steps portrayed in Table 7.4.

Process Interventions. Interventions that focus on aspects such as planning and evaluation, decision making, and communication can be seen as *process interventions.* As described previously, organizational processes involve patterned behavioral regularities that occur as the organization seeks to accomplish its mission. In dysfunctional organizations, there are breakdowns in cooperation and collaboration, resulting in inefficiency and ineffectiveness. These problems are especially problematic in the human service arena, where productive interactions are central to mission attainment. Considerable attention has therefore been devoted to "organization development" or process interventions (Schein, 1969; Schmuck & Miles, 1971).

The focus of process interventions has centered on variables such as teamwork, conflict, creative problem solving, trust and cooperation, attitudes and values, leadership styles, and listening and communication. These interventions assume that by improving the capabilities of individuals in the organization to work together along these dimensions, the overall productivity and health of the organization will be improved. Not surprisingly, the field has drawn heavily from social psychology and group dynamics. In fact, much of the early work grew out of the sensitivity training and "t-group" literature (Bradford, Gibb, & Benne, 1964).

Methods of process interventions can be subcategorized into four types:

TABLE 7.4
Components of an Organizational Needs Assessment

1. *Select a needs assessment committee*—the committee represents multiple perspectives and constituencies within the organization and assumes responsibility for the design and conduct of the needs assessment.
2. *Determine the unit(s) of analysis which will focus the needs assessment*—the committee will ascertain which units and aspects of the organization need to be assessed in order to obtain reliable and valid information for the intervention (e.g., staff members and clients, classroom, school building, school system), which will be perceived as useful by planners. Specified evaluation questions provide focus to this analysis.
3. *Design and conduct the needs assessment*—the committee gathers information relevant to the evaluation questions through methods such as observation, interview, document review, and surveys, and synthesizes this information to form operating hypotheses about the present state of affairs within the organization in relation to the problem area.
4. *Disseminate the needs assessment information*—the committee reports the information gleaned from the preceding activities to program planners in a format that lends itself to decision making, including: (a) the priority needs of clients and client systems, (b) present service delivery system information, (c) recommendations for planning and development of new services and/or alterations to present programming, and (d) suggestions for allocation of resources.

survey feedback, group development and team building, intergroup development, and process consultation (Illback & Zins, 1984). *Survey feedback* methods involve the use of systematic data collection about the variables of concern (e.g., morale, job satisfaction), followed by summarization of the data to organizational members as a means to clarify the nature and scope of the problems that the group may then discuss and attempt to resolve. Survey feedback is most effectively used as a component of a larger change process; when used in isolation it appears to be insufficient to promote lasting change.

Group development and team building methods are based on principles and procedures of group dynamics. Work groups (teams) are formed in organizations for explicit purposes, especially when there is a belief that a situation needs to change and no one individual can effect that change (Zander, 1985). In schools, work groups form for various reasons, such as when a problem arises (e.g., increase in substance abuse), a new mandate arrives (e.g., preschool handicapped services), or unexpected opportunities emerge (e.g., enhanced revenue availability). Some work groups are derived from Federal, state, and local laws, regulations, or policies (e.g., multidisciplinary teams under Public Law 94–142, student assistance teams), whereas others appear on an ad hoc basis and are more time limited (e.g., a committee to identify priority needs for a special services department). However, all work groups, formal or informal, proceed through stages of development that must be facilitated if the group is to accomplish its ultimate objectives (Dimock, 1987).

When the possibility of forming a work group is initially discussed, one or more individuals in the school community suggest that a purpose for group formation exists. Attendant to this purpose statement is a suggestion that certain individuals should be included as members of the group due to their particular expertise or role in the setting. In the *forming* stage of development, these individuals come together to explore whether the basis for an ongoing group exists.

There are a number of salient issues at this stage, such as who should properly be included in the group, what criteria should be used for inclusion, and what boundaries are recognized by group members and the organization (e.g., who is excluded, scope of group content and mission). Additionally, the forming group discusses its mission and goals and formulates clear statements about these to provide focus to subsequent activity. Group interaction focuses on problem definition, sharing information, and expressing opinions.

Group members also assess one another's degree of commitment to the overall purpose of the group, as a prerequisite to their further involvement. Further, group members are concerned with sanctions the group has to accomplish its assigned objectives (e.g., from management) and specific expectations others may have regarding group processes, procedures, and products. In this initial stage, work group behavior is often tenuous, as group members assess the viability of the group in relation to the task. To the extent that a common point of view regarding group purpose is arrived at, however, the group is ready to move on to other issues.

The second phase of typical work group development involves conflict (*storming*) about issues of power, prestige, decision making, and goals. In this stage, group members gradually establish implicit interpersonal hierarchies as individuals acquire various roles (e.g., leader). In some groups, a select few dominate the discussion early on, although an important goal for group development is involvement of all group members in discussion and decision making.

In the storming stage, group members not only provide information and express opinions about tasks; they begin to focus on process variables and group building. Issues such as who should speak, who should lead, and how decisions should be made (e.g., majority vote versus consensus) become real concerns (Bion, 1961). As these issues are worked through, patterns of communication and decision making evolve, which can lead to either dysfunction or collaboration.

Facilitation of the storming stage is crucial because the manner in which it is resolved dictates the parameters within which the work group will ultimately operate. Successful resolution can lead to a group that shares responsibilities, is open to input, manages conflict, is goal directed, and has a positive sense of group identity.

As the work group moves beyond the conflict stage, productivity relative to the group task becomes paramount. Effective work groups establish routines (*norming*) that allow for the efficient processing of a broad range of information and clear decisions about how to proceed. They also establish an atmosphere in which group members share leadership responsibilities in problem solving, with trust in one another's abilities and judgments. In effective work groups, individual differences and unique abilities are recognized and capitalized on, and a certain amount of deviation is tolerated. Rather than an aggregate of individuals working at cross purposes, effective (*performing*) work groups are interdependent, flexible, and cohesive.

Intergroup development methods focus not on the development of individual working groups but rather on the interdependency of subunits within the organization. For example, teacher, administrator, and parent groups, or persons belonging to various professional specialties (e.g., psychologists, occupational therapists, counselors) may be worked with to promote improved communication, role definition, and intergroup perceptions, especially where conflict and dysfunction exists.

An example of the relevance of intergroup development methods can be seen in the call for alternative service delivery systems currently debated within special education and school psychology. In order to decrease instructional fragmentation and rigidity, increase and improve social and academic experiences, and better utilize resources for mildly handicapped pupils, it has been recommended that the focus of intervention programs move away from strictly special educational environments, through a "regular education initiative" (Will, 1986). This requires various role groups, such as special and remedial education teachers, school psychologists, speech clinicians, and general education personnel, to alter their roles, responsibilities, and relationships. Considerable intergroup development will be necessary to accomplish this objective. (See Graden, Zins, & Curtis, 1988, for a thorough discussion of alternative educational delivery systems and approaches to facilitate intergroup development in this context.)

A more general category of intervention is termed *process consultation*, in which the consultant seeks to help clients and client systems behave more effectively within the social ecology of the organization. Many of the methods associated with the preceding process interventions can be subsumed by this approach. In essence, the process consultant is the mental health consultant/therapist to the organization, building relationships, facilitating interaction, giving process feedback, and suggesting alternative means for communicating and collaborating. Broad-based interventions focusing on school climate, interpersonal relationships, moral issues, and community concerns are examples of this mode of functioning.

Given the problem of organizing for preschool handicapped services, process interventions may begin with surveys to all relevant staff members about their knowledge, skills, and attitudes regarding the coming program. This might reveal that staff (e.g., early childhood teachers, psychologists) perceive that they have limited knowledge about the learning and behavior characteristics of developmentally delayed children, and even less knowledge of curricular and instructional issues. Whereas they are challenged by the task at hand, they may feel they also have skill deficits in certain areas, such as teaching, assessing, or making decisions. By conducting a systematic survey, including both a questionnaire and structured interviews, the facilitator may be able to help the group delineate the kinds of training and experiences needed to help them feel more competent and prepared.

Relatedly, it may become clear that programming for preschool services requires a higher degree of team interaction and collaboration than other, more established, services. Therefore, it may be useful to establish an ongoing process through which group goals and activities can be developed and revised, and conflicts can be managed or resolved. The relationship of this team to other groups within the organization will also need to be addressed.

Structural Interventions.   A third category of organizational intervention strategy is oriented toward "redesigning" fundamental aspects of policies, procedures, reward systems, service and program configurations, and other such mechanisms within the organization. Changes in organizational structure are presumed to alter organizational behavior and process.

Organizational design (and redesign) may take a variety of forms, such as reward systems, performance management/control systems, and task/organizational design (Beer, 1980). Each is discussed in the context of organizing to deliver preschool handicapped services.

Within all organizations, including schools, implicit and explicit *systems of reward and punishment* exist. Staff members receive salaries, benefits, and job security as compensation for the services they provide; in some organizations, they may receive bonuses for exemplary performance (e.g., merit pay). Additionally, praise, recognition, and approval serve as social reinforcers to develop and maintain desired behaviors. When persons in the organizations deviate significantly from expectations, they may receive mild reprimands, poor evaluations, suspension, or termination. In addition to these formalized rewards and punishments, typically administered by authority figures, there is an informal school culture in which other staff members provide reinforcement (and punishment) by recognizing special efforts and ignoring or criticizing deficient performance or unwanted actions.

Structural interventions seek to capitalize on both formal and informal reward systems in organizations. With regard to the preschool handicapped example, formal approaches may include: (a) providing special incentives to attract and retain staff (e.g., extra planning time, bonus pay, recognition), (b) emphasizing positive accomplishments through intermittent, regular performance feedback, and (c) providing clear feedback about practices that may be negative to the growth and development of the program (e.g., teacher becoming too isolated). Informal reward system strategies may focus on developing a sense of collegiality amongst team members so that they are prone to reinforce one another and by arranging for reinforcement to be delivered by others in the organization (e.g., superintendent).

Effective organizations are likely to also use *performance management and control systems* to enhance the behavior of organization members. This involves delineating and describing key goals and activities for individuals, groups, and subunits, followed by measurement, feedback, and modification. Numerous systems have been used by schools in this regard, including management by objectives (Bell, 1974), goal attainment scaling (Kiresuk & Sherman, 1968), performance appraisal (Beer, 1980), and program analysis and review (Maher & Bennett, 1984). The chapter by Williams and Johnson in this volume covers performance appraisal in detail.

In organizing for preschool services, key target behaviors may center on effective team planning, thorough assessment, competent instruction, and home–school coordination/communication to insure generalizability of the intervention program. Within these broad areas, more specific indicators of adequate and exemplary performance could be developed, along with a complete description of the activities they imply (e.g., obtaining training, conducting parent support groups, organizing team meetings).

Another means to structure interaction and behavior is through *task and organization design* methods. Most employees have job descriptions that set parameters on their behavior; task design is more explicit, undertaking to analyze and alter physical and psychological aspects of the work task so as to enhance worker productivity, collaboration, and satisfaction. Suggestions for effective task design include grouping tasks so that they relate naturally to one another and to the overall mission; establishing task identity by combining similar tasks; insuring that staff members have direct contact with those who will ultimately receive services; allowing staff members to perceive a sense of ownership of their work environment; and opening feedback channels (Beer, 1980). For preschool services, this may mean that assessment and evaluation need to be more clearly linked, with teachers taking primary responsibility for this continuous process. Also, the preschool team may need to be given sufficient latitude to make certain decisions about a range of operational issues, such as through a "quality circle" (Maher & Illback, 1984). Finally, specialists (e.g., psychologists, physical therapists) may profit from direct instructional involvement with the children being served to enhance their understanding of the impacts of decisions the team may make.

In contrast with task design, organization design is more global and far reaching. Schools (and other human service organizations) are prone to engage in reorganization when faced with internal (often political) problems. This may mean shifting lines of authority, moving subunits of the organization, or adding/deleting programs and services. For example, within school organizations, there is often debate about the amount of centralization of authority that may be necessary. Some programs, such as personnel services, special education, and maintenance of buildings and grounds, may function more smoothly when centrally coordinated. Others, such as instruction, may be more effective when decision making is centered at the building and classroom levels.

Another debate centers around the amount of specialization necessary in an organization. For example, should there be a number of separate, "pull out" programs in reading, such as Chapter I, learning disabilities, migrant program, remedial/basic skills education, or should all reading instruction be conducted within the general education program. In special education, decisions need to be made about the organization of programs for exceptional students.

Organization design for preschool services is crucial. It involves determining how the program will operate in the context of already existing programs and services, who will be responsible for direction and supervision (e.g., principal, special education supervisor), what ongoing system of planning and evaluation will be used, and how the physical and social environment for the program will be organized.

Individual Interventions.   A final domain of intervention strategies focuses attention on the individual. If a particular problem within an organization is conceptualized as pertaining specifically to a person or subunit, it may be most efficient to develop an intervention targeted toward modifying the behavior of this person or unit. Approaches associated with this domain include personnel recruitment and selection, remedial and disciplinary actions, continuing professional development, personal counseling, and self-supervision.

When an organization determines that a need exists within a program (e.g., preschool services) for a person who is trained and capable to perform the tasks of a key position (e.g., teacher, psychologist), it specifies the required level of training, experience, general competencies, and related characteristics of the person it is seeking. People in organizations are not interchangeable; they cannot be "slotted" into positions without regard to their particular professional strengths and weaknesses. *Personnel recruitment and selection* methods consider the idiosyncratic nature of particular roles and responsibilities and strive for goodness–of–fit between the job candidate and the job.

When a person has been found deficient in the performance of duties, the organization has a special obligation to its clients to improve performance through *remedial actions,* and, failing that, to remove the ineffective staff member from the position through *disciplinary actions.* Due process requires that administrative assistance, coupled with a remedial plan of action, be developed in conjunction with the deficient staff member. If, after a reasonable period of time, the person does not improve, management must choose among options of reassignment, suspension, or termination.

On a more positive note, the organization is also required to provide for the ongoing professional development needs of its members to enhance and maintain skills, develop new knowledge, and self-renew. This is done through a program of *continuing professional development*. Many school organizations are recognizing that personal problems can greatly affect workplace functioning and are offering *personal counseling* through employee assistance programs (EAP) (Farkas, 1989; Klarreich, DiGuiseppe, & DiMattia, 1987; Myers, 1984). Ultimately, staff members should be encouraged to engage in *self-supervision*, a process of self-monitoring, self-evaluating, and personal goal setting.

SUMMARY

This chapter has described the characteristics of schools organizations that influence the practice of psychology. School psychologists are encouraged to consider organizational perspectives that can contribute to problem conceptualization and intervention planning. Organizational-level interventions, which may be relevant to proactive efforts by the psychologist to enhance organizational functioning, are also presented.

School psychologists play a unique role in schools as they cross multiple systemic boundaries within and outside the organization, such as between the home and school, teacher and child, administrator and teacher, and building and central office (Illback & Maher, 1984). By taking an organizational perspective, psychologists who practice in schools can help clients by facilitating the improvement of organizational structures, processes, and behavior.

REFERENCES

American Psychological Association. (1981). Specialty guidelines for the delivery of services by industrial/organizational psychologists. *American Psychologist, 36,* 664–669.

Baker, F. (1974). From community mental health to human service ideology. *American Journal of Public Health, 64,* 576–581.

Beer, M. (1980). *Organization change and development: A systems view.* Santa Monica, CA: Goodyear.

Bell, T. H. (1974). *A performance accountability system for school administrators.* West Nyack, NY: Parker.

Berrien, F. K. (1976). A general systems approach to organizations. In M. D. Dunnette (Ed.), *Handbook of industrial and organizational psychology.* Chicago: Rand-McNally.

Bertalanffy, L. von. (1950). *General systems theory.* New York: Brazillier.

Bion, W. R. (1961). *Experiences in groups.* New York: Basic Books.

Bradford, L. P., Gibb, J. R., & Benne, K. D. (Eds.). (1964). *T-group theory and laboratory method.* New York: Wiley.

Brophy, J., & Good, T. L. (1986). Teacher behavior and student achievement. In M. C. Wittrock (Ed.), *Handbook of research on teaching* (3d ed., pp. 328–375). New York: Macmillan.

Cooke, R. A., & Coughlan, R. J. (1979). Developing collective decision-making and problem solving structures in schools. *Group and Organization Studies, 4,* 71–92.

Derr, C. B. (1976). "OD" won't work in schools. *Education and Urban Society, 8*(2), 227–241.

Dimock, H. G. (1987). *Groups: Leadership and group development.* San Diego: University Associates.

Dunnette, M. D. (Ed.). (1976). *Handbook of industrial and organizational psychology.* Chicago: Rand-McNally.

Epstein, J. L., & McPartland, J. M. (1976). The concept and measurement of the quality of school life. *American Educational Research Journal, 13,* 15–30.

Farkas, G. M. (1989). The impact of federal rehabilitation laws on the expanding role of employee assistance programs in business and industry. *American Psychologist, 12,* 1482–1490.

Fimian, M. J. (1985). The development of an instrument to measure occupational stress in teachers: The Teacher Stress Inventory. *British Journal of Occupational Psychology, 57,* 277–293.

Forman, S. G. (1981). Stress-management training: Evaluation of effects on school psychological services. *Journal of School Psychology, 19,* 233–241.

Forman, S. G., & Cecil, M. A. (1986). Teacher stress: Causes, effects, intervention. In T. R. Kratochwill (Ed.), *Advances in school psychology* (Vol. 5). Hillsdale, NJ: Lawrence Erlbaum Associates.

Fullan, M., Miles, M. B., & Taylor, G. (1980). Organization development in schools: The state of the art. *Review of Educational Research, 50,* 121–183.

Gottfredson, G. D. (1984). *Effective school battery.* Odessa, FL: Psychological Assessment Resources.

Graden, J. L., Zins, J. E., & Curtis, M. J. (1988). *Alternative educational delivery systems: Enhancing instructional options for all students.* Washington, DC: National Association of School Psychologists.

Hall, R. H. (1977). *Organizations: Structure and process.* Englewood Cliffs, NJ: Prentice-Hall.

Halpin, A. W., & Croft, D. B. (1962). *The organizational climate of schools.* Washington, DC: United States Office of Education.

Herman, J. L. (Ed.). (1988). *Program Evaluation Kit* (2nd ed.). Newbury Park, CA: Sage.

Hersey, P., & Blanchard, K. H. (1982). *Management of organizational behavior: Utilizing human resources.* Englewood Cliffs, NJ: Prentice-Hall.

Illback, R. J., & Maher, C. A. (1984). The school psychologist as an organizational boundary role professional. *Journal of School Psychology, 22,* 63–72.

Illback, R. J., & Zins, J. E. (1984). Organizational interventions in educational settings. In C. A. Maher, R. J. Illback, & J. E. Zins (Eds.), *Organizational psychology in the schools: A handbook for professionals.* Springfield, IL: Charles C. Thomas.

Illback, R. J., Zins, J. E., Maher, C. A., & Greenberg, R. (1989). In T. Gutkin & C. Reynolds (Eds.), *Handbook of school psychology* (2d ed., pp. 801–822). New York: Wiley.

Institute for Development of Educational Activities. (Undated). *Survey of effective school processes.* Dayton, OH: Author.

Katz, D., & Kahn, R. L. (1966). *The social psychology of organizations.* New York: Wiley.

Kiresuk, T. J., & Sherman, R. E. (1968). Goal attainment scaling: A general method for evaluating comprehensive mental health programs. *Community Health Journal, 4,* 443–453.

Klarreich, S. H., DiGuiseppe, R., & DiMattia, D. J. (1987). Cost-effectiveness of an employee assistance program with rational-emotive therapy. *Professional Psychology: Research and Practice, 18,* 140–144.

Likert, J. G., & Likert, R. (1978). *Profile of a school.* Ann Arbor, MI: Rensis Likert Associates.

Maher, C. A., & Bennett, R. E. (1984). *Planning and evaluating special education services.* Englewood Cliffs, NJ: Prentice-Hall.

Maher, C. A., & Illback, R. J. (1982). Planning for the delivery of special services in public schools: A multidimensional needs assessment framework. *Evaluation and Program Planning, 4,* 249–259.

Maher, C. A., & Illback, R. J. (1983). Planning for organizational change in schools: Alternative approaches and procedures. *School Psychology Review, 12,* 460–466.

Maher, C. A., & Illback, R. J. (1984). The Quality Circle: An approach to improving educational services in public schools. In C. A. Maher, R. J. Illback, & J. E. Zins (Eds.), *Organizational psychology in the schools: A handbook for professionals.* Springfield, IL: Charles C. Thomas.

Maher, C. A., Illback, R. J., & Zins, J. E. (Eds.). (1984). *Organizational psychology in the schools: A handbook for professionals.* Springfield, IL: Charles C. Thomas.

McInerney, J. F. (1985). Authority management. In C. A. Maher (Ed.), *Professional self-management: Techniques for special services providers.* Baltimore: Brookes.

Miller, J. G. (1965). Living systems. *Behavioral Science, 10,* 193–237.

Moos, R. H. (1979). *Evaluating educational environments.* Palo Alto, CA: Consulting Psychologists Press.

Myers, D. W. (1984). *Establishing and building employee assistance programs.* Westport, CT: Quorum.

National Commission on Excellence in Education. (1983). *A nation at risk: The imperative for educational reform.* Washington, DC: U.S. Government Printing Office.

Public Law 99–457. *Education of the Handicapped Act Amendments of 1986.*

Schein, E. H. (1969). *Process consultation.* Reading, MA: Addison-Wesley.

Schmuck, R. A., & Miles, M. B. (Eds.). (1971). *Organization development in schools.* Palo Alto, CA: National Press Books.

Schmuck, R., Runkel, P., Arends, J., & Arends, R. (1977). *The second handbook of organization development in schools.* Palo Alto, CA: Mayfield.

Schmuck, R., Runkel, P., & Langmeyer, D. (1969). Improving organizational problem solving in a school faculty. *Journal of Applied Behavioral Science, 5,* 455–483.

Stern, G. G. (1970). *People in context: Measuring person–environment congruence in education and industry.* New York: Wiley.

Will, M. (1986). *Educating students with learning problems: A shared responsibility.* Washington, DC: United States Department of Education.

Zaltman, G., Florio, D., & Sikorski, L. (1977). *Dynamic educational change.* New York: The Free Press.

Zander, A. (1985). *The purposes of groups and organizations.* San Francisco: Jossey-Bass.

8

CONTRIBUTIONS OF SOCIAL PSYCHOLOGY TO SCHOOL-BASED RESEARCH AND EVALUATION

Frederic J. Medway
Paula Skedsvold
University of South Carolina

No plan is perfect, yet plans are necessary if we are to avoid complete chaos.
—Edward T. Hall (in Rosenberg, 1978a, p. 121)

The first thing to realize is that there are no easy solutions.
—Stanley Milgram (in Rosenberg, 1978b, p. 150)

Man grasps reality, and can predict and control it, by referring transient and variable behavior and events to relatively unchanging underlying conditions.
—Fritz Heider (1958)

These three, seemingly disparate quotes by psychologists Hall, Milgram, and Heider summarize much of how we feel about the purpose and function of research in school psychology. To us, research involves a systematic plan to formulate a question and to discover one or more possible answers to it. The answers to human problems may be readily apparent or not, but rarely are they simple. Research plans and methods are necessary to understand the world in which we live and the people in it, to discover new laws, and verify ones that we suspect from common sense and observation. Our definition of research is intentionally broad and not limited to controlled experimentation. It does involve the motivation to accumulate facts and subsequently to link, sort, and analyze them, and a willingness to describe the process. Without plans to solve problems and a knowledge of how to conduct, evaluate, and apply research to find answers, the practice of school psychology would be chaotic.

Research in school psychology rests on the methodological foundations of experimental design, statistics, and measurement theory (cf. Bailey, 1987; Barlow, Hayes, & Nelson, 1984; Campbell & Stanley, 1963; Cook & Campbell, 1979; Mason & Bramble, 1989; Selltiz, Wrightsman, & Cook, 1976). Numerous books and articles have been written in the last 15 years on conducting and implementing research in school psychology (Kratochwill, 1978; Kratochwill, Schnaps, & Bissell, 1985; Phillips, 1987, 1990) and an entire issue of the *School Psychology Review* edited by Witt in 1987 was devoted to the topic. Rather than reviewing a wide variety of social research methods or covering the implementation and acceptability of research findings (cf. Reimers, Wacker, & Koeppl, 1987), issues that have been adequately covered in the school and educational psychology literature, in this chapter, we focus on the specific application of social psychological research to school psychology.

Our coverage begins by looking briefly at the present status of research in school and social psychology. We examine the extent to which school psychologists make use of social psychological research methods and attempt to address some reasons accounting for this historical lack of cross fertilization. Before turning to specific research issues and methods, we first look at the nature of research "paradigms" and review the assumptions of research in social and school psychology. Next, we consider the social psychology of school experimentation, including the effects of context and cognition on our data. And finally, we provide an overview of social psychological research methods that have particular relevance for school psychologists. Our review here is selective due to space considerations. However, we attempt to cover areas, such as qualitative methodologies and content analysis, that have not been reviewed for school psychologists.

RESEARCH ISSUES IN SCHOOL AND SOCIAL PSYCHOLOGY

Research in School Psychology

The last 25 years have been an unprecedented period of growth in the school psychology literature (Fagan, 1986), a growth attributable to a burgeoning research literature and accompanying research syntheses, critiques, and forecasts of future trends (e.g., French & Raykovitz, 1984; Medway & Updyke, 1985; Phillips, 1989, 1990; Reynolds & Clark, 1984; Witt, 1987). The emphasis on empirical research in school psychology has helped legitimize the field as an independent, unique discipline rather than as simply a professional digression of clinical psychology.

On the other hand, within school psychology, the gap between research and practice has been growing, and there is increasing disatisfaction with the payoffs from research ventures. School psychology research has been criticized as fragmented, lacking direction, largely atheoretical (Witt, 1987), and often irrelevant to daily school problems. School research is not considered a high priority by school administrators (Hartshorne & Johnson, 1985), and there are few external resources and little acknowledgment for conducting research for applied psychologists (Haynes, Lemsky, & Sexton-Radek, 1987). Some solutions to elevating the status of school research have been offered (Bardon, 1987; Martens & Keller, 1987; Phillips, 1987, 1989). For example, Bardon (1987) notes that research methods in school psychology have been overly traditional (cf. Shemberg, Keeley, & Blum, 1989) and recommends consideration of some of the qualitative research methodologies that increasingly are being used by social psychologists. Later in this chapter we review some of these techniques.

Research in Social Psychology

I guess that they are as far above us on the evolutionary scale as we are above the amoeba.
—"Mr. Spock" in The Devil in the Dark episode of "Star Trek"
created by Gene Roddenberry (in Rosenberg, 1978c, p. 67)

For students in school psychology training programs, the prospect of having to do a research project often provokes much anxiety in terms of choosing a topic, deciding how to study it, finding data analysis procedures, and logically accounting for the results. One wonders if students, and some practitioners, view social psychologists as masters of an art in which school psychologists are mere dabblers or, in Mr. Spock's words, low on the evolutionary scale.

Social psychology, at least since the late 1950s, has been dominated by the controlled laboratory investigation method to the exclusion of field studies. This has resulted simply from historical circumstances. Social psychology essentially began with Triplett's (1897) experiment dealing with how children's behavior was influenced by those around them and, except for the period immediately surrounding World War II, maintained this orientation. Among the major stimuli to this research thrust was the commitment of researchers trained in the 1960s and beyond to make social psychology a hard-nosed science, the ready availability of college student research subjects, and research funding through the National Science Foundation (NSF). When NSF first began to fund social research in the late 1950s, a decision was made to fund basic rather than applied studies, and it was not until 1975 that NSF began to fund developmental projects. By contrast, school psychologists, starting with Witmer whose psychoeducational clinic opened at the same time Tripplett was conducting his studies and proceeding through Gesell (see Fagan, 1987), carved out roles for themselves where practice and service delivery dominated, and where research was done for application rather than for scientific value. In fact, Witmer's philosophy was to study individual children in depth rather than collect normative data on groups (Fagan, 1985). The inception of scientist–practitioners models of training, growing out of the Boulder and Thayer conferences, did little to change the basic applied nature of school psychology even though both conferences touted the scientist role as the primary one (Parker & Detterman, 1988). To this day practitioners still want to know more about diagnosis and intervention than they do about research (Copeland & Miller, 1985).

Yet, despite the long history of research emphasis in social psychology, it too, like school psychology, is in a period of self-criticism (Israel & Tajfel, 1972) and "crisis" (Minton, 1984). Social psychologists are challenging the value of artificial laboratory experiments; questioning the subtle influences of the experimenter (Orne, 1962, Rosenthal, 1966) and subject biases (Sears, 1986) on data collection; raising ethical issues; and noting that social data has been accumulated without regard to the historic and cultural milieu, thus resulting in findings that are often irrelevant to real-world concerns (Gergen, 1973).

Close inspection of research in school psychology, especially over the last decade, raises similar concerns. For example, whereas the initial studies of consultation examined process dynamics in field settings (Kenney, 1986), recent research involves discrete, controlled investigation, often analogue in nature (Alpert & Yammer, 1983; Duncan & Pryzwansky, 1988). It is our hope that by highlighting research paradigms and methods in social psychology this chapter will encourage a similar examination of research in school psychology, hopefully sooner than later.

How Much Has Social Psychology Influenced Research in School Psychology?

Research Topics. Recently, Medway and Cafferty (1990) discussed several areas in which social psychology has relevance for school psychologists. However, a review of the prevailing literature in school psychology indicates that, with few exceptions discussed later, school psychology researchers have not pursued social psychological topics or methods to a great degree.

Several surveys of school psychology research bear this out. In 1984 Reynolds and Clark categorized the topics chosen by school psychologists in articles from 1974–1980 in their five primary journals. Only 6% of the articles dealt with "social-educational" themes, a category that included studies of classroom ecology and group problems. French and Raykovitz (1984) found that, over a 3-year period, only 13% of the dissertations in school psychology conducted were in a social area. However, neither of the two studies just mentioned limited social research to traditional areas of social psychology (e.g., attitudes, attraction, aggression, etc.). Further indirect evidence for the limited impact of social psychology theory in school psychology was provided by Oakland (1984). Of the 100 most frequently cited authors in the *Journal of School Psychology* in a 20-year period, only two, Kurt Lewin and Richard Schmuck, can be considered research social psychologists. Collaboration among school and social psychologists is probably rare. Of the top 25 universities as judged by publications in social psychology (Gordon & Smith, 1989), only six have APA-approved school psychology programs (Universities of Texas, Indiana, North Carolina, Kansas, Minnesota, and Wisconsin), and none of these programs are located within the psychology department.

Research Methods. Perhaps more important than whether school psychologists research social topics is whether school psychologists are aware of, and make proper use of, social psychological research methods and tools. In order to assess this we examined all research studies published in the *Journal of School Psychology* from 1980 through 1989, excluding all studies dealing with test reliability and validity. Each study was classified according to whether it employed a standard social psychological method or not (Bailey, 1987), and if so, which one. These data are shown in Table 8.1.

Table 8.1 shows that, broadly speaking, school psychologists have employed just three social psychological methods: surveys, observational techniques, and content analysis. Questionnaires have been frequently used to assess interventions, consultation effects (Duncan & Pryzwansky, 1988), perceptions of role and function, and interpersonal relations among children (i.e.,

TABLE 8.1
Percentage of Research Articles in the *Journal of School Psychology* (1980–1989)
Using Major Social Psychological Research Methods

Observational measures	17%
Survey methods	
Questionnaires	42%
Interviews	5%
Sociometric methods	7%
Attitude scales	6%
Archival research	
Content analysis	3%
Unobtrusive measures	2%

Note: Based on a total of 151 research studies excluding all studies involving assessment (i.e., test development, validation; prediction studies). Observational methods include behavioral observational studies.

sociometrics). The percentages of observational studies and content analysis research is misleading because the former typically involve observations of discrete behavioral units rather than molar social behaviors and the latter has generally been limited to studies of verbalizations during consultation. By contrast, interviews, unobtrusive measures, historical research, archival research, and cross-cultural studies are infrequent in school psychology journals. In this chapter we devote coverage to interviews, social observational methods, and other social research methods that have not been reviewed for school psychologists. First, however, we turn to look at some of the assumptions underlying research in school psychology and examine some nontraditional paradigms.

THE PHILOSOPHY OF SCHOOL AND
SOCIAL PSYCHOLOGICAL RESEARCH

> *I wished, by treating Psychology like a natural science, to help her to become one.*
> —William James (in McConnell & Gorenflo, 1989, p. 11)

School psychologists ask and are asked researchable questions every day. Having a question that leads to a search for relationships among phenomenon or variables is the hallmark of research (Kerlinger, 1979). That search, and it's method, is guided by a research "paradigm" or set of assumptions that can serve to both enlarge and restrict our research procedures. A paradigm is a general way of looking at the world, a set of assumptions expressing what is important and reasonable. Consider the following by Reedy (1989): "Any research effort . . . should be able to be repeated by any other researcher at any other time under *precisely the same conditions*" (p. 87). Selltiz Wrightsman, and Cook (1976) stated: "Only empirically based evidence counts (p. 22). And from Phillips (1982): "It is . . . important to know that one can generalize from a particular population, situation, or historical period to others" (p. 44).

Most psychologists, starting from their undergraduate days, have been taught these principles, which are considered part of the positivistic tradition in the natural and social sciences. Among other things, positivism assumes that large, complex events can be understood by breaking them down to their component parts, that these facts can be observed and objectively described, that broad theories can be derived from repeated confirmations and disconfirmations of data, that these theories are ahistorical, and that the researcher can observe and record and not influence the course of events (see Lincoln & Guba, 1985 for a comprehensive account of positivism).

A study by Medway and Forman (1980) is illustrative of classical positivistic thinking. The purpose of this study was noteworthy and significant, namely to determine the type of consultation preferred by teachers and psychologists. Teachers and psychologists viewed videotapes of a staged interaction between a consultant and a teacher regarding a child's behavior. Two different consultation models were shown in three vignettes lasting a total of 15 minutes. Teachers then judged the effectiveness of the consultation on a series of questions and rating scales. The researchers assumed that their sample was representative, that the vignette was relevant and realistic, and ultimately that there would be some relation between the data obtained (actually fashioned by the particular questions posed) and actual consultation in schools. It was assumed that a tightly controlled investigation of one small aspect of consultation would illuminate a corner of the field. A telling positivistic air is evident in the discussion of the study (Medway & Forman, 1980): "Actual consultation situations do not allow for control of these variables; on the other hand, examination of the individual components of the consultation session is a necessary first step in determining the effect of a complex set of interactions" (p. 347).

Rather than the exception, studies like this are increasingly the rule in school psychology as researchers attempt to add experimental control (Duncan & Pryzwansky, 1988). However, within social psychology, there is at least some recognition of the value of alternative conceptions of science that are relativistic and view data within a sociohistorical context.

Alternatives to Positivism

> *Nature and society are full of contradictions. As soon as one is resolved, another one appears.*
> —Mao Tse-tung (in Rosenberg, 1978d, p. 46)

Several writers have advocated shifts away from positivism and its transhistorical perspective to alternative paradigms in which facts are viewed as embedded within a sociohistorical context (Gergen, 1973). Lincoln and Guba (1975) propose a "naturalistic" paradigm derived from the work of Schwartz and Ogilvy (1979). The naturalistic paradigm is based on the following assumptions:

1. Complex social behaviors and systems cannot be understood as just a sum of the discrete parts; rather, they have unique properties that cannot be predicted by studying the isolated units. The thinking here is not unlike general systems theory and its particular application to areas such as family therapy (see Barbarin's chapter in this volume).

2. Social units should not be viewed as having a hierarchical arrangement in which influence and power emanates from the top down; rather, systems move as a result of shifting forces at levels sharing dominance, and move-

ment cannot be predicted examining just a few subunits. The thinking here is not unlike ecological psychology notions, as in Bronfenbrenner's (1979) analysis of sociocultural influences on adolescents.

3. Precise outcomes cannot be predicted. Observation influences present results and unexpected developments influence future conditions.

4. The causes of phenomenon are multiple, complex, and interacting. Distinctions between causes and effects blur due to reciprocal influence. A system cannot be understood without regard to its history.

5. Fluctuations in systems are important data, not simple random error (variance) that must be minimized.

6. No one model or theory is complete. Objective observation is an illusion. Multiple perspectives are needed to more fully understand phenomenon.

Naturalistic research and evaluation (Guba & Lincoln, 1989) proceeds, as does conventional research, with specifying a problem, determining data collection procedures, conducting data analysis etc.; however, the ordering of these steps is fluid and adapted according to context and constraint. Unlike traditional, positivistic research, emphasis is placed on human observation of rich social behavior (as opposed to observations of narrow behavioral units). Built into naturalistic research are methods to increase data credibility and trustworthiness so as to increase the chances of results influencing policy decisions. This latter procedure is in contrast to traditional methodologies that have collected "truths" in an impartial way and then, often unsuccessfully, tried to convince constituents to change their behavior. To choose but one illustration from many, despite a wealth of research and position statements by the National Association of School Psychologists, the practices of grade retention and corporal punishment continue in schools. Although the reasons for this are complex, a central reason is that many school personnel trust their own eyes, experiences, and comments from colleagues far more than they do published data based on aggregate cases collected in distant localities by strangers. We explore naturalistic inquiry methods in a later section of this chapter.

A similar paradigm known as the contextualist viewpoint has been proposed by Rosnow (Georgoudi & Rosnow, 1985; Rosnow, 1981). This view holds that sociopsychological events are specific to a certain context, are variable and in a state of perpetual change, and represent dynamic relations made up of personal factors (intentions, plans) and environmental conditions that give rise to these goals and impact on their attainment. The emphasis is on carefully specifying the context in which a human action occurs. Explanation, therefore, cannot be based solely on controlled experimentation but also must take into account the cultural, historical, and biographical methods. According to this view, an attribution cannot be considered a discrete event based either on motivational or informational considerations (Medway & Cafferty, 1990) but rather must incorporate cultural norms, context, and intentions.

To illustrate, a nationally known university recently had to replace it's football coach. In asking who might make the best coach from a list of candidates, attribution theorists (see Levesque and Lowe in this volume) would want to look at candidates' past coaching and recruiting records and their experience with a major program. The university, however, went beyond consideration of candidates' ability to coach and motivation and weighed reputation untarnished by NCAA investigations, "name" appeal, offensive and defensive philosophy, whether the person had previously coached in a highly disciplined program, the record of the applicant against this particular university, and finally, whether the applicant grew up in the state in which the university was located. The act of selecting a new coach can be perceived as both an end of a process (the job search) and the start of another one (coaching), and the final judgment was uniquely tied to the context. In short, the best coach for this college might well be very different than the one for another college. Similarly, there are probably certain school consultants who will outperform others who have received better training (based on empirical data), depending on the demands of the job and school culture.

RESEARCH AS A SOCIAL PHENOMENON AND PROCESS

> *The scientist has no corner on wisdom or morality.*
> —David Krech (in Rosenberg, 1978e, p. 142)

Both positivistic and naturalistic research paradigms recognize that researcher and subject have goals and motivations that influence the research process. Further, research occurs within a certain setting and this too will influence data collected. Major contributions of social psychology are the analysis of methodological issues common to contrived experiments, the role of the powerless subject and its potential for abuse, and, most recently, the role of cognitive biases in interpreting data.

Experimental Roles

Much of the research in both school and social psychology can be viewed as a scripted event, with both the experimenter and subject enacting both prescribed and implicit roles. The experimenter decides when the study begins and ends, selects the procedures and materials, etc. Subjects typically volunteer on the basis of limited information and are expected to passively accommodate to all experimenter's requests. One example, among many that might be chosen, is a study in which teachers taking a graduate course volunteered to read a case study about a child with behavior problems. Using different vignettes certain variables were manipulated. Following this, subjects rated the acceptability of a treatment strategy (Martens & Meller, 1989). Readers of these and similar studies naturally assume that all teachers compiled, responded honestly, and didn't question the purpose or value of the study, the realism of the vignettes, or the wording of the questionnaire. If any subject had, the data might be considered suspect and discarded.

Orne (1962) initially described the roles taken in an experiment and also introduced the idea of the "good subject" whose task is to discover the experimental hypotheses and assist the experimenter in their validation. "Demand characteristics" refer to the cues inherent in the situation that subjects use to understand their role and to formulate guesses as to the experimenter's hypotheses. Orne demonstrated that subjects would work for hours on a tedious task that required them to do pages of math calculations, tear up each page, and then start another. Although the situation was designed to be meaningless, the subjects persisted because they believed that the study measured their endurance. Fillenbaum (1966) described the role of the "faithful subject" who carefully follows the experimenter's requests and is less concerned with the reasons. One wonders what subjects might be thinking when asked to take long test batteries, especially those consisting of similar questions. For example, Niemenen and Matson (1989) were able to successfully administer scales encompassing more than 160 items dealing with depression and conduct to seriously behaviorally disturbed adolescents who, at least in this setting, faithfully followed study requests. Or, returning to the Martens and Meller (1989) study cited before, some teachers rated the acceptability of in-class response cost and others a home-based reinforcement program. Could these experienced teachers guess that different vignettes were being used (especially if there were instructions not to talk during the study)? Could they guess or partially figure out what the hypotheses were? Did they care? And, if so, would they respond in such a way as to give the experimenters what they wanted? Even if these questions are answered in the negative, it is still incumbent on researchers to consider the possibility.

Adair (1973) described the role of the "apprehensive" subject whose concern is with looking good and maintaining self-esteem. For these subjects research provides an atmosphere of evaluation and raises concerns over negative appraisal. The notion of the apprehensive subject is particularly useful in school consultation research. Increasingly, such research has been employing past or present students in graduate consultation courses taught by the researchers. One wonders if concerns about doing well when observed by one's course instructor or other member of a graduate faculty will influence the behaviors of these subjects even more than if it has been observed to affect undergraduate subjects drawn from introductory psychology courses.

Another important issue is the possibility of the experimenter unwittingly providing cues to subjects about the nature of the hypotheses, thus distorting the data. This has been labeled "experimenter expectancy effects" (Rosenthal, 1966). Employing experimenters who are "blind" as to the nature of the study will not entirely avoid this problem because they too, like subjects, may attempt to deduce the study's true nature (Aronson, Brewer, & Carlsmith, 1985). A better procedure is to allow researchers to know the hypotheses but remain blind as to which experimental condition the subject is assigned. Expectancy effects can influence a wide variety of research in school psychology, including assessment research as discussed in the chapter by Goh and Yoshida in this volume.

Collaborative Roles

In an attempt to control for some of the experimental biases described previously, some writers have suggested that a collaborative relationship occur between researcher and subject (Carlson, 1971). Jourard (1967) claimed: "If people show only certain of their possibilities to investigators who relate to human subjects in a prescribed, impersonal way, it is possible that if a . . . mutually revealing . . . relationship between experimenters and subjects were established, different facets of the latter's beings would be disclosed" (p. 109).

Further, Jourard (1967) advocated that investigators show research participants "how we have recorded his responses and tell him what we think they mean. We can ask him to examine then authenticate or revise our recorded version of the meaning of his experience for him. We can let him cross-examine us . . . to find out what we are up to" (p. 113).

Experimental and Mundane Realism

Typically, as experimenters attempt to control more and more variables in a study, they run the risk of reducing the realism of the situation and with it generalizability. The well-controlled study on intervention acceptability by Martens and Meller (1989) is an example of this and one the authors acknowledge: "subjects' perceptions based on written case descriptions may or may not be representative of behavior during actual consultative interactions" (p. 244).

When a study is involving to participants, when they take it seriously, and when it has an impact on them, the study is said to involve "experimental realism." It is relatively easy to design a realistic experiment involving children but more difficult with adults. To illustrate, in a study by Henry, Medway, and Scarbro (1979), first-grade students were asked to complete a series of problems while being "watched" and given feedback on their performance by either two children or two adults. The observers appeared on a TV set placed near the children, and children were told that the equipment actually allowed the observers to see the children work even though they were in another room. In actuality, the feedback was controlled using videotape. However, the situation was so real to the children that most talked to the taped observers and all agreed to share some of the money they had earned in the experiment with those watching them. The Henry et al. (1979) experiment, however, lacked "mundane realism" (Aronson & Carlsmith, 1968). Mundane realism refers to the extent to which events that occur in a research setting also occur in the real world; that is, although involving, the Henry et al. experimental setting was unlike any that children had previously encountered and probably unlike any that they would encounter in the future. Similarly, the Martens and Meller (1989) study, and other analogue studies, lack a degree of mundane realism. In laboratory investigations it is important to try to have high degrees of experimental and mundane realism.

Deception

Institutional Review Boards are required by law (National Research Act, PL 93-348) to review a proposed study in which something artificial is done to or for a person. These boards review requirements for using special populations such as children, prisoners, and the mentally and physically disabled, assess potential risks including possible legal liability of administering questionnaires asking someone to admit to a crime (e.g., using illegal drugs, committing criminal sexual assault), and require *informed consent* on the part of participants. Consent forms should instruct children and parents of procedures that might affect their willingness to participate and detail the level of confidentiality maintained. Confidential information gathered from adolescents may need to be released to parents to prevent some greater harm to the subjects (American Psychological Association, 1982). Subjects also may be required to be debriefed if there is deception involved and, if not required, researchers certainly have an ethical responsibility to do so. During the 1960s the number of deception studies reported in the *Journal of Personality and Social Psychology* increased over 300%. One out of two studies employed some form of deception (Christensen, 1988). The use of deception in psychological research has been debated over the past 25 years (Baumrind, 1979, 1985; Ring, 1967). It has been argued that deception undermines trust in psychological research and that the pool of naive participants is virtually exhausted (Baumrind, 1985). Deception itself has no negative consequences for participants (Christensen, 1988); however, experimenter inconsideration does result in a devaluing of psychological research (Aitkenhead & Dorday, 1985).

At present deception does not appear to be a major problem in school psychology research, although it is unknown how many studies do not fully inform adult subjects or children's parents and guardians. Bradley and Lindsay (1987), in writing about child abuse research, warn against any deception because abusive families already may be quite suspicious of researchers' motives. They also note that the intrusion of researchers into an already stressful family environment may negatively affect future family functioning. Alternatively, sharing information about family functioning with a researcher may lead to less stress and improved functioning (Boss, 1987).

A related issue for the field is whether subjects in school psychology experiments are in a position to grant truly voluntary informed consent. Teachers and psychologists themselves may feel pressures and obligations to volunteer so as to not alienate colleagues, supervisors, and professors. Students may feel compelled to participate because of teacher or peer pressure. Families recruited through social service agencies may not perceive their participation as strictly voluntary (Bradley & Lindsay, 1987). And families, especially of disadvantaged, minority, or low-achieving children may consent because of misunderstanding, fear of causing trouble with the school, or simply for the desire of receiving payment for their time. Likewise parents may assume that the university researcher, who has the school's permission, is in fact an agent of the school, thus limiting their ability to say no to intrusive research.

Social Hypothesis Testing

Research in social cognition has shown that under certain conditions there is a preference for seeking and using hypothesis-confirming information when testing theories of social behavior. In one study Snyder and Swann (1978) told subjects to get diagnostic information on a person who was suspected to be introverted or extroverted. Subjects testing the hypothesis that the person was introverted asked questions such as, "What factors make it hard for you to open up to other people?, whereas subjects in the extroverted hypothesis condition asked questions about instances of extroverted behavior. A subsequent study by Snyder and Cantor (1979) found that subjects recalled more information consistent with the original hypothesis than discordant information. This research has special significance for school psychologists given the overwhelming tendency for children referred for a particular problem to be diagnosed as having that problem. Such findings may simply reflect referrer diagnostic accuracy. However, school psychologists need to be sensitive to tendencies to try to fit incoming information into an already existing cognitive framework.

Borgida and DeBono (1989) questioned whether an expert testing a hypothesis in his or her domain of expertise would show less of a preference for hypothesis-confirming information than would novices. Their results did, in fact, show that experts were less likely to engage in hypothesis-confirming behaviors but only when operating within their domain of expertise. When outside their domains they were as susceptible to cognitive biases as novices. This research has interesting implications in light of newly emerging research looking at the problem-solving strategies of experts and novices (Pryzwansky, 1989).

Illusory Causation and Correlation

Other concepts that have emerged from the study of cognitive process are illusory causation—the tendency to ascribe social causation to salient persons—and illusory correlation—an erroneous perception of correlation between two uncorrelated events (McArthur, 1980).

Illusory causation was demonstrated by Taylor and Fiske (1975). In this study subjects watched an interaction between two people, one of whom faced them and one of whom did not. Subjects saw the salient, more forward-looking actor as causing the action more than the nonsalient actor. Illusory causation has implications for any research where school psychologists observe a target child and compare his or her behavior with a control student.

Illusory correlation has been demonstrated in several studies by Chapman. In one (Chapman & Chapman, 1967) undergraduates examined clients' lists of symptoms and drawings from the Draw-A-Person Test, supposedly belonging to the same clients. Subjects showed a tendency to make a connection between drawing characteristics and symptoms (e.g., large hands attributed to "aggressive" patients) even though the drawings and symptoms were independent. In a later study (Chapman & Chapman, 1969) experienced diagnosticians reported signs of male homosexuality that were invalid but had a high "verbal associative connection" to homosexuality, whereas ignoring empirically associated signs. Perceivers actively extract information from their social environments that they consider useful. This perception then appears difficult to contradict (McArthur, 1980).

Heuristics

Heuristics, or shortcut decision rules, in social cognition have been studied by Kahneman and Tversky (1973), Kahneman, Slovic, and Tversky (1982), and Nisbett and Ross (1980). Kahneman and Tversky found that predictions about social behavior are influenced by representativeness (or similarity) criteria rather than probability (or base rate) data. In one study subjects were told that they were to review five thumbnail descriptions drawn from a larger sample of 30 engineers and 70 lawyers (or vice versa). For example, one description that was designed to be compatible with an engineer stereotype read:

> Jack is a 45-year-old man. He is married and has four children. He is generally conservative, careful, and ambitious. He shows no interest in political and social issues and spends most of his free time on his many hobbies which include carpentry, sailing, and mathematical puzzles.

Subjects then rated the likelihood that the description was of an engineer or lawyer, and most chose engineer. The results showed that the personality descriptions themselves carried more weight than the base rates (participants given no descriptions used the base rates).

Fischhoff (1975) explored another heuristic that he described as "creeping determinism" and is often referred to as "hindsight bias." This refers to the tendency of subjects to overestimate the probabilities for events that have occurred. The study of heuristics has provided examples of how individuals, including researchers, can process information without reference to objective data.

SOCIAL PSYCHOLOGICAL RESEARCH METHODS

> *All the world, all of experience must be open to study.*
> —Abraham Maslow (1968)

There are a wide variety of research methods and strategies used in social psychology, many of which also are used in related social science fields (e.g., sociology, anthropology, political science, business, economics). Due to space limitations we have chosen four methods to review: observational techniques, survey research (including questionnaires, interviews, and rating scales), archival research including content analysis, and naturalistic inquiry. Coverage of the first two methods is more cursory than we would like, so we have provided a list of relevant additional readings. The last three methods, having been underutilized in school psychology, have promise to enrich the field's data base in the future. Other research methods are reviewed in a new volume by Hendrick and Clark (1990).

Observational Methods

Weick (1968) defined social psychological observational methods as "the selection, provocation, recording, and encoding of that set of behaviors and settings concerning organisms 'in situ' which is consistent with empirical aims"

(p. 360). Observational methods are used to study people in settings and situations that are common and familiar to them. Observational methods can be used in solely descriptive studies, in initial attempts to generate hypotheses, and as a data collection method in traditional experiments. However, this discussion is limited to observation in natural settings.

Observational methods are useful when behavior needs to be studied in context. The researcher may make changes in a natural setting, causing minimal interference, and observe if the change makes a difference. There are several approaches to observational research. Tinbergen (1963), taking an ethological perspective, recommended that behavior first be observed in the natural environment as it unfolds rather than trying to categorize behavioral units. Weick (1968) distinguished between a rational and an empirical approach to observational methodology. In the rational approach the investigator starts with a conceptual definition of the behavior and then moves toward specifying the measurement procedures. In the empirical approach the investigator selects the behavioral indicators and, after it is determined that something stable is being measured, attempts to determine what it is, much in the manner of factor analysis.

An example of the ethological approach is Whyte's (1943) classic study of Italian–American gangs in Boston. Whyte, a social scientist, literally moved to a Boston slum neighborhood, participated in gang life, and made extensive observations of gang society. However, Whyte chose not to disguise his identity and his presence in the group, as "participant–observer" had an impact on other members who modified their behavior according to his presence. This was one of the first demonstrations of the "Hawthorne effect" (Mayo, 1945). In the last 50 years, it has been well documented that commonly observers serve to inhibit natural behavior and also may cause changes in the tempo of behavior.

Observational methods are used in experiments and naturalistic studies. They also are widely used in role-playing research. Role playing involves a deliberate attempt to script a scenario and then assign persons to various roles that are loosely guided by the script. The subjects' reactions are observed in situ or recorded for future analysis (see Mixon, 1971 for a complete review).

Some biases that can effect the recording process in observation include:

1. In reconstructing an event, observers can produce simpler, less detailed, more coherent information than the actual event.
2. Observers may forget the middle portion of messages more frequently than beginning or end.
3. Observers may attempt to put closure or provide symmetry to events.
4. Extreme events may be distorted by observers to the mean.
5. Standards used to categorize events may change in the process of recording.

6. Satiation may cause unique events to be seen as typical.

Observational Records

Much of the observational research in school psychology is done using paper and pencil to record instances of discrete behavior. In social psychology, however, the concern is often with complex behavioral interactions (e.g., where the actor is looking, what he/she is saying, what he/she is holding, what reactions he/she is eliciting in another, etc.) rather than discrete instances of a given behavior (e.g., being off-task). Social psychologists also have been concerned with tracing the origins of behavior to examine causal chains. Because of this, much observational research in social psychology uses film and video recording. Film and video allow one to speed up or slow down events; allow comparisons of the actor in different settings; and allow one to study temporal sequences. Disadvantages are that camera placement influences the observational record, voices may not be clear, and different camera angles can create different meanings. The reader familiar with the problems of using videotaped replays to decide calls in professional football can readily appreciate the difficulties of using video in research settings.

In addition to film and video, two other methods have been used to record complex behavior: specimen records, which involve highly detailed descriptions of naturally occurring behavior and sign analysis, which involve generating a priori lists of behavioral categories and indicating which occur over time. One of the most useful and well-known, structured, sign systems is Bales' Interaction Process Analysis, a system designed to classify group member behavior into one of 12 categories. Half these categories assess actions aimed at group interpersonal relations (socioemotional activity) and the other half assess actions that focus on problem solving (task activity). The newest version of this system is called SYMLOG, an acronym for System of Multiple Level Observation of Groups (Bales, 1980).

Survey Research

Surveys are self-report methods of obtaining information on the behavior of a representative sample of the population. Surveys include questionnaires and interview procedures. Surveys do not require the control of experiments and are helpful in answering research questions that begin with "who," "what," "where," and "how." In addition to the references cited next, other key sources of survey research methods appear in volumes by Fowler (1984), Converse and Presser (1986), Kidder and Judd (1986), Oppenheim (1966), Marsh (1982), Bradburn and Sudman (1979), and Sudman and Bradburn (1982).

Questionnaires

As shown in Table 8.1 questionnaires have been frequently used in school psychology research. Questionnaires have been used practically exclusively in studies of psychologist role and function because (a) they do not require a trained experimenter to be present (b) they are inexpensive to produce, (c) they can be administered to groups or individuals, (d) they can be mailed, and (e) responding can be done anonymously. However, questionnaires sent through the mail do require motivation on the part of the respondent to fill them out and do so completely. They also require that the questionnaire developer write clear questions and know in advance areas relevant for questioning.

Constructing Questionnaires. People are most willing to answer questionnaires they see as relevant, of value, and that do not require an inordinate amount of time. Actual questions can be open-ended or closed-ended. With the former no response categories are specified and respondents are free to express whatever information, attitudes, and emotions they wish. These questions are useful when possible answers do not fit neatly into just a few categories or when the investigator is not sure of the possible answers (e.g., in the exploratory phase of a study). Closed-ended questions are used (a) when response categories are few and distinct, (b) when variables are well defined, (c) in later phases of social research, (d) when quantifying data is important, and (e) in self-administered surveys.

Open-ended questions can be easy to construct (e.g., "Describe the type of internship model endorsed by your training program") but difficult to code in a reliable fashion. Respondents need to be willing to express themselves and have sufficient language skills to do so. By contrast, although easier to code, it is harder to write closed-ended questions and alternative answers. The key is in specifying enough categories to cover nearly all responses while not overspecifying. It is often wise to include categories that allow the respondent to indicate "don't know" or "not applicable." Questionnaires often are developed by giving open-ended questions to a sample of respondents, analyzing the answers, and then constructing close-ended questions and response categories.

Another issue is actual question wording. Questions should not inquire two things at once because the answers to different aspects of a question may be different. An example of such a question is: "Do you feel that your pay and working conditions are satisfactory?" Researchers also must be cautious about using technical terms and slang. As school psychologists well recognize from psychological report writing, many words differ in meaning according to age, educational level, and ethnicity. Researchers must avoid leading questions that increase the probability of a response bias or "response set" (the tendency for questions to be answered in a particular way). One type of response set, "social desirability," is evident when a respondent answers questions in the most socially desirable manner rather than truthfully. Other response sets, "yea saying," and "nay saying," involve the tendency for respondents to consistently agree or disagree with questions. Accordingly, well-designed questionnaires have items phrased in both the positive and negative direction. Finally, presentations of earlier items in questionnaires have been shown to influence the interpretation of and affect generated by later items (Ottati, Riggle, Wyer, Schwarz, & Kuklinski, 1989).

When questions deal with personal or sensitive topics, respondents are less likely to be truthful and more likely to provide an answer they view as normative. The use of the randomized response technique (Warner, 1965) has been suggested to increase true responding for sensitive questions. Here the respondent is randomly asked either a sensitive question (e.g., Have you ever smoked marijuana?) or the same question worded negatively (e.g., Have you never smoked marijuana?). Interestingly, short questions of 12 words or less tend to be more threatening than longer questions of 33 words or more.

In finalizing a questionnaire the researcher must decide on the number of questions and their order. Questionnaires should be brief and to the point. Questions that are clear and easy to answer, such as providing background or demographic information, should be placed near the beginning, and sensitive and open-ended questions should be placed near the end. Response sets can be avoided by varying question format, response format, and length. Also, this maintains interest. Researchers can use the "funnel technique" that involves asking broad questions initially and subsequently asking more specific ones for narrower information.

The entire questionnaire should be pretested on a group of respondents for a critical analysis of wording, meaning, order, redundant information, etc. The number of "don't knows" chosen can be analyzed to see if any questions need to be reworded or discarded. Patterns of responses can be examined for response sets. Pilot testing is time consuming but important. A nationwide survey of graduate training in school psychology conducted in 1979 (Pfeiffer & Marmo, 1981) took about a half year to pilot test using eight training programs before nearly 200 universities received a final version.

The final task is to write a cover letter identifying the persons conducting the study or the institution sponsoring the research, describing the relevance of the study to convincingly justify it to the respondent, and explaining the importance of the respondent's compliance. The cover letter should also assure confidentiality, explain that there are no right and wrong answers (if applicable), specify that the questionnaire will not take long to complete, and encourage a prompt return. It is important to indicate how the data will be used and offer to send the respondent a copy of study results on completion.

However, unless the questionnaire itself is free of irrelevant and confusing questions, a persuasive cover letter is not likely to increase response rates.

It is usually recommended that a questionnaire take less than 30 minutes to complete and that a sample size of at least 150 people be obtained. There are several types of sampling procedures available to ensure representativeness and precision (Fowler, 1984).

Mailed Questionnaires. Questionnaires can be sent through the mail or administered in person in group administration or as part of a personal interview. Mailed questionnaires:

1. Cost less than interviews.
2. Can be completed at respondents' convenience.
3. Provide anonymity.
4. Reduce the potential for experimenter bias.
5. Allow for standardization of responses across diverse groups of people.
6. Allow one to obtain information from people in diverse geographical regions.

However, the response rates for mailed questionnaires are low and those who respond may be different from those who do not. In surveys of school psychologists only 30%–40% of potential respondents actually return the questionnaire, and respondents who do not belong to professional associations are rarely identified (Carroll, Bretzing, & Harris, 1981). Response rates are highest when questionnaires come from well-known groups or persons, when they are short, attractive, and easy to complete, when an addressed, stamped envelope is provided, when there is incentive to return it such as the chance to win a prize (Selltiz, Wrightsman, & Cook, 1976), and when respondents have a chance to take a telephone survey instead (Carroll, Bretzing, & Harris, 1981). Sending an informational letter in advance also helps reduce nonresponse. Follow ups by letter or telephone serve to increase compliance. A common procedure is sending two reminder letters followed by a telephone call. Follow ups may be difficult if questionnaires contain sensitive information and anonymity has been assured. However, a follow-up letter can still be sent to all participants stating that those who already returned the questionnaire can disregard the letter.

Interviews

Interviews, compared to questionnaires, allow one to probe for details, repeat and explain questions, and observe and record respondents' behavior during the interview. Question ordering can be varied and the interview can contain more complex questions than mailed questionnaires. Interviews are useful for subjects, such as young children and illiterate adults, who have reading and writing limitations.

Compared to questionnaires, interviews take more time and require more money to pay for interviewer training, interviewing time, and travel. They are less anonymous, a concern when the interview deals with sensitive topics.

Because the interview is a social situation (cf. Bailey, 1987), interviewers can influence the respondent through the inflection used in reading questions, through their nonverbal behavior, and through their physical characteristics (e.g., age, sex, race, appearance, etc). Additionally, the respondent can influence the researcher, leading to inaccurate recording of data. Children, in particular, may be more shy or hesitant in this questioning situation than when taking more structured intelligence and achievement tests. However, interviews have been used successfully with young children (Rich, 1968).

In most cases, interview questions are chosen in advance, although the degree of structure will vary depending on the number of open-ended and closed-ended items. Open-ended questions require respondents to produce an immediate answer regarding a topic they might not have thought about previously. These types of questions also may yield lengthy answers that are difficult to record without mechanical devices such as audio and video equipment. LaGreca (1983) and Paget (1984) provide additional reviews of this literature.

Telephone Interviews. An alternative to the face-to-face interview is the telephone interview (Lavrakas, 1987). With telephone interviews researchers can get immediate reactions to some situation, can control interviewer effects, and can monitor data collection. The cost is relatively low because travel is not involved and it is easier to train interviewers than for personal interviews. Personal and telephone interviews have similar response rates, and both have higher response rates than mailed questionnaires. Telephone interviews must be short and simple, and the caller must be convincing enough to keep the potential respondent from hanging up. Telephone interviews are more susceptible to social desirability biases than mailed questionnaires (Fowler, 1984).

Rating Scales

Much of the social psychologically oriented research in school psychology has used sociometric methods in which children are asked to rate or rank order others in their peer group in terms of attractiveness or desirability on certain interpersonal dimensions. Sociometry uses survey research methods but focuses on a certain subject matter and deals with a related type of analysis. The subject matter provides information about a person's position in a group, subgroupings, the relations among the subgroups, and group cohesiveness. The data has been used in studies dealing with leadership popularity, ethnic group relations, and the effects of certain experimental interventions on group structure (see Maruyama and LeCount's chapter in this volume).

The earliest studies using sociometry typically were done in schools. Criswell (1937) asked children to choose two classmates they would like to sit next to. She found that, up until fifth grade, sex segregation was more marked than racial segregation. Jennings (1943) studied companionship choices for girls in a residential school and found that leadership was not determined by any particular personality type but rather by the contribution the individual made to the group. To this day, sociometry is widely used in school psychology (Bullock, Ironsmith, & Poteat, 1988; Martin, 1986).

Several techniques have been suggested to reduce the generally cumbersome data generated by sociometric choices. These are graphical methods, including the sociogram technique originally described by Moreno (1934), simple quantitative methods, statistical methods, matrix methods, and fractionation of groups (Lindzey & Byrne, 1968).

Archival Research

Archival research involves answering research questions through the use of existing information such as Census records, health and crime statistics, school records, unemployment data, and information contained on computer files. Archival data allow researchers to study questions that cannot be studied using traditional methods, and because the data is already collected there is less chance of introducing new bias. However, the accuracy of the original data may be suspect, the records may be difficult to obtain, important information may not have been recorded (selective deposit), and information may have been destroyed (selective survival). Archival research may be used as part of historical research (i.e., examinations of historical documents over time in order to elucidate cause and effect relationships).

Kidder and Judd (1986) distinguished between three types of archival data: statistical records, survey archives, and written records. Statistical records are those collected by organizations such as schools, the US Census Bureau, the National Archives, the Educational Testing Service, and the National Assessment of Educational Progress. Survey archives consist of data gathered by polling agencies and stored on computer tapes such as the Gallup agency, the National Science Foundation, and the Institute of Social Research at the University of Michigan. Written records consist of documents such as diaries, letters, speeches, newspapers, ethnographies, books, and movies.

Archival research has not been prevalent in school psychology even though it may be easier for practitioners to pursue this than experimental research. A study by Moskowitz (1985) illustrates this method. Moskowitz used interviews along with archival data to evaluate the effectiveness of school-based parent groups on substance abuse in Georgia and Florida. The archival measures examined by Moskowitz included student achievement records, absenteeism, vandalism counts, discipline problems, and course enrollment.

Content Analysis.   Content analysis, often considered a subarea of archival research, includes various quantitative and qualitative methods for understanding the content of communication, including media. Content analysis involves the development of clear and explicit analysis categories that are then applied to the entire communications sample, which may include print media, radio, TV, film, and so forth. Within psychology, and school psychology in particular, content analysis has been applied primarily to the analysis of verbal interchanges (e.g., communication patterns in small groups, between consultant and consultee).

Although the systematic analysis of print media dates back about a century, the impetus for major advances in content analysis techniques was World War II when large-scale studies of German propaganda were initiated. Over the last 40 years major contributors to this field have been linguists and communication specialists rather than psychologists.

Contemporary content analysis techniques are concerned with symbolic meaning and perceiver inferences as conveyed through context, images, signs, and other sensory data. Although content analysis does include simple counting of words, images, and pictures (e.g., the number of intact, nuclear families portrayed in television shows from 1950–1960), what is often more important is the overall impression conveyed by artifacts, interpersonal encounters, linguistic meanings, attributions, signs, etc. (e.g., the impression that nuclear family structure is normative and that such families interact in certain ways; the mother wearing pearls while serving dinner to the whole family). For example, the impression conveyed by two images of the same person differing only in that one is seen "close up, face only" and the other "full figure" is different, the former being perceived as more intimate.

Readable books by Krippendorff (1980) and Berger (1982) provide excellent introductions to content analysis and media analysis, respectively. The rationale for these techniques has been succinctly described by Culler (1976): "Social and cultural phenomenon are not simply material objects or events but objects and events with meaning, and hence signs; . . . they do not have essences but are defined by a network of relations" (p. 4).

Semiological analysis is the study of such signs, their relationships, and what they signify. Syntagmatic analysis is the study of sequences of events in narratives. Paradigmatic analysis is the search for the hidden pattern of meaning as revealed through metaphor, analogy, codes, and figures of speech.

Why is it important for school psychologists to begin to study meaning as transmitted through media, narrative, signs, and even art? Simply because this is the way that most people come to know and have images of "psychologist," "school," "teacher," and "student," images that have a profound impact on role and function (cf. Webb, 1989).

Similarly, media shapes the average person's notions of teachers and schools, and this too can be studied in systematic ways. Vladimir Propp (1968), a Russian folklorist, offered a method of analyzing tales and stories to assess the parts and their relationships that makes use of 31 story "functions."

Many of Propp's functions appear in contemporary books and films about schools such as *Stand and Deliver* (Edwards, 1988), the true story of high school math teacher Jaime Escalante's dedication and success teaching Hispanic ghetto students. Among Propp's functions (see Berger, 1982) in this story are: (a) family members lacking something (students lacking self-confidence, school interest, and math background); (b) the testing of the hero (the task of preparing an unmotivated class; giving up a higher paying corporate job to teach); (c) combat between hero and villian (Escalante's anger at representatives of Educational Testing Service who imply that students' success on the Advanced Placement Calculus test was due to cheating); (d) a difficult task is presented to the hero (Escalante has few days to prepare students for a retest and the group is now very discouraged at their accusal); (e) the solution of the task (all students successfully pass the retest); and (e) recognition of the hero (Escalante demands reinstatement of original scores; he is seen as competent and honest; he continues to train more and more students to pass the test in succeeding years).

Stand and Deliver imparts powerful messages about schools and teaching. The messages themselves are not new for school psychologists. For example, 20 years earlier, Jackson (1968), in *Life in Classrooms*, interviewed a group of outstanding teachers many of whom were similar to the portrayal of Escalante. But compared to the film Jackson's book had minimal impact and probably has been read by few school psychologists, let alone many average citizens whose views shape the day-to-day activities of school psychologists. Archival research in general, and media analysis in particular, offer great promise for understanding many areas relevant to school psychology.

Naturalistic Inquiry

Naturalistic inquiry refers to a strategy for doing research rather than a specific data collection technique. As such, it makes use of surveys, interviews, and other methods. Traditional experimental inquiry requires the experimenter to state in advance how the research will be conducted. This includes specifying the problem, the theoretical rationale underlying the hypotheses, the methods and statistical procedures employed, and considering practical elements such as time schedules for data collection, resources, and finances. By contrast, naturalistic observation assumes that precise specification is not possible for all elements, and that the design must emerge and unfold given the territory and context (Lincoln & Guba, 1985).

Naturalistic inquiry involves certain steps and stages that we review next; however, these stages are not necessarily linear. Rather, there is ongoing accommodation of the research design to the data collection process. This is not unlike a student learning that therapy involves certain stages (e.g., rapport building, diagnosis, initial treatment, etc.) but realizing that human interaction rarely allows for these steps to unfold in the manner in which they are described in textbooks. Whereas a good therapist would not force a stage on a client, a good researcher should not force a stage on a research participant. In describing the 10 stages of naturalistic inquiry, we draw, where informative, some examples from our research examining the reactions of family members to job-related travel (Medway, 1989), specifically, an initial study of how expectations about travel influence coping styles (Shoultz, 1990).

Determining a Focus for Inquiry. Determining a focus for a study is important because it establishes the boundaries of inquiry and the relevancy of information (i.e., what data to include and what to discard). When we (Medway, 1989) set out to study the phenomenon of short-term separation due to job responsibilities, we found that our study would only involve companies where frequent travel was the norm and those that had an interest in working along with us for mutual advantage. This was about 10% of the companies we contacted. Further, our study was constrained by the fact that the company dictated who traveled, how long, and how much. Additionally, individuals who could not handle the stress of frequent traveling at all would not apply with these companies or would drop out naturally. Finally, we often found that interviewees wanted to talk about more than what was of interest to us (i.e., relationships).

Determining Fit of Paradigm to Focus. This step involves considering the degree of indeterminacy introduced by research intrusion, for example, respondents' degree of honesty, and the degree to which context and values will influence the data. Earlier we reviewed deception and providing incomplete information to subjects, procedures typically associated with the controlled, traditional experimental method. Deception is often justified on the grounds that it reduces dishonesty and possible demand characteristics. However, it has been argued that the methods of naturalistic inquiry—particularly prolonged engagement and persistent observations—are useful in detecting false data and dealing with it.

Determining the Fit of the Paradigm to the Theory. Phenomenon that are conceptualized according to traditional research assumptions will be poorly investigated if approached through naturalistic methods.

Determining Where and From Whom Data will be Collected. One of the key principles of naturalistic inquiry is to use maximum sampling variation. Gatekeepers and experts are used to nominate the sample (e.g., having reading consultants nominate reading disordered children for study). Naturalistic observation may start by extensive interviews and assessments of a relatively few participants rather than limited evaluations with large samples. In our pilot research on separation we did extensive interviews with about 25 travelers drawn from diverse companies with subjects providing leads on subsequent possible interviewees. Using this data the follow-up studies employed larger, discrete samples using questionnaires developed and refined by examining interview responses.

Determining Successive Inquiry Phases. There are three major phases to initial naturalistic inquiry. The first involves an exploration of the situation or site to determine what needs to be followed up. Lincoln and Guba (1985) give a relevant example taken from their research assessing the delivery of services under PL 94–142. Rather than make generalizations across sites in rural areas of the United States, they decided to construct a series of case studies and give consumers of this research the chance to select the case and site that appeared more like their own. The second phase involves focused exploration and in-depth assessment. The third involves writing a case study or report and submitting it to informants for review so that inaccuracies can be spotted prior to determining precise instrumentation. These stages are similar to pilot work in traditional experimentation; however, it is rare in pilot research for representative participants to critique the instrument and initial data.

Determining Instrumentation. Human observers are the primary data collection tool in naturalistic studies. Teams from various disciplines, with varying specialties, playing various roles are employed. Team members receive ongoing training and instruments receive ongoing refinement. The team members may use observational techniques, interviews, surveys, or other methods.

Planning Data Collection. Often naturalistic inquiry proceeds from unstructured interviews with general questions to structured ones with specific questions. Field notes, video, and audiorecording also are used to generate data in early stages and provide a basis for structured evaluation.

Planning Data Analysis.   Data analysis is not left for the final phases of the study, rather this process too is ongoing. As results come in, new questions may be raised or new forms of instrumentation required.

Planning the Logistics.   This stage is an important one for school psychologists who often do research in the "field." This stage involves scheduling contacts, forecasting and budgeting costs involved, arranging for an overseeing policy board, arranging for peer debriefers, organizing the responsibilities of the research effort, and producing final reports (often much lengthier and detailed than the usual experiment write-up). Decisions may need to be made regarding "minority opinions" or data that is nonmodal, data often viewed as variance or outlier in more traditional research paradigms.

Establishing Trustworthiness.   Whereas the traditional experimenter is concerned with issues of internal and external validity, the naturalistic researcher is concerned with persuading his or her audience that the findings are worth their attention. This issue is probably at the core of much criticism of school psychology research: criticism of the findings as irrelevant to practice and thus a denigration by research users (e.g., school administrators and policy makers) of the value of school psychology research. This problem has been addressed in several ways ranging from recommendations for more applicable data to studies that originate in field questions, the latter point of view articulated in several papers by Phillips (1989, 1990). The naturalist, however, might argue that research questions and methods cannot really originate in the field without consideration of paradigmatic concerns and intensive exploration of an issue using data from many parties to formulate the questions. For the naturalistic researcher the whole process of research is designed to facilitate the data being used, especially this final stage, trustworthiness.

In an attempt to ensure data trustworthiness, the researcher attempts to ensure: (a) that the data are credible to the parties who will have to use them, (b) that they can be readily transferred and applied to the context, and (c) that the findings are dependable and confirmable. This is accomplished through the use of techniques such as prolonged engagement (as compared to entering a research site, quickly collecting data, and then leaving with data in hand never to return), persistent observation (identifying salient elements and exploring them indepth), and triangulation (the use of multiple and different sources, methods, investigators, and theories). In our separation research we view our relationship with our sponsoring companies as a long-term consultant might. Our research agreement required us to provide a workshop based on the data once collected, and the feedback we receive from the workshop illuminates future research questions as does noting other areas that respondents want to talk about besides those of theoretical interest to us.

CONCLUDING COMMENTS

> Groucho to Gummo Marx: *If you had 10 apples and you wanted to divide them among six people, what would you do?*
> Gummo: *Make applesauce*
> —Marx Brothers (in Adamson, 1973, p. 49)

In this chapter we have examined the application of social research methods to educational settings. We have reviewed some methods, such as surveys, that have been widely used by school psychologists and highlighted others, such as archival research and naturalistic inquiry, which can only enrich the research base in school psychology. As we have seen, during the past two decades both social and school psychologists have become increasingly comfortable with controlled laboratory methods dealing with narrow topics and less inclined to tackle socially important issues in naturalistic settings. As researchers retreated more into the laboratory and designed ways to precisely quantify social behavior, practitioners ventured further out into the field and became merely consumers of occasionally relevant findings. Thus, communication between researchers and practitioners was reduced (cf. Phillips, 1989), resulting in less socially relevant research and practical settings that greeted new research pronouncements with skepticism.

It is our contention that social psychology offers many methods that are compatible with the roles of both academic and applied psychologists; and some methods, such as naturalistic inquiry, where the roles of investigator, facilitator, and intervener are deliberately obscured. However, returning to the themes of our opening quotations and the message of our final one, it is also our belief that it is not the use of any particular research method that will advance the profession but rather the adoption of an overriding creative plan to address, what may seem to be, difficult questions. Here we can learn from social psychology's unmistakable track record. In that field, the return from "one shot" studies has been negligible whereas the return from theoretically grounded research and planned problem solving has been considerable, especially when applied settings are used to develop frameworks (Rodin, 1985). Clearly, in the final analysis, advances in school psychology will not be exclusively in the hands of researchers or practitioners but rather will come from those individuals who are aware of methods that go beyond ones traditionally used in their field and can apply these methods in an innovative manner to the illumination of educational issues.

REFERENCES

Adair, J. G. (1973). *The human subject: The social psychology of the psychological experiment.* Boston: Little, Brown.
Adamson, J. (1973). *Groucho, Harpo, Chico, and sometimes Zeppo.* New York: Simon and Schuster.

Aitkenhead, M., & Dorday, J. (1985). What the subjects have to say. *British Journal of Social Psychology, 24*, 293–305.

Alpert, J. L., & Yammer, M. D. (1983). Research in school consultation: A content analysis of selected journals. *Professional Psychology: Research and Practice, 14*, 604–612.

American Psychological Association, Committee for the Protection of Human Research Participants in Research (1982). *Ethical principles in the conduct of research with human participants* (2d ed.). Washington, DC.

Aronson, E., Brewer, M., & Carlsmith, J. M. (1985). Experimentation in social psychology, In G. Lindzey & E. Aronson (Eds.), *Handbook of social psychology* (Vol. 1, 3d ed., pp. 441–486). New York: Random House.

Aronson, E., & Carlsmith, J. M. (1968). Experimentation in social psychology. In G. Lindzey & E. Aronson (Eds.), *The handbook of social psychology* (Vol. 2, pp. 1–79). Reading, MA: Addison-Wesley.

Bailey, K. D. (1987). *Methods of social psychological research* (3d ed.). New York: Free Press.

Bales, R. F. (1980). *SYMLOG case study kit.* New York: Free Press.

Bardon, J. I., (1987). The translation of research into practice in school psychology. *School Psychology Review, 16*, 317–328.

Barlow, D. H., Hayes, S. C., & Nelson, R. O. (1984). *The scientist–practitioner: Research and accountability in clinical and educational settings.* New York: Pergamon.

Baurmind, D. (1979). IRB's and social science research: The cost of deception. *IRB: A Review of Human Subjects Research, 1*(6), 1–4.

Baumrind, D. (1985). Research using intentional deception: Ethical issues revisited. *American Psychologist, 40*, 165–174.

Berger, A. A. (1982). *Media analysis techniques.* Beverly Hills: Sage.

Borgida, E., & DeBono, K. G. (1989). Social hypothesis testing and the role of expertise. *Personality and Social Psychology Bulletin, 15*, 212–221.

Boss, P. G. (1987). The role of intuition in family research: Three issues of ethics. *Contemporary Family Therapy, 9*(1–2), 146–159.

Bradburn, N. M., & Sudman, S. (1979). *Improving interview method and questionnaire design.* San Francisco: Jossey-Bass.

Bradley, E. J., & Lindsay, R. C. L. (1987). Methodological and ethical issues in child abuse research. *Journal of Family Violence, 2*, 239–255.

Bronfenbrenner, U. (1979). Contexts of child rearing. *American Psychologist, 34*, 844–850.

Bullock, M. J., Ironsmith, M., & Poteat, G. M. (1988). Sociometric techniques with young children: A review of psychometrics and classification schemes. *School Psychology Review, 17*, 289–303.

Campbell, D. T., & Stanley, J. C. (1963). *Experimental and quasi-experimental designs for research.* Chicago: Rand McNally.

Carlson, R. (1971). Where is the person in personality research? *Psychological Bulletin, 75*, 203–219.

Carroll, J. L., Bretzing, B. H., & Harris, J. D. (1981). Psychologists in secondary schools: Training and present patterns of service. *Journal of School Psychology, 19*, 267–273.

Chapman, L. J., & Chapman, J. P. (1967). Genesis of popular but erroneous psychodiagnostic observations. *Journal of Abnormal Psychology, 72*, 193–204.

Chapman, L. J., & Chapman, J. P. (1969). Illusory correlation as an obstacle to the use of valid psychodiagnostic signs. *Journal of Abnormal Psychology, 74*, 271–280.

Christensen, L. (1988). Deception in psychological research: When is its use justified? *Personality and Social Psychology Bulletin, 14*, 664–675.

Converse, J. M., & Presser, S. (1986). *Survey questions: Handcrafting the standardized questionnaire.* Beverly Hills, CA: Sage.

Cook, T. D., & Campbell, D. T. (1979). *Quasi-experimentation: Design and analysis issues for field settings.* Chicago: Rand McNally.

Copeland, E. P., & Miller, L. F. (1985). Training needs of prospective school psychologists: The practitioners' viewpoint. *Journal of School Psychology, 23,* 247–254.

Criswell, J. H. (1937). Racial cleavages in Negro–White groups. *Sociometry, 1,* 87–89.

Culler, J. (1976). *Structuralistic poetics: Structuralism, linguistics, and the study of literature.* New York: Cornell University Press.

Duncan, C. F., & Pryzwansky, W. B. (1988). Consultation research: Trends in doctoral dissertations 1978–1985. *Journal of School Psychology, 26,* 107–119.

Edwards, N. (1988). *Stand and deliver.* New York: Scholastic.

Fagan, T. K. (1985). Sources for the delivery of school psychological services during 1890–1930. *School Psychology Review, 14,* 378–382.

Fagan, T. K. (1986). The evolving literature of school psychology. *School Psychology Review, 15,* 430–440.

Fagan, T. K. (1987). Gesell: The first school psychologist, Part II. Practice and significance. *School Psychology Review, 16,* 399–409.

Fillenbaum, S. (1966). Prior deception and subsequent experimental performance: The "faithful" subject. *Journal of Personality and Social Psychology, 4,* 532–537.

Fischhoff, B. (1975). Hindsight = foresight: The effect of outcome knowledge on judgment under uncertainty. *Journal of Experimental Psychology: Human Perception and Performance, 1,* 288–299.

Fowler, F. J., Jr. (1984). *Survey research methods.* Beverly Hills, CA: Sage.

French, J. L., & Raykovitz, J. (1984). Dissertation research in school psychology, 1978–1980. *Journal of School Psychology, 22,* 73–82.

Georgourdi, M., & Rosnow, R. L. (1985). Notes toward a contextualist understanding of social psychology. *Personality and Social Psychology Bulletin, 11,* 5–22.

Gergen, K. J. (1973). Social psychology as history. *Journal of Personality and Social Psychology, 26,* 309–320.

Gordon, G. A., & Smith, C. J. (1989). Research productivity in social psychology. *Personality and Social Psychology Bulletin, 15,* 463–472.

Guba, E. G., & Lincoln, Y. S. (1989). *Fourth generation evaluation.* Newbury Park, CA: Sage.

Hartshorne, T. S., & Johnson, M. C. (1985). The actual and preferred roles of the school psychologist according to secondary school administrators. *Journal of School Psychology, 23,* 241–246.

Haynes, S. N., Lemsky, C., & Sexton-Radek (1987). Why clinicians infrequently do research. *Professional Psychology: Research and Practice, 18,* 515–519.

Heider, F. (1958). *The psychology of interpersonal relations.* New York: Wiley.

Hendrick, C., & Clark, M. S. (1990). *Research methods in personality and social psychology.* Newbury Park, CA: Sage.

Henry, S. E., Medway, F. J., & Scarbro, H. A. (1979). Sex and locus of control as determinants of children's responses to peer versus adult praise. *Journal of Educational Psychology, 71,* 604–612.

Israel, J., & Tajfel, H. (Eds.) (1972). *The context of social psychology.* London: Academic Press.

Jackson, P. W. (1968). *Life in classroom.* New York: Holt, Rinehart, & Winston.

Jennings, H. H. (1943). *Leadership and isolation.* New York: Longmans.

Jourard, S. M. (1967). Experimenter–subject dialogue: A paradigm for a humanistic science of psychology. In J. F. T. Bugental (Ed.), *Challenges of humanistic psychology* (pp. 109–116). New York: McGraw-Hill.

Kahneman, D., Slovic, P., & Tversky, A. (1982). *Judgment under uncertainty: Heuristics and biases.* Cambridge: Cambridge University Press.

Kahneman, D., & Tversky, A. (1973). On the psychology of prediction. *Psychological Review, 80,* 237–251.

Kenney, K. C. (1986). Research in mental health consultation: Emerging trends, issues, and problems. In F. V. Mannino, E. J. Trickett, M. F. Shore, M. G. Kidder, & G. Levin (Eds.), *Handbook of mental health consultation* (pp. 435–469). Washington, DC: U.S. Department of Health and Human Services.

Kerlinger, F. N. (1979). *Behavioral research: A conceptual approach.* New York: Holt, Rinehart, & Winston.

Kidder, L. H., & Judd, C. M. (1986). *Research methods in social relations* (5th ed.). New York: Holt, Rinehart, & Winston.

Kratochwill, T. R. (Ed.). (1978). *Single subject research: Strategies for evaluating change.* New York: Academic Press.

Kratochwill, T. R., Schnaps, A., & Bissell, M. S. (1985). Research design in school psychology. In J. R. Bergan, (Ed.), *School psychology in contemporary society* (pp. 58–91). Columbus, OH: Merrill.

Krippendorff, K. (1980). *Content analysis: An introduction to it methodology.* Beverly Hills, CA: Sage.

LaGreca, A. M. (1983). Interviewing and behavioral observations. In C. E. Walker & M. C. Roberts (Eds.), *Handbook of clinical child psychology* (pp. 109–131). New York: Wiley.

Lavrakas, P. J. (1987). *Telephone survey methods: Sampling, selection, and supervision.* Newbury Park, CA: Sage.

Lincoln, Y. S., & Guba, E. G. (1985). *Naturalistic inquiry.* Beverly Hills, CA: Sage.

Lindzey, G., & Byrne, D. (1968). Measurement of social choice and interpersonal attractiveness. In G. Lindzey & E. Aronson (Eds.), *The handbook of social psychology* (Vol. 2, pp. 452–425). Reading, MA: Addison-Wesley.

Marsh, C. (1982). *The survey method.* London: Allen & Unwin.

Martens, B. K., & Keller, H. R. (1987). Training school psychologists in the scientific tradition. *School Psychology Review, 16,* 329–337.

Martens, B. K., & Meller, P. J. (1989). Influence of child and classroom characteristics on acceptability of interventions. *Journal of School Psychology, 27,* 237–246.

Martin, R. P. (1986). Assessment of the social and emotional functioning of preschool children. *School Psychology Review, 15,* 216–232.

Maslow, A. H. (1968). *Toward a psychology of being.* New York: Van Nostrand Reinhold.

Mason, E. J., & Bramble, W. J. (1989). *Understanding and conducting research: Applications in education and the behavioral sciences.* New York: McGraw-Hill.

Mayo, E. (1945). *The social problems of an industrial civilization.* Cambridge, MA: Harvard University Press.

McArthur, L. Z. (1980). Illusory causation and illusory correlation: Two epistomological accounts. *Personality and Social Psychology Bulletin, 6,* 507–519.

McConnell, J. V., & Gorenflo, D. W. (Eds.). (1989). *Classic readings in psychology.* Forth Worth: Holt.

Medway, F. J. (August, 1989). (Chm.). *Intermitted separation and mobility: School and clinical perspectives.* Symposium presented at the meeting of the American Psychological Association. New Orleans.

Medway, F. J., & Cafferty, T. P. (1990). Contributions of social psychology to school psychology. In T. B. Gutkin & C. R. Reynolds (Eds.), *The handbook of school psychology* (2d ed., pp. 175–197). New York: Wiley.

Medway, F. J., & Forman, S. G. (1980). Psychologists' and teachers' reactions to mental health and behavioral school consultation. *Journal of School Psychology, 4,* 338–348.

Medway, F. J., & Updyke, J. F. (1985). Meta-analysis of consultation outcome studies. *American Journal of Community Psychology, 13,* 485–501.

Minton, H. L. (1984). J. F. Brown's social psychology of the 1930s: A historical antecedent to the contemporary crisis in social psychology. *Personality and Social Psychology Bulletin, 10,* 31–42.

Mixon, D. (1971). Behavior analysis treating subjects as actors rather than organisms. *Journal for the Theory of Social Behavior, 1,* 19–32.

Moreno, J. L. (1934). *Who shall survive?* Washington, DC: Nervous and Mental Disease Monograph, No. 58.

Moskowitz, J. M. (1985). Evaluating the effects of parent groups on the correlates of adolescent substance abuse. *Journal of Psychoactive Drugs, 17,* 173–178.

National Research Act, PL 93–348 (July 12, 1974).

Niemenen, G. S., & Matson, J. L. (1989). Depressive problems in conduct-disordered adolescents. *Journal of School Psychology, 27,* 175–188.

Nisbett, R. E., & Ross, L. (1980). *Human inference: Strategies and shortcomings in social judgment,* Englewood Cliffs, NJ: Prentice-Hall.

Oakland, T. (1984). The *Journal of School Psychology's* first twenty years: Contributions and contributors. *Journal of School Psychology, 22,* 239–250.

Oppenheim, A. N. (1966). *Questionnaire design and attitude measurement.* New York: Basic Books.

Orne, M. (1962). On the social psychology of the psychological experiment. *American Psychologist, 17,* 776–783.

Ottati, V. C., Riggle, E. J., Wyer, Jr., R. S., Schwarz, N., & Kuklinski, J. (1989). Cognitive and affective bases of survey opinion responses. *Journal of Personality and Social Psychology 57,* 404–415.

Paget, K. D. (1984). The structured assessment interview: A psychometric review. *Journal of School Psychology, 22,* 415–427.

Parker, L. E., & Detterman, D. K. (1988). The balance between clinical and research interest among boulder model graduate students. *Professional Psychology, 19,* 342–344.

Pfeiffer, S. I., & Marmo, P. (1981). The status of training in school psychology and trends toward the future. *Journal of School Psychology, 19,* 211–216.

Phillips, B. N. (1982). On reading and evaluating research in school psychology. In C. R. Reynolds & T. B. Gutkin (Eds.), *The handbook of school psychology* (1st ed., pp. 24–47). New York: Wiley.

Phillips, B. N. (1987). On science, mirrors, lamps, and professional practice. *Professional School Psychology, 2,* 221–229.

Phillips, B. N. (1989). Role of the practitioner in applying science to practice. *Professional Psychology: Research and Practice, 20,* 3–8.

Phillips, B. N. (1990). Reading, evaluating, and applying research in school psychology. In T. B. Gutkin & C. R. Reynolds (Eds.), *The handbook of school psychology* (2d ed., pp. 53–73). New York: Wiley.

Propp, V. (1968). *Morphology of the folk tale.* Austin: University of Texas Press.

Pryzwansky, W. B. (1989). School consultation: Some considerations from a cognitive psychology perspective. *Professional School Psychology, 4,* 1–14.

Reedy, P. D. (1989). *Practical research: Planning and design.* New York: Macmillan.

Reimers, T. M. Wacker, D. P., & Koeppl, G. (1987). Acceptability of behavioral interventions: A review of the literature. *School Psychology Review, 16,* 212–227.

Reynolds, C. R., & Clark, J. H. (1984). Trends in school psychological research (1974–1980). *Journal of School Psychology, 22,* 43–52.

Rich, J. (1968). *Interviewing children and adolescents.* London: Macmillan.

Ring, K. (1967). Experimental social psychology: Some sober questions about some frivolous values. *Journal of Experimental Social Psychology, 3,* 113–123.

Rodin, J. (1985). The application of social psychology. In G. Lindzey & E. Aronson (Eds.), *Handbook of Social Psychology* (Vol. 2, 3d ed., pp. 805–881). New York: Random House.

Rosenberg, M. S. (Ed.). (1978a). *Quotations for the new age.* Secaucus, NJ: The Citadel Press.

Rosenberg, M. S. (Ed.). (1978b). *Quotations for the new age.* Secaucus, NJ: The Citadel Press.

Rosenberg, M. S. (Ed.). (1978c). *Quotations for the new age.* Secaucus, NJ: The Citadel Press.

Rosenberg, M. S. (Ed.). (1978d). *Quotations for the new age.* Secaucus, NJ: The Citadel Press.

Rosenberg, M. S. (Ed.). (1978e). *Quotations for the new age.* Secaucus, NJ: The Citadel Press.

Rosenthal, R. (1966). *Experimenter effects in behavioral research.* New York: Appleton-Century-Crofts.

Rosnow, R. L. (1981). *Paradigms in transition: The methodology of social inquiry.* New York: Oxford University Press.

Shoultz, D. E. (1990). *The effects of intermittent job-related marital separations upon marital satisfaction: A cognitive perspective.* Unpublished doctoral dissertation, University of South Carolina.

Schwartz, P., & Olgivy, J. (1979). *The emergent paradigm: Changing patterns of thought and belief.* Analytical Report 7, Values and Lifestyles Program. Menlo Park, CA: SRI International.

Sears, D. O. (1986). College sophomores in the laboratory: Influences of a narrow data base on Social Psychology's view of human nature. *Journal of Personality and Social Psychology, 51,* 515–530.

Selltiz, C., Wrightsman, L. S., & Cook, S. W. (1976). *Research methods in social relations.* New York: Holt, Rinehart, & Winston.

Shemberg, K., Keeley, S. M., & Blum, M. (1989). Attitudes toward traditional and nontraditional dissertation research: A survey of directors of clinical training. *Professional Psychology: Research and Practice, 20,* 190–192.

Snyder, M., & Cantor, N. (1979). Testing hypotheses about other people: The use of historical information. *Journal of Experimental Social Psychology, 15,* 330–342.

Snyder, M., & Swann, W. B., Jr. (1978). Hypothesis-testing in social interaction. *Journal of Personality and Social Psychology, 36,* 1202–1212.

Sudman, S., & Bradburn, N. M. (1982). *Asking questions.* San Francisco: Jossey-Bass.

Taylor, S. E., & Fiske, S. T. (1975). Point of view and perceptions of causality. *Journal of Personality and Social Psychology, 32,* 439–445.

Tinbergen, N. (1963). On the aims and methods of ethology. *Zeitschrift Tierpsychology, 20,* 410–433.

Triplett, N. (1897). The dynamogenic factors in pacemaking and competition. *American Journal of Psychology, 9,* 507–533.

Warner, S. L. (1965). Randomized response: A survey technique for eliminating evasive answer bias. *Journal of the American Statistical Association, 60,* 63–69.

Webb, A. R. (1989). What's in a question? Three methods for investigating psychology's public image. *Professional Psychology: Research and Practice, 20,* 301–304.

Weick, K. E. (1968). Systematic observational methods. In G. Lindzey & E. Aronson, *The handbook of social psychology* (Vol. 2, pp. 357–451). Reading, MA: Addison-Wesley.

Whyte, W. F. (1943). *Street corner society.* Chicago: University of Chicago Press.

Witt, J. R. (Ed.) (1987). Research in school psychology. *School Psychology Review, 16,* 274–347.

PART

II

APPLYING SOCIAL PSYCHOLOGY TO CLINICIAL INTERVENTIONS IN THE SCHOOLS

The chapters preceding detail how many of the social psychological principles and theories discussed in Part 1 can be applied by school psychologists. Four chapters deal with processes of assessment, direct and indirect clinical interventions, and educational change strategies. The final chapter discusses the evaluation of the performance of school psychologists.

Chapter 9 by Goh and Yoshida reviews the many social variables that impact on the referral and assessment of children. These factors include expectations and attributions about children, their characteristics such as gender, race, language patterns, and test-taking skills, and the nature of diagnoses made in team settings. This chapter complements nicely the earlier chapters by Levesque and Lowe, and Henning-Stout and Conoley.

In Chapter 10 Sandoval and Davis deal with the social psychology of school counseling. Sandoval and Davis highlight the importance of several theories, most notably dissonance and reactance, to the counseling process. They also briefly discuss gender issues in counseling and family therapy, thus building on the earlier chapters of Henning-Stout and Conoley, and Barbarin.

In Chapter 11 Hughes discusses the social psychological principles inherent in school consultation. Consultation is an area in which social psychological theories have made major inroads, particularly attribution theory, dissonance, and reactance. Hughes makes uses of similar theoretical models as does Sandoval and Davis, and these two chapters nicely compliment one another.

Chapter 12 by Gettinger discusses social psychological variables that influence classroom performance and schooling. Gettinger covers cooperative learning models, adaptive education, and teacher perceptions. Her chapter builds on the earlier chapter on attribution and expectation by Levesque and Lowe and reviews principles relevant to the integration of special students discussed in Chapter 18 by Weyant.

In Chapter 13, Kevin Williams, an industrial-organizational psychologist, and his wife Gwen Williams, a practicing school psychologist, describe the evaluation and appraisal of school psychologists' performance from a social-cognitive framework. A model of performance appraisal is described and applied to school psychology evaluation. This is an important, cutting-edge area given the recent emphasis on school staff accountability. The Williams' assess the available appraisal techniques for school psychologists and highlight key variables that affect the accuracy of rater judgments.

9

THE INFLUENCES OF SOCIAL PSYCHOLOGICAL VARIABLES ON THE REFERRAL AND ASSESSMENT OF SCHOOL CHILDREN

David S. Goh
Roland K. Yoshida
Queens College, City University of New York

The basic tenents of social psychology and how social psychological variables affect the development of human behavior have been discussed in previous chapters. In this chapter, we examine the influences of some of these variables on the referral, testing, and evaluation of schoolchildren. Particular emphases are given to cultural, social interpersonal, and organizational factors in our discussion.

In recent years, the nature of testing and evaluation in the schools have gradually evolved from the traditional clinical model that focuses on the individual child, to a broader framework that seeks to assess both children and their social and learning environments (Carlson, Scott, & Eklund, 1980; Goh, Teslow, & Fuller, 1981). Within this framework, assessment is viewed as a process of data collection for decision-making/problem-solving purposes. This process encompasses several stages including referral, instrument selection, test administration and scoring, interpretation and use of assessment results, and multidisciplinary team decision making. We discuss the influence of several social psychological variables relevant to each of these stages in the following sections.

REFERRAL

Elementary and secondary teachers are most influential in determining which students are labeled handicapped and placed into special education programs. They begin the evaluation process by referring children. Their reasons for referrals are most likely to be confirmed. Mehan, Hertweck, and Meihls (1986) observed in their ethnographic study that psychologists chose assessment instruments that were consonant with the teachers' reasons for referral. In one study special education directors estimated that, on the average, more than 75% of students referred received some type of special education service (Algozzine, Christenson, & Ysseldyke, 1982). Actual counts from New York City showed that 95% of the students referred were found eligible for special education in 1983 and 85% in 1984 (Beattie, 1985). The significance attached to referral reasons warrants an analysis of how teachers make referral decisions.

Kelley's (1973) attribution theory provided an understanding of how individuals such as teachers decide that students are incapable of adequately achieving and/or appropriately behaving in particular classroom settings. Teachers are conceived as hypothesis testers who attempt to formulate stable explanations for outcomes according to three rules. First, they ask, how unusual are students' behaviors when compared to others? Students reading at the second-grade level in a fifth-grade class would be considered different from the majority of students who read at grade level. This discrepancy may be viewed as large enough to conclude that these "different" students need to be referred. Second, they ask how consistently do students demonstrate behaviors? Students' performance is judged to be at the same level regardless of context such as size of learning group (whole class, small group, individual group). Finally, they ask, do others such as colleagues perceive similar levels of performance? If so, consensus is high and teachers can have confidence in their conclusions.

Causal attributions (see Levesque & Lowe in this volume) can be either internal to the student (meaning learner characteristics) or external (signifying the students' school and home environment). Teachers cite most often internal attributions such as students' potential handicapping condition (learning disabled or mental retardation), their general lack of achievement or ability, and their behavioral problems when referring students (Anderson, Cronin, & Miller, 1986; Harris, Gray, Rees-McGee, Carroll, & Zaremba, 1987; Ownby, Wallbrown, D'Atri, & Armstrong, 1985; Potter, Ysseldyke, Regan, & Algozzine, 1983; Pugach, 1985; Ysseldyke, Christenson, Pianta, & Algozzine, 1983). However, many referral reasons documented in studies are general, vague, and without substantiating data.

Although referred students may demonstrate the problems as perceived by the teacher, the focus on internal attributions may also be symptomatic of what Gergen and Gergen (1986) termed self-serving bias. Johnson, Feigenbaum, and Weiby (1964) asked teachers to rate whether students' success or failure was due primarily to the students' abilities and efforts or to their own teaching skills. When students succeeded, teachers claimed credit; when students failed, teachers mentioned students' lack of ability or effort.

Once such judgments are made, they tend to be stable and lead to differences in some teachers' behaviors toward students (Brophy & Good, 1986; Jones & Nisbett, 1971). For example, Brophy and Good (1970) asked four teachers to rank students in order of expected achievement. Three boys and three girls who were high on each teacher's list were chosen and labeled as high achievers; the same number were selected from the bottom of the lists and named low achievers. High achievers received more positive and supportive feedback than low achievers from their teachers. Such differential interactions could suppress the low achievers' performance, thus reinforcing their teachers' expectations towards them.

In addition to findings of the potential influences of teacher expectations, the teacher effectiveness literature has shown considerable variability in teacher behavior to create desirable learning environments (Brophy & Good, 1986). Yoshida, Lopez, Friedman, and Matalon (1991) asked 10 teachers to nominate nine students, three of whom the teachers judged to be average; three, low achieving; and three in need of special education services. The students were interviewed to determine whether they could identify inappropriate classroom behaviors and whether they were able to role play "paying attention" behaviors. All but one student was able to do so. However, students in four classrooms regardless of their achievement status were on-task less than 50% of the time during observation sessions. In the remaining six classrooms, students identified as requiring special education services were on-task at higher rates than average learners in four classrooms with low overall on-task rates. Teachers differed in how they addressed students when inappropriate behaviors occurred. Teachers in low on-task classrooms tended to shout at students and hit desks to gain students' attention. The students themselves independently reported these behaviors. Although no differences were found in referral rates among the 10 teachers, these results raise the alternative hypothesis that low performance may be due not only to internal causes such as student ability and effort but also to external ones such as the quality of instruction given to the students.

In short, internal causes are most often stated when teachers refer students for special education. Yet the teacher effectiveness literature has consistently shown the considerable variation in the ways teachers manage their classes, an external cause. Even if we assume that teachers manage their classes equally well, Friedman, Cancelli, and Yoshida (1988) found that students labeled learning disabled showed very different on-task behavior rates depending on whether they were observed in small-group or large-group lecture settings. Although teachers' attributions of internal causes may be valid, Kelley's (1971) three questions provide a useful guide for school psychologists to evaluate alternative causes of students' performance.

TEST SELECTION

Selection of appropriate instruments is one of the most important considerations in the testing and evaluation of schoolchildren. Upon receiving the referral, the school psychologist reviews the available case information and determines the techniques and instruments to be used for data gathering. Essential to this deliberation are the purposes of testing and the characteristics of the individual or group being tested. The selected tasks must have the ability to produce valid information that is useful for dealing with children's problems either in terms of problem solving or decision making.

The need to consider the purposes of testing in instrument selection is obvious. Of equal importance are the characteristics of the children to be tested. Standardized tests are developed for certain age, educational, and cultural groups. These tests are suitable for use with particular children, only when they possess the same characteristics as those of the norm groups. Brown (1976) indicates that whenever test performance varies as a function of some characteristic, that characteristic should be considered when selecting the test. As much as a test may report satisfactory reliabilities and validities, these data would not equally apply to individuals who have personal characteristics or backgrounds different from that of the population for which the test was developed.

Particular concern should be given to selection of tests for use with children from ethnic/racial, handicapped, or other minority groups. The socialization process these children experience often fosters cognitive styles, communicative patterns, personality traits, values, and other psychological attributes different from those of the majority population. Such differences become a systematic source of error in many standardized tests, when they are used with ethnic minority children. For example, traditional intelligence tests that rely heavily on the values and experiences of the White, middle-class culture would not be equally suitable measures for culturally disadvantaged or linguistically different minority children. Likewise, Diamond and Tittle (1985) found that many achievement tests were biased against females due to unequal distribution of sex referents in test items. Thus, females are less likely to do as well as males on these tests (Brown, 1980; Green, 1987).

The issue of test bias has been a prominent concern and controversy during the past two decades. Green (1975) suggested that bias was "the expression in tests of racism, sexism, and other inappropriate attitudes" (p. 35). Numerous measurement specialists and psychologists (e.g., Berk, 1982; Cole, 1981; Diamond & Elmore, 1986; Flaugher, 1978; Green, 1978; Jensen, 1980; Reschly, 1979; Reynolds, 1982) have conducted investigations on detecting test bias, on designing methods for reducing test biases, and on fairly using tests in different settings. In the meantime, federal and state legislation has focused on tests to ensure their fairness when assessing women and men, ethnic and minority groups, and handicapped persons (Berk, 1982). For example, PL 94–142, the Education of All Handicapped Children Act of 1975, mandates that testing and evaluation materials must be selected so as not to be racially or culturally discriminatory.

Bias exists in any culture. No psychological test is either culture free or culture fair. It is impractical to expect all tests to be equally valid for all individuals from different subgroups of a population. Researchers, test publishers, and professional organizations are all making efforts to minimize bias in tests. Through judicious selection of test instruments, psychologists attempt to ensure the first step of nonbiased assessment of a child of any cultural origin or handicapping condition.

ADMINISTRATION AND SCORING OF TESTS

Psychological tests are administered according to standardized procedures. These procedures are designed so that all individuals who are taking the test receive the same treatment. Thus, the results are comparable from person to person and group to group. The ideal testing situation requires examiners to adopt an objective and scientific attitude towards the persons they are testing, whereas at the same time maintaining an emotionally supportive rapport with the examinees. This rapport is essential to elicit valid performance on psychological tests and measures. The testing situation, like other interpersonal situations, involves a social relationship between people. The interpersonal relationship and dynamics between examiners and examinees are influenced by the personal qualities they each bring to the situation. Although optimum standardization is the goal, one cannot overlook the effects of these interpersonal variables.

Examiner Characteristics

Examiners can have a significant effect on both cognitive and personality types of tests. Individually administered tests appear more subject to such effects than group tests (Graham & Lilly, 1984). A large number of examiner variables have been researched with individually administered tests, including age, sex, socioeconomic status, race/ethnicity, temperament, expectancy, familiarity with the examinee, and behavior during test administration. Three examiner variables have attracted the most research attention: (a) expectancy of examiners, (b) race/ethnicity of examiners, (c) and familiarity of examiners with examinees.

Examiner Expectancy. In social psychology, research has shown that experimenters' expectations can influence the behavior of a subject in a variety of psychological research (Rosenthal, 1966). Rosenthal and Jacobson (1968) conducted a study in which teachers were given a list of students who were expected to greatly improve their cognitive ability during the course of the year. Student names were actually selected randomly, but the teachers were incorrectly told the list was generated by means of a special pretest. The results of this experiment supported the "self-fulfilling prophecy." Although this study has been severely criticized for methodological problems (e.g., Cronbach, 1975), researchers have applied the conceptualization of expectancy effects to other settings.

Examiner expectancy appears to affect testing results. Sattler (1988) reviewed studies in this area and found that (a) pretest information (being bright or dull) about examinees influenced examiners' scoring of responses, especially if the responses were ambiguous, but (b) no consistent findings could be concluded on expectancy effects on the administration of intelligence tests. Sattler reasons that for an expectancy effect to occur examiners have to ignore children's actual performance, which is less likely to be observed during the administration of more structured tests such as intelligence tests. Klopfer and Taulbee (1976) indicated that examiner expectancy may have more of an effect on projective tests than intelligence tests. Wheeler, Adams, and Nielson (1986) designed a study to investigate whether physical attractiveness versus unattractiveness tended to elicit differential expectations and influence test evaluation. They found that examiners tended to attribute more positive personality and social characteristics to attractive than to unattractive children. These research findings lead to an apparent suggestion that examiners should guard against expectancy effects in test administration and scoring.

Examiner Familiarity. Examiner familiarity is defined as the degree to which examiners are acquainted with examinees prior to testing. A series of studies (Fuchs, Featherstone, Garwick, & Fuchs, 1984; Fuchs & Fuchs, 1989; Fuchs, Fuchs, Garwick, & Featherstone, 1983; Fuchs, Fuchs, Power, & Daily, 1985) have consistently reported that handicapped as well as minority children (African Americans and Hispanics) scored significantly higher when tested by familiar examiners. To account for the positive effect, Fuchs and Fuchs (1989) reasoned that, in a situation in which one feels more vulnerable or less adequate, having familiar examiners can optimize performance because anxiety may be lessened and the overall threat of the task is less. They further suggest that, because it has been shown that both minority and handicapped children's test performance improve when such a prior relationship has been established with examiners, perhaps examinees who feel at a disadvantage can benefit from being acquainted with examiners prior to testing.

Examiner Race/Ethnicity. The issue of whether or not the race of examiners affects examinees' test performance has long been an area of concern and much controversy. Graziano, Varca, and Levy (1982) reviewed 29 studies conducted from 1966 to 1982 and concluded that, taken as a whole, the research provided no consistent evidence that examiners of different races systematically elicit different performances in African American and Caucasian examinees. Sattler and Gwynne (1982) in their review of the literature concluded that the majority of research results did not reveal a significant effect of the race of examiners on children's test outcomes. However, Graziano, Varca, and Levy (1982) concluded that there were no effects in these studies because in some cases examiners' race enhanced test performance, whereas at other times it suppressed performance. Cronbach (1984) commented that "One reason that studies (in this area) add up to no rules or generalizations is that average is beside the point. Test takers react to what the examiner does and to immediate circumstances" (p. 66). When one thinks of the potential complexities involved in racial relations, it seems too simplistic to assume that within testing situations examiners' race will either have no effect or the same effect at all times.

The research previously cited shows that examiners possess qualities that may affect test outcomes for some children. These variables are likely to affect minority and handicapped children to a greater extent than normal children. However, one should not overgeneralize about examiner effects. Further, it is important to bear in mind that there may be significant interactions between examiner and examinee characteristics, in the sense that the same examiner characteristics or testing manner may have different effects on different examinees as a function of the examinees' own personal characteristics (Anastasi, 1988).

Examinee Characteristics

As testing is a reciprocal interaction between two individuals, it is obvious that contamination may also rise from personal characteristics of the test taker. Most notable among the examinee variables are attitude, language, test-taking skills, and self-concept.

Attitudes. The phenomenon of attitudes influencing test situations and scores can be found in all cultures. Some population characteristics may cause a subject to react rather than to respond in a testing situation. Watson (1972) reported on a series of studies that indicated high stress affected performance when African American examinees took tests with Caucasian examiners. Other examples about attitude dependent bias on the part of examinees are easily found in the literature of cross-cultural psychology. For example, Vernon (1982) maintained that the Chinese culture approves of a lack of equality between the sexes, thus adversely affecting the willingness of female

Chinese to actively participate and accept risk-taking responses in test interaction. Others (Goh, 1986; Leong & Huang, 1987) have discussed that Asian–American children in general are apprehensive about responding to non-Asian evaluators and thus do not fully respond under standard testing conditions.

Language.   Language can significantly affect test performance. Socialinguists indicate that the measurement of linguistic abilities may involve biases when the examinees' language differs from the examiners' verbal language and nonverbal behavior (Hoover, Politzer, & Taylor, 1987). This includes the more subtle wording connotations and uses within subcultures, and differing communicative styles. Kagan (1975) gave examples of how dialectical differences may affect test performance in cross-ethnic combinations of middle-class, Caucasian examiners and African–American examinees. In many instances, examiners and examinees are unaware of the dialectical differences with their hidden nuances of meaning thereby increasing the dangers of misinterpretation of utterances.

Language differences pose a more serious problem in the testing of language-minority children when using translators or translated versions of tests. Goh (1984) and Olmedo (1981) indicated that such practices present methodological problems that are not always treated properly. For example, translations do not ordinarily yield technically equivalent forms between different languages. The translated items may exhibit psychometric properties substantially different from those of the original English version. In addition, children from different social and cultural backgrounds may have a communicative style that is different from that of examiners. They may be uncomfortable answering questions that are in direct conflict with the rules of their culture. As a result, examiners may develop low expectations of examinees. More research is clearly needed in this area because the need for properly assessing bilingual and limited English proficiency students is rapidly increasing.

Test-Taking Skills.   Test-taking skills include examinees' motivation, adaptive strategies, response styles, test anxiety, and self-concept. Deficiencies in test-taking skills are observed in ethnic minority and nonminority children (Sattler, 1988). The professional literature (e.g., Anastasi, 1988; Cronbach, 1984) is filled with discussion about how these variables may affect examinees' performance in testing situations. For example, Graham and Lilly (1984) stated that testing situations involve many unpleasant characteristics (i.e., the testing is not sought out by the examinees, especially if they are children; personality tests sometimes pose embarrassing questions). These characteristics may present some threat to subjects' self-esteem and subsequently affect their performance. Karmos and Karmos (1984) suggested that persons' attitudes toward themselves affect every aspect of their lives, including testing situations. In a study examining the relationships among self-concept, attitude toward test, and test performance, Karmos and Karmos (1984) found that both examinees' attitudes about themselves or about the test's importance were significantly correlated to achievement test scores.

The preceding discussion reflects the sociopsychological complexities involved in a testing situation. The complexity of the issue increases as we recognize that both between- and within-group differences exist in many of the variables mentioned earlier. Skilled psychologists should be sensitive to the social dynamics involved in the testing environment. They should be able to minimize those influences interfering negatively with the examinees' performance. They should nurture those influences that are contributing positively to valid and ethical data gathering. As Cronbach (1984) correctly pointed out, an effective test administration calls for examiners, of whatever social and family origins, to discover styles that reach persons from different backgrounds.

INTERPRETATION AND USE OF TEST RESULTS

Too often, test results in education are used to label and categorize children so they can be placed in special classes. The issue of labeling children has been frequently discussed and criticized in recent years (e.g., Fernald, Williams, & Droescher, 1985; Smith, Osborne, Crim, & Rhu, 1986; Strenio, 1980). Whereas labeling may be necessary for government funding and may be publicly supported, many believe that labeling children has detrimental effects (Graham & Dwyer, 1987; Strenio, 1980), arguing that the labels lower teachers' expectations about students and cause them to behave in ways that fulfill those low expectations. Therefore, labels or categorizations perpetuate failure in these children.

Mislabeling is an even more severe problem. Mislabeling or misclassification represents by far a major error in interpreting and using test results. This occurs when students are categorized into special education programs not because of their performance but some other characteristic or external factors. For example, Smith, Osborne, Crim, and Rhu (1986) found that school officials gave greater surveillance to children who were not performing well academically and were also perceived as lower or working class Blacks and/or products of "poor" home environments; also, these children were more likely to be labeled learning disabled. As mentioned earlier, the nature of teacher referral may exert considerable influence on psychologists' evaluations of children. Similarly, stereotypic attitudes and inadequate knowledge about examinees also influence the interpretation and use of test results.

Stereotypes are preconceived perceptions of different characteristics (e.g., sex, racial/ethnicity status, communication patterns, and physical attractiveness) of certain individuals or groups. According to Koenig and Juni (1985), stereotyping is a process of hypothesizing that is socially designed to compensate for minimal, specific information about individuals. The notions of stereotyping and labeling are particularly pertinent to the evaluation of ethnic minority children and culturally disadvantaged children. Inexperienced psychologists often use test scores in a rigid manner. They ignore the experiential background of examinees or make erroneous interpretations based on stereotyped information about children's racial or ethnic status. Consequently, test scores are often misused to label minority students as uneducable, denying them appropriate educational opportunities and services.

Numerous studies have documented that a disproportionate number of racial and language minority students are assigned to certain education classes (Maheady, Towne, Algozzine, Mercer, & Ysseldyke, 1983). Communication patterns are also culturally based. Deviations from the expected pattern of communication often result in a judgment of low performance or low ability. Individuals who manifest such patterns are stereotyped as being different because they lack the ability to respond to obvious questions with obvious answers. Physical attractiveness or unattractiveness has long been documented in social psychological research as a social cue for stereotyping. Research indicates that individuals with high physical attractiveness are more likely to be rated high on attributes such as personality, performance, and ability (Benassi, 1982).

Several contributing factors can be identified for such misinterpretation or bias in the use of test results. Two major problems are lack of sufficient information for decision making and inadequate training of psychologists. Fernald, Williams, and Droescher (1985) found that mislabeling occurred primarily when little or no other information than test scores was available to form perceptions. They also maintained that mislabeling was more likely to occur when the criteria for decision making were vague and incomplete. Graham and Dwyer (1987) examined how examiners' evaluations were influenced by a label, examiners' expertise, and performance of the person who was labeled. The results showed that labels did have a negative impact on the evaluation of children's performance, but this effect was successfully attenuated by providing additional training to the examiners in the use of evaluation procedure. Examiners with additional practice and training were not influenced by a label.

Grant (1988) pointed out that examiners needed to consider simultaneously the effects of race, class, and gender in an attempt to understand schooling. Considering the child's experiential background and cultural context is particularly important in interpreting test scores. By not collecting information on these variables and paying attention to them, we are perpetuating biases and stereotypes.

Understanding cultural characteristics is essential for distinguishing differences from handicapping conditions. Whereas some behaviors do not conform to the desired or expected behaviors of the majority society, they may, nevertheless, be "normal" given a student's ethnic or cultural group (Carlson & Stephens, 1986). Such behaviors are best characterized as differences rather than handicapping conditions. Further, knowing how subcultural groups differ in their characteristics can help us learn important things about the relationship between socialization and behavior. This information should prove valuable in the development of appropriate and effective educational programs for these children.

MULTIDISCIPLINARY TEAM (MDT) DECISION MAKING

Once assessment data have been collected, multidisciplinary groups are used to make decisions about students' handicapping conditions, and educational programs and placements. The rationale for using multidisciplinary groups in evaluating students rests on the belief that team members will have the benefit of weighing data based upon different perspectives. Some variability in the restrictiveness of placements (e.g., regular class, resource room, special class, special school) was found when school administrators, school psychologists, and teachers selected placements of differing degrees of restrictiveness depending on whether those students were described as learning disabled, mentally retarded, or emotionally disturbed (Pfeiffer & Naglieri, 1984; Semmel, Yoshida, Fenton, & Kaufman, 1978). When judgments of individual team members were compared with team decisions, individual ratings were fairly comparable to team placement selections (Pfeiffer, 1982; Pfeiffer & Naglieri, 1983; Vautour & Rucker, 1977). The lack of strong evidence for the superiority of team decisions may be due to the limited placement options that could have been selected; MDTs make several other judgments such as eligibility and elements of the educational plans that could produce more variance.

In making group decisions, Yoshida, Fenton, Maxwell, and Kaufman (1978) applied social psychological theory from organizations to MDTs. Specifically, participation in the group process was hypothesized to be related to member satisfaction with decisions that should result in their commitments to implement them (Cooper & Wood, 1974). This relationship was confirmed; more participation led to increased levels of satisfaction (Yoshida, et al., 1978). However, MDTs do not operate as a participatory group but rather as organizational units in which powerful individuals impose or develop consensus for their opinions. Evaluation personnel, particularly school psychologists, contribute the most to the discussion, and classroom teachers and parents, the least (Goldstein, Strickland, Turnbull, & Curry, 1980; Pugach, 1982; Yoshida, Fenton, Maxwell, & Kaufman, 1978; Ysseldyke, Algozzine, & Allen, 1982; Ysseldyke, Algozzine, & Mitchell, 1982).

Fiorelli (1988) applied French and Raven's (1968) classic typology of power bases to group decision making in order to explain the strong effects of status on participation. French and Raven identified five types of power: (a) expert based upon expertise and knowledge, (b) legitimate based upon authority and position, (c) reward based upon positive reinforcement, (d) coercive based upon punishment, and (e) referent based upon others identifying and modeling powerful individuals (see also Erchul's application of this typology to parent participation in this volume). Fiorelli (1988) found that high-status members tended to refrain from using their legitimate power in favor of persuasion, a form of expert power, to influence team decisions. Nevertheless, these data indicate that expert power or any other type of power was not distributed equitably among participants.

In order for MDTs to function as a team, Kaiser and Woodman (1985) and Fiorelli (1988) suggested that more powerful members must recognize their authoritative position and strive to work with others to redistribute power. These steps are fundamental to any team-building activity. Given the lack of administrative support for team building, the burden is on high-status members such as school psychologists to provide leadership in developing functional team relationships.

CONCLUSION

The prevalent use of tests in determining who will be educated in what way is an important issue. Sedlacek (1977) points out that tests are a direct reflection of the attitudes held by a society. Overuse and misuse of tests have serious educational and social implications. This is particularly noteworthy with regard to culturally diverse, minority-group children. Misplacement of minority students into special education programs severely limits their educational and vocational opportunities, because identified children become socialized for a role of lower expectations. Psychologists need to adopt a wide range of assessment procedures and instruments that will provide nonbiased information for making educational decisions for all referred children.

Traditionally, testing and evaluation have not been a focus of social psychological research. Little research has been generated directly linking the two areas. However, many findings in social psychology have indirect implications for the assessment of children. We have discussed in this chapter the influences of some cultural, social interpersonal, and organizational variables that are most relevant to the assessment of children. Clearly, more research is needed in this area, and social psychology principles are important in understanding the nature of assessment.

REFERENCES

Algozzine, B., Christenson, S., & Ysseldyke, J. E. (1982). Probabilities associated with the referral to placement process. *Teacher Education and Special Education, 5,* 19–23.

Anastasi, A. (1988). *Psychological testing* (6th ed.) New York: Macmillan.

Anderson, P. L., Cronin, M. E., & Miller, J. H. (1986). Referral reasons for learning disabled students. *Psychology in the Schools, 23,* 388–395.

Beattie, R. I. (1985). *Special education: A call for quality.* New York: Office of the Mayor, City of New York: Commission on Special Education.

Benassi, M. (1982). Effects of order of presentation, primacy, and physical attractiveness on attributions of ability. *Journal of Personality and Social Psychology, 43,* 48–58.

Berk, R. A. (1982). *Handbook of methods for detecting test bias.* Baltimore: Johns Hopkins.

Brophy, J., & Good, T. (1970). Teachers' communication of differential expectations for children's classroom performance: Some behavioral data. *Journal of Educational Psychology, 61,* 365–374.

Brophy, J., & Good, T. L. (1986). Teacher behavior and student achievement. In M. C. Wittrock (Ed.), *Handbook of research on teaching* (3d ed., pp. 328–375). New York: MacMillan.

Brown, G. F. (1976). *Principles of educational and psychological testing.* New York: Holt, Rinehart, & Winston.

Brown, G. F. (1980). Sex bias in achievement test items: Do they have any effect on performance? *Teaching of Psychology, 7,* 24–26.

Carlson, C. I., Scott, M., & Eklund, S. J. (1980). Ecological theory and method for behavioral assessment. *School Psychology Review, 9,* 75–82.

Carlson, E. P., & Stephens, M. T. (1986). Cultural bias and identification of behaviorally disordered children. *Journal of Behavioral Disorders, 11,* 191–199.

Cole, S. N. (1981). Bias in testing. *American Psychologist, 36,* 1067–1077.

Cooper, M. R., & Wood, M. T. (1974). Effects of member participation and commitment in group decision making on influence, satisfaction, and decision riskiness. *Journal of Applied Psychology, 59,* 127–134.

Cronbach, L. J. (1975). Five decades of public controversy over mental testing. *American Psychologist, 31,* 1–14.

Cronbach, L. J. (1984). *Essentials of psychological testing* (4th ed.). New York: Harper & Row.

Diamond, E. E., & Elmore, B. P. (1986). Bias in achievement testing: Follow-up report of the AMECD Commission on bias in measurement. *Measurement and Evaluation in Counseling and Development, 19,* 102–112.

Diamond, E. E., & Tittle, C. K. (1985). Sex equity in testing. In S. Klein (Ed.), *Handbook for achieving sex equity through education* (pp. 163–188). Baltimore: Johns Hopkins.

Fernald, C. D., Williams, E. A., & Droescher, S. D. (1985). Actions speak louder . . . : Effects of diagnostic labels and child behavior on perceptions of children. *Professional Psychology: Research and Practice, 16,* 648–660.

Fiorelli, J. S. (1988). Power in work groups: Team member's perspectives. *Human Relations, 41,* 1–12.

Flaugher, R. L. (1978). The many definitions of test bias. *American Psychologist, 33,* 671–679.

French, J. R., & Raven, B. H. (1968). The bases of social power. In D. Cartwright & A. Zander (Eds.), *Group dynamics: Research and theory* (3d ed., pp. 259–269). New York: Harper & Row.

Friedman, D. L., Cancelli, A. A., & Yoshida, R. K. (1988). Academic engagement of elementary school children with learning disabilities. *Journal of School Psychology, 26,* 327–340.

Fuchs, D., Featherstone, N., Garwick, D. R., & Fuchs, L. S. (1984). Effects of examiner familiarity and task characteristics on speech and language-impaired children's test performance. *Measurement and Evaluation in Guidance, 16,* 198–204.

Fuchs, D., & Fuchs, L. (1989). Effects of examiner familiarity on Black, Caucasian, and Hispanic children: A meta-analysis. *Exceptional Children, 55,* 303–308.

Fuchs, D., Fuchs, L. S., Garwick, D. R., & Featherstone, N. (1983). The performance of language handicapped children with familiar and unfamiliar examiners. *Journal of Psychology, 114,* 37–46.

Fuchs, D., Fuchs, L. S., Power, M. H., & Daily, A. M. (1985). Bias in the assessment of children. *American Educational Research Journal, 22,* 185–198.

Gergen, K. J., & Gergen, M. M. (1986). *Social psychology.* New York: Springer–Verlag.

Goh, D. S. (1984, August). *Psychological measurement in cross-ethnic research.* Paper presented at the annual convention of the American Psychological Association, Toronto, Canada.

Goh, D. S. (1986). Identifying psychological needs of Asian American children. *Asian American Psychology Journal, 11,* 7–10.

Goh, D., Teslow, C., & Fuller, G. B. (1981). The practice of psychological assessment among school psychologists. *Professional Psychology, 12,* 696–706.

Goldstein, S., Strickland, B., Turnbull, A. P., & Curry, L. (1980). An observational analysis of the IEP conference. *Exceptional Children, 46,* 278–286.

Graham, S., & Dwyer, A. (1987). Effects of the learning disability label, quality of writing performance, and examiner's level of expertise on the evaluation of written products. *Journal of Learning Disabilities, 20,* 319.

Graham, J. R., & Lilly, R. S. (1984). *Psychological testing.* Englewood Cliffs, NJ: Prentice-Hall.

Grant, C. A. (1988). Race, class, gender, and schooling. *Education Digest, LI,* 15–18.

Graziano, W. G., Varca, P. E., & Levy, J. C. (1982). Race of examiner effect and the validity of intelligence tests. *Review of Educational Research, 52,* 469–497.

Green, B. F., Jr. (1978). In defense of measurement. *American Psychologist, 33,* 664–670.

Green, D. R. (1975). What does it mean to say a test is biased. *Education and Urban Society, 8,* 33–52.

Green, R. D. (1987). *Sex differences in item performance on a standardized achievement battery.* Paper presented at the annual convention of the American Psychological Association, New York.

Harris, J. D., Gray, B. A., Rees-McGee, S., Carroll, J. L., & Zaremba, E. T. (1987). Referrals to school psychologists: A national survey. *Journal of School Psychology, 25,* 343–354.

Hoover, R. M., Politzer, R. L., & Taylor, O. (1987). Bias in reading tests for black language speakers: A socialinguistic perspective. *Negro Educational Review, 38,* 81–98.

Jensen, A. R. (1980). *Bias in mental testing.* New York: Free Press.

Johnson, T. J., Feigenbaum, R., & Weiby, M. (1964). Some determinants and consequences of the teacher's perception of causality. *Journal of Educational Psychology, 55,* 237–246.

Jones, E. E., & Nisbett, R. E. (1971). The actor and the observer: Divergent perceptions of the causes of behavior in E. E. Jones, D. E. Kanouse, H. H. Kelley, R. E. Nisbett, S. Valin, & B. Weiner (Eds.), *Attribution: Perceiving the causes of behavior* (pp. 79–94). Morristown, NJ: General Learning Press.

Kagan, J. (1975). The magical aura of the IQ. In A. Montagu (Ed.), *Race and IQ* (pp. 52–58). New York: Oxford.

Kaiser, S. M., & Woodman, R. W. (1985). Multidisciplinary teams and group decision-making problems: Possible solutions to decision-making technique. *School Psychology Review, 14,* 457–470.

Karmos, A. H., & Karmos, J. S. (1984). Attitudes toward standardized achievement tests and their relation to achievement test performance. *Measurement and Evaluation in Counseling and Development, 17,* 55–66.

Kelley, H. H. (1971). Causal schemata and the attribution process. In E. E. Jones, D. E. Kanouse, H. H. Kelley, R. E. Nisbett, S. Valins, & B. Weiner (Eds.), *Attribution: Perceiving the Causes of Behavior* (pp. 151–174). Morristown, NJ: General Learning Press.

Kelley, H. H. (1973). The processes of causal attribution. *American Psychologist, 28,* 107–128.

Klopfer, W. G., & Taulbee, E. S. (1976). Projective tests. *Annual Review of Psychology,* 543–562.

Koenig, E. J., & Juni, S. (1985). Perceived personnel suitability: A function of job sex type, sex role, and sex. *Journal of Employment Counseling, 22,* 166–169.

Leong, F., & Huang, K. (1987, August). *Psychological assessment of Asian American children.* Paper presented at the annual convention of the American Psychological Association, New York.

Maheady, L., Towne, A., Algozzine, B., Mercer, B., & Ysseldyke, J. (1983). Minority overrepresentation: A case for alternative practices prior to referral. *Learning Disability Quarterly, 6,* 448–456.

Mehan, H., Hertweck, A., & Meihls, J. L. (1986). *Handicapping the handicapped: Decision making in students' education careers.* Stanford: Stanford University Press.

Olmedo, E. (1981). Psychological testing in educational classification and placement. *American Psychologist, 36,* 1078–1086.

Ownby, R. L., Wallbrown, F., D'Atri, A., & Armstrong, B. (1985). Patterns of referrals for school psychological services: Replication of the referral problems category system. *Special Services in the Schools, 1,* 53–66.

Pfeiffer, S. I. (1982). Special education placement decisions made by teams and individuals: A cross-cultural perspective. *Psychology in the Schools, 19,* 335–340.

Pfeiffer, S. I., & Naglieri, J. A. (1983). An investigation of multidisciplinary team decision making. *Journal of Learning Disabilities, 16,* 588–590.

Pfeiffer, S. I., & Naglieri, J. A. (1984). Special education placement decisions as a function of professional role and handicapping children. *Psychology in the Schools, 21,* 61–65.

Potter, M. L., Ysseldyke, J. E., Regan, R. R., & Algozzine, B. (1983). Eligibility and classification decisions in educational settings: Issuing "passports" in a state of confusion. *Contemporary Educational Psychology, 8,* 146–157.

Pugach, M. L. (1982). Regular classroom teacher involvement in the development and utilization of IEP's. *Exceptional Children, 48,* 371–374.

Pugach, M. L. (1985). The limitations of federal special education policy: The role of classroom teachers in determining who is handicapped. *Journal of Special Education, 19,* 123–137.

Reschly, D. J. (1979). Nonbiased assessment. In G. D. Phye & D. J. Reschly (Ed.), *School psychology: Perspectives and issues* (pp. 215–253). New York: Academic Press.

Reynolds, C. (1982). The problem of bias in psychological assessment. In C. R. Reynolds & T. B. Gutkin (Ed.), *The handbook of school psychology* (pp. 178–208). New York: Wiley.

Rosenthal, R. (1966). *Experimenter effects in behavioral research.* New York: Appleton-Century-Crofts.

Rosenthal, R. & Jacobson, L. (1968). *Pygmalion in the classroom.* New York: Holt, Rinehart, & Winston.

Sattler, J. M. (1988). *Assessment of children* (3d ed.) San Diego: Jerome Sattler.

Sattler, J. M., & Gwynne, J. (1982). White examiners generally do not impede test performance of black children: To debunk a myth. *Journal of Consulting and Clinical Psychology, 50,* 196–208.

Sedlacek, W. W. (1977). Test bias and the elimination of racism. *Journal of College Student Personnel, 18,* 16–20.

Semmel, D. S., Yoshida, R. K., Fenton, K. S., & Kaufman, M. J. (1978). *The contribution of professional role to group decision-making in a simulated pupil-planning team setting.* Washington, DC: U.S. Office of Education, Bureau of Education for the Handicapped, Division of Innovation and Development.

Smith, R. W., Osborne, L. T., Crim, D., & Rhu, H. A. (1986). Labeling theory as applied to learning disabilities: Survey findings and policy suggestions. *Journal of Learning Disabilities, 19,* 195–202.

Strenio, A. J., Jr. (1980). *The testing trap.* New York: Rawson, Wade.

Vautour, J. A. C., & Rucker, C. N. (Eds.). (1977). *Child study team training program: Book of readings.* Austin, TX: Special Education Associates.

Vernon, P. (1982). *The abilities and achievement of orientals in North America.* New York: Academic Press.

Watson, P. (1972). Can racial discrimination affect IQ? In R. Richardson & D. Spears (Eds.), *Race and intelligence* (pp. 56–67). Baltimore: Penguin.

Wheeler, P. R., Adams, G. R., & Nielson, E. C. (1986). Effect of a child's physical attractiveness on verbal scoring of the Wechsler Intelligence Scale for Children—Revised and personality attributions. *Journal of General Psychology, 2,* 109–116.

Yoshida, R. K., Fenton, K. S., Maxwell, J. P., & Kaufman, M. J. (1978). Group decision making in the planning team process: Myth or reality? *Journal of School Psychology, 16,* 237–244.

Yoshida, R. K., Lopez, E. C., Friedman, D. L., & Matalon, T. (1991). *Improving methods for appropriately identifying handicapped children.* Final report Grant #H023C70300, U.S. Department of Education, Special Education Programs.

Ysseldyke, J. E., Algozzine, B., & Allen, D. (1982). Participation of regular education teachers in special education team decision making. *Exceptional Children, 48,* 365–366.

Ysseldyke, J. E., Algozzine, B., & Mitchell, J. (1982). Special education team decision making: An analysis of current practice. *Personnel and Guidance Journal, 60,* 308–310.

Ysseldyke, J. E., Christenson, S., Pianta, B., & Algozzine, B. (1983). An analysis of teachers' reasons and desired outcomes for students referred for psychoeducational assessment. *Journal of Psychoeducational Assessment, 1,* 73–83.

10

APPLICATIONS OF
SOCIAL PSYCHOLOGY TO
SCHOOL COUNSELING AND THERAPY

Jonathan Sandoval
John M. Davis
University of California, Davis

A primary role besides testing and consultation for school psychologists is providing counseling services to children in the schools (Carroll, Harris, & Bretzing, 1979; Lacayo, Sherwood, & Morris, 1981). Although there are a number of other student services workers who counsel children, notably school counselors, elementary counselors, and school social workers, school psychologists also offer counseling.

The kinds of counseling that school psychologists provide differs somewhat from that provided by other personnel workers, although there is much overlap. Our position is that the primary counseling roles for school psychologists are crisis counseling, brief counseling, brief family therapy, vocational counseling for special education children, and social and other skills training. All these types of counseling can take place in groups; accordingly, school psychologists must have group work skills. Because there are so few school social workers and elementary school-level counselors, in most districts, the school psychologist is the only mental health professional with sufficient training and legislative authority to perform all these counseling roles.

Crises such as parental divorce, child maltreatment and abuse, experiencing the death of a loved one, attempted suicide, or adolescent parenthood have been shown to be related to disruption in a child's learning progress (Sandoval, 1988). Because they are often traumatic events and need to be responded to immediately, school psychologists, particularly in elementary schools, are often called upon to help children through a crisis or to prepare them for an impending crisis through a counseling intervention.

Another counseling role that often falls to the school psychologist is that of providing some form of brief therapy to children. Some school psychologists argue that mental health or adjustment counseling has no place in schools. These activities should go on outside the school and should not be funded with educational moneys. School psychologists are funded to deal directly with educational problems and difficulties only. They argue that school psychologists should not be involved in any form of psychotherapy, brief or long term. However, school psychologists do end up doing mental health counseling (Bernstein, 1976; Shaffer, 1985; Tharinger, 1985). For one reason, there often are no other mental health services available, or parents are only willing to permit the counseling in a school setting and will not follow through with an outside referral. When sanctioned and supported by school district administration, the school can be an ideal place to conduct counseling because it is a real-life setting with which the child must cope, as Bernstein (1976) points out. There are, as mentioned, others in the school whose responsibilities include counseling, notably the school counselor. However, much of the counseling done by school counselors is centered on discipline, attendance, and educational decision making. Many school counselors do not have sufficient time or may not be well enough trained to do long-term or brief mental health-oriented psychotherapy. School psychologists, by virtue of their typically more lengthy training, are somewhat better prepared to provide therapeutic interventions to children. However, because of cost difficulties and other demands on the school psychologists' time, it is clear that long-term counseling models are not feasible. Recent developments in the field of brief psychotherapy are creating options to permit therapists to intervene meaningfully in a few sessions (e.g., Bellak & Small, 1978; Davanloo, 1978). This trend towards brief psychotherapy in mental health settings and health maintenance organizations is a result of many variables, two of which are cuts in the finding of mental health programs, and the realization that treatment duration is generally less than 12 sessions (Garfield, 1978; Koss, 1979). In response to these realities, new techniques and theories aimed at helping clients resolve their conflicts in 6 to 20 sessions have emerged and have applications to work with children in schools.

Another way that school psychologists cope with the great demands on their time is to provide group services rather than individual one-to-one counseling (Claiborn & Strong, 1982). Group work may involve children experiencing a similar problem, for example, experiencing a parental divorce or coping with a learning disability, or groups may involve learning new skills such as assertiveness or prosocial behaviors. Group work may be done in classrooms or with specially constituted groups and may be applied to any of the types of counseling performed by school psychologists.

A growing movement in school psychology suggests that practitioners must understand family systems. Moreover, any therapy focusing on children in a school setting should include family involvement, when possible. The notions that children exist in a family network and fulfill particular roles within the family have led to new innovations in the schools where school psychologists work with all family members around family and school issues (Carlson, 1987; Conoley, 1987; Fine & Holt, 1983; Okun, 1984).

Finally, school psychologists increasingly are acknowledging their responsibility to provide vocational counseling to handicapped pupils. The Education for All Handicapped Children Act (PL 94–142) and the Rehabilitation Act of 1974 explicitly spells out the right of handicapped children for vocational education, and the Carl D. Perkins Act (PL 98–524) requires that an assessment of vocational interests and aptitudes be part of the placement process for handicapped students joining vocational training programs. School counselors also have some responsibilities for vocational counseling (Phelps & Lutz, 1977) but often do not have the time or training to deal with handicapped youngsters. Counseling special education populations, particularly around vocational issues, is an important but often neglected role for school psychologists (Hohenshil, 1982; Hohenshil, Levinson, & Heer, 1985).

In spite of these arguments favoring the school psychologist's counseling role, there are limits. One problem with the concept of school psychologists' counseling is the vagueness of the term. Many individuals define counseling as any conversation with a child concerning the child's feelings or behavior. Because of the time and resource constraints mentioned before, school psychologists are not afforded the luxury of, in our view, spending time with children where the goal is not made explicit, and where personality reorganization or personal adjustment is the goal. Many requests made to school psychologists focus on providing counseling to a child to make that child adjust better to a school situation. Acceding to these requests implies that the child is the one that needs to adjust, whereas in many cases it is the classroom or the school that needs to accommodate the child's needs. Counseling should not be a substitution for other interventions in the school designed both to improve the instructional program for the child and to alter the environment so that the probability of educational success is enhanced (Tharinger, 1985). Fine and Holt (1983) outlined a number of other issues in counseling, not the least of which is the often involuntary nature of counseling in the school. We expand on the topic of required counseling in a later section on reactance. This chapter is, however, devoted to discussing a number of applications of social psychological theory to the various kinds of counseling that is appropriate for school psychologists. Our focus is on the applications of theory to the counseling process rather than on the theories themselves, inasmuch as they have been covered in other chapters. Although we discuss the implications of a number of theories to counseling in general, we have noted that each of the theories has a more or less special application to a particular kind of counseling done by school psychologists. We take up attribution theory, dissonance theory, group process theory, self-theory, so-cial influence theory, reactance theory, and socialization theory related to gender and ethnicity. Relatively more weight is given to group process the-ory and group counseling than to the other forms of counseling, because these theories have not been covered elsewhere in this volume.

ATTRIBUTION AND ATTRIBUTION CHANGE IN COUNSELING

General Applications

Attribution theory (see Levesque & Lowe in this volume), exploring as it does how individuals attribute causality to others and to themselves, offers a poten-tially rich number of applications to the counseling process. Typically, a client comes to counseling in a state of confusion and disorganization. For adults, Freud noted that a healthy individual was one who was able to "love and work"; that is, a fully functioning person is capable of caring and satisfying interpersonal relations with others and is able to focus energies and talents on accomplishing tasks. Generally speaking, clients coming to the counselor have difficulties in either interpersonal relations or in understanding why they are unable to be successful at work or leisure activities (including learning). However, children, and some adolescents, often do not come to counseling of their own accord. Usually it is others who note their distress or inappropri-ate behaviors and then refer children to counselors so that changes may come about in cognition, emotion, or overt behavior (Group for the Advancement of Psychiatry, 1982). The child may or may not be aware that his or her be-haviors are not leading to satisfactory outcomes.

The first phase of counseling often consists of rapport building and an ex-ploration of the client's problems (Egan, 1986). The techniques the counselor uses during this stage are to establish rapport and listen actively to the client's concerns. In doing so the counselor attempts to build an understanding of how the client views her or himself and other persons. A useful conceptual framework for the counselor to organize these understandings is attribution theory. The counselor helps the client examine his or her attributions for both other individual's behavior and his or her own. By continuing to make the client's view of the world explicit and understanding *with* the client (as Carl Rogers, 1961, would have it), the counselor can check the rationality of these attributions. The counselor can challenge the client to examine the evidence in support of his or her attributions. This examination of client at-tributions is central to rational-emotive therapy (Ellis, 1967), reality therapy (Glasser, 1965), and some cognitive behavioral therapies (e.g., Beck, 1976).

One aspect of attribution theory is the subjective perception of the causes of school success and failure (Weiner, 1979). Clients see success or failure as either a function of their own efforts (personal control or internal causation) or of luck or other's efforts (external causation). Many systems of counseling emphasize that helping a client achieve a sense of internal causality is a particularly important goal. Glasser's (1965) reality therapy, for example, emphasized that the client must accept responsibility for what is occurring, and that the counselor's role is to reject statements that imply external causation for some aspects of the situation. For example, a child may blame a "mean" teacher for his or her refusal to do homework rather than to admit he or she does not have the skills necessary to complete the assignment. In fact, the client's explanations are examined until some behavior or feeling is acknowledged as being in the client's realm of responsibility and therefore modifiable. In the example, the child might finally acknowledge he or she does not know how to ask the teacher for help. Carkhuff and Berenson (1977) referred to this phenomenon as personalizing a situation and recommended a technique of changing a client's statement from external to internal causation. The counselor would shift reflective responses to a client's statement from, for example, "you feel confused because they have made all of your decisions for you" (reflecting external causation) to "you feel furious because you did not take advantage of the opportunity when you had it" (reflecting internal causation).

Gestalt therapists, too, examine their client's language and demand that it be changed to reflect an internal cause. A Gestalt counselor might suggest a client substitute "won't" for "can't" or use the pronoun "I" rather than "it" (Passons, 1975). These counseling interventions are to make the client aware of attributions.

Some children come to counseling with inappropriate internal attributions. They often assume that they are the cause of other's problems, as when a child believes he or she is responsible for a divorce or death in the family. Examining and confronting these mistaken beliefs is also important. Reality-based attributions are part of the goal of counseling.

Other children come to counseling with completely inappropriate external causation often derived from conditions producing learned helplessness (see chapter 14 in this volume). These maladaptive, almost pathological, patterns of attribution may be changed with great effort by teaching children directly to attribute their failures in school or social situations to effort or strategy instead of to ability (Dweck, 1975, 1986).

A special case of external attribution is children who have been given a medical diagnosis of hyperactive and prescribed medication (Whalen & Henker, 1976). If not handled correctly, these children may attribute their condition to forces beyond their control. These children are best treated by letting them know that medication can only *help* them, and their efforts are necessary if they are to control their symptoms. In other words, they must see themselves as having control over their behavior and attribute their successes to their efforts at self-control.

Thus the counseling process can be seen as one of attempting to change client attributions for their own behavior and to get the client to understand that others may have legitimate reasons for behaving as they do and that these reasons have nothing to do with the client's needs or wishes.

Specific Applications to Crisis Counseling

In the aftermath of a crisis two of the most prevalent reactions by clients are a feeling of helplessness and victimization or a feeling of guilt. Both are a result of attributional processes. Many clients feel that they have lost control over their lives and become extremely fatalistic, attributing what has happened to forces beyond their influencing. Others respond by dwelling on how some behavior or thought either caused the crisis or could have prevented it and subsequently take responsibility for the crisis. In most cases, what has happened to them is completely beyond their control and could not have been avoided by any positive action. On the one hand, clients in crisis need to appreciate the causes of their situation, which often involves confronting a fear of lack of control. On the other hand, it is important not to encourage or support blaming on the client's part (Sandoval, 1988). Again, the counselor aims to assist the client to achieve realistic attributions.

In those cases where the client is feeling helpless, in order to instill hope and to foster client coping behaviors, there is a need for the counselor to move the counselee quickly from a passive position to an active one. Clients must be helped to realize that if they are to heal from a crisis they must reassume control over those parts of their lives where they can realistically exert some control. A counselor working with a victim of assault, for example, might note the positive things the client did do to avoid or lessen the impact of the assault, such as save his or her life by being passive. Such inputs are important to restore some sense of control.

For those clients feeling overly responsible for what has happened, it is useful for the counselor to challenge such attributions and collect data regarding those beliefs. In general, the counselor must be wary of the "all or nothing" thinking that characterizes mistaken attributions. Beck and his associates (Beck, Rush, Shaw, & Emery, 1979) very specifically refer to the use of reattribution techniques and state that "the point is not to absolve the patient of all responsibility but to define the multitude of extraneous factors contributing to an adverse experience" (p. 158).

ATTITUDE CHANGE AND DISSONANCE THEORY IN COUNSELING

General Applications

One view of counseling is that it is focused on changing client attitudes and behaviors. A general principle from social psychology posits that to change attitudes one must first change behaviors. This is also a central tenent in almost all behaviorally based counseling theories (although, of course, orthodox behaviorists do not attend to attitudes). Behaviorists are confident that if they change behavior appropriate attitude change will occur by itself.

It has been observed by dissonance theorists that there is a drive for an individual to maintain cognitions that are logically consistent with one another and to be aversively motivated to reduce dissonance whenever there is inconsistency between cognitions or between cognitions and behaviors (Festinger, 1957). A number of studies have shown that if the behavior is changed attitudes will come to be changed so that they are consistent with or explain the particular behavior (see chapter 2 in this volume). The notion that there is a motive for cognitive consistency has had a great use in counseling procedures. In some situations it is useful for the counselor to create dissonance in the client, and in other situations it is possible a counselor might help reduce dissonance in a client.

Creating Dissonance as a Counseling Focus.   Nondirective counseling and psychotherapy, as outlined by Carl Rogers (1942, 1957), has as its goal the creation of a relationship between the counselor and the client where the counselee's feelings and attitudes may be freely explored. As the empathetic, warm, and genuine counselor listens to the client and reports back his or her understanding of what the client has said or implied, the effect often is to create dissonance. In fact the counselor may purposely point out ambivalence when the client expresses it or may note specific discrepancies in actions and beliefs or in one belief and another or in one action and another. Egan (1986) has termed this counselor action *challenging*. By pointing out discrepant thoughts and behaviors, the counselor motivates the client to reconcile the dissonance created. This reconciliation, or dissonance reduction, can be accomplished automatically by changing behavior, changing attitudes, or gaining a new insight into a situation or self so that the dissonance is no longer apparent. Alternatively, the client may advance to a new cognitive construction or schema that brings the cognitions into consistency.

Reducing Dissonance as a Counseling Focus.   Dissonance can often be reduced by changing behaviors or attitudes. The counselor may assist be-

SANDOVAL AND DAVIS

havior change by helping create a readiness to change or by giving the client new skills. These new skills can be explicitly taught through such methods as psychoeducation, role playing or observation, or the client may have the new behaviors in his or her repertoire but simply needs encouragement to try them. Dissonance theory predicts that with the change in behavior a change in attitude will also occur. Changes in behavior for most counseling theorists are the *sine quo non* of effective counseling.

Specific Applications to Brief Therapy

As previously mentioned, we believe brief therapy to be applicable to school-based populations and theoretically manageable within the job demands of many, but certainly not all, school psychologists. However, most brief therapy theorists writing about children and adolescents, except perhaps for radical behaviorists and the more extreme strategists, view some form of concurrent work with the parents (e.g., counseling, consultation, education) as essential.

Brief therapy is most appropriate and successful when motivation has been enhanced by stress, when pressure to adapt is high (Berlin, 1970), and when there exists a low level of child or family psychopathology (Dulcan, 1984). Specific "criteria" for selecting clients for brief treatment differ from theorist to theorist; however, there are a few general contraindicators. Brief treatment is not recommended during a crisis, when psychosis is present, with very unmotivated clients, when there is evidence of potential for homocidal or suicidal behavior, when sociopathy or severe personality disorders are present, or when no problem focus can be agreed upon.

Brief psychotherapy is much more problem focused than long-term therapy. The counselor and the client (preferably the family) jointly determine what problem needs to be addressed (problem definition) and then move on to problem-solving strategies. The process is also distinguished by a higher degree of directing, structuring, and challenging behavior on the part of the counselor than is seen in longer term work. Through creating a strong but realistic relationship with the counselor, as opposed to transference based work, the here and now relationship is used to create a situation in which the client will be led to self-confrontation. This movement can be facilitated by the counselor pointing out discrepancies between the client's stated goal and the client's current actions and professed attitudes (e.g., Ivey, 1986).

One could easily argue that many schools of brief therapy exist. For our purposes, we consider three basic groups: dynamic, cognitive behavioral, and strategic. In accord with our thinking, the dynamic and cognitive behavioral best fit the attitude change scheme. We discuss the strategic school of brief therapy when we present reactance theory.

First and foremost, brief dynamic therapy is a dissonance-increasing venture. Historically there has been an emphasis on challenging existing problem conceptualizations that interfere with progress (e.g., Davanloo, 1980; Sifneos, 1979). The conservative theorists of the dynamic group have developed their thoughts primarily from their analytic training and usually make the assumption that underlying the "problem" is a dynamic focus or central issue that may or may not be shared with clients. As Flegenheimer (1982) stated: "The central issue should reflect a theme that connects the presenting symptoms with other difficulties experienced in the past and with conflicts in the [client's past] that can be seen by the therapist to be dynamically related to the current problem" (p. 84). More systems and child-oriented practitioners from the dynamic school agree a focus in needed but do not insist that it be so analytically based (e.g., Rosenthal, 1979).

The creation of dissonance helps the therapist and client explore new conceptualizations of the problem, which enables them to move beyond their present position. This new understanding, besides allowing for new behaviors and reducing anxiety, also provides a new paradigm that theoretically allows for less constricted future problem solving.

The cognitive behavioral counselor can also function from a dissonance-creating position. By challenging "self messages" (Beck, 1976) or illogical inferences (Ellis, 1967), dissonance can be created that would force self-confrontation and lead to change. However, this group of theorists might also employ dissonance-reduction techniques. For instance, one might employ the techniques suggested by Forehand and McMahon (1981) or Kendall and Braswell (1985), not to challenge current cognitive constructs but rather to employ psychoeducational methodologies to teach someone to be more like what they want to be (e.g., better parents) and reduce their levels of cognitive dissonance through new learning. Following Meichenbaum (1974), a counselor might help a child develop a set of self-statements to make when confronted with a difficult problem in school, statements such as "Be creative, be unique," "Break away from the obvious, the commonplace," "Don't worry about what others think," "Go slow, don't hurry." Such statements help a child develop a set to handle life situations in a more creative and potentially effective manner. By creating these new attitudes through direct instruction, the client may achieve consistency in behavior and belief. The choice of the particular form of brief treatment, either dissonance increasing or reducing, usually depends on counselor orientation and client values.

GROUP PROCESS AND GROUP COUNSELING

Social psychologists studying group processes usually investigate group phenomena related to perception of others in a group, expectations of others, perceptions of self, and communication among members of a group. They also explore group roles and types of group membership and identification (Cartwright & Zander, 1953; Napier & Gershenfeld, 1985). A primary set of theories about group process have to do with the setting of group norms, pressures to adhere to group norms and factors underlying deviancy from group norms (see classic works by Berkowitz, 1978; Steiner, 1972; and Triandis, 1977). Also studied are how a groups' goals are set and under what conditions groups may act productively (see Zander, 1982). Within a group certain members emerge as leaders. Researchers also study the traits and behaviors of leaders (e.g., Stogdill, 1981). Social psychologists studying groups also look at group problem solving and decision making (Fox, 1987). A review of the theories and research related to all these lines of investigation is beyond the scope of this chapter. Nevertheless, a knowledge of this research and theory is useful in conducting group counseling.

Groups are used in counseling often because they permit the psychologist to have an impact on more than one individual at a time. However, a better rationale for the use of groups is that groups take advantage of the unique psychology of a group to bring about individual change in the members. Studies of group communication and perception suggest that group attractiveness, physical size, environment, and status of membership can all facilitate communication (Shaw, 1981). The existence of group norms and group pressures suggests that the counselors must work hard to enforce rules and norms that will help the group accomplish its particular goals. Deviance from group norms may result from true independence of an individual, that is, one individual may be indifferent to the expectations of the group, as opposed to rebellious. A rebel goes against group norms; although aware of norms, the rebel makes an explicit decision not to comply with them. The counselor must distinguish between these two kinds of nonconformity.

Studies of group productivity suggest that productivity is a function of group cohesiveness as well as the clarity and degree of commitment to group goals (Zander, 1982). A group counselor seeks to create a cohesive and goal-oriented group by providing feedback about group goals and working to increase the cohesiveness of the group. This can be done by establishing normative behaviors of giving constructive feedback and encouragement and being nonjudgmental as well as emphasizing the need for confidentiality.

Group problem-solving and decision-making activity research suggest that problem solving can be done in a rational manner, and that a group leader can encourage rational decision making in the group through enforcing particular kinds of rules and procedures (Fox, 1987).

Applications

Clinicians and clinical researchers agree that group norms are essential for productive work (Gazda, 1989; Ginott, 1961; Moos, 1974). The existence of group norms and group pressures suggests that much of the initial therapeutic work must be to aid in the development of and initiate the enforcement of those group norms that will be most beneficial to the style and goals of the group. Concurrently, the group members must begin to experience cohesion or an attraction to the group, a wanting to belong. Support and universalization (Yalom, 1985) are useful techniques for working on these issues especially in the less structured group experiences. As the clinician provides emotional support to group members and clarifies the many similarities and human communalities among group members (universalization), cohesion is facilitated. With these experiences the members become more desirous of belonging to the group. Out of questions regarding what kinds of behavior and attitudes are needed to be members of the group, norms are formed. As this is happening the clinician, through his or her behaviors, attitudes, and interventions (e.g., tolerance, empathy, openness, etc.), helps lay some of the basic groundwork necessary for positive group experiences.

The next set of issues to emerge in a group usually reflect the areas of problem definition and role clarity. These issues can be handled very differently depending on theoretical orientation and overall therapist goals. A Slavson play group (Slavson & Shiffer, 1975) would be very different from a psychoeducational skills group (May, Powell, Gazda, & Hauser, 1985; Rubin, 1969). Whereas the play group would allow the agenda to emerge from the interactions among members, the psychoeducational group would have preestablished goals and agendas and group members would have been selected as individuals whose functioning would be enhanced by these specific skills. One issue that is resolved similarly among the different group approaches but is not frequently addressed in group counseling is that of group roles. Group roles are those functions that are played out by group members in interaction with the group's dynamics. Horwitz (1977) wrote about how every group therapist must resolve for him or herself the individual–group dialectic issue. The counselor should ask: How much does the individual influence the group and how much does the group influence the individual? How much should I focus on the individual, and how much should I focus on the individual's role or functioning in the group?

Historically, clinical group work has focused on the individual dynamics, and social psychology has focused on the group dynamics. Agazarian and Peters (1981) helped bring these views together. They suggested that the choice is not of one or the other but that multiple perspectives are necessary, and they offered a multilevel model. The model consists of four levels that they refer to as the person, member, group role, and group-as-a-whole perspectives. Basically, the person level focuses on the intrapsychic dynamics of the individual; the member level focuses on the person's pull on the group; the group role level focuses on the group's pull on the person; and the group-as-a-whole perspective focuses on the total groups' dynamics. They argue that no one perspective captures the whole picture, and that the therapist must attempt to process the data provided by the group at a variety of levels simultaneously. Because any particular piece of data can be interpreted from all perspectives at the same time, the clinical question is which perspective would best fit the goal of the clinician at that point in time.

Let us illustrate by means of a clinical example. We are in the fourth session of a group for adolescents whose parents have recently divorced. Although Diane had been saying nothing in the group, outside the group she has been requesting to be seen individually to discuss dropping out of the group. The counselor has been empathic but suggested that she bring this up in the group. During the fifth session she reveals that she does feel and has felt alienated in the group and wants to discontinue. The group, with seeming empathy, agreed that seeing the counselor alone might be better for her.

According to the Agazarian and Peters' model, the counselor could intervene from any of the four perspectives they have conceptualized. At the *person* level, the counselor could attempt to offer insight about Diane's intrapsychic dynamics regarding her conflict about group membership. At the *member* level, the counselor could focus on Diane's interpersonal dynamics. How had Diane convinced the group to not provide support and instead encourage her to leave? At the *group role* level, the intervention would focus on the group gaining insight into how the role played by Diane was serving the group; for instance, had members been unable to talk about their own difficulties in joining the group and projected these onto Diane so that she could serve

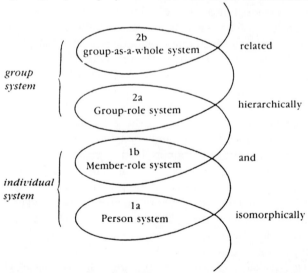

FIG. 10.1. Group and individual perspectives representing different levels of conceptual abstraction defined via general systems theory as: (1) individual system with subsystems (1a) person and (1b) member-role; and (2) group system with subsystems (2a) group-role and (2b) group-as-a-whole; related hierarchically and isomorphically. (Adapted from Agazarian & Peters, 1981).

a scapegoating function, one of the more common roles available. Finally, there is the *group-as-a-whole* interpretation. Here the counselor offers insight into the dynamics of the group. Thus, the counselor might ask: What is causing conflict within the group, and what is the group acting out by encouraging Diane to leave.

As social psychologists have found, common group roles are the scapegoat, the task leader, the socioemotional leader, and the "rebel" or deviant leader. However, any "role" can develop out of the needs of the group. The interaction of group and individual dynamics creates the role. The model allows the counselor to choose the perspective he or she believes will best further the group's development towards its particular goals.

As a special case of group counseling, family therapists have also been interested in the dynamics and roles among family members. A variety of roles seen as indicative of family dynamics have been postulated. For instance, Satir (1972) described *distracters, blamers, computers,* and *placaters;* Ackerman (1966) talked about the disturbed family triangle of *victim, persecutor,* and *healer;* and Minuchin (1974) wrote about the *identified patient* and the *parentified child.* All these roles describe processes that are interacted within a particular family and present the clinician with clues about where and how to intervene. Again, as in group counseling, the counselor must decide from which theoretical levels and perspectives he or she is going to function.

If one wanted to go one step further, multiple family therapy, or group family therapy, is possible (Laquer, 1976; Strelnick, 1977). Laquer maintained that multiple family therapy is more or less a hybrid of group and family therapy. These groups usually consist of four to five nuclear families who have children presented as the identified patient. As groups become larger and larger, it becomes clear that intrapsychic work becomes more problematic, and more of a focus on interpersonal and group dynamics and relationships is developed.

APPLICATIONS OF SELF-THEORY

General Applications

We have already discussed some of the applications of self-theory under the section of Attributions and Attributional Restructuring. An individual's conceptualization of self—attributes, values, and talents—is used in a number of ways in counseling.

Carl Rogers (1961) based his theory of personality development and therapeutic change on a self-theory. Rogers phenomenological theory held that every individual exists in a continually changing world of experience, at which he or she is the center. The organism reacts to the field as experienced and

perceived. Over time, the organism develops a sense of self as the movement towards actualization progresses. In time the sense of self in turn governs
what is perceived. Maladjustment, according to Rogers, exists when the organism denies to awareness those sensory experiences that are not included
in the sense or concept of self. Adjustment occurs when the self-concept is
roughly congruent with all the experiences the organism has had. Many of
Rogers' ideas about self are close to those articulated by Kurt Lewin (1951),
one of social psychology's pioneers.

The general application of self-theory to the counseling process is the recognition that individuals, as a function of their interactions with environments,
come to see the world and themselves in a unique idiosyncratic way (Kelly,
1955). The counseling process is directed at helping the client explore and
modify understandings of the self and the world. The tools the counselor uses
according to those who analyze the counseling process systematically (e.g.,
Egan, 1986; Ivey, 1986) are such techniques as attending, active listening,
probing, focusing, and counselor self-disclosure. Tests and other assessment
techniques also play a part in uncovering aspects of self.

Specific Applications to Vocational Counseling

Besides the general use of self in Rogers' theory, the most specific applications in self-theory have been by Donald Super (1957). Super (Super,
Starishevsky, Matlin, & Jordaan, 1963) focused on self-concept as a key to
vocational counseling: "A self concept is the individual's picture of himself,
the perceived self with accrued meanings. Since the person cannot ascribe
meanings to himself in a vacuum, the concept of self is generally a picture
of the self in some role, some situation, in a position, performing some set
of functions, or in some web of relationships" (p. 18). Self-concepts hierarchically develop from lower order self-descriptions. They may also come, in part,
from the process of identification with parents and from exploratory behavior
in the real world. Super's pioneering work in vocational counseling focused
on the process of assisting a person put into occupational terms his or her
idea of self. In the process, a vocational self-concept is created that Super
(Super et al., 1963) defined as "The constellation of self attributes considered
by the individual to be vocationally relevant, whether or not they have been
translated into a vocational preference" (p. 20). At the same time, the counselor helps clients to be aware of occupations in which their self-concept may
be most easily expressed, that is, to find occupational settings that would permit an adequate outlet for abilities, interests, values, and personality traits.
Super (1957) posited that the degree of satisfaction individuals derive from
work is related to the opportunities available to implement their self-concepts.
One of the primary ways that an occupational counselor or vocational counselor, including school psychologists working with special education young-

sters, proceeds is in helping the client engage in reality testing and exploratory behavior (Super et al., 1963). Another important device is the use of various psychological tests, particularly tests related to vocational-oriented abilities, tests related to identifying interests (Spitzer & Levinson, 1988), and tests related to personality (Hohenshil et al., 1985). The results of tests are used to help the client explore abilities, attitudes, interests, and values they may hold and to predict success in various occupations.

Besides knowledge of self-concepts, the school psychologist engaged in vocational counseling also needs to discuss issues coming from research on gender and ethnicity stereotyping with the client. Helping children examine and challenge stereotypes associated with vocations and with themselves as members of a gender or ethnic group is a necessary part of vocational planning. The client's as well as society's views are important.

ATTRACTION AND INFLUENCE THEORY

General Applications

Another set of research with implications for the counseling school psychologists are attraction and social influence theory (Dorn, 1984) on the one hand, and their opposite, reactance theory (Brehm, 1966), on the other. First, social psychologists are interested in what makes various individuals more attractive than others and able to influence attitudes and opinions. Counselors who, according to Strong (1968), are expert, attractive, and trustworthy are most credible to clients and are able to produce therapeutic personality change. As a result many feel that counselors should increase their interpersonal attractiveness in the early stages of counseling so that these positive feelings of regard for the counselor become part of the means by which counselors in the next stages of counseling are able to provide direction and assist counselees in changing their behaviors. Presumably, clients are more willing to cooperate with attractive counselors and to initiate new behavior (Strong & Claiborn, 1982).

Counselor attractiveness is related to perceived similarity between the counselor and the child, physical attractiveness, attractiveness of role, reputation for honesty, sincerity, and reputation as an expert, among other traits (Strong, 1968). More research needs to be done on what constitutes attractiveness for *children* because almost all the studies of this phenomenon have been done on adults (Corrigan, Dell, Lewis, & Schmidt, 1980). (The topic of interpersonal attraction is discussed in detail by Maruyama and LeCount in this volume.)

Whether intentionally or not, the counselor models many of the behaviors in which the counselee should engage. The counselor who is curious, open, honest, and open to change will pass these attitudes on to the client (Carkhuff & Berenson, 1977). A great deal of research has focused on the counselor's willingness to disclose things about him or herself appropriately (termed research on self-disclosure). In feeling comfortable in talking about him or herself, and being genuine about his or her emotions or feelings, the counselor is able to demonstrate and model appropriate behaviors for the counselee to engage in during the counseling process. Of course, the counselor need not be the only person who is attractive and influential. Groups may contain a number of attractive and influential members. In a group, credible and trustworthy members contribute to the positive behavior change of other members.

Attractiveness is a two-way street, of course. Counselors will be attracted to clients and influenced by them. Counselor training and supervision should explicitly deal with this phenomenon (part of the countertransference process), and counselors need to learn to monitor their objectivity in dealing with attractive or unattractive clients.

Specific Applications

One application of attraction and influence theory is facilitating prosocial behavior, under the assumption that a client's attractiveness and consequently success will be improved by growth in such skills. The research on attraction has indicated that specific behaviors are viewed more positively by others, and clients who learn them can be made particularly effective. School psychologists who are interested in screening may use sociometric techniques to identify children who are isolates or are overlooked by classmates. Other techniques to identify social skills problems are self-report measures, ratings by others, and behavioral role-play tasks (Gresham & Elliott, 1984). From these assessments, children at risk of social failure may be included in groups designed to facilitate prosocial behavior. A number of group curriculums on social skills enhancement in the schools have been developed, and there is a definite role for the school psychologist in implementing these kinds of programs. Much more is covered in these programs, of course, than simple assertiveness.

School-based programs are beginning to appear that have as their goals the improvement of children's social and coping skills in general (e.g., Matson & Ollendick, 1988; Meichenbaum, 1985). This general class of programs, often termed competence enhancement training (Cowen, 1985), combine didactic training with role playing and simulation to establish specific habits and dispositions. Examples are Spivack and Shure's Interpersonal Cognitive Problem-Solving (Spivack & Shure, 1984), Elias' Improving Social Awareness-Social Problem-Solving (Elias, Gara, Ubriaco, Rothbaum, Clabby, & Schuyler, 1986), Gesten and Weissberg's Social Problem-Solving Training (Gesten, Weissberg, Amish, & Smith, 1987), and Botvin's Life Skills Training (Botvin,

1983). Although some, like the last, are aimed at preventing drug abuse or other later problems, all help children acquire skills that increase their attractiveness among peers.

One of the earlier applications of changing client behavior in the social domain but not aimed directly at increasing attractiveness is in the development of responsible assertiveness on the part of clients. Creating skills of assertiveness in contrast to aggressiveness or passivity has been particularly effective for working with the complaints of young women (Bower, 1976). Assertiveness training often is done in a group setting but can also be part of an individual counseling session. Improving assertiveness skills makes clients feel better about themselves and ultimately makes them perceived as more open and confident to others, traits that are related to interpersonal attraction.

REACTANCE THEORY AND COUNSELING

General Applications

Attraction may lead to positive social influence, but another body of research, termed reactance theory (Brehm, 1966), points out people do not always do what others wish or suggest. Because children in school are often involuntary participants in counseling, this aspect of social psychology is also worth mentioning. J. W. Brehm argued that a person will experience psychological reactance whenever an optional behavior (called *free behavior*) is eliminated or threatened with elimination. The magnitude of reactance is a function of the importance and number of freedoms threatened and the magnitude of the threat. Brehm (1976) stated that the effect of reactance is "a motivational state that will be directed toward the restoration of the threatened or eliminated freedom" (p. 19). The person may restore the freedom by acting directly in opposition to the threat. If a teacher tells a child to raise his hand instead of talking out, the child may oppose the teacher and continue talking out. Another response is to restore freedom indirectly by an action that reestablishes the freedom by implication. Thus the child might raise his hand but find another situation in which to talk aloud. Other responses are to accept the reactance but do nothing overt, or to behave generally aggressively toward the person (e.g., teacher or counselor) who threatens the freedom (Brehm, 1976). Reactance theory has been studied in the context of attitude change and group behavior but has a number of implications for the counseling process in addition to understanding that some children will naturally resist the process.

Specific Applications to Brief Therapy

Although strategic brief psychotherapy's development has not directly been tied into the social psychological theory of reactance, it and reactance are quite complimentary. There is even a small body of literature focused on how to utilize reactance theory to enhance clinical strategic work (Brehm, 1976; Rohrbaugh, Tennen, Press, & White, 1981; Tennen, Rohrbaugh, Press, & White, 1981; Weeks & L'Abate, 1982).

Many subschools of strategic psychotherapy exist, but reactance theory has been most aligned with the brief therapy model developed at the Mental Research Institute (MRI) (see Watzlawick, Weakland, & Fisch, 1974). Simply stated, their view is that "problems" are brought about by "solutions" that are ineffective. Either because the ineffective solutions have a common-sense appeal or because there is a good fit with the dynamics of the person (or family), the client perseveres with the "solution" that continues or maintains the problem. The basic intervention, then, is to get the client to stop the ineffective solution. Rohrbaugh et al. (1981) suggested that the strategic approaches to helping the client stop, as outlined by the MRI theorists, can be conceptualized as compliance-based and defiance-based strategies. Compliance-based interventions bring about change when the client tries to obey a paradox, and defiance-based strategies are effective when the client rejects the paradox (Weeks & L'Abate, 1982).

How this more directly fits the reactance model was described by Rohrbaugh et al. (1981) as:

> In general, defiance-based interventions are used when the probability of reactance is high and the target behavior is perceived as free. Compliance-based paradoxical strategies are most helpful with unfree or bound target behavior, usually symptoms maintained by attempts to stave them off, and are most readily implemented when reactance potential is low . . . With compliance-based strategies, the therapist takes steps to maximize the likelihood of compliance; with defiance-based strategies, the therapist tries to maximize rebellion. (p. 458)

A common example of a compliance-based paradox is symptom prescription (Watzlawick et al., 1974). The clinician tells the client to enact or continue with the symptomatic behavior. The paradox is that when the client does so the "symptom" is no longer out of control. For instance, if an insomniac is instructed to stay awake, not only is the insomnia now more under control, but the instructions also interfere with the usual "solution" of trying to fall asleep.

A typical defiance-based strategy utilized by MRI is to ask clients to increase the symptom. For instance, often with fighting siblings who are locked in covert power struggles, counselors suggest that they should not stop fighting but rather increase their fighting because it is their only way of negotiating (if this is the case). The paradox is that if they increase their fighting they are losing the power struggle with the therapist, and that the only way to enhance their power with the therapist is to cooperatively reduce their fighting.

Most children seen by school psychologists are not voluntary clients and do not perceive themselves initially as having a problem. It is natural for them to be resistant, and the counselor might as well acknowledge it without giving in to it (Egan, 1986). To the extent the counselor is able to draw the child into the counseling process and not be perceived as an authority figure imposing change and limiting the freedom of the child, reactance will be minimized. Much is made about resistance in the counseling literature (e.g., Cormier & Cormier 1985), but much behavior termed resistance may be better conceptualized as reactance.

GENDER AND ETHNICITY IN COUNSELING

General Applications

The research on both gender and ethnicity in social psychology has pointed out important ways that the different genders and different ethnic groups are socialized in our culture and in the various subcultures that make up our society. Individuals, as part of the developmental process, take on different attitudes, behaviors, and perhaps even abilities as their experiences are dictated by their culture during their formative years (see Henning-Stout & Conoley in this volume). Value differences certainly have been explicated for both the different genders (Schlossberg & Kent, 1979) and for different cultures (Atkinson, Morten, & Sue, 1982; Sue, 1977, 1981). In counseling it is important to assist clients in evaluating the various gender roles that have been reinforced for them, because they may not wish to change them. Other clients may be helped by helping them to explore the appropriateness of the various expectations they have for themselves and that others have placed on them.

Some theorists, such as Gilligan (1982), have pointed out that women develop different ways of thinking about and evaluating moral dilemmas than men. As a result, counselors must be aware of gender differences in value and facilitate moral reasoning in different clients without imposing their own gender-based values. Similarly, counselors need to be aware of ethnic or culturally based differences in values and attitudes and adopt a pluralistic stance (Niemeyer & Fukuyama, 1984). Counselors must be able to keep their own value systems in check and work within the framework of the clients and families they are seeing (Benjamin, 1981).

Specific Applications to Family Therapy

The specific application of research on gender particularly, but to some extent on ethnicity as well, falls in the area of family therapy. Family therapy is a form of group counseling, a special focus that can evaluate and help clients review how gender roles and other roles are developed in the family setting. The structural-functional (Hill & Hansen, 1960) and structural-functional plus developmental (Parsons & Bales, 1955) social psychological models of the family provide ways of conceptualizing the family very similar to some family therapy writers (Bell & Vogel, 1968; Minuchin, 1974).

For instance, the social psychological and clinical models are both very concerned with the organizational structure of the family. Other similarities include interest in the examination of subsystems in terms of their functional relationships and complimentary natures, interest in multilevel perspectives of the family and its members in relation to themselves and society, and an emphasis on the stable or homeostatic properties of a family.

However, because the goal of family counseling is to improve the functioning of the family group, clinical models such as Minuchin's (1974) also try to provide an understanding of family change processes more than, for instance, the Parsons and Bales' (1955) model. Some of the clinical processes related to these issues would then be to make explicit the family- and gender-related roles for its members, to improve communication, and to foster appropriate emotional support for development.

CONCLUSION

The social psychological theories discussed in this and other chapters in this book provides a rich, empirical, and theoretical grounding for a number of counseling activities undertaken by school psychologists. The applications that have been discussed in these chapters are not always easy to implement in counseling and have a number of issues attached to them related to their ethical use. In general, an ethical issue in social psychology that has been discussed at some length is the appropriateness of deceiving individuals. Some, but not all, social psychologists believe deception to be a necessary feature of their experimental designs (see Baron, 1981; Baumrind, 1979). This difficulty manifests itself in counseling more as a problem in influencing individuals without their permission or knowledge, or in being untruthful. The counselor armed with a number of techniques for behavior change may consciously or unconsciously change attitudes, beliefs, values, and behaviors of clients in directions not in their own best interests and without their knowledge. Studies in social psychology suggest that individuals can tell when others are deceiving them (De Paulo, Stone, & Lassiter, 1985), so perhaps Carl Rogers' (1957) injunction that counselors be honest and genuine is particularly appropriate. For a complete discussion of the ethics of manipulation in the service of behavioral change, see Herbert Kelman's (1965) classic article.

The issue of undue influence also raises its head in dealing with clients in different social and ethnic groups from the client, and the solution to the dilemma usually involves increasing the sensitivity on the part of the counselor. Most of these ethical dilemmas, to the extent that they can be resolved, depend on an increase in counselor awareness and provide for some forms of peer review for the counselor's work.

In general, however, the power of the social psychological theories in either supporting traditional effective counselor behavior or in suggesting alternative counseling behaviors is great. School psychologists working in counseling roles with children can facilitate both the personal and the educational development of youngsters with a counseling technique grounded in modern social psychological theory and research.

REFERENCES

Ackerman, N. W. (1966). *Treating the troubled family.* New York: Basic Books.

Agazarian, Y., & Peters, R. (1981). *The visible and invisible group: Two perspectives on group psychotherapy and group process.* London: Routledge & Kegan Paul.

Atkinson, D. R., Morten, G., & Sue, D. W. (1982). *Counseling American minorities* (2d ed.). Dubuque, IA: Brown.

Baron, R. A. (1981). The "costs of deception" revisited. *IRB: A review of human subjects research, 3,* 8–10.

Baumrind, D. (1979). The costs of deception. *IRB: A review of human subjects research, 1,* 1–4.

Beck, A. (1976). *Cognitive therapy and emotional disorders.* New York: International Universities Press.

Beck, A. T., Rush, A. J., Shaw, B. F., & Emery, G. (1979). *Cognitive therapy of depression.* New York: The Guilford Press.

Bell, N. W., & Vogel, E. F. (Eds.) (1968). *A modern introduction to the family.* New York: The Free Press.

Bellak, L., & Small, L. (1978). *Emergency psychotherapy and brief psychotherapy* (2d ed.). New York: Grune & Stratton.

Benjamin, A. (1981). *The helping interview* (3d ed.). Boston: Houghton–Mifflin.

Berkowitz, L. (Ed.). (1978). *Group process.* New York: Academic Press.

Berlin, I. N. (1970). Crisis intervention and short-term therapy: An approach to a child psychiatric clinic. *Journal of the American Academy of Child Psychology, 9,* 595–606.

Bernstein, M. E. (1976). Psychotherapy in the schools: Promise and perplexity. *Journal of School Psychology, 14,* 314–321.

Bower, S. (1976). Assertiveness training for women. In J. Krumboltz & C. Thoresen (Eds.), *Counseling methods* (pp. 467–474). New York: Holt, Rinehart, & Winston.

Botvin, G. J. (1983). *Life skills training.* New York: Smithfield Press.

Brehm, J. W. (1966). *A theory of psychological reactance.* New York: Academic Press.

Brehm, S. S. (1976). *The application of social psychology to clinical practice.* Washington: Hemisphere. (Halsted Press, dist.)

Carkhuff, R., & Berenson, B. (1977). Beyond counseling and therapy (2nd. ed.). New York: Holt, Rinehart, & Winston.

Carlson, C. I. (1987). Resolving school problems with structural family therapy. *School Psychology Review, 16,* 457–468.

Carroll, J. L., Harris, J. D., & Bretzing, B. H. (1979). A survey of psychologists serving secondary schools. *Professional Psychology, 10,* 766–770.

Cartwright, D., & Zander, A. (1953). *Group dynamics,* Evanston, IL: Row, Peterson.

Claiborn, C. D., & Strong, S. R. (1982). Group counseling in the schools. In C. R. Reynolds & T. B. Gutkin (Eds.), *The handbook of school psychology* (pp. 530–553). New York: Wiley.

Conoley, J. C. (1987). Schools and families: Theoretical and practical bridges. *Professional School Psychology, 2,* 191–203.

Cormier, W. H., & Cormier, L. S. (1985). *Interviewing strategies for helpers* (2d ed.). Monterey, CA: Brooks/Cole.

Corrigan, J. D., Dell, D. M., Lewis, K. N., & Schmidt, L. D. (1980). Counseling as a social influence process: A review. *Journal of Counseling Psychology Monograph, 27,* 395–431.

Cowen, E. (1985). Person-centered approaches to primary prevention in mental health: Situation-focused and competence-enhancement. *American Journal of Community Psychology, 13,* 31–48.

Davanloo, H. (1978). *Basic principles and techniques in short-term dynamic psychotherapy.* New York: Spectrum.

Davanloo, H. (Ed.) (1980). *Short-term dynamic psychotherapy.* New York: Jason Aronson.

De Paulo, B. M., Stone, J. L., & Lassiter, G. D. (1985). Deceiving and detecting deceit. In B. R. Schlenker (Ed.), *The self and social life* (pp. 323–370). New York: McGraw–Hill.

Dorn, F. J. (1984). *Counseling as applied social psychology:* An introduction to the social influence model. Springfield, IL: Charles C. Thomas.

Dulcan, M. K. (1984). Brief psychotherapy with children and their families: The state of the art. *Journal of the American Academy of Child Psychology, 23,* 544–551.

Dweck, C. S. (1975). The role of expectations and attributions in the alleviation of learned help-lessness. *Journal of Personality and Social Psychology, 31,* 674–685.

Dweck, C. S. (1986). Motivational processes affecting learning. *American Psychologist, 41,* 1040–1048.

Egan, G. (1986). *The skilled helper* (3d ed.). Monterey, CA: Brooks/Cole.

Elias, M. J., Gara, M., Ubriaco, M. Rothbaum, P. A., Clabby, J. F., & Schuyler, T. (1986). Impact of a preventive social problem solving intervention on children's coping with middle-school stressors. *American Journal of Community Psychology, 14,* 259–275.

Ellis, A. (1967). Rational-emotive psychotherapy. In D. Arbuckle (Ed.), *Counseling and psychotherapy* (pp. 78–95). New York: McGraw–Hill.

Festinger, L. (1957). *A theory of cognitive dissonance.* Stanford, CA: Stanford University Press.

Fine, M. J., & Holt, P. (1983). Intervening with school problems: A family system's perspective. *Psychology in the Schools, 20,* 59–66.

Flegenheimer, W. V. (1982). *Techniques of brief psychotherapy.* New York: Jason Aronson.

Forehand, R. L., & McMahon, R. J. (1981). *Helping the noncompliant child: A clinician's guide to parent training.* New York: The Guildford Press.

Fox, W. M. (1987). *Effective group problem solving.* San Francisco: Jossey–Bass.

Garfield, S. L. (1978). Research on client variables in psychotherapy. In S. L. Garfield & A. E. Bergin (Eds.), *Handbook of psychotherapy and behavior change* (2d. ed., pp. 191–232). New York: Wiley.

Gazda, G. M. (1989). *Group counseling: A developmental approach* (4th ed.). Boston: Allyn & Bacon.

Gesten, E. L., Weissberg, R. P., Amish, P. L., & Smith, J. K. (1987). Social problem-solving training: A skills-based approach to prevention and treatment. In C. A. Maher & J. E. Zins (Eds.), *Psychoeducational interventions in the schools* (pp. 26–45). New York: Pergamon.

Gilligan, C. (1982). *In a different voice.* Cambridge, MA: Harvard University Press.

Ginott, H. (1961). *Group psychotherapy with children.* New York: McGraw–Hill.

Glasser, W. (1965). *Reality therapy.* New York: Harper & Row.

Gresham, F. M., & Elliott, S. N. (1984). Assessment and classification of children's social skills: A review of methods and issues. *School Psychology Review, 13,* 292–301.

Group for the Advancement of Psychiatry (1982). *The process of child therapy.* New York: Brunner/Mazel.

Hill, R., & Hansen, D. A. (1960). The identification of conceptual frameworks utilized in family study. *Marriage and Family Living, 22,* 299–311.

Hohenshil, T. H. (1982). School psychology and vocational counseling–vocational school psychology. *The Personnel and Guidance Journal, 61*(1), 11–13.

Hohenshil, T. H., Levinson, E. M., & Heer, K. B. (1985). Best practices in vocational assessment for handicapped students. In A. Thomas & J. Grimes (Eds.), *Best practices in school psychology* (pp. 215–228). Kent, OH: National Association of School Psychologists.

Horwitz, L. (1977). A group centered approach to group psychotherapy. *International Journal of Group Psychology, 27,* 423–439.

Ivey, A. (1986). *Developmental therapy: Theory into practice.* San Francisco: Jossey-Bass.

Kelly, G. (1955). *The psychology of personal constructs* (Vols. I and II). New York: Norton.

Kelman, H. C. (1965). Manipulation of human behavior: An ethical dilemma for the social scientists. *Journal of Social Issues, 27,* (2), 31–46.

Kendall, P. C., & Braswell, L. (1985). *Cognitive-behavioral therapy for impulsive children.* New York: Guildford Press.

Koss, M. P. (1979). Length of psychotherapy for clients seen in private practice. *Journal of Consulting and Clinical Psychology, 47,* 210–212.

Lacayo, N., Sherwood, G., & Morris, J. (1981). Daily activities of school psychologists: A national survey. *Psychology in the schools, 18,* 184–190.

Laquer, H. P. (1976). Multiple family therapy. In P. J. Guerin (Ed.), *Family therapy: Theory and practice* (pp. 405–416). New York: Gardner Press.

Lewin, K. (1951). *Field theory in social science; selected theoretical papers.* D. Cartwright (Ed.). New York: Harper.

Matson, J. L., & Ollendick, T. H. (1988). *Enhancing children's social skills.* New York: Pergamon Press.

May, H. J., Powell, M., Gazda, G. M., & Hauser, G. (1985). Life skill training: Psychoeducational training as mental health treatment. *Journal of Clinical Psychology, 41,* 359–367.

Meichenbaum, D. (1974). *Cognitive behavior modification.* Morristown, NJ: General Learning Press.

Meichenbaum, D. (1985). *Stress inoculation training.* New York: Pergamon Press.

Minuchin, S. (1974). *Families and family therapy.* Cambridge, MA: Harvard University Press.

Moos, R. (1974). *The social climate scales: An overview.* Palo Alto, CA: Consulting Psychologists Press.

Napier, R. W., & Gershenfeld, M. K. (1985). *Groups: Theory and experience* (3d ed.). Boston: Houghton–Mifflin.

Niemeyer, G., & Fukuyama, M. (1984). Exploring the content and structure of cross-cultural attitudes. *Counselor Education and Supervision, 23,* 216–224.

Okun, B. F. (1984). Family therapy in the schools. In J. C. Hansen & B. F. Okun (Eds.), *Family therapy with school related problems* (pp. 1–12). Rockville, MD: Aspen Systems.

Parsons, T., & Bales, R. F. (1955). *Family, socialization and interaction process.* New York: The Free Press.

Passons, W. R. (1975). *Gestalt approaches in counseling.* New York: Holt, Rinehart, & Winston.

Phelps, L. A., & Lutz, R. J. (1977). *Career exploration and preparation for the special needs learner.* Boston: Allyn & Bacon.

Rogers, C. (1942). *Counseling and psychotherapy.* Cambridge, MA: Houghton–Mifflin.

Rogers, C. (1957). The necessary and sufficient conditions of therapeutic personality change. *Journal of Consulting Psychology, 21,* 95–103.

Rogers, C. R. (1961). *On becoming a person.* Boston: Houghton–Mifflin.

Rohrbaugh, M., Tennen, H., Press, S., & White, L. (1981). Compliance, defiance, and therapeutic paradox. *American Journal of Orthopsychiatry, 51,* 454–467.

Rosenthal, A. J. (1979). Brief focused psychotherapy. In J. D. Noshpitz & S. I. Harrison (Eds.), *Basic handbook of child psychiatry* (Vol. 3, pp. 57–72). New York: Basic Books.

Rubin, L. J. (Ed.) (1969). *Life-skills in school and society: 1969 yearbook.* Washington, DC: Association for Supervision and Curriculum Development, National Education Association.

Sandoval, J. (1988). Conceptualizations and general principles of crisis counseling, intervention, and prevention. In J. Sandoval (Ed.), *Crisis counseling, intervention and prevention in the schools* (pp. 3–20). Hillsdale, NJ: Lawrence Erlbaum Associates.

Satir, V. (1972). *People making.* Palo Alto, CA: Science and Behavior Books.

Schlossberg, N. K., & Kent, L. (1979). Effective helping with women. In S. Eisenberg & L. E. Patterson (Eds.), *Helping clients with special concerns* (pp. 263–286). Chicago: Rand McNally.

Shaffer, M. B. (1985). Best practices in counseling senior high school students. In A. Thomas & J. Grimes (Eds.), *Best practices in school psychology* (pp. 393–400). Kent, OH: The National Association of School Psychologists.

Shaw, M. E. (1981). *Group dynamics: The psychology of small group behavior.* New York: McGraw-Hill.

Sifneos, P. (1979). *Short-term dynamic psychotherapy.* New York: Plenum Press.

Slavson, S. R., & Shiffer, M. (1975). *Group psychotherapies for children: A text book.* New York: International Universities Press.

Spitzer, D., & Levinson, E. M. (1988). A review of selected vocational interest inventories for use by school psychologists. *School Psychology Review, 17,* 673–693.

Spivack, G., & Shure, M. B. (1984). *Social adjustment of young children: A cognitive approach to solving real-life problems.* San Francisco: Jossey-Bass.

Steiner, I. D. (1972). *Group process and productivity.* New York: Academic Press.

Stogdill, R. M. (1981). *Handbook of leadership* (rev. ed.) (B. M. Bass, Ed.). New York: Free Press.

Strelnick, A. H. (1977). Multiple family group therapy: A review of the literature. *Family Process, 16,* 307–325.

Strong, S. R. (1968). Counseling: An interpersonal influence process. *Journal of Counseling Psychology, 15,* 215–224.

Strong, S. R., & Claiborn, C. D. (1982). *Change through interaction: Social psychological processes of counseling and psychotherapy.* New York: Wiley.

Sue, D. (1977). Counseling the culturally different. *Personnel and Guidance Journal, 55,* 422–425.

Sue, D. W. (1981). *Counseling the culturally different.* New York: Wiley.

Super, D. E. (1957). *The psychology of careers.* New York: Harper & Bros.

Super, D. E., Starishevsky, R., Matlin, N., & Jordaan, J. P. (1963). Career development: Self-concept theory. New York: College Entrance Examination Board.

Tennen, H., Rohrbaugh, M., Press, S., & White, L. (1981). Reactance theory and therapeutic paradox: A compliance-defiance model. *Psychotherapy, 18,* 14–22.

Tharinger, D. (1985). Best practices in counseling elementary students. In A. Thomas & J. Grimes (Eds.), *Best practices in school psychology* (pp. 447–459). Kent, OH: The National Association of School Psychologists.

Triandis, H. C. (1977). *Interpersonal behavior.* Monterey, CA: Brooks/Cole.

Watzlawick, P., Weakland, J., & Fisch, R. (1974). *Change: Principles of problem formation and problem resolution.* New York: W. W. Norton.

Weeks, G. R., & L'Abate, L. (1982). *Paradoxical psychotherapy: Theory and practice with individuals, couples, and families.* New York: Bruner/Mazel.

Weiner, B. (1979). A theory of motivation for some classroom experience. *Journal of Educational Psychology, 71,* 3–25.

Whalen, C. K., & Henker, B. (1976). Psychostimulants and children: A review and analysis. *Psychological Bulletin, 83,* 1113–1130.

Yalom, I. D. (1985). *The theory and practice of group psychotherapy* (3d ed.). New York: Basic Books.

Zander, A. (1982). *Making groups effective.* San Francisco: Jossey-Bass.

11

SOCIAL PSYCHOLOGY FOUNDATIONS OF CONSULTATION

Jan N. Hughes
Texas A & M University

A psychological consultant attempts to influence professional caregivers, who have responsibility to their clients to adopt more effective strategies in their dealings with clients. Consultation is a collaborative problem-solving relationship in which a nonpsychological professional (consultee) voluntarily approaches the psychologist (consultant) for assistance with a work-related problem. Rather than referring the child to the psychologist, consultation is a request for assistance in carrying out the consultee's responsibility to the client. Thus, the consultee continues to be responsible for the problem and is free to accept or to reject the consultant's help (Brown, Pryzwansky, & Schulte, 1987; Caplan, 1970; Conoley & Conoley, 1982).

In teacher consultation, the focus of this chapter, the teacher–consultee is responsible for implementing recommendations that emerge from the consultation process. Thus, psychological consultants are successful only to the degree they influence teachers to adopt more effective approaches. In this model, the teacher is the target of the consultant's change efforts. Any psychologist who has engaged in consultation can attest to the difficulty of such efforts to effect generalizable and durable change in teachers' behaviors. Teacher behavior is in no small measure determined by what teachers think, and what they think is determined by a myriad of variables, including their attributions for pupils' behavior, personal sense of competency, implicit theories of teaching, and perceptions of the consultant's motives, credibility, and trustworthiness. Influencing the teacher to implement a specific strategy with a child is more than a manner of accurately diagnosing the child's problem and prescribing a technologically "correct" intervention. Rather, the consultant must carefully attend to a host of interpersonal, intrapersonal, and situational variables that determine the success of the consultant's efforts to influence the teacher to adopt a particular approach with a child. The premise of this chapter is that consultation is an interpersonal influence process and that the extensive literature on interpersonal influence in social psychology and, more recently in counseling and clinical psychology, is relevant to consultation.

CONSULTATION AS AN INTERPERSONAL INFLUENCE PROCESS

The view that consultation is an interpersonal influence process is not new. Gerald Caplan, the father of mental health consultation, emphasized the interpersonal aspects of consultation in several chapters of his seminal book, *The Theory and Practice of Mental Health Consultation* (1970). Caplan's relationship-building techniques, such as onedownsmanship, are entirely consistent with theories of interpersonal influence based on such social psychological processes as reactance (Brehm, 1966) and cognitive dissonance (Festinger, 1957). The consultation literature recognizes that the collaborative, nonhierarchial relationship in consultation necessitates the exercise of relationship-building skills and indirect-influence strategies (Brown et al., 1987; Conoley & Conoley, 1982; Parsons & Meyers, 1984).

The consultation relationship shares important similarities with counseling and psychotherapy. Both are helping processes in which the helper relies on social influence to bring about change in another person. The helpee's perceptions of the helper's expertise, interpersonal qualities, and motives determine the amount of resultant change. Both consultation and counseling involve the application of psychological principles to the resolution of problems. The client's problems discussed in counseling often involve the client's unsuccessful attempts to exert interpersonal control over a third person, just as teachers' problems are often a result of their unsuccessful attempts to influence pupils. However, consultation is carried out for the benefit of a third person, whereas the client in counseling is the expected beneficiary.

The parallels between counseling and consultation are important because an extensive literature has developed during the past 20 years on the applications of social psychology to counseling. In a landmark paper in 1968, Stanley Strong argued that counseling is an interpersonal influence process and that the burgeoning research on opinion change is relevant to counseling. In 1978 Strong expanded the areas of social psychology that are relevant to counseling to include attribution theory (see Levesque & Lowe in this volume). Strong (1978) stated:

Psychotherapy can be viewed as a branch of applied social psychology. Psychotherapy is a setting for interpersonal influence, an area of study in social psychology. The major targets for change in psychotherapy are client behaviors in social interactions. How clients feel about themselves (vis-a-vis others), how effective they are in controlling themselves (in social interaction), and how effectively they control their environments (mostly other people) are aspects of behavior in social interaction, which is the major focus of social psychology. (p. 101)

Since 1968 the view that research on social psychology informs clinical practice has gained widespread acceptance, as evidenced by more than a dozen books on social psychological processes in counseling and psychotherapy and a journal devoted to social processes in therapy, the *Journal of Social and Clinical Psychology.*

Whereas virtually all authors in consultation mention the importance of the consultant–consultee relationship, few have explicitly applied principles of attitude change to consultation. There are some exceptions. In 1974 Reppucci and Saunders reflected on their experiences as external behavior consultants to the Connecticut School for Boys, a state training school for adjudicated adolescent male delinquents. Their experiences taught them that good technology is not enough for effecting durable, system-wide changes, and that behavior modifiers must attend to social processes in natural settings. They elaborated eight obstacles they encountered in their attempt to implement a token economy. Two of these, the problems of language and consultees' perceptions of the personal characteristics of the consultant, are currently active research topics in school consultation (e.g., Gutkin, 1986; Rhoades, 1989; Witt, Moe, Gutkin, & Andrews, 1984). Reppucci and Saunders urged behavior modifiers to confront the theoretical limitations of behavior modification and to integrate it with theories of social psychological phenomena.

Other consultation theorists have applied specific principles and theories derived from social psychology to consultation. Martin (1978) was the first to define consultation as an interpersonal influence process and applied French and Raven's (1959) classification relationship. French and Raven defined social power as the potential of one person (Person A) to affect the attitudes, behaviors, or beliefs of another (Person B). Of the five sources of power potentially available in interpersonal relationships identified by French and Raven, Martin argued that three (reward, coercive, and legitimate) are not available to the consultant.

Reward power depends on Person B's perception that Person A has the ability to administer rewards and to remove punishers. Whereas reward power is based on Person A's ability to manipulate positive outcomes, coercive power is based on the manipulation of negative outcomes. Thus, Person A has coercive power in relationship to Person B, when Person B perceives that he or she will be punished by Person A if he or she fails to conform to Person A's influence attempt.

Legitimate power is a more complex base of influence, as it entails role theory and group norms. Person A has legitimate power when Person B believes that Person A has a legitimate right to influence Person B, and that Person B has an obligation to accept this influence. Legitimate power is based on the notion of the legitimacy of authority and carries with it an "oughtness." A principal has the right to require teachers to attend faculty meetings. Legitimate power is usually narrow in scope and attempts by a person to exercise it outside that range decrease the legitimate power of the authority figure (French & Raven, 1959).

Because reward, coercive, and legitimate sources of power are present in supervisory, hierarchical relationships, they are unavailable to the consultant. The consultant relies on the two remaining sources of influence, expert and referent power.

The consultant has expert power to the degree that the consultee attributes to the consultant knowledge or skill that the consultee feels he or she needs to meet personal goals. A great deal of literature in social psychology, summarized later in this chapter, describes the conditions under which a person attributes expert power to another. Because expert power is highly specific, Martin suggests that consultants who must deal with a wide variety of problems establish expert power in a few specific areas and strive to maximize referent power.

The consultant accrues referent power when the consultee identifies with the consultant and is attracted to the consultant's values, beliefs, and behaviors. Martin (1978) reinterpreted the consultation literature on the importance of the consultation relationship as demonstrations of the importance of maximizing referent power. Because referent power is based on a more global identification process, it requires frequent opportunity for interaction with the consultant. However, its effects are broader, and the consultant who accrues referent power has the potential to influence a broader range of consultee behaviors and attitudes. Martin suggested that referent and expert power are dependent, so that it is difficult to maintain high levels of each. Additionally, a primary reliance on expert power is likely to be ineffective because problems in consultation require the application of a wide range of approaches toward effecting changes in important beliefs and attitudes, and consultants who try to solve these problems with a range of solutions emanating from a single theoretical base will be perceived as doctrinaire and inflexible.

In the decade since Martin's article, consultation theorists have applied attribution theory (Martin, 1983), cognitive dissonance theory (Hughes, 1983), social exchange theory (Erchul & Chewning, 1990), and psychological reactance (Hughes & Falk, 1981) to consultation. Additionally, researchers have investigated the role of teachers' subjective perceptions of the acceptability of interventions recommended by consultants on their willingness to initially implement and subsequently continue with recommended strategies (Witt et al., 1984).

Despite these several attempts to apply social psychological principles to both consultation and counseling, to date there is no single, systematic account of the applications of social psychology to consultation. The purpose of this chapter is to provide such an account. No pretense is made that this account is comprehensive. Topics included under the rubric of social psychology are too numerous and diverse to permit anything approaching comprehensive coverage. The third edition of the venerable *Handbook of Social Psychology* (Lindzey & Aronson, 1985), published in two large volumes, includes 30 chapters. Several chapter topics that are relevant to consultation (e.g., decision making and decision theory, role theory, conformity, interpersonal attraction) are not mentioned or are mentioned briefly in this chapter. The selection of topics was based on the author's idiosyncratic interests and subjective evaluation of the utility of topics to consultation. Neither is this account integrative. Social psychology is not a unified theory that permits application "in totem." For example, Petty and Cacioppo (1981), in the preface to their book on attitude change and persuasion, reviewed seven theories, all of which have some explanatory power and none of which have been discarded or replaced. Rather, different theories predict different phenomena best.

To further complicate matters, often the same phenomenon can be explained by more than one theory, or two theories predict opposite effects in a given situation. An example of the former is found in a classical study involving the effects of a mild and severe threat given children not to play with a desired toy (Aronson & Carlsmith, 1963). Children in the mild threat condition showed less liking for the toy later, when given permission to play with the toy, compared to children in the severe threat condition. Dissonance theory, which is discussed later, explains these results in terms of the inconsistency between liking the forbidden toy and choosing not to play with it under the mild threat condition. Children resolve this inconsistency by derogating the toy. Children in the severe threat condition experience no inconsistency between choosing not to play with the forbidden toy and liking the toy. These same results, however, have been interpreted by self-perception theory (Bem, 1972). Self-perception theory predicts that the child in the mild threat condition observes his or her behavior in a manner similar to that of a third party observer and attributes his or her choice not to play with the forbidden toy to low liking for the toy.

An example of two principles of attitude change predicting different results is the finding that persuaders with high credibility produce more attitude change (Kelman & Hovland, 1953) and the incompatible finding that high credibility persuaders create more psychological reactance, limiting the amount of attitude change (Brehm, 1966). The implication of such apparent inconsistencies is that social interaction is complex and no single principle gains predictive supremacy. Which principle has the greatest predictive power in a given situation depends on characteristics of that situation. This chapter attempts to clarify the applications and limitations of the principles discussed.

The principles discussed are grouped into two types of factors, intrapersonal and interpersonal. Intrapersonal factors refer to consultee characteristics that have implications for what the consultant recommends and how the consultant presents the recommendation. Because these factors influence the consultant's behavior, they are interpersonal, too, and the division is somewhat arbitrary. Factors identified as interpersonal are clearly interactive and cannot be considered outside the relationship.

INTRAPERSONAL FACTORS

Attributions

Research interest in teachers' attributions reflects an increased appreciation for the role of teachers' thought processes in determining their classroom behaviors (Clark & Peterson, 1984; Shavelson & Stern, 1981). The cognitive view of teaching posits that cognitive processes (e.g., expectations, perceptions, judgments), behavior, and the environment form a reciprocal influence process (Bandura, 1977). According to this view, a teacher's attributions, judgments, decisions, and problem-solving processes mediate the teacher's behaviors, which in turn influence the environment and the teacher's perceptions of the environment. Although a discussion of teachers' thought processes is beyond the scope of this chapter, the following discussion of attributions illustrates the benefits derived from this line of inquiry and the importance of consultees' cognitions in consultation (Medway, 1989).

Attributional theories of behavior posit that people make hypotheses about why they and others behave the way they do (Heider, 1958; Weiner, 1979). Such hypotheses help the person understand, predict, and control events. There is no single, coherent attribution theory but a number of individual theories that attempt to explain the attributions people make in different situations. This section discusses the implications for consultation of teachers' causal attributions about pupils' behaviors, their own behavior, and the consultant's behavior.

Attributions about Pupils' Behaviors. Interest in teachers' attributions for pupils' behaviors is based on the premise that such attributions influence the way teachers attempt to modify behavior. Indeed, researchers have documented relationships between teachers' attributions for children's behaviors and teachers' preferred and actual strategies for resolving problems (Brophy & Rohrkemper, 1981; Medway, 1979).

Research on students' attributions for their own performance, reviewed by Levesque and Lowe earlier in this volume, demonstrate the influence of students' attributions for success and failure on subsequent effort and, thus, future success. Attributions to external/unstable causes (such as effort) may result in greater effort, and attributions to internal/stable causes (such as ability) may result in a state referred to as learned helplessness (Seligman et al., 1984). (This is discussed in greater detail in C. Peterson's chapter in this volume.) Similarly, it is reasonable to expect that teachers' attributions regarding students' successes or failures will affect their behaviors toward students. If a teacher attributes a student's failure or misbehavior to factors external to the teacher (e.g., factors within the child or home), the teacher may be less likely to work to improve the student's performance. Furthermore, attributions to different types of child variables (effort versus ability) are likely to result in different teacher responses. Considerable research evidence supports both lines of reasoning. First, types of attributions for pupils' behaviors that teachers make are discussed, followed by research on the effect of attributions on teachers' behavior. This review is necessarily brief, and the reader interested in a more complete review of this research is referred to Peterson and Barger (1985).

When pupils are performing poorly, teachers tend to attribute pupils' academic and behavioral difficulties to factors external to the teacher (Brophy & Rohrkemper, 1981; Christenson, Ysseldyke, Wang, & Algozzine, 1983); that is, teachers typically do not accept responsibility for pupils' poor performances. (Research demonstrates that consultants are also unlikely to accept responsibility for failures; Short & Ringer, 1987; Smith & Lyon, 1986.) A survey by the National Education Association (1979) found that 95% of teachers questioned attribute academic and behavioral difficulties to within-student characteristics and to factors in the child's home life, 4% to the school system, and only 1% to inappropriate instruction. Medway (1979) investigated actual attributions of teachers for problems of students referred for special education services. After initiating a referral, teachers were individually interviewed by school psychology interns. During the interview, teachers were asked to name specific problems or concerns they had regarding the referred student and to indicate what they felt was the primary cause of the major problem. After the open-ended portion of the interview, teachers were asked to rate each of 11 potential causes of the problem. Analyses of interview responses revealed that teachers' attributions varied as a function of the type of student problem (i.e., learning or behavior problem). Ability factors were cited as the major cause for 67% of the children with learning problems, but ability factors were not cited as causes for any children with behavior problems.

In contrast, home problems were seen as primarily responsible for 67% of the children with behavior problems. Teachers did not spontaneously mention their own teaching or peer influences in the classroom. The ratings revealed that teachers rated home and family factors significantly more responsible than teacher-related factors.

Researchers have offered several explanations for teachers' overwhelming tendency to attribute problems to factors external to the teacher. One explanation involves actor-observer attributional differences (Jones & Nisbett, 1971). Specifically, actors (students in this case) tend to attribute their own actions to situational influences, whereas observers (teachers in this case) tend to attribute the actors' actions to personality dispositions of the actors. Jones and Nisbett explained these attributional differences in terms of actors having access to information not possessed by observers, such as the actors' intentions and historical information, and to differences between actors and observers in what they focus on in the situation. Actors focus on the environment so that they can respond to it. For observers, the actor is part of the environment and the observer's attention is focused on the actor, as part of the environment. In addition to cognitive factors, observer–actor differences are explained in terms of motivational biases. Actors are reluctant to explain their behavior in terms of enduring personality characteristics. Such explanations may threaten actors' perceptions of themselves as free to choose how to behave (reactance theory is discussed later). For the observer, trait explanations are a convenient way of organizing others' behavior, increasing their ability to predict behavior.

Kelley's (1971) principle of covariance is also relevant to teachers' tendencies to make within-the-child attributions. Persons attribute causality to a person, versus the person's situation, when the person's behavior is distinctive and consistent over time, modality, and interactants. Chronic student problems are distinctive (other students in class do not present the problem) and consistent over time and modality (occurs regardless of the teacher's way of interacting with the pupil). The teacher may not have the opportunity to determine if other teachers experience the same effect when interacting with the pupil. Medway (1979) stated: "Thus, based merely on differential covariation information available to teachers an attribution to student factors for the failure of problem children would be most likely" (p. 815).

Kelley's (1971) discounting principle is relevant, too. When specific information about a plausible cause of a given effect is present, a person discounts the role of other possible causes in producing the effect. If ability or motivation is a plausible explanation, the teacher is not likely to give serious consideration to other causes. Therefore, teachers may attribute unitary causes for students' behavior versus multiple and interactive causes.

Finally, teachers' attributional tendencies may serve an ego-enhancing function (Bradley, 1978). Individuals tend to deny personal responsibility for failure as a means of preserving their self-image. Because teachers invest a great deal of energy in referred pupils and value their teaching competence, externalizing failure is an especially likely occurrence.

The finding that teachers attribute student problem behaviors to factors external to teachers is important because teachers behave differently to pupils depending on their attributions for their behavior. Specifically, several researchers demonstrate that teachers' attributions to effort are highly predictive of teachers' use of praise and criticism (see Clark & Peterson, 1984). For example, Medway (1979) observed teachers' use of praise and criticism following correct/appropriate and incorrect/inappropriate pupil behaviors. Teacher–pupil interactions were observed for the referred child and for a nonproblem child. Although teacher attributions were not related to teacher praise, attributions were significantly related to teacher criticism, accounting for 63% of the overall variability in teacher criticism. Over half of this variability was uniquely due to attributions to effort. Teachers who attributed student problems to a lack of motivation were more likely to criticize the pupil's inappropriate or incorrect behavior than they were to criticize a nonreferred child's inappropriate or incorrect behavior. This finding, taken in combination with the finding that 61% of referred children were rated by teachers as low on motivation (Christenson et al., 1983), explains why children with academic and behavior problems receive a disproportionate amount of negative feedback, even taking into account their higher rate of inappropriate behaviors (Brophy & Good, 1974).

Brophy and Rohrkemper (1981) examined the relationship among teachers' attributions, the goals they set for children, and likely control strategies. When teachers believed students' problems were intentional (under the student's control), they were less likely to use rewards and supportive teacher responses (i.e., preventive or remedial attempts to address the problem) and relied on punishment or threats as control strategies. When teachers attributed behavior to pupils' characteristics that were not within the pupils' ability to control (ability, "label"), teachers were more likely to provide support, nurturance, and instruction rather than administer rewards or punishments.

The relationship between teachers' attributions and behavior may be mediated by teacher affect. Different attributions for achievement outcomes elicit different affective responses on the part of teachers (see Graham, 1984). Sympathy is elicited when failure is attributed to ability (an uncontrollable, internal, stable cause), whereas anger is elicited when effort attributions are made (controllable, internal, and unstable). Furthermore, teachers' affective responses serve as cues to students that they use to make causal inferences about themselves (Graham, 1984). Teacher displays of sympathy and anger affect students' attributions for their own behaviors, and these self-ascriptions influence other achievement-related cognitions such as expectancies for success (Graham, 1984; Weiner, Graham, Stern, & Lawson, 1982). For example, a teacher who responds with sympathy toward a failing student might be motivated by the desire to protect the self-esteem of the failing student. Yet research findings indicate that sympathetic displays can lead to low-ability self-ascriptions and to a decline in expectancies for success (Graham, 1984). Rather than protecting the self-esteem of a failing student, sympathy might actually undermine it. Anger, on the other hand, is an emotional reaction to failure that teachers more typically avoid because of its presumed threat to the self-esteem of the low-ability student. But the attributional message communicated by this emotion may have positive consequences inasmuch as effort rather than ability is the inferred cause of failure.

Implications for the Consultant. Given the overwhelming tendency on the part of teachers to attribute pupils' problems to within-child and family factors, the consultant who believes classroom factors may be responsible, in whole or in part, for children's problems will have difficulty establishing common ground or a shared understanding of the problem with the teacher. The consultant's and the teacher's goals and preferred strategies are likely to be mismatched. Yet, the consultant wants the teacher to change his or her causal attributions in the direction of increased emphasis on factors under the teachers' control. Medway (1989) suggested that the best consultants are those who are able not only to generate "good" solutions to problems but also able to generate solutions that can be assimilated into a teacher's existing cognitive schemata.

Assuming that teachers' prevalent attributional tendencies serve an ego-enhancing function, the consultant might eliminate the teacher's motivation to externalize responsibility for the problem by reviewing the teacher's success with similar problems, emphasizing differences in student response to different classroom situations (peer influences, nature of task) and instructional strategies, empathizing with the teacher's sense of frustration, reframing frustration as an indicator of the teacher's investment in finding ways to help the student, discussing one's own failures in parallel situations, and avoiding evaluative comments (which may trigger the teacher's need to engage in ego-protecting maneuvers).

The consultant would be wise to accept the teacher's initial attributions in order to establish shared meaning and then seek additional but not mutually exclusive causal attributions. If the consultant's attributions of the pupils' problems are too discrepant with those of the teacher, the consultant is less likely to influence the teacher (Claiborn, Ward, & Strong, 1981).

The consultant might also present the teacher information about the importance of the teacher's cues on the student's self-ascriptions. A combination of teacher use of prompts, curriculum revision, mild displays of anger or disappointment, the moderate use of praise, and the establishment of performance expectations that are just ahead of the student's current performance levels produce more effort self-ascriptions on the part of students.

There is some evidence that the consultation process, with its emphasis on formulating more specific and concrete definitions of children's problems and assessing a range of factors that may influence the problems, changes teachers' attributions. Wehmann, Zins, and Curtis (1989) investigated the effect of participating in 10 weeks of consultation on teachers' attributions for children's behaviors. They analyzed audiotapes of the first and last consultation session and found a significant decrease in teachers' statements ascribing the problem to within-child factors and an increase in the proportion of statements ascribing problems to interactional causes. At the end of the consultation, teachers indicated they felt more control over problems and expected to achieve problem resolution.

Teacher Attributions Regarding Consultation Outcomes.   When teachers implement a recommendation that emerges from the consultation process, teachers will infer reasons for their own behaviors. These self-ascriptions may affect whether the changes in behaviors are durable or generalizable to other pupils or situations (the goal of consultation). Bem's (1972) self-perception theory explains how people come to attribute attitudes to themselves. Bem suggested that every person, be he actor or observer, discriminates as well as possible behavior that is under specific reinforcement contingencies (demanding behavior) from behavior that is a result of generalized social reinforcement (tacting behavior). If a person views his behavior as manding, that is, occurring under conditions of external reinforcement contingencies, the person concludes that his behavior does not reflect his true attitudes. But if the behavior is perceived as tacting (occurring in the absence of strong environmental rewards or punishers), the person views his behavior as conveying information about his attitudes. "Do I like spinach? I guess, I'm always eating it" captures the reasoning behind self-perception theory. Lepper (1973) replicated the Aronson and Carlsmith (1963) forbidden toy study, described earlier, and provided support for self-perception theory. This study had been interpreted as a demonstration of dissonance theory. Children who refrained from playing with the forbidden toy under the mild threat condition devalued this toy much more than children who refrained under the severe threat condition. Lepper reasoned that children who see themselves refrain from playing with the toy in conjunction with a mild threat infer that they have good self-control. The children in the high threat condition have ample justification for not playing with the toy and cannot make this self-ascription. Indeed, they may deduce they need strong external justification to resist the toy. Three weeks later children who had refrained from playing with the forbidden toy under mild threat conditions engaged in less cheating behavior than children who refrained under the severe threat. Children's attributions of self-control in the first experiment influenced their self-perceptions in a way that generalized to another situation requiring self-control.

External justification can also alter one's intrinsic motivation to engage in an activity. In a laboratory investigation (Lepper, Greene, & Nisbett, 1973), children were provided an opportunity to engage in an interesting activity (drawing with colored markers). Some of the children were told they would receive a reward for engaging in the task. A second group of children were not told to expect a reward but received one anyway. A third group of children neither expected nor received a reward. Later, children were given an opportunity to color in a free-choice situation, with no rewards being offered. As predicted by self-perception theory (as well as by dissonance theory), children who expected and received a reward engaged in less drawing than the other children. The authors suggested these children attributed their behavior as occurring because of the reward, whereas the other children attributed it to their own preferences (intrinsic interest). Thus, they continued to engage in drawing when no external reinforcement was available. S. Brehm (1976) concluded that when a person engages in a behavior under conditions of external justification, the short-term goal of having the person engage in a certain way is realized. But the goal of long-term, generalizable change may be jeopardized.

The implications of this line of research for consultation are straightforward. When the consultant wants a teacher to engage in a certain behavior, the consultant should use only that amount of external justification necessary to influence the teacher to try the new behavior. Sources of external justification that need to be considered include the consultant's interpersonal attractiveness (an empathic, warm, accepting listener is rewarding), promises of large improvements in the problem (it works every time), personal appeals (do it for me), and promises of future assistance (I will help you set up learning centers). The consultant should minimize the importance of external justifications by attributing the teacher's behavior to his or her own values, beliefs, or other personal qualities (e.g., "I can understand why you would prefer a strategy that permits you to nurture children's self-esteem").

Indirect experimental support for this last suggestion was provided by Miller, Brickman, and Bolen (1975). In their study teachers implemented a "tidy campaign" to encourage pupils to keep their rooms neat. Teachers in a "persuasion" condition relied on their social power and gave frequent exhortations in the form of "How messy this room is. Pick up all these papers. How could you be so untidy! You simply must be more tidy." Teachers in an attribution condition interpreted children's tidy behaviors as reflective of children's personal choices. "I am impressed by how tidy you are. You are very ecologically minded and keep your classroom clean." Although all conditions led to neat classrooms during the tidy campaign, only the attribution condition resulted in neat classrooms after the campaign ended. Apparently students in the attribution condition attributed their tidiness to their own values, beliefs, and attitudes, and these personal characteristics, being enduring, maintained the tidy behavior. Strong (1982) referred to such a change as spontaneous compliance, defined as "behavior that is emitted in compliance to external factors but is attributed to personal causes." (p. 200–201)

In consultation, the consultant's social power (combination of expert and referent power) may result in the teacher engaging in the recommended behavior; however, if the intervention is to be maintained or generalized, the consultant must encourage consultees to own the change in terms of attributing their behavior to personal characteristics (values, dispositions, beliefs, personal growth, attitudes). Consultants must influence consultees to accept personal responsibility for their actions. Fortunately, much of the literature on rapport building in consultation and counseling suggests ways to minimize the overtness of the consultant's (or counselor's) persuasive attempts. Addressing the counselor's role in therapy, Strong (1982) stated:

> While change in therapy results from compliance pressures and demand characteristics, therapists go to great lengths to draw client attention away from these pressures and avoid providing explicit justifications for change in therapy. Therapeutic dictums that therapists never tell clients what to do, never give advice, and never directly tell clients to stop symptomatic behaviors, avoid giving clients external justifications to account for induced change. The dictums function to allow personal attributions for change and thus help generate generalized and persistent therapeutic change. (p. 202)

The consultant not only wants to encourage teachers to attribute their positive behaviors to personal characteristics but also wants to influence teachers to attribute undesired (i.e., not recommended) behaviors to external causes. If a person engages in an undesired behavior and is provided external justification, the person is less likely to change his or her attitude in the direction of supporting the unacceptable behavior (Strong, 1982). For example, the consultant might want the teacher to discontinue use of publicly stigmatizing punishments (e.g., nose to the blackboard). The consultant might change the teacher's use of this approach through his or her exercise of social power. However, the teacher's underlying beliefs and attitudes that supported this disciplinary strategy (e.g., children need to be published for bad behavior) will not be affected by the consultant's intervention. A more effective approach for the consultant interested in generalizable and durable change is to attribute the teacher's use of punishment to external causes, such as the lack of support from the administration or the child's tendency to elicit power control discipline approaches. The consultant points out that the teacher wants to find ways to be less punitive and more reinforcing to children. The consultant understands that the teachers chose their profession because they want to help children grow into capable and happy individuals. The consultant might point out that the teacher's participation in consultation is, in itself, a demonstration of his or her desire to employ different strategies. Of course, the consultant wants to tailor the message to the teacher, and an exaggerated argument would probably alter the teacher's attributions about the consultant's behavior that would be antagonistic to the consultation process.

TEACHER SELF-EFFICACY

Teachers' beliefs about their ability to influence students' problems are likely to affect the amount of effort they expend in helping students, the persistence of these efforts, and the types of strategies for resolving student problems. An emerging literature has documented relationships between teachers' self-efficacy beliefs and teachers' behaviors (Brophy & Evertson, 1977; Gibson & Dembo, 1984; Gutkin & Ajchenbaum, 1984; Gutkin & Hickman, 1988).

Just as there is no single attribution theory, there is no single definition of self-efficacy. Gibson and Dembo (1984) identified two factors on their 30-item measure of teacher self-efficacy. One factor, labeled Personal Teaching Efficacy, represents a teacher's belief that he or she has the skills and abilities to bring about student learning. An item loading on this factor is "When the grades of my students improve it is usually because I found more effective teaching approaches." The second factor represents a teacher's sense of teaching efficacy, or "belief that any teacher's ability to bring about change is significantly limited by factors external to the teacher, such as the home environment, family background, and parental influences" (p. 574). An example item on this factor is "A teacher is very limited in what he/she can achieve because a student's home environment is a large influence on his/her achievement."

Gibson and Dembo suggested that personal teaching efficacy is similar to Bandura's (1977) construct of self-efficacy. The second factor Gibson and Dembo identified, General Teaching Efficacy, is similar to the construct locus of control (Rotter, 1966). Persons with an internal locus of control (internals) believe they are responsible for consequences, whereas externals believe fate or change determines consequences. Whereas locus of control is a global personality construct, general teaching efficacy is specific to teaching outcomes.

Gutkin and Ajchenbaum (1984) found a relationship between teachers' perceptions of control over pupil problem behaviors and their preferences for consultation versus referral. Consistent with their prediction, teachers who perceived themselves as exercising control over problem behaviors preferred consultation, which requires continued teacher responsibility and involvement with the problem, to referring the child for special education. Gutkin and Hickman (1988) reported that manipulating teachers' sense of control over problems increased their preference for engaging in consultation.

Teachers' personal teaching efficacy has received less research attention than has their general teaching efficacy. Hughes, Grossman, and Barker (1990) reported a negative relationship between teachers' personal self-efficacy (expectation they could successfully resolve pupil behavior problems on their own) and positive expectations for consultation. Furthermore, teachers with high personal self-efficacy tended to report less change in their professional behaviors, following consultation.

Implications for Consultation. Teacher self-efficacy is a new research topic in school psychology, and any suggested applications of this research to consultation are necessarily offered as tentative hypotheses. It appears that consultants should attempt to increase teachers' sense of control over presenting problems. Providing information about successful classroom interventions with similar problems is likely to increase teachers' sense of controllability and, consequently, their willingness to grapple with the problem in consultation (Gutkin & Hickman, 1988). If teachers believe they are able to successfully implement a given intervention, or to resolve a problem on their own, they are likely to initiate and persist with an intervention. The consultant might increase teachers' personal self-efficacy for specific interventions by modeling the intervention or asking the teacher to try it out in a role-play situation. For example, if the consultant wants the teacher to use self-instructional training (Meichenbaum & Goodman, 1971), the consultant might model the approach with a child or invite the teacher to practice it in an analogue situation. Additionally, the consultant might emphasize how the intervention is similar to what the teacher has done in the past.

There is some evidence that teachers with high personal teaching efficacy tend not to participate in consultation or tend to report not changing their behavior as a result of consultation. Some of this evidence is indirect. For example, teaching self-efficacy tends to increase with years of experience (Safran, 1985), and more experienced teachers are less likely to participate in consultation (Gutkin & Bossard, 1984; Iscoe, Pierce-Jones, McGehearty, & Friedman, 1967), rate consultants' intervention less acceptable (Witt et al., 1984), and report less professional growth resulting from consultation (Weissenburger, Fine, & Poggio, 1982). Hughes et al. (1990) found that teachers with higher self-efficacy valued consultation less and tended to report less change in their behaviors as a result of consultation. One explanation for these findings is that experienced teachers, who have developed a greater sense of self-efficacy (confidence in their abilities), value their teaching behaviors more highly and value their freedom to engage in these behaviors more than less experienced teachers. As discussed in a later section, the importance of a behavior and the importance of the freedom to engage in it predict higher levels of reactance when that behavioral freedom is threatened. Thus, experienced teachers may resist the consultant's influence attempts, especially if the teacher perceives the consultant's persuasive intent. Therefore, consultants need to employ Caplan's (1970) onedownsmanship strategies with experienced, high self-efficacy teachers. These strategies include asking for the teacher's observations, inferences, and suggestions prior to offering one's own, giving the credit for his or her unique perspective on the problem, freely admitting to one's lack of knowledge, and asking for instruction from the teacher. The consultant avoids overt attempts to persuade and encourages consultee ownership of recommendations emerging from consultation. Because a person's prior expectation that a communicator intends to persuade influences the arousal of reactance (Strong & Claiborn, 1982), the consultant will want to present consultation as a collaborative problem-solving relationship in which the teacher is an active participant and shares responsibility for the problem and its resolution.

ACCEPTABILITY OF INTERVENTIONS

Recently, much research attention has focused on factors that affect teachers' judgments of the acceptability of interventions (Elliott, 1988; Witt & Elliott, 1985; Witt, Martens, & Elliott, 1984). This research is an outgrowth of research on clients' acceptability of psychotherapy treatments (Kazdin, 1980; Kazdin & Cole, 1981). These researchers have argued that perceptions of intervention acceptability influence teachers' adherence to the intervention, affecting the integrity of treatment implementation and, therefore, increasing treatment effectiveness.

Not surprisingly, teachers' perceptions of intervention acceptability for recommendations made by consultants are influenced by teachers' perceptions of aspects of the intervention (e.g., the amount of time and teacher skill required, the risk to the target child, effects on other children) as well as perceptions of the intervention's effectiveness. Important to this discussion is research demonstrating how the manner of intervention presentation affects teachers' perceptions of acceptability.

One aspect of the manner of presentation is the language used to describe the intervention. Several investigators have found that teachers prefer a behavioral intervention when it is described or labeled in humanistic versus behavior terms (Kazdin & Cole, 1981; Woolfolk, Woolfolk, & Wilson, 1977). Witt et al. (1984) found that when an intervention was described in pragmatic terms it was rated more acceptable by teachers than when it was described in either behavioral or humanistic terms.

Rhoades (1989) investigated two aspects of intervention presentation, language and teacher involvement, on teacher ratings of intervention acceptability. Rhoades found no main effect on teachers' acceptability ratings for language (jargon versus ordinary language) or teacher involvement. She did, however, find an interesting interaction between teacher involvement and language. In the low-involvement condition, teachers rated the intervention more acceptable when the consultant used technical language. In the high-teacher involvement condition, there was no difference in acceptability ratings between the jargon and ordinary language conditions. Rhoades concluded that when consultants assume expert versus collaborative roles, their use of technical language bolsters their credibility, leading to higher acceptability ratings. It is important to note that in Rhoades' simulation study the consultant's opportunity to exercise referent power was very minimal. Thus, the study's findings may be limited to situations in which the only source of influence available to the consultant is expert power. In natural consultations, the sources of influence available to the consultant include interpersonal (referent) power, too, and technical language may detract from the consultant's referent power.

INTERPERSONAL FACTORS

Whereas self-efficacy, attributions, and perception of acceptability might be thought of as consultee characteristics, other variables affecting the consultant's influence on the consultee reside either in the consultant or in the consultant–consultee interaction. First, research on characteristics of communicators (message source) that affect the persuasiveness of an interpersonal influence attempt are reviewed, with an emphasis on studies on communication in helping relationships. Next, two motivational theories, cognitive dissonance theory and reactance theory, are described and applied to consultation. Finally, Strong and Claiborn's (1982) social influence model of change in psychotherapy is presented as a framework for applying the various theories discussed in this chapter to effecting change in consultation.

Characteristics of the Communicator

Communicators with high perceived credibility, trustworthiness, and attractiveness are more successful in influencing audiences (Hovland & Weiss, 1951; Petty & Cacioppo, 1981). Over 100 studies have investigated factors that affect clients' perceptions of counselors' expertness, trustworthiness, and attractiveness and the role of these factors in client change (Corrigan, Dell, Lewis, & Schmidt, 1980; Strong, 1968; Strong & Claiborn, 1982). These studies have generally upheld the assertion that client perceptions of these characteristics predict clients' satisfaction with counseling and client changes in target attitudes and behaviors. Strong (1968) summarizes factors that influence clients' perceptions of expertness, trustworthiness, and attractiveness.

Expertness. Perceptions of expert status is influenced by "(a) objective evidence of specializing training such as diplomas, certificates, and titles, (b) behavioral evidence of expertness such as rational and knowledgeable arguments and confidence in presentation, and (c) reputation as an expert" (p. 216). One of the behaviors that leads to judgments of expertness is structuring (Strong & Schmidt, 1970). Therapists who structure the interview are perceived as most expert. Similarly, behavioral consultants who use structuring techniques (i.e., ask questions and seek or offer specifics about the problem) are more effective (Bergan & Tombari, 1976; Erchul, 1987). This same finding may explain Medway and Forman's (1980) finding that teachers prefer a videotape presentation of behavior consultation to mental health consultation. The behavioral consultant was more directive and used more specifications and verbal structuring techniques.

Trustworthiness. Strong (1968) also described factors influencing perceptions of trustworthiness. "Communicators' trustworthiness is a function of: (a) reputation for honesty, (b) social role, such as physician, (c) sincerity and openness, and (d) perceived lack of motivation for personal gain" (p. 218).

Attractiveness. In general, attractiveness refers to the audience's liking for the communicator. Similarities in class membership (i.e., similarity in the social group to which persons belong) is less important than perceived similarities in issue-relevant attitudes and beliefs (Simons, Berkowitz, & Moyer, 1970). Attractiveness in counseling is primarily a function of therapist warmth and the client's perceptions of therapist liking for the client (see Strong & Claiborn, 1982) rather than similarity to the counselor. Moderate use of counselor self-disclosure enhances attractiveness perceptions (Cozby, 1972; Worthy, Gary, & Kahn, 1969). Self-disclosure permits identification with the consultant, which is the basis for referent power. Although self-disclosure generally enhances perceptions of attractiveness and expertness, too much self-disclosure can reduce the counselor's influence, and the amount of optimal self-disclosure may differ for men and women. In one counseling study, more self-disclosure reduced client perceptions of trustworthiness for women, but not for men (Merluzzi, Banikiotes, & Missbach, 1978). (The social basis of counseling is discussed in Sandoval and Davis' chapter in this book.)

These findings on counselor characteristics are consistent with the literature of consultant characteristics. Gutkin (1986) found that consultees' perceptions of the consultant's communication skills and knowledge of psychological principles were related to consultees' evaluations of the success of consultation. Silverman (1974) found that teacher liking for the consultant and liking to work with the consultant were the most important factors related to satisfaction with consultation.

Trustworthiness may be an aspect of credibility. When a consultant enters a system, the consultant is confronted with multiple, and often conflicting, service expectations. Given the importance of being perceived as trustworthy, it is critical that the consultant adequately educate all parties to his or her role, goals, the nature of the type of help offered, the degree of confidentiality afforded, etc. Much of the literature on entry in consultation (e.g., Caplan, 1970; Conoley & Conoley, 1982) addresses the importance of establishing and communicating shared expectations regarding the consultant's services.

Dissonance Theory

Festinger's theory of cognitive dissonance (1957) has generated an enormous literature. Although his original formulation has been refined by several others, most notably Brehm and Cohen (1962) and Wicklund and Brehm (1976), the basic tenets of the original theory remain the same. Research interest in dissonance is a result of its ability to predict important and varied beliefs and behaviors (see Brehm & Cohen, 1962). The power and breadth of application of dissonance led Sharon Brehm in her 1976 book, *The Application of Social Psychology to Clinical Practice,* to state the cognitive dissonance theory may be the most powerful theory for affecting client change in therapy.

First, the basic elements of contemporary dissonance theory are described. Although even a summary of research supporting each element of dissonance theory is beyond the scope of this discussion, selected investigations are described to illustrate the types of research generated by the theory. After this overview is presented, specific applications of dissonance to consultation are suggested.

Basic Elements of Dissonance Theory. A cognition is any bit of knowledge a person possesses about the world. Cognitions can refer to behaviors (I attended an Aggie baseball game), attitudes (I like guacamole), or beliefs (I believe women are capable of assuming positions of leadership). Cognitions can be specific or general in scope and can refer to unimportant or central attitudes or beliefs. Cognitions are related to each other in one of two ways. Cognitions are in an *irrelevant* relationship to each other when Cognition A does not imply anything about Cognition B. Persons have an enormous number of cognitions, and the vast majority of them are irrelevant to each other. The cognitions "I like the color blue" and "I buy American cars" are in an irrelevant relationship. When cognitions are in a *relevant* relationship to one another, such relationship is either consonant or dissonant. Cognitions A and B are in a *consonant* relationship when Cognition A implies Cognition B. Stated differently, given Cognition A, Cognition B follows. Knowing I believe in supporting American manufacturers is consistent with my knowledge that I bought a Ford Bronco. Cognitions A and B are in a *dissonant* relationship when Cognition A implies the obverse of Cognition B. Knowing that I believe in supporting American manufacturers is inconsistent with knowing that I bought a Honda. Dissonant cognitions involve contradiction. Given A, one expects Cognition B, but A occurs and not-B actually exists.

A central premise of dissonance theory is that dissonant cognitions create a state of tension called dissonance, which motivates the person to change at least one cognition to reduce the dissonance. According to Festinger (1957), the amount of dissonance experienced is a function of (a) the importance of the cognitions and (b) the proportion of dissonant to consonant cognitions. When the dissonant cognitions are important and when the number of dissonant cognitions increases in relation to consonant ones, dissonance arousal is greatest. The greater the dissonance arousal, the more likely are dissonance reduction attempts.

Festinger applied his theory to three major areas: selective exposure to information, decision-making processes, and forced compliance. The third area is the most relevant to processes occurring in counseling and consultation. In a forced compliance situation, a person is induced to behave in a manner that is inconsistent with a person's attitudes and beliefs. If the induction (persuasive attempt) is successful, and the person engages in counterattitudinal behavior, dissonance may be aroused. Consider, for example, the situation in which a person who believes in a woman's right to seek an abortion is induced to write a "prolife" essay. The person's behavior is inconsistent with the person's attitudes. Dissonance may be aroused in this situation, depending on certain other cognitions. For example, if the person made the decision to write the essay under conditions of low choice (high external justification, such as having to write the essay to pass a speech class or receiving $100 for writing the essay), little dissonance is aroused. When dissonance is aroused, the person engages in one or more dissonance-reduction attempts. In the forced choice paradigm, two of the most likely dissonance-reduction strategies are changing one's private opinion to be consistent with one's behavior (the desired outcome in counseling and psychotherapy, when the therapist/consultant has induced the client to engage in the recommended behavior), and magnifying the importance of the external justification for the behavior.

The reader may be bothered by the view that consultation shares similarities with the forced compliance situation. After all, consultation is a voluntary relationship, and the consultee is free to accept or to reject the consultant's recommendations. However, the consultant often hopes to influence the consultee to adopt different behaviors with a particular child. Presumably, the reason consultees are not engaging in the desired behaviors is that they have opinions, attitudes, and beliefs that are not supportive of performing the desired behavior. Dissonance theory predicts that when consultees do perform the desired behaviors, their performances will be dissonant with those cognitions that prevented them from performing the behaviors in the absence of the consultant's assistance. It is in this sense that the desired behaviors are counterattitudinal. The "forced" aspect refers to the inducements the consultant provides for engaging in the behavior. These inducements might be rational arguments supportive of the behavior, the interpersonal attractiveness of the consultant, the hope of problem resolution, or a host of other variables, both logical and affective, that influence the consultee's decision to engage in the desired behavior.

People go around with inconsistent beliefs and attitudes all the time, and there is no evidence people are motivated to change them. Behavioral commitments, however, are more difficult to ignore and are more resistant to change. For example, if a teacher uses a contingency management strategy for modifying a student's behavior, and the teacher believes it is wrong to reward children for doing what they are supposed to do, the teacher experiences dissonance. The cognition, "I used a contingency management strategy," cannot easily be changed. Therefore, the teacher is most likely to change the other cognitions in the dissonant relationship and believe it is appropriate, under some conditions, to reward children for "good behavior." The behavioral commitment does not require actually engaging in the counterattitudinal behavior but may consist of publicly declaring one's intention to engage in the behavior (Brehm & Cohen, 1962).

However, for a change in beliefs and attitudes more supportive of the behavioral commitment to occur, two conditions must be present (Wicklund & Brehm, 1976). First, the person must feel responsible when commitment is voluntary and when the consequences of behavior can be foreseen. If a person chooses an activity and foresees its consequences, the person feels more responsible for the decision and more dissonance is created. Foreseeable negative consequences increase dissonance arousal and subsequent attitude change. Thus, if a teacher uses extinction and expects the problem will worsen, and it does, the teacher's sense of responsibility for the behavioral commitment increases, and he or she feels more favorable to the extinction procedures. Unforeseeable negative consequences reduce responsibility and attitude change.

The second variable, *justification,* has been extensively researched (Brock, 1968; Freedman, 1963). Justifications in terms of incentives for engaging in the counterattitudinal behavior or threats or punishment for not engaging in the counterattitudinal behavior act to reduce perceived responsibility for the behavior and reduce attitude change. When a person engages in a counterattitudinal behavior for which there is strong external justification, dissonance arousal is minimal. For example, if the teacher who dislikes a phonetic approach is paid $100 for using it as part of a study, little dissonance is expected and there is little likelihood the person will change liking of the phonetic approach.

Next, three elements of dissonance theory, (i.e., commitment, choice, and justification) are applied to consultation. Research illustrative of the empirical basis for each element is described, followed by suggested practical applications to consultation.

Applications to Consultation

Behavioral Commitment. Commitment to behavior discrepant from attitudes the individual holds produces dissonance. This is especially true if the commitment is public because it is difficult to discount or revoke the behavior (Kiesler, Pollak, & Kanouse, 1968). Not only does commitment to a dissonant behavior (counterattitudinal behavior) produce attitude change, but commitment to a consonant behavior (i.e., one consistent with one's attitudes) strengthens the attitude, rendering it more resistant to change.

Commitment is relevant both to situations in which the consultant wishes to change a consultee's attitudes or beliefs and to situations in which the consultant wants to strengthen an existing attitude or belief. In the former situation, the consultant would be wise to obtain a clear, public commitment to engage in the recommended behavior. The following statements elicit public commitments: "Is this something you plan to try?"; "When do you think would be the best time to begin this plan?"; "What changes in your usual routine will this plan necessitate?"; "How can we best plan for those changes?"; "So, when I come back next week, we can assess how Alvin responded to this plan." The consultant, in obtaining the commitment, must be careful not to exert too much direct influence, because the consultee will feel the commitment was made under conditions of low choice, which reduces responsibility for the commitment and subsequent attitude change.

Perhaps the most important application of commitment in consultation concerns behaviors consonant with existing, but weak, attitudes. By encouraging the consultee to publicly endorse desired attitudes, behaviors, and beliefs, the saliency of these beliefs and attitudes is enhanced, leading to more consistency between behavior and expressed attitudes. Thus, when a teacher expresses belief in students learning from each other, the consultant might encourage the teacher to cite examples of actual peer-learning opportunities or information showing the effectiveness of this approach. A major tenet of client-centered counseling is that, by helping the client clarify existing beliefs and attitudes, the counselor helps the client achieve greater consistency between behavior, beliefs, and feelings.

Choice. When a person engages in attitude-discrepant behavior under perceived coercion, there is little dissonance arousal and subsequent attitude change (Brock, 1962, 1968; Brock & Buss, 1962). The results of an early study on choice (Cohen & Latane, in Brehm & Cohen, 1962) are instructive. Yale undergraduates who were initially opposed to the institution of a compulsory religious course at Yale were given either a high or low degree of choice in making a speech advocating a compulsory religious course. Subjects in the high-choice condition were in a dissonance-producing situation. They freely chose to make a public statement that was inconsistent with their attitudes on an important issue with potentially serious consequences. As expected, subjects in the high-choice group showed more attitude change than subjects given low choice.

In another study on choice (Cohen, Terry, & Jones, 1959), subjects were given high or low choice in hearing a counterattitudinal message. The choice manipulation produced significant differences in attitude change toward the message for subjects whose original attitudes were extreme.

The application of these studies on choice to consultation is straightforward and is consistent with the emphasis in the consultation literature on the voluntary, nonhierarchial, and collaborative nature of the consultation relationship (Brown et al., 1987; Caplan, 1970). Parsons and Meyers (1984) stated that the consultant can increase consultee involvement in consultation, and subsequent responsibility for implementing the recommendations emerging from consultation, by asking the consultee to make suggestions, providing verbal recognition of the consultee's contributions to the intervention plans, emphasizing the consultee's freedom to accept or to reject the consultant's suggestions, and encouraging the consultee to make decisions. The consultant should attempt to discover any pressure to seek consultation that the consultee may be experiencing by making comments such as, "Tell me how you came to be interested in the possibility of obtaining consultation?" "Did anyone suggest to you that you might talk with me about this situation?" If pressure is uncovered, the consultant might agree to satisfy the perceived external pressure for the consultee to seek assistance by meeting with the consultee once, while indicating that the consultant is available to participate in a different type of problem-solving relationship.

Research on consultee preferences for different models of consultation demonstrates consultees' preferences for high teacher involvement (collaborative consultation) versus low involvement (Babcock & Pryzwansky, 1983; Fine, Grantham, & Wright, 1979; Rhoades, 1989; Wenger, 1979). Teachers prefer to be involved in the development of remedial plans (Gutkin, 1980, 1986), and teachers find the solutions generated through collaborative consultation processes more acceptable than solutions generated by someone else (Fairchild, 1976; Reinking, Livesay, & Kohl, 1978). The voluntary nature of consultation should be emphasized throughout the consultation process. "We have talked about several different approaches. Why don't you think about these for now, and when we meet next week you can decide which direction you want to take." The decision to continue in consultation serves as a cognition dissonant with the belief that consultation is unhelpful. Therefore, the consultant would emphasize the voluntariness of participation throughout the process: "Do you want to continue to work together on this problem, or do you think you would prefer to work on it by yourself now?"

Justification. External justification for engaging in a counterattitudinal behavior reduces dissonance and attitude change. In Festinger and Carlsmith's (1959) classical study on monetary inducement, college subjects were offered either \$1.00 (low justification) or \$20.00 (high justification) to tell another subject that a boring and tedious task was interesting and enjoyable. Subjects in the low-justification condition changed their personal evaluation of the task in a favorable direction more than did subjects offered high justification. In one of the few studies of dissonance effects in a clinical situation, Bogart, Loeb, and Rutman (1969; cited in Brehm, 1976) examined the effect of magnitude of inducement to participate in a rehabilitative program on continued participation in the program, after inducements were removed. Although both inducements resulted in some increase in participation in the program, a higher percentage of patients provided with a small monetary inducement continued their participation after the inducement was removed than patients provided a large monetary inducement.

Other research on positive and negative consequences of the discrepant behavior shows that for consequences to affect dissonance the person must be aware of the consequences of his behavioral commitment prior to the commitment (Brehm & Jones, 1970; Freedman, 1963). Positive and negative consequences can have a paradoxical effect on behavior. Expected positive consequences of a commitment decrease linking for the commitment, whereas expected negative consequences may increase liking for the commitment (Wicklund & Brehm, 1976). Unexpected positive consequences increase liking for the commitment, whereas unexpected negative consequences decrease liking for the behavior. Even if consequences are unforeseen, they will affect dissonance reduction if the person views the consequences as an outcome of his or her efforts or ability or if the person believes the consequences were foreseeable at the time of the commitment (Wicklund & Brehm, 1976).

Research on external justification suggests that the consultant would want to minimize external justification for entering into consultation and for implementing any recommendations emerging from consultation. Seymour Sarason, in his school faculty speech introducing consultation, underscores the fact that the consultant does not guarantee answers to the problems teachers bring to consultation (Sarason et al., 1960): "We do not know to what extent we can be of help to you. We do not present ourselves as experts who have answers. We have much to learn about this helping process. . . The only thing we can guarantee you is that we want to learn and to help. We have much to learn from you, and together we may be able to be of help to children in school" (pp. 58–62).

Because unexpected negative consequences increase dissonance reduction, the consultant should make certain that the consultee is aware of the possibility of negative consequences of the commitment. For example, in recommending an operant strategy, the consultant should be certain that the consultee anticipated the amount of effort involved, the likely increase in the undesirable behavior following the withdrawal of reinforcement, and any likely negative effects on other children. When unexpected negative consequences follow, the consultant might attempt to prevent a decrease in the consultee's liking for the commitment by emphasizing the foreseeability of the outcome at the time of the commitment: "Of course, we might have expected this would occur."

REACTANCE

J. Brehm presented his theory in 1966, in his book, *A Theory of Psychological Reactance*. Briefly, Brehm postulated that "people have the subjective experience of freedom to do what they want, to do it the way they want, and to do it when they want in regard to limited and specifiable areas of behavior" (p. 118). Further, when an individual's experience of freedom is limited or threatened with limitation (or elimination), the individual will react in such a way as to restore the experience of freedom. Thus, when people experience threats to their freedoms, they will experience psychological reactance. The magnitude of the reactance depends on the unique instrumental value of the freedom (i.e., the importance of that freedom in satisfying important needs), the proportion of freedoms eliminated or threatened with elimination, the implication of possible future elimination of free behaviors, and the magnitude of the pressure to comply with a threat to the elimination of free behaviors. Free behaviors include not only observable behaviors but also emotions, attitudes, and beliefs. Thus, greatest reactance occurs when the threatened freedom is one of only a few freedoms, is instrumental in satisfying an important need, when complying with the threat has implications for future behaviors (this is the first in a series of threats to behave freely), and when the pressure to comply is great. S. Brehm and J. Brehm (1981) provide a comprehensive review of Brehm's theory.

When reactance is aroused, the individual is motivated to restore the threatened or eliminated freedom. Several modes of restoration are possible. The individual may attempt to restore freedom by directly engaging in the threatened behavior. This course of action is possible only when the behavior is threatened, not eliminated. The individual may use indirect action to decrease reactance, such as engaging in a similar behavior or encouraging someone else, an equivalent person, to engage in the threatened or eliminated behavior. Also, when these two avenues are not available, the motivation toward restoring freedom may be expressed through increased desire for the behavior.

Furthermore, reactance may be accompanied by aggression, which may serve to restore the freedom or may occur when no restorative purposes are served (Worchel, 1974).

Reactance theory has been used to explain resistance in psychotherapy (S. Brehm, 1976) and in consultation (Hughes & Falk, 1981). When a consultant suggests a course of action to the consultee, the consultee may experience a threat to the freedom to engage in other behaviors or not to engage in the suggested behavior. Reactance is aroused, and the consultee restores the perceived freedom by rejecting the consultant's recommendation. Furthermore, when reactance is aroused, the behavior threatened with elimination increases in attractiveness.

If one assumes a teacher's teaching behaviors are important to him or her and that the teacher has a small number of strategies (behaviors) for responding to atypical student behaviors, one would expect a forceful consultant would elicit reactance on the part of this teacher. This reactance would likely result in the teacher expressing a greater value for the threatened approach to the problem and resistance to following the consultant's approach. Additionally, the teacher might derogate the consultant (an aggressive response that also reduces dissonance aroused by not following the advice of a designated expert).

Two types of reactance-based approaches are described in the literature applying reactance to therapy and consultation: reactance suppression approaches and reactance utilization approaches.

Reactance Suppression. Some applications of reactance are identical to dissonance applications. Both theories suggest the importance of minimizing inducements to behave in the recommended way and communicating the collaborative, nonhierarchial aspect of the consultation relationship. Some additional implications of reactance suppression are presented next.

Research on reactance suggests the consultant should avoid doing favors for consultees. Brehm and Cole (1966) found subjects who received an unrequested favor from another student (confederate) were less likely to subsequently offer to help the student.

Consultants with high authority should use the onedownsmanship techniques recommended by Caplan (1970). J. W. Brehm (1966) reported college students who received a threat to their freedom to agree with a position advocated by a college professor showed less attitude change than students who received the same threat from another college student.

Several researchers have found that it is more difficult to develop effective consultation with experienced teachers. More experienced teachers are less likely to participate in consultation (Gutkin & Bossard, 1984; Iscoe et al., 1967), less likely to change their behavior as a result of consultation (Weissenburger et al., 1982), and less likely to accept the consultant's suggestions

(Witt et al., 1984). Martin and Curtis (1980) found that consultants had more failure experiences with older, more experienced teachers than with younger, less experienced teachers. These results may be explained in terms of reactance theory. It is plausible that more experienced teachers feel more competent to decide how to teach. Wicklund and Brehm (1968) found the more competence a person felt on an important issue, the more likely that person was to experience reactance in response to a threat to that freedom. Experienced teachers may experience greater reactance arousal when a consultant threatens that freedom by suggesting alternative behaviors with a child. Thus, reactance suppression techniques may be especially necessary when consulting with more experienced teachers.

Research on the effect of the implication for future behavior on reactance arousal (Brehm, 1966) has implications for the consultant. Consultants should reduce the threat of future implications of the consultee accepting the consultant's advice. (If I accept the consultant's advice this time, will she expect me to accept it next time?) If the consultee believes the consultant's attempt to persuade is the first in a series of attempts, future freedoms are implicated and reactance will be higher.

When the consultant supports the consultee's initial position, the consultant should avoid strongly supporting it and encourage the consultee to state the benefits of a contrary position. Strong support for the consultee's belief may arouse reactance, especially if the consultee has not exercised his or her freedom to hold a contrary belief by stating the pros of a contrary belief. In two studies discussed in Wicklund (1974), college subjects who were given an opportunity to state their position on an issue demonstrated more reactance following a subsequent communication advocating the same position than did subjects who received a communication advocating a position contrary to the subjects' previously stated one. Subjects who had stated a contrary position had already demonstrated their freedom to take that position and, consequently, experienced less of a threat to the freedom to take that position. Subjects having the opportunity to state the pros of the position with which they disagreed prior to receiving the one-sided communication advocating the position they held demonstrated little reactance (i.e., they did not change toward the position with which they originally disagreed).

A final implication concerns minimizing the perceived threat to engage in the old behavior. The consultant should point out that engaging in the new behavior does not threaten old behaviors. The consultant might point out that the new behavior is an addition to the consultee's behavioral repertoire rather than a substitute for existing behaviors.

Reactance Utilization. Paradoxical injunctions (Haley, 1963) utilize reactance to promote desired change in psychotherapy. In a situation where the therapist wants the client to discontinue symptomatic behavior (behavior Y) and encourages the client to stop doing Y and to do X, reactance may be aroused and the client will resist doing X. When the therapist believes the resistance is a result of reactance arousal, the therapist tells the client to engage in the symptomatic behavior (Y). The client will perceive his or her freedom to engage in non-Y threatened and will restore his sense of freedom by engaging in X. This approach has been applied to a wide variety of problems in therapy (Haley, 1968; Madanes, 1981).

Hughes and Falk (1981) demonstrated the application of reactance utilization to consultation. The case involved an experienced teacher who engaged in excessive nurturing behaviors with a child with a history of neglect. The teacher resisted the consultant's interpretation of the problem as the child needing to learn more independence and rejected the consultant's observations concerning the child's capabilities. The paradoxical injunction involved telling the teacher that the child probably needed more nurturing, and signaling the teacher to hover and protect more, offering a strong rationale for this recommendation, and visiting the classroom to develop a system for signaling the teacher to hover. The teacher resisted the consultant's recommendation by hovering less and stating that she was not able to respond to the child's every need and that he was capable of doing many things on his own.

Although reactance utilization can be effective, there certainly are risks to this approach that probably render it unacceptable in school consultation. First there is the ethical issue of the consultee's freedom to accept or to reject the consultant's influence. Although deception is present in many consultant strategies (e.g., Caplan's methods of theme interference are based on deception), the deception inherent in paradoxical strategies is more obvious, and the consultee is less able to resist the influence attempt. The primary reason paradox is not appropriate in consultation, however, is the effect such strategies might have on the consultant's credibility and trustworthiness, essential aspects of referent power. Because consultants work in social systems, it is unlikely their recommendations will remain confidential. The possibility of effecting an improvement in one pupil's situation must be weighed against the risk to the consultant's social influence with other consultees within the system.

Consultation and The Social Influence Model

Stanley Strong and Charles Claiborn (1982; Strong, 1982) state that change in counseling is the result of two factors: social power and discrepancy. The counselor's task is to use his or her social power (primarily referent, expert, and legitimate power) to manage discrepancy between the client's existing attitudes and behaviors and those recommended by the counselor. Counselors with more social power can manage larger discrepancies than counselors with less social power. If the counselor is perceived as having little expert power, for example, the client is likely to resolve the dissonance created by the discrepant message by derogating the counselor rather than by changing important attitudes or behaviors. Generally, small discrepancies produce greater change in counseling. For example, Claiborn, Ward, and Strong (1981) found congruence between the counselor's interpretations and the client's beliefs to be more facilitative of change than large discrepancies in content. Additionally, the more the client is invested in a position the smaller the optimal discrepancy. Strong and Claiborn (1982) said: "If the client is committed to a position on an issue, interventions of small discrepancy are warranted since larger discrepancies are likely to produce resistance" (p. 64). An essential aspect of managing discrepancy to promote client change is blocking other ways of resolving dissonance created by the discrepancy, making it more likely the client will change his or her attitudes, beliefs, and values in a direction supportive of the recommended change. Thus, the counselor attempts to obtain a behavioral commitment and blocks ways the client might minimize responsibility for the commitment.

Strong and Claiborn note that the exercise of social power in counseling does not always involve discrepant information. Instead, social power might be exercised by manipulating client commitment to a position of involvement in an issue or helping the client to see previously unnoticed relationships among attitudes. These counselor approaches do not seem like influence, and the client attributes change to intrapsychic rather than interpersonal processes. Strong and Claiborn (1982) stated: "Attitude change in counseling and psychotherapy is seldom the consequence of overt persuasion; it results from the therapist creating the conditions for change which, in turn, appears spontaneous to the client" (p. 54).

The consultant, too, attempts to exercise social influence to change another's attitudes or behaviors that are important to the other person and in which the person is highly invested. Often this influence is one of strengthening consultee commitment to a behavior consonant with other relevant consultee attitudes and beliefs. Thus, the consultant provides the consultees with an opportunity to publicly commit to an approach, increase their investment in the approach, recognize previously unnoticed consonant relationships among the approach and other attitudes and beliefs, and increase their self-efficacy for engaging in the behavior. At other times the consultant desires to weaken consultee commitment to an approach and uses his or her social influence to create dissonance while blocking undesired modes of dissonance reduction, so that these consultee beliefs and attitudes consonant with the recommended behavior are strengthened. The consultant accomplishes this by introducing small discrepancies rather than by introducing discrepancies that may result in relationship termination.

SUMMARY

When the psychologist views consultation as an interpersonal influence process, the psychologist must focus attention simultaneously on two aspects of consultation: the problem to be solved in consultation and the consultee's thought processes. The first task entails providing the most technically sound assessment of the problem situation and generating the best solution to the problem (i.e., a solution that is supported by an empirical and/or theoretical literature). A hallmark of behavior consultation is its quest for scientifically valid (technologically correct) problem solutions. The second task for the consultant is assessing the relevant consultee cognitions (i.e., about the student, about teaching, about the consultant) and presenting his or her observations and recommendations in a manner acceptable to the teacher. This second aspect of consultation is not less scientific than the first, and a considerable empirical literature on interpersonal influence and attitude change exists. However, the application of this body of research to consultation practice is in an embryonic state.

This chapter has reviewed research in social psychology and, to a lesser degree, in cognitive psychology that is relevant to the second task in consultation. Although the research reviewed is relevant to consultation, the implications offered are based on extrapolation of research findings in contexts different from consultation. There exists a clear need for research on the role of consultee cognitions in consultation. This research should include both research on consultation strategies that are effective in changing consultee cognitions and investigations of ways the consultant can use information about consultees' cognitions to effect a better match between the consultant's recommendations and the consultee's cognitive schemata (Shavelson & Stern, 1981).

The types of consultee cognitions that might be targeted for change in consultation include teachers' attributions, expectations, attitudes, cognitive differentiation and complexity, and problem-solving behaviors. Two studies follow this line of investigation (Cleven & Gutkin, 1988; Curtis & Watson, 1980).

The research on intervention acceptability (e.g., Witt, Martens, & Elliott, 1984) illustrates the importance of taking consultees' cognitions into consideration in selecting an intervention in consultation. The consultation research agenda for the 1990s should expand on this start by addressing questions such as the following: Do teachers differing in self-efficacy perform differently in consultation? Are different consultation approaches differentially effective with experienced, confident teachers and novice teachers? At the end of successful consultations, are teachers' and consultants' attributions for the problem more similar than they are at the end of unsuccessful consultations? What types of external justifications present in consultation minimize consultee dissonance and subsequent attitude change? What consultant behaviors minimize consultee reactance and promote consultee acceptance of the consultant's recommendations?

REFERENCES

Aronson, E., & Carlsmith, J. M. (1963). Effect of severity of threat on the valuation of forbidden behavior. *Journal of Abnormal and Social Psychology, 66,* 584–588.

Babcock, N. L., & Pryzwansky, W. B. (1983). Models of consultation: Preferences of educational professionals at five stages of service. *Journal of School Psychology, 21,* 359–366.

Bandura, A. (1977). *Social learning theory.* Englewood Cliffs, NJ: Prentice-Hall.

Bem, D. J. (1972). Self-perception theory. In L. Berkowitz (Ed.), *Advances in experimental social psychology* (Vol. 6 pp. 2–62). New York: Academic Press.

Bergan, J. R., & Tombari, M. L. (1976). Consultant skill and efficiency and the implementation and outcomes of consultation. *Journal of School Psychology, 14,* 3–14.

Bradley, G. W. (1978). Self-serving biases in the attribution process: A reexamination of the fact or fiction question. *Journal of Personality and Social Psychology, 36,* 56–71.

Brehm, J. W. (1966). *A theory of psychological reactance.* New York: Academic Press.

Brehm, J. W., & Cohen, A. R. (1962). *Explorations in cognitive dissonance.* New York: Wiley.

Brehm, J. W., & Cole, A. H. (1966). Effect of a favor which reduces freedom. *Journal of Personality and Social Psychology, 3,* 420–426.

Brehm, J. W., & Jones, R. A. (1970). The effect on dissonance of surprise consequences. *Journal of Experimental Social Psychology, 6,* 420–431.

Brehm, S. S. (1976). *The application of social psychology to clinical practice.* New York: Wiley.

Brehm, S. S., & Brehm, J. W. (1981). *Psychological reactance: A theory of freedom and control.* New York: Academic Press.

Brock, T. C. (1962). Cognitive restructuring and attitude change. *Journal of Abnormal and Social Psychology, 64,* 264–271.

Brock, T. C. (1968). Relative efficacy of volition and justification in arousing dissonance. *Journal of Personality, 36,* 49–66.

Brock, T. C., & Buss, A. H. (1962). Dissonance, aggression, and evaluation of pain. *Journal of Abnormal and Social Psychology, 65,* 197–202.

Brophy, J. E., & Everston, C. (1977). Teacher behaviors and student learning in second and third grades. In G. D. Borich (Ed.), *The appraisal of teaching: Concepts and process* (pp. 79–95). Reading, MA: Addison-Wesley.

Brophy, J., & Good, T. (1974). *Teacher–student relationships: Causes and consequences.* New York: Holt, Rinehart, & Winston.

Brophy, J. E., & Rohrkemper, M. M. (1981). The influence of problem ownership on teachers' perceptions of and strategies for coping with problem students. *Journal of Educational Psychology, 73,* 295–311.

Brown, D., Pryzwansky, W. B., & Schulte, A. C. (1987). *Psychological consultation: Introduction to theory and practice.* Boston: Allyn & Bacon.

Caplan, G. (1970). *The theory and practice of mental health consultation.* New York: Basic Books.

Christenson, S., Ysseldyke, J., Wang, J., & Algozzine, B. (1983). Teacher's attributions for problems that result in referral for psychoeducational evaluation. *Journal of Educational Research, 76,* 174, 180.

Claiborn, C. D., Ward, S. R., & Strong, S. R. (1981). Effects of congruence between counselor interpretation and client beliefs. *Journal of Counseling Psychology, 28,* 101–109.

Clark, C. M., & Peterson, P. L. (1984). *Teachers' thought processes.* Institute for Research on Teaching, Michigan State University, East Lansing, MI. [ERIC ED 251449]

Cleven, C. A., & Gutkin, T. B. (1988). Cognitive modeling of consultation processes: A means for improving consultees' problem definition skills. *Journal of School Psychology, 26,* 379–390.

Cohen, A. R., Terry, H. I., & Jones, C. B. (1959). Attitudinal effects of choice in exposure to counterpropaganda. *Journal of Abnormal and Social Psychology, 58,* 388–391.

Conoley, J. C., & Conoley, C. W. (1982). *School consultation: A guide to practice and training.* New York: Pergamon.

Corrigan, J. B., Dell, D. M., Lewis, K. N., & Schmidt, L. D. (1980). Counseling is a social influence process: A review. *Journal of Counseling Psychology, 27,* 395–441.

Cozby, P. C. (1972). Self-disclosure and liking. *Sociometry, 35,* 151–160.

Curtis, M. J., & Watson, K. L. (1980). Changes in consultee problem clarification skills following consultation. *Journal of School Psychology, 18,* 210–221.

Elliott, S. N. (1988). Acceptability of behavioral treatments: Review of variables that influence treatment selection. *Professional Psychology: Research and Practice, 19,* 68–80.

Erchul, W. (1987). A relational communication analysis of control in school consultation. *Professional School Psychology, 2,* 113–124.

Erchul, W., & Chewning, T. (1990). Behavioral consultation from a request-centered relational communication perspective. *School Psychology Quarterly, 5,* 1–20.

Fairchild, T. N. (1976). School psychological services: An empirical comparison of two models. *Psychology in the Schools, 13,* 156–162.

Festinger, L. (1957). *A theory of cognitive dissonance.* Eranston, IL: Row, Peterson.

Festinger, L., & Carlsmith, J. M. (1959). Cognitive consequences of forced compliance. *Journal of Abnormal and Social Psychology, 58,* 203–210.

Fine, M. J., Grantham, V. L., & Wright, J. G. (1979). Personal variables that facilitate or impede consultation. *Psychology in the Schools, 16,* 533–539.

Freedman, J. L. (1963). Attitudinal effects of inadequate justification. *Journal of Personality, 31,* 371–385.

French, J. P. Jr., & Raven, B. (1959). The basis for social power. In D. Cartwright (Ed.), *Studies in social powers* (pp. 118–149). Ann Arbor: Institute of Social Research, University of Michigan.

Gibson, S., & Dembo, M. (1984). Teacher efficacy: A construct validation. *Journal of Educational Psychology, 76,* 569–582.

Graham, S. (1984). Teacher feelings and student thoughts: An attributional approach to affect in the classroom. *The Elementary School Journal, 85,* 91–104.

Gutkin, T. (1980). Teacher perceptions of consultation services provided by school psychologists. *Professional Psychology, 11,* 637–642.

Gutkin, T. B. (1986). Consultees' perceptions of variables relating to the outcomes of school-based consultation interactions. *School Psychology Review, 15,* 375–382.

Gutkin, T. B., & Ajchenbaum, M. (1984). Teachers' perceptions of control and preferences for consultative services. *Professional Psychology: Research and Practice, 15,* 565–570.

Gutkin, T. B., & Bossard, M. D. (1984). The impact of consultant, consultee, and organizational variables on teacher attitudes toward consultation services. *Journal of School Psychology, 22,* 251–258.

Gutkin, T. B., & Hickman, J. A. (1988). Teachers' perceptions of control over presenting problems and resulting preferences for consultation versus referral services. *Journal of School Psychology, 26,* 395–398.

Haley, J. (1963). *Strategies of psychotherapy.* New York: Grune & Stratton.

Haley, J. (1968). *Problem-solving therapy.* San Francisco: Jossey-Bass.

Heider, F. (1958). *The psychology of interpersonal relations.* New York: Wiley.

Hovland, C. I., & Weiss, W. (1951). The influence of source credibility on communication effectiveness. *Public Opinion Quarterly, 15,* 635–650.

Hughes, J. N. (1983). The application of cognitive dissonance theory to consultation. *Journal of School Psychology, 21,* 349–357.

Hughes, J. N., & Falk, R. S. (1981). Resistance, reactance, and consultation. *Journal of School Psychology, 19,* 134–142.

Hughes, J., Grossman, P., & Barker, D. (1990). Teachers' expectancies, participation in consultation, and perceptions of consultant helpfulness. *School Psychology Quarterly, 5,* 167–179.

Iscoe, I., Pierce-Jones, J., McGehearty, L., & Friedman, S. (1967). Some strategies in mental health consultation: A brief description of a project and some preliminary results. In E. L. Cowen, E. Garner, & M. Zax (Eds.), *Emergent approaches to mental health problems* (pp. 307–330). New York: Appleton-Century-Crofts.

Jones, E. E., & Nisbett, R. E. (1971). The actor and the observer: Divergent perceptions of the causes of behavior. In E. E. Jones, D. Kanouse, H. H. Kelley, R. E. Nisbett, S. Valins, & B. Weiner (Eds.), *Attributions: Perceiving the causes of behavior.* Morristown, NJ: General Learning Press.

Kazdin, A. E. (1980). Acceptability of time-out from reinforcement procedures for disruptive child behavior. *Behavior Therapy, 11,* 329–344.

Kazdin, A. E., & Cole, P. M. (1981). Attitudes and labeling biases toward behavior modification: The effects of labels, content, and jargon. *Behavior Therapy, 12,* 56–68.

Kelley, H. H. (1971). Attributions in social interaction. In E. E. Jones, D. Kanouse, H. H. Kelley, R. E. Nisbett, S. Valins, & B. Weiner (Eds.), *Attribution: Perceiving the causes of behavior.* Morristown, NJ: General Learning Press.

Kelman, H. C., & Hovland, C. I. (1953). "Reinstatement" of the communication in delayed measurement of opinion change. *Journal of Abnormal and Social Psychology, 48,* 327–335.

Kiesler, C. A., Pollak, M. S., & Kanouse, D. E. (1968). The interactive effects of commitment and dissonance. *Journal of Personality and Social Psychology, 8,* 331–338.

Lepper, M. (1973). Dissonance, self-perception and honesty in children. *Journal of Personality and Social Psychology, 25,* 65–79.

Lepper, M., Greene, D., & Nisbett, R. E. (1973). Undermining children's intrinsic interest with extrinsic rewards: A test of the overjustification hypothesis. *Journal of Personality and Social Psychology, 28,* 129–137.

Lindzey, G., & Aronson, J. E. (1985). *Handbook of social psychology* (3d ed.). New York: Random House.

Madanes, C. (1981). *Strategic family therapy.* San Francisco: Jossey-Bass.

Martin, R. (1978). Expert and referent power: A framework for understanding and maximizing consultation effectiveness. *Journal of School Psychology, 16,* 49–55.

Martin, R. P. (1983). Consultant, consultee, and client explanations of each other's behavior in consultation. *School Psychology, 12,* 35–41.

Martin, R. P., & Curtis, M. (1980). Effects of age and experience of consultant and consultee on consultation outcome. *American Journal of Community Psychology, 8,* 733–736.

Medway, F. (1979). Causal attributions for school-related problems: Teacher perceptions and teacher feedback. *Journal of Educational Psychology, 71,* 809–819.

Medway, F. (1989). Further considerations on a cognitive problem-solving perspective on school consultation. *Professional School Psychology, 4,* 21–27.

Medway, F. J., & Forman, S. G. (1980). Psychologists' and teachers' reactions to mental health and behavioral school consultation. *Journal of School Psychology, 18,* 338–348.

Meichenbaum, D., & Goodman, J. (1971). Training impulsive children to talk to themselves: A means of developing self-control. *Journal of Abnormal Psychology, 77,* 115–126.

Merluzzi, T. V., Banikiotes, P. G., & Missbach, J. W. (1978). Perceptions of counselor characteristics: Contributions of counselor sex, experience, and disclosure level. *Journal of Counseling Psychology, 25,* 479–482.

Miller, R. L., Brickman, P., & Bolen, D. (1975). Attribution versus persuasion as a means for modifying behavior. *Journal of Personality and Social Psychology, 31,* 430–441.

National Education Association (1979). Teacher opinion poll. *Today's Education, 68,* 10.

Parsons, R. D., & Meyers, J. (1984). *Developing consultation skills.* San Francisco: Jossey-Bass.

Peterson, P. L., & Barger, S. A. (1985). Attribution theory and teacher expectancy. In J. B. Dusek, V. C. Hall, & W. J. Meyer (Eds.), *Teacher expectancies.* Hillsdale, NJ: Lawrence Erlbaum Associates.

Petty, R. E., & Cacioppo, J. T. (1981). *Attitudes and persuasion: Classic and contemporary approaches*. Dubuque, IA: William C. Brown.

Reinking, R. H., Livesay, G., & Kohl, M. (1978). The effects of consultation style on consultee productivity. *American Journal of Community Psychology, 6,* 283–290.

Reppucci, N. D., & Saunders, J. T. (1974). Social psychology of behavior modification: Problems of implementation in natural settings. *American Psychologist, 29,* 649–660.

Rhoades, M. (1989, April). *Teacher acceptability of behavioral consultation*. Paper presented at annual meeting of the National Association of School Psychologists, Boston.

Rotter, J. B. (1966). Generalized expectancies for internal versus external control of reinforcement. *Psychological Monographs, 80* (1, Whole No. 609).

Safran, S. P. (1985). Correlates of special educators' self-efficacy beliefs. *Journal of Special Education, 9,* 61–67.

Sarason, S. B., Levine, M., Goldenberg, I. I., Cherlin, D. L., & Bennett, E. M. (1960). *Psychology in community settings: Clinical, educational, vocational, social aspects*. New York: Wiley.

Seligman, M. E. P., Kaslow, N. J., Alloy, L. B., Peterson, C., Tannenbaum, R. L., & Abramson, L. Y. (1984). Attributional style and depressive symptoms in children. *Journal of Abnormal Psychology, 93,* 235–238.

Shavelson, R. J., & Stern, P. (1981). Research on teachers' pedagogical thoughts, judgments, decisions, and behavior. *Review of Educational Research, 51,* 455–498.

Short, R. J., & Ringer, M. M. (1987). Consultant experience and attributions in school consultation. *Professional School Psychology, 2,* 273–279.

Silverman, W. H. (1974). Some factors related to consultee satisfaction with consultation. *American Journal of Community Psychology, 2,* 303–310.

Simons, H. W., Berkowitz, N. N., & Moyer, R. J. (1970). Similarity, credibility, and attitude change: A review and a theory. *Psychological Bulletin, 73,* 1–16.

Smith, D. K., & Lyon, M. A. (1986). School psychologists' attributions for success and failure in consultations with parents and teachers. *Professional Psychology: Research and Practice, 17,* 205–209.

Strong, S. R. (1968). Counseling: An interpersonal influence process. *Journal of Counseling Psychology, 15,* 215–224.

Strong, S. R. (1978). Social psychological approach to psychotherapy research. In S. L. Garfield & A. E. Bergin (Eds.), *Handbook of psychotherapy and behavioral change*. New York: Wiley.

Strong, S. R. (1982). Emerging integrations of clinical and social psychology: A clinician's perspective. In G. Weary & H. L. Mirels (Eds.), *Integrations of clinical and social psychology* (pp. 181–213). New York: Oxford.

Strong, S. R., & Claiborn, C. D. (1982). *Changing through interaction: The social psychology of counseling and psychotherapy*. New York: Wiley.

Strong, S. R., & Schmidt, L. D. (1970). Expertness and influence in counseling. *Journal of Counseling Psychology, 17,* 81–87.

Wehmann, B. A., Zins, J. E., & Curtis, M. J. (1989, April). *The effects of consultation on teachers' perceptions of the causality of children's school-related problems*. Paper presented at annual meeting of the National Association of School Psychologists, Boston.

Weiner, B. (1979). A theory of motivation for some classroom experiences. *Journal of Educational Psychology, 71,* 3–25.

Weiner, B., Graham, S., Stern, P., & Lawson, M. (1982). Using affective cues to infer causal thoughts. *Developmental Psychology, 18,* 278–286.

Weissenburger, J., Fine, J. W., & Poggio, J. (1982). The relationship of selected consultant/teacher characteristics to consultation outcomes. *Journal of School Psychology, 20,* 263–270.

Wenger, R. D. (1979). Teacher responses to collaborative consultation. *Psychology in the schools, 16,* 127–131.

Wicklund, R. A. (1974). *Freedom and reactance.* Hillsdale, NJ: Lawrence Erlbaum Associates.
Wicklund, R. A., & Brehm, J. W. (1976). *Perspectives on cognitive dissonance.* New York: Lawrence Erlbaum Associates.
Witt, J. C., & Elliott, S. N. (1985). Acceptability of classroom management strategies. In T. R. Kratochwill (Ed.), *Advances in school psychology* (Vol. 4, pp. 251–288). Hillsdale, NJ: Lawrence Erlbaum Associates.
Witt, J. C., Martens, B. K., & Elliott, S. N. (1984). Factors affecting teachers' judgments of the acceptability of behavioral interventions: Time involvement, behavior problem severity, type of intervention. *Behavior Therapy, 15,* 204–209.
Witt, J., Moe, G., Gutkin, T., & Andrews, L. (1984). The effect of saying the same thing in different ways: The problem of language and jargon in school-based consultation. *Journal of School Psychology, 22,* 361–367.
Woolfolk, A. E., Woolfolk, R. C., & Wilson, G. T. (1977). A rose by any other name . . . : Labeling bias and attitudes toward behavior modification. *Journal of Consulting and Clinical Psychology, 45,* 184–191.
Worchel, S. (1974). The effect of three types of arbitrary thwarting on the instigation to aggression. *Journal of Personality, 42,* 300–318.
Worthy, M., Gary, A., & Kahn, G. (1969). Self-disclosure as an exchange process. *Journal of Personality and Social Psychology, 3,* 59–63.

12

APPLICATIONS OF SOCIAL PSYCHOLOGY TO LEARNING AND INSTRUCTION

Maribeth Gettinger
University of Wisconsin-Madison

There is a growing awareness among educational researchers and practition-ers that a number of social psychological variables can affect classroom per-formance. Classrooms are social environments that involve interactions among teachers and students within the context of various structured activi-ties. Viewed in this way, the teaching–learning process can be conceptualized as a social psychological phenomenon with interactive and structural charac-teristics of the instructional environment affecting student performance. The purpose of this chapter is to examine how principles and concepts of social psychology may apply to classroom learning and instruction. Specifically, it examines how interactions and organizational aspects of schooling affect stu-dent learning and perceptions of both teachers and students. The emphasis is on school-based research that has direct relevance for student learning. First, critical structural and interactional dimensions of schooling are reviewed. The effects of these dimensions on student learning are also discussed. The bulk of this chapter offers descriptions of the application of social psycholo-gy to learning and implications for designing classroom instruction.

SOCIAL PSYCHOLOGICAL ASPECTS OF CLASSROOM INSTRUCTION

There are many social psychological aspects of classroom instruction that may affect student outcomes. Research into the application of social psychol-ogy to learning and instruction has focused primarily on two aspects of teach-ing: the nature of teacher–student interactions (e.g., Brophy & Good, 1974) and the structural organization of classrooms (e.g., Bossert, 1979). What children gain from instruction—their interpretation and understanding of their social world, their acquisition of knowledge and skills, and even their evaluation and perception of themselves—is influenced by the structure of their daily classroom experiences. The way in which classroom activities are structured, in turn, determines how students interact with the teacher and with each other. Thus, both structural and interaction patterns may influence the cognitive and affective outcomes of instruction.

Slavin (1983) referred to the structure of classroom activity as the instructional system. According to Slavin (1980a, 1983), an instructional system combines two critical elements: the instructional task structure and the student reward or incentive structure. Although task structure has been defined in different ways in the literature (Berliner, 1983; Bossert, 1979; Doyle, 1983), it generally reflects the various types of teaching formats and instructional activities (including pace and content) used in a classroom. Group lecture versus individual seatwork, oral discussion versus written responses, and memorization versus problem-solving content are all examples of dimensions along which instructional task structure may vary.

The second element of an instructional system, the reward structure, may be characterized by the frequency, magnitude, and type of extrinsic rewards used (e.g., grades, teacher praise, evaluative feedback), the functional relation between performance and rewards, and the degree to which individual students' rewards are dependent on classmates' performance. Reward structures are generally categorized as being: (a) cooperative, or positive reward interdependent, when one student's success helps others to be successful; (b) competitive, or negative reward interdependent, when one student's success means another student is less successful (e.g., grading curve); and (c) individualistic, or reward independent, when students' rewards are unrelated to each other (Ames & Ames, 1984; Michaels, 1977; Slavin, 1977). This conceptualization of how an individual's consequences relate to classmates' performance corresponds to what Johnson and Johnson (1974) described as the instructional goal structure. Johnson and Johnson (1974) identified five types of goal structures: (a) individual noncompetitive structure; (b) individual competitive, where rewards are achieved independently; (c) cooperative, where goals are interdependent; (d) cooperative within groups and competitive between groups; and (e) competitive within and between groups.

There are additional parameters beyond task and reward or goal structures that also characterize the overall system of instructional activities in a classroom. Marshall and Weinstein (1984) offered an analysis of classroom activity structures that adds a third dimension—specifically, student grouping patterns. Placing children in small groups for instruction is a common practice in elementary schools. There are a variety of formal grouping techniques (e.g., whole-group, ability grouping) that reflect a critical element of a classroom's activity structure and student–student interactions. Rosenholtz and Simpson (1984) consider similar dimensions in their analysis of classroom environments and add a fourth dimension, the classroom authority structure. Authority structure refers to the extent to which students have autonomy in controlling their own learning, including choice of activities, pace of learning, and criteria for rewards.

Collectively, these dimensions (task, reward or goal, grouping, and authority structures) reflect the structural and interactional complexity of classroom life. This analysis of the instructional system is an appropriate framework for discussing the application of social psychology to instruction and learning. In effect, classroom procedures derived from social psychological principles implicate changes in one or more of these structural elements and concomitant interactional patterns.

Traditionally, the effects on student performance of a single variable, such as the grouping or reward structure, have been studied. Marshall (1981), however, suggested that an interactive model, one that considers multiple structural and communication aspects of classrooms, may be more appropriate for understanding how social psychological determinants of student performance operate. Brophy (1979) also emphasized the need for classrooms to be viewed as dynamic contexts within which variables interrelate with one another. Although relevant for a variety of cognitive and affective outcomes, Marshall and Weinstein (1984) described the application of an interactive model specifically to the development of students' self-evaluation as a result of instructional grouping. According to Marshall and Weinstein (1984), social comparison among students may be heightened under certain kinds of classroom organization, such as instructional grouping. Comparison to high-achieving peers can be particularly detrimental for low achievers by leading to feelings of inferiority, low aspirations, and lack of motivation. Ability grouping has been specifically criticized because of the potentially detrimental effects of social comparison on students' self-evaluations (Filby & Barnett, 1982; Levine, 1983; Rosenbaum, 1980). When groups are homogeneously and hierarchically arranged according to ability and remain stable over time, children can easily compare themselves to others in their class. In Marshall's (1981) interactive model, however, grouping is viewed as just one structural variable that functions in relation to other aspects of the classroom environment. In other words, additional interactive variables may operate to either increase or minimize the potentially negative effects of grouping practices. For example, if grouping is flexible rather than static, thereby pulling together different sets of students for different instructional purposes, and if groups work under cooperative rather than competitive goal structures, then students are afforded a broader range of comparison with a variety of peers. Under these circumstances, students are able to observe and evaluate their own and others' strengths in a variety of areas. The reward structure is another dimension that may interact with grouping practices to minimize social comparison. In classrooms where different students are praised for different types of accomplishments, the distribution of rewards will be less differentiated between high- and low-ability students. Thus, social comparison is less likely to lead to consistently negative self-evaluations. In sum, it is the totality of the classroom environment—in this case, grouping as well as task and reward structures— that determines how social psychological variables operate. What may be detrimental in one setting may be neutral or even positive in another context.

Rosenholtz and Simpson (1984) offered another relevant perspective for considering the social psychological aspects of classroom instruction. They view students as active participants in their own socialization whose interpretations are influenced by the structure of daily classroom experiences and by interactions with teachers and peers. Consistent with Slavin (1983) and Marshall (1981), Rosenholtz and Simpson (1984) theorized that characteristics of classroom organization influence student outcomes, in particular the process by which students' self-perceptions evolve. The quality of classroom instruction most likely to affect student perceptions has been termed dimensionality. Classroom structure may vary from being unidimensional, or undifferentiated, to multidimensional depending on whether activities are organized around a single or multiple dimensions of comparison. Task structures, for example, are unidimensional when all students work on the same tasks and when a limited range of standard, instructional materials and methods are used. Multidimensional task structures, on the other hand, encourage students to work on several different types of tasks (depending on their ability and interest) and consider a variety of individual task performances as acceptable. Similarly, authority structures are unidimensional when there is low student autonomy and high teacher directiveness; multidimensional authority structures, in contrast, allow students to make independent choices about what work to do and when or how to do it, thus increasing performance options. In terms of grouping, unidimensional grouping occurs when students work as a whole class or in homogeneous ability groups, whereas multidimensional grouping occurs when children work as individuals or in varying groups not defined by a single dimension such as ability. Research by Rosenholtz and Rosenholtz (1981) and Simpson (1981) confirms that negative self-evaluations occur more readily in unidimensional than in multidimensional classes. Rosenholtz and Simpson (1984) hypothesize that alternative bases of interpretation are more limited in unidimensional than multidimensional classroom organizations, thereby maximizing the detrimental effects of social comparison.

In sum, Slavin's (1983) concept of an instructional system with a variety of structures and related interaction patterns, Marshall and Weinstein's (1984) model underscoring the interactive nature of classroom variables, and Rosenholtz and Simpson's (1984) quality of classroom dimensionality are all important for understanding the complexity of the social psychological aspects of instruction and learning. The following sections focus in greater detail on three general applications of the principles and concepts of social psychology to instructional practices—specifically, cooperative learning, adaptive instruction, and teacher and student perceptions.

COOPERATIVE LEARNING

The development, implementation, and evaluation of cooperative learning programs represent one of the most widespread applications of social psychology to learning and instruction. Cooperative learning refers to instructional methods in which students work together in small groups toward a group goal. Unlike traditional competitive classroom structures, an essential feature of cooperative learning is that an individual student's success in some way contributes to the success of the group.

Whereas research on cooperative learning in classrooms began in the 1970s, laboratory-based social psychological research on cooperation dates back to the 1920s (e.g., Maller, 1929). Social psychologists who studied cooperation identified several positive outcomes that result when individuals work cooperatively rather than competitively toward a common goal. Subsequently, educational psychologists hypothesized that similar benefits would accrue for students engaged in cooperative classroom activities. For example, social psychologists found that, in cooperative situations, a group norm often developed sanctioning individual behavior directed toward helping the group achieve its goal (Deutsch, 1949a). The instructional analogue to this finding from social psychology is that, through cooperative learning, peers convey to one another that engaging in appropriate goal-oriented behaviors (e.g., completing assignments, staying on-task) is important and valued by the group (Slavin & Turner, 1979). Like social psychologists, cooperative learning researchers have studied the effects of individuals' working together in small groups in which tasks and rewards are interdependent among group members.

Cooperative Learning Methods

The most popular cooperative methods for classroom instruction are derived from four different models of cooperative learning (Slavin, Sharan, Kagan, Hertz-Lazarowitz, Webb, & Schmuck, 1985). From a social psychological perspective, these cooperative learning paradigms synthesize small-group dynamics and social-interaction principles. Each model is predicated on the assumption that the way in which learning is structured largely determines how students interact with one another, and that student–student interactions, in turn, may influence instructional as well as social outcomes (Johnson, 1980).

Thus, face-to-face interaction among students is a salient characteristic of cooperative learning. Furthermore, there is a set of basic structural elements central to all cooperative learning strategies that theoretically underlie the effectiveness of cooperative learning in enhancing student performance (achievement, motivation) and cohesiveness (positive interpersonal relations). Specifically, some degree of positive interdependence in task and/or reward structures is inherent in cooperative learning strategies. Individual accountability for mastering the learning material also occurs in cooperatively structured learning activities. Combining positive interdependence and individual accountability means that a group's success depends on the learning and performance of all group members (Slavin, 1983). According to Slavin (1987), this type of classroom structure fosters peer tutoring, increases the amount of time spent giving and receiving explanations among students, focuses the activities of group members on ensuring that each group member learns the material, and engenders an interest among students in each other's achievement.

Despite these commonalities, Slavin (1980a) noted that the major types of cooperative learning techniques do differ in terms of the extent to which various structural elements exist. Specifically, the degree of interdependence and individual accountability as well as the extent to which the teacher imposes structure on students' assignments differentiate cooperative learning strategies. Perhaps the most controversial point of departure among various methods is the amount of competition that exists between groups (Bossert, 1988). For comparison of cooperative learning methods, a brief description of each basic approach is presented next, with particular emphasis on the differentiating dimensions. Detailed books or manuals have been written about each technique (see reference citations following).

Student Team Learning. Student Team Learning methods (STL; Slavin, 1980c, 1980d, 1983) emphasize the use of team goals and team success that can be achieved only if all team members learn the objectives being taught (high reward interdependence). Using STL, students are assigned to small, heterogeneous groups. After the teacher presents the material to be learned (high teacher-imposed structure), students work on the same material within their teams to ensure that all members have mastered the lesson content (low task interdependence). In Student Teams-Achievement Divisions (STAD; Slavin, 1978a, 1978b, 1980b), students are quizzed, and their quiz scores contribute to team scores using a system termed achievement divisions (high individual accountability). Achievement divisions among students are based on their performance on preceding quizzes. For example, scores of the highest six students on previous quizzes are compared; then scores of the next highest students are compared, and so on. The top scores in each achievement division earn the greatest number of points for their team. In Teams-Game-

Tournament (TGT; DeVries & Edwards, 1973; DeVries & Slavin, 1978; DeVries, Slavin, Fennessey, Edwards, & Lombardo, 1980) quizzes are replaced with tournaments in which students compete to earn points for their team. Similar to the notion of achievement divisions in STAD, competitors are matched on the basis of previous tournament performance. In all STL methods, high-performing teams earn certificates, recognition in a weekly newsletter, or other forms of team rewards (intergroup competition).

Two additional STL methods employ the same organization as STAD and TGT; however, each is designed for use in a particular content area and combines cooperative learning with individualized instruction. Team Assisted Individualization (TAI; Slavin, Leavey, & Madden, 1981) is built on a programmed mathematics series covering concepts from addition through introductory algebra (grades 3 through 6). Cooperative Integrated Reading and Composition (CIRC; Johnson & Johnson, 1975) is designed for teaching reading and writing skills in grades 3 through 5.

Jigsaw. Jigsaw (Aronson, Stephan, Sikes, Blaney, & Snapp, 1978; Aronson, Bridgeman, & Geffner, 1978) is a cooperative learning method in which individuals cooperate to learn a task (high task interdependent), but their performance is evaluated on an individual basis (low reward interdependence). In this method, students are assigned to small, heterogeneous teams to work on academic material that is broken down into sections, one section per team member (high teacher-imposed structure). Team members first read their sections, then meet with members from other teams who have the same sections ("expert groups"), and finally return to their teams to teach their sections to other members. Although there is no team goal or reward as in STL methods, students are still motivated to support and show interest in each other's work in that this is the only way they can learn about sections other than their own. The element of individual accountability is present to the extent that positive learning behaviors of individual team members help others to be rewarded. In Jigsaw, intergroup competition is not used.

Slavin (1978b) developed a modification of Jigsaw, called Jigsaw II, in which all students are assigned all sections of material, thereby reducing task interdependence, with each member receiving one topic on which to become an expert. As in Jigsaw, expert groups meet to discuss their topics and then students return to their teams to teach their sections to teammates. Reward interdependence and intergroup competition are increased by adding a team reward component; individual quiz scores are translated into team scores similar to the procedures used in STAD.

Learning Together. In this model of cooperative learning (Johnson & Johnson, 1975; Johnson, Johnson, Holubec, & Roy, 1984), students work in small groups collectively to complete a single assignment (low individual accountability and low task interdependence). Although students are instructed to learn specific material, the degree of teacher-imposed structure on cooperative groups is minimal. Student autonomy is fostered by instructing students in group-process skills and encouraging students to monitor their own functioning as a group. Although a group reward is not offered, students are praised for how well they work cooperatively and accomplish the group task (low reward interdependence). Groups do not compete against one another in this approach to cooperative learning.

Group Investigation. In Group Investigation (GI) or Small Group Teaching (Sharan, 1980; Sharan & Sharan, 1976), considerable autonomy is given to student groups to choose their own topics and organize their own work roles (low teacher-imposed structure). This approach to cooperative learning encourages groups to solve problems by gathering and synthesizing different information among individual group members. There is a high degree of task interdependence in that students are assigned special data-gathering tasks within the group and then communicate information and share their ideas to produce a group report. Cooperative group inquiry and discussion are more prominent features of this model than intergroup competition or interdependent group rewards.

Mediating Processes

Cooperative learning methods have been evaluated extensively over the last 15 years as alternatives to more traditional classroom instruction. In general, the research documents the effectiveness of cooperative strategies for affecting a variety of cognitive and affective outcomes of instruction, including student achievement and motivation, intragroup relations, relationships between mainstreamed and regular education students, and students' self-esteem (Johnson, Johnson, & Maruyama, 1983; Johnson, Maruyama, Johnson, Nelson, & Skon, 1981; Sharan, 1980; Slavin, 1980a; see also chapter 18 in this volume). The degree of social interdependence among group members appears to be an important variable in cooperative learning. When interactions are structured so that each student's participation is essential to reaching the group goal, there is an increase in the contact among group members and an improvement in individuals' self-esteem (Johnson & Johnson, 1975). Cooperative learning experiences have been found to promote greater cognitive and emotional perspective-taking ability among students than either competitive or individualistic learning experiences (Johnson, 1975). Furthermore, there is evidence that students perceive a greater likelihood of success in cooperative learning situations. For example, inherent in all STL methods is the concept of equal opportunities for success. This means that high, average, and low achievers contribute to their teams by improving their own past performance. By competing with students of comparable ability, all students are challenged to do their best and all students have the opportunity to be a team "star." This particular aspect of cooperative learning has implications for students' perceptions of success in that each student has an equal opportunity to achieve (Slavin, 1980b). Finally, cooperative learning experiences have been found to promote greater liking for peers and encourage the development of more positive interpersonal relationships, particularly among heterogeneous groups, in terms of ability, gender, racial–ethnic background, and socioeconomic status (Johnson, Johnson, Johnson, & Anderson, 1976).

Aside from traditional social psychological explanations for cooperative activities and their effects (Deutsch, 1949b; Miller & Hamblin, 1963; Sherif & Sherif, 1956), classroom researchers generally have not examined systematically the underlying processes that mediate the positive effects of cooperative learning strategies on students' achievement and prosocial behavior just described. Researchers have described several different mediating mechanisms that may occur within cooperative learning groups. Johnson and Johnson (1985b) suggested that the achievement outcomes of cooperative techniques may be attributed, in part, to more advanced cognitive processing that derives from working with peers. For example, cooperative learning, especially within heterogenous groups, may promote higher order reasoning strategies and increase opportunities for oral rehearsal of information among students. Johnson and Johnson (1985a) also claimed that a cooperative social context facilitates constructive controversy, which, in turn, fosters academic as well as social problem-solving skills. In any learning situation, conflicts among ideas and opinions will arise that must be reconciled to reach a group solution or achieve a group goal. Social psychological research comparing competitive versus cooperative contexts has found that cooperation provides a more supportive climate, promotes accurate and complete communication among group members, and leads to the perception that conflicts are problems to be jointly solved (Deutsch, 1973; Rubin & Brown, 1975). When these findings are extended to cooperative learning contexts in classrooms, Johnson and Johnson (1985a) theorized that the process of controversy leads constructively to improved decision making and problem solving as well as more accurate cognitive perspective taking among students. Sharan and his colleagues (Sharan, 1980; Sharan, Hertz-Lazarowitz, & Ackerman, 1980) found, for example, that the GI method was superior to a control group in affecting higher order cognitive skills. They attribute these effects to the fact that sharing ideas and communication are encouraged within a cooperative context in the GI approach.

A somewhat different mediating process was suggested by Slavin (1983, 1985). In his review of research on cooperative learning techniques, Slavin

(1980a) concluded that methods with high reward interdependence have a greater positive effect on achievement than those with lower interdependence. He speculates that this interdependence activates peer pressure or a group norm that increases both students' learning and social cohesion. When team structures in STL motivate students toward a reward, students review the material among themselves until everyone has mastered it. The individual accountability and group reward structure of STL do not necessarily foster sharing and combining of individual ideas as in the GI approach. In this regard, STL may be most effective when the academic objective is learning basic skills or acquiring factual information.

Finally, cooperative learning studies have suggested that peer interaction, encouragement, and involvement in learning that result when children work together on academic tasks in themselves facilitate learning and increase friendship and acceptance among students (Johnson, 1980, 1981). Descriptive research addressing the specific nature of peer interactions in cooperative groups, however, documents that the quality of interaction (giving and receiving explanations) varies among students in groups and may have differential effects on learning (Cazden, 1986; Cohen, 1984; Peterson, Janicki, & Swing, 1981; Webb, 1982, 1985; Webb & Kenderski, 1984). For example, Webb (1985) found that giving explanations to peers relates to achievement, whereas simply providing them with correct answers does not. Peterson et al. (1981) found that receiving help from peers does not consistently relate to improved performance. Finally, Cazden (1986) offered additional evidence that elementary schoolchildren may simply not know how to provide helpful explanations to peers. Thus, the increased student–student interaction engendered by cooperative learning alone may not account for positive learning outcomes. It appears that the quality of interactions is equally important.

Conclusions

Several conclusions regarding cooperative learning strategies emerge from this review. First, cooperation in the classroom leads to increased academic performance, more liking for classmates (cf. chapter 4 in this volume), and improved self-esteem and attitudes toward school. Although limited in scope, some investigations have begun to explore the interrelationships among the social psychological aspects of cooperation and the underlying mechanisms that lead to positive academic and social outcomes. One implication from research on interactional processes is that it may be helpful to teach students how to interact effectively in small groups so that, when cooperative learning is used in classrooms, students will gain maximum benefits cognitive and socially. Instructing students to cooperate and to help one another may not enhance learning if students do not know how to give and receive assistance effectively. Another implication from research on cognitive processes is that basic skills and higher order skills may be differentially affected by the type of cooperative learning method used. If children's low achievement is linked to a lack of basic skills, STL methods are likely to improve academic functioning, whereas low achievement stemming from deficits in higher order cognitive skills may improve through a GI or Learning Together approach. Finally, research on grouping practices suggests that the development of accepting and supportive student–student relationships, as well as positive learning outcomes, can be enhanced through cooperative grouping procedures (Wilkinson, 1988). Positive student–student interactions are particularly enhanced when teachers encourage constructive resolution of controversies within groups and the development of classroom norms supporting achievement and appropriate behavior.

ADAPTIVE EDUCATION

Adaptive education refers to the design and implementation of instructional environments that are flexible and adaptive to accommodate individual differences among students. Adapting instruction to individual differences requires a consideration of social psychological factors as well as cognitive and conative variables. According to Bloom (1976), individual differences among students manifest themselves along a variety of dimensions categorized primarily as cognitive entry behaviors (ability, prior knowledge, prerequisite skills) or affective entry behaviors (interests, attitudes, self-perceptions). Corno and Snow's (1986) conceptualization of learning aptitude included three types of aptitude variables: intellectual abilities, learning styles, and academic motivation and related interpersonal characteristics. Corno and Snow (1986) hypothesized that different types of learner aptitude affect different aspects of educational performance. For example, intellectual ability may influence the quality of students' performance (e.g., level and type of learning task), whereas interpersonal factors influence the quantity of performance (e.g., persistence and effort).

The fundamental objective underlying models of adaptive education (i.e., to adapt to individual differences) evolved from the writings of Bloom and Glaser on student diversity and school learning. According to Bloom (1968) and Glaser (1972), differences in student outcomes, such as achievement, are a function of the learning environment as well as individual learner characteristics. Insofar as learning reflects the learner's response to the environment, instruction is viewed as a deliberate manipulation of the learning environment to adapt to diversity among students and facilitate appropriate responding (Wang & Lindvall, 1984). Based on these views, models of adaptive education (Bloom, 1976; Glaser, 1977; Wang & Walberg, 1985) conceptualize the process of learning and instruction as incorporating dual, interactive adaptation—adaptation within instruction to accommodate student differences and adaptation among students to respond to instruction.

Recently, there has been a shift in research on individual differences to move beyond cognitive characteristics of learners to a consideration of social psychological characteristics as well. Increasingly, learner differences are being viewed in terms of motivation, attitudes, self-perceptions, and affective responses involved in the acquisition and retention of knowledge (Gordon, 1983; Messick, 1979). Although a variety of individual-difference variables have been identified in the literature as correlates of learning (Gagne, 1967; Snow, Federico, & Montague, 1980), most programs of adaptive instruction are still concerned with a limited number of instructionally relevant variables, those being primarily cognitive in nature (e.g., intelligence, prior achievement).

One social psychological determinant of variability in student learning that has important implications for instructional design and adaptation is students' perception of personal control over their learning. According to Stipek and Weisz (1981), perceived control of events appears to affect children's academic achievement. Students' perception of control over learning is one of the few social psychological factors that has been considered in the design of extant adaptive education programs.

Characteristics of Adaptive Education

Research syntheses of recent studies evaluating the effectiveness of adaptive education methods have identified several critical design features that characterize the most effective programs (Wang, 1987; Waxman, Wang, Anderson, & Walberg, 1985). Seven salient program features have been delineated. Two of these characteristics—(a) students assuming responsibility for diagnosing their own needs, planning learning activities, and evaluating mastery, and (b) students determining goals, outcomes, and activities—underlie the development of students' sense of personal control indigenous to adaptive education.

According to Glaser (1977), adaptive education is most importantly learner-centered education. In adaptive education programs, instruction is essentially controlled by the learner. Control by the student occurs in two interactive ways, thus reflecting the reciprocal nature of adaptation. First, the child's individual needs and abilities are taken into consideration when planning and carrying out learning activities and, as such, may be viewed as shaping instruction. Second, learning environments are designed so that children are able to make decisions and plan their instructional time and activities themselves. While adjusting to the individuality of children, adaptive education also fosters a sense of personal control of learning among students (Resnick, 1972). Adaptive teaching is, therefore, a dynamic process. Instruction both adapts to the learner and allows the learner to adapt to instruction.

Given these salient characteristics, adaptive education can be conceptualized as an application of social psychological principles targeting primarily a change in the authority structure of traditional classrooms. As described earlier, authority structure is one dimension along which classroom activities can vary. Conventional classrooms tend to impose an organization and social climate emphasizing directive, decision-making roles for teachers. A change in the authority structure is inherent in adaptive education programs. This change is achieved through the development of self-management capabilities and a concomitant increase in personal control among students.

Learner Control and Adaptive Education

Corno and Snow (1986) offered a conceptualization of classroom instruction that implicates adaptive teaching methods in the development of students' sense of personal control. In their model, instruction varies along a continuum representing the degree to which it mediates the learning process. Mediation may focus on cognitive aptitudes or social psychological variables such as learner control. In the same way that instruction varies in the cognitive demands placed on learners, it may also differ in the extent to which students are required to control their own learning (Snow, 1980). As instructional mediation increases, learning depends less on students' abilities. For example, as instruction takes more responsibility for controlling learning and behavior through teacher-directed instruction and teacher-imposed contingencies, learning depends less on students' self-control. In adaptive teaching, instruction is conceptualized as moving along this continuum of mediation depending on individual needs.

From the perspective of personal control, low instructional mediation is associated with high learner control. In other words, little mediation affords students the opportunity for self-direction. More intrusive instruction that involves a high degree of mediation circumvents students' inability to manage their own learning by limiting the opportunities for self-control. According to Salomon (1979), instruction at the most intrusive end of the mediation continuum "short-circuits" student control whereas the least intrusive mediation "activates" student control. Adaptive teaching rests on the notion that as instruction matches learners' need for direction, learners will gain in their personal control. Subsequently, teaching continues to adapt to learners' increase in self-management capabilities by becoming gradually less intrusive. The underlying hypothesis is that adaptation promotes development of self-management so that mediation is eventually removed (Wang, Reynolds, & Schwartz, 1988).

Advocates of adaptive education assume that students' perceptions of personal control is related to school learning and that it is important to incorporate this variable into the design of adaptive learning environments (Wang

& Walberg, 1985). Students' perception of personal control refers to their belief that they are responsible for their school learning. Social psychological studies investigating Rotter's (1966) concept of locus of control have influenced recent work addressing the implications of locus of control for instructional design. Social psychological research during the 1960s found that internal locus of control was positively related to such outcomes as resisting group pressures (Crowne & Liverant, 1963), actively trying to change the environment (Gore & Rotter, 1963), making realistic bets in high-risk situations (Liverant & Scodel, 1960), and using previously learned skills to acquire new ones (Holden & Rotter, 1962). Parallel investigations examining students' perceptions of personal control in school situations have documented that students' positive perceptions of self-competence and self-control are associated with motivation and success in school learning (Crandall, Katkovsky, & Preston, 1962; Felixbrod & O'Leary, 1974; Hansford & Hattie, 1962; Stipek & Weisz, 1981; Thomas, 1980). Researchers have generated a variety of theoretical concepts of self-perception and school learning, including self-efficacy (Bandura, 1981), self-worth (Covington & Berry, 1976), attributions of causality (Weiner, 1979), self-evaluation (Tesser & Campbell, 1982), and self-responsibility (Wang, 1983). Furthermore, instructional intervention studies have focused on fostering the development of students' perceptions of control over their learning (deCharms, 1976; Heckhausen & Krug, 1982; McLaughlin, 1976; Nowicki & Barnes, 1973; Wang & Stiles, 1976; Weiner, 1983). In general, educational research suggests that students' sense of control can be modified through instructional intervention and that a relationship exists between changes in student perceptions of personal control and improvements in school performance.

Adaptive Teaching Methods

The preceding conclusions emerging from research on personal control and school learning provide the basic rationale underlying the development of adaptive teaching methods (Wang, 1980). Adaptive instruction incorporates two critical design characteristics: (a) instruction and practice in self-management skills, and (b) mastery of basic academic skills. The development of competence in self-management and academic skills results in an increased sense of personal control in an interactive manner. As basic skills are mastered, teachers' perceptions of student competence and teachers' behavior towards students are altered, resulting in changes in students' perceptions of their own competence. In adaptive teaching programs, students function in a structured environment that provides opportunities for acquiring skills and emphasizes self-direction and self-evaluation. As a result, students gain an increased sense of self-efficacy and personal control. Academic successes are more likely to increase students' perceptions of control if they are achieved with minimal mediation or dependence on the teacher.

The Adaptive Learning Environments Model (ALEM; Wang, Gennari, & Waxman, 1985) is one educational program designed to develop students' personal control through a combination of individualized learning experiences that assure mastery of basic skills and an instructional management system that provides for the development of self-management skills, called the Self-Schedule System (Wang, 1974, 1976). This system requires that students share the control of and responsibility for their own learning. Students in classrooms operating under the Self-Schedule System obtain assignments of structured, prescriptive learning tasks and decide with the teacher how much time to allocate for completing the assigned tasks. Students may choose to work on these tasks in any order and mix them with self-selected, open-ended projects or activities. The system is built on a hierarchy of levels of students' competence in planning their own learning. As students progress through the hierarchy, the choices become more complex (e.g., number of tasks to be completed and range of task options increase, and the time period to be planned is lengthened), and the degree of teacher guidance or mediation decreases. Thus, each child plans his or her learning that includes tasks prescribed by the teacher to focus on basic skill acquisition as well as student-selected exploratory activities such as writing plays, preparing reports, conducting experiments, and so forth. Self-scheduling not only affords flexibility in matching instruction to students' needs and interests, but also an increased responsibility among students for their own learning.

Glaser (1977) has documented that educational responsibility can be fostered even among kindergarten and early elementary grade children through adaptive classroom environments. For example, classrooms can be structured to teach simple self-management skills such as preparing for, carrying out, and evaluating instructional activities. Glaser (1975) described one kindergarten classroom in which instructional materials were stored and coded (according to difficulty level) on open shelves. When children were assigned tasks, they exercised responsibility by selecting their own coded materials, determining what was to be done and whether assistance was needed, checking their own work, and returning materials appropriately when completed. In an adaptive classroom environment such as this, children are not passive learners, constrained in physical activity and dependent on teacher direction; instead, they function as responsible individuals participating in decisions about their own instruction and learning.

Conclusions

In sum, social psychology can contribute to the development of adaptive instructional practices by providing information about how learners may be taught in ways that meet their individual needs and characteristics. Collectively, research evaluating the effectiveness of various adaptive education approaches has documented that the program features characteristic of adaptive teaching, when implemented consistently, predict students' perceptions of personal control (reflected in their responses to structured interviews and measures of locus of control) as well as achievement outcomes (see review by Wang, 1987). As with the effectiveness research on cooperative learning, several classroom processes that mediate these effects on achievement and personal control have been suggested (Wang et al., 1985, 1988; Waxman et al., 1985). For example, analyses of classroom processes under ALEM reveal a positive change in the nature and patterns of interactions between students and teachers, interactions among peers, and the manner in which classroom time is spent by students. Specifically, classroom observations reveal a higher frequency of student-initiated and instruction-related interactions with teachers, more constructive peer interactions, and a higher engagement rates among students in ALEM classrooms compared to control classrooms. The self-regulated aspect characteristic of most adaptive programs is also critical to the maintenance of student motivation in classrooms. Thus, implementation of adaptive education appears to lead to positive changes in classroom processes, which, in turn, influence achievement and achievement-related social psychological outcomes.

TEACHER AND STUDENT PERCEPTIONS

The nature of teacher and student perceptions and associated classroom expectations have been examined extensively as social psychological determinants of student performance (Brophy & Good, 1974; see chapter 3 in this volume). Research has explored a variety of issues surrounding teacher–student relationships including the extent to which teachers communicate performance expectations to students and how expectations are responded to and/or influence performance among students. The literature generally has documented effects on student performance when teacher–student interactions include teachers' communication of their goals for performance to students. If teachers set high but attainable goals for performance and communicate these to students, achievement usually increases. Conversely, if teachers set goals that are low, achievement tends to decrease (Good, 1979). The results of this research offer some implications for teaching practices in terms of both communication and classroom structure. An awareness of the process by which academic expectations are communicated to students can help teachers create positive educational environments for all students.

Teaching Behaviors Related to Performance Expectations

Although the self-fulfilling effects of performance expectations on human behavior have long been addressed in the social psychological literature, the publication of *Pygmalion in the Classroom* (Rosenthal & Jacobson, 1968) initiated the possibility of a self-fulfilling prophecy as being an educational issue. Many classroom observational studies have investigated the ways in which performance expectations are communicated to students. A variety of observable teacher behaviors have been found to vary depending on induced or naturalistic performance expectations (Braun, 1976; Brophy, 1985; Brophy & Good, 1970). For example, a pattern of differential feedback to high- and low-expectation students has been observed among many elementary classroom teachers. Specifically, teachers tend to criticize low-expectation students more frequently than high-expectation students, whereas high-expectation students receive more frequent praise and more detailed, accurate, and frequent feedback about their responses (accurate or inaccurate) than low-expectation students (Brophy & Good, 1970). Teacher interactions with high- and low-expectation students appear to differ in additional ways: Teachers have been observed to pay less attention to lows, call on lows less often to answer questions, wait less time for lows to answer questions, seat lows farther from the teacher, and demand less work and effort from lows than highs (Good, 1980).

Rosenthal (1974) provided a categorization scheme for summarizing behaviors associated with teachers' expectations concerning student performance. Rosenthal's four-factor categorization includes climate, verbal input, verbal output, and feedback components. Cooper (1979) reviewed research investigating the operation of each factor to support Rosenthal's (1974) contentions that (a) teachers create a warmer socioemotional climate for high-expectation students, (b) the quality and quantity of teachers' input to students are greater for highs, (c) teachers create more output opportunities for highs through more frequent interactions and greater willingness to pursue answers with highs, and (d) high-expectation students receive more praise and constructive feedback from teachers than do low-expectation students.

In sum, the teacher expectation literature has documented that some teachers do exhibit differential behavior toward high- and low-expectation students. Not all teachers, however, exhibit a consistent pattern of differentiated interaction toward low and high students. Studies based on both student perceptions of differential teacher treatment (Brattesani, Weinstein, & Marshall, 1984) and direct observations (Brophy & Good, 1974) noted that, although all teachers held expectations for their students, only some actually discriminated in their treatment of high and low achievers. Summarizing findings across several studies, Good (1980) estimated that approximately one-third of the observed teachers were what he described as being overreactive. These teachers clearly overreacted to students based on their performance expectations; they provided fewer educational opportunities for lows and responded in a more critical fashion to the same behaviors among lows (incorrect responses, disruptive behaviors) as highs. Other teachers were described as being reactive in that their differential treatment of high- versus low-expectation students was prompted by the behavior of high students. For example, highs were given more opportunities to respond in part because they raised their hand or initiated interactions with the teacher more often than lows did. Finally, the third category of teachers, proactive teachers, had classroom structures and communication patterns that allowed them to respond to all students with similar amounts and types of feedback and to teach all students without being affected by their performance expectations. Thus, it appears that the extent to which teachers demonstrate differential behavior toward high and low students is an individual-difference variable in itself (Brophy & Good, 1974).

Factors Mediating Differential Treatment

The conclusion that not all classroom teachers show strong expectation effects in their instructional practices promulgated the development of several different theoretical models and empirical investigations of teacher behavior during the 1970s. Some of this work retained a social psychological perspective in explaining teacher behavior (e.g., Ames, 1983; Cooper, 1979), whereas other research focused more on classroom management and effective teaching behaviors (e.g., Berliner, 1988; Brophy & Good, 1986).

From a social psychological vantage, Cooper (1977, 1979, 1983) contended that behavior toward low students is influenced by teachers' personal control needs. Cooper suggests that teachers have fewer interactions with and dispense more criticism to low-expectation students in an attempt to gain control over the classroom process. Teachers may respond differently to high- and low-expectation students depending on whether they have relatively high or low control needs. For example, teachers with greater control needs are more likely to discourage low-achieving students from initiating contacts with them in whole-group situations because those interactions tend to be longer, less rewarding in terms of correct student responding, and, consequently, more disruptive to the teacher's control. Ames (1983) offered a social psychological framework that is similar to Cooper's. Ames believes that teachers make attributions about their own performance, in part, in response to student performance. Some teachers view their teaching to be more strongly related to student outcomes than others. Failure, which is more common among low-achieving students, is construed as negative performance feedback for teachers who take primary responsibility for student outcomes. Thus, differential treatment of low-expectation students may reflect teachers' efforts to affect their own experience of success and failure. Both Cooper and Ames posit that social psychological factors (i.e., personal needs for classroom control or success attribution) underlie the observed variations in frequency of interaction and performance feedback in classrooms.

The teacher effectiveness literature (see review by Brophy & Good, 1986) has adopted a somewhat different perspective from that of Cooper or Ames. Researchers in the area of teaching effectiveness (e.g., Anderson, Evertson, & Emmer, 1980; Doyle, 1979; Good & Grouws, 1977; Stallings, Robbins, Presbrey, & Scott, 1986) are interested in identifying observable classroom processes or behaviors that are associated with desirable products or student outcomes (e.g., high achievement and engagement) among both high- and low-achieving students. In general, this research has found that teachers' level of management skills (e.g., structuring and using classroom time efficiently, implementing standard rules and procedures, consequating student behaviors immediately), and ability to anticipate and meet the instructional needs of all students (e.g., being alert to and intervening with students who do not understand task demands, providing corrective feedback, directing the pace and content of instruction) are the individual-difference variables that underlie differential teacher behavior. In other words, low-achieving students may receive different (and ineffective) treatment from teachers who simply do not possess specific skills for dealing with academic failure or inappropriate behavior. Teachers exhibiting effective management and teaching skills are less discriminating in their treatment of high- versus low-expectation students.

Student Expectations

It has been argued that student perceptions and expectations also influence classroom learning. Weiner, Graham, Taylor, and Meyer (1983) stated that students abstract meaning from teachers' behaviors, and these interpretations may affect students' classroom performance. Research addressing students' awareness of teachers' communications about expectations has documented that: (a) students do perceive differential teacher treatment on observed behaviors (Brophy & Good, 1974); (b) classrooms differ in the extent to which students perceive differential treatment (Weinstein, Marshall, Brattesani, & Middlestadt, 1982); and (c) when students perceive high levels of differential treatment, teacher expectations are more strongly associated with student expectations and achievement (Brattesani et al., 1984). Braun (1976) claimed, furthermore, that low student expectations for themselves help perpetuate low expectations of teachers.

Differential behaviors in which teachers have been observed to engage can serve to reinforce inappropriate attributions or negative self-evaluations among students. Weiner et al. (1983) identified the differential nature of performance feedback given to high- versus low-ability students as critical in both shaping and confirming student expectations. For example, when feedback does not realistically match student performance (e.g., praise for success on an easy task, criticism for failure on a difficult task), students often infer that such communications carry messages that they are low in ability.

Even communications that might be deemed appropriate for low-ability students (e.g., providing correct answers without taking time to help students arrive at the answer themselves) can be interpreted by students to mean that they are unable to do the work.

Student perceptions play a critical role in models describing how teacher perceptions may be fulfilled in the classroom. Teacher expectations are not automatically self-fulfilling; an expectation requires more than its existence to become fulfilled. Most importantly, teachers' expectations must be communicated to students (through differential treatment and/or through student interpretations). It is students' perceptions of teacher behaviors that affect students' academic self-concepts and attributions and, in turn, shape their achievement and behavior.

Conclusion

We know that teachers form expectations for student performance on the basis of variations in student functioning and background. For a significant number of teachers, these differential expectations often translate into differential treatment of high- and low-expectation students. Several individual-difference characteristics may render teachers more susceptible to expectation effects. Regardless of whether these characteristics reflect social psychological variables or management skills, most models of how teachers' expectations may be fulfilled in classrooms and related research (e.g., Brophy & Evertson, 1981; Good, 1980; Good & Brophy, 1974) suggest that differential treatment may affect students' self-concepts, achievement motivation, and levels of aspiration. The extent to which students themselves are susceptible to expectation effects in turn may relate to various student characteristics, including students' subjective interpretation of successful performance (Frieze, Francis, & Hanusa, 1983), their effort–outcome covariation beliefs (Cooper, 1977), and self-concept (Braun, 1976). Thus, the ultimate effects of differential treatment as an expression of teacher expectations on student achievement are either indirect, involving student interpretive processes such as self-concept or motivation, or direct, affecting achievement directly without implicating mediating processes (Cooper & Good, 1983). Although the evidence on the differential treatment accorded to high- and low-ability students has been established in teacher expectation research, there remains a need for more information regarding teacher and student characteristics that make them more or less vulnerable to expectation effects as well as the extent to which achievement is affected.

IMPLICATIONS FOR INSTRUCTIONAL DESIGN

A number of implications for classroom practices emerge from an analysis of how social psychology may apply to learning and instruction. First, from the adaptive instruction literature, it appears that functioning in a structured environment, where opportunities for skill mastery are provided and self-regulated learning is emphasized, leads to an increased sense of personal control and self-efficacy among students (Wang, 1983). Personal control may be further enhanced if children achieve their successes without a high degree of dependence on the teacher (e.g., for rewards or incentives). Attribution theorists (Stipek & Weisz, 1981; Weiner, 1979) suggest that students' personal control is associated with achievement-related outcomes, such as greater task persistence and more openness to modifying inappropriate behaviors or inaccurate responses when confronted with failures. Thus, the incorporation of adaptive educational program characteristics into the schooling process—specifically, design features that attempt to transfer responsibility for learning from the teacher to the student—represents one application of social psychological principles.

Findings from both the social psychological and teacher effectiveness perspectives on teacher and student perceptions accord well with the implications derived from the adaptive instruction literature. According to Blumenfeld, Pintrich, Meece, and Wessels (1982), an important objective for educators is not necessarily to restructure or change children's self-perceptions directly (e.g., attribution training); rather it is to provide effective, proactive management and instruction that enable children to acquire academic skills (Gettinger, 1988; Good, 1979). In other words, insofar as classroom teachers are reactive in their instructional practices and enable existing differences among students to actualize through differential treatment, then the negative influence of certain social psychological variables will be heightened. Conversely, teachers who are more proactive, through structuring instruction and interacting appropriately and consistently with students, can minimize such negative effects.

Two different perspectives offer suggestions for achieving a more proactive approach to classroom instruction. First, the effective teaching literature focuses on the development of specialized skills, such as organizing classroom activities so that teachers are able to interact with and establish appropriate goals for all students and monitoring student progress regularly (Brophy & Good, 1986). For example, in order for students to direct their efforts appropriately, teachers should be clear about the purposes of academic tasks and grading criteria. Similarly, feedback should be instructive for students, addressing both weak and strong aspects of performance, rather than praising incorrect responses or misguided work in an effort to boost self-esteem. Additional effective teaching strategies concerned with social psychological variables include: (a) noncompetitive learning environments, (b) flexible grouping, (c) providing opportunities for success in a variety of areas (academic as well as nonacademic), (d) mastery-oriented learning, and (e) evaluation based on comparison with prior achievement (Rosenholtz & Rosenholtz, 1981).

A social psychological perspective suggests that encouraging teachers' personal views of children's abilities as being multifaceted and, to a certain degree, externally controlled can influence their use of teaching and management practices that are congruent with these views (Swann & Snyder, 1980). Helping teachers become more aware of their own behaviors and potential biases, emphasizing the importance of positive, but realistic, expectations for all students, and encouraging teachers to take time to know students as individuals can often lead to the development of more proactive teaching strategies. Brophy and Good (1974), for example, suggested that teachers might hold individual conversations with students to increase their understanding of the different ways in which students define their own success. This may enable teachers to broaden the range of successful task performance in classrooms to accommodate students' individual definitions of success.

The cooperative learning research suggests that instructional grouping in classrooms need not be problematic in terms of social comparison. Grouping that consistently segregates students by ability can exaggerate the perceptions and role of ability in classrooms. Conversely, heterogeneous groups that are treated equally in terms of opportunities for learning and success not only minimize the detrimental effects of comparison but also enhance social acceptance and personal esteem. In addition, cooperative group structures facilitate teachers' efforts at socializing children to value learning opportunities for their own sake rather than for competition or rewards, which is a critical component of classroom motivation.

SUMMARY

Learning and instruction take place in a social context, with structural characteristics and interactional patterns with peers and teachers defining the social psychological nature of classrooms. Social psychological variables are an inherent part of the educational process and, as such, the principles and concepts of social psychology can provide input for both educational research and applications to classroom learning.

Recent research evaluating the benefits of procedures such as cooperative learning and adaptive instruction raises an important question regarding the application of social psychology to classroom learning (e.g., Slavin et al., 1985). Specifically, are the positive effects derived from these applications on both cognitive and affective outcomes due to social psychological variables or instructional variables? Slavin and Karweit (1985), for example, speculated that the relative success of cooperative learning methods results from their systematic, effective teaching practices and not from their underlying cooperative processes. The implications and recommendations for designing classroom instruction that were addressed in the preceding section potentially lead to an overall improvement in instructional quality as well as a consideration of social psychological factors. The suggestions concerning classroom management, well-specified routines for students, and continuous performance feedback are all examples in which the instructional aspects of teaching, not necessarily the social psychological aspects, may have produced the positive achievement and interpersonal results. A closer examination of the social psychological versus instructional variables related to the success of classroom applications of social psychology is certainly plausible. Nonetheless, given the interactive and social nature of schooling, it may be difficult to disassociate these factors in classroom designs. Clearly, student outcomes are linked to both instructional practices and social psychological factors.

REFERENCES

Ames, C., & Ames, R. (1984). Goal structures and motivation. *Elementary School Journal, 85,* 39–52.

Ames, R. (1983). Teachers' attributions for their own teaching. In J. M. Levine & M. C. Wang (Eds.), *Teacher and student perceptions: Implications for learning* (pp. 105–123). Hillsdale, NJ: Lawrence Erlbaum Associates.

Anderson, L. M., Evertson, C. M., & Emmer, E. T. (1980). Dimensions in classroom management derived from recent research. *Journal of Curriculum Studies, 12,* 343–356.

Aronson, E., Bridgeman, D. L., & Geffner, R. (1978). The effects of a cooperative classroom structure on student behavior and attitudes. In D. Bar-Tal & L. Saxe (Eds.), *Social psychology of education: Theory and research* (pp. 257–272). New York: Wiley.

Aronson, E., Stephan, C., Sikes, J., Blaney, N., & Snapp, M. (1978). *The jigsaw classroom.* Beverly Hills, CA: Sage.

Bandura, A. (1981). Self-referent thought: A developmental analysis of self-efficacy. In J. H. Flavell & L. R. Ross (Eds.), *Cognitive social development: Frontiers and possible futures* (pp. 175–202). New York: Cambridge University Press.

Berliner, D. C. (1983). Developing conceptions of classroom environments: Some light on the T in classroom studies of ATI. *Educational Psychologist, 18,* 1–13.

Berliner, D. C. (1988). Effective classroom management and instruction: A knowledge base for consultation. In J. L. Graden, J. E. Zins, & M. J. Curtis (Eds.), *Alternative educational delivery systems: Enhancing instructional options for all students* (pp. 309–325). Washington, DC: National Association of School Psychologists.

Bloom, B. S. (1968). Learning for mastery. *Evaluation Comment, 1*(2), 74–86.

Bloom, B. S. (1976). *Human characteristics and school learning.* New York: McGraw-Hill.

Blumenfeld, P. C., Pintrich, P. R., Meece, J., & Wessels, K. (1982). The formation and role of self perceptions of ability in elementary classrooms. *Elementary School Journal, 82,* 401–420.

Bossert, S. T. (1979). *Tasks and social relationships in classrooms.* Cambridge: Cambridge University Press.

Bossert, S. T. (1988). Cooperative activities in the classroom. In E. Z. Rothkopf (Ed.), *Review of research in education* (Vol. 15, pp. 225–250). Washington, DC: American Educational Research Association.

Brattesani, K. A., Weinstein, R. S., & Marshall, H. H. (1984). Student perceptions of differential teacher treatment as moderators of teacher expectation effects. *Journal of Educational Psychology, 76,* 236–247.

Braun, C. (1976). Teacher expectation: Socio-psychological dynamics. *Review of Educational Research, 46,* 185–213.

Brophy, J. E. (1979). Teacher behavior and its effects. *Journal of Educational Psychology, 71,* 733–750.

Brophy, J. E. (1985). Teacher–student interaction. In J. Dusek (Ed.), *Teacher expectancies* (pp. 43–92). Hillsdale, NJ: Lawrence Erlbaum Associates.

Brophy, J. E., & Evertson, C. M. (1981). *Student characteristics and teaching.* New York: Longman.

Brophy, J. E., & Good, T. L. (1970). Teachers' communication of differential expectations for children's classroom performance: Some behavioral data. *Journal of Educational Psychology, 61,* 365–374.

Brophy, J. E., & Good, T. L. (1974). *Teacher–student relationships: Causes and consequences.* New York: Holt, Rinehart, & Winston.

Brophy, J. E., & Good, T. L. (1986). Teacher behavior and student achievement. In M. C. Wittrock (Ed.), *Handbook of research on teaching* (3d ed., pp. 328–375). New York: Macmillan.

Cazden, C. (1986). Classroom discourse. In M. Wittrock (Ed.), *Handbook of research on teaching* (3d ed., pp. 432–463). New York: Macmillan.

Cohen, E. (1984). Talking and working together: Status, interaction, and learning. In P. Peterson, L. C. Wilkinson, & M. Hallinan (Eds.), *The social context of instruction: Group organization and group processes* (pp. 171–188). New York: Academic Press.

Cooper, H. M. (1977). Controlling personal rewards: Professional teachers' differential use of feedback and the effects of feedback on student's motivation to perform. *Journal of Educational Psychology, 69,* 419–427.

Cooper, H. M. (1979). Pygmalion grows up: A model for teacher expectation communication and performance influence. *Review of Educational Research, 49,* 389–410.

Cooper, H. M. (1983). Communication of teacher expectations to students. In J. M. Levine & M. C. Wang (Eds.), *Teacher and student perceptions: Implications for learning* (pp. 193–211). Hillsdale, NJ: Lawrence Erlbaum Associates.

Cooper, H. M., & Good, T. L. (1983). *Pygmalion grows up: Studies in the expectation communication process.* New York: Longman.

Corno, L., & Snow, R. E. (1986). Adapting teaching to individual differences. In M. C. Wittrock (Ed.), *Handbook of research on teaching* (3d ed., pp. 605–629). New York: Macmillan.

Covington, M. V., & Berry, R. (1976). *Self-worth and school learning.* New York: Holt, Rinehart, & Winston.

Crandall, V. J., Katkovsky, W., & Preston, A. (1962). Motivational and ability determinants of young children's intellectual academic behaviors. *Child Development, 33,* 643–661.

Crowne, D. P., & Liverant, S. (1963). Conformity under varying conditions of personal commitment. *Journal of Abnormal and Social Psychology, 66,* 547–555.

deCharms, R. (1976). *Enhancing motivation: Change in the classroom.* New York: Wiley.

Deutsch, M. (1949a). An experimental study of the effects of cooperation and competition upon group process. *Human Relations, 2,* 199–231.

Deutsch, M. (1949b). A theory of cooperation and competition. *Human Relations, 2,* 129–151.

Deutsch, M. (1973). *The resolution of conflict.* New Haven, CT: Yale University Press.

DeVries, D., & Edwards, K. (1973). Learning games and student teams: Their effects on classroom process. *American Educational Research Journal, 10,* 307–318.

DeVries, D., & Slavin, R. (1978). Teams-Games-Tournament: A research review. *Journal of Research and Development in Education, 12,* 356–362.

DeVries, D., Slavin, R., Fennessey, G., Edwards, K., & Lombardo, M. (1980). *Teams-Games-Tournament: The teaming approach.* Englewood Cliffs, NJ: Educational Technology.

Doyle, W. (1979). Classroom tasks and students' abilities. In P. L. Peterson & H. J. Walberg (Eds.), *Research on teaching: Concepts, findings and implications* (pp. 183–209). Berkeley, CA: McCutchan.

Doyle, W. (1983). Academic work. *Review of Educational Research, 53,* 159–200.

Felixbrod, J. J., & O'Leary, K. D. (1974). Self-determination of academic standards by children: Toward freedom from external control. *Journal of Educational Psychology, 66,* 845–850.

Filby, N., & Barnett, B. (1982). Student perceptions of better readers in elementary classroom. *Elementary School Journal, 82,* 435–450.

Frieze, I. H., Francis, W. D., & Hanusa, B. H. (1983). Defining success in classroom settings. In J. M. Levine & M. C. Wang (Eds.), *Teacher and student perceptions: Implications for learning* (pp. 3–27). Hillsdale, NJ: Lawrence Erlbaum Associates.

Gagne, R. M. (Ed.). (1967). *Learning and individual differences.* Columbus, OH: Merrill.

Gettinger, M. (1988). Methods of proactive classroom management. *School Psychology Review, 17,* 227–242.

Glaser, R. (1972). Individuals and learning: The new aptitudes. *Educational Researcher, 1,* 5–13.

Glaser, R. (1975). The school of the future: Adaptive environments for learning. In L. Rubin (Ed.), *The future of education: Perspectives on tomorrow's schooling* (pp. 147–191). Boston: Allyn & Bacon.

Glaser, R. (1977). *Adaptive education: Individual diversity and learning.* New York: Holt, Rinehart, & Winston.

Good, T. L. (1979). Teacher effectiveness in the elementary school: What we know about it now. *Journal of Teacher Education, 30,* 52–64.

Good, T. L. (1980). Classroom expectations: Teacher–pupil interactions. In J. H. McMillan (Ed.), *The social psychology of school learning* (pp. 72–122). New York: Academic Press.

Good, T. L., & Grouws, D. (1977). Teaching effects: A process-product study in fourth grade mathematics classrooms. *Journal of Teacher Education, 28,* 49–54.

Gordon, E. W. (Ed.). (1983). *Human diversity and pedagogy.* Westport, CT: Mediax.

Gore, P. M., & Rotter, J. B. (1963). A personality correlate of social action. *Journal of Personality, 31,* 58–64.

Hansford, B. C., & Hattie, A. J. (1982). The relationship between self and achievement-performance measures. *Review of Educational Research, 52,* 123–142.

Heckhausen, H., & Krug, S. (1982). Motive modification. In A. Steward (Ed.), *Motivation and society* (pp. 34–76). San Francisco: Jossey-Bass.

Holden, K. B., & Rotter, J. B. (1962). A non-verbal measure of extinction in skill and chance situation. *Journal of Experimental Psychology, 63,* 519–520.

Johnson, D. W. (1975). Cooperativeness and social perspective-taking. *Journal of Personality and Social Psychology, 31,* 241–244.

Johnson, D. W. (1980). Group processes: Influences of student–student interactions on school outcomes. In J. McMillan (Ed.), *The social psychology of school learning* (pp. 123–168). New York: Academic Press.

Johnson, D. W. (1981). Student–student interaction: The neglected variable in education. *Educational Researcher, 10,* 5–10.

Johnson, D. W., & Johnson, R. T. (1974). Instructional goal structure: Cooperative, competitive, or individualistic. *Review of Educational Research, 44,* 213–240.

Johnson, D. W., & Johnson, R. T. (1975). *Learning together and alone.* Englewood Cliffs, NJ: Prentice Hall.

Johnson, D. W., & Johnson, R. T. (1985a). Classroom conflict: Controversy versus debate in learning groups. *American Educational Research Journal, 22,* 237–256.

Johnson, D. W., & Johnson, R. T. (1985b). The internal dynamics of cooperative learning groups. In R. Slavin, S. Sharan, S. Kagan, R. Hertz-Lazarowitz, C. Webb, & R. Schmuck (Eds.), *Learning to cooperate, cooperating to learn* (pp. 103–124). New York: Plenum Press.

Johnson, D., Johnson, R., Holubec, E., & Roy, P. (1984). *Circles of learning.* Washington, DC: Association for Supervision and Curriculum Development.

Johnson, D., Johnson, R., Johnson, J., & Anderson, D. (1976). The effects of cooperative vs. individualized instruction on student prosocial behavior. *Journal of Educational Psychology, 68,* 446–452.

Johnson, D., Johnson, R., & Maruyama, G. (1983). Interdependence and interpersonal attraction among heterogeneous and homogeneous individuals: A theoretical formulation and a meta-analysis of the research. *Review of Educational Research, 53,* 5–54.

Johnson, D., Maruyama, G., Johnson, R., Nelson, D., & Skon, L. (1981). Effects of cooperative, competitive, and individualistic goal structures on achievement: A meta-analysis. *Psychological Bulletin, 89,* 47–62.

Levine, J. M. (1983). Social comparison and education. In J. M. Levine & M. C. Wang (Eds.), *Teacher and student perceptions: Implications for learning* (pp. 22–55). Hillsdale, NJ: Lawrence Erlbaum Associates.

Liverant, S., & Scodel, A. (1960). Internal and external control as determinants of decision making under conditions of risk. *Psychological Reports, 7,* 59–67.

Maller, J. B. (1929). *Cooperation and competition.* New York: Teachers College, Columbia University.

Marshall, H. H. (1981). Open classrooms: Has the term outlived its usefulness. *Review of Educational Research, 51,* 181–192.

Marshall, H. H., & Weinstein, R. S. (1984). Classroom factors affecting students' self-evaluations: An interactional model. *Review of Educational Research, 54,* 301–325.

McLaughlin, T. F. (1976). Self-control in the classroom. *Review of Educational Research, 46,* 631–663.

Messick, S. (1979). Potential uses of noncognitive measurement in education. *Journal of Educational Psychology, 71,* 281–292.

Michaels, J. W. (1977). Classroom reward structures and academic performance. *Review of Educational Research, 47,* 87–98.

Miller, L., & Hamblin, R. (1963). Interdependence, differential rewarding, and productivity. *American Sociological Review, 28,* 768–778.

Nowicki, S., & Barnes, J. (1973). Effects of a structured camp experience on locus of control orientation of inner-city children. *Journal of Genetic Psychology, 122,* 247–262.

Peterson, P., Janicki, T., & Swing, S. (1981). Ability by treatment interaction effects on children's learning in large-group and small-group approaches. *American Educational Research Journal, 18,* 452–474.

Resnick, L. B. (1972). Open education: Some tasks for technology. *Educational Technology, 12,* 70–76.

Rosenbaum, J. E. (1980). Social implications of educational grouping. In D. Berliner (Ed.), *Review of research in education* (Vol. 8, pp. 361–401). Washington, DC: American Educational Research Association.

Rosenholtz, S. J., & Rosenholtz, S. H. (1981). Classroom organization and the perception of ability. *Sociology of Education, 54,* 132–140.

Rosenholtz, S., & Simpson, C. (1984). The formation of ability conceptions: Developmental trend or social construction? *Review of Educational Research, 54,* 31–63.

Rosenthal, R. (1974). *On the social psychology of the self-fulfilling prophecy: Further evidence for Pygmalion effects and their mediating mechanisms.* New York: MSS Modular Publications.

Rosenthal, R., & Jacobson, L. (1968). *Pygmalion in the classroom: Teacher expectation and pupils' intellectual development.* New York: Holt, Rinehart, & Winston.

Rotter, J. B. (1966). Generalized expectancies for internal versus external control of reinforcement. *Psychological Monographs, 80* (609).

Rubin, J., & Brown, B. (1975). *The social psychology of bargaining and negotiation.* New York: Academic Press.

Salomon, G. (1979). *Interaction of media, cognition and learning.* San Francisco: Jossey-Bass.

Sharan, S. (1980). Cooperative learning in small groups: Recent methods and effects on achievement, attitudes, and ethnic relations. *Review of Educational Research, 50,* 241–271.

Sharan, S., Hertz-Lazarowitz, R., & Ackerman, Z. (1980). Academic achievement of elementary school children in small-group versus whole-class instruction. *Journal of Experimental Education, 48,* 125–129.

Sharan, S., & Sharan, Y. (1976). *Small-group teaching.* Englewood Cliffs, NJ: Educational Technology.

Sherif, M., & Sherif, C. (1956). *The outline of social psychology.* New York: Harper & Row.

Simpson, C. (1981). Classroom structure and the organization of ability. *Sociology of Education, 54,* 120–132.

Slavin, R. (1977). Classroom reward structure: An analytical and practical review. *Review of Educational Research, 47,* 633–651.

Slavin, R. (1978a). Student teams and achievement divisions. *Journal of Research and Development in Education, 12,* 39–49.

Slavin, R. (1978b). Student teams and comparison among equals: Effects on academic performance and student attitudes. *Journal of Educational Psychology, 70,* 532–538.

Slavin, R. (1980a). Cooperative learning. *Review of Educational Research, 50,* 315–342.

Slavin, R. (1980b). Effects of individual learning expectations on student achievement. *Journal of Educational Psychology, 72,* 520–524.

Slavin, R. (1980c). Student team learning: A manual for teachers. In S. Sharan, P. Hare, C. Webb, & R. Hertz-Lazarowitz (Eds.), *Cooperation in education* (pp. 82–135). Provo, UT: Brigham Young University Press.

Slavin, R. (1980d). *Using student team learning* (rev. ed.). Baltimore: Johns Hopkins University, Center for the Social Organization of Schools.

Slavin, R. (1983). *Cooperative learning.* New York: Longman.

Slavin, R. (1985). An introduction to cooperative learning research. In R. Slavin, S. Sharan, S. Kagan, R. Hertz-Lazarowitz, C. Webb, & R. Schmuck (Eds.), *Learning to cooperate, cooperating to learn* (pp. 5–16). New York: Plenum Press.

Slavin, R. (1987). Cooperative learning: Where behavioral and humanistic approaches to classroom motivation meet. *Elementary School Journal, 88,* 29–37.

Slavin, R., & Karweit, N. (1985). Effects of whole class, ability grouped, and individualized instruction on mathematics achievement. *American Educational Research Journal, 22,* 351–367.

Slavin, R., Leavey, M., & Madden, N. (1981). *Student teams and individualized instruction: Effects on student achievement, attitudes, and behavior.* Baltimore: Johns Hopkins University, Center for the Social Organization of Schools.

Slavin, R., Sharan, S., Kagan, S., Hertz-Lazarowitz, R., Webb, C., & Schmuck, R. (Eds.). (1985). *Learning to cooperate, cooperating to learn.* New York: Plenum Press.

Slavin, R., & Tanner, A. M. (1979). Effects of cooperative reward structures and individual accountability on productivity and learning. *Journal of Educational Research, 72,* 294–298.

Snow, R. E. (1980). Aptitude, learner control, and adaptive instruction. *Educational Psychologist, 15,* 151–158.

Snow, R. E., Federico, P-A., & Montague, W. E. (Eds.). (1980). *Aptitude, learning, and instruction.* Hillsdale, NJ: Lawrence Erlbaum Associates.

Stallings, J., Robbins, M., Presbrey, L., & Scott, J. (1986). Effects of instruction based on the Madeline Hunter model on students' achievement: Findings from a Follow-Through Project. *Elementary School Journal, 86,* 571–587.

Stipek, D. J., & Weisz, J. R. (1981). Perceived personal control and achievement. *Review of Educational Research, 51,* 101–137.

Swann, W., & Snyder, M. (1980). On translating beliefs into actions: Theories of ability and their application in an instructional setting. *Journal of Personality and Social Psychology, 38,* 879–888.

Tesser, A., & Campbell, J. A. (1982). A self-evaluation maintenance approach to school behavior. *Educational Psychologist, 17,* 1–12.

Thomas, J. (1980). Agency and achievement: Self-management and self-regard. *Review of Educational Research, 50,* 213–240.

Wang, M. C. (1974). *The rationale and design of the Self-Schedule System* (LRDC Publication 1974/5). Pittsburgh: University of Pittsburgh, Learning Research and Development Center.

Wang, M. C. (1976). *The Self-Schedule System for instructional-learning management in adaptive school learning environments* (LRDC Publication 1976/9). Pittsburgh: University of Pittsburgh, Learning Research and Development Center.

Wang, M. C. (1980). Adaptive instruction: Building on diversity. *Theory into Practice, 19,* 122–128.

Wang, M. C. (1983). Development and consequences of students' sense of personal control. In J. Levine & M. C. Wang (Eds.), *Teacher and student perceptions: Implications for learning* (pp. 213–247). Hillsdale, NJ: Lawrence Erlbaum Associates.

Wang, M. C. (1987). Individual differences and effective schooling. *Professional School Psychology, 2,* 53–66.

Wang, M. C., Gennari, P., & Waxman, H. C. (1985). The Adaptive Learning Environments Model: Design, implementation, and effects. In M. C. Wang & H. J. Walberg (Eds.), *Adapting instruction to individual differences* (pp. 191–235). Berkeley, CA: McCutchan.

Wang, M. C., & Lindvall, C. M. (1984). Individual differences and school learning environments. In E. W. Gordon (Ed.), *Review of research in education* (Vol. 11, pp. 161–225). Washington, DC: American Educational Research Association.

Wang, M. C., Reynolds, M. C., & Schwartz, L. L. (1988). Adaptive instruction: An alternative educational approach for students with special needs. In J. L. Graden, J. E. Zins, & M. J. Curtis (Eds.), *Alternative educational delivery systems: Enhancing instructional options for all students* (pp. 199–220). Washington, DC: National Association of School Psychologists.

Wang, M. C., & Stiles, B. (1976). An investigation of children's concept of self-responsibility for their school learning. *American Educational Research Journal, 13,* 159–179.

Wang, M. C., & Walberg, H. J. (Eds.). (1985). *Adapting instruction to individual differences.* Berkeley, CA: McCutchan.

Waxman, H. C., Wang, M. C., Anderson, K. A., & Walberg, H. J. (1985). Adaptive education and student outcomes: A quantitative synthesis. *Journal of Educational Research, 78,* 228–236.

Webb, N. (1982). Student interaction and learning in small groups. *Review of Educational Research, 52,* 421–445.

Webb, N. (1985). Student interaction and learning in small groups: A research summary. In R. Slavin, S. Sharan, S. Kagan, R. Hertz-Lazarowitz, C. Webb, & R. Schmuck (Eds.), *Learning to cooperate, cooperating to learn* (pp. 147–172). New York: Plenum Press.

Webb, N., & Kenderski, C. (1984). Student interaction and learning in small-group and whole-class settings. In P. Peterson, L. C. Wilkinson, & M. Hallinan (Eds.), *The social context of instruction: Group organization and group processes* (pp. 153–170). New York: Academic Press.

Weiner, B. (1979). A theory of motivation for some classroom experiences. *Journal of Educational Psychology, 71,* 3–25.

Weiner, B. (1983). Speculations regarding the role of affect in achievement-change programs guided by attributional principles. In J. M. Levine & M. C. Wang (Eds.), *Teacher and student perceptions: Implications for learning* (pp. 250–278). Hillsdale, NJ: Lawrence Erlbaum Associates.

Weiner, B., Graham, S., Taylor, S. E., & Meyer, W-U. (1983). Social cognition in the classroom. *Educational Psychologist, 18,* 109–124.

Weinstein, R. S., Marshall, H. H., Brattesani, K. A., & Middlestadt, S. E. (1982). Student perceptions of differential teacher treatment in open and traditional classrooms. *Journal of Educational Psychology, 74,* 678–692.

Wilkinson, L. C. (1988). Grouping children for learning: Implications for kindergarten education. In E. Z. Rothkopf (Ed.), *Review of research in education* (Vol. 15, pp. 203–223).

13

APPLICATIONS OF
SOCIAL PSYCHOLOGY
TO SCHOOL EMPLOYEE
EVALUATION AND APPRAISAL

Kevin J. Williams
The University at Albany, State University of New York

Gwen M. Williams
Fonda-Fultonville Central School, Fonda NY

Performance appraisal, the evaluation of work behavior along job dimensions, is not typically high on school psychologists' research or practice agendas. Industrial and organizational (I/O) psychologists have been interested in this topic because of the centrality of performance appraisal to an organization's functioning. Extensive research has been conducted on the method and process of evaluating work performance (Borman, 1974; DeNisi & Williams, 1988; Landy & Farr, 1980). There are a number of reasons, however, why school psychologists may want to take a more active interest in performance appraisal research. First, valid performance appraisal systems are pivotal in demonstrating the worth and contribution of the school psychologist to the organization. The issue of accountability has received much attention within the field of school psychology recently (Fairchild, 1975; Maher, 1979; National Association of School Psychologists (NASP), 1985), and an understanding of the appraisal process may help direct efforts to address this issue (Bennett, 1980). Second, training and accreditation policies (Curtis & Zins, 1989; HASP, 1984) require accurate methods of appraising the school psychologist's performance. Third, as this chapter addresses in its final section, research in I/O psychology has not addressed specific concerns of school psychologists and is unlikely to do so in the future.

This chapter integrates theory in social psychology, social cognition, and I/O psychology to provide a model of the performance appraisal process. Empirical work is reviewed and critical individual, social, and organizational factors affecting performance evaluation are identified. The review of empirical work presented here is not meant to be exhaustive (for such a review see DeNisi & Williams, 1988; Landy & Farr, 1980), but concentrates on research most relevant to the model presented here. In the following sections, we (a) discuss the nature of performance appraisals in organizations, (b) present a social-cognitive model of the appraisal process, and (c) discuss the implications of the model for performance appraisal in schools and for school psychologists.

THE NATURE OF PERFORMANCE APPRAISAL

Types of Performance Measures

Although there are many ways to measure job behavior, it is useful to break performance appraisals down into two types: nonjudgmental and judgmental (Landy, 1989). Nonjudgmental methods of appraisal rely on objective data rather than subjective ratings. Production data are the most common objective measures of performance, but personnel information such as absences, promotions, and safety records are also used. Time elapsed from the beginning of a referral to its completion is a nonjudgmental measure of school psychologists' effectiveness (Fairchild, 1975). Whereas objective production data may seem easy and fair measures of job performance, there are a number of factors that make them problematic. Production measures are frequently contaminated by situational and organizational variables (e.g., resource availability, equipment failure, work group characteristics) and hence highly unreliable (Landy & Farr, 1983). "Lag time," for example, is affected by the number of referrals a school psychologist is presented with at a particular time, student absenteeism, and the schedules of teachers, parents and other professionals who need to be interviewed. Also, there are many jobs (e.g., administrator and, perhaps, school psychologist) for which there are no readily available objective data. Accordingly, judgmental methods are the most common method of appraisal in organizations (Landy & Farr, 1983) and are the primary focus of the present chapter. Judgmental methods require raters to subjectively evaluate a target other's standing on an underlying attribute. Rating scales are the most typical judgmental measure of work performance. It is human nature to readily judge the performance of others, whether they are co-workers, elected officials, the school's new coach, or ourselves. Such judgments help us navigate our social environments. The nature of these judgments, about both self and others, will also affect our perceptions, behavior, and interactions in the workplace.

It is important to note that whatever measure of work performance is used, it must be relevant to successful performance on the job. Rating individuals on performance dimensions unrelated to success will defeat the objectives of the organization's performance appraisal system. For example, evaluating filing clerks on neatness of their desks will decrease accurate filing (i.e., the relevant criterion measure) if, to ensure favorable evaluations, clerks remove files from the tops of their desks at the end of each day and hide them. Likewise, evaluating teachers on the basis of how well their students perform on standardized tests will encourage teaching students how to take tests rather than master subject material.

Purposes of Performance Appraisal

Performance appraisals are used in organizations for a variety of purposes: administrative and personnel decisions (e.g., salary increments, promotions, transfers, and terminations), training assessment and referrals, and feedback for employee development (Cleveland, Murphy, & Williams, 1989). The most common use is for personnel decisions (Bernardin & Villanova, 1986).

Despite the different objectives of these appraisal purposes, organizations rarely conduct separate appraisals for each purpose. Time constraints and organizational priorities may encourage the use of performance appraisals conducted for one purpose for other purposes as well. Often a yearly comprehensive appraisal is used for all purposes (Bernardin & Villanova, 1986; Meyer, Kay, & French, 1965). Using the same performance evaluation for different purposes, however, reduces the effectiveness of the appraisal system (Meyer et al., 1965). Cleveland et al. (1989) have argued that different appraisal purposes are incompatible. Personnel decisions emphasize between-individual comparisons whereas employee development concerns emphasize within-individual comparisons. Focusing on one type of information will decrease the quality of the other. Because personnel decisions usually receive highest priority in organizations, between-individual information is likely to be emphasized at the expense of within-individual information. Employee development will likely suffer as a result (Meyer et al., 1965). Organizations should be encouraged to conduct separate appraisals for separate purposes.

Common Problems with Judgmental Measures of Performance

Distributions of performance ratings often display leniency, halo bias, and range restriction (Bernardin & Beatty, 1984). Leniency refers to ratings that are consistently too positive. Halo bias refers to (Bernardin & Beatty, 1984) "a tendency to rate a person similarly across traits in accordance with an overall or global impression" (p. 173). Range restriction refers to ratings that fail to encompass the complete rating scale. As a result of these tendencies, discrimination among ratees is often poor; ratings may fail to adequately distinguish between ratees of differing performance levels.

Traditional approaches to addressing these problems have focused on the method of appraisal such as the development of better rating scale formats and better training for users of rating scales. These approaches, however, failed to lead to any real improvement in appraisal validity (Landy & Farr, 1980). Much discussion and research has revolved around the validity of appraisal instruments. Many different rating scale formats have been introduced (for a comprehensive review, see Bernardin & Beatty, 1984) and format comparison studies have been numerous (for reviews see Bernardin & Villanova, 1986; Landy & Farr, 1983). Although graphic rating scales, consisting of trait or job dimension labels and a varying number of numeric or adjective anchors (e.g., "poor," "average," "outstanding"), are the most common type of rating scales in organizations, many have expressed dissatisfaction with these instruments (Landy & Farr, 1983). Behavioral rating scales, such as Behaviorally Anchored Rating Scales (BARS; Smith & Kendall, 1963), behavior checklists, and Behavior Observation Scales (Latham & Wexley, 1977), have become popular with organizations and researchers. Some evidence suggests that BARS are more acceptable to raters and ratees than graphic rating scales (Bernardin & Beatty, 1984), but overall the evidence suggests that they are not much better in terms of accuracy than other methods (Landy & Farr, 1980). It is our opinion that the type of instrument used by raters will not significantly influence accuracy and that the sources of rating "errors" occur earlier in the judgment process. By focusing on the method of appraisal, little was learned about *how* raters reached their judgments (DeNisi & Williams, 1988). As a result, research in I/O psychology now focuses on the process of performance appraisal.

A PROCESS MODEL OF PERFORMANCE APPRAISAL

The following model focuses on the cognitive, affective, and contextual factors influencing the rater's judgment of others' performance. It is a general model that is applicable to any setting that involves the evaluation of others. As such, it can be extended to a number of appraisal situations in school systems: ratings of school personnel, evaluation and assessment of students, and evaluations of interns and training programs.

Researchers studying performance appraisal have been concerned mainly with the factors influencing the accuracy of performance ratings (e.g., Borman, 1978; McIntyre, Smith, & Hassett, 1984). Evidence of halo and leniency have been used as indicators of inaccuracy, despite evidence that they are sometimes unrelated to accuracy (Murphy, Garcia, Kerkar, Martin, & Balzer,

1982). Recently, questions about the usefulness of the strict accuracy paradigm have been raised (Kavanagh, 1982), and investigators have expanded the scope of their research to include systems variables.

Accuracy is one component of the model presented next, but we also incorporated *employee acceptance* and *utility* of appraisals as outcome variables. Appraisal acceptance refers to the attitudes employees have regarding the validity of the organization's performance appraisal system, and whether or not they recognize it as indicative of actual performance. Ratings, even accurate ones, will be of limited value if employees do not accept them as valid or useful. Factors influencing employee acceptance of the appraisal system are perceived fairness and accuracy of appraisal, frequency of appraisal, credibility of the rater, presence of clear performance standards, and satisfaction with supervisor's performance (Kavanagh, Hedge, & DeBiasi, 1985; Landy, Barnes-Farrell, & Cleveland, 1980). Appraisal utility refers to the extent to which the performance appraisal system increases an organization's functioning.

Information Processing Stages

Cognitive models of the rater usually present a series of stages through which performance information is processed to produce a rating (DeNisi, Cafferty, & Meglino, 1984; Ilgen & Feldman, 1983; Landy & Farr, 1980). These stages are: information acquisition, encoding, storage in memory, retrieval from memory, and judgment. These stages are represented in the center box in Fig. 13.1. The rater is seen as a "cognitive filter" through which performance information must pass before a rating is produced (Landy & Farr, 1980). Each stage of the model in Fig. 13.1 presents cognitive obstacles to the accurate portrayal of ratee performance.

Information Acquisition. The manner in which raters acquire performance information will influence their final ratings. Raters must be able to identify and attend to relevant information, they must be accurate and efficient in observing behavior, and they must acquire adequate amounts of data to form valid representations of ratee performance. Murphy et al. (1982) found that overall rating accuracy was related to rater's accuracy in observing ratee behaviors. Raters who do not correctly identify relevant behaviors or draw incorrect inferences from behaviors cannot form valid representations of performance. Furthermore, Murphy et al. (1982) found that observational accuracy was not a generalized ability.

A series of studies by DeNisi and his colleagues (DeNisi, Cafferty, Williams, Blencoe, & Meglino, 1983; Williams, DeNisi, Blencoe, & Cafferty, 1985) examined raters' strategies for acquiring appraisal information in the presence

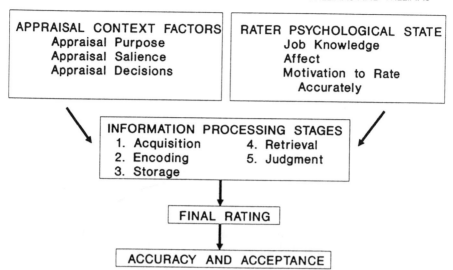

FIG. 13.1.   A social-cognitive model of the performance appraisal process.

and absence of situational constraints. When raters were unconstrained in their search (i.e., they were allowed to search for as much information as they wanted before rating workers), one search strategy was preferred. Raters observed one worker at a time, searching just once for information on how each performed the different tasks. In attribution theory terms (see Chapter 3 in this volume), this "person-blocked" strategy yields *distinctiveness* information (i.e., how individuals behave in different situations). However, when raters were constrained in their search by only allowing them a fraction of available information, a much different strategy was preferred. In this situation, most raters adopted a "maximizing" strategy. They observed the performance of one worker on one task and then switched to another worker performing a different task (DeNisi et al., 1983). Raters seemed to be trying to maximize information about the different tasks and workers. A more efficient strategy might have been to compare the workers' performances on one important task. Because the acquisition of performance information in organizations is typically constrained, this finding has important implications for appraisals conducted for different purposes. School administrators pressed for time may not gather enough information to make valid between- or within-ratee comparisons. Comparisons between teachers, for example, would be deficient because they were not observed performing the same tasks; differing levels of task difficulty or varying strengths of teachers may unduly influence the results of such comparisons. Within ratee comparisons would suffer because the rater was not able to observe the teacher performing all tasks.

Two other findings are important to note. First, raters rarely search for consistency information—how a worker performs the same task on different occasions (Williams et al., 1985). Instead, they are content to use a single specific performance to make generalizations about overall ability on that task, a variant of the base-rate fallacy common to person perception literature (Nisbett & Ross, 1980). Second, even when raters are unconstrained in their search, they choose to observe relatively little (less than 50%) of the available information (Williams et al., 1985). These findings suggest a general willingness on the part of raters to make judgments with partial data.

Encoding and Storage. The manner in which ratee performance is represented and stored in memory will also determine ratings. Social cognition research demonstrates that observers are active interpreters of behavior (Nisbett & Ross, 1980; Wyer & Srull, 1981). Observers use schemata, or knowledge structures, to make sense of new information they receive and assimilate it into memory (Wyer & Srull, 1981). The use of schemata, such as a performance schema relating hard work to successful performance, allows the observer to "go beyond the information given" (Nisbett & Ross, 1980, p. 17) and infer unobserved qualities (e.g., job success) from observed events (e.g., hard work). Self or "like-me" schemata are activated when observers use knowledge of how they perform(ed) a job or task to judge the performance of others on that job or task (Zalesny & Highhouse, in press). Principals, for example, may rate teachers by comparing observed teaching methods to those that they themselves use(d).

Ratings are also influenced by the way in which raters categorize and organize information in memory. A consistent finding has been the use of person categories to store information (Cafferty, DeNisi, & Williams, 1986; Feldman, 1981; Nathan & Lord, 1983). Observers tend to organize and combine bits of information about individuals into general categories reflecting overall behavior. The use of person categories or prototypes facilitates impression formation but obscures behavioral detail (DeNisi & Williams, 1988). As a result, raters rely extensively on global impressions for their ratings of others (Nathan & Lord, 1983). Relying on global impressions rather than behavioral detail masks true performance levels.

Retrieval and Judgment. Finally, the nature of recalled events will influence performance ratings. Recalled events are likely to diverge from observed events, in part, because of encoding and categorization tendencies. Also, raters are more likely to recall global impressions and affective summaries of ratee behavior than behavioral detail (DeNisi et al., 1984; Nathan & Lord, 1983). Recent research has found low correlations between a rater's recall of specific performance episodes and ratings (Murphy, Philbin, & Adams, 1989; Williams, Cafferty, & DeNisi, 1990), suggesting that raters base their ratings on global impressions of ratees rather than on behavioral detail.

When raters do rely on recalled information, events that are readily accessible in memory will have a disproportionate effect on ratings. Raters may use the availability heuristic (Tversky & Kahneman, 1973) and quickly assume that recalled behaviors are valid representations of overall ability. In many instances, however, easily accessible information is not a true reflection of observed behavior. Information consistent with global impressions is more easily recalled by raters than inconsistent information (DeNisi et al., 1984). Memories can also be reconstructed to fit with newly formed impressions or second-hand knowledge. This is likely to happen when raters have limited access to information about ratees. Administrators, for example, may rely on comments by teachers or parents for appraisals of school psychologists rather than actual data. Thus, school psychologists, as well as other workers affected by second-hand information, should make it their responsibility to educate those they interact with about their professional duties and goals.

Summary of Information-Processing Stages. The major findings regarding the processing of performance information for appraisals are presented in Table 13.1. As a whole, these findings demonstrate cognitive economy on the part of the rater and the "rush to judgment" (Ilgen & Feldman, 1983). There are obvious cognitive constraints on the rater's information processing capabilities (Nisbett & Ross, 1980); raters cannot attend to and process all possible performance information about ratees. Thus raters restrict the extent of their search for information and ignore certain types of information. They use effort-reducing heuristics to encode, categorize, and retrieve information. These tendencies reduce the cognitive load for the rater and facilitate the formation of general impressions. Global impressions rather than behavioral detail are primarily used to produce ratings.

These economical strategies may decrease accuracy because the representation of performance formed by raters is not likely to reflect actual performance. The ratee's acceptance of the appraisal is also likely to decrease. Acceptance of appraisal increases as the frequency of observation and evaluation increases (Landy, Barnes, & Murphy, 1978). If workers are aware that they have not been observed on multiple occasions performing all the tasks they are responsible for but are still evaluated on all tasks, they are not likely to accept the ratings as valid or informative. The emphasis on global evaluations also is likely to reduce acceptance of the appraisal system. Appraisals that are too general in nature will lose their informational or feedback value (Meyer et al., 1965). Global impressions do not lend themselves well to specific recommendations for the future.

Influence of Contextual Factors

Figure 13.1 also identifies several contextual factors that influence the information-processing tendencies outlined before. The purpose of appraisal affects both the type of information sought by raters (Williams et al., 1985)

TABLE 13.1
Summary of Findings on Information-Processing Stages

Information Acquisition

- Raters choose to observe limited amount of performance.
- Raters' search for information is not conducive to within- or between-ratee comparisons.
- Consistency information ignored.

Encoding and Storage in Memory

- Person categorization.
- Schematic processing.
- Abstraction of global impressions.

Information Retrieval and Judgment

- Impressions recalled more easily than behavioral detail.
- Reliance on cognitive heuristics, such as the availability heuristic.
- Ratings based on impressions.

and the way performance information is utilized in reaching appraisal decisions (Zedeck & Cascio, 1982). Different information is seen as important for different purposes. Information selected and encoded on the basis of an upcoming appraisal may not be relevant, or may not be stored in a manner conducive, to future appraisal decisions. Also, it is doubtful, given the limited search strategies demonstrated by raters, that enough information is initially collected to suit all potential purposes of appraisal.

Appraisal purpose has also been found to affect rating outcomes, with appraisals for administrative purposes displaying more leniency than appraisals for development or research purposes (DeCotiis & Petit, 1978). One reason for this difference may be that motivational factors cause raters to inflate their ratings. This explanation for rating distortion is examined further in the following section. Previous appraisal decisions also influence the processing of performance information. Previous ratings may act as schemata for future ratings: Rater may selectively attend to, encode, and recall information that confirms established impressions (Lingle & Ostrom, 1979; Wyer, Srull, & Gordon, 1984). Williams, DeNisi, Meglino, and Cafferty (1986) found that initial appraisal decisions influenced the categorization of information about ratees in memory as well as subsequent judgments.

The saliency of the appraisal task to raters during observation of ratee performance also affects ratings. Raters have many organizational responsibilities in addition to appraisal and thus may not be thinking of appraising performance when relevant information is encountered. Attention to and encoding of relevant appraisal information decreases when appraisal salience is low (Balzer, 1986; Murphy et al., 1989). Different types of information processing have been documented under different levels of appraisal saliency (Murphy et al., 1989; Williams et al., 1990). When salience is high, raters make "on-line" judgments of ratees (Hastie & Park, 1986), demonstrating person categorization process and independence of recall and ratings. When salience is low, however, raters use information recalled from memory for their ratings (i.e., memory-based judgments; Hastie & Park, 1986) but the quality of recalled information is low because relevant information was not initially attended to; hence ratings are of inferior quality. Williams et al. (1990) found ratings made under conditions of low salience to be restricted in range and lacking in differentiation.

Rater Psychological States

The psychological state of the rater will affect ratings. Figure 13.1 identifies the rater's knowledge of the ratee's job, the rater's affective or emotional state, and his or her motivation to rate accurately as psychological variables impinging on the appraisal process.

Job Knowledge. The extent to which the rater is familiar with the ratee's job influences both appraisal accuracy and the ratee's acceptance of the appraisal. Raters are more likely to rely on preexisting cognitive schemata when they lack knowledge about the job performed by the ratee (Cooper, 1981; Kozlowski, Kirsch, & Chao, 1986). Raters who do not understand the interrelatedness and relative importance of job dimensions are likely to assume that performance on one dimension is predictive of performance on another, or that certain job dimensions outweigh others. Such assumptions are seldom correct. Nonpsychologists often are responsible for evaluating school psychologists (Zins, Murphy, & Wess, 1989) and, to the extent that they lack detailed knowledge of the school psychologist's job and its relation to organizational effectiveness, ratings distortions such as halo are likely to be high.

The rater's knowledge of the ratee's job is apt to affect the ratee's acceptance of his or her ratings. Landy et al. (1978) found that the supervisor's knowledge of the ratee's job duties was positively related to ratees' acceptance of performance ratings. Raters lacking job knowledge are likely to be seen as lacking credibility, thus decreasing the perceived validity of their ratings.

Affect. Individuals responsible for appraisals often report feeling uncomfortable and anxious about having to rate others (Bernardin & Villanova, 1986; Cayer, DiMattia, & Wingrove, 1988). Recent studies of rater mood states during the appraisal process suggest that raters in positive moods recall more positive information about others, are more lenient, and display greater halo bias than raters in negative moods (Sinclair, 1988; Williams & Keating, 1987).

Williams and Keating (1987) found that raters in negative moods were poorer discriminators of overall performance than those in positive moods.

The rater's self-efficacy (i.e., the extent to which one perceives that he or she can make fair and accurate ratings) may moderate the affect-rating relationship. Alliger and Williams (in press; Williams, Alliger, & Pullium, 1989) found that for raters high in self-efficacy positive affect was related to higher levels of leniency and halo. For raters low in self-efficacy, negative affect was related to higher levels of leniency and halo. Also, raters low in self-efficacy responded more negatively to the appraisal setting than raters high in self-efficacy. These findings are significant because they indicate that raters who are uncomfortable and unsure of themselves in the rating task are likely to experience negative affect and produce ratings of inferior quality. Because uncomfortable and unsure raters may be quite prevalent (Cayer et al., 1988), steps should be taken to increase their feelings of competence.

Motivational Influences. An implicit assumption of the cognitive research just discussed is that, if raters could process performance information "correctly," accuracy would increase. At times, however, raters may be able to accurately access the performance of others but not be willing to assign an accurate rating. Supervisors have reported deliberately altering performance appraisals when they consider the consequences of ratings for the ratee and themselves (Longenecker, Sims, & Gioia, 1987).

The motivation to provide accurate evaluations of others may be low for a number of reasons. First, evidence suggests that raters dislike giving poor ratings to workers, especially when ratings are to be made available to ratees (Fisher, 1979; Sharon & Bartlett, 1969). To avoid possible confrontation or feelings of guilt, supervisors may inflate ratings of below-average performers. In addition, when performance appraisals are tied to benefits such as salary increases or promotions (e.g., merit or performance-based pay plans in schools; Wood & Baldwin, 1988), raters may not want to be seen as responsible for employees losing such benefits (DeCotiis & Petit, 1978; Longenecker et al., 1987). Often raters and ratees are involved in working relationships that must continue after appraisals are conducted (Bernardin & Villanova, 1986). Raters may feel pressure to provide ratings pleasing to ratees in order to maintain effective relationships. Alternatively, they may want to avoid documenting poor performance that would become part of an employee's permanent file (Longenecker et al., 1987). All these factors create pressure to inflate ratings, pressures that become stronger when interpersonal liking exists (Tsui & Barry, 1986).

Pressures to deflate ratings also exist in organizations. The executives in Longenecker et al.'s (1987) study reported that they assign lower than justified ratings in order to speed up the employee-termination process, encourage an employee to quit, or to punish rebellious workers. One can also imagine supervisors using low ratings to motivate workers or to provide a "kick-in-the-pants." Disliking the ratee may make these alternatives more attractive to raters.

The motivation to distort ratings may also be influenced by beliefs raters have about other raters in the organization and the utility of the organization's appraisal system. Research evidence suggests that rating distortions increase as raters' trust in others to provide accurate ratings decreases (Bernardin & Beatty, 1984). To the extent that one believes that others are providing inaccurate ratings, he or she is likely to distort the ratings of his or her own subordinates (Bernardin & Beatty, 1984). Recently, Schulman (1989) examined the relation between beliefs about the usefulness of the organization's appraisal system and performance ratings in a manufacturing firm. He found that perceived utility was negatively related to halo and leniency indices. Step-pay programs, where salary and raises are based on level of training and tenure rather than performance (Wood & Baldwin, 1988), may be linked with low perceptions of appraisal utility. Raters are not apt to perceive useful consequences of their ratings and thus not be motivated to provide accurate ratings.

In sum, the social and organizational context of performance appraisal influences the rater's motivation to provide accurate ratings. Table 13.2 summarizes the major findings in this area. Concern over relations with others or consequences for oneself, along with perceptions of how other raters approach the rating task, will sometimes eliminate accuracy as a goal for raters.

TABLE 13.2
Summary of Effects of Rater's Psychological State on Performance Ratings

Job Knowledge

- Unknowledgeable raters rely on pre-existing schemata more than knowledgeable raters.
- Ratings by unknowledgeable raters are less likely to be accepted by ratees.

Rater Affect

- Raters report feeling uncomfortable about rating others.
- Negative affect plus low self-efficacy results in range restriction.

Motivation to Inflate Ratings

- When perceived utility of ratings is low.
- When ratings are made known to ratees.
- When used for raises, promotions, etc.
- When rater and ratee must work together.
- When rater likes ratee.

Motivation to Deflate Ratings

- In order to speed up termination process.
- In order to punish workers.
- When rater dislikes ratee.

EXTENSIONS OF THE MODEL
TO SCHOOLS AND SCHOOL PSYCHOLOGISTS

The remainder of this chapter examines critical concerns in the design of performance appraisal systems in schools. We draw on the process model to offer suggestions on how to make school performance appraisal systems more constructive, relevant, and acceptable. Although the suggestions are appropriate for all school personnel, the evaluation of school psychologists is our main focus. This section should appeal to those concerned with appraisal of their own performance as well as to individuals responsible for supervising and evaluating interns and other personnel. As evidenced by the establishment of more rigorous training and credentialing standards (Curtis & Zins, 1989), performance appraisal is likely to be a continuing concern for school psychologists throughout their training and careers.

Criterion Issues: What Should Be Rated

Identifying performance criteria in school settings presents a formidable obstacle to effective appraisal. What is successful teaching, therapy, consultation, or assessment? Disagreement within a profession over job criteria is likely and disagreement is even more likely across professions. Studies report low levels of agreement in schools over important school psychologist activities (Hughes, 1979; Medway, 1977). School psychologists need to be involved in the establishment of criteria upon which they will be rated (Stratford, 1987). For example, Cobb and Stacey (1987) identified seven major functions for school psychologists: assessment, direct intervention for students, program development, program implementation, consultation and training, professional practice and development, and communication skills. School psychologists should work with administrators in determining competency and success criteria on these dimensions. Once the criteria of success have been established, attention can shift to data collection and judgment concerns (Kruger, 1987).

Process Issues: How Personnel Should Be Rated

The research reviewed earlier suggests that effective personnel evaluations occur when relevant information is accessible to raters who use appropriate rating schemata and are motivated to accurately rate workers, and ratees accept the appraisal system as fair. Applications of our model to the evaluation of school psychologists revolves around these themes.

Frequent and Structured Performance Observation. In order to accurately evaluate workers, supervisors must be able to observe or obtain performance information that is representative of the tasks performed or behaviors exhibited by them (Bernardin & Beatty, 1984). Supervision of school psychologists, however, appears to be restricted (Milofsky, 1989; Zins et al., 1989). Zins et al. (1989) found that less than 25% of school psychologists surveyed reported receiving any supervision. In addition, supervision was often provided by a nonschool psychologist (e.g., administrators with education degrees). Unfortunately, school psychology internship supervision suffers from similar problems (Alessi, Lascurettes-Alessi, & Leys, 1981). Work characteristics also limit the extent to which school psychologists can be observed by raters. Confidentiality issues often impede observations of counseling sessions or consultation with parents and teachers. Likewise, observation conducted during individual assessment raises concerns about how students may be influenced by the administrator's presence. As a result, direct observations of school psychologists are often confined to presentations or meetings where the behaviors displayed, although important, may not be critical determinants of job success.

Administrators and school psychologists should arrange for periodic observation of relevant job activities, with performance assessment and feedback as the intended goal. If opportunity for observation is severely limited, raters should observe psychologists perform more than once a few mutually agreed upon critical tasks.

Along with increased supervision time, observation training should be given to those responsible for rating school psychologists. Raters should be trained in tactics for gathering information. They should be encouraged to seek greater amounts of information, rather than jumping to conclusions, and to seek information that can disconfirm expectations (Ilgen & Feldman, 1983). Because nonpsychologists frequently act as raters of school psychologists, they may not feel qualified to provide ratings of psychologists or understand the nature of their work. Two types of rater training that may be useful for nonpsychologists are "frame-of-reference" training (Bernardin, 1979), which attempts to provide raters a standard performance schema for observing and rating workers, and "rater accuracy training" (Pulakos, 1984), which instructs raters on the multidimensional nature of the performance being observed and rated. If properly constructed, such training programs would provide supervisors with a proper schema for observing and evaluating school psychologists.

Use Multiple Data Collection Methods.   As mentioned earlier, the job of school psychologist is not one in which important tasks are readily observable. Thus, there is still a need to develop other methods of data collection. School psychologists should actively provide performance information to raters (Bennett, 1980; Fairchild, 1975; Sandoval & Lambert, 1977). Fairchild (1975) suggested that time elapsed from the beginning of a referral to its completion can be used as a measure of effectiveness. Other forms of diary keeping, such as logging time engaged in various tasks, may be appropriate in documenting one's contribution to the organization. These "production" data may be particularly useful when supplemented with judgmental information.

Accountability interviews (Fairchild, 1975) provide a method for eliciting information from school staff members. Principals are encouraged to meet with their faculty and others who have professional contact with the school psychologist to gather information about the psychologist's performance. Principals then share this information with the school psychologist. Alternatively, the school psychologist can be included in the initial meetings. One advantage of this method is that it provides raters and ratees with performance information from multiple sources. It also provides the opportunity for establishing goals for future performance. Subsequent interviews could assess goal attainment. Combining goal-setting with performance appraisal resembles "Management-by-Objectives" programs that are common methods of appraisal in organizations (Bretz & Milkovich, 1989; Szilagyi & Wallace, 1983). Humes (1975) has outlined such a goal-setting and evaluation program for school psychologists.

Caution is advised, however, in the use of accountability interviews. First, nonpsychologists are providing information about performance. They may lack a proper understanding of the nature of school psychologists' work (Hughes, 1979; Medway, 1977). They may also provide general rather than specific feedback. Second, motivational pressures are likely to be high. Ratees may inflate the significance of their activities and raters may be motivated to avoid confrontation. Thus, accountability interviews may suffer from the same problems as other forms of appraisal interviews (Meyer et al., 1965).

Zins (1985) suggested that school psychologists develop rating scales to distribute to consumers of psychological services. Specifically, these rating scales target areas where the school psychologist feels the need for professional development or areas that are of concern to administrators. Zins (1985), however, cautions against the use of global ratings in favor of observable behaviors. Whereas self-developed appraisals may be accurate, there may be some problems with others' acceptance of these ratings if there is lack of agreement over the role of the school psychologist and the behaviors to be rated. In addition, self-developed appraisal systems without input from other personnel within the school system may not be efficient in terms of increasing the functioning of the organization. These methods of appraisal gain credibility when incorporated into an organization-wide appraisal system, or when seen as originating with the administration rather than the school psychologist.

Work-sample tests or exercises provide another means of evaluating job skills. They also provide added opportunity to observe relevant skills and to appraise the psychologists' behavior (cf. Alessi et al., 1981). For instance, audiotapes and videotapes have been used to increase the opportunity to observe intern behaviors (Engin & Klein, 1975). The technology now exists to make use of interactive videotape simulations (Alliger, Serbell, & Vodas, 1989). A microcomputer can be used to present taped vignettes (e.g., consultation with teachers) stored on video discs to psychologists or trainees and record their responses on a videocamera. A variety of teacher responses can be stored on the video disc, cued by responses of the ratee. Organizations now use such simulations to train salesmen (Alliger et al., 1989); such techniques could easily yield between- and within-ratee information and reduce observation demands on supervisors.

   Table 13.3 summarizes the various alternative appraisal techniques available to school psychologists. Advantages and disadvantages of each method are presented. The method used should yield information related to areas targeted for professional development or areas that are of concern to organizations.

Establish an Environment Conducive to Rating.   A rating environment that circumvents cognitive and motivational barriers to accurate ratings facilitates effective appraisal in organizations. From a cognitive perspective, this would require situations to be such that the rater's "rush to judgment" is halted or slowed. Relatively simple techniques such as the careful review and recall of observed behaviors have been found to increase rating accuracy (Murphy

TABLE 13.3
Alternative Methods of Gathering Performance Appraisal Data
for School Psychologists

Method	Advantages	Disadvantages
Accountability Interview	1. Multiple feedback sources.	1. Lacks common frame of reference.
	2. Goal-setting used in conjunction with appraisal.	2. Motivational pressures are high.
	3. Rater-ratee-client involvement.	3. Tendency toward global evaluations.
Self-Generated Rating Scales	1. Target specific areas for professional development.	1. Acceptance by others may be low.
	2. High content validity.	
Interactive Simulations/Work Samples	1. Standardized observation.	1. Costly in terms of money and time.
	2. Variety of skills/activities can be observed.	2. Ratee reactance.
	3. Within and between ratee information.	
Diaries/Logs	1. Behavioral information.	1. Frequently contaminated.
	2. Effectiveness criteria.	2. Motivational pressures high.
	3. Compatible with goal setting programs.	

et al., 1989; Zalesny & Highhouse, 1989), especially when rating salience is low during initial observation of performance (Williams et al., 1990). Reflecting on observed performance will increase the behavioral basis of ratings, thereby limiting the influence of global impressions. Rating procedures and instructions should also encourage raters to test initial expectations by seeking disconfirming evidence (Ilgen & Feldman, 1983).

From a motivational perspective, school systems need to design performance appraisal systems that allay raters' fears or concerns about upsetting workers (and themselves) and disrupting harmonious work relations. Principals need the trust and support of teachers; school psychologists need the trust and support of students, teachers, administrators, and parents; teachers need support of each other, etc. Raters may be reluctant to damage working relationships by assigning average or subpar ratings to others, even if they accurately reflect that person's performance. School administrators may also wish to avoid aggrevating "us" versus "them" climates, or avoid confrontations with teacher and employee unions that may be caused by critically evaluating teachers or staff. To avoid these problems, schools should establish a climate of trust, where raters and ratees alike perceive that ratings are fair and accurate reflections of performance.

Our review suggests that organizations can increase perceptions of performance appraisal fairness by attending to due process or procedural justice issues. The fairness of the procedures used to determine ratings greatly influence overall acceptance of the appraisal system. Specific recommendations for increasing perceived fairness of appraisals include: soliciting input prior to evaluation and using it, allowing ratees the chance to rebut an evaluation, and increasing the rater's familiarity with the ratee's work (Greenberg, 1986).

Increase Participant Involvement. One way of increasing the amount and quality of information available to raters and establishing a conducive rating environment is to involve raters and ratees in the construction and implementation process and make them responsible for its use. Bretz and Milkovich (1989) surveyed Fortune 100 companies and found that in the vast majority of them managers did not participate in system design and were not held responsible for their ratings. Employees also were not involved in the development process and did not use appraisal feedback for developmental or advancement purposes. Commitment and trust in the appraisal system should be low in such cases. Organizations should make clear the responsibility of raters to provide ratees with accurate ratings and of ratees to use appraisal information for self-development. Ratee involvement will ensure that relevant job dimensions and criteria are used in performance appraisal; rater involvement will increase perceived utility of the system. Participation by both parties will broaden perspectives of how each other's jobs relate to overall organizational functioning and goals.

Encouraging self- and co-worker appraisal systems may be one way of encouraging employee development. Co-worker and self-appraisals were linked to positive work perceptions of school psychologists in a recent study (Williams, Williams, & Ryer, 1990). School psychologists in New York State were surveyed as to the frequency and types of feedback they receive on the job. Results demonstrated that, whereas feedback from administrators was infrequent and unrelated to job satisfaction, frequent positive self-appraisal and co-worker feedback were related to work self-efficacy as well as job satisfaction.

Performance Appraisal and Pay Systems

A final consideration is how a school's appraisal system relates to compensation plans. Earlier we alluded to the effects of compensation plans on raters' motivation to rate accurately. It was argued that step programs may reduce perceptions of rating utility, thus decreasing the incentive to rate accurately. With such programs, the focus of performance appraisals should shift from between-person comparisons to within-person comparisons, and raters and ratees should relate evaluation information to professional development.

Recently, performance-based pay systems in education have received increased attention from educators and politicians, leading to a re-examination of such programs by researchers (Wood & Baldwin, 1988). Merit pay systems base salary increments or bonuses on performance levels or contributions to the organization. Under such programs, the link between performance appraisals and outcomes is more obvious to all members of an organization, but raters still may not be motivated to rate accurately. Rating inflation is a concern when subjective evaluations are tied closely to monetary allocations (Bernardin & Villanova, 1986). There are other potential dysfunctional consequences of merit-pay systems for organizations. For example, competition among staff members may arise, eroding group morale and cooperation. To prevent such negative consequences, organizations have to link rewards closely to job performance in the eyes of its members. Both distributive justice (perceived fair allocation of rewards) and procedural justice (perceived fairness of the methods by which rewards are allocated) have to be established in order for merit-pay systems to work. This has severe implications for a school's performance appraisal system. If rewards are to be allocated based on subjective ratings of workers supplied by supervisors who rush to judgment in situations where the motivation to rate accurately is low, perceptions of procedural and distributive justice will be low.

There are labor issues to consider as well when implementing merit-pay systems. If merit pay or bonuses are considered part of wages, then they may have to be negotiated issues with teachers' unions (Wood & Baldwin, 1988), and thus the performance appraisal system becomes part of the negotiation process; that is, how performance ratings relate to wages will have to be identified and rating validity demonstrated. Present performance appraisal systems may not be up to that challenge. We urge caution in advocating merit-pay plans until effective performance appraisal systems are implemented and accepted by workers.

CONCLUSIONS

We have presented a model of the job performance appraisal process with the intention of stimulating school psychologists' interest and involvement in developing appraisal systems in schools. Cognitive, motivational, and contextual factors influencing rating accuracy and acceptance have been examined. Rating situations in organizations are cognitively and motivationally complex. The rater is an active, thinking, and feeling participant in the appraisal process. The development of sound appraisal systems within organizations and for professional purposes will require attention to the psychological aspects of appraisal. This is not an easy task, but effective appraisal systems will facilitate skill development among professionals and promote organizational efficiency.

REFERENCES

Alessi, G. J., Lascurettes-Allessi, K. J., & Leys, W. L. (1981). Internships in school psychology—supervision issues. *School Psychology Review, 10*, 461–469.

Alliger, G. M., Serbell, C., & Vodas, J. (1989). *Evaluation of a simulation to teach soft skills.* Paper presented at the 7th annual Computer-Based Training Conference, Nashville, TN.

Alliger, G. M., & Williams, K. J. (in press). Affective congruence and the employment interview. In *Advances in information processing* (Vol. 4). Greenwich, CT: JAI Press.

Balzer, W. K. (1986). Biases in the recording of performance-related information: The effects of initial impression and centrality of the appraisal task. *Organizational Behavior and Human Decision Processes, 37*, 329–347.

Bennett, R. E. (1980). Methods for evaluating the performance of school psychologists. *School Psychology Monograph, 4*, 45–59.

Bernardin, H. J. (1979). Rater training: A critique and reconceptualization. *Proceedings of Academy of Management*, 216–220.

Bernardin, H. J., & Beatty, R. W. (1984). *Performance appraisal: Assessing human behavior at work.* Boston: Kent.

Bernardin, H. J., & Villanova, P. (1986). Performance appraisal. In E. A. Locke (Ed.), *Generalizing from the laboratory to field settings* (pp. 43–62). Lexington, MA: Lexington.

Borman, W. (1974). The rating of individuals in organizations. *Organizational Behavior and Human Performance, 12*, 105–124.

Borman, W. (1978). Exploring the upper limits of reliability and validity in job performance ratings. *Journal of Applied Psychology, 63*, 135–144.

Bretz, R. D., Jr., & Milkovich, G. T. (1989). *Performance appraisal in large organizations: Practice and research implications* (Working paper #89-17). Center for Advanced Human Resource Studies, School of Industrial and Labor Relations, Cornell University, Ithaca, NY.

Cafferty, T. P., DeNisi, A. S., & Williams, K. J. (1986). Search and retrieval patterns for perfor-mance information: Effects on evaluations of multiple targets. *Journal of Personality and Social Psychology, 50,* 676–683.

Cayer, M., DiMattia, D. J., & Wingrove, J. (1988). Conquering evaluation fear. *Personnel Ad-ministrator, 33,* 97–107.

Cleveland, J. N., Murphy, K. R., & Williams, R. E. (1989). Multiple uses of performance appraisal: Prevalence and correlates. *Journal of Applied Psychology, 74,* 130–135.

Cobb, C. T., & Stacey, D. C. (1987, March). *Performance appraisal and accountability for school psychologists: Issues and procedures.* Paper presented at the Annual Meeting of the National Association of School Psychologists, New Orleans.

Cooper, W. H. (1981). Ubiquitous halo. *Psychological Bulletin, 90,* 218–244.

Curtis, M. J., & Zins, J. E., (1989). Trends in training and accreditation. *School Psychology Review, 18,* 182–202.

DeCotiis, T. A., & Petit, A. (1978). The performance appraisal process: A model and some testa-ble hypotheses. *Academy of Management Review, 21,* 635–646.

DeNisi, A. S., Cafferty, T. P., & Meglino, B. M. (1984). A cognitive model of the performance appraisal process: A model and research propositions. *Organizational Behavior and Human Performance, 33,* 360–396.

DeNisi, A. S., Cafferty, T. P., Williams, K. J., Blencoe, A. G., & Meglino, B. M. (1983). Rater infor-mation acquisition strategies: Two preliminary experiments. *Proceedings of the Academy of Management,* 169–172.

DeNisi, A. S., & Williams, K. J. (1988). Cognitive approaches to performance appraisal. In G. R. Ferris & K. M. Rowland (Eds.), *Research in personnel and human resources management* (Vol. 6, pp. 109–155). Greenwich, CT: JAI.

Engin, A. W., & Klein, I. R. (1975). The effectiveness of simulation technique as an integral part of a school psychology training program. *Journal of School Psychology, 13,* 171–183.

Fairchild, T. N. (1975). Accountability: Practical suggestions for school psychologists. *Journal of School Psychology, 13,* 149–159.

Feldman, J. M. (1981). Beyond attribution theory: Cognitive processes in performance appraisal. *Journal of Applied Psychology, 66,* 127–148.

Fisher, C. D. (1979). Transmission of positive and negative feedback to subordinates: A laborato-ry investigation. *Journal of Applied Psychology, 64,* 533–540.

Greenberg, J. (1986). Determinants of perceived fairness of performance evaluations. *Journal of Applied Psychology, 71,* 340–342.

Hastie, R., & Park, B. (1986). The relationship between memory and judgment depends on whether the judgment task is memory-based or on-line. *Psychological Review, 93,* 256–268.

Hughes, J. (1979). Consistency of administrators' and psychologists' actual and ideal perceptions of school psychologists' activities. *Psychology in the Schools, 16,* 234–239.

Humes, C. W., II (1974). School psychologist accountability via PBBS. *Journal of School Psychol-ogy, 12,* 40–45.

Ilgen, D. R., & Feldman, J. L. (1983). Performance appraisal: A process focus. In B. M. Staw & L. L. Cummings (Eds.), *Research in organizational behavior* (Vol. 5, pp. 141–197). Greenwich, CT: JAI Press.

Kavanagh, M. J. (1982). Evaluating performance. In K. Rowland & G. Ferris (Eds.), *Personnel management: New perspectives* (pp. 127–226). Boston: Allyn & Bacon.

Kavanagh, M. J., Hedge, J., & DeBiasi, G. (1985). *Clarification of some empirical issues in regard to employee acceptability of performance appraisal: Results from five samples.* Paper presented at the annual meeting of the Eastern Academy of Management, Albany, NY.

Kozlowksi, S. W. J., Kirsch, M. P., & Chao, G. T. (1986). Job knowledge, ratee familiarity, con-ceptual similarity and halo error: An exploration. *Journal of Applied Psychology, 71,* 45–49.

Kruger, L. J. (1987, March). *A functional approach to performance appraisal of school psychologists.* Paper presented at the annual meeting of the National Association of School Psychologists, New Orleans.

Landy, F. J. (1989). *Psychology of work behavior* (4th ed.). Pacific Grove, CA: Brooks/Cole.

Landy, F. J., Barnes-Farrell, J. R., & Cleveland, J. N. (1980). Perceived fairness and accuracy of performance evaluation: A follow-up. *Journal of Applied Psychology, 65,* 355–356.

Landy, F. J., Barnes, J. R., & Murphy, K. R. (1978). Correlates of perceived accuracy and fairness of performance evaluations. *Journal of Applied Psychology, 63,* 751–754.

Landy, F. J., & Farr, J. L. (1980). Performance rating. *Psychological Bulletin, 87,* 72–107.

Landy, F. J., & Farr, J. L. (1983). *The measurement of work performance: Methods, theory, and applications.* New York: Academic Press.

Latham, G., & Wexley, K. (1977). Behavioral observation scales for performance appraisal purposes. *Personnel Psychology, 30,* 255–268.

Lingle, J. H., & Ostrom, T. M. (1979). Retrieval selectivity in memory-based judgments. *Journal of Personality and Social Psychology, 37,* 180–194.

Longenecker, C. O., Sims, H. P., Jr., & Gioia, D. A. (1987). Behind the mask: The politics of employee appraisal. *Academy of Management Executive, 1,* 183–193.

Maher, C. A. (1979). Guidelines for planning and evaluating school psychology service delivery systems. *Journal of School Psychology, 17,* 203–212.

McIntyre, R. M., Smith, D. E., & Hassett, C. E. (1984). Accuracy of performance ratings as affected by rater training and perceived purpose of rating. *Journal of Applied Psychology, 69,* 147–156.

Medway, F. J. (1977). Teachers' knowledge of school psychologists' responsibilities. *Journal of School Psychology, 15,* 301–307.

Meyer, H. H., Kay, E., & French, J. (1965). Split roles in performance appraisal. *Harvard Business Review, 43,* 123–129.

Milofsky, C. (1989). *Tester and testing: The sociology of school psychology.* New Brunswick, NJ: Rutgers University Press.

Murphy, K. R., Garcia, M., Kerkar, S., Martin, C., & Balzer, W. K. (1982). Relationship between observational accuracy and accuracy in evaluating performance. *Journal of Applied Psychology, 67,* 320–325.

Murphy, K. R., Philbin, T. A., & Adams, S. A. (1989). Effect of purpose of observation on accuracy of immediate and delayed performance ratings. *Organizational Behavior and Human Decision Processes, 43,* 336–354.

Nathan, B. R., & Lord, R. G. (1983). Cognitive categorization and dimensional schemata: A process approach to the study of halo in performance rating. *Journal of Applied Psychology, 68,* 102–114.

National Association of School Psychologists (1984). *Standards for training and filed placement programs in school psychology.* Washington, DC: Author.

National Association of School Psychologists (1985, January). *Professional conduct manual.* Washington, DC: Author.

Nisbett, R., & Ross, L. (1980). *Human inference: Strategies and shortcomings of social judgment.* Englewood Cliffs, NJ: Prentice-Hall.

Pulakos, E. D. (1984). A comparison of rater training programs: Error training and accuracy training. *Journal of Applied Psychology, 69,* 581–588.

Sandoval, J., & Lambert, N. M. (1977). Instruments for evaluating school psychologists' functioning and service. *Psychology in the Schools, 14,* 172–179.

Schulman, D. (1989). *The effects of trust in the performance appraisal system of ratings.* Unpublished master's thesis, Rensselaer Polytechnic Institute, Troy, NY.

Sharon, A. T., & Bartlett, C. J. (1969). Effect of instructional conditions in producing leniency on two types of rating scales. *Personnel Psychology, 22,* 252–263.

Sinclair, R. C. (1988). Mood, categorization breadth, and performance appraisal: The effects of order of information acquisition and affective state on halo, accuracy, information retrieval, and evaluations. *Organizational Behavior and Human Decision Processes, 42*, 22–46.

Smith, P. C., & Kendall, L. M. (1963). Retranslation of expectations: An approach to the construction of ambiguous anchors for rating scales. *Journal of Applied Psychology, 47*, 149–155.

Stratford, R. (1987). Evaluating psychologists' performance: A procedural guide to appraisal. *Educational and Child Psychology, 4*, 74–81.

Szilagyi, A. D., Jr., & Wallace, M. J., Jr. (1983). *Organizational behavior and performance* (3rd ed.). Glenview, IL: Scott, Foresman.

Tsui, A. S., & Barry, B. (1986). Interpersonal affect and rating errors. *Academy of Management Journal, 29*, 586–599.

Tversky, A., & Kahneman, D. (1973). Availability: A heuristic for judging frequency and probability. *Cognitive Psychology, 5*, 207–232.

Williams, K. J., Alliger, G. M., & Pulliam, R. (1989). *Rater affect and performance ratings: Evidence for the moderating effects of rater perceptions.* Unpublished manuscript, University at Albany, Albany, NY.

Williams, K. J., Cafferty, T. P., & DeNisi, A. S. (1990). The effect of appraisal salience on recall and ratings. *Organizational Behavior and Human Decision Processes, 46*, 217–239.

Williams, K. J., DeNisi, A. S., Blencoe, A. G., & Cafferty, T. P. (1985). The role of appraisal purpose: Effects of purpose on information acquisition and utilization. *Organizational Behavior and Human Decision Processes, 35*, 314–329.

Williams, K. J., DeNisi, A. S., Meglino, B. M., & Cafferty, T. P. (1986). Initial decisions and subsequent performance evaluations. *Journal of Applied Psychology, 71*, 189–195.

Williams, K. J., & Keating, C. W. (1987). Affect and the processing of performance information. In G. H. Dobbins (Chair.), *Affect in Human Resource Management: Implications for appraisals, promotions, and sanctions.* Symposium presented at the annual meeting of the Society of Industrial and Organizational Psychology.

Williams, K. J., Williams, G. M., & Ryer, J. (1990). The relation between performance feedback and job attitudes among school psychologists. *School Psychology Review, 19*, 550–563.

Wood, R. C., & Baldwin, G. H. (1988). Legal challenges to merit pay programs. *Journal of Educational Finance, 14*, 135–155.

Wyer, R. S., & Srull, T. K. (1981). Category accessibility: Some theoretical and empirical issues concerning the processing of social stimulus information. In E. T. Higgins, C. P. Herman, & M. P. Zanna (Eds.), *Social cognition: The Ontario symposium* (pp. 161–197). Hillsdale, NJ: Lawrence Erlbaum Associates.

Wyer, R. S., Srull, T. K., & Gordon, S. (1984). The effects of predicting a person's behavior on subsequent trait judgments. *Journal of Experimental Social Psychology, 20*, 29–46.

Zalesny, M., & Highhouse, S. (in press). Accuracy in performance evaluation. *Organizational Behavior and Human Decision Processes.*

Zedeck, S., & Cascio, W. (1982). Performance appraisal decisions as a function of rater training and purpose of appraisal. *Journal of Applied Psychology, 67*, 752–758.

Zins, J. E., (1985). A scientific problem-solving approach to developing accountability procedures for school psychologists. *Professional Psychology: Research and Practice, 16*, 56–67.

Zins, J. E., Murphy, J. J., & Wess, B. P. (1989). Supervision in school psychology: Current practices and congruence with professional standards. *School Psychology Review, 18*, 56–63.

PART

III

APPLICATIONS TO CLINICAL AND SOCIAL PROBLEMS

This final section of the book provides some social psychological perspectives on a broad range of clinical and social problems that may be of concern to the school psychologist. The variety of topics and approaches represented are intended to suggest ways in which the social psychological perspective can enrich our understanding of many school-related problems. It should be noted that several social psychological concepts employed in earlier chapters emerge again in the different contexts represented by this section.

In chapter 14, Peterson takes an extended look at ways in which learned helplessness may play a key role in various school problems. In doing so, he raises a number of important issues for those interested in this literature. He identifies learned helplessness (as opposed to simple passivity) as consisting of: (1) maladaptive passivity stemming from (2) a history of uncontrollability and involving processes of (3) cognitive mediation. He also identifies two research traditions distinguished by a focus on how uncontrollability produces passivity versus a focus on individual differences in attributional explanations for negative outcomes. With respect to second tradition, there are three dimensions of explanatory style: (1) locus of causality (internal vs. external), (2) stability (stable vs. unstable), and (3) extent (global vs. specific). Peterson applies learned helplessness to classroom situations, particularly to underachievement, mental retardation, teacher burnout, and absenteeism and illness. He also discusses ways to combat learned helplessness, including environmental enrichment (making the classroom environment more responsive), attribution retraining, and parental intervention.

Chapter 15, by Johnson, Rose, and Russell, is a review of the literature on loneliness across the school years, highlighting some interesting findings and some directions for research. The authors raise two important points for those interested in this developing area: (1) Young children may not understand the concept of loneliness as distinct from aloneness the way older children and adults do; and (2) the circumstances that lead to feelings of loneliness—such as the people without whom we feel lonely—may change over the life-span. In their discussion of these issues, the authors indicate the importance of other distinctions in this literature, particularly Weiss' distinction between social and emotional isolation.

Chassin, Presson, Sherman, and Curran, in chapter 16, deal with some social psychological factors that can contribute to an understanding of adolescent substance abuse. The chapter raises several interesting issues. First, what is the goal of substance use prevention programs? Is it to prevent initial use or movement from experimentation to habitual use? Also it makes the distinction between "personal" and "social" effects of substance use, where personal effects use is more predictive of later problem use. Second, who is at risk? There may be different types of at-risk students. Third, what are the benefits and functions of use? This is most important because it highlights social psychological models of substance use that stress the various functions that use serves including: (1) self-verification, (2) self-enhancement, (3) self-handicapping, (4) self-awareness reduction, and (5) precocity and pseudomaturity assertion.

These issues are followed by an evaluation of various school-based intervention strategies, some traditional and some innovative. Among traditional strategies are traditional health education approaches, affective education, and provision of alternatives to substance use. All these have had limited success in part due to lack of specificity. Among innovative approaches based in part on social psychological theory are social influence approaches involving effective techniques for resisting peer influence, use of commitment strategies for decisions, and better development of persuasive communications, and social and personal skills training programs. The authors point out some difficulties evaluating these programs and review some current experimental programs. They conclude with some provocative comments on issues facing the school psychologist involved in the implementation of substance use prevention programs.

In chapter 17, Erchul examines some social psychological perspectives that may prove valuable in meeting the growing need for school psychologists to deal with families in handling school problems. The chapter focuses on issues of social power and interpersonal influence. The discussion of power is oriented around Olsen and Cromwell's (1975) domains of social power: power base, power process, and power outcomes. Power base is derived from the five bases of social power proposed by French and Raven (1959). Power process is discussed in terms of the Theory of Reasoned Action (as applied to getting people to follow through on recommendations), Social Exchange Theory (as applied to parents remaining in psychologist/parent relationship), Foot-in-the-Door and Door-in-the Face techniques (as applied to getting parents to comply with recommended actions), and the Theory of Schismogenesis (as applied to developing a mutually satisfying relationship between psychologist and parents). Power outcome is discussed in terms of enablement and empowerment of parents.

Chapter 18 is a review by Weyant of approaches derived from social psychology for achieving integration of culturally different and handicapped students into the dominant educational milieu. Cultural integration and mainstreaming of handicapped students comprise the two major divisions of the chapter.

Referring to racial and ethnic integration, Weyant points out the lack of strong results. Then he discusses Allport's contact hypothesis, specifying the conditions under which contact should reduce prejudice. The major cooperative learning techniques (student teams, the jigsaw classroom, group-investigation, and learning together) are described and evaluated, followed by description and evaluation of another technique involving contact in cooperative games.

Next, the chapter turns to mainstreaming problems and the use of techniques such as modified versions of cooperative learning and cooperative games techniques to meet the special problems of the handicapped student. A further set of treatments for the handicapped situation involves social skills training.

Taken as a whole, this section illustrates the potential for applying a variety of social psychological concepts—some old and some new—to a wide range of issues of concern to the school psychologist. Note, however, that whereas the emphasis in this section and indeed in the entire book has been on social psychological applications to school psychological problems, benefits flow both ways. In the application of social principles derived from theory and laboratory tests, the school psychologist can identify gaps and weaknesses in the original formulations and can suggest ways in which such formulations can be strengthened. Moreover, collaboration between social and school psychologists may well shed new light on old problems and suggest new areas for scientific advance.

14

LEARNED HELPLESSNESS AND SCHOOL PROBLEMS

Christopher Peterson
University of Michigan

In this chapter I discuss how the learned helplessness model, in both its original and reformulated versions, might apply to a variety of school problems: underachievement, mental retardation, burnout, absenteeism, and illness. Because learned helplessness can be prevented or undone, its potential applicability to common problems encountered in school is exciting. I close by sketching several strategies that might be used to combat learned helplessness in the classroom.

INTRODUCTION

Learned helplessness was described more than 20 years ago by animal learning psychologists (Overmier & Seligman, 1967; Seligman & Maier, 1967). These investigators immobilized a mongrel dog and exposed it to a series of electric shocks that it could neither avoid nor escape. Although the dog was not physically traumatized by these shocks, 24 hours later it showed a set of striking deficits.

Here are the details of this procedure. The dog was placed in a shuttlebox, in which the simple response of moving from one end to the other would terminate electric shock. A typical animal has no trouble learning to make the correct escape response in a shuttlebox, but the dog previously exposed to shocks simply sat there and acted helplessly. More exactly, three related difficulties were shown. First, the dog initiated few attempts to escape. Second, it showed few overt signs of emotionality while being shocked. Third, when it occasionally did make a successful escape response, it was not likely to follow it with another escape response on the next trial. It was as if the dog did not notice that its previous response had turned off the shock.

The deficits shown by the dog implicate impaired motivation, emotion, and cognition. Taken together, these difficulties have come to be known as the *learned helplessness phenomenon.* Learned helplessness reveals itself most obviously by passive behavior in situations where active responses would win reward or avoid punishment.

The researchers who originally described learned helplessness in animals proposed an explanation of the phenomenon that stresses the role played by expectations (Maier & Seligman, 1976). According to this explanation, the animal learns that it cannot control shock exposure; the shocks come and go regardless of its behavior. This learning of response–outcome independence is represented as a belief in helplessness that is then generalized to new situations where responses do affect outcomes and thus produce the observed deficits. This cognitive explanation is the core of the *learned helplessness model.*

It is important to emphasize that what is learned in learned helplessness is the expectation of response–outcome independence and not passive behavior per se. This confusion occurs with some frequency in the learned helplessness literature, as described by Peterson and Bossio (1989). The danger of course is that sometimes passivity is produced directly, by trauma or coercion. To regard passivity of this kind as learned helplessness is to miss its essence. Preventative or ameliorative interventions will be ineffective, perhaps even counterproductive.

Two Research Traditions

Shortly after learned helplessness was described in animals, researchers wondered if an analogous phenomenon could be demonstrated in people. This indeed proved to be the case: People exposed to uncontrollable events later showed motivational, emotional, and cognitive deficits akin to those produced in animals by exposure to uncontrollable events (e.g., Hiroto & Seligman, 1975). However, learned helplessness in people proved more complicated than in animals due to the greater cognitive capacities of human beings. Various findings accumulated that were difficult to accommodate within the framework of the original helplessness model. Many of these anomalous findings had to do with the boundary conditions of helplessness. Sometimes uncontrollable events led to widespread problems; sometimes difficulties were more circumscribed or altogether absent.

Theorists therefore modified the learned helplessness model as it applied to people to take into explicit account exactly how the helpless person interprets the original uncontrollable events (Abramson, Seligman, & Teasdale, 1978). This *reformulated helplessness model* specifically emphasizes people's causal attributions for uncontrollability. Depending on the nature of these attributions, different types of helplessness are expected.

Three dimensions of causal attributions are deemed important (see Chapter 3 in this volume). First, is the cause of uncontrollability internal ("it's me") or external? Internal attributions presumably lead to self-esteem loss following uncontrollable events. Second, is the cause stable ("it's going to last forever") or is it unstable? A stable cause for uncontrollability leads to chronic helplessness. Third, is the cause global ("it's going to undercut everything that I do") or specific? A global attribution is associated with pervasive deficits following uncontrollable events.

The reformulated model also hypothesizes that people show habitual tendencies to explain events in a consistent way. Someone who typically explains bad events with internal, stable, and global causes is more at risk for helplessness following uncontrollability than someone who favors external, unstable, and specific causes. This individual difference is termed one's *explanatory style*, and a great deal of research has been devoted to developing measures of explanatory style and assessing its relationship to failures of adaptation that involve passivity (Peterson & Seligman, 1984).

When we speak of learned helplessness in people, we thus refer to two different research traditions. The first stems from the original model and looks at how uncontrollable events produce passivity. The second tradition stems from the reformulated model and concerns itself with the relationship between explanatory style and passivity. These research traditions are not incompatible (Peterson, 1985). Indeed, they should be more integrated than they actually are. The reformulated helplessness model did not replace the original model. As just explained, it merely highlighted the mediating role played by one's causal attributions.

But two separate research traditions nonetheless developed, probably because wholly different methods and techniques are needed to investigate the role of situational factors on the one hand versus dispositional factors on the other (cf. Cronbach, 1957). When learned helplessness ideas are applied to different social problems, psychologists tend to draw on one research tradition or the other, and seldom on both simultaneously. Nonetheless, the learned helplessness model with its explicit concern with explanatory style is very much a diathesis-stress account of passivity. The learned helplessness model has rarely been tested in its entirety (Abramson, Metalsky, & Alloy, 1988).

For our purposes, the existence of these different research traditions has two important implications. The first is that most attempts by theorists and researchers to apply helplessness ideas to school problems have drawn only on one tradition or the other. Either uncontrollable events are stressed, or individual differences in explanatory style are emphasized. Although each set of influences bears a relationship to passivity, surely their joint effect deserves examination.

The second implication is that the enormous research literature concerned with learned helplessness in people is fragmented. In the best of all worlds, applied research stands firmly on the foundation of basic findings. But in the case of learned helplessness, practitioners necessarily find themselves straddling the basic work rather than standing upon it. This is not the insurmountable problem it might seem, because the different research traditions do converge in their support for the helplessness model. Documenting this convergence is one of my goals in this chapter.

However, in designing interventions based on the helplessness model, perhaps the school psychologist can go beyond the history sketched here. To address both the person and the person's environment is necessary. This embodies a "true" social psychological perspective as originally articulated by Kurt Lewin (1935, 1951). Such a perspective is the most important contribution that social psychologists have to make to the field of school psychology. Learned helplessness is simply one example of this approach.

Recognizing Learned Helplessness

How can one recognize learned helplessness? As the term is used, learned helplessness can be recognized by three criteria (Peterson, 1985).

First and most obviously is *maladaptive passivity*. Passivity is easy to recognize, but before one identifies passivity as a reflection of learned helplessness, one must ascertain that it is maladaptive. In other words, sometimes passivity can be instrumental, winning reward or avoiding punishment for the passive individual. This passivity may produce problems for the individual, to be sure, but it still is not what is meant by learned helplessness. We know that learned helplessness is present only when we can be sure that active responding would be better for the individual than holding still, metaphorically or literally.

Second is a *history of uncontrollability*. The learned helplessness model, in both versions, is an account of how helplessness develops. Critical in arguing that learned helplessness is present is knowing that uncontrollable events have preceded observed passivity. Physical or psychological trauma may produce an unresponsive individual, but if trauma is the critical factor rather than response–outcome independence, learned helplessness cannot be said to be present.

Third is *cognitive mediation* of observed deficits. Remember that the learned helplessness account of passivity is a cognitive theory. Expectations of response–outcome independence are assigned a causal role in producing helplessness. If an individual believes that responses indeed influence outcomes, then—whether or not this believe is accurate—learned helplessness cannot be said to be present.

Cognitive mediation is often difficult to demonstrate, because people's responses to point-blank questions about their perceptions of control do not always prove valid, for a variety of reasons. People may be defensive, or grandiose, or simply unable to report on beliefs that nonetheless dictate how they behave (Nisbett & Wilson, 1977). One research strategy is to ascertain someone's explanatory style for bad events; to the degree that the person invokes internal, stable, and global causes, an expectation of helplessness is plausibly inferred (Peterson & Seligman, 1984). This strategy admittedly is one step removed from actual expectations, but we have found it difficult to phrase questions for subjects about response–outcome independence so that they know what we mean.

If it seems that I am belaboring the meaning of learned helplessness, it is only because the term has apparently been difficult for many to grasp (Peterson & Bossio, 1989). The consequences of misidentifying passivity as learned helplessness can be dire. Only when all three criteria of learned helplessness are arguably present in an instance of passivity can we undertake theory-based interventions to prevent or undo the problem it poses.

LEARNED HELPLESSNESS IN THE CLASSROOM

If learned helplessness is to be found in the classroom, then what does it look like? Remember the three criteria. Any classroom phenomenon that involves passivity is the first place to search for learned helplessness. Students as well as teachers may act in a passive way, and by their very passivity they may not attract as much attention as their rambunctious counterparts. Once passivity is identified, we must ask if it is maladaptive. Here we must pose a frank question about our particular school environment. Do we punish, intentionally or unintentionally, students or teachers who make waves? If the answer is yes, perhaps the passivity we observe is simply the result of someone learning to sit still and shut up or else.

But suppose the school environment indeed is a responsive one and suppose the individuals within it are inappropriately passive. Then we must see if uncontrollable events plausibly preceded the observed passivity. Students and teachers live simultaneously in several settings, and uncontrollability in any of these may produce helplessness in another. Uncontrollability may befall someone at home or at school, or even in society as a whole.

Learned helplessness is very much a psychological phenomenon, but these ideas find a ready parallel in the sociological literature on alienation as produced by social institutions. In both cases, events are seen as independent of the person's actions; estrangement is represented in cognitive terms;

and passivity ensues. Indeed, research shows that some institutions more than others produce listlessness, apathy, and poor morale.

Thoreson and Eagleston (1983) observed that many schools pose tasks for children that they lack the resources to meet. They cite in particular the example of athletics. Schools do not emphasize jogging, swimming, or bicycling—activities that all students can do—but rather competitive sports like football, basketball, and baseball that can be mastered only by the physically elite. What can result from this emphasis is helplessness vis-a-vis physical fitness, which shows up later in life as a failure to exercise and otherwise engage in health-promoting activities.

A similar argument can be made for other academic programs that only few students can master, no matter how hard they try. This may produce a tendency to be helpless in the face of later frustration. Winefield and Fay (1982) conducted an experiment with students in a traditional high school versus those from a school with an "open" format (who had an enhanced sense of their own efficacy). Students from both schools were given problems to work, which either did or did not have solutions. Then they were all given a second set of problems, all of which could be solved.

The results should give us pause. If they had first worked at solvable problems, students from both schools did well on the second set of problems. But if they had first worked at unsolvable problems, students from the traditional school did not do well on the second set. They gave up. Students from the open school persisted, presumably because they were less susceptible to the effects of learned helplessness.

If we find that maladaptive passivity is preceded by experience with uncontrollable events, then we must look for the final criterion of learned helplessness: cognitive mediation. This can be shown by questioning students about their beliefs in control or causal attributions. If their answers vary systematically with observed deficits on the one hand and uncontrollable experiences on the other, we can assume that learned helplessness is present in the classroom.

Teachers as well as students may be inappropriately passive, and it is possible that learned helplessness is implicated in poor teaching, discipline problems, withdrawal, dissatisfaction, absenteeism, and turnover on the part of teachers (cf. Martinko & Gardner, 1982). Related research looking at work organizations, in general, suggests that individuals are most likely to perceive no relationship between their actions and outcomes when the organizations are run as highly centralized bureaucracies with formal rules (Aiken & Hage, 1966; Blauner, 1964). Particularly salient in underscoring one's helplessness is the sense that salaries and benefits are unrelated to one's performance (Kerr, 1975; Lawler, 1966). The implications for contemporary educational administration are obvious, and there are clear suggestions for how to design and run a school so that learned helplessness on the part of teachers is made less likely.

APPLICATION TO PARTICULAR SCHOOL PROBLEMS

So far I've discussed learned helplessness in the classroom in general terms. There is every reason to believe that learned helplessness can be found in at least some classrooms throughout the country. With the three criteria kept in mind, one can recognize instances of learned helplessness. In this section, I discuss particular school problems in light of these criteria. Can we conclude that learned helplessness is implicated?

Underachievement

I start with school underachievement, one of the most frequently examined topics in the entire learned helplessness literature. More so than many domains, school courses represent a situation where one's efforts often matter. Accordingly, learned helplessness induced elsewhere might be clearly evident in the classroom. Indeed, school as a whole is a good approximation to the laboratory where learned helplessness was first discovered.

Dweck (1975) was among the first researchers to look at academic achievement explicitly in learned helplessness terms. She characterized students as "helpless" versus "mastery-oriented" according to their responses to a questionnaire asking about the reasons for academic success and failure. Helpless children attribute failure to lack of ability (an internal, stable, and global cause). These children employ ineffective strategies when trying to solve problems, report negative feelings, expect to do poorly, and ruminate excessively about irrelevant matters (Diener & Dweck, 1978). Helpless children respond to failure by doing even worse when given subsequent opportunities; success just rolls off their back with no effect (Dweck & Reppucci, 1973). Mastery-oriented children show just the opposite characteristics. Dweck's findings suggest the relevance of learned helplessness to understanding school underachievement, because the problems of underachieving students cohere exactly as they do in the learned helplessness phenomenon.

Additional research by Butkowsky and Willows (1980) examined reading difficulties in light of the learned helplessness model. Regardless of whatever else may be going on when a student has trouble reading, these researchers argued that learned helplessness exacerbates the problem, as failure begets helplessness that begets further failure. They demonstrated that fifth-grade boys with reading problems expressed negative expectations concerning their future success at reading. These students also explained their failures with internal and stable causes, and they failed to persist at reading.

Studies also show a link between helplessness constructs and academic outcomes among college students (for a review, see Peterson, 1990). For instance, Peterson and Barrett (1987) had freshman students at the beginning of a school year complete a measure of explanatory style for bad academic events. This individual difference predicted grades during their first year at college. The more someone favored internal, stable, and global causes, the worse were his or her grades, regardless of his or her SAT scores. Further, students who explained bad events with internal, stable, and global causes did *not* visit an advisor as frequently as their more efficacious counterparts.

A study by Peterson, Colvin, and Lin (1989) extended these results. College students completed a measure of explanatory style at the beginning of a school term and then kept track of academic disappointments and failures in a weekly diary. When a bad event occurred in the classroom, they were asked to report what—if anything—they did to bolster their performance. Those students who explained bad events with internal, stable, and global causes were less likely to take active steps in the wake of bad events than were those who used external, unstable, and specific causes.

The research reviewed shows that school underachievement satisfies two criteria of learned helplessness: passivity and cognition. Does experience with uncontrollability precede these problems? Relevant here is an investigation of sixth graders by Kennelly and Mount (1985). They measured the degree to which students believed that teachers delivered rewards and punishments in a contingent fashion as well as whether or not they were seen by their teachers as helpless. Perceptions of noncontingency were correlated with helplessness. These two variables in turn predicted actual academic performance. Analogous findings have been reported by other investigators (Johnson, 1981; Kennelly & Kinley, 1975; Yates, Kennelly, & Cox, 1975). In all, learned helplessness provides a good explanation of school underachievement.

School underachievement in turn leads to other difficulties: low self-esteem, depression, and failure to pursue higher education. Perhaps the problem of school dropouts involves learned helplessness. Perhaps alcohol and substance abuse have their roots in problems originally brought about by learned helplessness (see Chassin et al., this volume).

Mental Retardation

Another classroom phenomenon that may involve learned helplessness is the passivity common among mentally retarded and learning-disabled individuals. Weisz (1979) showed that retarded individuals experience accumulated failure as they aged, more so than nonretarded individuals, by observing feedback given to individuals by teachers. Relative to nonretarded students, retarded students were given much more negative feedback, both relatively and absolutely. In the long run, this feedback undercuts the individual's sense of efficacy.

DeVellis (1977) similarly has argued that the passivity, submissiveness, and learning difficulties often seen among retarded individuals who are institutionalized is in part a product of the institution itself. Uncontrollability abounds. The staff may attend not to the needs of individuals but to matters of convenience. Institutionalized individuals may be unresponsive to each other, mutually exacerbating the helplessness that produced passivity in the first place. Finally, seizures and other negative physical conditions may be imposed on the person and further lead him or her to expect future response–outcome independence.

These experiences produce a susceptibility to helplessness, a finding confirmed in subsequent research by Raber and Weisz (1981), who found that retarded students were increasingly disrupted by failure as they got older. This interaction is important in arguing that learned helplessness is present, because it shows that as experience with uncontrollability accumulates, so too does the propensity to be helpless in the face of failure.

Teacher Burnout

Burnout is the emotional and physical exhaustion sometimes befalling those who provide services to other people. Burnout appears to be determined chiefly by direct contact of an intense nature, when immediate needs exceed the resources to meet them. Teachers are at obvious risk for burnout. The symptoms of burnout overlap considerably with those of depression, except that in most cases, burnout is work related. In a sense, burnout is an 8-hour per day depression, and its context-specific nature suggests that learned helplessness might indeed be operating.

Greer and Wethered (1984) concurred with this suggestion, and they survey studies of burnout that implicate all three criteria of learned helplessness. Investigations converge to show that all three criteria for learned helplessness are present in cases of burnout. First, burnout involves maladaptive passivity. Those experiencing work-related exhaustion are rigid and do not seek solutions to their problems. Second, burnout is preceded by uncontrollable events, particularly lack of progress on the part of those one is trying to help—students, patients, or clients (Sarata, 1974). Third, burnout is accompanied by cognitions of helplessness (Cherniss, 1980). Teacher burnout therefore is an excellent example of learned helplessness.

Absenteeism and Illness

One of the most recent applications of learned helplessness ideas is to physical illness. Helplessness appears related to poor health (Peterson & Seligman, 1987), so student or teacher absenteeism from school due to illness may be yet another instance of learned helplessness. Needless to say, absenteeism can compound the other problems already discussed in this section.

This line of work results from a convergence between research with animals and research with human beings. Studies with animals show that uncontrollable events but not controllable ones suppress the immune system and render an animal less capable of fighting off disease (Laudenslager et al., 1983). Similar results have been found with people (for a review, see Peterson & Bossio, 1991).

Different studies show that explanatory style is a risk factor for illness. Peterson (1988) measured the explanatory style of college students at one point in time. Students who habitually explained bad events with internal, stable, and global causes experienced more days of illness in the following month and made more doctor visits in the following year than did students who favored external, unstable, and specific causes.

In a 35-year longitudinal study of 99 men, Peterson, Seligman, and Vaillant (1988) replicated these findings. Subjects were participants in the well-known Harvard Study of Adult Development (Vaillant, 1977). Explanatory style was assessed by a content analysis procedure from open-ended questionnaires completed when subjects were in their middle twenties. Thirty-five years later, the overall health status of these same subjects was ascertained by physician examinations buttressed with objective medical tests. The more pessimistic an individual as a young adult, the less healthy he was decades later. These results remained even when initial health status was held constant statistically.

As intriguing as these correlations between explanatory style and health may be, they provide no hint at the mechanism that links one's way of explaining bad events with physical well-being. Mundane behavior may be a pathway between explanatory style and illness. In particular, passive behavior in the realm of health promotion can result from a fatalistic explanatory style, eventually taking a toll on health.

Three studies support this contention. Peterson (1988) found that students who explained bad events with internal, stable, and global causes tended not to engage in behaviors like eating sensibly, exercising, sleeping at least 8 hours a night, and refraining from excessive drinking. Peterson and Lin (1987) found that fatalistic individuals who fell ill were less likely to take active steps in order to feel better. Finally, Lin and Peterson (1990) clarified their previous study by showing that the inactivity of individuals when they fell ill was associated with an inability to believe that they could cope actively with the demands of illness.

COMBATTING LEARNED HELPLESSNESS IN THE CLASSROOM

Granted that learned helplessness is implicated to varying degrees in a spectrum of classroom problems, involving both students and teachers, what can be done? As stressed throughout this chapter, the practical benefit of correctly identifying manifestations of learned helplessness is the ability to use what is already known about how to combat helplessness. Because learned helplessness is a cognitive phenomenon, ~~the target for intervention should be the individual's beliefs concerning response–outcome independence~~. These can be bolstered before people experience uncontrollability, which should confer immunity in the face of bad events (cf. Seligman & Maier, 1967). Or they can be changed after people have experienced uncontrollability and developed helplessness, which should reverse the passivity displayed (cf. Seligman, Maier, & Geer, 1968). Needless to say, prevention is a more efficient strategy than remediation. Regardless, the same kinds of specific techniques should prove useful in either case.

Environmental Enrichment

The best way to combat helplessness is to eradicate the situational factors that produce it. Environments must be enriched, and this means two things. ~~First, there must be adequate rewards available in a setting. Second, these rewards must be contingent on what a person does~~. An enriched environment is not simply lavish but additionally responsive. There must be a clear connection between what one does and what ensues.

There are important qualifications here, particularly as this recommendation might be put into effect within a school setting. An enriched environment is not limited to a school's physical plant and material goods. High-tech doodads are neither necessary nor sufficient for an enriched school environment. Indeed, as social psychologists regard the environment, the most important part of it is other people. ~~Students and teachers must be responsive to each other, and it is praise rather than material goods that should be present in abundance~~. Helpless people are not responsive to the world, so of course they are not responsive to each other. Helplessness and passivity may be contagious, just as depression and demoralization can be (cf. Seligman et al., 1984).

A responsive world is not a permissive one. The benefits of making rewards available all vanish if these are handed out indiscriminately. Rewards must follow what a person does, and so too must punishment. The rules that govern outcomes in school must be clear, fair, and consistent. It is difficult for a teacher to be fair in every detail, but this is the best way to combat learned helplessness in students.

Finally, if an enriched environment is created around individuals who are already helpless, this may be insufficient to undo their helplessness, simply because part of their problem entails not noticing that the prevailing conditions have changed. What must be done in these cases is repeatedly to call the individual's attention to the changes and then encourage him or her to test the reality. The helpless individual should not be told to change her thoughts but to ~~test new beliefs against the evidence of the world~~. The practitioner who arranges such tests had better be sure what the results of such an "experiment" will show, of course, because an experience like this can backfire easily and thereby strengthen helplessness.

Several years ago I worked in conjunction with a program in a junior high school that attempted to bolster the sense of efficacy among students in the "middle" of the class ranks. In other words, these children were neither exceptionally good nor exceptionally problematic. Mainly they were passive, at a young age merely going through the emotions at school, creating no waves and reaching no heights.

The school system devised a program for these students that enriched their school environment in just the way I have sketched. The major innovation was to have the different classroom teachers of the students meet together daily, coordinating their lesson plans as well as team-teaching various classes. The goal was to make the different parts of the curriculum cohere and to provide a series of integrated challenges for each individual student. For example, if one student showed a flair for numbers in math class, then this information would be passed on to the social studies teacher, who would ask the student to prepare a report stressing statistics.

I evaluated whether a student's sense of perceived control increased. I administered measures of explanatory style to participants before and after the year-long program, as well as to a comparison group of students. I found that the program did encourage students to explain events more optimistically (Peterson, 1990). Whether this change led to long-term benefits is still under investigation.

Attribution Retraining

Another way to combat learned helplessness in the classroom is to change the way that students and teachers explain bad events. If someone who usually employs internal, stable, and global causes to account for the occurrence of bad events can be induced instead to use external, unstable, and specific causes, then the prevalence of learned helplessness should be decreased— even if the objective environment has not been changed at all.

Critical in implementing this recommendation is the realization that many of the causal explanations that people offer are not appropriately judged as correct or incorrect. To be sure, there are some events that have true causes that can readily be identified. One should not tell someone to fly in the face of reality and change these causal beliefs. But there are also many events that are too singular and/or too complexly determined to say with certainty exactly why they occurred. Why did a student spell a given word wrong on a spelling test? Why did someone's parents fight the day before? Why did one teacher get a large raise and a second teacher none at all? ~~When causal~~

ambiguity exists, someone should fill it with an optimistic explanation. There is everything to gain by doing so, namely the avoidance of all the difficulties that can follow in the wake of fatalistic explanations.

How can someone's attributions be changed? It is not enough just to tell a person to think differently. Explanatory style cannot be altered as readily as a mistaken telephone number (Peterson, 1982). However, cognitive therapy for depression is known to be an effective way to change entrenched beliefs, including explanatory style (cf. Seligman, 1981; Seligman et al., 1988). The general procedure can easily be adapted to a classroom setting (Beck, Rush, Shaw, & Emery, 1979):

- Instruct the individual about the relationship between thoughts on the one hand and motivation, emotion, and behavior on the other.
- Introduce the notion of explanatory style and the idea that it works automatically.
- Train the individual to interrupt the automatic process of offering pessimistic explanations for bad events as they occur.
- Show the individual how to test an explanation against the facts of the matter if possible.
- If not possible, tell the person to substitute a more upbeat interpretation of what is going on.

Beck et al. call cognitive therapy a process of collaborative empiricism, meaning that the therapist and client work together as if they were a scientific team: testing negative thoughts against evidence. Attribution training in the classroom should be approached in the same collaborative spirit, with the teacher and student working together to devise explanations of performance and test these against available evidence.

One important implication of attribution retraining is that teachers and students have to attend not only to "correct" and "incorrect" answers on assignments and tests but also to *why* some answers are better than others and to *how* students can produce these better answers. Attention to the process of achievement should bolster a student's sense of efficacy as well as his or her self-conscious use of strategies.

Cecil and Medway (1986) surveyed the literature on attribution retraining among schoolchildren, and they offered concrete advice about how best to proceed with these interventions. The typical intervention encourages students to explain failure in terms of lack of effort. As already shown in this chapter, children who tend not to make effort attributions (which are unstable and specific) show more school problems than children who do offer such attributions for failure. When students start to explain failure in terms of their own lack of effort, then their school performance indeed often improves.

For instance, Dweck (1975) has shown that when students who habitually attribute failure to a lack of ability are taught instead to attribute failure to a lack of effort, they end up responding more vigorously to academic set-backs and disappointments. Other interventions showing that attributional retraining is effective against school failure have been discussed by Brustein (1978), Sowa and Burks (1983), and Wilson and Linville (1982, 1985).

In undertaking attribution retraining, we must be alert to the possibility that the changes thereby induced can be fragile (Cecil & Medway, 1986). One obvious pitfall occurs when effort attributions prove untenable, either because of the school environment or the child's actual abilities. Needless to say, the teacher who encourages effort attributions must take reality into account. The teacher must be sure that a particular child urged to explain failure as due to insufficient effort has *not* been making an effort. Otherwise, attribution retraining can backfire, undercutting even further the underachieving student.

Attribution retraining is most likely to yield long-term benefits when the classroom teacher incorporates it into his or her everyday instructional reper-toire (Cecil & Medway, 1986). Feedback should be accompanied by "help-ful" attributions, explicit or implicit. Criticism should involve circumscribed explanations ("you didn't spend enough time on that math problem"); praise should entail highly general attributions ("you are a very conscientious in-dividual"). Students should be reinforced for making appropriate attributions and challenged when they offer explanations likely to induce helplessness.

Parental Intervention

It is a truism to urge that the parents of students should be involved in their education, but a recent study by Vanden Belt and Peterson (in press) gave a specific rationale in learned helplessness terms for this recommendation. We were interested in exploring the contribution of parental beliefs to the failure of some students to work up to their potential in the classroom. In particular, we wondered if explanatory style of the parents would relate to poor performance and academic adjustment by their children.

Approximately 100 grade school children and their parents participated in the study. Parents completed a measure of explanatory style asking them how they would explain various bad events that might befall their child. The teachers of these children then rated their classroom performance, relative to their apparent potential, along a variety of dimensions. Results were straightforward and striking. Those parents who explained bad events involv-ing their children with internal, stable, and global causes had children who consistently failed to live up to their potential.

One may argue that the direction of causality actually might run in the opposite direction, from classroom performance to parental explanations. However, this is not a sound good argument. First, studies show that explanatory style is a stable characteristic of an individual. Without intervention, explanatory style can persist in the same form for decades (e.g., Burns & Seligman, 1988). Second, by design, we included in our sample of students a number of students with physical and mental handicaps. If "reality" in the form of actual student performance dictated the way parents explained events involving their children, surely the parents of handicapped students would view the world differently than parents of nondisabled students. However, the pattern of results was exactly the same for both groups. Parental explanatory style predicted classroom performance to the same degree. Presumably these beliefs are transmitted to the children, who live up (or down) to them.

The practical implication of Vanden Belt and Peterson's (in press) results is the suggestion of yet one more way to combat learned helplessness in the classroom: parental intervention. A goal of parent–teacher conferences and similar activities in which the school system comes into contact with the home should be to legitimize more optimistic explanations by parents, particularly among those parents whose children are not working up to their potential. Parents want to view their children in the best possible light. Some may simply not know how to do so, and here is a task with which the school can help them. Workshops or lectures on the actual determinants of child behavior, the malleability of school skills, and the importance of optimism can be undertaken with the hope that they will decrease learned helplessness in the classroom.

CONCLUSION

Learned helplessness entails maladaptive passivity. It is preceded by uncontrollable events and mediated by the expectation that responses and outcomes are unrelated. Although one would not want to attribute all the ills found in the classroom to learned helplessness, certainly this phenomenon plays a role in some of the striking failures of adaptation that can be observed in the school setting.

Learned helplessness is a psychological phenomenon, and there is always a danger when explaining school problems in psychological terms that one will be heard as "blaming the victim" for his or her difficulties. A careful reading of this chapter reveals that helpless students and teachers are not to blame in any sense of the term. Learned helplessness is a product of particular social environments. Anyone placed in these situations would eventually act in a helpless way. If one wishes to point a finger of blame, turn it away from the victims of helplessness. But a better use of one's energy is to devise solutions that involve changing how people think and act, particularly in relationship to one another.

REFERENCES

Abramson, L. Y., Metalsky, G. I., & Alloy, L. B. (1988). The hopelessness theory of depression: Does the research test the theory? In L. Y. Abramson (Ed.), *Social cognition and clinical psychology* (pp. 33–65). New York: Guilford.

Abramson, L. Y., Seligman, M. E. P., & Teasdale, J. D. (1978). Learned helplessness in humans: Critique and reformulation. *Journal of Abnormal Psychology, 87,* 49–74.

Aiken, M., & Hage, J. (1966). Organizational alienation: A comparative analysis. *American Sociological Review, 31,* 497–507.

Beck, A. T., Rush, A. J., Shaw, B. F., & Emery, G. (1979). *Cognitive therapy of depression.* New York: Guilford.

Blauner, R. (1964). *Alienation and freedom: The factory worker and his industry.* Chicago: University of Chicago Press.

Brustein, S. C. (1978). Learned helplessness. *Journal of Instructional Psychology, 5,* 6–10.

Burns, M. O., & Seligman, M. E. P. (1989). Explanatory style across the life span: Evidence for stability over 52 years. *Journal of Personality and Social Psychology, 56,* 471–477.

Butkowsky, I. S., & Willows, D. M. (1980). Cognitive-motivational characteristics of children varying in reading ability: Evidence for learned helplessness in poor readers. *Journal of Educational Psychology, 72,* 408–422.

Cecil, M. A., & Medway, F. J. (1986). Attribution retraining with low-achieving and learned helpless children. *Techniques: A Journal for Remedial Education and Counseling, 2,* 173–181.

Cherniss, C. (1980). *Staff burnout: Job stress in the human services.* Beverly Hills: Sage.

Cronbach, L. J. (1957). The two disciplines of scientific psychology. *American Psychologist, 12,* 671–684.

DeVellis, R. F. (1977). Learned helplessness in institutions. *Mental Retardation, 15,* 10–13.

Diener, C. I., & Dweck, C. S. (1978). An analysis of learned helplessness: Continuous changes in performance strategy and achievement cognitions following failure. *Journal of Personality and Social Psychology, 36,* 451–462.

Dweck, C. S. (1975). The role of expectations and attributions in the alleviation of learned helplessness. *Journal of Personality and Social Psychology, 31,* 674–685.

Dweck, C. S., & Reppucci, N. D. (1973). Learned helplessness and reinforcement responsibility in children. *Journal of Personality and Social Psychology, 25,* 109–116.

Greer, J. G., & Wethered, C. E. (1984). Learned helplessness: A piece of the burnout puzzle. *Exceptional Children, 50,* 524–530.

Hiroto, D. S., & Seligman, M. E. P. (1975). Generality of learned helplessness in man. *Journal of Personality and Social Psychology, 31,* 311–327.

Johnson, D. S. (1981). Naturally acquired learned helplessness: The relationship of school failure to achievement behavior, attributions, and self-concept. *Journal of Education Psychology, 73,* 174–180.

Kennelly, K. J., & Kinley, S. (1975). Perceived contingency of teacher-administered reinforcements and academic performance of boys. *Psychology in the Schools, 12,* 449–453.

Kennelly, K. J., & Mount, S. A. (1985). Perceived contingency of reinforcements, helplessness, locus of control, and academic performance. *Psychology in the Schools, 22,* 465–469.

Kerr, S. (1975). On the folly of rewarding A, while hoping for B. *Academy of Management Journal, 18,* 769–783.

Laudenslager, M. L., Ryan, S. M., Drugan, R. C., Hyson, R. L., & Maier, S. F. (1983). Coping and immunosuppression: Inescapable but not escapable shock suppresses lymphocyte proliferation. *Science, 221,* 568–570.

Lawler, E. E. (1966). The mythology of management compensation. *California Management Review, 9,* 11–22.

Lewin, K. (1935). *A dynamic theory of personality.* New York: McGraw-Hill.

Lewin, K. (1951). *Field theory in social science: Selected theoretical papers*. New York: Harper.

Lin, E. H., & Peterson, C. (1990). Pessimistic explanatory style and response to illness. *Behaviour Research and Therapy, 28*, 243–248.

Maier, S. F., & Seligman, M. E. P. (1976). Learned helplessness: Theory and evidence. *Journal of Experimental Psychology, 105*, 3–46.

Martinko, M. J., & Gardner, W. L. (1982). Learned helplessness: An alternative explanation for performance deficits? *Academy of Management Review, 7*, 195–204.

Nisbett, R., & Wilson, T. D. (1977). Telling more than we can know: Verbal reports on mental processes. *Psychological Review, 84*, 231–259.

Overmier, J. B., & Seligman, M. E. P. (1967). Effects of inescapable shock upon subsequent escape and avoidance learning. *Journal of Comparative and Physiological Psychology, 63*, 23–33.

Peterson, C. (1982). Learned helplessness and attributional interventions in depression. In C. Antaki & C. Brewin (Eds.), *Attributions and psychological change: A guide to the use of attribution theory in the clinic and classroom* (pp. 97–115). London: Academic Press.

Peterson, C. (1985). Learned helplessness: Fundamental issues in theory and research. *Journal of Social and Clinical Psychology, 3*, 248–254.

Peterson, C. (1988). Explanatory style as a risk factor for illness. *Cognitive Therapy and Research, 12*, 117–130.

Peterson, C. (1990). Explanatory style in the classroom and on the playing field. In S. Graham & V. S. Folkes (Eds.), *Attribution theory: Applications to achievement, mental health, and interpersonal conflict* (pp. 53–75). Hillsdale, NJ: Lawrence Erlbaum Associates.

Peterson, C., & Barrett, L. C. (1987). Explanatory style and academic performance among university freshmen. *Journal of Personality and Social Psychology, 53*, 603–607.

Peterson, C., & Bossio, L. M. (1989). Learned helplessness. In R. C. Curtis (Ed.), *Self-defeating behaviors* (pp. 235–257). New York: Plenum Press.

Peterson, C., & Bossio, L. M. (1991). *Health and optimism*. New York: Free Press.

Peterson, C., Colvin, D., & Lin, E. H. (1989). *Explanatory style and helplessness*. Unpublished manuscript, University of Michigan.

Peterson, C., & Lin, E. H. (1987). [*Explanatory style and response to illness: Study One*]. Unpublished data, University of Michigan.

Peterson, C., & Seligman, M. E. P. (1984). Causal explanations as a risk factor for depression: Theory and evidence. *Psychological Review, 91*, 347–374.

Peterson, C., & Seligman, M. E. P. (1987). Explanatory style and illness. *Journal of Personality, 55*, 237–265.

Peterson, C., Seligman, M. E. P., & Vaillant, G. E. (1988). Pessimistic explanatory style is a risk factor for physical illness: A thirty-five year longitudinal study. *Journal of Personality and Social Psychology, 55*, 23–27.

Raber, S. M., & Weisz, J. R. (1981). Teacher feedback to mentally retarded and nonretarded children. *American Journal of Mental Deficiency, 86*, 148–156.

Sarata, B. P. V. (1974). Employee satisfactions in agencies serving retarded persons. *American Journal of Mental Deficiency, 79*, 434–442.

Seligman, M. E. P. (1981). A learned helplessness point of view. In L. P. Rehm (Ed.), *Behavior therapy for depression: Present status and future directions* (pp. 123–142). New York: Academic Press.

Seligman, M. E. P., Castellon, C., Cacciola, J., Schulman, P., Luborsky, L., Ollove, M., & Downing, R. (1988). Explanatory style change during cognitive therapy for unipolar depression. *Journal of Abnormal Psychology, 97*, 13–18.

Seligman, M. E. P., & Maier, S. F. (1967). Failure to escape traumatic shock. *Journal of Experimental Psychology, 74*, 1–9.

Seligman, M. E. P., Maier, S. F., & Geer, J. (1968). The alleviation of learned helplessness in the dog. *Journal of Abnormal Psychology, 73*, 256–262.

Seligman, M. E. P., Peterson, C., Kaslow, N. J., Tanenbaum, R. L., Alloy, L. B., & Abramson, L. Y. (1984). Attributional style and depressive symptoms among children. *Journal of Abnormal Psychology, 93,* 235–238.

Sowa, C. J., & Burks, H. M. (1983). Comparison of cognitive restructuring and contingency-based instructional models for alleviation of learned helplessness. *Journal of Instructional Psychology, 10,* 186–191.

Thoreson, C. E., & Eagleston, J. R. (1983). Chronic stress in children and adolescents. *Theory into Practice, 22,* 48–56.

Vaillant, G. E. (1977). *Adaptation to life.* Boston: Little, Brown.

Vanden Belt, A., & Peterson, C. (in press). Parental explanatory style and its relationship to the classroom performance of disabled and non-disabled children. *Cognitive Therapy and Research.*

Weisz, J. R. (1979). Perceived control and learned helplessness among retarded and nonretarded children: A developmental analysis. *Developmental Psychology, 15,* 311–319.

Wilson, T. D., & Linville, P. W. (1982). Improving the academic performance of college freshmen: Attribution therapy revisited. *Journal of Personality and Social Psychology, 42,* 367–376.

Wilson, T. D., & Linville, P. W. (1985). Improving the performance of college freshmen with attributional techniques. *Journal of Personality and Social Psychology, 49,* 367–376.

Winefield, A. H. & Fay, P. M. (1982). Effects of an institutional environment on responses to uncontrollable outcomes. *Motivation and Emotion, 6,* 103–112.

Yates, R., Kennelly, K., & Cox, S. H. (1975). Perceived contingency of parental reinforcements, parent–child relations, and locus of control. *Psychological Reports, 36,* 139–146.

15

LONELINESS AND INTERPERSONAL RELATIONSHIPS ACROSS THE SCHOOL YEARS

Ruth Ann Johnson
Jayne Rose
Augustana College

Daniel W. Russell
University of Iowa

Development is a cumulative process involving an interplay between the individual and the social environment. The school years, in particular, encompass changes in a multitude of domains (i.e., physical, cognitive, affective, and interpersonal). These changes do not take place in isolation nor do they necessarily proceed at the same pace. Maturation, environmental factors, asynchronies in development, and antecedent experiences may all serve to facilitate or impede the successful transition from childhood to adulthood.

Nowhere is the interaction among developmental influences as evident as in the interpersonal realm. As children move from the microcosmic world of the family into the expanding context of school, they are confronted with increasing complexity in the nature and scope of their social relationships. Failure to adapt to the changing demands of the social environment at any point in development may lead to isolation, rejection, and loneliness.

Loneliness has been characterized as the unpleasant or distressing state that arises from a perceived deficiency in the quantity or quality of one's social relationships (Peplau & Perlman, 1982). Inherent in this definition are the following three elements: (a) the experience is aversive; (b) existing relationships are seen as lacking in some way; and (c) the evaluation is subjectively determined independent of one's objective social status.

The aversiveness of loneliness is supported by its consistent association with a variety of unpleasant emotions, including depression (Levin & Stokes, 1986; Russell, Peplau, & Cutrona, 1980), anxiety (Russell et al., 1980), and low self-esteem (Levin & Stokes, 1986). These relations have been observed in people of varying ages (e.g., Brennan & Auslander, 1979; Perlman, Gerson, & Spinner, 1978) and racial groups (e.g., Hojat, 1983). Although loneliness and other negative affective states are similar in their manifestations and frequently occur together, their conceptual distinctiveness has been demonstrated in a number of studies (e.g., Bell, 1985; Russell et al., 1980).

Studies have shown repeatedly that lonely people are not lacking in social contacts or social activities per se (Chelune, Sultan, & Williams, 1980), although they do tend to spend more time alone and engage in more solitary activities (Russell et al., 1980). The literature is not entirely consistent regarding the relation between loneliness and the size of one's social network. Although some authors report an inverse relationship between loneliness and number of friends (Levin & Stokes, 1986), others do not (Williams & Solano, 1983). The operative factor appears not to be the objective/quantitative aspects of one's social status, but rather the subjective/qualitative dimension. Compared to nonlonely people, lonely individuals consistently report their social contacts and relationships to be less satisfying (Cutrona, 1982), less intimate (Russell et al., 1980), less helpful (Schultz & Saklofske, 1983), and less emotionally supportive (Corty & Young, 1981; Levin & Stokes, 1986). In all cases where quantitative and qualitative factors have been compared, relational *quality* has been significantly more predictive of loneliness (Cutrona, 1982).

Although loneliness may have immediate precipitating causes (e.g., loss of a close friend), other factors play a role in increasing or decreasing a person's vulnerability to loneliness and ability to cope. One such factor is the individual's level of development. Throughout the life-span, variations occur in the types of relationships deemed important, the functions relationships serve, and the cognitive processes available to evaluate social relationships.

The purpose of this chapter is to examine loneliness in its association with the dynamic processes of development over the school years. We take a chronological approach and examine factors implicated in the experience of loneliness at three developmental periods, early school age, adolescence, and college. After reviewing relevant literature, we conclude with a discussion of implications for interventions to prevent loneliness among students across the school years.

LONELINESS AMONG SCHOOL-AGED CHILDREN

Children are born into relationships. Typically a mother and father, as well as other family members and friends, welcome the newborn's arrival. Theorists have emphasized the importance of establishing optimal relationships with caregivers early in life. For example, Erikson (1963) maintained that infants are confronted with the psychosocial crisis of trust versus mistrust.

Sensitive, consistent caregiving promotes a sense of trust that enables the child to approach the world in a positive, hopeful way. In the absence of such caregiving, children develop the notion that the world is unpredictable and inhospitable and ultimately are led to mistrust it. This not only contributes to relationship difficulties between the child and his/her caregiver, but also sets the stage for future social impairments.

Support for this notion comes from many studies. For example, children who were securely attached to their mother at 18 months were found to be more popular with their peers in preschool (Sroufe, 1983). In addition, their preschool teachers rated them as having fewer behavior problems and more positive affect. Another study found abused children to be significantly lower on a variable representing "secure readiness to learn and explore in the company of unfamiliar adults" (Aber & Allen, 1987, p. 410). The authors proposed that the early relationship with an abusive parent contributed to insecure relationships later with other adults.

Because deficits in relationships can occur at an early age, some theorists have proposed that infants and young children are capable of experiencing loneliness. Illingsworth (1955, cited in Ellison, 1978) claimed that the "first signs of separation anxiety, or loneliness, appear during the first three months of life" (p. 7). Z. Rubin (1982) argued that "children as young as three, and I suspect, children even younger than that can feel what Robert Weiss calls 'the loneliness of social isolation' " (p. 266). Theorists who discuss loneliness in young children typically relate it to deficiencies in relationships with parents (Shaver & Rubinstein, 1980). Evidence of the association between current loneliness and poor early relations with parents has been found in retrospective studies of Iranian and American college students as well as adults (Lobdell & Perlman, 1986). However, because the measures of loneliness were obtained concurrently with measures of parental involvement, it could be argued that the association merely reflects a tendency for lonely people to negatively evaluate both past and current relationships. The case for early parental influences exerting a direct effect on later loneliness would be strengthened by prospective studies utilizing more objective assessments of parental behavior.

Among older, elementary-aged children, the focus of loneliness research has been on deficits in peer relationships. A recent review (Parker & Asher, 1987) concluded that, although low peer acceptance does not always result in later adjustment difficulties, it is unusual for high school dropouts and juvenile delinquents not to have experienced problems with their peers during the elementary and early adolescent grades. The authors found no consensus regarding the effects of peer relations on adult psychopathology. They suggested that this was most likely due to methodological problems in existing research rather than an absence of effects.

Measurement of Loneliness in Children

The majority of empirical studies of loneliness among school-aged children employ the children's loneliness scale developed by Asher and his colleagues (e.g., Asher & Wheeler, 1985). This is a 24-item measure that includes 16 items pertinent to loneliness and social dissatisfaction. The items directly assess feelings of loneliness (e.g., "I'm lonely"), appraisals of current peer relationships (e.g., "I don't have any friends"), perceptions of the degree to which important interpersonal needs are being met (e.g., "There's no other kids I can go to when I need help in school"), and perceptions of social skills (e.g., "I'm good at working with other children"; Asher, Parkhurst, Hymel, & Williams, in press).

Theorists and researchers of adult loneliness are very clear in distinguishing between loneliness and aloneness or social isolation (Peplau & Perlman, 1982). Consequently, even though objective measures of social activity and relationships (e.g., frequency of social activities with friends) are correlated with scores on measures of loneliness designed for adults, there is still a large portion of the variance in loneliness scores that is not explained by these variables. It has not been established that respondents to the children's loneliness scale are responding on the basis of the quality, rather than the quantity, of their relationships. For example, the item, "I have nobody to talk to," seems to reflect an objective lack of social contact rather than perceived deficits in the quality of relationships. Other items seem more appropriate (e.g., "I feel alone"), but it is difficult to determine how children interpret those items. Even if, from an adult viewpoint, we are measuring loneliness, that does not guarantee that children interpret an item in the same way as an adult. Asher et al. (in press) report that when kindergarten and first-grade children are asked what loneliness is, they indicate that it is a "feeling of being sad and alone" (p. 9). When asked the cause of such feelings, they respond that loneliness occurs "when you have nobody to play with" (p. 9). Such responses suggest that in children the distinction between loneliness and being alone may be blurred.

Related to this point are the results of factor analyses of the children's loneliness scale. As noted earlier, this scale contains items assessing feelings of loneliness, perceptions of relationships, perceptions of social competence, and feelings regarding whether one's relationship needs are being met. When factor analyzed, these items all loaded on one factor (Asher et al., in press). This suggests that children are not making the same distinctions between loneliness and related constructs as adults and therefore leads one to question whether children are experiencing the same thing as adults when they are "lonely."

Loneliness and Childhood Relationships

Studies of children have found that 8% to 10% report being lonely (Asher & Wheeler, 1985). Although some studies do not find grade-level differences in the incidence of loneliness (Asher & Wheeler, 1985), other studies do report age differences. A questionnaire study comparing second, fourth, and sixth graders found that younger children experience significantly more loneliness (Luftig, 1987). However, Wallerstein and Kelly's (1980) report of children experiencing the divorce of their parents revealed that 9- to 10-year-olds (typically 3rd or 4th graders) were most likely to explicitly use the term loneliness to describe their emotional state. Different modes of response in the two studies may explain the discrepancy in findings. Specifically, younger children may endorse more items indicative of loneliness when prompted by the stimulus of a loneliness question, whereas older children may spontaneously use the term lonely to describe themselves. Such age-related differences may reflect developmental changes in the ability to label emotional experience (e.g., Lewis & Rosenblum, 1978).

One approach to understanding loneliness in children has been to identify characteristics of lonely children. Studies of sociometric status have revealed that children who are rejected by their peers report greater loneliness (Asher & Wheeler, 1985). Because studies have found that peer rejection is moderately stable through the elementary school years (Coie & Dodge, 1983), this suggests that loneliness may also be stable. Although studies have not assessed loneliness over time among children, other measures of negative affect (i.e., depression, anxiety, dissatisfaction) have been found to be highly stable in children (e.g., $r = .97$; Lerner, Hertzog, Hooker, Hassibi, & Thomas, 1988).

A second approach to understanding loneliness in children has involved longitudinal, prospective studies of factors that predict loneliness. A significant portion of the variance in loneliness scores among fourth and fifth graders was explained by observational measures of their social behavior (e.g., group play, conversation with peers) in kindergarten and second grade. Peer ratings of sensitivity and isolation explained additional variance in fifth graders' scores (K. H. Rubin, Hymel, & Mills, 1988). Research with preschoolers has revealed that peer acceptance is significantly predicted by behavioral observations of their positive social interactions (Quay & Jarrett, 1984). Furthermore, children who are rejected in kindergarten are more frequently rated as having poor social adjustment by their third-grade teachers (Li, 1985). These findings suggest that social behavior, peer acceptance, and loneliness are closely interrelated. An important issue regards the temporal relations among these variables. Ladd, Price, and Hart (1988) investigated the association between social behavior and peer acceptance. They proposed that either (1) a child's behavior contributes to changes in his/her peer status (e.g., being aggressive leads one to be rejected), or (2) one's status in the peer group leads to changes in one's behavior (e.g., if rejected, one responds by becoming aggressive). Their longitudinal study supported the first hypothesis, that the child's social behavior contributes to peer status. They also found that once a child had a negative reputation, that reputation remained intact even if his/her behavior changed. This testifies to the importance of identifying rejected children as early as possible, before their peer status has been firmly established.

Determining that children's behavior contributes to their status leads to an examination of behaviors that promote peer acceptance. Results from studies employing direct observations, teacher ratings, and peer assessments of behavior are fairly consistent in their appraisal of rejected children's behavior with peers. Rejected children are more aggressive, inattentive, and nervous, and less likely to engage in appropriate behavior. They make fewer prosocial advances, but those they do initiate tend to occur at inappropriate times. Consequently, these approaches are more likely to be spurned. Teachers initiate more negative contact with rejected children than with other students (K. H. Rubin & Daniels-Beirness, 1983). Even when placed in a new group of unfamiliar agemates, rejected children quickly reestablish the same status (Coie & Kupersmidt, 1983).

Social-Cognitive Factors and Loneliness

It has been found that as children grow older they make clearer distinctions between friends and acquaintances and also see relationships as multidimensional (Berndt & Perry, 1986). For example, younger children cannot conceive of friends engaging in conflict, whereas older children and adolescents recognize that friendships can include disagreements. Age differences have also been found in children's expectations of friends. Generally, these reflect increasing emphasis on internal, psychological aspects and decreasing emphasis on situational bases of friendship (Bigelow, 1977). This trend is also seen in the knowledge children have about their friends. Although there are no age differences in the external knowledge they have, older children have significantly more knowledge of internal characteristics (Diaz & Berndt, 1982).

Barenboim (1981) related this growth in children's knowledge of the internal characteristics of people to general cognitive development as described by Piaget. He found that concrete operational children can use behavioral comparisons and psychological constructs, but formal operational skills are necessary for psychological comparisons because they require abstract thought.

Models of the information-processing steps individuals must negotiate to achieve successful social interactions have been developed (K. H. Rubin &

Krasnor, 1986). According to this approach, children with relationship problems have difficulty with these steps. As a test of this hypothesis, Feldman and Dodge (1987) related the model directly to sociometric status. Results revealed that low-status children were more likely to attribute a hostile intention to a peer and generate an aggressive response than children of higher status. Further analyses revealed that the differences were significant for boys but not girls. Boys processed information in a way that intensified conflict, whereas girls' information processing tended to minimize it. Furthermore, older children were better able to generate and evaluate the effectiveness of response.

Additional support for the role of information-processing deficiencies was reported by K. H. Rubin and Krasnor (1986). They also found differences in social problem solving among children in different sociometric categories. In addition, they found that social problem-solving skills assessed in kindergarten were predictive of popularity in second grade.

Information-processing approaches are helpful because they target specific skills for intervention. Asher and Renshaw (1981) reported that efforts to teach these social skills to low-status children have generally proven successful. As the authors indicated, social skills involve cognitions as well as behaviors.

Summary

Although it seems clear that children can and do experience deficiencies in their relationships with family members and friends, the available evidence suggests that their cognitive processing abilities may prohibit them from experiencing loneliness in a manner comparable to adolescents or adults. Retrospective studies of college students and older adults suggest that early attachment relationships with parents may be associated with loneliness. However, prospective studies of the effects of disruptions in early attachment relationships on childhood and adult loneliness are necessary before these findings can be interpreted as reflecting causal relationships. Peer rejection has been found to be associated with childhood loneliness, suggesting that interpersonal behaviors (e.g., aggressiveness, inappropriate behaviors) and cognitive processes (e.g., attributing hostile intent to others) that are associated with peer rejection may also be implicated in childhood loneliness.

Our interpretation of these findings is weakened by the lack of research directly addressing loneliness among young school-aged children. Future studies should evaluate whether the meaning of the term *loneliness* is comparable for young children and older adults. The role of interpersonal behaviors and social-cognitive processes in determining childhood loneliness should also be examined. Findings from such investigations may provide useful information in designing cognitive and behavioral interventions focused on loneliness among school-aged children.

LONELINESS DURING ADOLESCENCE

Brennan (1982) has stated that "adolescence seems to be the time of life when loneliness first emerges as an intense, recognizable phenomenon" (p. 269). Social relationships may be insufficient or unsatisfying at any age, but there is no question that adolescents *perceive* this deficiency more acutely than do persons at any other stage of life. Although Brennan and Auslander (1979) estimated the incidence of serious loneliness to be only 10% to 15% of the adolescent population, they observed that more than half their sample agreed with the statement, "I often feel lonely."

In a series of studies that compared high school students to adults, Larson and Csikszentmihalyi (1978) found that the two groups did not differ in the frequency with which they were alone (approximately 25% of the time). However, adolescents reported feeling much more lonely at these times. In fact, feelings of loneliness and detachment were the most intense reactions to being alone reported by adolescents, regardless of the nature of their activities or the fact that their solitude was usually by choice.

Loneliness within the adolescent population appears to correlate with many of the same affective, attitudinal, and behavioral characteristics that are found in studies of older age groups. Loneliness in adolescents has been linked to such negative emotions as depression, anxiety, and boredom (Brennan & Auslander, 1979; Moore & Schultz, 1983). Lonely adolescents have lowered self-esteem and perceive themselves to be less attractive and likeable (Moore & Schultz, 1983). In addition, they believe that others (e.g., teachers, parents, peers) are not interested in them or will not accept them (Brennan & Auslander, 1979; Goswick & Jones, 1982). Lonely adolescents may lack the requisite social skills to initiate and maintain satisfying relationships. They tend to be shy (Ishiyama, 1984), self-conscious, socially anxious, and hesitant to take social risks (Moore & Schultz, 1983). Loneliness is inversely related to the amount of time spent with peers and dating frequency (Brennan & Auslander, 1979). Finally, young people report that when they are lonely, they tend to engage in passive solitary activities (e.g., watching TV) that have little likelihood of improving either their mood or their social involvement (Brennan & Auslander, 1979; Moore & Schultz, 1983).

For some adolescents, loneliness is a recurring but transient state. Subjects in one sample (Moore & Schultz, 1983) reported feeling lonely about three times a month, but the duration averaged only half a day. For others, however, loneliness may take a more chronic form and be symptomatic of poor adjustment. Adolescent loneliness has been associated with delinquency and psychological disturbance (Ostrov & Offer, 1980), suicide (Neiger & Hopkins, 1988), and school failure (Brennan & Auslander, 1979).

Much of our understanding of loneliness during the adolescent period is based on limited data or research on related constructs. Relatively few empirical studies have examined a representative sample of adolescents. A further complication is that loneliness has been assessed in a variety of ways, ranging from a single self-labeling item (e.g., "I am so very lonely"; Ostrov & Offer, 1980) to multiple-item instruments designed to identify separate components of loneliness (e.g., loneliness with parents vs. peers; Marcoen, Goosens, & Caes, 1987).

Changes in Relationships

Most of the explanations for the higher incidence of loneliness among young people compared to older adults have centered around the developmental changes that occur at this age (cf., Brennan, 1982). Important relationships are transformed as parents and peers assume differential significance and functions. Weiss (1973) distinguished between loneliness due to social isolation (i.e., deficiencies in network size) and loneliness due to emotional isolation (i.e., lack of a strong sense of attachment; see Russell, Cutrona, Rose, & Yurko, 1984). Adolescents may be at particular risk for both types of loneliness as they outgrow childhood patterns of relating to parents and peers (for reviews of relationship changes in adolescence, see Reisman, 1985).

Regarding their relationships with parents, lonely adolescents tend to feel emotionally isolated from their parents and to perceive them as rejecting, negative, unsupportive, and dissatisfied (Brennan & Auslander, 1979). There is ample data to suggest that adolescence is accompanied by an increase in parent–child conflict (Steinberg, 1987), mutual dissatisfaction (Papini & Sebby, 1987), and feelings of emotional distance on the part of both parent and child (Steinberg, 1987). In fact, Marcoen et al. (1987) found an overall linear increase in parent-related loneliness from fifth to eleventh grade in their large sample of Belgian adolescents.

Although parental divorce during childhood or adolescence is associated with loneliness in adulthood (Shaver & Rubenstein, 1980), familial disruption per se may be less important than the atmosphere surrounding the change in family status. Among adolescents whose parents were divorced within the preceding year, only those who were exposed to high levels of parental conflict were found to be less socially competent, lower in social problem-solving skills, and more depressed, anxious, and withdrawn (Forehand, McCombs, Long, Brody, & Fauber, 1988). Adolescents whose parents remained together demonstrated no measured ill effects from parental conflict in either this or a second study (Forehand, Brody et al., 1988). Stability in family structure may compensate to some degree for unpleasantness in the family atmosphere. However, an alternative hypothesis may be drawn from Cohen, Burt, and Bjork (1987), who observed that adolescent adjustment (i.e., anxiety, depression, and self-esteem) was relatively independent of the stresses experienced by their parents.

It appears that adolescents become less attached to parents as friends gain importance. Adolescents are much more likely to spend time with peers than with family (Larson & Csikszentmihalyi, 1978), and time with parents continues to decrease across the adolescent years (Brennan, 1982). Consistent with studies of younger children, early adolescents who were rejected by their peers scored highest on a measure of peer social loneliness (i.e., perceived isolation; Goff & Bukowski, 1989). However, the observed association between rejection and two other forms of self-reported loneliness (i.e., general emotional and family loneliness) reinforces the notion that rejected children fare less well overall than their better integrated peers. Similarly, Goswick and Jones (1982) found that 72% of the variance in high school students' loneliness scores was explained by negative feelings and perceptions associated with peer relationships. Family experiences did not add significantly to the regression equation predicting loneliness.

Weiss (1973) proposed that a variety of relationships are required in order to meet different interpersonal needs. Parents do not become unimportant in the lives of adolescents. Instead, there is likely to be greater differentiation in the functions served by each type of relationship. Young people perceive greater mutuality with friends than with parents across the adolescent years (Hunter, 1985). Intimacy and self-disclosure between friends increases from fourth grade to college, surpassing intimacy with parents by middle high school (Franzoi & Davis, 1985).

Summary

Adolescents appear to be the population subgroup at greatest risk for loneliness. Studies have indicated that loneliness may be an important etiological factor for a number of problems associated with the teen years, such as failure in school, delinquency, and suicide. Surprisingly, however, there has been no research evaluating possible interventions to address loneliness among adolescents.

Changes in focus from the family to the peer culture appear to precipitate the high rates of loneliness among this age group. Developing a network of peer relationships and the initiation of dating relationships requires the application of new social skills by the adolescent, which may leave many junior high and high school students vulnerable to loneliness.

LONELINESS AMONG COLLEGE STUDENTS

Because of their ready availability, college students are the group from which most conclusions about loneliness have been drawn. The factors related to loneliness among college students have much in common with those of adolescence, but two developmental issues are more pronounced for the older group. First, college attendance often requires a physical separation from parents, old friends, and familiar routines, and an integration into a new social environment. Second, heterosexual relationships assume greater importance and become increasingly different from relationships with friends of the same sex.

Changes in Relationships

For new students, feelings of loneliness may be particularly acute as they leave established relationships and face a campus of strangers. Although all significant relationships (e.g., family, romantic involvements) are implicated in loneliness (Corty & Young, 1981; Cutrona, 1982), integration with peers seems to figure most strongly for first-year students (Cutrona, 1982). Fortunately, loneliness appears to decline during the freshman year without intervention. A longitudinal study of new students at UCLA found that 75% of the students reported feeling lonely during their first 2 weeks on campus, with the incidence of loneliness declining to 25% by the end of the first year on campus (Cutrona, 1982).

Individual factors may mediate the degree to which college students are able to adapt to the new social context. A number of the personal dispositions associated with loneliness (e.g., self-consciousness, social anxiety, low self-esteem, introversion, low social risk taking, and a low need for affiliation) may decrease the probability that these students will initiate or reciprocate social overtures (Levin & Stokes, 1986; Russell et al., 1980). Shyness may serve as a similar impediment, although its impact may be lessened with time as students become more familiar with their social milieu (Cheek & Busch, 1981). Finally, loneliness has been linked with low interpersonal acceptance and negative views of human nature (Levin & Stokes, 1986). Because lonely students often avoid situations where they risk rejection, embarrassment, or disappointment, these attitudes may further hinder the development of satisfying relationships.

Initiation skills are likely to be crucial in early social contacts, but other areas of competence may become more important over time. Buhrmester, Furman, Wittenberg, and Reis (1988) found that satisfaction with friendships was linked to those skills that help to maintain a positive affective climate (e.g., emotional support, self-disclosure, and conflict management). Loneliness has been related to rigid patterns of self-disclosure that do not match the demands of the situation (Chelune et al., 1980) and to low levels of attention and responsiveness in conversations (Bell, 1985; Jones, Hobbs, & Hockenbury, 1982). Such behaviors undoubtedly lead to less rewarding encounters as indicated by subjects' reports that, following interactions with lonely and nonlonely partners in a laboratory setting, they liked their lonely partners less well and had little desire to interact with them in the future (Bell, 1985). However, Gerson and Perlman (1979) observed that college women whose loneliness was situational in nature demonstrated more nonverbal expression than did subjects who were either chronically lonely or not lonely at all. It is difficult to tell from these data whether loneliness is the result of deficient social ability or whether persistent disappointment leads to lower expectations of success and a consequent lack of effort. Regardless of the direction of causality, however, training in conversational skills appears to be effective in decreasing loneliness and some of its negative interactional accompaniments (Jones et al., 1982).

Heterosexual Relationships

Relationships with members of the opposite sex become more significant during the college years. Lonely students report less satisfaction with their romantic partners and tend to date less frequently (Cutrona, 1982; Russell et al., 1980). Those who do not date at all tend to be more lonely than are students whose dating relationships are only casual (Russell et al., 1980). Romantic disappointments may yield a different type of loneliness than dissatisfaction with friendships (Russell et al., 1984). Perceived deficiencies in heterosexual relationships have been associated with emotional loneliness (i.e., lack of a secure attachment) and depression. This is in contrast to the social loneliness and anxiety that appear to accompany dissatisfaction with friendships.

There appears to be a developmental change over the college years in the types of interpersonal relationships that are most important to students (Russell et al., 1984). During the freshman and sophomore years, loneliness is primarily related to the perceived adequacy of relationships with friends. For older college students who are facing graduation and adult responsibilities, heterosexual relationships are of paramount importance, with loneliness being most strongly related to the perceived adequacy of romantic or dating relationships.

Self-reported social competence, particularly initiation, was found to be predictive of college students' dating frequency and perceived popularity (Buhrmester et al., 1988). However, students do not necessarily see themselves as equally competent in all relationships. When dealing with romantic partners, as compared to same-sex friends, students see themselves as less assertive, initiating, self-disclosing, and poorer at conflict management. College students of both sexes who report moderate levels of self-disclosure seem to be more satisfied with their romantic relationships than are those whose patterns of disclosure are more extreme (Lombardo & Wood, 1979). Men are more confident than women about initiating relationships (Buhrmester et al.,

1988). In one study, actual initiation of contact with members of the opposite sex was negatively related to loneliness for men, but not for women (Craig-Bray & Adams, 1986).

Summary

Entering college represents for most students a transition from the home community to a new social context. As would be expected, this disruption of social ties results in a high incidence of loneliness, from which most students recover. In contrast to other school-aged populations, intervention studies for loneliness have been conducted with college student samples, indicating the efficacy of social skills training.

Research with college students also suggests a developmental transition in the types of interpersonal relationships that are most critical to the individual. Younger students appear to be focused on the development of a network of friendships, whereas for older students intimate heterosexual relationships are most important. These latter findings have important implications for interventions to assist lonely college students, suggesting that the focus of intervention may need to change over the college years.

IMPLICATIONS FOR INTERVENTIONS

Our analysis of loneliness across the school years suggests two important conclusions. First, with increasing age the nature and meaning of the term *loneliness* may change. For the school-aged child, loneliness and aloneness may be synonymous. With increasing age and cognitive sophistication, loneliness for the adolescent and college student appears to reflect important distinctions in the type and quality of desired interpersonal relationships. Thus, for older students, one can be alone but not lonely.

There also appear two developmental changes in the types of interpersonal relationships that are most important to the student. For the young school-aged child, parents and family along with playmates represent key interpersonal relationships. During the junior high and high school years, a transition from family to peer relationships occurs, with concomitant changes in the sources of loneliness. The focus on peer friendships changes to an emphasis on the development of an intimate heterosexual relationship by the end of college.

These changes over time in the nature and sources of loneliness have important implications for attempts to intervene with the lonely student. For younger students, the simple presence of playmates may be sufficient to prevent loneliness, whereas more subtle qualitative issues in relationships become important for the adolescent and college student. Similarly, the types of relationships that are important to the student also appear to change with age, indicating a need to tailor interventions to the developmental stage of the student.

Interventions with School-Aged Children

Although it is unreasonable to expect that a child will never be lonely, it is important to identify children at risk for chronic or intense loneliness, because it has been linked to depression and other aversive emotional states among adults. However, such identification may prove to be difficult for two reasons. First, it has not been clearly established that what children and adults experience as loneliness are comparable, nor that children who are lonely develop into lonely adults. Consequently, until research more clearly establishes the construct of loneliness in children and its relationship to that state in adults, we may be either over or under identifying children at risk. The problems inherent in missing children who could use help are obvious. However, singling out a child for help may be stigmatizing (Matter & Matter, 1985) and, therefore, overidentification is also problematic.

Second, a consistent correlate of loneliness in children has been sociometric status. Children who are rejected by their peers on average are more lonely than those in other sociometric status groups (Asher & Wheeler, 1985). Consequently, one might think that rejected children should be the ones targeted for intervention strategies to prevent loneliness. However, the rejected group has also been found to be the most heterogeneous in terms of loneliness (Asher & Wheeler, 1985). This suggests that there are subgroups of rejected children, some who experience feelings of loneliness and others who do not. By targeting all rejected children for loneliness prevention programs, we would again be running the risk of misidentification. Williams and Asher (1987) have begun to disaggregate rejected children into subgroups. They have found that the rejected children who were most lonely were those who received no friendship nominations from their classmates even when an unlimited number of nominations were allowed. Future research should be directed towards greater specification of those children at risk for loneliness.

To date, intervention programs with children have been directed towards those children without friends rather than those identified as lonely. Programs designed to teach children social skills have generally proven to be successful. Asher and Renshaw (1981) found that 75% of the studies showed improved sociometric status for subjects who had social skills training that emphasized cognitive as well as behavioral modifications.

Matter and Matter (1985) provided suggestions for elementary school counselors working with lonely children. They emphasize teaching social skills that will enable the child to be more successful in interactions with others as well as helping the child to overcome self-defeating beliefs and thoughts. They indicate that counselors should also strive to modify the school environment so that fewer pupils are excluded. Suggestions on how this might be accomplished include decreasing competition among students and increasing the amount of time spent in shared activities.

Clearly, we must be cautious in designing intervention strategies for lonely children, because the meaning of "loneliness" for this age group has not been clearly delineated. However, available research suggests that behavioral and cognitive programs are effective in helping rejected children gain greater acceptance from classmates. How this influences their emotional state, or level of loneliness, has not been assessed.

Intervening with Adolescents and Young Adults

Because the loneliness of older students appears to be most closely linked to changes in relational needs and more sophisticated perceptions of relationships, it follows that intervention should be geared toward these issues. Little empirical work has addressed the alleviation of loneliness among adolescents. However, the developmental similarities between teenagers and college students make it likely that findings from interventions with the older age group would be applicable to both populations.

Recommendations for addressing loneliness in young people tend to fall into two general categories, social skills training and cognitive modifications. In one of the few reports of intervention with adolescents, Franco, Christoff, Crimmins, and Kelly (1983) described the case study of a 14-year-old boy who was referred for outpatient skills training because of excessive shyness and poor peer relations. In twice-weekly sessions spanning 15 weeks, the boy received instruction, modeling, and rehearsal in four social skills (e.g., asking questions and maintaining eye contact). When training was complete, his performance in all areas was rated as significantly better than baseline by both peers (strangers) and adults (parents and teachers). He also demonstrated improved social integration (e.g., dating, activities with friends) more than a year after the end of the program.

Positive effects of social skills training have also been reported for male college students whose initial loneliness scores were two and a half standard deviations above the mean for that population (Jones et al., 1982). In this comparative study, subjects who received instruction and practice in specific behaviors (e.g., attention to partner) were significantly less lonely, shy, and anxious at the end of 3 weeks of training than were subjects who participated in unguided interaction or who received no intervention at all. It should be noted that, although improvement was seen, subjects' loneliness scores remained significantly elevated. It is unclear from these results whether a longer period of training is needed to produce a greater reduction in loneliness or whether it takes more time for the benefits to impact on ongoing relationships.

Because of the subjective nature of loneliness, cognitive interventions are appropriate when existing interpersonal skills are adequate. A variety of authors (cf., Bandura, 1977; Beck, Rush, Shaw, & Emery, 1979) have suggested that beliefs and expectations mediate between behavior potential and actual performance. When individuals expect their efforts to fail, they are unlikely to try. Young (1982) has applied the principles of cognitive therapy to the treatment of loneliness in college students. In his approach, intervention is directed toward correcting the perceptual distortions and erroneous interpretations that lead people to negatively evaluate their behaviors, relationships, and probabilities of success.

Conclusions

Rook (1984) identified three goals of interventions for loneliness that are applicable to people of all ages: (a) the development of satisfying relationships, (b) intervention to minimize the sequelae of loneliness (e.g., depression) and (c) prevention of loneliness in the first place. During the school years, the following recommendations are most applicable. First, meaningful relationships may be facilitated through the development of social skills, realistic expectations for self and others, and opportunities for interpersonal contact and cooperative activities. Adolescents, in particular, may need guidance in learning the skills that are important for dating and heterosexual relationships. Structured activities that emphasize the sharing of feelings may also help adolescents to find areas of similarity with others and reduce the perception of emotional isolation that seems to be so common at this age. Second, the negative effects of loneliness may be minimized if young people have access to support networks during times of social loss and if they have been helped to develop solitary skills (i.e., constructive uses for time alone). Finally, helping parents to understand and support their children at all stages of development may better prepare these young people to cope with the changes that occur in their interpersonal and intrapersonal experience.

ACKNOWLEDGMENTS

The authors would like to thank Carolyn Cutrona for her comments on an earlier version of this chapter. Preparation of this chapter was supported by program project grant P01-AG07094 from the National Institute on Aging (R. Wallace, PI). Correspondence should be sent to Daniel W. Russell, Center for

Health Services Research, College of Medicine, University of Iowa, Iowa City, IA 52242.

REFERENCES

Aber, J. L., & Allen, J. P. (1987). Effects of maltreatment on young children's socioemotional development: An attachment theory perspective. *Developmental Psychology, 23*, 406–414.

Asher, S. R., Parkhurst, J. T., Hymel, S., & Williams, G. A. (in press). Peer rejection and loneliness in childhood. In S. R. Asher & J. D. Coie (Eds.), *Peer rejection in childhood*. New York: Cambridge University Press.

Asher, S. R., & Renshaw, P. D. (1981). Children without friends: Social knowledge and social-skill training. In S. R. Asher & J. M. Gottman (Eds.), *The development of children's friendships* (pp. 273–296). Cambridge: Cambridge University Press.

Asher, S. R., & Wheeler, V. A. (1985). Children's loneliness: A comparison of rejected and neglected peer status. *Journal of Consulting and Clinical Psychology, 53*, 500–505.

Bandura, A. (1977). Self-efficacy: Toward a unifying theory of behavior change. *Psychological Review, 84*, 191–215.

Barenboim, C. (1981). The development of person perception in childhood and adolescence: From behavioral comparisons to psychological constructs to psychological comparisons. *Child Development, 52*, 129–144.

Beck, A. T., Rush, A. J., Shaw, B. F., & Emery, G. (1979). *Cognitive therapy of depression*. New York: Guilford Press.

Bell, R. A. (1985). Conversational involvement and loneliness. *Communication Monographs, 52*, 218–235.

Berndt, T. J., & Perry, T. B. (1986). Children's perceptions of friendships as supportive relationships. *Developmental Psychology, 22*, 640–648.

Bigelow, B. J. (1977). Children's friendship expectations: A cognitive-developmental study. *Child Development, 48*, 246–253.

Brennan, T. (1982). Loneliness at adolescence. In L. A. Peplau & D. Perlman (Eds.), *Loneliness: A sourcebook of current theory, research, and therapy* (pp. 269–290). New York: Wiley Interscience.

Brennan, T., & Auslander, N. (1979). *Adolescent loneliness: An exploratory study of social and psychological pre-dispositions and theory*. Boulder, CO: Behavioral Research Institute.

Buhrmester, D., Furman, W., Wittenberg, M. T., & Reis, H. T. (1988). Five domains of interpersonal competence in peer relationships. *Journal of Personality and Social Psychology, 55*, 991–1008.

Cheek, J. M., & Busch, C. M. (1981). The influence of shyness on loneliness in a new situation. *Personality and Social Psychology Bulletin, 7*, 572–577.

Chelune, G. J., Sultan, F. E., & Williams, C. L. (1980). Loneliness, self-disclosure, and interpersonal effectiveness. *Journal of Counseling Psychology, 27*, 462–468.

Cohen, L. H., Burt, C. E., & Bjork, J. P. (1987). Life stress and adjustment: Effects of life events experienced by young adolescents and their parents. *Developmental Psychology, 23*, 583–592.

Coie, J. D., & Dodge, K. A. (1983). Continuities and changes in children's social status: A five year longitudinal study. *Merrill-Palmer Quarterly, 29*, 261–282.

Coie, J. D., & Kupersmidt, J. B. (1983). A behavioral analysis of emerging social status in boys' groups. *Child Development, 54*, 1400–1416.

Corty, E., & Young, R. D. (1981). Social contact and perceived loneliness in college students. *Perceptual and Motor Skills, 53*, 773–774.

Craig-Bray, L., & Adams, G. R. (1986). Measuring social intimacy in same-sex and opposite-sex contexts. *Journal of Adolescent Research, 1*, 95–101.

Cutrona, C. E. (1982). Transition to college: Loneliness and the process of social adjustment. In L. A. Peplau & D. Perlman (Eds.), *Loneliness: A sourcebook of current theory, research, and therapy* (pp. 291–309). New York: Wiley Interscience.

Diaz, R. M., & Berndt, T. J. (1982). Children's knowledge of a best friend: Fact or fancy? *Developmental Psychology, 18,* 787–794.

Ellison, C. W. (1978). Loneliness: A social-developmental analysis. *Journal of Psychology and Theology, 6,* 3–17.

Erikson, E. H. (1963). *Childhood and society* (2nd ed.). New York: Norton.

Feldman, E., & Dodge, K. A. (1987). Social information processing and sociometric status: Sex, age, and situational effects. *Journal of Abnormal Child Psychology, 15,* 211–227.

Forehand, R., Brody, G., Slotkkin, J., Fauber, R., McCombs, A., & Long, N. (1988). Young-adolescent maternal depression: Assessment, interrelations, and family predictors. *Journal of Consulting and Clinical Psychology, 56,* 422–426.

Forehand, R., McCombs, A., Long, N., Brody, G., & Fauber, R. (1988). Early adolescent adjustment to recent parental divorce: The role of interparental conflict and adolescent sex as mediating variables. *Journal of Consulting and Clinical Psychology, 56,* 624–627.

Franco, D. P., Christoff, K. A., Crimmins, D. B., & Kelly, J. K. (1983). Social skills training for an extremely shy young adolescent: An empirical case study. *Behavior Therapy, 14,* 568–575.

Franzoi, S. L., & Davis, M. H. (1985). Adolescent self-disclosure and loneliness: Private self-consciousness and parental influences. *Journal of Personality and Social Psychology, 48,* 768–780.

Gerson, A. C., & Perlman, D. (1979). Loneliness and expressive communication. *Journal of Abnormal Psychology, 88,* 258–261.

Goff, J. F., & Bukowski, W. M. (1989, April). *A multidimensional study of children's loneliness and their social relationships.* Paper presented at the meeting of the Society for Research in Child Development, Kansas City.

Goswick, R. A., & Jones, W. H. (1982). Components of loneliness during adolescence. *Journal of Youth and Adolescence, 11,* 373–383.

Hojat, M. (1983). Comparison of transitory and chronic loners on selected personality variables. *British Journal of Psychology, 74,* 199–202.

Hunter, F. T. (1985). Individual adolescents' perceptions of interactions with friends and parents. *Journal of Early Adolescence, 5,* 295–305.

Ishiyama, F. I. (1984). Shyness: Anxious social sensitivity and self-isolating tendency. *Adolescence, 19,* 903–911.

Jones, W. H., Hobbs, S. A., & Hockenbury, D. (1982). Loneliness and social skills deficits. *Journal of Personality and Social Psychology, 42,* 682–689.

Ladd, G. W., Price, J. M., & Hart, C. H. (1988). Predicting preschoolers' peer status from their playground behaviors. *Child Development, 59,* 986–992.

Larson, R., & Csikszentmihalyi, M. (1978). Experiential correlates of time alone in adolescence. *Journal of Personality, 46,* 677–693.

Lerner, J. V., Hertzog, C., Hooker, K. A., Hassibi, M., & Thomas, A. (1988). A longitudinal study of negative emotional states and adjustment from early childhood through adolescence. *Child Development, 59,* 356–366.

Levin, I., & Stokes, J. P. (1986). An examination of the relation of individual difference variables to loneliness. *Journal of Personality, 54,* 717–733.

Lewis, M., & Rosenblum, L. A. (1978). *The development of affect.* New York: Plenum Press.

Li, A. K. F. (1985). Early rejected status and later social adjustment: A three-year follow-up. *Journal of Abnormal Child Psychology, 13,* 567–577.

Lobdell, J., & Perlman, D. (1986). The intergenerational transmission of loneliness: A study of college females and their parents. *Journal of Marriage and Family, 48,* 589–595.

Lombardo, J. P., & Wood, R. D. (1979). Satisfaction with interpersonal relations as a function of self-disclosure. *Journal of Psychology, 102,* 21–26.

Luftig, R. L. (1987). Children's loneliness, perceived ease in making friends, and estimated social adequacy: Development and social metacognition. *Child Study Journal, 17,* 35–53.

Marcoen, A., Goosens, L., & Caes, P. (1987). Loneliness in pre- through late adolescence: Exploring the contributions of a multidimensional approach. *Journal of Youth and Adolescence, 16,* 561–577.

Matter, D. E., & Matter, R. M. (1985). Children who are lonely and shy: Action steps for the counselor. *Elementary School Guidance and Counseling, 20,* 129–135.

Moore, D., & Schultz, N. R., Jr. (1983). Loneliness at adolescence: Correlates, attributions, and coping. *Journal of Youth and Adolescence, 12,* 95–100.

Neiger, B. L., & Hopkins, R. W. (1988). Adolescent suicide: Character traits of high-risk teenagers. *Adolescence, 23,* 469–475.

Ostrov, E., & Offer, D. (1980). Loneliness and the adolescent. In J. Hartog, J. R. Audy, & Y. A. Cohen (Eds.), *The anatomy of loneliness* (pp. 170–185). New York: International Universities Press.

Papini, D. R., & Sebby, R. A. (1987). Adolescent pubertal status and effective family relationships: A multivariate assessment. *Journal of Youth and Adolescence, 16,* 1–15.

Parker, J. G., & Asher, S. R. (1987). Peer relation and later personal adjustment: Are low-accepted children at risk? *Psychological Bulletin, 102,* 357–389.

Peplau, L. A., & Perlman, D. (1982). Perspectives on loneliness. In L. A. Peplau & D. Perlman (Eds.), *Loneliness: A sourcebook of current theory, research, and therapy* (pp. 1–20). New York: Wiley Interscience.

Perlman, D., Gerson, A. C., & Spinner, B. (1978). Loneliness among senior citizens: An empirical report. *Essence, 2,* 239–248.

Quay, L. C., & Jarrett, O. S. (1984). Predictors of social acceptance in preschool children. *Developmental Psychology, 20,* 793–796.

Reisman, J. M. (1985). Friendship and its implications for mental health or social competence. *Journal of Early Adolescence, 5,* 383–391.

Rook, K. A. (1984). Promoting social bonding: Strategies for helping the lonely and socially isolated. *American Psychologist, 39,* 1389–1407.

Rubin, K. H., & Daniels-Beirness, T. (1983). Concurrent and predictive correlates of sociometric status in kindergarten and grade one children. *Merrill-Palmer Quarterly, 29,* 337–351.

Rubin, K. H., Hymel, S., & Mills, R. S. L. (1989). Sociability and social withdrawal in childhood: Stability and outcomes. *Journal of Personality, 57,* 237–255.

Rubin, K. H., & Krasnor, L. R. (1986). Social-cognitive and social behavioral perspectives on problem solving. *Minnesota Symposium on Child Psychology, 18,* 1–68.

Rubin, Z. (1982). Children without friends. In L. A. Peplau & D. Perlman (Eds.), *Loneliness: A sourcebook of current theory, research, and therapy* (pp. 255–268). New York: Wiley Interscience.

Russell, D., Cutrona, C. E., Rose, J., & Yurko, K. (1984). Social and emotional loneliness: An examination of Weiss's typology of loneliness. *Journal of Personality and Social Psychology, 46,* 1313–1321.

Russell, D., Peplau, L. A., & Cutrona, C. E. (1980). The revised UCLA Loneliness Scale: Concurrent and discriminant validity evidence. *Journal of Personality and Social Psychology, 39,* 472–480.

Schultz, B. J., & Saklofske, D. H. (1983). Relationship between social support and selected measures of psychological well-being. *Psychological Reports, 53,* 847–850.

Shaver, P., & Rubinstein, C. (1980). Childhood attachment experience and adult loneliness. In L. Wheeler (Ed.), *Review of personality and social psychology* (Vol. 1, pp. 42–73). Newbury Park, CA: Sage.

Sroufe, L. A. (1983). Infant-caregiver attachment and patterns of adaptation in preschool: The roots of maladaptation and competence. *Minnesota Symposium on Child Psychology, 16,* 41–81.

Steinberg, L. (1987). Impact of puberty on family relations: Effects of pubertal status and pubertal timing. *Developmental Psychology, 23,* 451–460.

Wallerstein, J. S., & Kelly, J. B. (1980). The effects of parental divorce: Experiences of the child in later latency. In J. Hartog, J. R. Audy, & Y. A. Cohen (Eds.), *The anatomy of loneliness* (pp. 148–169). New York: International Universities Press.

Weiss, R. S. (1973). *Loneliness: The experience of emotional and social isolation.* Cambridge, MA: MIT Press.

Williams, G. A., & Asher, S. R. (1987, April). *Peer- and self-perceptions of peer rejected children: Issues in classification and subgrouping.* Paper presented at the Society for Research in Child Development, Baltimore.

Williams, J. G., & Solano, C. H. (1983). The social reality of feeling lonely: Friendship and reciprocation. *Personality and Social Psychology Bulletin, 9,* 237–242.

Young, J. E. (1982). Loneliness, depression, and cognitive therapy: Theory and application. In L. A. Peplau & D. Perlman (Eds.), *Loneliness: A sourcebook of current theory, research, and therapy* (pp. 379–406). New York: Wiley Interscience.

16

SOCIAL PSYCHOLOGICAL FACTORS IN ADOLESCENT SUBSTANCE USE AND ABUSE

Laurie Chassin
Clark C. Presson
Arizona State University

Steven J. Sherman
Indiana University

Patrick J. Curran
Arizona State University

Substance use is one of the most highly publicized and salient issues of the 1980s. Steroid use among Olympic stars, drug-related deaths of college athletes, and disqualification of Supreme Court and cabinet level nominees for current or past substance use have all contributed to a public perception of drug use as one of the nation's most critical issues. Because most drug use starts in adolescence, the schools have been identified as important resources in substance use prevention campaigns. However, the sensationalization of drug use and the emotionalism of the issues has led to demands for actions in the "war on drugs" that are not always well grounded in a thorough understanding of the phenomenon.The purpose of this chapter is to illustrate ways in which social psychology can help provide this understanding and thus guide prevention efforts.

In rejecting the current sensationalism surrounding adolescent drug use, we do not mean to deny the importance of the problem or to deny that adolescents are an appropriate target group for preventive intervention. Substance use and abuse constitute one of the most significant threats to public health in the United States. Cigarette smoking is currently the largest single preventable cause of death in the United States (U.S. Surgeon General, 1986) and is initiated largely during adolescence. Use of licit or illicit substances is thought to be a factor in up to half of adult deaths from cardiovascular disease and in the majority of adolescent deaths by violence (Blum, 1987; Pentz et al., 1989). Alcohol has been implicated in 55% of fatal automobile accidents (National Institute on Drug Abuse, 1984). Recent data suggest that 11% of pregnancies were affected by maternal drug use (National Association for Perinatal Research and Education, 1988). From a public health standpoint, mortality and morbidity would be significantly reduced if drug use were deterred. From an economic standpoint, annual costs of substance use have been estimated at $100 billion dollars (National Institute on Drug Abuse, 1987). This includes costs from lost productivity, health care, social services, and the criminal justice system.

Not only is adolescent substance use an important public health problem, but it is a problem of particular concern to school systems for several reasons. First, school is a good setting within which to have impact on substance use because schools have easy access to the adolescent population that is in the period of risk for substance use initiation. Available data suggest that cessation of already established substance use is difficult to achieve, and therefore that primary prevention is an important goal (Botvin, 1987). School settings are an obvious place for such prevention efforts. Second, schools are a source of both risk and protective factors in the development of substance use. For example, school success and high academic aspirations are protective factors that insulate adolescents from substance use problems (Johnston, O'Malley, & Bachman, 1988; Kandel, 1980). On the other hand, academic failure and peer school environments where drug use is prevalent raise risk for substance use initiation. Third, substance use has direct relevance to the academic mission of the schools. For example, substance use increases the risk for subsequent absenteeism, school failure, and school dropout (Newcomb & Bentler, 1986; Pirie, Murray, & Leupker, 1988).

Given the complexity of drug use behavior, and given the potential consequences, it is important to approach adolescent substance use from a rational, scientific basis. Social psychology has been able to provide useful conceptual tools, theoretical frameworks, and empirical results that allow us to understand adolescent drug use and to devise strategies for prevention. The purpose of this chapter is to highlight the contributions of social psychology to answering some of the important questions facing school psychologists. An exhaustive review of all the theories and correlates of adolescent substance use is beyond the scope of this chapter. We focus on social psychological models and issues that are most relevant to schools. Other types of models, for example those that emphasize family factors or biological factors, are not covered (see Baumrind, 1985; Bry, 1983; and Pickens & Svikis, 1988 for reviews).

THE SCOPE OF THE PROBLEM: HOW PREVALENT IS ADOLESCENT SUBSTANCE USE?

Given the public perception of a drug use epidemic, it might be surprising to note that national data suggest a recent overall decline in adolescent drug use. Perhaps the best way to describe briefly the epidemiology of adolescent drug use is to examine the data from the Monitoring the Future Study (Johnston et al., 1988), which annually surveys a nationally representative sample of high school seniors. The 30-day prevalence figures from this study from 1978–1987 are presented in Table 16.1. It should be noted that these figures must be considered underestimates of use because they are obtained from high school seniors in a school-based data collection, and thus they do not reflect use among dropouts and truants (subsamples in which drug use is more prevalent; Pirie et al., 1988). Nevertheless, an understanding of trends over time can be gained from these data.

The general pattern of adolescent drug use has been to show stable increases in prevalence during the 1970s and a rather consistent downward trend throughout the 1980s. Thus, for example, the percentage of high school seniors who reported use of any illicit drug in the past 30 days rose from 55.2% in 1978 to 65.8% in 1982 and decreased to 56.6% in 1988. The trend is also seen in marijuana use (which is the most commonly used illicit drug among high school seniors). Daily marijuana use increased almost twofold between 1975 and 1978, and, at its peak, 1 out of 9 high school seniors reported using marijuana on a daily basis. In 1979 this dramatic rise stopped, and by 1988 only 1 in 30 reported daily use of marijuana. Trends in drug use vary by type of drug, with dramatic declines in the use of sedatives, stimulants, tranquilizers, and PCP, moderate declines in marijuana and (most recently) in cocaine, but stable use or increases in the use of heroin, opiates, alcohol, and inhalants (Johnston et al., 1988).

Despite the public emphasis on illicit drug use, the licit drugs are the ones that are most commonly used. The vast majority of high school seniors have used alcohol (92% reported some use in 1988). Moreover, 38% of high school seniors report heavy drinking (5 or more drinks in a row) in the past 2 weeks. Cigarettes are the most commonly reported drug that is used on a daily basis. Highest levels of daily cigarette use were reported in 1977 (29% of high school seniors). This level gradually declined until 1983, at which point it stabilized at the current level of 19%.

The epidemiology of adolescent drug use also varies with both age and gender. Generally, there is a higher proportion of males than females reporting drug use, especially when considering heavy levels of use. Cocaine, inhalants, hallucinogens, heroin, methaqualone, and LSD show use rates by males from 1.3 to 3.5 times higher than for females. The only illicit drugs used more frequently by females than males are stimulants and tranquilizers (Johnston et al., 1988). Gender differences in stimulant use may be due to females' use of stimulants for weight loss. Females also show higher cigarette smoking rates than males.

Retrospective data from the Monitoring the Future Study suggest that initial experiences with cigarettes, alcohol, and marijuana tend to occur prior to entrance into high school (i.e., before 10th grade). For the majority of illicit drugs other than marijuana, between 40% and 56% of those individuals

TABLE 16.1

Trends in Thirty-Day Prevalence of Eighteen Types of Drugs

Percent who used in last thirty days

	Class of 1975 (9400)	Class of 1976 (15400)	Class of 1977 (17100)	Class of 1978 (17800)	Class of 1979 (15500)	Class of 1980 (15900)	Class of 1981 (17500)	Class of 1982 (17700)	Class of 1983 (16300)	Class of 1984 (15900)	Class of 1985 (16000)	Class of 1986 (15200)	Class of 1987 (16300)
Approx. N =													
Marijuana/Hashish	27.1	32.2	35.4	37.1	36.5	33.7	31.6	28.5	27.0	25.2	25.7	23.4	21.0
Inhalants[a]	NA	0.9	1.3	1.5	1.7	1.4	1.5	1.5	1.7	1.9	2.2	2.5	2.8
Inhalants Adjusted[b]	NA	NA	NA	NA	3.2	2.7	2.5	2.5	2.5	2.6	3.0	3.2	3.5
Amyl & Butyl Nitrites[c,h]	NA	NA	NA	NA	2.4	1.8	1.4	1.1	1.4	1.4	1.6	1.3	1.3
Hallucinogens	4.7	3.4	4.1	3.9	4.0	3.7	3.7	3.4	2.8	2.6	2.5	2.5	2.5
Hallucinogens Adjusted[d]	NA	NA	NA	NA	5.3	4.4	4.5	4.1	3.5	3.2	3.8	3.5	2.8
LSD	2.3	1.9	2.1	2.1	2.4	2.3	2.5	2.4	1.9	1.5	1.6	1.7	1.8
PCP[c,h]	NA	NA	NA	NA	2.4	1.4	1.4	1.0	1.3	1.0	1.6	1.3	0.6
Cocaine	1.9	2.0	2.9	3.9	5.7	5.2	5.8	5.0	4.9	5.8	6.7	6.2	4.3
"Crack"[g]	NA	NA	NA	NA	NA	NA	NA	NA	NA	NA	NA	NA	1.5
Other cocaine[c]	NA	NA	NA	NA	NA	NA	NA	NA	NA	NA	NA	NA	4.1

Heroin	0.4	0.2	0.3	0.3	0.2	0.2	0.2	0.2	0.2	0.3	0.3	0.2	0.2
Other Opiates[e]	2.1	2.0	2.8	2.1	2.4	2.4	2.1	1.8	1.8	2.3	2.0	1.8
Stimulants[e]	8.5	7.7	8.8	8.7	9.9	12.1	15.8	13.7	12.4	NA	NA	NA	NA
Stimulants Adjusted[e,f]	NA	NA	NA	NA	NA	NA	NA	10.7	8.9	8.3	6.8	5.2	NA
Sedatives[e]	5.4	4.5	5.1	4.2	4.4	4.8	4.6	3.4	3.0	2.3	2.4	2.2	1.7
Barbiturates[e]	4.7	3.9	4.3	3.2	3.2	2.9	2.6	2.0	2.1	1.7	2.0	1.8	1.4
Methaqualone[e]	2.1	1.6	2.3	1.9	2.3	3.3	3.1	2.4	1.8	1.1	1.0	0.8	0.6
Tranquilizers[e]	4.1	4.0	4.6	3.4	3.7	3.1	2.7	2.4	2.5	2.1	2.1	2.1	2.0
Alcohol	68.2	68.3	71.2	72.1	71.8	72.0	70.7	69.7	69.4	67.2	65.9	65.3	66.4
Cigarettes	36.7	38.8	38.4	36.7	34.4	30.5	29.4	30.0	30.3	29.3	30.1	29.6	29.4

[a] Data based on four questionnaire forms. N is four-fifths of N indicated.
[b] Adjusted for underreporting of amyl and butyl nitrites.
[c] Data based on a single questionnaire form. N is one-fifth of N indicated.
[d] Adjusted for underreporting of PCP.
[e] Only drug use that was not under a doctor's orders is included here.
[f] Based on the data from the revised question, which attempts to exclude the inappropriate reporting of nonprescription stimulants.
[g] Data based on two questionnaire forms. N is two-fifths of N indicated.
[h] Question text changed slightly in 1987.

NOTE: NA indicates data not available.

From: Johnston, O'Malley, and Bachman (1988).

reporting use by the end of their senior year had initiated use prior to beginning high school. The exception to this pattern is the initiation rates of cocaine use, which were highest in the final 2 years of high school (Johnston et al., 1988). These data suggest that middle school years are the period of risk for initiation of substance use experimentation.

What is the Goal of Substance Use Prevention in the Schools?

In adopting prevention as a goal, it is important to clarify the target behavior to be prevented. Substance use prevention has been commonly interpreted to mean advocating absolute abstinence (i.e., preventing even an initial experiment with any substance). Thus, most prevention programs focus on deterring adolescents' initial experimentation with substance use. There are several rationales for this emphasis on initial experimentation. First, empirical evidence has shown systematic progressions in adolescent substance use in that the use of legal "gateway" drugs (such as beer, wine, cigarettes, and hard liquor) raises risk for later use of illicit drugs (Kandel & Faust, 1975). Accordingly, prevention researchers have suggested that preventing experimentation with the gateway drugs may deter use of substances that follow in the progression.

Another rationale for a focus on preventing initial experimentation points to the benefits of successfully delaying onset. First, delaying onset of substance use directly and simply reduces the amount of exposure to dangerous substances (e.g., less exposure to carcinogens in tobacco smoke). This will delay the onset of drug-related disease. More optimistically, delaying onset of use might ultimately reduce onset because some early motivations for drug use will no longer be present. For example, older adolescents and adults may be less likely than younger adolescents to adopt cigarette smoking as a way of being rebellious. For some substances, our system of laws already implicitly conveys delayed onset as a goal. For example, substances like alcohol and tobacco are prohibited for adolescents but are legal for adults.

Despite these rationales, some prevention researchers question whether an exclusive focus on first experiments is warranted. First, given the prevalence data just cited, it is evident that some experimentation is statistically normative. Some substances are clearly part of the larger social fabric, and eradication of all adolescent experimentation would be unrealistic to achieve (Newcomb & Bentler, 1988). Developmentally, adolescent substance use experimentation may serve a function in the transition from childhood to adulthood. One of the mechanisms available to facilitate this transition involves boundary testing—that is, engaging in behaviors that are generally restricted for children. Thus, regardless of what rules or laws are applied, some boundary testing will occur as a part of the natural process of establishing adult identities and roles (Erikson, 1962). This also suggests that complete elimination of adolescent experimentation may be an unrealistic goal. In addition, some forms of adolescent experimentation may not have long-term negative implications. One must distinguish use from abuse. For example, recent longitudinal data suggest that long-term negative consequences of adolescent drug use are associated with regular and committed use and not with adolescent experimentation (Newcomb & Bentler, 1988).

Finally, if prevention programs focus exclusively on deterring adolescents' initial experimentations with substances, there is a danger that they will fail to address the later (and more problematic) transitions from experimental to regular use. These later transitions to more advanced stages of use may serve different functions and be motivated by different factors than is early experimentation. Social psychological models of behavioral adoption suggest this (Abelson, 1982). Early stages of behavioral adoption seem to be based more on compliance and concern with rewards and punishments, whereas later stages are more likely to involve acts of internalized beliefs and values and commitments (Abelson, 1982; Kelman, 1958). Prevention programs that aim to deter transitions from experimental to regular use will have to combat different factors than those designed to prevent initial experimentation (e.g., Leventhal, Fleming, & Glynn, 1988). Thus, researchers have suggested that prevention programs should be broadened away from an exclusive focus on initial experimentation to try to deter transitions from experimental to more regular use.[1]

An additional alternative prevention goal follows from the fact that some substance use etiologies are thought to be more prognostic of later difficulties than are other etiologies. For example, Carman (1979) argued that substance use that is motivated by its "personal" effects (rather than its social effects) leads to more negative outcomes; that is, substance use that is motivated by a need to transform one's mood or to relieve distress has more negative implications than use that is motivated by social factors such as peer pressure. Some indirect evidence for this hypothesis was provided by recent longitudinal data (Newcomb & Bentler, 1988). Similarly, Mann, Chassin, & Sher (1987) found that alcohol use among high-risk subjects (adolescent children of problem drinking parents) was more closely tied to personal effects motives than was alcohol use among low-risk subjects. Conversely, alcohol use among low-risk subjects was more closely tied to social motives than was alcohol use among children of alcoholics. Thus, not only are certain levels

---

[1]The idea that prevention programs should focus on the later transitions from experimental to regular use does *not* mean that experimentation should be publicly labeled as acceptable, but rather that prevention programs should expand their focus to deal with the determinants of moves from experimental to regular use. Moreover, accepting experimentation as inevitable is not appropriate for highly addictive substances.

of consumption particularly problematic, but the use of substances to relieve personal distress may warrant concern. In terms of prevention goals, rather than focusing on substance use in general, it might be more important to focus on the personal distress-relieving functions of substance use.

Who is at Risk for Substance Use?

If effective school-based prevention programs are to be designed, it is important to consider characteristics of the target audience. Very general, omnibus programs that try to reach all adolescents may be ineffective and, in fact, may fail to influence those adolescents who are most at risk. Prospective research has helped to identify the characteristics of high-risk adolescents (Brook, Whiteman, Gordon, & Cohen, 1986; Chassin et al., 1984; Jessor & Jessor, 1977; Kandel, 1978). One important factor to consider is the change in risk across time and situation. Substance use initiation is most common at the entrance to middle school or junior high school (with another risk period at entrance to high school). The transition to middle or junior high school constitutes a stressor for early adolescents (Simmons, Rosenberg, & Rosenberg, 1973). It is a time of threat to self-image and change in peer environment. Peer pressure is likely to be influential because of the need to integrate into a new social network. Because of this timing, prevention programs are often aimed at early seventh-grade audiences.

It is also important to remember that high-risk adolescents can be characterized as unconventional and rebellious and loosely tied to conventional social institutions. Adolescents who have poor school grades and lowered aspirations for academic success are more likely to use substances. One challenge for school-based prevention programs is to tailor their programs to influence and involve these unconventional "deviance prone" adolescents.

Other important risk factors that have been identified include peer and parent substance use, positive attitudes and beliefs about use, familial alcoholism or criminality, and dysfunctional parenting (such as a lack of discipline, or excessive or inconsistent discipline; Botvin, 1987). Detailed reviews of these risk factors are available elsewhere (Chassin, 1984; Kandel, 1980).

It is important to remember that, although the established risk factors for substance use primarily relate to rebellious, nonconventional adolescents who are alienated from school or who fail in school, there are more "successful" or "conventional" adolescents who use drugs as well. For example, Mosbach and Leventhal (1988) found that the two adolescent groups or "cliques" in which cigarette use was most common were the "dirts" or the "freaks," who could best be described as unconventional and rebellious, and the "hot shots" who were described as leaders in academic and extracurricular activities. To understand substance use among these varied types of teenagers, it is necessary to understand the functions that substance use serves. Substance use is motivated by different functions and benefits in different types of adolescents.

Benefits and Functions of Use: Social Psychological Models

Social psychology teaches us the importance of understanding the functions served by a given behavior. Smith, Bruner, and White (1956) and Katz (1960) identified several different functions served by attitudes, opinions, and behaviors. For example, opinions might serve an ego-defensive function such that their expression helps protect a person from acknowledging basic and painful truths about him or herself. Alternatively, opinions can serve a value-expressive function in allowing a person to give positive expression to her or his central values or self-concept. What is important is that attitudes and opinions that serve different functions are not changeable by the same influence techniques. Insight approaches are more effective for changing attitudes serving an ego-defensive function, whereas information-based approaches work better for attitudes based on a value-expressive function (McClintock, 1958). Thus, if substance use would serve different functions for different adolescents, it would take different prevention approaches to change their relevant attitudes and opinions (see Chassin, Presson, & Sherman, 1985, for a discussion of how prevention programs for substance use should be guided by an understanding of the antecedents and functions of such use).

Substance use prevention programs have not always paid adequate attention to the psychological benefits and functions that substance use can serve for adolescents. For example, teaching adolescents to "just say no" will help a student who is already motivated to abstain from drugs but who lacks only the social skill to refuse peer offers. However, because substance use can serve important positive social and psychological functions for adolescents, they may not always be motivated to "say no" (Leventhal & Cleary, 1980). Here we discuss some of the important functions of adolescent substance use that prevention programs must combat.

Several recent social psychological theories highlight the motives and functions that adolescent substance use may serve. On a global level, expectancy theory (Goldman, Brown, & Christiansen, 1987) and the theory of reasoned action (Ajzen & Fishbein, 1980) have demonstrated that adolescents who believe that substance use leads to positive consequences are more likely to begin to use drugs later (Chassin et al., 1984; Christiansen, Smith, Roehling, & Goldman, 1989; Norman & Tedeschi, 1989). For example, adolescents who believe that substance use will help celebrate social occasions, enhance "highs", alter experience, and satisfy curiosity may be more likely to initiate substance use than are adolescents who do not believe that substance use will produce these positive outcomes. Cognitive models focus on attitudes and beliefs that adolescents hold and the role that attitudes, beliefs, and expectations have in determining subsequent behavior. (A more detailed discussion of the role of the theory of reasoned action can be found in chapter 2 in this volume.)

On a more specific level, social psychological theories have identified several functions of substance use that help us better understand the motives for this behavior.

Self-Verification Functions.   Self-verification theory suggests that individuals are motivated to express and affirm their existing self-concepts and to behave in ways that are consistent with the images that they hold of themselves. For example, individuals may prefer to receive feedback that is consistent with their own views of themselves, even if that feedback is negative (Swann, 1983). Theoretically, these positions suggest that individuals require stability in their self-perceptions and that people are therefore motivated to maintain existing self-images.

Adolescent substance use may serve self-verification functions. If there are distinct social images that are associated with substance use behavior, and if these images include traits or behaviors that are consistent with certain adolescents' pre-existing self-concepts, then those adolescents will be motivated to use substances in order to express and affirm their self-images. For example, if an adolescent male has a self-concept as a tough, "cowboy" type and if chewing tobacco is associated with this kind of image, then he may chew tobacco as a way of expressing this image. Moreover, social psychological research suggests that the tendency to choose behaviors that are consistent with self-concept is even stronger when important aspects of the self-concept are threatened (Greenberg & Pyszczynski, 1985). Given that adolescent substance use occurs during times of threat to self-concept (social transitions between elementary and middle school and between middle and high school), self-verification motives may be particularly important.

Research in the area of cigarette smoking, smokeless tobacco use, and alcohol use has been consistent with these self-verification mechanisms (Barton, Chassin, Presson, & Sherman, 1982; Burton et al., 1989; Chassin, Tetzloff, & Hershey, 1985). For example, our studies have found that the social image associated with cigarette smoking was an ambivalent one. Smoking carried many negative associations such as ill health, foolishness, disobedience, and not acting one's age. However, smokers were also seen as having desirable qualities, including toughness, sociability, and interest in the opposite sex. This social image of smoking was related to smoking behavior and intentions. Adolescents whose actual self-concepts were consistent with the prototypic smoker were more likely to smoke, and, among nonsmokers, were more likely to intend to smoke in the future (Barton et al., 1982; Chassin et al., 1981).

Self-Enhancement Functions. A second way in which the self determines behavioral decisions is through self-enhancement motives. In contrast to self-verification theories, self-enhancement theories argue that there is a motive for self-concept change rather than for self-concept stability. Self-enhancement theories are based on the premise that individuals are motivated to improve their self-concepts, both in order to maintain a positive image of themselves (Tesser, 1986) and to engage in strategic self-presentation to project a favorable impression in the eyes of others (Schlenker, 1980). These theories suggest that adolescents who aspire to the traits and characteristics associated with the images of substance users adopt substance use as a way of attaining an idealized self-concept either in their own eyes or the eyes of others.

Self-enhancement motives may be particularly powerful in the adolescent age period. Adolescence is a time of heightened awareness and preoccupation with self-concept. Young adolescents are acutely aware of the image that they project to other people. Elkind and his colleagues (Elkind, 1967; Elkind & Bowen, 1979) coined the term *imaginary audience* to describe adolescents' beliefs that others are preoccupied with their behavior and appearance. Given the importance of the self-concept during adolescence, self-concept motivations may be particularly powerful determinants of adolescents' decisions.

Kaplan (1980) presented an interesting variant of the self-enhancement model. In common with self-enhancement theories, he views individuals as being motivated to raise or increase their level of self-esteem. Adolescents who receive negative feedback from their usual social environments are motivated to increase their self-esteem by seeking positive feedback from others. In order to do this, they reject the norms of the conventional, mainstream group and affiliate with alternative, deviant groups. These groups reject conventional norms and reinforce counternormative behaviors such as substance use. In this way, substance use serves the function of raising self-esteem through acceptance by members of a deviant group. Kaplan's (1980) longitudinal study of seventh graders provides support for such a mechanism. Adolescents who initially showed low self-esteem were later likely to engage in deviant behavior, to affiliate with deviant peers, and to show increases in self-esteem.

Self-Handicapping Functions. According to this model, substances are used to protect a fragile but positive self-image in the face of an upcoming challenge to self-concept. When people feel good about themselves in some sphere of behavior but have uncertainty about their competence, an upcoming testing situation poses a great threat. In this situation, a self-handicapper may choose a strategy that actually impairs performance on the test, but one that will allow perceptions of underlying competence to go unchallenged. Perhaps the example most familiar to school settings is underachievement, where effort is not exerted so that failure cannot be attributed to a lack of ability. If a student fails an exam because he or she did not study, the student can still maintain that "I could have gotten an A if I wanted to." The failure is attributed to the lack of effort and not to the lack of ability (see Chapter 3 in this volume). Self-handicapping behaviors seem irrational, paradoxical, and self-destructive, but actually they serve a self-protective function. Even while they increase the likelihood of failure, they protect the self-concept from the implications of that failure.

In a similar way, drugs or alcohol can, because of perceptions of their performance-inhibiting qualities, help people avoid negative implications of failure as well as enhance the positive impact of success. Drug use does this by shaping and controlling the attributions that are made for failure and success. In the case of failure, personal competence won't be challenged. It is due to the effects of the drug. In the case of success, perceptions of personal competence may even be enhanced because the success occurred in the face of the drug induced inhibitory factors. Thus, drug use as a self-handicapping strategy can protect the self-image by structuring the context of behavior in a threatening situation.

Self-handicapping strategies involving drug and alcohol use have been demonstrated empirically. In several studies, subjects were induced to adopt positive but uncertain self-concepts in an area of intellectual performance. This was done by administering noncontingent success feedback to subjects (they were told they were correct no matter what answer they arrived at) on a series of very difficult problems where subjects were unlikely to feel that they had mastered the problem-solving process. Following this, if given the opportunity prior to another testing phase, subjects chose performance-impairing drugs as a way to avoid implications of possible failure (Berglas & Jones, 1978)—especially if no performance-enhancing option was available (Tucker, Vuchinich, & Sobell, 1981).

The use of drugs as a self-handicapping strategy also serves an anxiety-reducing function. In a situation of upcoming challenge to the self-concept, anticipatory anxiety is present because of the impending evaluation. By choosing a self-handicapping option, the adolescent reduces anticipatory anxiety about the event because failure loses its threatening quality. This anxiety-reduction benefit places self-handicapping theories of substance use in the broader tradition of tension-reduction models.

As described, self-handicapping is a strategy that is adopted not by failing or low self-esteem students by rather by successful students who do care about their performance. Self-handicapping is initiated by burdensome expectations placed on successful students who have some doubts about their abilities to continue to succeed. Burdensome expectations might be instilled in children of highly successful parents or children who have had successful siblings but who are unsure themselves about whether or not they can live up to these expectations. More important from an educational standpoint, Berglas (1987) theorized that self-handicapping can be created by praise that is not tied to actual performance. Noncontingent reward can create doubt about one's abilities. Thus, well-meaning but noncontingent praise and rewards delivered by parents and teachers can actually create burdensome expectations, which in turn establish the conditions under which adolescents may choose self-handicapping behaviors including substance use.

Interestingly, self-handicapping strategies involving drug and alcohol have been demonstrated only with males (Berglas, 1987). One reason for this may be that alcohol and drug use is not yet seen as an acceptable behavior for females. However, just as smoking has recently become more acceptable and more prevalent among females, an increase in the social acceptability of drug and alcohol use may lead to an increase in the adoption of substance use as a self-handicapping strategy for females. Also interesting is the fact that self-handicapping strategies in the laboratory are adopted when other more adaptive, performance-enhancing coping options are unavailable. For substance use prevention, these data suggest that providing positive alternative coping options can deter the self-handicapping functions of substance use. Finally, it is important to note that self-handicapping strategies involving drug and alcohol use will fail if that use becomes a dependency or regular pattern. Once one is labelled as an alcoholic, for example, then expectations of successful performance cannot be maintained.

Self-Awareness-Reducing Functions. Whereas self-handicapping is a strategy that may lead to substance use in the face of upcoming challenge, a somewhat different basis for alcohol use is suggested by self-awareness theory (Hull, 1987). This theory applies to individuals who are experiencing some degree of perceived failure from their environments. Hull (1987) suggested that alcohol use is motivated by the avoidance of a painful state of self-awareness. Individuals who are highly self-aware and who receive failure feedback from the environment may use alcohol to decrease their awareness of such negative self-relevant information. Thus, according to this theory, individuals with high levels of dispositional self-awareness who are experiencing failure feedback will be most likely to use alcohol. Laboratory studies provide support for this model with adult subjects. Subjects high or low in dispositional self-awareness were assigned to receive either success or failure feedback on laboratory tasks. Among subjects who were high in self-awareness, those who received failure feedback consumed more alcohol in a subsequent wine-tasting task than did those who received success feedback. Among those who were low in self-awareness, the feedback had no significant effect on consumption (Hull & Young, 1983).

Although the self-awareness model of alcohol use has had empirical support for adult subjects, there is reason to be cautious in applying the model to adolescents. In a survey of high school students, Chassin, Mann, and Sher

(1988) failed to find support for this model. Instead, high self-aware students drank at lower levels. In interpreting these findings, Chassin et al. (1988) turned to a body of social psychological knowledge that has linked high self-awareness with an acute sensitivity to social norms and proscriptions. Highly self-aware adolescents may be dissuaded from use by the illegal nature of alcohol consumption and the social proscriptions against adolescent alcohol use. Moreover, in the natural environment (as opposed to the laboratory), adolescents may have a variety of ways of coping with failure feedback without resorting to alcohol use. Thus, it is possible that alcohol use will result only when these other coping options are blocked. Although the self-awareness model may not explain the most typical path into adolescent alcohol use, it may still apply to those adolescents who are highly self-aware, who experience failure feedback, and who have a narrow range of alternative coping options for dealing with this failure.

These last two models (self-handicapping and self-awareness) indicate that it is not always the "down and out" or low self-esteem adolescents who are at risk for alcohol and drug abuse. These models show how relatively successful, high self-esteem adolescents might engage in substance use under the appropriate triggering circumstances—perceived failure in the case of self-awareness and anticipated failure in the case of self-handicapping.

The self-handicapping and self-awareness models are also special cases of more general stress reduction models. In both cases, the substance use behavior serves to reduce perceived personal distress. More general models of stress and coping have also been applied to adolescent substance use (e.g., Wills, 1986). In these models, negative environmental stress events precede the use of substances, which then serve a coping function and act to reduce negative affect. For example, stress events may decrease adolescents' sense of perceived control over their lives. Substance use can then serve to increase perceived control (Newcomb & Harlow, 1986). These models suggest that intervention efforts should include attempts to increase available coping strategies as a way of deterring adolescent substance use.

Precocity and Pseudomaturity Functions.   Another social psychological approach to adolescent substance use has been problem behavior theory (Jessor & Jessor, 1977). This theory notes that adolescent substance use behaviors co-vary and are also associated with minor delinquent behaviors and early sexual experience. These problem behaviors are characterized as involving a premature transition to adult activities in violation of age norms. The characteristics of such "transition-prone" adolescents include personality factors (e.g., high tolerance for deviance, low expectations for attaining academic success, high value on independence) and perceived environment factors (e.g., low perceived supportiveness and low perceived strictness by friends and parents). Problem behavior theory has been successfully applied to the initiation of alcohol and marijuana use in adolescence (Jessor & Jessor, 1977). One important contribution of this model has been in the description of the high-risk "deviance prone" adolescent who is the best target audience for preventive interventions. Given that "deviance prone" adolescents are relatively unconventional and alienated from school settings, it is a challenge for school-based substance use prevention programs to construct persuasive messages that will be effective for this group.

A recent, related model of substance use has been presented by Newcomb and Bentler (1988). Their model characterizes drug and alcohol use as behaviors adopted in order to accelerate social development. These activities enable students to "grow up" quickly. According to this model, students most likely to be at risk for substance use are those least able to delay gratification. Such students are prone to seek out immediate benefits in life, despite possible long-term costs. Indeed, regular use of drugs in adolescence is associated with an early entry into work and marital roles (Newcomb & Bentler, 1988). Unfortunately, this kind of precocious development is not associated with competent handling of adult roles and tasks. Thus, regular substance use in adolescence is also associated with instability in marital and work roles. Thus, adolescent substance use involves only a "pseudomaturity" and a foreshortening of appropriate developmental sequences.

In sum, substance use can serve a wide variety of positive functions for adolescents. Substance use can provide novel experiences and new sensations; it can serve to express and verify an existing self-image; it can enhance self-image through positive reinforcement from a deviant peer group. Substance use can convey a social image of precocity and maturity; it can decrease painful self-awareness of negative environmental feedback; and it can serve as a self-handicapping strategy. Given these various functions, it is inappropriate to view substance use initiation only as involving passive adolescents who are pressured to use drugs against their will. Rather adolescents may be attracted to substance use for a variety of reasons. This discussion has also highlighted the complexity of adolescent substance use behavior. There are multiple pathways into substance use. Different adolescents are at risk for different reasons. Different levels of use may be motivated by different factors. The complex and multivariate nature of adolescent drug use makes it difficult to develop intervention programs. As we see next, those programs that have been most promising have attempted to take into account the complex functions that substance use can serve.

SCHOOL-BASED PROGRAMS FOR SUBSTANCE USE PREVENTION: AN EVALUATION

Just as our understanding of adolescent substance use has been enhanced by social psychological research and theory, so too has the development of prevention programs. We describe the major approaches to school-based programs and show how they have been guided by social psychological thinking and research, and we evaluate the impact of these programs in light of the ideas that we have presented about substance use behaviors.

Traditional Health Education Approaches

Traditional health education programs attempted to teach students about the health relevant effects of substance use. They were based on social psychological models of rational decision making, that is, that substance use is in large part a consequence of a lack of appropriate information. By presenting the health facts, it was assumed that adolescents would change their beliefs and attitudes and that correspondent behavioral change would follow (Ajzen & Fishbein, 1980). There were several shortcomings of these initial approaches. First, there was a narrow focus on the negative long-term health effects of drugs. Such messages ignored the positive social and interpersonal benefits of substance use. Adolescents might still choose to use substances because to them the positive immediate social benefits outweigh the long-term negative health effects and the latter effects are so psychologically distant. Moreover, these messages about long-term health consequences lack credibility with an adolescent audience (Bell & Battjes, 1985).

Not only did the content of traditional health education limit its effectiveness, but the form of presentation was also problematic. Early programs typically presented facts without consideration for the packaging of these messages. One early attempt to take into account message presentation based on social psychological theorizing assumed that high fear appeals would best motivate people to change their health behaviors. However, social psychologists soon demonstrated that high fear messages were in fact unlikely to be successful in changing health behaviors (Janis & Feshbach, 1953; Leventhal, 1968). Rather, high fear appeals produced defensive avoidance. Thus, early health education methods of presentation were ineffective.

Finally, even with a sophisticated presentation of a wide variety of information, information alone is unlikely to be effective because presenting information does not teach adolescents the relevant behavioral skills. Information may change adolescents' attitudes and beliefs about substance use and may produce a motive to avoid substance use. However, if adolescents lack skills to cope with stress or skills to resist peer offers of use, they may still adopt substance use behaviors. If adolescents do not have behavioral alternative ways of dealing with stressors or with failure situations or with peer substance use situations, they will still use substances despite having appropriate information and attitudes.

Affective Education

In some ways, affective education approaches to substance use prevention grew out of disillusionment with traditional health education and a fear that traditional information-only programs might even increase substance use (Stuart, 1974). Instead, educators sought to raise self-esteem through a series of values clarification and decision-making exercises. No explicit mention of substance use was included in these programs. A social psychological analysis reveals several reasons why affective education by itself should be an unsuccessful strategy to prevent substance use. First, as we have seen, substance use is not necessarily initiated only by adolescents who are low in self-esteem. Thus, raising self-esteem addresses only a limited aspect of risk factors. Second, social psychological theory suggests that it is necessary to focus on specific beliefs and attitudes in order to change specific behaviors (Fishbein & Ajzen, 1974; Heberlein & Black, 1976). Affective education attempts to change very general attitudes as a way of changing a specific (drug use) behavior. Finally, social psychological theories of self-consistency (as described earlier) suggest that achieving self-concept change is not an easy task. Self-verification and self-consistency theories indicate that individuals are motivated to maintain stability of self-concept even in the face of countervailing evidence.

Providing Alternatives to Substance Use

Another approach to substance use prevention has been termed the provision of *alternatives* (Swisher & Hu, 1983). As with affective education, these programs recognize that drug use serves important social and psychological functions for adolescents. However, unlike affective education, these programs attempt to deter drug use by providing alternative activities and skills that represent more positive ways to achieve these same social and psychological benefits. Some alternatives that have been used include recreational activities, jobs, and training in personal competencies such as reading skills and job skills (Bry, 1982; Swisher & Hu, 1983). As with affective education, however, the content of these programs is not made specific to substance use.

Social Psychologically Based Prevention Programs

Recently, researchers have used social psychological theory and research to develop preventive interventions in the area of adolescent drug use. The first of these programs was introduced by Richard Evans and his colleagues at the University of Houston and was designed to deter adolescent cigarette smoking. This program attempted to combat the important social forces that might lead adolescents to begin to smoke (i.e., peer pressure, parent model-ing, and media pressure). The basic premise of this program is derived from the social psychological concept of "social inoculation" (McGuire, 1964). Ac-cording to McGuire, many persuasion attempts are difficult to resist because people have never thought about the issue and are unpracticed in resisting the arguments. McGuire thus suggested that a mild influence attempt might help build resistance against future strong attempts—especially if one is taught to refute or counterargue against the mild attack. Following this line of thought, Evans et al. (1978) presented videotapes of peer pressures to smoke and taught young adolescents ways to resist these pressures. Although the results of this program were disappointing (Evans et al., 1981; Flay, 1985), its theoretical basis and its innovative approach provided a model for fur-ther social psychologically based prevention efforts. These efforts can be divid-ed into two types: social influence programs (Flay et al., 1985; Pentz et al., 1989) and social and personal skills training programs (Botvin, 1987). Most of the programs have concentrated on preventing cigarette smoking, although, most recently, they have been applied to other substance use as well (Bot-vin, Baker, Renick, & Fizzola, 1984; Pentz et al., 1989).

Social Influence Approaches

Social influence approaches stem most directly from Evans' initial work and continue to rely on McGuire's concept of social inoculation to help adoles-cents develop counterarguments against social pressures to use drugs. These programs have elaborated on Evans' initial work by training specific skills that students can use to resist social pressures and by incorporating new com-ponents. For example, peer leaders have been used as well as more tradi-tional teacher-led formats (e.g., Murray, Johnson, Luepker, & Mittelmark, 1984). In addition, these programs have drawn on Kiesler's (1971) notion of public commitment and have had adolescents reach a decision about their own substance use behavior and publicly announce this decision to the class. Finally, these new social influence programs have attempted to correct stu-dents' overestimations of drug use prevalence among their peers. Research has shown not only that adolescents overestimate the extent of substance use, but that those who make the highest overestimations are more likely to begin substance use (Chassin et al., 1984; Leventhal et al., 1988), perhaps because they view substance use as more normative and acceptable. By presenting accurate information about the infrequency of substance use, it is hoped that adolescents will be deterred from experimentation. As this ex-ample illustrates, these social psychologically based programs do not reject the idea of presenting drug-related information to students, and thus they share this in common with health education programs. Many of these pro-grams also present information about the short-term health effects of drug use as well. What is different about the social influences approaches is the type of information that is presented. Information about social consequences of use, information about true prevalence, and information about short-term consequences have replaced a traditional emphasis on the long-term health consequences that are considered less salient and important to young adolescents.

What is also different about the social influence approaches is that, rather than simply using didactic presentation of information, they have drawn on social psychological research in formulating the ways in which persuasive messages are delivered. Thus, social psychology has shaped not only the content of these programs but also the methods and techniques by which that content is communicated. One prominent example of this is the Waterloo Smoking Project (Flay et al., 1983; Flay et al., 1985). Drawing on the information-processing model of Hovland, Janis, and Kelley (1953), messages are repeated in multiple channels (e.g., videotapes, posters, discussion) to increase the probability that adolescents will attend to the information and comprehend it. Information is elicited from subjects besides being provided to them. This process should be more likely to change beliefs and attitudes than simply to provide information from outside sources. The idea that active participation in a program will be more effective is consistent with social psychological research showing that self-generated material is processed more deeply than externally presented material (Slamecka & Graf, 1978). Moreover, the program also relies on decision-making theory (Janis & Mann, 1977), in which subjects are asked to use the material from the program to reach their own decision concerning cigarette smoking. Finally, the program uses role-playing techniques derived from social psychology (King & Janis, 1956) to train students in specific skills to resist peer pressure.

Social and Personal Skills Training Programs

Another recent social psychologically based type of prevention program relies on training social and personal skills (Botvin, 1987; Botvin et al., 1984; Schinke & Gilchrist, 1983). The theoretical bases of these programs lie in social learning theory and in problem behavior theory. Social and personal skills programs rest on the assumption that adolescents use drugs in order to attain any one of a variety of desirable benefits including those described above (self-definition, enhanced self-esteem, regulation of anxiety or negative affect). They note that the social influence programs described previously do not give adolescents alternative ways of attaining these personal and social benefits and thus do not address some of the important motives and functions of substance use. Moreover, these researchers argue that adolescents who are low in self-esteem and autonomy will also be more vulnerable to external social pressures to smoke. By increasing self-esteem and autonomy, personal skills training programs are thought to reduce vulnerability to social influence.

According to Botvin (1987), the hallmarks of these programs include developing general problem-solving abilities, developing resistance skills, increasing self-control and self-esteem through goal setting and self-reinforcement, learning coping strategies (such as relaxation training) for dealing with anxiety, learning new social skills such as conversational skills and dating skills, and assertiveness training. These skills are taught both on a general level and as applied specifically to situations that involve drug use. One prominent example of this approach is Life Skills Training (Botvin et al., 1984), which has shown promising results in reducing substance use among young adolescents. Issues related to the implementation of such programs were reviewed by Forman and Linney (1988).

Personal and social skills programs have some features in common with the older affective education approaches, in that they recognize the importance of self-protective motives and they teach general personal and social skills (e.g., decision-making skills, self-esteem enhancement strategies). However, the two approaches also have important differences. The older affective education programs did not mention substance use and did not teach skills that were specific to substance use situations. Personal and social skills approaches include specific information about substances as well as specific skills for dealing with substance use situations.

Evaluations of Program Success

In a recent meta-analysis, Tobler (1986) compared the impact of five substance use prevention modalities: traditional health education, affective education, a combination of these two, social psychologically based programs, and the provision of alternatives. In terms of their impact on actual adolescent substance use behavior, Tobler found that traditional health education, affective education, and their combination were ineffective. She concluded that there was no supporting evidence for continuing these programs. The social psychologically based programs, however, had the largest impact, followed by the programs that provide alternatives to substance use. The results for the alternatives programs were particularly interesting because they had their largest impact on high-risk adolescents such as delinquents and those with school problems. Thus, although the recent social psychologically based programs are clearly empirically the most promising, the alternatives programs may still have an important role.

From a social psychological perspective, the success of the more recent social psychologically based programs is predictable. These programs are multifaceted and attempt to combat some of the social and personal functions of substance use (e.g., Life Skills Training). The programs attempt to train specific behavioral skills to combat social pressures to use drugs. Moreover, the programs attempt to implement their messages using techniques that have been empirically determined to achieve a persuasive effect. However, even though these approaches have a promising beginning, their effectiveness is by no means definitively established or well understood. Many of the empirical evaluations of these programs have had serious methodological flaws that make it impossible to draw definitive conclusions, and no comparative tests among the social psychological approaches (e.g., Life Skills Training versus a social influence approach) have been performed. Moreover, because many of the evaluations have been done on applications to adolescent cigarette smoking, there are only limited data concerning the impact of these programs on broad categories of adolescent drug use. In addition, long-term program impacts are unknown.

What is also important from the point of view of this chapter is the question of how much of these programs' impact can be traced to their reliance on social psychological theory and research. These programs are multidimensional and extremely complex in content. Empirical evaluations have assessed global effectiveness, but they are unable to reveal which specific program components are actually impactful. Moreover, there have been disappointingly few documented effects on the theoretical mediators of behavior change. Thus, it is impossible to identify with certainty the active ingredients in program success. It must also be remembered that these programs are being administered in a larger social climate in which there is growing emphasis on "healthy life styles" and considerable media attention to antidrug campaigns (such as "just say no"). Given this "social boost" from the larger environment, a variety of program components could be responsible for program effects. Thus, there are many unanswered questions concerning the actual magnitude of program impact on drug use, the long-term program impact, and the active ingredients in program success.

Some Current Directions in School-Based Substance Use Prevention

Some interesting programs that have recently been initiated include an attempt to integrate family and community resources with social influences programs (Pentz et al., 1989), an attempt to integrate a reframing of adolescents' initial experiences with substance use with social influences programs (Leventhal et al., 1988), and an attempt to draw on computer technology to deliver health education (Bosworth, Gustafson, Hawkins, & Gustafson, 1983).

Pentz et al. (1989) reported an innovative attempt to expand the social influences approach to prevention by adding family and community components. Obviously, substance use prevention is a difficult undertaking for the schools if support from the family and larger community is lacking. Family and community influences on adolescent substance use are substantial. Pentz et al. (1989) added a family "homework" component by having adolescents do a series of family interviews about topics such as methods that the family could use to counteract drug use influences. Community components included mass media coverage of the school-based prevention program, press conferences, and regular meetings with community leaders. Initial program results showed a significant decrease in substance use onset in the treated group compared to a control condition.

Another addition to the social influences approach has been proposed by Leventhal and his colleagues (Leventhal et al., 1988) and has been tested with respect to adolescent cigarette smoking. Leventhal argues that social influence approaches are confined to dealing with initial smoking experimentation and lack techniques for preventing transitions from experimental to more regular use. These transitions are (in part) related to adolescents' initial experiences with the substance (Hirschman, Leventhal, & Glynn, 1984). Thus, in the case of cigarette smoking, adolescents who experienced negative physical sensations when first experimenting with cigarettes were less likely to continue use. Based on these findings, Hirschman and Leventhal (1989) incorporated a prevention component in which they reframed adolescents' interpretations of their physiological sensations to attempt to deter further use. For example, when adolescents stop coughing in response to cigarettes, they may view this as becoming adapted and adjusted to smoking. Leventhal et al. reframe this experience as the failure of the body's physical defense mechanisms so that damage from smoking is now possible. This reframing of ambiguous physical sensations has a long history within social psychology (Schachter & Singer, 1962). Promising initial results of this program have been reported (Leventhal et al., 1988).

The advent of computer technology has led to attempts to introduce substance use prevention into the schools through a computer-based format. The assertion here is that the novelty and appeal of computer games makes the experience more interesting for students, and that program branching makes it possible to deliver only relevant programs to particular students (Bosworth et al., 1983). In one example of computer-based drug prevention, Bosworth and her colleagues (Bosworth et al., 1983) have taken content from existing approaches (e.g., training in refusal skills, decision-making skills, knowledge of high-risk situations) and integrated this content into a computer-based format. Both individual programs and programs designed for family use are available, and initial tests have shown reductions in substance use as a result of this program.

SUMMARY AND CONCLUSIONS

In this chapter we have tried to illustrate the ways in which social psychology has contributed to our understanding of the antecedents of substance use, the functions of substance use, and the likely effectiveness of programs to prevent such use. Social psychological research and theory suggest that substance use is not simply adopted by powerless adolescents who cannot "say no." Although some substance use experimentation can occur in this way, substance use also serves many different positive social and psychological functions for adolescents. We have also seen the complexity of substance use behaviors. It is not simply the low self-esteem, failing adolescent who uses drugs. Rather, there are multiple pathways into drug use, and different adolescents will use drugs for different reasons. We have seen some of the limitations of earlier school-based substance use prevention programs, as well as some promising results of recent social psychologically based interventions. It is still unknown, however, how school-based prevention programs can reach some of the highest risk "deviance prone" adolescents who are relatively unconventional and alienated from traditional school values. Perhaps community programs of the type that provide alternatives to substance use would be important for these adolescents.

Throughout this chapter, we have stressed the benefits of applying a social psychological perspective to the issue of adolescent drug use. However, there are also cautions and limitations that must be raised in applying basic research to real world problems. Effects that are found in the laboratory cannot simply be expected to occur in a less controlled naturalistic setting (cf., Higginbotham, West, & Forsyth, 1988). One relevant example of this problem can be found in the literature on role playing (which is a popular technique in recent substance use prevention programs). Janis and Gilmore (1965) found that role playing was less effective when the experimenter aroused hostility or suspicion than when the experimenter was seen as acting from benign motives. When prevention programs are implemented in a school setting led by either teachers or high achieving and conventionally "popular" peer leaders, the perceptions and evaluations held by the adolescents may undermine the effectiveness of role-playing techniques that previously succeeded in laboratory settings. In general, as researchers and practitioners try to apply social psychological findings from the laboratory to field interventions, it is important to attend to the boundary and limiting conditions that moderate the effects of interventions.

Finally, we should realize that there are limits to what social psychology can provide to the school psychologist in terms of decisions about the specifics of substance use programs. Social psychology can provide only the theory and data to help understand the factors that underlie substance initiation, and, in so doing, can suggest strategies that are likely to be effective in the prevention of substance use. However, decisions about the development and implementation of drug programs must be based on more than an abstract understanding of the processes involved in substance use initiation and the likely effectiveness of prevention programs. Decisions about the specific features of programs must also involve considerations of an ethical, philosophical, and political nature. For example, we must ask ourselves what are the values and goals that are being reflected in the drug prevention programs? Is it simply an issue of licit versus illicit substances? If so, then the so-called "hard drugs" should be the main targets of programs. If physical harm and general long-term health concerns are the issues, however, then the legal drugs of alcohol and cigarettes, which have the greatest potential for damage, should be the main targets of intervention. Even when the goals and values are decided, the strategies and tactics chosen must also involve questions that go beyond simple probabilities of effectiveness. For example, programs that rely on mass conformity and public commitment may be effective, but the ways in which these programs are implemented might result in implicit threats of public ridicule. The ethical and social appropriateness of such a program must be considered. Similarly, a decision about whether to have a smoking area in a school may have to balance notions of the right to smoke with notions about whether smoking areas encourage students to adopt or continue to use tobacco. Finally, it is necessary to examine the underlying messages that may be inadvertently communicated in substance use prevention campaigns. Along with effective drug prevention, campaigns may engender fear among adolescents or may reinforce a feeling of powerlessness or lack of control through images of inevitable addiction (Peele, 1987). Thus, although social psychology can tell us about the processes of substance use initiation and about program effectiveness, school psychologists must carefully consider the ethical implications of prevention goals and programs. It is in fact these ethical and philosophical considerations that will prove more difficult for the school psychologist to resolve (Gottlieb, Burdine, & McElroy, 1987).

ACKNOWLEDGMENTS

Preparation of this chapter was supported by grant HD13449 to the first three authors and by grant DA05227 to the first author.

REFERENCES

Abelson, R. P. (1982). Three models of attitude-behavior consistency. In M. P. Zanna, E. T. Higgins, & C. P. Herman (Eds.), *Consistency in social behavior: The Ontario Symposium* (Vol. 2, pp. 131–146). Hillsdale, NJ: Lawrence Erlbaum Associates.

Ajzen, I., & Fishbein, M. (1980). *Understanding attitudes and predicting social behavior.* Englewood Cliffs, NJ: Prentice-Hall.

Barton, J., Chassin, L., Presson, C. C., & Sherman, S. J. (1982). Social image factors as motivators of smoking initiation in early and middle adolescence. *Child Development, 53,* 1499–1511.

Baumrind, D. (1985). Familial antecedents of adolescent drug use: A developmental perspective. In C. L. Jones & R. J. Battjes (Eds.), *Etiology of drug abuse: Implications for preventive intervention* (pp. 13–44). NIDA Research Monograph 56, DHHS Publication No. (ADM) 85-1335. Washington, DC: U. S. Government Printing Office.

Bell, C. S., & Battjes, R. (1985). *Prevention research: Deterring drug abuse among children and adolescents.* NIDA Research Monograph 63, DHHS Publication No. (ADM) 85-1334. Washington, DC: U.S. Government Printing Service.

Berglas, S. (1987). Self-handicapping model. In H. T. Blane & K. Leonard (Eds.), *Psychological theories of drinking and alcoholism* (pp. 305–345). New York: Guilford Press.

Berglas, S., & Jones, E. E. (1978). Drug choice as a self-handicapping strategy in response to noncontingent success. *Journal of Personality and Social Psychology, 36*, 405–417.

Blum, R. (1987). Contemporary threats to adolescent health in the United States. *Journal of the American Medical Association, 257*, 3390–3395.

Bosworth, K., Gustafson, D., Hawkins, R., & Gustafson, D. (1983). Adolescent health information and computers: The Body Awareness Resource Network (BARN). *Health Education, 14* (5).

Botvin, G. J. (1987). Prevention research. *Drug and drug abuse research: Second Triennial Report to Congress.* National Institute on Drug Abuse, DHHS Pub. No. (ADM) 87-1486, Washington, DC: U.S. Government Printing Office.

Botvin, G. J., Baker, E., Renick, N., & Fizzola, A. (1984). A cognitive-behavioral approach to substance abuse prevention. *Addictive Behaviors, 9*, 137–147.

Brook, J., Whiteman, M., Gordon, A., & Cohen, P. (1986). Dynamics of childhood and adolescent personality traits and adolescent drug use. *Developmental Psychology, 22*, 403–414.

Bry, B. (1982). Reducing the incidence of adolescent problems through preventive intervention: One and five year follow-up. *American Journal of Community Psychology, 10*, 265–275.

Bry, B. (1983). Empirical foundations of family-based approaches to adolescent substance use. In T. Glynn, C. Leukefeld, & J. Ludford (Eds.), *Preventing adolescent drug abuse: Intervention strategies* (pp. 154–172). NIDA Research Monograph 47, DHHS (ADM)83-1280. Washington, DC: U.S. Government Printing Office.

Burton, D., Sussman, S., Hansen, W., Johnson, C., & Flay, B. (1989). Image attributions and smoking intentions among seventh grade students. *Journal of Applied Social Psychology, 19*, 656–66.

Carman, R. S. (1979). Motivations for drug use and problematic outcomes among rural junior high school students. *Addictive Behaviors, 4*, 91–93.

Chassin, L. (1984). Adolescent substance use and abuse. In P. Karoly & J. Steffen (Eds.), *Advances in child behavioral analysis and therapy* (pp. 99–152). Lexington, MA: Heath.

Chassin, L., Mann, L., & Sher, K. J. (1988). Self-awareness theory, family history of alcoholism, and adolescent alcohol involvement. *Journal of Abnormal Psychology, 97*, 206–217.

Chassin, L., Presson, C., & Sherman, S. J. (1985). Stepping backward in order to step forward: An acquisition-oriented approach to primary prevention. *Journal of Consulting and Clinical Psychology, 53*, 612–622.

Chassin, L., Presson, C. C., Sherman, S. J., Corty, E., & Olshavsky, R. (1981). Self-images and cigarette smoking in adolescence. *Personality and Social Psychology Bulletin, 7*, 670–676.

Chassin, L., Presson, C. C., Sherman, S. J., Corty, E., & Olshavsky, R. (1984). Predicting the onset of cigarette smoking in adolescents: A longitudinal study. *Journal of Applied Social Psychology, 14*, 224–243.

Chassin, L., Tetzloff, C., & Hershey, M. (1985). Self-image and social image factors in adolescent alcohol use. *Journal of Studies on Alcohol, 46*, 39–48.

Christiansen, B., Smith, G., Roehling, P., & Goldman, M. (1989). Using alcohol expectancies to predict adolescent drinking behavior after one year. *Journal of Consulting and Clinical Psychology, 57*, 93–99.

Elkind, D. (1967). Egocentrism in adolescence. *Child Development, 38*, 1025–1034.

Elkind, D., & Bowen, D. (1979). Imaginary audience behavior in children and adolescents. *Developmental Psychology, 15*, 38–44.

Erikson, K. T. (1962). Notes on the sociology of deviance. *Journal of Social Problems, 9*, 307–314.

Evans, R., Rozelle, R., Mittelmark, M., Hansen, W., Bane, A., & Havis, J. (1978). Deterring the onset of smoking in children: Knowledge of immediate physiological effects and coping with peer pressure, media pressure, and parent modeling. *Journal of Applied Social Psychology, 8*, 126–135.

Evans, R. I., Rozelle, R. M., Maxwell, S. E., Raines, B. E., Dill, C. A., Guthrie, T. J., Henderson, R. H., & Hill, P. C. (1981). Social modeling films to deter smoking in adolescents: Results of a three-year field investigation. *Journal of Applied Social Psychology, 66,* 399–414.

Fishbein, M., & Ajzen, I. (1974). Attitudes toward objects as predictors of single and multiple behavioral criteria. *Psychological Review, 81,* 59–74.

Flay, B. R. (1985). What we know about the social influences approach to smoking prevention: Review and recommendation. In C. S. Bell & R. Battjes (Eds.), *Prevention research: Deterring drug abuse among children and adolescents.* NIDA Research Monograph 63, pp. 67–112. Washington, DC: U.S. Government Printing Office.

Flay, B. R., Ryan, K. B., Best, J. A., Brown, S., Kersell, M. W., d'Avernas, J. R., & Zanna, M. P. (1985). Are social-psychological smoking prevention programs effective? The Waterloo study. *Journal of Behavioral Medicine, 8,* 37–59.

Flay, B. R., d'Avernas, J. R., Best, J. A., Kersell, M. W., & Ryan, K. B. (1983). Cigarette smoking: Why young people do it and ways of preventing it. In P. J. McGrath & P. Firestone (Eds.), *Pediatric and adolescent behavioral medicine* (pp. 132–181). New York: Springer.

Forman, S. G., & Linney, J. A. (1988). School-based prevention of adolescent substance abuse: Programs, implementation, and future directions. *School Psychology Review, 17,* 550–558.

Goldman, M., Brown, S., & Christiansen, B. (1987). Expectancy theory; Thinking about drinking. In H. T. Blane & K. Leonard (Eds.), *Psychological theories of drinking and alcoholism* (pp. 181–227). New York: Guilford Press.

Gottlieb, N., Burdine, J., & McElroy, K. (Eds.) (1987). Ethical dilemmas in health promotion. *Health Education Quarterly, 14,* 1–111.

Greenberg, J., & Pyszczynski, T. (1985). Compensatory self-inflation: A response to the threat to self-regard of public failure. *Journal of Personality and Social Psychology, 49,* 273–280.

Heberlein, T. A., & Black, J. (1976). Attitudinal specificity and the prediction of behavior in a field setting. *Journal of Personality and Social Psychology, 33,* 474–479.

Higginbotham, H., West, S., & Forsyth, D. (1988). *Psychotherapy and behavior change: Social, cultural, and methodological perspectives.* New York: Pergamon.

Hirschman, R. S., & Leventhal, H. (1989). Preventing smoking behavior in school children: An initial test of a cognitive developmental program. *Journal of Applied Social Psychology, 19,* 559–583.

Hirschman, R. S., Leventhal, H., & Glynn, K. (1984). The development of smoking behavior: Conceptualization and supportive cross-sectional data. *Journal of Applied Social Psychology, 14,* 184–207.

Hovland, C. I., Janis, I. L., & Kelley, H. H. (1953). *Communication and persuasion.* New Haven: Yale University Press.

Hull, J. G. (1987). Self-awareness model. In H. T. Blane & K. E. Leonard (Eds.), *Psychological theories of drinking and alcoholism* (pp. 272–304). New York: Guilford Press.

Hull, J. G., & Young, R. D. (1983). The self-awareness-reducing effects of alcohol: Evidence and implications. In J. Suls & A. G. Greenwald (Eds.), *Psychological perspectives on the self* (Vol. 2, pp. 159–190). Hillsdale, NJ: Lawrence Erlbaum Associates.

Janis, I. L., & Feshbach, S. (1953). Effects of fear-arousing communications. *Journal of Abnormal and Social Psychology, 48,* 78–92.

Janis, I. L., & Gilmore, J. B. (1965). The influence of incentive conditions on the success of role-playing in modifying attitudes. *Journal of Personality and Social Psychology, 1,* 17–27.

Janis, I. L., & Mann, L. (1977). *Decision-making: A psychological analysis of conflict, choice, and commitment.* New York: The Free Press.

Jessor, R., & Jessor, S. L. (1977). *Problem behavior and psychosocial development: A longitudinal study of youth.* New York: Academic Press.

Johnston, L., O'Malley, P., & Bachman, J. (1988). *Illicit drug use, smoking, and drinking by America's high school students, college students, and young adults 1975–1987.* National Institute on Drug Abuse, DHHS Pub. No. (ADM)89-1602. Washington, DC: U.S. Government Printing Office.

Kandel, D. B. (1978). Convergences in prospective longitudinal surveys of drug use in normal populations. In D. Kandel (Ed.), *Longitudinal research on drug use: Empirical findings and methodological issues* (pp. 3–38). Washington, DC: Hemisphere.

Kandel, D. B. (1980). Drug and drinking behavior among youth. *Annual Review of Sociology, 6*, 235–285.

Kandel, D. B., & Faust, R. (1975). Sequences and stages in patterns of adolescent drug use. *Archives of General Psychiatry, 32*, 923–932.

Kaplan, H. B. (1980). *Deviant behavior in defense of self*. New York: Academic Press.

Katz, D. (1960). The functional approach to the study of attitudes. *Public Opinion Quarterly, 24*, 163–204.

Kelman, H. C. (1958). Compliance, identification and internalization: Three processes of attitude change. *Journal of Conflict Resolution, 2*, 51–60.

Kiesler, C. A. (1971). *The psychology of commitment*. New York: Academic Press.

King, B. T., & Janis, I. L. (1956). Comparison of the effectiveness of improvised versus non-improvised role-playing in producing opinion changes. *Human Relations, 9*, 177–186.

Leventhal, H. (1968). Experimental studies of anti-smoking communications. In E. F. Borgatta & Robert R. Evans (Eds.), *Smoking, health, and behavior* (pp. 95–122). Chicago: Aldine.

Leventhal, H., & Cleary, P. (1980). The smoking problem: A review of research and theory in behavioral risk modification. *Psychological Bulletin, 88*, 370–405.

Leventhal, H., Fleming, R., & Glynn, K. (1988). A cognitive-developmental approach to smoking intervention. In S. Maes, C. D. Spielberger, P. Defares, & I. G. Sarason (Eds.), *Topics in health psychology* (pp. 79–105). New York: Wiley.

Mann, L., Chassin, L., & Sher, K. J. (1987). Alcohol expectancies and risk for alcoholism. *Journal of Consulting and Clinical Psychology, 55*, 411–417.

McClintock, C. G. (1958). Personality syndromes and attitude change. *Journal of Personality, 26*, 479–493.

McGuire, W. J. (1964). Inducing resistance to persuasion. In L. Berkowitz (Ed.), *Advances in experimental social psychology* (Vol. 1, pp. 191–229). New York: Academic Press.

Mosbach, P., & Leventhal, H. (1988). Peer group identification and smoking: Implications for intervention. *Journal of Abnormal Psychology, 97*, 238–245.

Murray, D., Johnson, C. A., Luepker, R. V., & Mittelmark, M. B. (1984). The prevention of cigarette smoking in children: A comparison of four strategies. *Journal of Applied Social Psychology, 14*, 274–289.

National Association for Perinatal Addiction Research and Education. (1988). *Innocent addicts: High rate of prenatal drug abuse found*. ADAHMA News. (October, 1989).

National Institute on Drug Abuse. (1984). *Drug abuse and drug abuse research: The first in a series of triennial reports to Congress*. DHHS Publication No. (ADM)85-1372. Washington, DC: U.S. Government Printing Office.

National Institute on Drug Abuse. (1987). *Drug Abuse and Drug Abuse Research: The second triennial report to Congress*. DHHS Publication No. (ADM)87-1486. Washington, DC: U.S. Government Printing Office.

Newcomb, M. D., & Bentler, P. M. (1986). Drug use, educational aspirations, and workforce involvement. *American Journal of Community Psychology, 14*, 303–321.

Newcomb, M. D., & Bentler, P. M. (1988). *Consequences of adolescent drug use: Impact on the lives of young adults*. Newbury Park, CA: Sage.

Newcomb, M. D., & Harlow, L. L. (1986). Life events and substance use among adolescents: Mediating effects of perceived loss of control and meaninglessness in life. *Journal of Personality and Social Psychology, 51*, 564–571.

Norman, N., & Tedeschi, J. (1989). Self-presentation, reasoned action, and adolescents' decisions to smoke cigarettes. *Journal of Applied Social Psychology, 19*, 543–559.

Peele, S. (1987). Running scared: We're too frightened to deal with the real issues in adolescent substance abuse. *Health Education Research: Theory and Practice, 2*, 423–432.

Pentz, M. A., Dwyer, J. H., MacKinnon, D. P., Flay, B. R., Hansen, W. B., Wang, E. Y. I., & Johnson, C. A. (1989). A multicommunity trial for primary prevention of adolescent drug use. *Journal of the American Medical Association, 261,* 3259–3267.

Pickens, R. W., & Svikis, D. S. (Eds.) (1988). *Biological vulnerability to drug abuse.* NIDA Research Monograph 89, National Institute on Drug Abuse, DHHS Publication No. (ADM)88-1590. Washington, DC: U.S. Government Printing Office.

Pirie, P. L., Murray, D. M., & Leupker, R. V. (1988). Smoking prevalence in a cohort of adolescents including absentees, dropouts, and transfers. *American Journal of Public Health, 78,* 176–178.

Schachter, S., & Singer, J. (1962). Cognitive, social, and physiological determinants of emotional states. *Psychological Review, 69,* 379–399.

Schinke, S. P., & Gilchrist, L. D. (1983). Primary prevention of tobacco smoking. *Journal of School Health, 53,* 416–419.

Schlenker, B. R. (1980). *Impression management: The self-concept, social identity, and interpersonal relations.* Monterey, CA: Brooks/Cole.

Simmons, R. G., Rosenberg, F., & Rosenberg, M. (1973). Disturbance in the self-image at adolescence. *American Sociological Review, 38,* 553–568.

Slamecka, N. J., & Graf, P. (1978). The generation effect: Delineation of a phenomenon. *Journal of Experimental Psychology, 4,* 592–604.

Smith, M. B., Bruner, J. S., & White, R. W. (1956). *Opinions and personality.* New York: Wiley.

Stuart, R. (1974). Teaching facts about drugs: Pushing or preventing. *Journal of Educational Psychology, 66,* 189–201.

Swann, W. B., Jr. (1983). Self-verification: Bringing social reality into harmony with the self. In J. Suls & A. G. Greenwald (Eds.), *Psychological perspectives on the self* (Vol. 2, pp. 33–66). Hillsdale, NJ: Lawrence Erlbaum Associates.

Swisher, J. D., & Hu, T-W. (1983). Alternatives to drug abuse: Some are and some are not. In T. Glynn, C. Leukefeld, & J. Ludford (Eds.), *Preventing adolescent drug abuse: Intervention strategies* (pp. 141–154). NIDA Research Monograph 47, National Institute on Drug Abuse, Washington, DC: U.S. Government Printing Office.

Tesser, A. (1986). Some effects of self-evaluation maintenance on cognition and action. In R. M. Sorrentino & E. T. Higgins (Eds.), *Handbook of motivation and cognition: Foundations of social behavior* (pp. 435–464). New York: Guilford.

Tobler, N. S. (1986). Meta-analysis of 143 adolescent drug prevention programs: Quantitative outcome results of program participants compared to a control or comparison group. *Journal of Drug Issues, 16,* 537–567.

Tucker, J., Vuchinich, R., & Sobell, M. (1981). Alcohol consumption as a self-handicapping strategy. *Journal of Abnormal Psychology, 90,* 220–230.

U.S. Surgeon General (1986). *The health consequences of involuntary smoking: A report of the Surgeon General.* Washington, DC: U.S. Government Printing Office.

Wills, T. (1986). Stress and coping in early adolescence: Relationships to substance use in urban school samples. *Health Psychology, 5,* 503–530.

17

SOCIAL PSYCHOLOGICAL PERSPECTIVES ON THE SCHOOL PSYCHOLOGIST'S INVOLVEMENT WITH PARENTS

William P. Erchul
North Carolina State University

School psychologists increasingly have been interested in expanding the scope of their services by assessing and treating a student's difficulties within the family context. This growing family focus by school psychologists may be partly attributed to societal trends such as the dramatic increase in the numbers of single-parent, step-, dual-earner, and minority group families, and to our heightened awareness of the family's influence on children's learning, behavioral, and emotional problems. Other signposts of school psychology's emerging interest in families can be observed in the publication of three special issues of the *School Psychology Review* that have addressed family issues (i.e., Erchul, 1987a; Guidubaldi, 1980; Shellenberger, 1981); results of national surveys (Carlson & Sincavage, 1987; Erchul, Scott, Dombalis, & Schulte, 1989) documenting school psychologists' eagerness to work with parents and families; and the creation in 1984 of the Family–School Interest Group within the National Association of School Psychologists.

With the recent passage of Public Law 99–457, the Preschool Education of the Handicapped Act, it can be expected that school psychological services to parents and their young children will be further legitimized. Considered a downward extension of P. L. 94–142, P. L. 99–457 in part requires the development of Individualized Family Service Plans (IFSP's) for families having developmentally delayed preschoolers. School psychologists would seem to be key personnel in the implementation of this legislation (Mcloughlin, 1988; Mowder, Widerstrom, & Sandall, 1989).

Given this strong interest in and impetus for working with parents and families, one might conclude there is a wealth of information within the school psychology literature regarding this topic. Unfortunately, this is not the case. The 26 articles contained in the three *School Psychology Review* special issues referred to before comprise almost half of all articles on family/parenting issues that have been published in the major school psychology journals since 1963. There are, however, some excellent books and chapters on parenting and family issues written by school psychologists, including those by Brassard (1986), Carlson (1988), Conoley (1989), Fine (1980, 1989), Kramer (1985), and Petrie and Piersel (1982). In addition, there are many books published in the field of family therapy that serve as valuable references for family-oriented school psychologists. A selective listing of these books is contained in Table 17.1.

Few would disagree that changing a dysfunctional family system requires one to wield social power and interpersonal influence. Fortunately, health care providers generally (Gaupp, 1966; Reiff, 1974) and school psychologists specifically (Lambert, 1973; Martin, 1978) have been regarded historically as having both power and influence. Conoley and Gutkin (1986) argued more recently that interpersonal influence processes should be emphasized to a greater degree in school psychology training because the provision of effective services "depend[s] to a large extent on psychologists' abilities to influence the behavior of third-party adults" (p. 403). In a related way, Simpson and Fiedler (1989) noted that parent–professional cooperation "extends beyond legislation and . . . *interpersonal*, not legislative conditions are the basis of

TABLE 17.1
A Selective Listing of Family Therapy Books for School Psychologists

Author(s)	Year Published	Title
Becvar & Becvar	1988	*Family therapy: A systematic integration*
Bowen	1978	*Family therapy in clinical practice*
Gurman & Kniskern (Editors)	1981	*Handbook of family therapy*
Haley	1976	*Problem-solving therapy*
Haley	1980	*Leaving home: The therapy of disturbed young people*
Hoffman	1981	*Foundations of family therapy*
Kerr & Bowen	1988	*Family evaluation: An approach based on Bowen theory*
Madanes	1981	*Strategic family therapy*
Minuchin	1974	*Families and family therapy*
Minuchin & Fishman	1981	*Family therapy techniques*
Nichols & Everett	1986	*Systemic family therapy: An integrative approach*
Satir	1972	*Peoplemaking*
Satir	1964	*Conjoint family therapy*
Selvini-Palazzoli, Boscolo, Cecchin, & Prata	1978	*Paradox and counterparadox*

cooperative involvement" (pp. 160–161, emphasis added). Thus, issues of social power and interpersonal relationships are seen as consistent with current thinking in both school psychology and parent education.

Given the many social psychological theories that might be applied to explain processes and outcomes relevant to the school psychologist's conduct of parent education, therapy, and training (cf. Fine, 1980), the aim of this chapter is rather modest. Specifically, this chapter presents aspects of social power and interpersonal influence and discusses them more generally in relation to the school psychologist's involvement with parents. The primary focus is on the psychologist/parent relationship, with a secondary focus on specific activities in which the two parties are frequently engaged (e.g., school-based conferences). Existing processes and outcomes are explained in light of selected social psychological theories, techniques, models, and research. In several instances, suggestions for practice are offered.

This chapter is structured around Olson and Cromwell's (1975) three domains of social power. These domains are: (a) *power base*, seen as the resources Person A can potentially use to effect behavioral change in Person B; (b) *power process*, which refers to the face-to-face interactions wherein influence is exerted by A and accepted or rejected by B; and (c) *power outcomes*, viewed as the consequences of influence attempts, such as who profited from the interaction, or "who won." Although Martin (1978) used a power base perspective and Erchul (1987b) used a power process perspective to explore aspects of school psychologist/teacher consultation, Olson and Cromwell's power domains to date have not been applied to examine the school psychologist/parent relationship.

DEFINITIONS AND ASSUMPTIONS

Before proceeding further, several terms require definitions. *Social influence* (Raven & Litman-Adizes, 1986), as used in this chapter refers to "change in belief, attitude or behavior of a person—the target of influence—which results from the action of some other person or a group of persons—the influencing agent" (p. 185). *Power*, the potential influence the agent can demonstrate over the target (French & Raven, 1959), is synonymous with Olson and Cromwell's (1975) power base. Similarly, *control* refers to successful interpersonal influence attempts and thus is closely related to Olson and Cromwell's power process. *Compliance* is a response by the target in agreement to a face-to-face request or demand made by the agent. Thus, the agent is in control to the extent he or she can induce compliance in the target.

Because some health care professionals, including school psychologists, may feel uneasy relating aspects of social power to their professional role, several of the author's assumptions need to be outlined. First, despite the often negative connotation associated with power, the fact remains that it is one of the most fundamental components of all human interaction (Leary,

1957; Strong & Hills, 1986) and significantly affects school psychologists' roles
and functioning. Second, there is great utility in examining the school psy-
chologist/parent relationship as an interpersonal influence process, just as
others (e.g., Martin, 1978; Zins & Ponti, 1990) have regarded the school psy-
chologist/teacher consulting relationship as an interpersonal influence
process.

Third, although this chapter discusses the school psychologist/parent relationship in light of social influence theories, in most cases empirical data are
lacking on the efficacy of these theories as applied to the practice of psychology. Although applications of these theories offer intriguing possibilities, one
must ultimately regard the author's extensions of these theories as suggestions—not prescriptions—for practice. Finally, on a related point, one should
be alerted to the ethical concerns raised by the use of influence strategies.
This issue is articulated well by Miller and Burgoon (1973) who have percep-
tively concluded, "ethical questions have always been linked with the persuasive process" (p. 104). Regrettably, it is beyond the scope of this chapter
to address issues of social influence in light of their ethical implications for
the practitioner. As a step in this direction, however, Hughes and Falk (1981)
and Hughes (1986) have provided insightful commentary on the ethical implications of the school-based consultant's use of influence attempts.

POWER BASE: ATTRIBUTIONS OF POWER
TO THE SCHOOL PSYCHOLOGIST BY PARENTS

Bases of Social Power

Because French and Raven's (1959) typology of social power bases has been
presented several other times in the school psychology literature (e.g., Hughes,
this volume; Martin, 1978; Zins & Curtis, 1984), its treatment here is brief.
Instead emphasis is placed on less well-known aspects of this typology and
its implications for the school psychologist/parent relationship.

In their classic work, French and Raven (1959) delineated five bases of
social power:

1. Reward power is founded on Person B's perception of Person A's ability to reward B for desired behavior.
2. Coercive power subsumes reward power and includes B's perception
that A is able to punish B for noncompliance.
3. Legitimate power is rooted in B's obligation to accept A's influence attempt because B believes A has a legitimate right to influence.
4. Referent power is A's ability to influence B based upon B's perception
of some desirable and/or similar personal quality in A.

5. Expert power is B's perception that A possesses knowledge or expertise in a designated area.

Raven later (1965) introduced an additional type: 6. Informational power is A's ability to influence B because of the judged relevance of the information contained in A's message.

Of the six bases of power, only informational power results in socially independent change in the target. That is, Person B's acceptance of Person A's influence attempt is solely dependent on the content of the message; B's assessment of A is irrelevant in informational power. If A is successful in influencing B, it is because B accepted the message on its own merit. ("Even though the school psychologist told me to take my son Jimmy to the pediatrician, I had made up my mind already to do it.") Because of the internal attribution made by the target (which often gives rise to greater confidence and enhanced self-efficacy), the use of informational power is seen as resulting in longer lasting change (Raven & Litman-Adizes, 1986).

When considering the six power bases, another factor to bear in mind is whether follow-up monitoring of the target is required in order to maintain the desired change. Surveillance of this kind is necessary for coercive and reward power but not for the other types of power. For example, parent education program enrollees who pay a "security deposit" upon registration may attend and participate regularly in sessions (i.e., when monitoring is possible) but may not retain the acquired knowledge and skills once the program ends. When the structure provided by rewards, punishments, and surveillance ends, it is unclear how long behavior change will last (Raven & Litman-Adizes, 1986).

Application of Theory to the School Psychologist's Involvement with Parents

What sources of power are available to the school psychologist in his or her interactions with parents? Earlier analyses that examined the school consultant's power bases indicated that expert, referent (Martin, 1978), legitimate (Gallessich, 1982), and informational (Parsons & Meyers, 1984) power bases could apply to that peer-professional working relationship. However, in examining their respective power bases, school psychologists and parents are by no means equal. Whereas school psychologists often can use any or all of the six types of social power, parents enter the relationship with no specific sources of power.

School psychologists exhibit referent power when they develop rapport with parents, engage in joint decision making, point out similarities between themselves and parents, and describe themselves or their work in ways that parents see as favorable. School psychologists are attributed expert power by parents when they offer recommendations, describe their professional training and experience, make unilateral decisions, and use technical language. It is the psychologist's expert power that often begins the relationship (i.e., when the results of testing conducted by the psychologist are shared with the parent). School psychologists are ascribed informational power by parents to the extent that their communications are consistent with parents' own beliefs or intended actions.

Less frequently present are coercive, reward, and legitimate power. Attributions of these to the school psychologist by parents may be expected to vary based on such status variables as the parents' level of income, years of formal education, etc. Parents attribute coercive and reward power to the school psychologist if they believe the psychologist can reward or punish them. Although these attributions would seem to occur infrequently, one should bear in mind that the psychologist's approval and disapproval of a parent's actions constitute forms of reward and coercive power, respectively. If a parent admires and respects the psychologist, attributions of reward and coercive power are more probable.

Because some parents associate the school psychologist with the medical community, they are likely to believe in medical traditions such as "the doctor knows best" and thus attribute legitimate power to the psychologist. Parents who perceive the psychologist as having legitimate power expect orders and generally will comply with those orders when given. It would seem a difficult task to engage parents in a more collaborative or egalitarian manner if their attributions of legitimate power to the school psychologist are firmly fixed.

It is evident that parents attribute considerable power to the school psychologist. But how much social power do *parents* possess? What social power bases do parents operate from when interacting with school psychologists? To answer these questions, it may be useful to examine parents' involvement in Individualized Education Plan (IEP) conferences. Specifically, despite the importance of IEP conferences relative to achieving educational goals, (a) some parents fail to attend (Goldstein, Strickland, Turnbull, & Curry, 1980); and (b) even when attending, most parents' participation has been documented as being very passive (Turnbull, 1983; Yoshida & Gottlieb, 1977). These findings can be interpreted within a social power framework. Although there may be many reasons why parents fail to attend or actively participate, one reason may be that they are simply overwhelmed and overpowered by the many professionals who comprise the multidisciplinary team. All team members are experts in their areas and additionally may be accorded coercive, reward, and legitimate power by parents. Often it seems that the school psychologist's comforting words and efforts to establish rapport fail to counteract the parents' perceptions of the school's authority. It is ironic that the P. L. 94–142-mandated multidisciplinary evaluation, which was intended to produce a comprehensive evaluation for suspected handicapped children, would result in an intimidating personal experience for many parents.

To bring closure to this section, Table 17.2 summarizes information pertaining to key characteristics of French and Raven's (1959) and Raven's (1965) bases of social power as well as their application to the school psychologist/parent relationship.

POWER PROCESS: FACE-TO-FACE INFLUENCE ATTEMPTS

Power base and power outcome are domains of the future and the past, respectively, and reflect relatively static operations. In contrast, power process describes an immediate, dynamic, and interactive mode of exchange (Olson & Cromwell, 1975). Because power process appears to be the power domain that has received the least research attention (Rogers-Millar & Millar, 1979), it is given special emphasis in this chapter. Next, three theories and two techniques relating to power process are outlined and then discussed in relation to the school psychologist's involvement with parents.

The Theory of Reasoned Action

The theory of reasoned action (Fishbein & Ajzen, 1975; Ajzen & Fishbein, 1980) attempts to specify the factors involved when one's attitudes predict the subsequent performance of specific behaviors. The term *reasoned action* refers to the theory's assumption that a person tends to act in a rational manner (i.e., he or she contemplates the probable consequences of behavior and acts to attain certain outcomes and avoid others). A second assumption made by the theory is that behavior can be predicted from intention. Thus, a mother who intends to monitor her son's completion of homework each night is more likely to follow through than one who does not have this intention. A third assumption is that specific behaviors can be predicted more accurately than can general behaviors. For example, the theory is likely to be more accurate in predicting whether a father will help his daughter with her language arts homework each Tuesday evening versus help her with some type of homework sometime during the week.

The theory has four major components: (1) attitude toward the behavior (Aact), (2) subjective norms (SN), (3) behavioral intention (BI), and (4) the behavior itself. The first component, *Aact*, is an individual's attitude toward engaging in a specific behavior. Aact is dependent on an individual's beliefs about the consequences of the specific behavior, and his or her assessment of the possible outcomes. For example, two mothers, Mary and Karen, agree

TABLE 17.2

A Comparison among Social Power Bases (French & Raven, 1959; Raven, 1965) with Implications for the School Psychologist/Parent Relationship

Power Base	Definition	Type of Resulting Change in Target	Need for Surveillance by Agent	Attributed to School Psychologists by Parents
Coercive	Target perceives that Agent is able to punish him or her for noncompliance; subsumes reward power.	Socially Dependent	Yes	In Some Cases
Reward	Target perceives that Agent can reward him or her for desired behavior.	Socially Dependent	Yes	In Some Cases
Legitimate	Target believes Agent has a legitimate right to influence.	Socially Dependent	No	In Some Cases
Expert	Target believes that Agent possesses knowledge or expertise in a specific area.	Socially Dependent	No	Yes
Referent	Target perceives some desirable and/or similar personal quality in Agent.	Socially Dependent	No	Yes
Informational	Target judges the content of Agent's message to be relevant to his or her situation.	Socially Independent	No	Yes

that monitoring their children's nightly homework completion will result in higher academic achievement, and that this extra effort will take away from their own time to relax. However, the mothers differ in terms of their evaluation of these outcomes. Mary may feel that her children's success in school is essential, so she will gladly forgo some of her free time each evening. On the other hand, Karen is a single parent who works fulltime; she may be less willing to spend her limited free time monitoring homework. Given this information, Mary's Aact is more positive than Karen's.

The second component, *SN* (subjective norms) is an individual's perception of what others think he or she should do, coupled with his or her motivation to comply with others' expectations. Continuing the preceding example, both Mary and Karen may sense that friends, peers, and school personnel want the nightly homework monitoring to take place. However, assuming that Karen is a more independent thinker than Mary, she may be less motivated to act on the wishes of others. Mary, who is active in the Parent–Teacher Association, may be more motivated to comply with others' expectations.

Aact and SN combine to predict a third component, *BI*, the behavioral intention. The relative importance of Aact versus SN as well as the relative emphasis a person places on Aact and SN to create the BI can be expected to vary based on the specific behavior involved. The BI consequently predicts the individual's performance of the specific behavior—the theory's fourth component. In the given example, Mary's behavioral intention appears to be stronger than Karen's and would likely lead to the prediction that Mary will monitor her children's completion of homework assignments more regularly than will Karen.

The theory of reasoned action has been utilized to predict a variety of behaviors, including weight loss (Schifter & Ajzen, 1985) and mothers' decisions to breast feed versus bottle feed their babies (Manstead, Profitt, & Smart, 1983). However, the theory clearly is not successful in accurately predicting all behaviors based on attitudes alone. One problem relates to the fact that in many instances one's past behavior, rather than one's current attitudes, is a better behavioral predictor. Another problem is that the model may accurately predict one's behavioral *intention*, but not one's ultimate behavior. Another indication that the theory lacks some explanatory power is that various modifications have been proposed to the original theory by Ajzen and others. These problems and refinements notwithstanding, the theory continues to be well regarded within social psychology (Chaiken & Stangor, 1987).

Application of Theory to the School Psychologist's Involvement with Parents

Most schools are not equipped with adequate resources or personnel to provide a full range of human services, so school psychologists often refer families to outside agencies and community professionals (Braden & Sherrard,

1987). Unfortunately, between 20% to 50% of recommendations made to parents to seek such services are not followed (Zins & Hopkins, 1981). Furthermore, only about half of those who do begin outside treatment go for more than one visit (Conti, 1973).

Using the theory of reasoned action, how might a school psychologist increase the chances of parents following through on recommendations to make initial contact with human service agencies? Acknowledging that forces other than attitudes influence eventual behavior, several suggestions are offered. First, because the theory is more successful in predicting specific than general behavior, it is suggested that a higher rate of follow-through may result if referrals to particular agencies or professionals are made by providing parents with names and telephone numbers of contact persons (Zins & Hopkins, 1981). Second, having parents acknowledge the importance of follow-up services and voice a firm commitment (i.e., intention) during a school-based conference to contact a specific agency or professional may be effective. This approach centers on making parents' Aact more positive. Finally, arranging circumstances so that parents seeking community services could talk with other parents who have had positive experiences with those services may be beneficial. This approach emphasizes the importance of SN as well as the potential attribution of referent power to the experienced parents from the parents who will hopefully seek services.

Social Exchange Theory

Social exchange theory (Thibaut & Kelley, 1959) views interpersonal relationships in light of the rewards and costs involved. Although few individuals keep meticulous records of the good and bad elements in a relationship, it is true that most tend to seek out and continue in relationships that offer profitable outcomes. Thibaut and Kelley (1959) proposed two processes that individuals use when evaluating the outcomes in a relationship. The first process is the individual's comparison level (CL), defined as the standard against which people judge the level of satisfaction with their outcomes. The CL serves as the baseline for what people have come to expect from relationships in terms of rewards and costs. Relationships with outcomes above the CL are viewed as positive and enjoyable, whereas those below the CL are viewed as negative and taxing. The second process is the comparison level for alternatives (CL alt). In the CL alt, people contrast the profits from a given relationship with the possible profits from other available relationships. Thus, the CL alt is the standard one uses when deciding whether to continue or end a relationship.

Application of Theory to the School Psychologist's Involvement with Parents

By applying social exchange theory, the psychologist/parent relationship may be viewed as one in which there is a trading off of rewards and costs by both parties. Using the school-based parent conference as a basis for discussion, some of the possible costs incurred by parents may be hypothesized. First, parent conferences are almost always held because of a child's academic or behavioral difficulties. Parents therefore often enter into these conferences feeling defensive, guilt ridden, or inadequate. Second, research (e.g., Goldstein et al., 1980) indicates that many parents, through their passivity, surrender control of the conference to school personnel. For some parents, this lack of input ("suffering in silence") may be difficult to endure. Third, parents may perceive a risk relating to the possibility that *their* deficiencies and not those of their child will be discussed at the conference. For example, a parent may feel the psychologist is "psychoanalyzing" him or her through the use of probing questions. The probability of this scenario occurring would seem to increase to the extent that the parent attributes legitimate and/or expert power to the psychologist.

These costs often are then balanced by the possibility of various rewards being presented to parents. Among these may be that the school conference provides a vehicle for parents: (a) to share ideas and concerns with trained professionals; (b) to gain information about their child's educational and psychological functioning; and (c) to begin taking steps that may lead to the successful resolution of their child's problems. Improvement in the home/school relationship and increased parental participation in school conferences may be achieved if the psychologist is successful in promoting these rewards over whatever costs parents perceive.

In analyzing this relationship further, it may be the case that the CL of cooperative, involved, and satisfied parents is modest, and their CL alt reflects their perception that the psychologist's assistance is unique—unavailable from other school personnel. On the other hand, the CL of resistant, uncooperative, or dissatisfied parents may be quite high, and their CL alt is based on the perception that help other than that which the psychologist can provide is readily available. Because parents weigh the relationship with the school psychologist in terms of costs and benefits, it is important that the psychologist emphasize the positive aspects of the relationship when possible.

The Foot-In-The-Door and Door-In-The-Face Techniques

The foot-in-the-door technique (FITD) (Freedman & Fraser, 1966) is an influence strategy intended to induce compliance in a target through the agent's use of two sequential requests. The first request is small, even insignificant, to ensure that the target will agree to it. The second request is always larger and reflects the behavior of real interest to the agent. It is expected that the target also will comply with the second request.

In their classic demonstration of FITD; Freedman and Fraser (1966, Experiment II) went from door to door asking California residents to sign a petition indicating support for a safe driving campaign. Nearly all who were approached complied with this first request. Two weeks later, a different set of interviewers arranged to meet individually with the original experimental subjects as well as a comparable number of control subjects who had not received the initial request. This time, all subjects were requested to place a very large, obtrusive sign reading "Drive Carefully" in their front yards for about 1 week. Interestingly, over 55% of the subjects who complied with the first request (signing the petition) also agreed to the second request (posting the sign). In contrast, less than 17% of the control subjects agreed to place the sign in their front yards. Freedman and Fraser (1966) concluded that subjects' compliance with the first request tended to increase their compliance with the second request.

The door-in-the-face technique (DITF) is a second interpersonal influence strategy that relies on the use of sequential requests to achieve behavioral compliance. Originally described by Cialdini, Vincent, Lewis, Catalan, Wheeler, and Darby (1975), DITF is the operational inverse of FITD; that is, the first request is large and demands a great deal of time, effort, and/or money and is rejected by the target. The second request makes smaller, though often still considerable, demands and it is expected that the target will comply.

Cialdini et al. (1975) first demonstrated DITF in a study in which college students were asked individually if they would serve as a volunteer counselor to a juvenile delinquent for 2 hours each week for a minimum of 2 years. Obviously, this constituted an extreme request and all subjects refused. A second request followed in which the same experimental group subjects were asked to chaperone (without pay) a group of juvenile delinquents on a day trip to the zoo. Fifty percent of the subjects agreed to become volunteer zoo chaperones. This finding is remarkable when compared to the 17% rate of compliance given by a group of control subjects who were asked only to chaperone the zoo trip. Thus, DITF resulted in a three-fold increase in the percentage of compliance to a smaller, yet still substantial, request.

It is important to evaluate both FITD and DITF in terms of their effectiveness in reliably inducing compliance. A meta-analysis conducted on both techniques (Dillard, Hunter, & Burgoon, 1984) revealed the effects of both to be relatively weak. Also, both strategies require a prosocial topic (e.g., helping a charitable cause) in order to work. Furthermore, effects for FITD are larger when there is no apparent incentive such as payment to perform the initial request. DITF is effective only when the delay between the requests is brief—less than one day. For FITD, the delay between requests does not appear to be a critical factor.

Application of Techniques to the School Psychologist's Involvement with Parents

Given these two sequential-request persuasive strategies, it would be tempting to describe how the psychologist could use them most effectively to induce greater compliance in parents. However, due to the ethical issues involved (e.g., use of deception) and the fact that the effects produced by the techniques are relatively weak, a prescriptive approach is not taken. Instead, hypotheses based on FITD and DITF are offered to explain the existing phenomenon of why parents follow or do not follow requests made by school personnel. In applying FITD and DITF to explore this phenomenon, it is worth noting first that neither technique will be effective unless a prosocial behavior is requested (Dillard et al., 1984). Fortunately, for the purpose of this discussion, all educational and psychological recommendations can be considered prosocial in nature because they have the intent of improving a student's academic achievement and/or emotional adjustment.

Knowing how FITD works may be useful in understanding parents' compliance with certain educational recommendations. For example, it is a common recommendation to have children bring home schoolwork completed during the week so that parents can see the learning activities in which their children have been involved. The request made of the parents at that time is to sign their children's work to verify that the assignments were received and reviewed. This is a minor request that few parents refuse. Parents of children who are experiencing some academic difficulties, however, often are asked to comply with another request. This second request takes the form of asking parents to assist their children with homework for some specified amount of time each evening. Although other factors could account for parents' compliance with the second request, FITD provides one explanation. In the example given, FITD assumes that successful entrée involving compliance with a minor request increases the chances that compliance with a second request requiring greater commitment also will be achieved. A second example of FITD is illustrated by having parents collect baseline data (Request 1) before asking them to take responsibility for a home-based behavior management program (Request 2).

DITF may operate similarly in explaining parents' follow through with specific recommendations. For instance, Mr. and Mrs. Smith have arranged to confer with Dr. Jones, the school psychologist, to discuss the results of the evaluation of their 9-year-old son Brian. Brian has been experiencing some behavior difficulties, and Dr. Jones recommends that Brian would benefit from the structure provided by a comprehensive behavior management program at home. During the parent conference, Dr. Jones explains the "ideal" program in detail and specifies that the Smiths would need to: (a) keep track of five of Brian's problem behaviors every 15 minutes each evening, (b) arrange to give Brian rewards daily if he displayed enough acceptable behaviors, (c) arrange to give him even larger rewards weekly if other criteria were met, and (d) keep the school regularly informed as to Brian's progress. Although the Smiths clearly see the need for such efforts to help their son, they see the outlined program as too complicated and one that would require too much commitment on their part. Because the Smiths do not accept this comprehensive program, Dr. Jones devises a scaled-down version that the parents see as workable. The Smiths agree to participate fully in this second behavior management program. Although one may certainly interpret the outcome of this example in terms of the treatment acceptability literature (Elliott, 1988), DITF provides one means of explaining the observed phenomenon.

Interestingly, FITD and DITF together help to explain why some parents fail to follow *any* recommendations. An important aspect of these strategies is that both involve a small request and a large request. FITD makes the small request first, then the large request; DITF reverses the sequence. When parents fail to comply with a series of recommendations made by the psychologist, it may be because they perceive *all* these recommendations to constitute large requests. It seems that the contrast principle is important not only in fundamental sensory processes (e.g., visual perception) but also in social influence (Cialdini, 1985).

The Theory of Schismogenesis

Gregory Bateson's (1935, 1958) theory of schismogenesis is another social psychological theory that can be meaningfully applied to study the school psychologist/parent relationship. Notable applications of this theory within the school psychology literature have been presented previously by Power and Bartholomew (1985, 1987). Interested readers are encouraged to consult these references for a more extensive discussion.

Bateson's theory evolved from analyzing the Iatmul tribe in New Guinea during the 1930s. In this field study, he sought to explore contact between different cultures and contact between differentiated groups (i.e., groups having different social roles or positions) within the Iatmul culture. When two differentiated groups exist in dynamic equilibrium, Bateson (1935) proposed that the relationship between them is characterized as symmetrical, complementary, or reciprocal. Furthermore, extreme patterns of symmetry and complementarity will lead to schismogenesis, a pathological pattern of interaction. Each relationship type as well as schismogenesis now is presented in greater detail.

A *symmetrical* relationship exists when members of Groups A and B hold similar goals and exhibit similar behaviors. As a result, individuals in Group

A will display behavior 1 when interacting with Group B. In reply, members of Group B will exhibit behavior 1. Over time, behavior 1 will become the standard response to behavior 1 for both groups. For example, if behavior 1 represents boasting, then boasting will be present in a cause–effect manner when Groups A and B interact.

A *complementary* relationship exists when members of Groups A and B differ with respect to goals and patterns of behavior. Consequently, individuals in Group A will display behavior 2 when interacting with individuals in Group B. In reply, members of Group B will exhibit behavior 3. In time, Group B's response to Group A's behavior 2 will be established firmly as behavior 3, and vice versa. For example, if Group A's behavior 2 is assertiveness and Group B's behavior 3 is submissiveness, then over time one behavior will trigger the other in a stimulus–response fashion when the two groups interact.

Symmetry and complementarity are not inherently good/bad or normal/abnormal but rather denote two basic ways in which relationships may be classified (Watzlawick, Beavin, & Jackson, 1967). However, both types lead to *schismogenesis*, "a process of differentiation in the norms of individual behavior resulting from cumulative interaction between individuals" (Bateson, 1958, p. 175). Unless corrected, schismogenesis will be detrimental to an established relationship because it introduces pathology into that relationship. For instance, using the earlier example of symmetry, boasting by Groups A and B will escalate to greater rivalry, then aggression, and eventually termination of the relationship. Citing the earlier example of complementarity, the progressively greater assertiveness of Group A and increasing submissiveness of Group B will create distance in the relationship, produce mutual hostility, and eventually undermine the relationship.

Bateson (1935) proposed a third type of relationship, *reciprocity*, that flexibly combines elements of symmetry and complementarity. In a reciprocal relationship, Group B sometimes responds with behavior 1 to Group A's behavior 1 (i.e., symmetry) but at other times responds with behavior 2 or 3 (i.e., complementarity). Likewise, Group A responds to Group B's behavior 1 with behavior 1, 2, or 3. For example, reciprocity will prevail between Groups A and B if the latter responds alternately with assertiveness and submissiveness to the former's assertiveness, and vice versa. Because the reciprocal relationship is compensated and balanced within itself, it does not result in schismogenesis. To integrate the preceding information, Table 17.3 provides a summary of the key constructs of Bateson's theory of schismogenesis.

Application of Theory to the School Psychologist's Involvement with Parents

To date, Bateson's theory has been adapted and applied to study various areas of human interaction, including international relations, home–school relations, marital and family communication, small group behavior, and care giver/care

TABLE 17.3
Key Components of Bateson's (1935, 1958) Theory of Schismogenesis

Component	Definition
Symmetry	A relationship type characterized by a minimization of behavioral differences between individuals; becomes dysfunctional (i.e., schismogenic) when escalation of behaviors occurs.
Complementarity	A relationship type characterized by a maximization of behavioral differences between individuals; becomes dysfunctional (i.e., schismogenic) when these differences become exaggerated and serve to polarize individuals.
Reciprocity	A relationship type that is balanced with regard to symmetry and complementarity; represents the best way to avoid schismogenesis.
Schismogenesis	A process, triggered by extreme types of symmetry and complementarity, which leads to dysfunctional relational outcomes. Schismogenesis can be avoided through the development of reciprocity and/or application of restraining factors.
Restraining Factor	An action that, when successful, lowers the probability of schismogenesis; introduces elements into a relationship that move it closer to reciprocity.

recipient relationships. The discussion that follows centers on how to develop and improve the school psychologist/parent relationship through the use of restraining factors—another means of staving off the harmful effects of schismogenesis. Several factors are presented followed by an example of how each factor could apply to the school psychologist/parent relationship.

First, promoting mutual dependence in an essentially complementary relationship will stabilize that relationship; that is, if Groups A and B realize they depend on each other for needed goods or services, then schismogenesis is not likely to occur. Within the psychologist/parent relationship, if parents are regarded as experts in their child's behavior across many settings and the school psychologist is regarded as an expert in mental health and education, then mutual respect will be present. A productive working relationship should ensue because each party depends on the other's expertise. However, given the earlier discussion of French and Raven's (1959) power bases, it may be difficult for parents to accept and use their expert power. For example, if a parent assumes a passive role during a school-based conference, the psychologist should ask questions and/or make statements that convey that the parent's input is essential in order to arrive at a realistic plan of action. After the parent responds, the psychologist should reinforce the parent's participation by acknowledging the importance of his or her unique contributions.

Second, uniting Groups A and B in loyalty or opposition to some external force (e.g., leader or issue) will prevent schismogenesis. The school psychologist might apply this restraining factor by commiserating with parents about rising taxes, rainy weather, poor produce at the supermarket, etc. By exercising referent power in this manner, the psychologist and parent will be drawn together on yet another level, which should bode well for the success of their working relationship.

Third, the course of schismogenesis may be controlled by educating the involved parties about the schismogenic pattern present in their relationship. Focusing on the process rather than the content of the interaction may facilitate this intervention (Watzlawick et al., 1967). For example, if the school psychologist detects signs of schismogenesis (e.g., extremes in parental behavior such as increased hostility, competitiveness, or withdrawal), he or she should act to defuse this situation. Engaging in reflective listening (e.g., responding directly to the emotion contained in the parents' messages) and tactfully pointing out to the parents the negative impact of their actions may be effective in this regard.

Fourth, schismogenic strain may be alleviated by altering the nature of a symmetrical rivalry, perhaps through "comic relief." For example, Bateson (1958) observed what he called "the diversion of harshness into buffoonery" (p. 194), a mechanism that was effective in reducing competitive symmetry in the Iatmul culture. Although the school psychologist/parent relationship may not be characterized as a "symmetrical rivalry," Bateson's suggestion that humor be used as an intervention is well taken. School psychologists should possess a variety of interpersonal skills and problem-solving techniques and, more importantly, know when to apply them. A part of this may include the occasional interjection of humor to demonstrate an awareness of the relationship itself.

Fifth, in a relationship based primarily on one pair of complementary behaviors, infusing a second pair of complementary behaviors into the relationship may forestall schismogenesis created by the first pair. For instance, an illness or accident may transform an assertion/submission complementary relationship into a caretaker/invalid complementary relationship. Within the school psychologist/parent relationship, a complementary relationship based on the psychologist's expert knowledge and the parents' initial willingness to accept this expertise eventually may result in resentment on the parents' part, due to their lack of input. Recognizing this schismogenic development, the psychologist might choose to shun the role of content expert and instead adopt a more facilitative role in order to reduce the parents' resentment. By redefining the relationship in this manner, the psychologist would be able to avoid the extreme complementarity encountered earlier.

Finally, the occurrence of complementary schismogenesis between Groups A and B will similarly distort intragroup relations; that is, if complementary relationships emerge between members of Group A, then certain Group A members will act and be viewed as similar to members of Group B. As a result, the essentially complementary relationship between Groups A and B then will contain elements of symmetry and therefore stabilize. Within the school psychologist/parent relationship, extreme complementarity can arise if parents view the psychologist as the "only one" who can help them. This situation increases frustration on both sides, as the psychologist cannot meet all the parents' needs and many parents feel they have been neglected by the psychologist. To solve this problem, the school psychologist might enlist the services of skilled parents who could assist other, less skilled parents. The establishment of a school-based mutual help group for parents is a way to formalize this arrangement. (See Killilea, 1976, for other examples of mutual help groups.) Bateson would claim such a mechanism for role-reversal would stop the original complementary schismogenesis.

POWER OUTCOME: MAKING PARENTS THE ULTIMATE VICTORS

Olson and Cromwell's (1975) third domain of power, power outcome, is concerned with the question, "Who won?" Unlike the previous two domains, power outcome would seem to apply more to the area of professional sports than to the school psychologist/parent relationship! It is not the author's intent to depict this relationship as a competition, despite our often keen awareness of the "winners" and "losers" in various help giver/recipient relationships. The position taken instead is that the school psychologist must use his or her sources of power and influence to enable and empower parents. Through our efforts in this regard, parents can become the ultimate "victors."

The Enabling Model of Helping and Its Application to the School Psychologist's Involvement with Parents

From their incisive review of the research literatures of helping relationships and social support, Dunst and Trivette (1987) proposed a model of helping parents based on the principles of enablement and empowerment. Briefly, the model posits that parents are *enabled* to the extent they are given opportunities to acquire and/or display their competence. Parents are *empowered* to the extent they attribute behavioral changes to their own efforts. Empowerment and informational power (Raven, 1965) are similar in that both foster socially independent change (see Table 17.2). According to Dunst and Trivette, it is up to the help giver to offer assistance in a manner that maximizes the enablement and empowerment of parents.

Regrettably, many time-honored attempts to help parents actually result in negative consequences that serve to decrease rather than increase parents' sense of empowerment. For example, if the help that is offered does

TABLE 17.4

Negative Consequences of Various Helping Approaches (Dunst & Trivette, 1987)

Help giving is likely to:

---

1. Result in learned helplessness if it undermines parental competence and control.
2. Foster dependencies when help givers take relative and, in some cases, absolute control over the presenting problem.
2. Lower parental self-esteem if the help giver acts in a patronizing way, or a way that suggests that the parent is inferior, incompetent, or inadequate.
4. Increase feelings of indebtedness if: (a) the benefits resulting from the services favor the parents, (b) the onus of help seeking rests with the parents, (c) the help giver's efforts are seen as altruistic, and (d) comparisons made by the parents suggest that they should be grateful.
5. Increase dependence and helplessness if it does not require the parents to acquire effective behaviors.
6. Result in harmful consequences if it is unsolicited and only reinforces parents' negative feelings toward themselves.
7. Trigger negative reactions if there is a mismatch or incongruence between help that is requested and that which is given.
8. Have debilitating effects and elicit negative reactions when the parents perceive no problems and have no self-identified need.

Note: From "Enabling and Empowering Families: Conceptual and Intervention Issues" by C. J. Dunst and C. M. Trivette, 1987, *School Psychology Review, 16*, pp. 446–447. Copyright 1987 by the National Association of School Psychologists. Adapted by permission.

not require a parent to develop necessary skills, he or she will continue to need that help indefinitely. The parent's immediate needs may be met but the opportunity for him or her to learn and develop self-reliance will be reduced considerably. Another example is offering assistance to a parent who sees no problems and has no apparent needs related to this unsolicited help. Parental resentment may follow from this seemingly unnecessary assistance (Dunst & Trivette, 1987). These and other negative consequences of various approaches to helping, as applied to parents-as-clients, are presented in Table 17.4.

In contrast, styles of helping based on principles of empowerment tend to make parents more competent and self-sufficient. For example, helping approaches that acknowledge the importance of and encourage parents' use of naturally occurring support networks (e.g., neighbors, church members) are empowering. The professional help giver's services also should not attempt to replace or downplay the significance of these community-based resources. A second example of a helping approach that fosters empowerment is offering assistance that is normative relative to the parents' own culture. Help that is perceived as "foreign" often is regarded as demeaning and may heighten status differences between the help giver and recipient (Dunst & Trivette, 1987). For example, a psychologist has encouraged an academically gifted high school senior to apply for admission to several highly competitive out-of-state universities. However, the psychologist's efforts are not seen as empowering because both the student and his parents have regarded it as a source of pride that, following high school graduation, the former would run the family business.

A more complete listing of principles of empowerment as related to working with parents is contained in Table 17.5.

Dunst and Trivette's (1987) model of helping parents through enablement and empowerment recently has been applied to the practice of school-based teacher consultation (see Witt & Martens, 1988; Zins & Ponti, 1990). Given the model's empirical support and intuitive appeal, it is likely to have an increasing impact on the practice of school psychology in the years to come.

CONCLUSIONS

The literature of social psychology has much to contribute to school psychology (Conoley & Gutkin, 1986). As school psychologists continue to expand their services to parents and families, they should consider principles and theories of social psychology as a means of enhancing their established approach to practice. This chapter has introduced a social psychological perspective on the school psychologist's working relationship with parents. Select-

TABLE 17.5
Principles of Empowerment (Dunst & Trivette, 1987)

The help giver will be empowering to the extent he or she:

1. Is both positive and proactive.
2. Offers help instead of waiting for the parents to request help.
3. Promotes a clear understanding that the parents are responsible for making major decisions regarding the help to be offered.
4. Offers assistance that is normative relative to the parents' own culture.
5. Offers help that is congruent with the parents' own assessment of their problem or need.
6. Offers help in which the parents' benefits are greater than their costs of seeking and accepting assistance.
7. Offers help that the parents can reciprocate in some way.
8. Enhances the self-esteem of the parents and helps them to experience some immediate success in solving a problem or meeting a need.
9. Acknowledges the importance of and encourages the parents' use of natural support networks.
10. Promotes a sense of cooperation and joint responsibility for solving problems or meeting needs.
11. Fosters the parents' acquisition of effective behaviors, thus making them more self-reliant.
12. Assists parents in realizing not only that problems were solved or needs met, but also that they achieved success through their own efforts.

Note: From "Enabling and Empowering Families: Conceptual and Intervention Issues" by C. J. Dunst and C. M. Trivette, 1987, *School Psychology Review, 16*, pp. 451–453. Copyright 1987 by the National Association of School Psychologists. Adapted by permission.

ed aspects of social power and interpersonal influence were presented and applied to explain existing phenomena and to offer suggestions for improving services.

Looking ahead to the development of this area over the next decade, the author speculates that two trends are likely to develop. First, future empirical work will test the usefulness of the theories and techniques presented here with regard to the school psychologist/parent relationship. Recent work conducted within counseling psychology (Sharkin, Mahalik, & Claiborn, 1989) provides a prime example of this type of research. Specifically, Sharkin et al. investigated the foot-in-the-door technique (FITD) with respect to the counselor/client relationship and found that clients' compliance with a small request had a significant effect on their motivation to change. A second predicted trend is that family-oriented school psychologists are likely to borrow increasingly from the growing research literature on school-based teacher consultation to derive bases for family–school practice. Some evidence for this assertion can be seen in the revised edition of a consultation textbook (Brown, Pryzwansky, & Schulte, 1991) that contains a chapter on methods for consulting with parents.

ACKNOWLEDGMENT

The author wishes to acknowledge Ann C. Schulte for her insightful comments on an earlier version of this chapter.

REFERENCES

Ajzen, I., & Fishbein, M. (1980). *Understanding attitudes and predicting behavior.* Englewood Cliffs, NJ: Prentice-Hall.

Bateson, G. (1935). Culture contact and schismogenesis. *Man, 35,* 178–183.

Bateson, G. (1958). *Naven* (2d ed.). Stanford, CA: Stanford University Press.

Becvar, D. S., & Becvar, R. J. (1988). *Family therapy: A systemic integration.* Boston: Allyn & Bacon.

Bowen, M. (1978). *Family therapy in clinical practice.* New York: Jason Aronson.

Braden, J. P., & Sherrard, P. A. D. (1987). Referring families to nonschool agencies: A family systems approach. *School Psychology Review, 16,* 513–518.

Brassard, M. R. (1986). Family assessment approaches and procedures. In H. M. Knoff (Ed.), *The assessment of child and adolescent personality* (pp. 399–449). New York: Guilford.

Brown, D., Pryzwansky, W. B., & Schulte, A. C. (1991). *Psychological consultation: Introduction to theory and practice* (2nd ed.). Boston: Allyn & Bacon.

Carlson, C. (1988). Family assessment and intervention for school psychologists. In T. R. Kratochwill (Ed.), *Advances in school psychology* (Vol. VI, pp. 81–129). Hillsdale, NJ: Lawrence Erlbaum Associates.

Carlson, C. I., & Sincavage, J. M. (1987). Family-oriented school psychology practice: Results of a national survey of NASP members. *School Psychology Review, 16,* 519–526.

Chaiken, S., & Stangor, C. (1987). Attitudes and attitude change. *Annual Review of Psychology, 38,* 575–630.

Cialdini, R. B. (1985). *Influence: Science and practice.* Glenview, IL: Scott, Foresman.

Cialdini, R. B., Vincent, J. E., Lewis, S. K., Catalan, J., Wheeler, D., & Darby, B. L. (1975). Reciprocal concessions procedure for inducing compliance: The door-in-the-face technique. *Journal of Personality and Social Psychology, 31,* 206–215.

Conoley, J. C. (1989). The school psychologist as a community/family service provider. In R. C. D'Amato & R. S. Dean (Eds.), *The school psychologist in nontraditional settings: Integrating clients, services, and settings* (pp. 33–65). Hillsdale, NJ: Lawrence Erlbaum Associates.

Conoley, J. C., & Gutkin, T. B. (1986). School psychology: A reconceptualization of service delivery realities. In S. N. Elliott & J. C. Witt (Eds.), *The delivery of psychological services in schools: Concepts, processes, and issues* (pp. 393–424). Hillsdale, NJ: Lawrence Erlbaum Associates.

Conti, A. P. (1973). A follow-up investigation of families referred to outside agencies. *Journal of School Psychology, 11,* 215–222.

Dillard, J. P., Hunter, J. E., & Burgoon, M. E. (1984). Sequential-request persuasive strategies: Meta-analysis of foot-in-the-door and door-in-the-face. *Human Communication Research, 10,* 461–488.

Dunst, C. J., & Trivette, C. M. (1987). Enabling and empowering families: Conceptual and intervention issues. *School Psychology Review, 16,* 443–456.

Elliott, S. N. (1988). Acceptability of behavioral treatments: Review of variables that influence treatment selection. *Professional Psychology: Research and Practice, 19,* 68–80.

Erchul, W. P. (Ed.) (1987a). Family systems assessment and intervention. (Special Issue). *School Psychology Review, 16*(4).

Erchul, W. P. (1987b). A relational communication analysis of control in school consultation. *Professional School Psychology, 2,* 113–124.

Erchul, W. P., Scott, S. S., Dombalis, A. O., & Schulte, A. C. (1989). Characteristics and perceptions of beginning doctoral students in school psychology. *Professional School Psychology, 4,* 103–111.

Fine, M. J. (Ed.). (1980). *Handbook on parent education.* New York: Academic Press.

Fine, M. J. (Ed.). (1989). *The second handbook on parent education.* San Diego: Academic Press.

Fishbein, M., & Ajzen, I. (1975). *Belief, attitude, intention and behavior: An introduction to theory and research.* Reading, MA: Addison-Wesley.

Freedman, J. L., & Fraser, S. C. (1966). Compliance without pressure: The foot-in-the-door technique. *Journal of Personality and Social Psychology, 4,* 195–202.

French, J. R. P., & Raven, B. H. (1959). The bases of social power. In D. Cartwright (Ed.), *Studies in social power.* Ann Arbor: University of Michigan Institute of Social Research.

Gallessich, J. (1982). *The profession and practice of consultation.* San Francisco: Jossey-Bass.

Gaupp, P. G. (1966). Authority, influence, and control in consultation. *Community Mental Health Journal, 2,* 205–210.

Goldstein, S., Strickland, B., Turnbull, A. P., & Curry, L. (1980). An observational analysis of the IEP conference. *Exceptional Children, 46,* 278–286.

Guidubaldi, J. (Ed.) (1980). Families: Current status and emerging trends. (Special Issue). *School Psychology Review, 9*(4).

Gurman, A. S., & Kniskern, D. P. (Eds.). (1981). *Handbook of family therapy.* New York: Brunner/Mazel.

Haley, J. (1976). *Problem-solving therapy.* San Francisco: Jossey-Bass.

Haley, J. (1980). *Leaving home: The therapy of disturbed young people.* New York: McGraw-Hill.

Hoffman, L. (1981). *Foundations of family therapy.* New York: Basic Books.

Hughes, J. N. (1986). Ethical issues in school consultation. *School Psychology Review, 15,* 489–499.

Hughes, J., & Falk, R. (1981). Resistance, reactance, and consultation. *Journal of School Psychology, 19,* 134–142.

Kerr, M. E., & Bowen, M. (1988). *Family therapy: An approach based on Bowen theory.* New York: W. W. Norton.

Killilea, M. (1976). Mutual help organizations: Interpretations in the literature. In G. Caplan & M. Killilea (Eds.), *Support systems and mutual help: Multidisciplinary explorations* (pp. 37–93). New York: Grune & Stratton.

Kramer, J. J. (1985). Best practices in parent training. In A. Thomas & J. Grimes (Eds.), *Best practices in school psychology* (pp. 263–273). Washington, DC: National Association of School Psychologists.

Lambert, N. M. (1973). The school psychologist as a source of power and influence. *Journal of School Psychology, 11,* 245–250.

Leary, T. (1957). *Interpersonal diagnosis of personality.* New York: Roland.

Madanes, C. (1981). *Strategic family therapy.* San Francisco: Jossey-Bass.

Manstead, A. S. R., Profitt, C., & Smart, J. L. (1983). Predicting and understanding mothers' infant-feeding intentions and behavior: Testing the theory of reasoned action. *Journal of Personality and Social Psychology, 44,* 657–671.

Martin, R. (1978). Expert and referent power: A framework for understanding and maximizing consultation effectiveness. *Journal of School Psychology, 16,* 49–55.

Mcloughlin, C. S. (1988). Provision of psychological services to very young children and their families. In J. L. Graden, J. E. Zins, & M. J. Curtis (Eds.), *Alternative educational delivery systems: Enhancing instructional options for all students* (pp. 269–290). Washington, DC: National Association of School Psychologists.

Miller, G. R., & Burgoon, M. (1973). *New techniques of persuasion.* New York: Harper & Row.

Minuchin, S. (1974). *Families and family therapy.* Cambridge, MA: Harvard Press.

Minuchin, S., & Fishman, H. C. (1981). *Family therapy techniques.* Cambridge, MA: Harvard Press.

Mowder, B. A., Widerstrom, A. H., & Sandall, S. (1989). School psychologists serving at-risk and handicapped infants, toddlers, and their families. *Professional School Psychology, 4,* 159–171.

Nichols, W. C., & Everett, C. A. (1986). *Systemic family therapy: An integrative approach.* New York: Guilford.

Olson, D. H., & Cromwell, R. E. (1975). Power in families. In R. E. Cromwell & D. H. Olson (Eds.), *Power in families* (pp. 3–11). Beverly Hills: Sage.

Parsons, R. D., & Meyers, J. (1984). *Developing consultation skills.* San Francisco: Jossey-Bass.

Petrie, P., & Piersel, W. C. (1982). Therapy 2: Family therapy. In C. R. Reynolds & T. B. Gutkin (Eds.), *The handbook of school psychology* (pp. 580–590). New York: Wiley.

Power, T. J., & Bartholomew, K. L. (1985). Getting uncaught in the middle: A case study in family-school system consultation. *School Psychology Review, 14,* 222–229.

Power, T. J., & Bartholomew, K. L. (1987). Family–school relationship patterns: An ecological assessment. *School Psychology Review, 16,* 498–512.

Raven, B. H. (1965). Social influence and power. In I. D. Steiner & M. Fishbein (Eds.), *Current studies in social psychology* (pp. 371–382). New York: Holt, Rinehart, & Winston.

Raven, B. H., & Litman-Adizes, T. (1986). Interpersonal influence and social power in health promotion. In W. B. Ward (Ed.), *Advances in health education and promotion* (Vol. 1, Pt. A, pp. 181–209). Greenwich, CT: JAI Press.

Reiff, R. (1974). The control of knowledge: The power of helping professions. *Journal of Applied Behavioral Science, 10,* 451–461.

Rogers-Millar, L. E., & Millar, F. E. (1979). Domineeringness and dominance: A transactional view. *Human Communication Research, 5,* 238–246.

Satir, V. (1964). *Conjoint family therapy.* Palo Alto, CA: Science and Behavior Books.

Satir, V. (1972). *Peoplemaking.* Palo Alto, CA: Science and Behavior Books.

Schifter, D. E., & Ajzen, I. (1985). Intention, perceived control, and weight loss: An application of the theory of planned behavior. *Journal of Personality and Social Psychology, 49,* 843–851.

Selvini-Palazzoli, M., Boscolo, C., Cecchin, G., & Prata, G. (1978). *Paradox and counterparadox.* New York: Aronson.

Sharkin, B. S., Mahalik, J. R., & Claiborn, C. D. (1989). Application of the foot-in-the-door effect to counseling. *Journal of Counseling Psychology, 36,* 248–251.

Shellenberger, S. (Ed.). (1981). Services to families and parental involvement with interventions. (Special Issue). *School Psychology Review, 10*(1).

Simpson, R. L., & Fiedler, C. R. (1989). Parent participation in individualized educational program (IEP) conferences: A case for individualization. In M. J. Fine (Ed.), *The second handbook on parent education* (pp. 145–171). San Diego: Academic Press.

Strong, S. R., & Hills, H. I. (1986). *Interpersonal Communication Rating Scale.* Richmond, VA: Virginia Commonwealth University.

Thibaut, J. W., & Kelley, H. H. (1959). *The social psychology of groups.* New York: Wiley.

Turnbull, A. P. (1983). Parental participation in the IEP process. In J. A. Mulick & S. M. Pueschel (Eds.), *Parent–professional partnerships in developmental disability services* (pp. 107–122). Cambridge, MA: Ware Press.

Watzlawick, P., Beavin, J., & Jackson, D. D. (1967). *Pragmatics of human communication.* New York: W. W. Norton.

Witt, J. C., & Martens, B. K. (1988). Problems with problem-solving consultation: A re-analysis of assumptions, methods, and goals. *School Psychology Review, 17,* 211–226.

Yoshida, R. K., & Gottlieb, J. (1977). A model of parental participation. *Mental Retardation, 15,* 17–20.

Zins, J. E., & Curtis, M. (1984). Building consultation into the educational service delivery system. In C. A. Maher, R. J. Illback, & J. E. Zins (Eds.), *Organizational psychology in the schools: A handbook for professionals* (pp. 213–242). Springfield, IL: Charles C. Thomas.

Zins, J. E., & Hopkins, R. A. (1981). Referral out: Increasing the number of kept appointments. *School Psychology Review, 10,* 107–111.

Zins, J. E., & Ponti, C. R. (1990). Best practices in school-based consultation. In A. Thomas & J. Grimes (Eds.), *Best practices in school psychology* (2d ed., pp. 673–693). Washington, DC: National Association of School Psychologists.

CHAPTER

18

SOCIAL PSYCHOLOGICAL APPROACHES TO THE INTEGRATION OF CULTURALLY DIFFERENT AND HANDICAPPED STUDENTS IN SCHOOLS

James M. Weyant
University of San Diego

> *desegregating a school system does not necessarily mean integrating its*
> *students. Indeed, if we were to take an aerial photograph of the playground*
> *or cafeteria at a recently desegregated school, it most frequently would*
> *reveal a striking pattern, depicting several discrete clusters of children*
> *gathered in their own ethnic groups. . . . when the children get up to talk*
> *with their friends, go outside to play, or sit down to eat, they tend to*
> *separate along ethnic lines.*
> —Aronson and Osherow (1980, p. 163)

This chapter deals with ways to achieve true integration in desegregated schools. As the preceding quotation expresses so well, integration of schools means more than putting diverse kinds of students into the same classrooms. When schools are truly integrated, students with dissimilar backgrounds and capabilities accept one another and interact in positive ways. In recent years, two broad kinds of school integration have been attempted. *Cultural integration* involves fostering greater appreciation and interaction among students of different races and ethnic backgrounds. *Mainstreaming* involves integrating handicapped students into classrooms with their nonhandicapped peers. These forms of integration present numerous and difficult challenges, and volumes have been written about how successful integration might best be achieved (e.g., Prager, Longshore, & Seeman, 1986; Berres & Knoblock, 1987). This chapter focuses on social psychological approaches to school integration that have been field tested.

RACIAL AND ETHNIC INTEGRATION OF SCHOOLS

Despite a considerable amount of research that social psychologists do on phenomena related to important social issues, they rarely have much impact on public policy (Hennigan, Flay, & Cook, 1980). To some extent desegregation of schools has been an exception to the rule. In the early 1950s, social scientists argued, through testimony and an amicus curiae (friend of the court) brief, against what was then the legally sanctioned doctrine of "separate but equal" education for various racial groups. Such racial segregation was ruled unconstitutional by the United States Supreme Court in the landmark case of *Brown v. Board of Education* (1954) on the grounds that it violated the equal protection clause of the Fourteenth Amendment. Thus, in effect, the court mandated the desegregation of schools. Although the extent to which the social science input influenced the court's decision has been questioned, Kenneth Clark (1979), a social psychologist who participated both with testimony and as a coauthor of the social science brief, later wrote: "this was probably the first time that a separate non-legal brief dealing with the social psychological aspects of a constitutional issue was submitted to *and accepted* by the United States Supreme Court" (p. 477).

In the amicus curiae brief presented to the Supreme Court in the *Brown* case, the social scientists advanced a theory about deleterious consequences of segregation and the potential benefits of desegregation (Stephan, 1978). The theory is that segregation sets in motion a vicious circle, as depicted in Fig. 18.1. As can be seen, it was hypothesized that segregation, which is caused by White prejudice toward Blacks, leads to lowered self-esteem among Blacks. Low self-esteem among Blacks results in low achievement. Frustration over low achievement then contributes to Black prejudice toward Whites. Black prejudice toward Whites feeds White prejudice toward Blacks and the circle continues. Desegregation, it was argued, would serve to break the vicious circle by providing the opportunity for greater understanding and less prejudice between Blacks and Whites. With this greater interracial acceptance, the self-esteem and achievement of Blacks would increase, which would further undermine the basis for prejudice. The idea that the vicious circle of segregation and prejudice can be broken by desegregation has come to be known as the contact hypothesis. It was hypothesized that interracial contact could achieve three goals: (1) the reduction of racial prejudice; (2) an increase in the self-esteem of Blacks; and (3) an increase in the academic achievement of Blacks. It seems reasonable to assume that, if the contact hypothesis were valid for desegregation of Whites and Blacks, then it would most likely hold for desegregation of other racial, ethnic, or culturally different groups.

Even the casual observer, who merely keeps abreast of major news stories, is likely to be aware that, unfortunately, busing and other means of

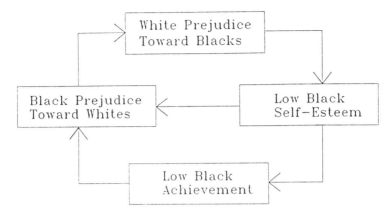

FIG. 18.1.   Causal model derived from social science testimony in *Brown v. Board of Education.*

school desegregation have not always achieved positive results and often seem to produce more problems than they solve. Taking a more scientific view, Walter Stephan (1978) reviewed the research literature on school desegregation more than 20 years after the *Brown* decision and concluded that the hypothesized benefits of desegregation were, for the most part, not achieved. Cautioning that there were flaws in many of the studies, Stephan concluded that desegregation does not generally reduce racial prejudice (and may even lead to increases in Black prejudice towards Whites) and does not reliably increase the self-esteem of Blacks. However, he did conclude that desegregation sometimes does increase the achievement of Blacks. In balance, these findings raise serious questions about the social science theory presented to the Supreme Court in the *Brown* case.

ALLPORT'S CONTACT HYPOTHESIS

In the 1970s and early 1980s, several researchers put forth the notion that school desegregation failed to provide the benefits promised in 1954 because not enough attention was paid to the conditions that facilitate constructive interracial contact (e.g., Aronson & Osherow, 1980; Schofield & Sagar, 1977; Slavin, 1979). Ironically, the facilitating conditions were stated quite clearly in Gordon Allport's book, *The Nature of Prejudice,* which was published in 1954. According to Allport, interracial contact is most likely to lead to reduced prejudice and provide related benefits when it occurs among racial and ethnic groups that have common (interdependent) goals and equal status and when such contact is sanctioned by authorities.

Schofield and Sagar (1977) were able to find a school in which the seventh-grade classes met Allport's criteria for constructive contact reasonably well.

School authorities clearly sanctioned and encouraged interracial activities. Black and White students shared goals, working together to form new special-interest organizations and to raise funds for those organizations. Equal status was fostered by having an equal proportion of Blacks in all classes, despite the fact that the average reading scores for the Blacks were clearly lower than for the Whites. In contrast, the eighth-grade class in the same school clearly violated Allport's equal status criterion in that a tracking system was used, and a greatly disproportionate number of students who were placed in the accelerated classes were White.

In what can best be classified as a nonequivalent control group design (Campbell & Stanley, 1966), Schofield and Sagar compared the seating patterns, both face-to-face and side-by-side, that occurred in the cafeteria over the course of the school year in the seventh-grade and eighth-grade classes. As expected, they found that interracially mixed seating increased significantly among the seventh graders but not among the eighth graders. In fact, interracial face-to-face seating decreased significantly in the eighth grade. In a follow-up study, Schofield (1979) found that when the seventh graders from the equal-status classes moved on to the tracking system in the eighth grade they began to resegregate in the cafeteria but nevertheless still engaged in more interracially mixed seating than did other students who entered the same eighth-grade classes from segregated classes in another school system. Thus, it seems that equal-status contact in schools, in the context of common goals and sanction by authority, can lead to spontaneous interracial interaction and that this effect is somewhat resistant to change, even when the school system is formally resegregated.

Schofield and Sagar (1977) considered the school system that they studied to be unusual in its efforts to make desegregation work. Even so, it seemed to make a critical error by using a tracking system in the eighth grade. Officials in other school systems may be even less aware of how to make desegregation work. Allowing schools to discover the ideal conditions for positive interracial contact has been a serious underutilization of social science knowledge (Hennigan, Flay, & Cook, 1980). Given the general failure of school desegregation to meet the goals that it was intended to accomplish, it is unfortunate that the social science input into the *Brown* decision did not emphasize more clearly how the ideal conditions for interracial contact can be brought about. Beginning in the 1970s, however, many social psychologists set about developing classroom techniques to apply Allport's facilitating conditions to achieve the goals of desegregation.

Cooperative Learning: Applying the Contact Hypothesis

One of the first applications of Allport's version of the contact hypothesis to desegregated schools was carried out by Weigal, Wiser, and Cook (1975). Each of 10 teachers of seventh- and tenth-grade classes in a newly desegregated school volunteered to teach one class with a small-group mode and one with a traditional whole-class mode. In the small-group mode, students were assigned to racially heterogeneous groups of five students each, with the modal group containing three Whites, one Black, and one Mexican–American. To foster interethnic interdependence, the small groups were instructed to discuss information and to share interpretations in their groups. Additionally, representatives from each group made presentations to the rest of the class and rewards were given on the basis of group performance. The small-group treatment was used for one period a day (out of seven) for 4 to 7 months. The whole-class method involved lectures by the teacher and discussion involving the entire class. It was found that, compared to students in the whole-class condition, students who participated in the small groups engaged in fewer cross-ethnic hostilities and more cross-ethnic helping. Also, White students in the small-group condition reported greater respect, liking, and friendship for Mexican–American classmates than did Whites in the whole-class condition.

In addition to the pioneering efforts of Weigal, Wiser, and Cook, Allport's contact hypothesis has been applied in a number of well-developed and extensively researched classroom interventions that are generally referred to as cooperative learning techniques (Slavin, 1985). Although the techniques vary in many respects, they all share some common elements. The most essential of these common elements is that students are assigned to racially heterogeneous groups and are given common goals that can be met best by working together. In most cases, care is taken to create some manner of equal status among the students. The manner in which common goals are established and equal status is fostered varies among the specific techniques. To organize the following review, the cooperative learning techniques that have been used in racially and ethnically desegregated classrooms are classified as (a) student teams, (b) the jigsaw classroom, (c) group investigation, and (d) learning together. Also, in reviewing evaluation studies of these techniques, particular attention is paid to outcome measures that are most relevant to the original goals of desegregation, which are reduction in prejudice of all students and increases in the self-esteem and academic achievement of minorities.

Student Teams

Student teams was one of the first cooperative learning techniques that was formally evaluated as a means of inducing positive interracial interaction in desegregated schools (DeVries & Edwards, 1974). The technique involves assigning students to racially mixed teams of about four or five members. The teams compete academically with other teams on material that is presented by the teacher. Students are given the opportunity to help their teammates to learn the material and are told that recognition will be given on the basis of team performance. Thus, the technique is designed to create interdependence within teams. It is assumed that the competition between teams will motivate the students to do well.

Two major variations of the technique that have been applied to racial and ethnic integration use slightly different ways to give all students an equal opportunity to earn points for their teams. In Teams–Games–Tournament (TGT) (DeVries & Slavin, 1978) academic tournaments are held. In the tournaments each member of a team competes against a member of another team who has similar ability. Individual scores are then added together to arrive at a team score. In Student Teams–Achievement Divisions (STAD) (Slavin, 1978) the technique is simplified by eliminating the tournaments and replacing them with quizzes. Each team member's performance is compared to his or her own past performance and team scores arrived at by adding together individual improvement scores. With both TGT and STAD team scores are reported in class newsletters.

The effects of TGT and STAD on desegregated classes were carefully evaluated in numerous field experiments. These studies occurred in actual classrooms, in classes ranging from grades two through 12, with regular classroom teachers, random assignment of whole classes or individual students to conditions, and use of the same curriculum objectives and materials in both the treatment and control conditions (DeVries, Edwards, & Slavin, 1978; DeVries & Slavin, 1978; Slavin, 1978, 1979; Slavin & Oickle, 1981; Widaman & Kagan, 1987). The studies most typically involved a comparison made between classes randomly assigned to use a student team technique for a few hours a week or to control classes in which the students both worked and were rewarded individually. Overall, compared to the control conditions, the effects of TGT and STAD were quite positive. In a review of 10 studies, DeVries and Slavin (1978) report that TGT typically led to significant increases in sociometric selections of cross-racial friendships and in academic achievement. Slavin (1978, 1979) found similar effects with STAD; however, the positive influence on academic achievement was not as consistent as it was with TGT.

The influence of STAD on academic performance now appears to be more complex than was originally hypothesized. Exploring an indication from an earlier pilot study, Slavin and Oickle (1981) did an experiment demonstrating that STAD interacts with race of students in influencing academic achievement. They found that Blacks experience large and significant gains in academic achievement with STAD as compared to a control condition, whereas Whites make a small, nonsignificant gain with STAD. Widaman and Kagan (1987) provided evidence indicating that the effects of student teams on academic achievement depend on both the social orientation, cooperative or competitive, of the students involved and the specific learning technique used. In a field experiment they found that initial cooperativeness of students was positively related to academic gains for students in STAD but negatively related to academic gains for students in TGT or traditional classrooms. They suggest that the face-to-face competition in the TGT tournaments may be compatible with the motives of competitive students but incompatible with the motives of cooperative students. In addition, they propose that minorities, who are relatively cooperative in their social orientation, should obtain their greatest academic gains in STAD, which is consistent with Slavin and Oickle's findings.

The Jigsaw Classroom

The jigsaw classroom is a social psychological technique that was designed with the expressed purpose of facilitating successful desegregation of schools (Aronson, Stephan, Sikes, Blaney, & Snapp, 1978). As with the application of student teams, the jigsaw technique is based in large measure on Allport's (1954) criteria for successful intergroup contact (Aronson & Osherow, 1980). First, students are divided into small racially heterogeneous groups of about four to seven students each. A lesson is then divided into as many parts as there are members in a group. Each group member is given only one part of the lesson to learn on his or her own, yet all students are eventually tested on the entire lesson. The students are supposed to fit together the pieces of the lesson by teaching each other their parts, metaphorically as if they were putting together a jigsaw puzzle. Equal status is achieved because each group members has an equally important part of the lesson to be learned. Interdependence is required for each student's own success as well as for the common goal of the group. To minimize the potential problem of students doing a poor job of learning and teaching their individual parts, students can be put into counterpart groups before presenting their parts to their jigsaw groups. A counterpart group consists of all students in the class from different jigsaw groups who have been assigned the same part of the jigsaw lesson. Through cooperative efforts the counterparts can help each other become competent teachers of their own parts; thus once again the students are interdependent.

Evaluation studies of the jigsaw classroom have yielded mixed results. The initial studies produced positive findings. Using what can best be described as a nonequivalent control group design (Campbell & Stanley, 1966), Blaney, Stephan, Rosenfield, Aronson, and Sikes (1977) compared fifth-grade classes that were exposed to the jigsaw technique with other fifth-grade classes who were not exposed to jigsaw learning. Teachers volunteered for the jigsaw condition and recommended highly competent teachers for the control condition. In the treatment condition, students participated in 45 minutes of jigsaw learning 3 times a week for 6 weeks. The material to be learned was the same for the treatment and control conditions. Analyses of pre and posttests indicated that the jigsaw technique had many positive effects. The two effects that are most relevant to the original goals of desegregation were that the jigsaw students came to like their groupmates better, perhaps indicating some reduction in prejudice, and jigsaw students increased in self-esteem, whereas the self-esteem of the control students actually decreased. Using a similar research design, Lucker, Rosenfield, Sikes, and Aronson (1976) found that minorities (Blacks and Mexican–Americans) in jigsaw classes made significantly greater academic gains than did minorities in traditional classes. Type of instruction had no significant effect on the academic performance of Whites. As possibly another indication of reduced prejudice, Bridgeman (1981) found that jigsaw students exhibited greater empathy for others than did control subjects.

Modifying the technique slightly, Ziegler (1981) found even more positive effects of jigsaw. Sixth-grade classes that had wide ethnic diversity—including Anglos, Italians, Chinese, Greeks, and West Indians—were randomly assigned to jigsaw learning or a control condition. The jigsaw students spent 40 minutes a week in counterpart groups and 80 minutes a week in jigsaw groups for 8 weeks. As a new aspect of the technique, each student's grade was a composite of his or her own quiz score and the average test score of his or her group, thus making one's own grade even more dependent on group performance. Teachers in the control condition were asked to de-emphasize small group activities and to assign individual projects for the same curriculum used in the jigsaw condition. Compared to the control subjects, the jigsaw students developed more casual and close cross-racial friendships, showed greater appreciation for social diversity, scored higher on cross-cultural role taking, and made significantly greater academic gains on tests of the curriculum. All these effects, except for appreciation of social diversity, held up 10 weeks after treatment.

Other studies shed doubt on the efficacy of the jigsaw classroom as a means of facilitating positive effects of desegregation in schools. In both a laboratory experiment and a reanalysis of the Blaney et al. (1977) data, Rosenfield, Stephan, and Lucker (1981) found evidence that incompetent groupmates are disliked in interdependent learning situations. They suggest that this is a serious limitation, because minority students often enter desegregated schools with low achievement levels. In two well-designed field studies, Moskowitz, Malvin, Schaeffer, and Schaps (1983, 1985) found no differences between jigsaw and control classes on attitudes towards peers, academic achievement, or self-esteem. Both of the studies by Moskowitz et al. involved process evaluations to determine which of the jigsaw classes were most faithfully carried out, and, even when only the most exemplary jigsaw classes were compared to control classes, no outcome differences were found. Moskowitz and his colleagues suggested that the failure of jigsaw to produce positive effects may be because of its individual reward structure and that the technique might be more effective if students were assigned grades on the basis of average test performance of their jigsaw groups. This proposed modification is quite similar to the one that had been so successfully employed by Ziegler (1981).

Group-Investigation

Another technique that somewhat conforms to Allport's (1954) criteria for successful desegregation is Group-Investigation (G-I) (Sharan, 1980), a method developed in Israel to help integrate students with Western and Middle Eastern ethnic backgrounds. In G-I students select subtopics within a general problem area defined by the teacher. After the subtopics are selected, the students then organize into ethnically heterogeneous groups of two to six students each. In consultation with the teacher, each group devises and carries out a plan for investigating one of the subtopics. When the investigation is completed, the groups make presentations of their subtopics to the rest of the class. Both students and the teacher evaluate each group's contribution to the class. More so than any other technique, G-I provides multiple opportunities to share goals and to cooperate, including the selection, investigation, presentation, and evaluation of material. It is less clear whether the technique establishes equal status among the students.

Evaluations studies indicate that G-I consistently produces positive outcomes. In a nonequivalent control group study with second through sixth graders, Sharan, Hertz-Lazarowitz, and Ackerman (1980) found that students who participated in 3 weeks of G-I outperformed students in traditional classes in academic tasks that require, according to Bloom's taxonomy (Bloom, Engelhart, Furst, Hill, & Krathwohl, 1956), high levels of cognitive functioning. Using the same research design with third through seventh graders, Hertz-Lazarowitz, Sharan, and Steinberg (1980) found that students who participated in G-I were more cooperative and altruistic than were students in traditional classes. The greater cooperativeness of the G-I students extended to interactions with students who were from other investigation groups and to situations that were not structured by the teacher.

The most extensive evaluation of G-I was a field experiment conducted in Israel with desegregated classes that included students with both Western and Middle Eastern ethnic backgrounds (Sharan, Kussel, Hertz-Lazarowitz, Bejarano, Raviv, & Sharan, 1984). Teachers of seventh-grade classes were randomly assigned to use G-I, STAD, or to traditional, whole-class instruction for 16 weeks. Compared to students in the traditional classes, the students in both G-I and STAD scored higher on achievement tests and exhibited more cooperative behavior. G-I was more effective than either STAD or traditional instruction in increasing both cross-ethnic interactions and academic achievement on tasks requiring high levels of cognitive functioning.

Learning Together

In their extensive work in desegregated schools, Johnson and Johnson (1975, 1981a, 1982a) emphasize the importance of providing opportunities for students to learn together interdependently through the use of cooperative goal structures. As earlier defined by Deutsch (1949), there are three types of goal structures that students may encounter in the classroom. With a cooperative goal structure, a student can obtain his or her goal if, and only if, other students obtain their goals. In direct contrast, with a competitive goal structure a student can obtain his or her goal if, and only if, other students fail to reach their goals. With the individualistic goal structure, the achievement of a goal by one student is independent of goal attainment by other students. Traditionally, teachers tend to use competitive and individualistic goal structures far more often than cooperative ones. Johnson and Johnson do not suggest that competitive and individualistic goal structures be eliminated but strongly advocate greater use of cooperative structures, especially in desegregated classrooms.

As implemented in research by Johnson and Johnson (1981a, 1982a), learning together is a simple procedure. Students are assigned to racially heterogeneous groups of four members each. For any given lesson, the teacher provides learning materials and instructs the students to work together as a group to complete a single assignment sheet while seeing to it that all the students in the group master the material. The students are also told that all group members are to provide ideas and to make suggestions. The teacher praises and rewards the group as a whole. For comparison purposes, other students are assigned to individualistic and competitive goal structures. In the individualistic structure, students are instructed to work on their own, avoiding interaction with one another, and the teacher praises and rewards individual performance. The competitive structure is the same as the individualistic structure except that each day the students are ranked and the teacher praises the top five students.

In a well-controlled experiment, Johnson and Johnson (1981a) randomly assigned fourth graders to either a cooperative or an individualistic condition. Each condition took 55 minutes a day for 16 days. To control for teacher effects, the teacher switched conditions halfway through the study. Behavioral observations revealed that during both the instructional sessions and free time there was more cross-racial interaction among students in the cooperative condition than there was in the individualistic condition. In a similar study that also included a competitive condition, Johnson and Johnson (1982a) found that even 5 months after the treatments there were more cross-racial nominations as preferred playmates among students who had been in the cooperative condition than among those who were in either the individualistic or competitive condition.

Using the same manipulations of cooperative and individualistic goal structures, Johnson, Johnson, Tiffany, and Zaidman (1983) replicated the positive effects of cooperative goal structures on cross-racial friendships and interactions. In addition, they found that students in the cooperative condition scored higher on achievement tests of the curriculum than did students in the individualistic condition. Greater liking for minorities by Whites in the cooperative condition than in the individualistic condition occurred even though Whites performed academically at a significantly higher level. Thus, Johnson et al. conclude that low achievers are not disliked in cooperative situations, as was feared even by advocates of cooperative goal structures (e.g., Deutsch, 1949), and that equal status, in the form of equal contributions to shared goals, is not essential for positive intergroup contact.

Contact in Cooperative Games

Rogers, Miller, and Hennigan (1981) extended the strategy of using interdependent interracial contact as a means of facilitating successful desegregation from the classroom to the playground. Earlier observational studies revealed that in desegregated elementary schools boys engage in more interracial interaction than do girls (Rogers & Miller, 1980, 1981). It was also observed that in the playground boys more often played team games (e.g., basketball, softball), which require more participants and more cooperation than do the games that girls play (e.g., hopscotch, jump rope). Also, when boys choose teams for their games, they tend to pick the best players first and race does not appear to be a prejudicial factor. These observations led to the prediction that, if girls were to engage in cooperative games that involved players of different races, then spontaneous cross-racial interactions among girls would increase.

To test their hypothesis Rogers et al. (1981) introduced an intervention that took place 2 days a week for 2 weeks on the playground during recess at a desegregated elementary school. The intervention, which was administered by female college students, involved encouraging the girls to play cooperative games using available equipment. Observations of interactions were made on days when the games were not in progress. During the 2-week period, cross-racial interactions increased dramatically, stayed at a high level 2 weeks after the intervention, and, although they declined somewhat, were still significantly more frequent 4 weeks after the intervention than they were before the intervention. This was, however, only a pilot study and did not include a control group. In a subsequent longer term study, which involved a control group that was encouraged to play individualistic games, no increases in spontaneous cross-racial interactions were observed (Miller, Rogers, & Hennigan, 1983). The investigators noted that several factors made the circumstances for their intervention less than ideal. For example, during the course of the study a district court reversed a lower court's desegregation order in one of the two schools. Thus, sanction for desegregation by authority, one of Allport's criteria for successful desegregation, was seriously undermined. Also, the cooperative games involved the use of expensive equipment (e.g., parachutes), which was not available to the subjects on days when observations of interaction were made. Unfortunately, the intervention, which seemed so promising in the pilot study, has not been replicated under more ideal conditions.

MAINSTREAMING HANDICAPPED STUDENTS INTO REGULAR CLASSROOMS

Consistent with the Supreme Court's decision to disallow racial segregation, a series of major court decisions in the early 1970s extended the Fourteenth Amendment's equal protection clause to disabled children (Berres & Knoblock, 1987). These decisions helped pave the way for the Education for All Handicapped Children Act (PL 94–142), which was passed by the U.S. Congress in 1975. This law mandates that handicapped children be educated in what is called the "least restrictive environment"; that is, to the maximum extent possible handicapped children are to be educated with nonhandicapped children, and special classes, separate schooling, or other forms of segregating handicapped from nonhandicapped children may occur only when a child's handicap is so severe that he or she could not achieve satisfactorily in regular classes.

The integration of handicapped children into regular classrooms is commonly referred to as "mainstreaming." Although there are numerous forms of handicaps, more than 80% of all the children affected by PL 94–142 fall into four categories: learning disabled (41.7%), speech impaired (26.0%), mentally retarded (17.3%), and emotionally disturbed (8.3%) (Reynolds & Birch, 1988). These figures are consistent with Madden and Slavin's (1983a) observation that mainstreaming has had its greatest impact, in terms of numbers, on children with mild academic handicaps, which helps explain why most of the social psychological approaches to mainstreaming deal with integrating such children into regular classrooms.

Besides merely placing handicapped and nonhandicapped in the same classrooms (physical integration), it is generally recognized by educators and researchers that successful mainstreaming also involves social and instructional integration (Berres & Knoblock, 1987; Madden & Slavin, 1983a; Reynolds & Birch, 1988). As with racial desegregation, contact between handicapped and nonhandicapped children has been shown to have inconsistent effects, unless the situation under which that contact occurs is carefully structured. Thus, the social psychological work on mainstreaming deals mainly with ways of structuring successful contact between handicapped and non-handicapped children in regular classrooms. Once again, interventions that emphasize interdependence and cooperation are applied.

Cooperative Learning Applied to Mainstreamed Classrooms

Two of the cooperative learning approaches that have been applied to racial and ethnic desegregation—student teams and learning together—have also been applied to mainstreaming.

Student Teams

To some extent the student team approaches that were successful in facilitating successful racial and ethnic desegregation may be helpful in the mainstreaming of handicapped students into the regular classroom. Slavin (1977) found that, in a special school for adolescents with emotional and behavioral problems, Teams–Games–Tournament (TGT) improved social relations. Madden and Slavin (1983b) demonstrated that, compared to individualized instruction, Student Teams–Achievement Divisions (STAD) led to less rejection of handicapped students by nonhandicapped peers and higher academic achievement and self-esteem. Nevertheless, in a review of research on the academic and social effects of mainstreaming, Madden and Slavin (1983a) acknowledge that both cooperative learning structures and carefully programmed individualized instruction produce positive outcomes. Thus, Slavin and his associates (Slavin, 1984; Slavin, Leavey, & Madden, 1984; Slavin, Madden, & Leavey, 1984a, 1984b) devised an intervention, called Team Assisted Individualization (TAI), which combines cooperative learning and individualized instruction.

TAI was designed to overcome a potential limitation of applying TGT and STAD to mainstreamed classes (Slavin, Madden, & Leavey, 1984a). The problem is that with TGT and STAD all students are to learn the same material at the same pace, and academically handicapped students are likely to have difficulties keeping up. Thus, the major modification of the student team approach in TAI is that, while working in teams whose members vary in ability, students are given their own individualized learning units. These units all cover the same basic material but are designed for the ability level of the individual students as determined by pretests of the subject matter. Similar to STAD, students in TAI work in teams of four or five students each to help prepare for tests that will be used to determine team scores and team recognition. While preparing for the tests, teams further break down into pairs or triads so that the students may exchange worksheets and check each other's work. If students have difficulties at this point, they are encouraged to seek help from teammates before asking the teacher for help. Once a student reaches a criterion level of performance on his or her individualized unit, then he or she takes a test on the unit. At the end of each week team scores are calculated on the basis of both the average number of units covered by each team and on test scores for those units. Given that the level of difficulty of the units and tests are individualized, all students have an equal chance to contribute to the team score. The technique also involves periodic teacher instruction, sometimes to small groups of students who are at about the same ability level and at other times to the entire class. More details on TAI may be found elsewhere (e.g., Slavin, 1984).

In a comprehensive evaluation of TAI in mainstreamed classrooms that included students with mild academic handicaps, 18 classes of third, fourth, and fifth graders were randomly assigned to 10 weeks of mathematics instruction with TAI, individualized instruction (II), or traditional methods (Slavin, Leavey, & Madden, 1984; Slavin, Madden, & Leavey, 1984a). TAI was implemented as described before. II involved the same kind of individualized learning units and procedure as in TAI, except that the students worked individually, not in teams. The control (traditional instruction) condition involved use of traditional textbooks, group-paced instruction, and teacher-directed, homogeneous math groups. The results indicated that, compared to the control condition, TAI led to greater gains in mathematics achievement, higher self-concept in math, and more liking and less social rejection of academically handicapped students. However, the TAI and II conditions were not significantly different on any of these measures. Also, whereas TAI led to significantly greater achievement for the combined sample of handicapped and nonhandicapped students, no significant gain was found when only the data for the handicapped students was analyzed. The latter shortcoming was overcome in a longer term study that showed that, after 24 weeks of exposure to TAI, both mildly academically handicapped and nonhandicapped students made significantly greater gains in math achievement than did students in a control condition (Slavin, Madden, & Leavey, 1984b). The long-term study did not include an II condition, and thus the question of whether TAI is more efficacious than II in bringing about positive effects in mainstreamed classrooms remains unresolved.

More recently, Slavin and his associates have turned their attention to adapting team approaches to reading and writing, two curriculum areas that had previously not been taught and evaluated with cooperative learning procedures (Slavin, Stevens, & Madden, 1988). Their approach, Cooperative Integrated Reading and Composition (CIRC), is highly structured and multifaceted. Only some of the basics of the technique are described here. CIRC combines the use of mixed-ability, cooperative learning teams with same-ability reading and writing groups. First students are assigned to same-ability reading groups of eight to 15 students each. From the reading groups pairs or triads of students are assigned to mixed-ability teams representing two different reading groups. The same teams are used for writing activities. Within teams the same-ability pairs carry out many activities together, such as reading to each other and giving each other feedback. Other activities, such as discussing stories, involve the whole team. The pairs check and initial each other's record forms as they complete weekly assignments. Team scores are based on quizzes, compositions, and book reports. All activities involve an initial presentation by the teacher, team practice, peer preassessment, more practice, and testing.

An evaluation in which 22 mainstreamed classes of third and fourth graders were matched and assigned either to 24 weeks of CIRC or to traditional instruction indicated that CIRC led to significantly greater gains in several measures of reading and writing (Slavin et al., 1988). These effects were found for students at all levels of ability. Most impressively, special education students in CIRC gained 1.92 grade equivalents more in reading comprehension than special education students in the control condition and 1.44 grade equivalents more in reading vocabulary. In addition, whereas both CIRC and individual learning with the CIRC materials led to greater gains in reading comprehension than did the control condition, CIRC significantly enhanced the positive effect beyond that found for the individual treatment.

Learning Together

Johnson and Johnson and their associates have approached the mainstreaming of academically handicapped students into regular classrooms with the same technique that they applied to racial desegregation (Armstrong, Johnson, & Balow, 1981; Johnson & Johnson, 1981b, 1981c, 1982b; Smith, Johnson, & Johnson, 1982). The key element of the technique is cooperative goal structures. Handicapped and nonhandicapped students in mainstreamed classrooms are assigned to small groups of about four students who vary in ability. The students in a group are given one set of curriculum materials and are instructed to work together with the common goal of having all group members master the information. All group members are to give ideas and to make suggestions. The teacher praises and rewards the group as a whole.

In evaluation studies, students were randomly assigned to learn together with the cooperative goal structure or to learn the same curriculum material while working individually. The results consistently indicate that the cooperative goal structures bring about positive outcomes on a number of objective and self-report measures. Observations of student behavior revealed that interaction between handicapped and nonhandicapped students was more frequent in the cooperative condition both during the treatments and during free time than it was in the individualistic condition (Johnson & Johnson, 1981b, 1981c). Self-report, sociometric measures also indicated more attraction between handicapped and nonhandicapped peers in the cooperative condition than in the individualistic condition (Armstrong, Johnson, & Balow, 1981; Johnson & Johnson, 1981c, 1982b). Achievement tests showed greater academic gains for students in the cooperative condition than for those in the individualistic condition (Armstrong, Johnson, & Balow, 1981; Smith, Johnson, & Johnson, 1982). Self-esteem was also higher in the cooperative condition (Smith, Johnson, & Johnson, 1982). Unfortunately, the sample sizes in the individual studies were so small, especially for handicapped students, that it is not clear whether the increases in achievement and self-esteem of cooperative learning were significant for both the handicapped and nonhandicapped students.

Cooperative Games

Rynders, Johnson, Johnson, and Schmidt (1980) provide evidence that a cooperative goal structure in a recreational setting can increase attraction between severely handicapped and nonhandicapped students. Their subjects were 30 junior high school students, 12 with Down syndrome and 18 non-handicapped, who participated in a bowling program that lasted for 8 weeks. After being stratified so that four handicapped and six nonhandicapped students were in each condition, the subjects were randomly assigned to three goal structures. In the cooperative condition, the students were instructed to maximize the group bowling score and to encourage, reinforce, and assist one another. Prizes were awarded on the basis of the group score. In the competitive condition, students were instructed to maximize their individual scores in order to outperform the other students in their group. They were to seek assistance only from the teacher and prizes were awarded to the highest individual scorers. In the individualistic condition students were instructed to maximize their own individual scores in order to reach a set criterion and to seek assistance only from the teacher. Prizes were awarded to any student who reached the criterion. Observations during the study revealed that there were more positive interactions between the handicapped and nonhandicapped students in the cooperative condition than in either the competitive or individualistic conditions. The same pattern of findings were found with self-report measures of attraction. There were no significant differences in the bowling scores among the three experimental conditions. As expected, the nonhandicapped students had significantly higher bowling scores than did the handicapped students. The investigators emphasize that, although it may seem counterintuitive, even though the lower bowling scores by the handicapped students adversely affected the chance for nonhandicapped students to receive prizes only with the cooperative goal structure, the nonhandicapped students liked the handicapped students best in the cooperative condition.

Social Skills Training for
Mainstreamed Handicapped Students

Academically handicapped students in mainstreamed classes are often rejected by their nonhandicapped peers (Gottlieb & Budoff, 1973; Porter, Ramsey, Tremblay, Iaccobo, & Crawley, 1978). To some extent this problem may be accounted for by prejudicial attitudes and biased perceptions of the nonhandicapped peers (Hollinger, 1987). There is also evidence that academically handicapped students tend to have poorly developed social skills (e.g., Gottlieb & Leyser, 1981). Thus, it has been suggested that social skills training may be effective in helping handicapped students adapt to the regular classroom (Gottlieb & Leyser, 1981; Gresham, 1981; Hollinger, 1987).

Madden and Slavin (1983a) reviewed several approaches to social skills training—coaching, direct reinforcement, modeling, counseling, and cognitive behavior modification—that could be applied to helping academically handicapped students to become socially integrated into mainstreamed classes. Among these techniques, the only social psychological approach is modeling, which has not actually been applied to helping academically handicapped students. Nevertheless, O'Connor (1969, 1972) did show that modeling of social skills helped shy normal-progress students to become more socially competent. It may be valuable to evaluate whether O'Connor's approach would work with academically handicapped students in mainstreamed classes. Hollinger (1987) suggests that, because nonhandicapped students so often have biased social perceptions of their handicapped peers, modeling or other forms of social skills training might be most effective in mainstreamed classes when all the students, handicapped and nonhandicapped, are exposed to the training.

CONCLUSIONS

Social psychological approaches to cultural integration and mainstreaming have centered on the application of Allport's (1954) criteria for positive intergroup contact, especially interdependence and, to a lesser extent, equal status. For the most part, these applications, collectively referred to as cooperative learning techniques, have been shown to be effective in reducing prejudice and in increasing the self-esteem and academic achievement of minority and handicapped students. These effects have occurred without any evidence of negative consequences for majority and nonhandicapped students. Indeed, there is much evidence that the academic achievement of majority and nonhandicapped students also is increased by cooperative learning. The positive effects of cooperative learning have been obtained by implementing the methods for only a few hours a week with teachers who have had only brief training with the techniques. Perhaps most impressive are the consistently positive findings in actual school settings with various grade levels, curricula, and types of students. Thus, there is good reason to believe that cooperative learning is a practical and robust approach to successful integration of schools.

Although the evidence supporting the efficacy of cooperative learning as a means to successful integration of schools is impressive, some issues regarding the application of these techniques are not clearly resolved. For example, studies investigating whether slow learners will be disliked in cooperative learning situations have yielded inconsistent and contradictory findings. Second, although there is some evidence that cooperative learning produces lasting benefits, there have only been a few studies that have measured long-term effects. Third, given that the cooperative learning techniques are multifaceted, it has been suggested that analyses of the components of each technique be examined, with either more precise field experimentation (Slavin, Stevens, & Madden, 1988) or laboratory experiments (Miller, Brewer, & Edwards, 1985), in order to determine which aspects of the techniques bring about the positive effects. Finally, although most of the studies produced positive results when cooperative learning was implemented by teachers with very little training, it is not clear how much training is adequate and whether teachers would be motivated to use the techniques as prescribed if they were not involved in an evaluation study.

The reader should keep in mind that only social psychological approaches to school integration have been reviewed here. Other approaches, including educational and legal interventions, no doubt have merit as well. A multidisciplinary approach might be most effective. Social psychologists did contribute to the Brown case, which mandated desegregation of schools. Although desegregation alone has not been effective in bringing about successful integration, use of cooperative learning techniques in desegregated schools has been shown to be quite effective. Perhaps social psychologists could contribute to other legal approaches, such as designing busing plans that will have the best possible psychological effects. Social psychological input into the designing of educational approaches, such as Black studies programs, might also prove fruitful.

REFERENCES

Allport, G. (1954). *The nature of prejudice*. Reading, MA: Addison-Wesley.
Armstrong, B., Johnson, D. W., & Balow, B. (1981). Effects of cooperative vs. individualistic learning experiences on interpersonal attraction between learning-disabled and normal-progress elementary school students. *Contemporary Educational Psychology, 6,* 102–109.

Aronson, E., & Osherow, N. (1980). Cooperation, social behavior, and academic performance: Experiments in the desegregated classroom. In L. Bickman (Ed.), *Applied social psychology annual* (Vol. 1, pp. 163–196). Beverly Hills, CA: Sage.

Aronson, E., Stephan, C., Sikes, J., Blaney, N., & Snapp, M. (1978). *The jigsaw classroom.* Beverly Hills, CA: Sage.

Berres, M. S., & Knoblock, P. (Eds.). (1987). *Program models for mainstreaming: Integrating students with moderate to severe disabilities.* Rockville, MD: Aspen.

Blaney, N. T., Stephan, C., Rosenfield, D., Aronson, E., & Sikes, J. (1977). Interdependence in the classroom: A field study. *Journal of Educational Psychology, 69,* 121–128.

Bloom, B. S., Engelhart, N. D., Furst, E. J., Hill, W. H., & Krathwohl, D. R. (1956). *Taxonomy of educational objectives. Handbook I: Cognitive domain.* Pacific Palisades, CA: Goodyear.

Bridgeman, D. L. (1981). Enhanced role taking through cooperative interdependence: A filed study. *Child Development, 52,* 1231–1238.

Brown v. Board of Education of Topeka, 347 U.S. 483 (1954).

Campbell, D. T., & Stanley, J. C. (1966). *Experimental and quasi-experimental designs for research.* Chicago: Rand McNally.

Clark, K. B. (1979). The role of social scientists 25 years after Brown. *Personality and Social Psychology Bulletin, 5,* 477–481.

Deutsch, M. (1949). An experimental study of the effects of cooperation and competition upon group process. *Human Relations, 2,* 199–231.

DeVries, D. L., & Edwards, K. J. (1974). Student teams and learning games: Their effects on cross-race and cross-sex interaction. *Journal of Educational Psychology, 66,* 741–749.

DeVries, D. L., Edwards, K. J., & Slavin, R. E. (1978). Biracial learning teams and race relations in the classroom: Four field experiments using teams–games–tournament. *Journal of Educational Psychology, 70,* 356–362.

DeVries, D. L., & Slavin, R. E. (1978). Teams–Games–Tournament: Review of ten classroom experiments. *Journal of Research and Development in Education, 12,* 28–38.

Gottlieb, J., & Budoff, A. (1973). Social acceptability of retarded children in nongraded schools differing in architecture. *American Journal of Mental Deficiency, 78,* 15–19.

Gottlieb, J., & Leyser, Y. (1981). Friendship between mentally retarded and nonretarded children. In S. Asher & J. Gottman (Eds.), *The development of children's friendships.* Cambridge: Cambridge University Press.

Gresham, F. (1981). Social skills training with handicapped children: A review. *Review of Educational Research, 51,* 139–176.

Hennigan, K. M., Flay, B. R., & Cook, T. D. (1980). "Give me the facts": Some suggestions for using social science knowledge in national policy-making. In R. F. Kidd & M. J. Saks (Eds.), *Advances in applied social psychology* (Vol. 1). Hillsdale, NJ: Lawrence Erlbaum Associates.

Hertz-Lazarowitz, R., Sharan, S., & Steinberg, R. (1980). Classroom learning style and cooperative behavior of elementary school children. *Journal of Educational Psychology, 72,* 97–104.

Hollinger, J. D. (1987). Social skills for behaviorally disordered children as preparation for mainstreaming: Theory, practice, and new directions. *Remedial and Special Education, 8,* 17–27.

Johnson, D. W., & Johnson, R. T. (1975). *Learning together and alone.* Englewood Cliffs, NJ: Prentice Hall.

Johnson, D. W., & Johnson, R. T. (1981a). Effect of cooperative and individualistic learning experiences on interethnic interaction. *Journal of Educational Psychology, 73,* 444–449.

Johnson, D. W., & Johnson, R. T. (1981b). Building friendships between handicapped and nonhandicapped students: Effects of cooperative and individualistic instruction. *American Educational Research Journal, 18,* 415–423.

Johnson, D. W., & Johnson, R. T. (1981c). The integration of the handicapped into the regular classroom: Effects of cooperative and individualistic instruction. *Contemporary Educational Psychology, 6,* 344–353.

Johnson, D. W., & Johnson, R. T. (1982a). Effects of cooperative, competitive, and individualistic learning experiences on cross-ethnic interaction and friendship. *Journal of Social Psychology, 118,* 47–58.

Johnson, D. W., & Johnson, R. T. (1982b). The effects of cooperative and individualistic instruction on handicapped and nonhandicapped students. *Journal of Social Psychology, 118,* 257–268.

Johnson, D. W., Johnson, R., Tiffany, M., & Zaidman, B. (1983). Are low achievers disliked in a cooperative situation? A test of rival theories in a mixed ethnic situation. *Contemporary Educational Psychology, 8,* 189–200.

Lucker, G. W., Rosenfield, D., Sikes, J., & Aronson, E. (1976). Performance in the interdependent classroom: A field study. *American Educational Research Journal, 13,* 115–123.

Madden, N, A., & Slavin, R. E. (1983a). Mainstreaming students with mild handicaps: Academic and social outcomes. *Review of Educational Research, 53,* 519–569.

Madden, N, A., & Slavin, R. E. (1983b). Effects of cooperative learning on the social acceptance of mainstreamed academically handicapped students. *Journal of Special Education, 17,* 171–182.

Miller, N., Brewer, M. B., & Edwards, K. (1985). Cooperative interaction in desegregated settings: A laboratory analogue. *Journal of Social Issues, 41,* 63–79.

Miller, N., Rogers, M., & Hennigan, K. (1983). Increasing interracial acceptance: Using cooperative games in desegregated elementary schools. In L. Bickman (Ed.), *Applied social psychology annual* (Vol. 4). Beverly Hills, CA: Sage.

Moskowitz, J., Malvin, J., Schaeffer, G., & Schaps, E. (1983). Evaluation of a cooperative learning strategy. *American Educational Research Journal, 20,* 687–696.

Moskowitz, J. M., Malvin, J. H., Schaeffer, G. A., & Schaps, E. (1985). Evaluation of jigsaw, a cooperative learning technique. *Contemporary Educational Psychology, 10,* 104–112.

O'Connor, R. D. (1969). Modification of social withdrawal through symbolic modeling. *Journal of Applied Behavioral Analysis, 2,* 15–22.

O'Connor, R. D. (1972). Relative efficiency of modeling, shaping, and combined procedure for modification of social withdrawal. *Journal of Abnormal Psychology, 79,* 327–334.

Porter, R., Ramsey, B., Tremblay, A., Iaccobo, M., & Crawley, S. (1978). Social interactions in heterogeneous groups of retarded and normally developing children: An observational study. In B. Sackett (Ed.), *Observing behavior: Theory and applications in mental retardation* (pp. 311–328). Baltimore: University Park Press.

Prager, J., Longshore, D., & Seeman, M. (Ed.). (1986). *School desegregation research: New directions in situational analysis.* New York: Plenum Press.

Reynolds, M. C., & Birch, J. W. (1988). *Adaptive mainstreaming: A primer for teachers and principals* (3rd ed.). New York: Longman.

Rogers, M., & Miller, N. (1980). *Quantitative and qualitative differences in peer selection in a desegregated school.* Paper presented at the annual meeting of the American Psychological Association, Montreal.

Rogers, M., & Miller, N. (1981). *The effect of school setting on the social interaction of children in a desegregated school.* Paper presented at the annual meeting of the American Psychological Association, Los Angeles.

Rogers, M., Miller, N., & Hennigan, K. (1981). Cooperative games as an intervention to promote cross-racial acceptance. *American Educational Research Journal, 18,* 513–516.

Rosenfield, D., Stephan, W. G., & Lucker, G. W. (1981). Attraction to competent and incompetent members of cooperative and competitive groups. *Journal of Applied Social Psychology, 11,* 416–433.

Rynders, J. E., Johnson, R. T., Johnson, D. W., & Schmidt, B. (1980). Producing positive interaction among Down syndrome and nonhandicapped teenagers through cooperative goal structuring. *American Journal of Mental Deficiency, 85,* 268–273.

Schofield, J. W. (1979). The impact of positively structured contact on intergroup behavior: Does it last under adverse conditions? *Social Psychology Quarterly, 42,* 280–284.

Schofield, J. W., & Sagar, H. A. (1977). Peer interaction patterns in an integrated middle school. *Sociometry, 40,* 130–138.

Sharan, S. (1980). Cooperative learning in small groups: Recent methods and effects on achievement, attitudes, and ethnic relations. *Review of Educational Research, 50,* 241–271.

Sharan, S., Kussel, P., Hertz-Lazarowitz, R., Bejarano, Y., Raviv, S., & Sharan, Y. (1984). *Cooperative learning in desegregated schools.* Hillsdale, NJ: Lawrence Erlbaum Associates.

Sharan, S., Hertz-Lazarowitz, R., & Ackerman, Z. (1980). Academic achievement of elementary school children in small group versus whole-class instruction. *Journal of Experimental Education, 48,* 125–129.

Slavin, R. E. (1977). A student team approach to teaching adolescents with special emotional and behavioral needs. *Psychology in the Schools, 14,* 77–84.

Slavin, R. E. (1978). Student teams and achievement divisions. *Journal of Research and Development in Education, 12,* 39–49.

Slavin, R. E. (1979). Effects of biracial learning teams on cross-racial friendships. *Journal of Educational Psychology, 71,* 381–387.

Slavin, R. E. (1984). Team Assisted Individualization: Cooperative learning and individualized instruction in the mainstreamed classroom. *Remedial and Special Education, 5,* 33–42.

Slavin, R. E. (1985). Cooperative learning: Applying contact theory in desegregated schools. *Journal of Social Issues, 41,* 45–62.

Slavin, R. E., Leavey, M., & Madden, N. A. (1984). Combining cooperative learning and individualized instruction: Effects on students' mathematics achievement, attitudes, and behaviors. *Elementary School Journal, 84,* 409–422.

Slavin, R. E., Madden, N. A., & Leavey, M. (1984a). Effects of cooperative learning and individualized instruction on mainstreamed students. *Exceptional Children, 50,* 434–443.

Slavin, R. E., Madden, N. A., & Leavey, M. (1984b). Effects of team assisted individualization on the mathematics achievement of academically handicapped and nonhandicapped students. *Journal of Educational Psychology, 76,* 813–819.

Slavin, R. E., & Oickle, E. (1981). Effects of cooperative learning teams on student achievement and race relations: Treatments by race interactions. *Sociology of Education, 54,* 174–180.

Slavin, R. E., Stevens, R. J., & Madden, N. A. (1988). Accommodating student diversity in reading and writing instruction: A cooperative learning approach. *Remedial and Special Education, 9,* 60–66.

Smith, K., Johnson, D. W., & Johnson, R. (1982). Effects of cooperative and individualistic instruction on the achievement of handicapped, regular, and gifted students. *Journal of Social Psychology, 116,* 277–283.

Stephan, W. G. (1978). School desegregation: An evaluation of predictions made in Brown v. Board of Education. *Psychological Bulletin, 85,* 217–238.

Weigal, R. H., Wiser, P. L., & Cook, S. W. (1975). The impact of cooperative learning experiences on cross-ethnic relations and attitudes. *Journal of Social Issues, 31,* 219–244.

Widaman, K. F., & Kagan, S. (1987). Cooperativeness and achievement: Interaction of student cooperativeness with cooperative versus competitive classroom organization. *Journal of School Psychology, 25,* 355–365.

Ziegler, S. (1981). The effectiveness of cooperative learning teams for increasing cross-ethnic friendship: Additional evidence. *Human Organization, 40,* 264–268.

AUTHOR INDEX

A

Abelson, R. P., 403, 420
Aber, J. L., 379, 393
Abramson, L. Y., 275, 302, 361, 369, 374, 376
Ackerman, N. W., 141, 159, 257, 265
Ackerman, Z., 313, 331, 457, 469
Adair, J. G., 202, 220
Adams, E. B., 118, 132
Adams, G. R., 96, 103, 106, 234, 244, 389, 393
Adams, J. S., 91, 106
Adams, S. A., 339, 341, 342, 348, 349, 353
Adamson, J., 220
Adler, T. F., 62, 79
Agazarian, Y., 255, 256, 265
Agnew, R., 96, 106
Aiken, M., 364, 374
Aitkenhead, M., 205, 221
Ajchenbaum, M., 282, 300
Ajzen, I., 26, 27, 40, 42, 43, 44, 45, 405, 412, 413, 420, 422, 431, 433, 445, 446, 447
Alessi, G. J., 346, 347, 351
Algozzine, B., 96, 110, 125, 135, 230, 238, 240, 241, 243, 244, 275, 277, 299

Ali, S. L., 115, 132
Allen, D., 240, 244
Allen, J. P., 379, 393
Alliger, G. M., 343, 348, 351, 354
Alloy, L. B., 275, 302, 361, 369, 374, 376
Allport, F. H., 15, 21, 30, 45
Allport, G. W., 6, 9, 21, 451, 455, 457, 465, 466
Alpert, J. L., 114, 117, 118, 132, 196, 221
Altman, M. A., 138, 159
Amerikaner, M. H., 137, 138, 159
Ames, C., 62, 65, 76, 306, 327
Ames, R., 62, 76, 306, 322, 327
Amish, P. L., 260, 266
Anastasi, A., 235, 236, 241
Anders, T., 116, 134
Anderson, D., 313, 329
Anderson, K. A., 316, 320, 332
Anderson, L. M., 323, 327
Anderson, P. L., 230, 241
Andrews, L., 271, 273, 283, 284, 303
Arends, J., 179, 191
Arends, R., 179, 191
Armstrong, Barbara, 463, 464, 466
Armstrong, Bruce, 230, 243
Aronson, E., 37, 45, 98, 107, 203, 204, 221, 273, 279, 299, 301, 311, 327, 449, 451, 455, 456, 467, 468

Shiffer, M., 255, 268
Shinn, M. R., 129, 135
Shonkoff, J. P., 157, 160
Short, R. J., 275, 302
Shoultz, D. E., 217, 225
Shultz, T. R., 57, 58, 79, 80
Shure, M. B., 260, 268
Sicoly, F., 89, 110
Siegler, R. S., 57, 58, 80
Sifneos, P., 253, 268
Sigall, H., 29, 45, 46
Sigler, E., 73, 77
Signorella, M. L., 127, 135
Sikes, J., 311, 327, 455, 456, 467, 468
Sikes, J. N., 73, 78
Sikora, D. M., 102, 107
Sikorski, L., 179, 191
Silverman, W. H., 286, 302
Silvern, L. E., 125, 135
Simmons, R. G., 404, 424
Simons, H. W., 286, 302
Simpson, C., 307, 308, 330, 331
Simpson, R. L., 426, 448
Sims, H. P., 343
Sincavage, J. M., 425, 445
Sinclair, R. C., 342, 354
Singer, J., 418, 424
Singer, M. T., 158, 159
Skon, L., 312, 330
Slamecka, N. J., 415, 424
Slavin, R. E., 306, 308, 309, 310, 311, 312,
313, 314, 326, 328, 331, 451, 453,
454, 460, 461, 462, 463, 465, 466,
467, 468, 469
Slavson, S. R., 255, 268
Slotkkin, J., 385, 394
Slovic, P., 206, 223
Small, L., 246, 265
Smart, J. L., 430, 447
Smith, C. J., 197, 222
Smith, D. E., 336, 353
Smith, D. K., 275, 302
Smith, E. R., 29, 46
Smith, G., 405, 421
Smith, J. K., 260, 266
Smith, K., 463, 464, 469
Smith, M. B., 405, 424
Smith, P. C., 336, 354
Smith, R. W., 237, 244
Smith, T. L., 26, 29, 45
Smollar, H., 99, 111

Snapp, M., 311, 327, 455, 467
Snarey, J. R., 128, 135
Snow, R. E., 315, 316, 317, 328, 331
Snyder, M., 84, 111, 205, 225, 326, 331
Sobell, M., 408, 424
Sockloff, A., 120, 135
Sohn, D., 61, 80
Solano, C. H., 378, 396
Sorensen, A. B., 124, 133
Sowa, C. J., 372, 376
Speck, R., 157, 160
Spinner, B., 378, 395
Spitzer, D., 259, 268
Spivack, G., 260, 268
Spratt, M. F., 66, 72, 77
Sroufe, L. A., 379, 395
Srull, T. K., 339, 341, 354
Stacey, D. C., 345, 352
Staffieri, J. R., 96, 111
Stallings, J., 323, 331
Stangor, C., 118, 135, 433, 446
Stanley, J. C., 115, 116, 132, 194, 221, 452,
455, 467
Starishevsky, R., 258, 259, 268
Stein, A., 61, 80
Steinberg, L., 385, 396
Steinberg, R., 457, 468
Steiner, I. D., 19, 23, 254, 268
Stenberg, C., 137, 159
Stephan, C., 311, 327, 455, 456, 467, 468
Stephan, W. G., 450, 451, 456, 469
Stephens, M. T., 239, 241
Stern, G. G., 181, 191
Stern, P., 274, 278, 298, 302
Stern, W., 124, 134
Stevens, R. J., 462, 463, 466, 469
Stewart, N. R., 122, 135
Stiles, B., 318, 332
Stipek, D. J., 64, 80, 124, 135, 316, 318,
325, 331
Stogdill, R. M., 254, 268
Stokes, J. P., 377, 378, 387, 394
Stokes, N. A., 96, 108
Stokes, S. J., 96, 111
Stone, J. L., 264, 266
Stratford, R., 345, 354
Strelnick, A. H., 257, 268
Strenio, A. J., 237, 244
Strickland, B., 240, 242, 430, 435, 446
Strong, S. R., 246, 259, 266, 268, 270, 271,
278, 281, 284, 285, 286, 296, 297,
299, 302, 428, 448

Subject Index